CRIMINAL JUSTICE

Mainstream and Crosscurrents

Second Edition

John Randolph Fuller

State University of West Georgia

Prentice Hall
Upper Saddle River, New Jersey
Columbus, Ohio

Library of Congress Cataloging-in-Publication Data

Fuller, John R.
  Criminal justice : mainstream and crosscurrents / John Randolph Fuller. — 2nd ed.
    p. cm.
  ISBN 0-13-504262-3 (978-0-13-504262-5)
  1. Criminal justice, Administration of—United States.
2. Crime—United States. I. Title.
  HV9950.F859 2010
  364.973—dc22

                                          2008041125

Editor in Chief: *Vernon Anthony*
Senior Acquisitions Editor: *Tim Peyton*
Development Editor: *Elisa Rogers*
Editorial Assistant: *Alicia Kelly*
Production Coordination: *Linda Zuk, WordCraft LLC*
Project Manager: *Holly Shufeldt*
Senior Operations Supervisor: *Pat Tonneman*
Art Director: *Diane Ernsberger*
Text Designer: *Kathryn Foot*

Cover Designer: *Mike Fruhbeis*
Cover photo: *Big Stock*
Manager, Image Resource Center,
  Rights and Permissions: *Zina Arabia*
Manager, Visual Research: *Beth Brenzel*
Image Permissions Coordinator: *Joanne Dippel*
Director of Marketing: *David Gesell*
Marketing Assistant: *Alicia Wosniak*

This book was set in Janson Text by S4Carlisle Publishing Services and
was printed and bound by Quebecor. The cover was printed by Phoenix
Color Corp.

Pearson Education Ltd., London
Pearson Education Singapore Pte. Ltd.
Pearson Education Canada, Inc.
Pearson Education—Japan

Pearson Education Australia Pty. Limited
Pearson Education North Asia Ltd., Hong Kong
Pearson Educación de Mexico, S.A. de C.V.
Pearson Education Malaysia Pte. Ltd.ii

Prentice Hall
is an imprint of

www.pearsonhighered.com

10 9 8 7 6 5 4 3 2 1
ISBN-13 978-0-13-504262-5
ISBN-10   0-13-504262-3

For Amy,

who made me rewrite everything. Several times.
Lupus grex grex lupus est.

WELCOME TO THE SECOND EDITION

The following pages will introduce you to what's new in the Second Edition, as well as to the hallmark features that have made *Criminal Justice: Mainstream and CrossCurrents* one of the best critical thinking introductory criminal justice textbooks on the market.

At the heart of this textbook are the **CrossCurrents,** which contrast the successes and reforms of the criminal justice system by emphasizing contemporary cases as well as the unpopular laws, ill-funded agencies, and honest mistakes that affect the quality of American justice. Linked closely to the theme of each chapter, the CrossCurrents feature reveals the multiple facets of crime and the solutions we are searching for in society.

New to the Second Edition

◄ MyCrimeKit

This student website and electronic study guide (www.mycrimekit.com) is filled with resources designed to enhance students' experience of the text through multimedia, practice quizzes, glossary flashcards, weblinks to external resources, and more.

► Paperback Cover

Moving from a hardback cover to a paperback cover has reduced the price of the book, making it more affordable for students.

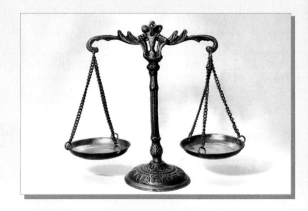

CrossCurrents

Legal Rights at Guantanamo Bay

One of the consistent criticisms of the war on terror has been the suspension of legal rights for "enemy combatants." The U.S. government has determined that those captured on the battlefield in Afghanistan and Iraq are not entitled to rights normally given to prisoners of war or U.S. citizens. By housing these individuals at a U.S. Navy base in Guantanamo Bay, Cuba, the administration has effectively kept suspected terrorists in a legal limbo that prevents them from challenging the reasons and conditions of their confinement.

The Supreme Court recently ruled in *Boumediene v. Bush* that these detainees are now entitled to the constitutional right of *habeas corpus*, which means they can challenge the legal basis of their detention in federal court. According to Human Rights Watch, it is unclear exactly what this will mean for the detainees. At the very least it means that some semblance of due process will be afforded them, but it is doubtful that they will be released anytime in the near future. There is considerable public pressure on the U.S. government to close down the Guantanamo Bay prison and give the detainees a hearing to determine whether they are legally held. The court held that Guantanamo cannot be all but two hours a day in small cells with no natural light or fresh air. Their meals are slipped through a slot in the door, and they are given little more than a single book and the Koran to occupy their time. Even their limited "recreation" time—which is sometimes provided in the middle of the night—generally takes place in single cell cages so that detainees can't physically interact with one another. None of these detainees have been allowed visits by family members, and very few have been able to make phone calls home.[3]

The future of the prison at Guantanamo Bay is uncertain. Public pressure is growing to close it down and provide a more humane form of detention and legal rights. Exactly what will become of these detainees remains in doubt. The home countries of some of them do not want them back, and it is difficult to find other countries willing to accept suspected terrorists. In many respects these are "men without a country," as the legal problems of releasing them are significant. Many wonder whether they have the requisite mental health to adjust to freedom after being incarcerated for more than six years in extremely difficult conditions.

◄ Expansion of Critical Perspective

Coverage of critical perspectives has been expanded throughout the text in order to provide a more even balance between mainstream and critical viewpoints.

► Maximum-Security Prisons

Expanded information on the history of supermax prisons, including a description of the federal penitentiary in Marion Illinois as the model for today's supermax prison, and a new CrossCurrents box that examines the possible reasons behind today's proliferation of supermax prisons.

Eye on Criminology

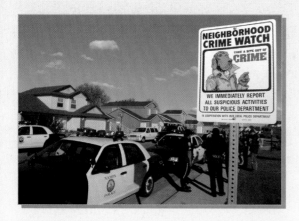

◀ Contemporary Models of Policing

Community policing, problem-oriented policing, and zero-tolerance policing are three organizational models that are challenging the traditional policing model, each suggesting a different level of interaction between the police and the public.

▼ New Challenges to Law Enforcement

Law enforcement constantly faces new challenges in the war on drugs, such as the steep rise in the usage and manufacture of methamphetamine.

▲ The Dark Figure of Crime

One of the difficulties inherent in attempting to measure crime is the fact that not all offenses are reported. The "dark figure of crime" is the name for all offenses that are committed but not reported. This text examines the reasons behind this phenomenon, an understanding of which is essential to an understanding of how to interpret crime statistics.

▶ Social Control and Social Justice

The criminal justice system seeks to maintain a balance between imposing order and preserving individual rights and freedoms. This text examines the issues that lawmakers, police officers, judges, and corrections officials face in striving to maintain this balance.

Key Features

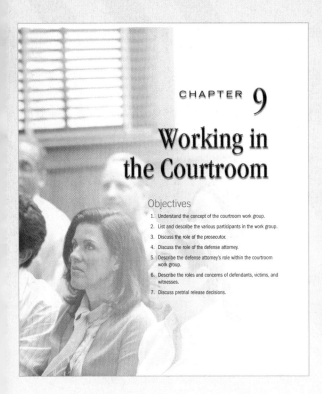

CHAPTER 9

Working in the Courtroom

Objectives

1. Understand the concept of the courtroom work group.
2. List and describe the various participants in the work group.
3. Discuss the role of the prosecutor.
4. Discuss the role of the defense attorney.
5. Describe the defense attorney's role within the courtroom work group.
6. Describe the roles and concerns of defendants, victims, and witnesses.
7. Discuss pretrial release decisions.

◀ **Chapter Objectives** at the beginning of each chapter highlight the important issues covered in the chapter.

▶ **CrossCurrents** boxes appear in every chapter and provide the student with concrete, real-life examples of how justice is administered in the United States. These examples highlight critical perspectives of the topics presented in the text, encouraging critical thinking and serving as the basis for exercises, class discussions, and projects.

9.2 *CrossCurrents*

How Much Justice Can You Afford?

Being accused of breaking the criminal law can be expensive. Even for those who are not indigent, the expense of hiring a lawyer can seem astronomical and can place severe limits on just how effective a defense can be pursued. Lawyers cost money. Just how much money can shock even the most cynical of us.

At the extreme end are the legal fees that resulted from the contingency fees claimed by some private attorneys who represented states in suits against the tobacco industry. According to an editorial in the *Rocky Mountain News*, "In Maryland . . . one attorney claimed his 25 percent fee entitled him to more than $1.1 billion of the state's $4.6 billion settlement. That came out to $30,000 for each hour he claimed to have worked." Of course, criminal defense attorneys do not receive that level of compensation, but even at $100 to $400 an hour, the expense of a full trial with all of its preparation can run into tens of thousands of dollars. Other expenses in addition to attorney's fees could include the following:

- Psychiatric evaluations
- Expert witnesses
- Polygraph tests
- Travel expenses for witnesses
- Expenses associated with the preparation of courtroom visual aids such as diagrams, maps, and charts

Expenses such as these can severely deplete the savings of most people and cause them to go into debt. However, when the client is indigent and has to rely on a public defender, the expenses for the case can quickly become limited. In Bend, Oregon, a defense attorney billed the state $1,500 for plane fare for a witness from England. After interviewing the woman, the attorney decided she would not help the case. After the newspaper reported the story, the attorney paid the expense out of his own pocket. When the cost of a criminal offense soars to more than $100,000, even prosperous individuals have difficulty achieving full justice. When court-appointed public defenders are compensated with as little as $65 per hour, it is understandable that each client is not going to be the beneficiary of an extensive defense.

Finally, what happens when the client runs out of money in the middle of the case or desires an appeal? Defense attorneys have the expenses of maintaining an office and paying secretaries and can afford to do only limited *pro bono* (non-paying) work. The result is that the quality of justice one receives can depend on how deep one's pockets are.

Think About It

1. Should attorneys' fees be capped?
2. Should the state provide the best attorneys available to defendants who cannot afford them?
3. Should all attorneys work for the state? Should they all be private?

Source: "Put Cap on Fees From State Lawsuits," *Rocky Mountain News*, February 17, 2003, http://rockymountainnews.com/drmn/opinion/article/0,1299,DRMN_38_1749940,00.html; Charles E. Beggs, "District Attorneys Question Spending," Associated Press/Worldlink.com, www.theworldlink.com/articles/2003/02/14/news/news03.txt.

6.1 FOCUS on ETHICS

IT'S ONLY MARIJUANA

As a city police officer, you are constantly called on to use your discretion in deciding when to invoke the criminal law. To be honest, you do not make an arrest every time you have the opportunity because you do not want to spend all your time processing petty cases.

One evening you and your partner are called to a fraternity house on the local university campus after neighbors complained of loud partying at 2 A.M. You are admitted into the house by an obviously intoxicated fraternity president, who says, "Come on in, officers. Look around all you want. There's nobody here but us chickens." As he giggles hysterically at his joke, you realize two things. First, he has given you permission to conduct a legal search of the house, and second, there is the unmistakable smell of marijuana emanating from both the fraternity house and its president.

As you and your partner conduct a cursory search, you easily find a water pipe, several half-full bags of high-grade marijuana, and about a dozen marijuana cigarettes that were tossed behind the couch, under chairs, and under the rug. You are about to cobble together all the marijuana to determine whether a felony case can be made when your partner takes you aside and informs you that his wife's little sister, a high school junior, is present but passed out cold in one of the bedrooms. Your partner says his wife would kill him if her sister gets arrested, and he begs you to let everyone go with just a warning. You are concerned about the number of youths who are engaged in underage drinking and drug use, but your partner is insistent and says, "Hey, it's only marijuana."

What Do You Do?

1. Tell your partner that "the law's the law" and arrest everyone in the house on whom you think you can make a good case, including his wife's little sister.
2. Warn everyone in the house to keep the noise down and that if the neighbors complain again and you have to come back, you will institute option 1.
3. Gather up all the marijuana and alcohol and flush them down the toilet while sending everyone home, thus ending the party.

◀ **Focus on Ethics** Scenarios ask students to make choices in ethically challenging situations that are routinely faced by criminal justice practitioners. These dilemmas are complex, requiring the student to consider the balance of values, procedures, and the law in arriving at solutions.

CASE IN POINT

TERRY V. OHIO

THE CASE	THE POINT
Terry v. Ohio, 392 U.S. 1, 88 S.Ct. 1868 (1968)	Police have the right to search suspects to ensure their own safety if they think that the suspects are armed.

A Cleveland police officer who was in an area that he had patrolled for many years saw two men, John Terry and a man surnamed Chilton, walking back and forth repeatedly in front of a store and pausing to stare in the window. The officer reported that they did this about 24 times. After each pass, they met and talked on a nearby street corner. They were joined by a third man, who left the group, but met up with them again a few blocks away from the store. The officer suspected the three men of inspecting the store in order to rob it later. The officer went up to the men and identified himself as a policeman. Suspicious, he checked Terry for weapons and felt a gun concealed in his coat pocket, and, in a further search, a gun in Chilton's pocket. Terry and Chilton were charged with and convicted of carrying concealed weapons. Terry appealed, the central argument in the case being whether police have the right to search people acting suspiciously if they believe a criminal offense is being planned. The Supreme Court upheld Terry's conviction.

◄ **Case in Point** boxes summarize major court cases that are the bedrock of the criminal justice for readers who do not have a legal education.

► **Review Questions** at the end of each chapter ask the student open-ended questions to help review the main ideas in the chapter.

REVIEW QUESTIONS

1. What two problems affect the image and functioning of the court?
2. Are courts purely a feature of European societies?
3. What system did Europeans use in lieu of violence to settle wrongs and disputes?
4. What was the first type of jury?
5. Why were the first grand juries and trial juries flawed?
6. What was the Court of the Star Chamber?
7. What served as the foundation for U.S. courts?
8. What is the only Bill of Rights item that is also included in all the state constitutions?
9. Name the three types of court jurisdiction.
10. What types of cases do federal courts hear? What levels constitute federal courts?
11. What is an inferior court?
12. Discuss the differences between trial courts of limited jurisdiction and trial courts of general jurisdiction.
13. What is the purpose of state intermediate courts of appeals? Do all states have them? Why or why not?
14. What do local and community courts do?

KEY TERMS

actual-seizure stop 214	reasonable stop standard 214	stop 213
grabbable area 210	reasonable suspicion 212	stop-and-frisk 214
legalistic style 194	seizure 213	watchman style 194
probable cause 207	service style 194	
racial profiling 205	show-of-authority stop 214	

◄ **Glossary** Key Terms identified in each chapter are defined in the text margin where the word appears and then again at the end of the book in an extensive glossary. This feature helps students identify the important terms and phrases used in the criminal justice system.

Supplements

The second edition of *Criminal Justice: Mainstream and CrossCurrents* is supported by a complete package of instructor and student resources.

INSTRUCTOR SUPPLEMENTS

Instructor's Resource CD (IM, PPT and TestGen)	0-13-504243-7
Instructor's Manual	0-13-504265-8
PowerPoint Presentations	0-13-504266-6
TestGen Computerized test Bank	0-13-504279-8
Test Item File for WebCT	0-13-504269-0
Test Item File for BlackBoard	0-13-504268-2

STUDENT SUPPLEMENTS

mycrimekit

MyCrimeKit, at www.mycrimekit.com, is an electronic study guide filled with chapter-specific media.

Other Student Supplements

Careers in Criminal Justice CD-ROM	0-13-119513-1
Ethics in Criminal Justice CD-ROM	0-13-204398-X
CJ Student Writer's Manual, 4/e	0-13-231876-8
CJ Dictionary	0-13-192132-0
CJ Systems Chart	0-13-170161-4

State-Specific Supplements

Arizona	0-13-225220-1
California	0-13-171954-8
Colorado	0-13-225219-8
Florida	0-13-171956-4
Illinois	0-13-171955-6
Indiana	0-13-170168-1
Maryland	0-13-170169-X
Massachusetts	0-13-170170-3
Michigan	0-13-114031-0
Nevada	0-13-225253-8
New York	0-13-171958-0
North Carolina	0-13-114030-2
Ohio	0-13-048312-5
Pennsylvania	0-13-170166-5
Texas	0-13-171957-2

Brief Contents

Contents

CHAPTER 2   The Nature and Measurement of Crime   41

CHAPTER 3   Theories of Crime   75

CHAPTER 4   Criminal Law   117

Part II   Enforcing the Law   151

Part III   The Role of the Courts   259

CHAPTER 8   History and Organization of Courts   261

CHAPTER 9   Working in the Courtroom   293

CHAPTER 10   The Disposition: Plea Bargaining, Trial, and Sentencing   325

Part V   Problems in the Crosscurrents   461

CHAPTER 14   Juvenile Delinquency and Juvenile Justice   463

CHAPTER 15   Victimless Crimes   499

Preface

Having taught the introduction to criminal justice course for many years using many books, I embarked on the journey to tell the story of criminal justice in a way that will help students grasp both the excitement of the field and the immense responsibility of serving the country and community. Although several fine books are already on the market, I have sought to provide a fresh approach to the teaching of the class, one that my students have found to be particularly relevant and interesting. To that end, I have written this book to reflect a theme that captures the excitement and potential of studying crime and the criminal justice system: the mainstream and crosscurrents.

The field of criminal justice is not a deep, still pond where one can see the bottom through crystal clear water. Rather, it is like a fast-moving stream with currents, crosscurrents, eddies, rapids, and hydraulics. Heraclitus' observation that one cannot step into the same stream twice is also true of the field of criminal justice, which can change just as dramatically. This book is intended to reflect those changes. Since the terrorist attacks of September 11, 2001, the field of criminal justice has become even more complex and challenging to study and to write about. The basic mission of some criminal justice agencies, such as the FBI, has been altered; a new cabinet-level department in the federal government, the Department of Homeland Security, has been created; and state and local criminal justice agencies now have the additional duties of being the first responders to terrorist attacks. Yet, in spite of this new and unprecedented threat, the fundamental job of the criminal justice system remains. Protecting individuals and property within the rule of law has always been a difficult mission. The delicate balance between public safety and individual rights and liberties is being stretched anew by the additional requirements of terrorist threats; the laws designed to address those threats, such as the USA Patriot Act; and the emotions of citizens, which range from legitimate concern to paranoia.

To develop a healthy perspective on the field of criminal justice, the student must have an appreciation for the history of social control, an understanding of the limits of science and the government, and a willingness to think critically about how the system might be reformed. It has been my experience that those who work in the criminal justice system often have practical ideas for its improvement. Many of my students and former students have been law enforcement officers, probation or parole officers, corrections workers, and rape crisis center employees. I continually learn from them about their successes, concerns, and frustrations of working in the criminal justice system. Having been there myself, I know that practical experience gives one a perspective that cannot be duplicated in the classroom. Therefore, this book is written with the view that the criminal justice system is not as neat and orderly as is often portrayed in textbooks. There are crosscurrents—extending the analogy—that must be put in context if we are to understand why people break the law and how the criminal justice system responds.

I hope that this fresh approach to criminal justice will find a space in criminal justice education. The book is designed to be, first and foremost, a mainstream text that covers the canon required in the first course that most criminal justice majors take. Additionally, the book serves as an introduction to the discipline for those students who have not yet chosen a major. In addition to these goals, the book offers a crosscurrents theme that extends the student's critical thinking skills beyond the memorization of dry facts and figures. The history and contemporary concerns of the discipline of criminal justice are among the most interesting and necessary fields of study offered at universities. It is somewhat regrettable that the employment opportunities in criminal justice are so plentiful: it would be better for us all if crime were less prevalent. Nevertheless, good people are needed to fill the many positions in the criminal justice system that require workers who can solve problems, act ethically, and be trusted to use power responsibly. To the extent that this book facilitates the development of those types of individuals, it will be judged a success. I remain committed to improving the integrated educational package that accompanies the book, and I eagerly solicit suggestions for improvement from both instructors and students. You can contact me at crosscurrent@comcast.net.

ORGANIZATION OF THE BOOK

The book is organized in a manner that introduces the student to the field of criminal justice, follows cases through the criminal justice process, and highlights some of the pressing unresolved issues and concerns that continue to challenge criminal justice practitioners. Part One features four chapters. The first chapter identifies some of the ways we understand crime, highlights the structure of the criminal justice system, and relates the system to other institutions that affect criminal justice. Chapter 2 deals with the history and issues concerning the measurement of crime and why this is such an important task. Chapter 3 reviews the major schools of criminology and the important biological, psychological, and sociological theories that attempt to explain crime. Chapter 4 provides an introduction to criminal law and identifies the different types of laws, sources of law, and features of what constitutes a crime.

Part Two is concerned with enforcing the law. Chapter 5 presents the history and organization of law enforcement. Chapter 6 highlights some of the issues and problems with controlling the police, and Chapter 7 considers some of the pressing issues facing contemporary law enforcement.

Part Three deals with the court system. Chapter 8 provides a history of how courts were developed and how they are currently organized. Chapter 9 covers the courtroom work group and explains the roles of the prosecutor, defense attorney, and judge. Chapter 10 covers plea bargaining, the trial, and sentencing.

Part Four deals with the correctional system. Chapter 11 covers the history of social control and capital punishment, and Chapter 12 deals with life in the contemporary prison. Chapter 13 explains how corrections are used in the community setting by covering probation, parole, and intermediate sanctions.

Finally, Part Five highlights some of the pressing problems that continue to challenge the criminal justice system. Chapter 14 deals with the special issues of juveniles who break the law and differentiates between the adult and juvenile criminal justice systems. Chapter 15 covers how personal and public values affect the criminal justice system, exploring how drug abuse, gambling, and sex work are sometimes considered criminal offenses and sometimes considered legitimate enterprises. Chapter 16 explores the future of criminal justice by contrasting the war-on-crime metaphor with the growing movement toward peacemaking criminology and restorative justice.

SUPPLEMENTS

This text is accompanied by an Instructor's Manual with Test Bank, TestGen, PowerPoints, Test Item File, Instructor Resource CD-ROM, and a MyCrimeKit website (www.mycrimekit.com).

To access supplementary materials online, instructors need to request an instructor access code. Go to www.pearsonhighered.com/irc where you can register for an instructor access code. Within 48 hours after registering you will receive a confirming e-mail including an instructor access code. Once you have received your code, go to the site and log on for full instructions on downloading the materials you wish to use.

Acknowledgments

I was lucky to have a set of reviewers who were not afraid to suggest ways that this edition could be improved. The following reviewers gave generously of their time and expertise, and I am grateful for their many wise suggestions:

Richard R. Becker
Lone Star College, Tomball

Ronald G. Burns
Texas Christian University

Scott E. Culhane
University of Wyoming

Richard D. Hartley
University of Texas at San Antonio

Ronnie Jones
Southeastern Louisiana University and Tulane University

Tina Lee
University of Tennessee at Martin

Robert Mutchnick
Indiana University of Pennsylvania

Mark Szolyga
Sanford-Brown College

Tracy F. Tolbert
California State University at Long Beach

I'm also indebted to the reviewers for the first edition of the text, and I have tried to maintain the high quality and readability that their input allowed me to obtain.

Frank Afflito
The University of Memphis, Memphis, TN

Jerry Armor
Calhoun County Community College, Decatur, AL

Beth Bailey
Charleston Southern University, Charleston, SC

Paul Becker
University of Dayton, Dayton, OH

Robert Bing
University of Texas, Arlington, TX

James Black
University of Tennessee, Knoxville, TN

Steve Brandl
University of Wisconsin-Milwaukee

Susan Brinkley
The University of Tampa, Tampa, FL

Steve Brodt
Ball State, Muncie, IN

Ronald Burns
Texas Christian University, Ft. Worth, TX

Kim Davies
Augusta State University, Augusta, GA

Alex delCarmen
University of Texas, Arlington, TX

Holly Dersham-Bruce
Dawson Community College, Glendive, MT

Dana DeWitt
Chadron State College, Chadron, NE

John Doherty
Marist College, Poughkeepsie, NY

Vicky Dorworth
Montgomery College, Rockville, MD

Dave Graff
Kent State University-Tuscarawas Campus, New Philadelphia, OH

Robert Griffiths
Suffolk County Community College, Selden, NY

Doris Hall
California State University, Bakersfield, CA

William Harver
Widener University, Chester, PA

Bill Head
Indiana University, Bloomington, IN

Chris Hertig
York College, York, PA

Denise Huggins
*University of Arkansas,
Fayetteville, AR*

Art Jipson
University of Dayton, Dayton, OH

Paul Katsampes
*Metropolitan State College of Denver,
Denver, CO*

Bill Kelly
Auburn University, Auburn, AL

Curt Kuball
Reedley College, Reedley, CA

Steve Light
SUNY, Plattsburgh, NY

Vivian Lord
*University of North Carolina,
Charlotte, NC*

Jeff Magers
*Stephen F. Austin State University,
Nacogdoches, TX*

A. L. Marstellar
Drury College, Springfield, MO

William McCamey
*Western Illinois University,
Macomb, IL*

David McElreath
Washburn University, Topeka, KS

Susan McGuire
San Jacinto College, Houston, TX

Kevin Meehan
*California State University,
Fullerton, CA*

Kenneth Mentor
*New Mexico State University, Las
Cruces, NM*

Patrick Mueller
*Stephen F. Austin State University,
Nacogdoches, TX*

Donna Nicholson
*Manchester Community College,
Manchester, CT*

Emmanuel Onyeozili
*University of Maryland-Eastern Shore,
Princess Ann, MD*

Michael Polakowski
University of Arizona, Tucson, AZ

John Race
*University of Pittsburgh,
Pittsburgh, PA*

Jeff Ross
*University of Baltimore,
Baltimore, MD*

Joe Schafer
*Southern Illinois University,
Carbondale, IL*

Barbara Sims
*Penn State University, University
Park, PA*

Jeffrey Spears
*University of North Carolina at
Wilmington, NC*

David Streater
*Catawba Valley Community College,
Hickory, NC*

Susette Talarico
University of Georgia, Athens, GA

Carol Thompson
*Texas Christian University,
Ft. Worth, TX*

Kim Tobin
Westfield State College, Westfield, MA

Kevin Walsh
*Texas A&M University, College
Station, TX*

Jeremy Wilson
*Catawba Valley Community College,
Hickory, NC*

Dawn Young
*Bossier Parish Community College,
Bossier, LA*

The professionals at Pearson Education have been delightful to work with. My editor, Tim Peyton, has been instrumental in helping me refine the focus of the book to appeal to a broad range of students and professors. His wise counsel and sound judgment mean a lot to me, and I will be forever indebted for his commitment to this project. My development editor, Elisa Rogers, has also provided extremely valuable advice. Additionally, her attention to detail has ensured that this text is both accurate and informative. Adam Kloza also deserves recognition for his tireless commitment to the marketing aspects of the project. Finally, the editor-in-chief, Vernon Anthony, has been a tireless supporter of my work over the years, and I appreciate it.

I'm also indebted to my colleagues at a University of West Georgia who have supported me and provided valuable insights into how this text could be improved. I have received advice from David Jenks, Cathi Jenks, Mike Johnson, Chris Williams, and Jane McCandless.

Finally, the person most responsible for the success of the first edition of this book and this revision is Amy Hembree. She has taught me everything I know about writing, but not everything she knows. I still have so much to learn from her.

About the Author

John Randolph Fuller has been a professor of criminology at the University of West Georgia for more than 27 years. He brings both an applied and theoretical background to his scholarship and has been recognized by his students and peers as an outstanding teacher and scholar. In 1991, the university student government association voted him College of Arts and Sciences faculty member of the year. In 2002, the student honors council recognized him as honors professor of the year. In 2006, he was selected for the distinguished scholar award, as well as being designated as a governor's teaching fellow in recognition of his commitment to students and innovative teaching techniques.

Dr. Fuller served as a probation and parole officer for the Florida Probation and Parole Commission in Broward County, Florida, where he managed a caseload of more than 100 felons. In addition, he served as a criminal justice planner for the Palm Beach County metropolitan criminal justice planning unit. In this capacity, he worked with every criminal justice agency in a three-county area and wrote grants for the Law-Enforcement Assistance Administration that funneled more than $1 million into local criminal justice agencies. By working directly with offenders as a probation and parole officer and with criminal justice administrators as a criminal justice planner, Dr. Fuller gained significant insights that inform his writing about the criminal justice system and have aided him in identifying both the mainstream practices and the crosscurrent issues that continue to prevent the achievement of justice for all.

Dr. Fuller has authored and edited numerous journal articles, chapters, and books on criminal justice, criminology, and juvenile delinquency. In 2009, he published *Juvenile Delinquency: Mainstream and Crosscurrents*, which extends the theme of this book into the juvenile justice system. The first edition of *Criminal Justice: Mainstream Crosscurrents* won the prestigious TEXTY award from The Text and Academic Authors Association.

PART ONE
Crime
Problems, Measurement, Theories, and Law

Chapter 1	*The Problem of Social Control*	
Chapter 2	*The Nature and Measurement of Crime*	
Chapter 3	*Theories of Crime*	
Chapter 4	*Criminal Law*	

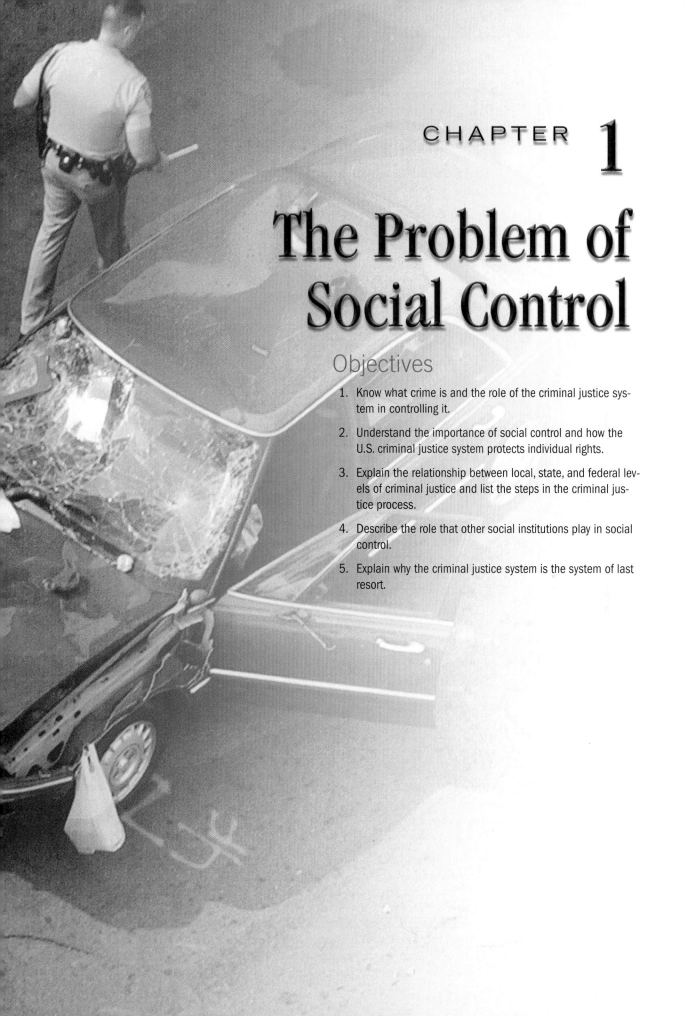

The Problem of Social Control

Objectives

1. Know what crime is and the role of the criminal justice system in controlling it.

2. Understand the importance of social control and how the U.S. criminal justice system protects individual rights.

3. Explain the relationship between local, state, and federal levels of criminal justice and list the steps in the criminal justice process.

4. Describe the role that other social institutions play in social control.

5. Explain why the criminal justice system is the system of last resort.

The academic discipline of criminal justice is an important and timely area of study in the contemporary world. It has taken on new meaning since the terrorist events of September 11, 2001, capturing the imagination of many students who otherwise would not consider criminal justice as a major field of study. Criminal justice programs across the country are growing in enrollment, and the demand for increased resources and faculty is at an all-time high. Criminal justice has become an important field of study for three main reasons:

- **Criminal justice deals with important issues**   The problems of maintaining order under the rule of law have long been sensitive issues that require an informed electorate and dedicated public servants. Protecting the public and depriving offenders of their liberty, and sometimes even their lives, are serious endeavors that require personnel who understand the implications of enforcing the law in fair and transparent way. Without a criminal justice system that has the support of the people, the nation would sink into chaos and violence. An important and delicate balance must be maintained between crafting and enforcing laws and preserving the liberties of citizens.

- **Criminal justice is an interesting field of study**   Because of the popularity of television programs depicting criminal justice issues, many students come to college with preconceived ideas about how justice should be achieved. Although many of their ideas are based on the fictions of popular entertainment, this does not diminish their interest. Criminal justice is an important field of study because it can correct some of the myths and misconceptions that students acquire from the media.

- **Criminal justice needs trained and skilled employees**   The final reason that criminal justice is such an important area of study is that there is a need for intelligent and level-headed individuals to fill important positions in the field. Criminal justice has drastically changed since September 11, 2001, requiring workers to have greater technological skills, good judgment, and a high degree of ethical integrity. Many criminal justice jobs have been upgraded to the point that they require a better educated and more socially sensitive worker. The professionalization of the criminal justice field is ongoing and will require college students to specialize in the criminal justice discipline rather than other majors.

The U.S. criminal justice system is undergoing rapid social change and requires new employees to be open to new ways of doing things and willing to challenge the status quo when it is ineffective. As the baby boom generation of Americans moves toward retirement, there are tremendous opportunities in the criminal justice system for a new generation to achieve leadership positions and chart a new course for the nation.

WHAT IS CRIME?

Crime can be described as an action taken by a person or a group of people that violates the rules of a given society to the point that someone is harmed or that society's interests are harmed. Most people envision crime as fairly straightforward, often sordid affairs, such as robbery, rape, and murder. For example:

- On July 22, 1991, police in Milwaukee, Wisconsin, found a man in handcuffs wandering on the street. The man claimed that he had escaped from another man who was trying to kill him and led the officers to an apartment littered with bones. Police arrested the apartment's owner, Jeffrey Dahmer, and began an investigation the next day. Clad in biohazard suits, officers removed evidence from the dwelling, including skulls found in the refrigerator, the freezer, and a filing cabinet; three headless torsos stashed in a 55-gallon drum; miscellaneous entrails and decomposing limbs; and photos of decaying corpses. The various

Rosa Parks is a hero of the civil rights movement. She showed that unjust laws can be changed by principled nonviolent protest.

Source: *Corbis/Bettmann*

body parts amounted to the remains of 11 people. Investigators later determined that Dahmer had killed 17 men and boys in a spree that had begun in 1978, during his first summer out of high school, with the murder of a young male hitchhiker.[1]

Many offenses do not involve the harming of other people, but the breaking of laws set up to keep a society in a certain order. Although order is a good thing to have in a society, sometimes the order itself is questionable.

- In December 1955, a young, black seamstress for a Montgomery, Alabama, department store got on a city bus and sat down in the "colored" section. When the "whites only" section filled up, a white man was left standing. The bus driver demanded that the woman, Rosa Parks, and three other patrons in the colored section give up their seats for the white man. Of the four black patrons, Parks was the only one who would not move. She was arrested; four days later she was found guilty of disorderly conduct, and the Montgomery bus boycott began. One year later, Montgomery's segregation of bus service was declared unconstitutional.[2]

Other offenses, such as espionage crimes, threaten not only a society's laws, but also its political stability. How these offenses are dealt with, however, is usually a result of the political mood of the times. In the last 10 years, those who have committed treasonous crimes have been sent to prison. The 1950s were a much different era, however.

- In 1950 the FBI arrested Julius Rosenberg, an electrical engineer who had worked for the U.S. Army during World War II, and his wife, Ethel. The couple was indicted for conspiracy to provide classified military information to the Soviet Union. In their 1951 trial, the government charged that in 1944 and 1945 the Rosenbergs had persuaded Ethel's brother, an employee at the Los Alamos atomic bomb project, to provide them and another person with top-secret data on nuclear weapons. The primary evidence against the Rosenbergs came from Ethel's brother and his wife. Both Julius and Ethel were found guilty and sentenced to death; their co-defendants received prison terms. Many people complained that the fervently anti-Communist political climate of the day made a fair trial impossible, and the Rosenbergs claimed innocence throughout the whole ordeal. Despite many appeals and pleas for clemency, the Rosenbergs were executed on June 19, 1953, becoming the first U.S. civilians to suffer the death penalty for espionage.[3]

Is crime the breaking of a moral principle? If so, whose morals? Is crime the breaking of a law? What if the law is immoral? Is crime the breaking of political laws or mores? What if those laws result in large numbers of people being imprisoned or even executed? Questions such as these make talking rationally about crime difficult. The personal nature of crime compounds this problem. Crime can be scary. Crime can hurt people. In a heterogeneous society such as the 21st-century United States, even the concept of *rational* is up for grabs. What is rational to one person might not be rational to another, and everyone has his or her own solution to crime based on what he or she considers rational.

Taking these factors into account, a student of criminal justice can begin to understand how the outwardly simple progression of crime → arrest → trial → punishment really represents a myriad of subtleties and complications. Still, as individuals, we hold tightly to the perspectives that support our personal notions of fairness, justice, and goodness, even when we know those notions might be grounded in the privilege of middle-class values concerning race, class, and gender. However, crime is a messy human problem that does not respond to simple, mechanical, or straightforward solutions.

By way of example, let me tell you about my neighbor, who is a pilot for a major airline. When he is at a gathering and someone becomes aware of his occupation, he seldom has to defend his area of expertise. No one tells him how to land his 747 at New York City's JFK International Airport; they do not offer advice on what to do in the event of a water landing, nor do they attempt to explain how to properly adjust the wing flaps. For the most part, they talk about how fascinating it must be to fly for a living and then try to find another topic of conversation. By contrast, when I am at such gatherings and people find out that I am a criminal justice professor, I get an earful of opinions about how to deal with criminals. Unfortunately, these opinions are uninformed by the research done in criminology and often reflect personal biases and ideas borrowed from talk radio and cable television programs that spin news to support political agendas. I smile politely when individuals say, "We should cut off thieves' hands like they do in the Mideast," or, "We should lock drug users up for the rest of their lives." I used to argue with them, but I seldom changed anyone's point of view.

To be fair, whereas flying a 747 is beyond the experience of most individuals, being a victim of a crime is not. Therefore, almost everyone has passionate opinions about what to do with the criminal justice system. Although I envy my neighbor the pilot for his unchallenged expertise, I would not trade occupations. Twenty-five years of studying crime and working with the criminal justice system has taught me one important lesson: the truth is not always clear. Truth is a shade of gray. So even though people sometimes have opinions about crime that I find ridiculous, I treat them with respect because I am uncertain about my own conclusions. I have strong opinions about crime and justice, but I try to keep an open mind because new research, changing political atmospheres, or my own personal experiences might affect the way I understand criminal justice issues.

The study of crime and the criminal justice system is not an exact science. No one has a lock on the truth, and each of us needs to be humble in how we assert our views. We need to use what C. Wright Mills called the **sociological imagination.**[4] Mills encouraged us to step back from our personal experiences and examine issues apart from our social location. For example, could a father of a murdered daughter reasonably sit on a jury of the accused killer? Of course not. Likewise, according to Mills, each of us should attempt to look at crime and criminal justice policy from a neutral and objective position. The key word here is *attempt*. It can be argued that no one can truly be neutral and objective when considering social issues. We must be honest and

sociological imagination
The idea that we must look beyond the obvious to evaluate how our social location influences how we perceive society.

acknowledge that our social class, race, gender, age, and other personal attributes affect our thinking. Only by explicitly stating our social location can we, and those we seek to convince, put our opinions in context and evaluate them.

Objectivity and neutrality are worthy goals, but beware of those who claim to have achieved them. Often these individuals represent the status quo. Their unexamined views might reflect the conventional wisdom of their particular occupation, religion, or social class.

The Approach of This Book

This book is designed with a special purpose: to make students think. Rather than presenting a selection of facts, dates, and names, this text requires critical thinking from the reader. Criminal justice as a discipline and as a system is open to many interpretations and viewpoints. Students who work through this text will realize that much of what passes for conventional wisdom is actually open to debate. This should not be surprising, given the problems of the criminal justice system and the difficulty of preventing crime and rehabilitating offenders. However, the limitations of the criminal justice system, as well as its successes, make criminal justice worthy of serious study. This book is intended for students who desire to learn, serve society, and make a difference in the lives of others.

This book has two primary and complementary purposes in delivering the information that an introductory criminal justice class requires: to present the mainstream approach that is found in most traditional criminal justice texts, as well as a crosscurrent approach that fosters critical thinking. Specifically, these two approaches can be explained this way:

- **The mainstream**   In order to prepare students for careers in the criminal justice system and to fully participate as citizens in United States, this text covers the traditional issues and concerns of the discipline of criminal justice. Students will find chapters on the major components of the criminal justice system—police, courts, and corrections—as well as a chapter on the juvenile justice system. These topics are covered in a comprehensive, balanced, and practical manner.

- **The crosscurrents**   In this text, *crosscurrents* are the controversial problems and solutions that run throughout the mainstream criminal justice system (see Figure 1-1). Although the mission of the criminal justice system—to deal with crime—is clear, this mission can be approached in many ways, none of them all "right" or all "wrong." The U.S. criminal justice system accomplishes some goals well; other approaches need improvement. Sometimes the criminal justice system seems less than fair to victims, offenders, and the accused. As a bureaucracy, it can be slow and inefficient. Sometimes injustice is done. The crosscurrents approach of this text addresses these issues and explores possible solutions. These issues can be controversial and political, and often there is no clear answer. But there are solutions, many of which are as complex as the problems they address, and reaching these solutions requires clear and critical thinking. This text addresses the crosscurrents of the criminal justice system primarily through boxes that highlight ethics, court cases, and criminal justice issues. These boxes often ask questions that do not have easy answers and are designed to explore the differences in opinion of students. An example of some of the issues that stimulate controversy are capital punishment, gun control, rehabilitation, police use of force, mandatory sentencing, and treating juveniles as adults. This text examines each of these issues, as well as many others, with the aim of allowing students to develop their own informed opinions and ideas.

Rigorous examination of the criminal justice system informed by research is the best way to understand and improve the system. One of the themes of this book is that

Figure 1-1   Criminal Justice: The Mainstream and Crosscurrents If you imagine criminal justice as a river, then traditional approaches to criminal justice problems can be considered the mainstream, while the controversial problems and solutions are the crosscurrents.

what people think they know about crime is often based on incomplete and inaccurate information. This is the case for several reasons:

1. **We tend to personalize.** We have experiences that are real and immediate, and we expect everyone else to be as concerned as we are. When crime affects us, we want others to be just as outraged and insulted. Relatively minor offenses against us are serious matters in our lives and inform our opinions. Nevertheless, the experiences of crimes done to us cannot reliably be extrapolated to all others.

2. **All crime is local crime.** One of the by-products of improved communications has been the perceived immediacy of crime.[5] In the past, we learned of crime from the newspaper and our local television stations. Now, cable television and the Internet connect us in such a way that we envision incidents that happen thousands of miles away as being a local danger. For example, the school violence that happened at Littleton, Colorado, was so thoroughly covered in the media that the tragedy began to seem like a local danger. Many schools now have emergency plans to respond to violent situations and practice

Police officers serve a wide range of functions in society besides arresting suspects. Here, a New York City police officer helps a woman hanging from a 16th-floor building balcony. Officers later rescued the woman, who had been on the ledge for about an hour.

Source: Corbis/Reuters America LLC

them much like fire drills. Although the threat of school violence is real, the likelihood of the threat is often exaggerated.

3. **Crime statistics do not tell the whole story.**   Measuring crime is a tricky business. Applying those measurements to our own situations can be even trickier. Crime is not evenly distributed over time and across jurisdictions. Not all of us are equally susceptible to crime or equally affected by it. We sometimes base our fears on a misreading of the actual threat of crime.

4. **Sometimes prejudices affect our thinking.**   Throughout history, social class and racism have influenced our thinking about crime. Control of the "dangerous classes" has sometimes created more injustices than it has solved.[6]

5. **We have a limited idea of the dangers to our safety.**   The barely visible crimes of corporations and governments often are not considered as serious as street crime, even though they might do more actual harm to society and individuals.[7] A good example of this is the Enron scandal in the early 2000s, in which corporate executives were convicted of various financial offenses, including fraud and conspiracy, that adversely affected the lives and finances of thousands of the company's employees.[8]

Crime in the United States

All crime is not created equal. Many offenses go undetected, and their harm to society is not generally perceived. Some offenses are just a step across the line of good and effective business practices and are considered the price we pay for a market economy. An example of this would be insider trading. Other offenses are sensationalized by the media and given such vast resources in their detection and prosecution that they distort the perception of the amount and seriousness of crime in society. Finally, there is the problem of street crime, of which everyone is afraid.

These broad categories of crime illustrate how complex and differentiated the issue really is. Making broad general statements about crime is difficult because so many behaviors are considered criminal offenses. It is useful, then, to distinguish general types of crime that excite popular imagination. In the next chapter, we will consider types of crime in a more detailed and legalistic manner. Keep in mind that the categories here are intended as a brief and introductory overview with the goal of showing that crime is a complex and confusing phenomenon.

STREET CRIME   Sensationalized crimes are fascinating, but the public's apprehensions are mostly focused on **street crime**.[9] Rape, assault, and robbery are real fears for many people, and most people take precautions to limit their chances of being victimized. However, street crime includes a wide variety of acts in both public and private spaces, including interpersonal violence and property crime (see Figure 1-2). These are the offenses most often included in measurements of crime. Homicide, rape, assault, larceny, arson, breaking and entering, and motor vehicle theft are offenses measured by the *Uniform Crime Reports* and the ones that are envisioned in discussions about the crime rate.

The effect of rape, assault, and especially homicide can alter how a person and his or her loved ones relate to others and can require many years of recovery, so a healthy fear of street crime is wise. For example, when searching for the car in a dark parking lot, we might look over our shoulder to assess whether a possible assailant is lurking in the shadows. However, street crime is still relatively rare. Most of us go about our daily lives without encountering danger, and we do not need to carry a weapon or to distrust people most of the time. In fact, most people feel safe most of the time.[10] Some studies have found that those with the least likelihood of being victimized fear crime the most. Elderly citizens demonstrate the greatest fear of street crime, yet they are the least likely to encounter it. Conversely, young males are the most victimized, yet they do not have a great fear of crime. In some ways, this disjuncture is understandable, but it also illustrates just how distorted our concept of crime has become.[11]

The crime rate is not always correlated with the public perception of the level of crime. During the 1990s, people felt that crime was one of the most important problems

street crime

Small-scale, person offenses such as single-victim homicide, rape, robbery, assault, burglary, and vandalism.

Figure 1-2   Percentage of Victimizations by Type of Offense, 2006.

Source: Bureau of Justice Statistics, "Criminal Victimization in the United States, Statistical Tables," www.ojp.usdoj.gov/bjs/pub/pdf/cvus06.pdf.

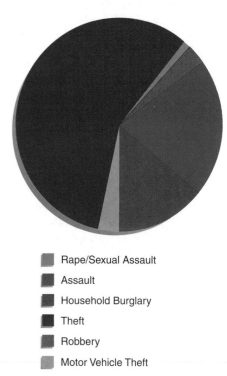

■ Rape/Sexual Assault

■ Assault

■ Household Burglary

■ Theft

■ Robbery

■ Motor Vehicle Theft

in society even as the crime rate declined.[12] Because the public is so concerned about street crime, many of our criminal justice resources are devoted to its prevention and prosecution. (See Crosscurrents 1.1 to learn more about how urban legends relate to our anxiety about street crime.) This emphasis on street crime is both understandable and problematic. We need to believe that the criminal justice system is doing all that can be done to protect innocent people from predatory criminals. To have communities in which individuals feel safe in public spaces, the police must engage in preventive patrol and make arrests when laws are violated. Although the merits of symbolic reassurance can be argued, clearly the public demands that the police "do something" to prevent crime and apprehend lawbreakers.[13] According to some criminologists, the aggressive control of the homeless is necessary for meaningful, safe communities. People who feel safe on the streets are engaged in public interaction to a greater degree, and this, in turn, means that the streets are populated by more and more lawful citizens.[14]

The emphasis on street crime is problematic because it drains resources from the prevention of other types of crime. Jeffrey Reiman contended that corporate crime is really much more harmful to society than street crime. He added that the preoccupation of the criminal justice system with street crime is fueled by a racist and class-conscious society. Although street crime is significant to individuals, corporate crime is much more damaging to society as a whole. Reiman argued that individuals with the most money and power define crime and use the criminal justice system to protect their own interests.[15]

CORPORATE CRIME, WHITE-COLLAR CRIME, AND ORGANIZED CRIME   Sometimes criminal offenders are conventional in all other aspects of their lives, and it is difficult to envision them as lawbreakers. Because harmful behaviors are not always defined as crimes, envisioning how otherwise honorable citizens can be considered criminals is sometimes difficult. So-called pillars of society known for their charity, public service, and conventional behavior are occasionally the biggest crooks. Some offenders do a great deal of harm to others even while they appear to be doing good deeds.

Corporate crime involves breaking laws in the otherwise lawful pursuit of profit. For example, an industrial company that does not follow safety standards in disposing of its industrial waste can do irreparable harm to the environment and to the health of thousands of people. Although the intent of the company's officers may be simply to maximize profits and not to hurt anyone, the result can be devastating. What is good for the company's shareholders might harm those who live in the community where the factory operates. The company's officers did not physically rob or

corporate crime
Offenses committed by the officers of a corporation who use that corporation's business to pursue illegal activity in the name of the corporation.

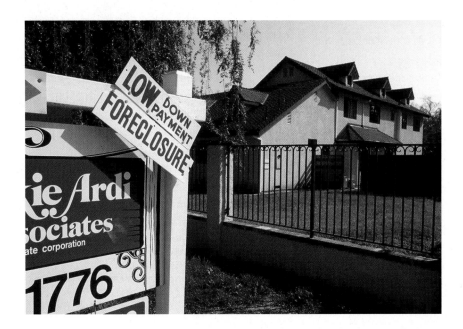

A real estate sign in Los Angeles, California, advertises a foreclosed home for sale. During the subprime mortgage crisis, some lenders were accused of conducting unethical lending practices with unqualified home buyers or for misrepresenting their financial conditions to stockholders.
Source: Michael Newman / PhotoEdit Inc.

CrossCurrents

Scary Stories

What do these crime warnings have in common?

- "Groups of teenagers have been caught . . . playing a new and dangerous game called Spunkball. Spunkball consists of a group of teens in a car pulling up to a stop light, and looking around for another car stopped nearby with an open window. When one is spotted, the teens shout, "Spunkball," and throw a gasoline-soaked rag wrapped in aluminum foil through the open window. On the outside of the foil is attached a small fire cracker, with the fuse lit. When the fire cracker explodes, it shreds the foil, and the rag is ignited, causing a large flame that may catch the interior of the car on fire."

- "Imagine: You walk across the parking lot, unlock your car and get inside. . . . You look into the rear-view window to back out of your parking space and you notice a piece of paper, some sort of advertisement stuck to your rear window. So, [you] jump out of your vehicle to remove that paper . . . when you reach the back of your car, that is when the car-jackers jump out of nowhere . . . jump into your car and take off."

- "[A woman] heard a crying baby on her porch the night before last and called the police. The police told her, "Whatever you do, do NOT open the door." . . . [A serial killer has been using a recorded baby's cry] to coax women out of their homes thinking that someone dropped off a baby. . . . Please pass this on and do not open the door for a crying baby."[1]

What these crime warnings have in common is that they are not true. These warnings, all collected off the Internet, came from e-mails that have been making the rounds of the nation's inboxes for several years. Although all of the reported incidents are possible, so far no police agency has reported any similar incidents, much less a series of them. E-mail has contributed to the popularity of "crime-warning urban legends" because forwarding these stories in an e-mail to a chain of friends is easy, free, and often anonymous. Crime-warning urban legends have grown so popular that Internet sites such as Snopes.com have been set up to debunk them.

Although many urban legends are fun or interesting, crime-warning urban legends reflect the public's real fear of street crime. Most crime-warning urban legends are about some kind of random victimization, such as rape, murder, or assault, often by serial killers, teenagers, or gangs. One of the first and most popular warnings to be distributed by e-mail warned motorists driving at night not to flash their headlights at other cars that had their headlights off. Those cars, according to the legend, might be full of gang members who, as part of an initiation, would chase down and assault or kill the well-meaning motorist. This urban legend combines a number of fears that many people have about street crime: gangs, violence, that nighttime is when the worst crimes happen, and that "do-gooders" needlessly put themselves at risk by trying to help strangers.

The incidents in crime-warning urban legends never happen to anyone traceable or specific. The victim is always a friend of a friend or a completely fictional person. Although street crime is real and everyone should take some preventive measures for personal safety, crime-warning urban legends can raise social anxiety about street crime to unrealistic levels by appealing to emotions rather than logic. According to one study, "irrational fears often propagate in the form of informal contemporary legends that use as experts only the ubiquitous 'friend of a friend.'"[2]

Crime-warning urban legends might serve much the same purpose that ghost stories do: to entertain us, to warn us of the unknown and remind us to be careful, and to help us confront our fears and anxieties. However, police agencies have reported that particularly potent or new urban legends have actually sparked "copycat crimes," hurt local businesses, or overloaded emergency lines with frightened callers who are worried that something like what is described in the urban legend might happen.[3]

Think About It

1. Which crime-warning urban legends have you heard or read that you at first thought were true?
2. Have you ever passed along a crime-warning urban legend?
3. If you receive a crime warning in your e-mail, do you check to see whether it is true?
4. Crime-warning urban legends can be considered as crosscurrents to mainstream criminal justice because they report incidents that never happened. However, do you think any of these urban legends are possible?

[1]All anecdotes collected from Snopes, "Crime Warnings," www.snopes.com/crime/warnings/warnings.asp.

[2]Chip Heath, Chris Bell, and Emily Sternberg, "Emotional Selection in Memes: The Case of Urban Legends," *Journal of Personality and Social Psychology* 81, no. 6 (December 2001): 1040.

[3]Mary Sanchez, "E-Mailed Urban Legends Do Harm to Plaza," *Kansas City Star*, metropolitan edition, March 1, 2000; "'Kidnap' Warning E-Mail Revealed as Hoax," *Evening Gazette* (Teesside, Middlesbrough, England), final edition, January 17, 2004; Eric J. S. Townsend, "Flier on Your Car? Don't Worry, Really," *Greensboro (NC) News-Record*, November 26, 2005.

assault the citizens, but the damage done to the community water supply can be immensely more harmful. Corporations can hurt individuals in an infinite variety of ways. Yet when we look at the law and the response by the criminal justice system, we see that street crime is treated with greater penalties.[16]

Sometimes the terms *corporate crime* and *white-collar crime* are used interchangeably, but there are important distinctions between them.[17] Corporate crime involves the purposeful commission or omission of acts by individuals acting as representatives of a business. Their goal is to make money for the business, and the offenses they commit are related to making the company profitable. White-collar crime, by contrast, is not necessarily aimed at the consumer. White-collar crime can involve employees harming the corporation. The treasurer who embezzles money and the office manager who makes excessive long-distance phone calls are harming the company.

Organized crime is committed by individuals working together systematically to break the law for profit. Organized crime in the United States can bring to mind the Mafia or similar ethnically based organizations. These organizations, which first gained notoriety during the **Prohibition** years, have been made famous in books, films, and television programs. However, many groups of people are engaged in organized crime.[18] Asian, Hispanic, and Russian peoples, former prison inmates, and a host of other groups engage in organized-crime activities. As in Prohibition, the **war on drugs** has provided opportunities and incentives for a wide variety of criminal organizations. Organized crime is different from corporate and white-collar crime in the way it interacts with the criminal justice system and the harm it does to society. Typical activities of organized-crime groups include narcotics trafficking, prostitution rings, and murders for hire.

SENSATIONALIZED CRIME   Much of what we think we know about crime comes to us from the media. Television news programs and dramas, newspapers, and reality-based television programs such as *COPS* tend to distort and sensationalize the picture of crime in the United States. There is an old newsroom saying: "If it bleeds, it leads." On one hand, we depend on the media to give us the truth in the news, but we must realize that the media have an agenda of their own that is concerned with selling news and advertising.[19] Although many journalists try to report the news fairly, the decision of exactly what is newsworthy is made at an executive level and often on grounds of how well it will sell.

Cases such as the O. J. Simpson trial and the JonBenet Ramsey murder have received an excessive amount of coverage far beyond their real news value. In many ways, cases such as these have transcended being news to become entertainment. These cases actually affected only a few individuals in a direct manner and normally would have been reported only in the local media, but because of some sensational or unusual feature, they became national news. The sensational treatment of a few high-profile offenses affects our perception of crime. When some local offenses become nationally reported to such an extreme extent, they take on the appearance that everyone, everywhere, should be concerned about their safety. For example, school shootings in Colorado, Tennessee, Oregon, Mississippi, Virginia, and Illinois have caused schools across the nation to prepare for potential violence. However, the truth is that children are safer in school than in their homes and always have been.

We must be careful when considering how the media report crime. The good news is that media outlets report the truth. The bad news is that often they do not report the whole truth. They do not put the news of crime in context for the viewer. In many ways, the media distort the context to make the news more immediate and personal. Certain offenses are selected for their sensational nature and made into national issues. Why was the Natalee Holloway case so widely and intensely reported? When we consider the thousands of other cases each year in which people mysteriously disappear, we must ask why this case, which took place in Aruba, interests the media so much. At the time of her disappearance, Holloway was a young blonde woman on a high school graduation trip. The case involves wealthy young people going to parties and clubs in an exotic tropical locale. The ability of the media to print photographs of Holloway and the young men suspected of being involved in her disappearance help keep the case in the spotlight.[20]

organized crime
Illegal activity by a group that is set up specifically to break the law in pursuit of profit.

Prohibition
The period from January 29, 1920, to December 5, 1933, during which the manufacture, transportation, and sale of alcoholic beverages was made illegal in the United States by the Eighteenth Amendment.

war on drugs
A policy aimed at reducing the sale and use of illegal drugs.

SOCIAL CONTROL AND SOCIAL JUSTICE

socialization

A process by which individuals acquire a personal identity and learn the norms, values, behavior, and social skills appropriate to their society.

Imagine how chaotic society would be if there were no rules and everyone did whatever they wanted. Meaningful communities would be impossible. To live with other people, individuals must curb their appetites, ambitions, and desires. The problems of maintaining individual freedoms within a group setting are the concerns of our systems of social control. The institutions in our society—religion, family, school, and community—all have, among other missions, the goals of socializing individuals into the group.

The importance of **socialization** cannot be overstated. People who are successfully socialized take their place in society as productive members and leaders. Socialization does not mean that new members simply replicate the patterns of the past, but rather that they understand the traditions and principles on which their society is based and adapt those values to emerging circumstances. Socialization is an imperfect process. Not all of us are socialized to the same degree, and in many societies, especially democracies, social value is attributed to being a maverick, rebel, or outsider.[21] These themes or roles often are played out in behavior such as eccentric apparel, tattoos, body piercing, or to a more extreme extent, crime. More than a simple quest for identity, breaking the law is often a calculated method to gain material possessions or demonstrate dominance.[22] Those who are inadequately socialized not only fail to contribute to society, but also can become so problematic that society believes they must be confined, exiled, or, in extremely rare cases, eliminated. How these decisions are made is the purview of the criminal justice system.

The amazing feature that sets the U.S. criminal justice system apart from those of many other countries is the way individual rights are protected as an integral part of the functioning of law enforcement. In the short run, it might be a lot easier, considerably more efficient, and a good bit less expensive to allow the criminal justice system to enforce the law without the restraints imposed by constitutional rights. Yet these restraints are precisely what make the United States such a beacon of freedom around the world. By protecting the rights of marginal individuals such as aliens, the impoverished, criminals, and even terrorists, the United States demonstrates a high level of respect for both people and laws. In the long run, this example of democracy in action shows the world that the response of a government to the problems of crime can be both dynamic and compassionate.

The criminal justice system must maintain a delicate balance between imposing order and preserving individual rights. This task, which is extremely difficult in the best of times, becomes even more problematic in times of war and terrorism. Yet it would be a grave mistake to think of these issues as mutually exclusive. In other words, keeping citizens safe does not require that they lose their constitutional rights. The successful creation and nurturing of meaningful communities require that the government serve citizens' interests by finding methods to control crime without allowing law enforcement agencies to turn the country into a police state. Achieving this delicate balance is part of the Herculean task of the criminal justice system.

As we construct new responses to the threats of terrorism, this task will challenge lawmakers, police officers, judges, corrections officials, and the rest of us to develop a new appreciation for the complexities and ambiguities of crime control in the 21st century. Criminal justice workers can see through the romantic and frivolous veneer of pundits who contend that waging a war on crime is the only way to ensure public safety. Although criminal behavior must be addressed within the rule of law, many practitioners recognize that more fundamental questions must be considered. These questions about the nature of justice in the United States include concerns of racial prejudice, economic inequality, and differential access to the decision-making processes in all aspects of society.

THE CRIMINAL JUSTICE SYSTEM

When the law is broken, the criminal justice system must respond in the name of society. As citizens in a democratic government, we elect officials to provide these services. The criminal justice system comprises a variety of agencies from different levels of government, each with a mission to deal with some aspect of crime. Although some of these agencies appear to overlap in duties, and the system appears to be inefficient and cumbersome, the system chugs along, processing a vast number of cases. However, the criminal justice system is criticized for being ineffective and failing to produce the justice that many people expect. To understand the system's inefficiencies, we must first realize that it is not exactly a system.

First, the system is not confined to one level of government. The criminal justice system spans the range from local governments to the federal government. The lines of authority and distinction between agencies is not always clear, and in some cases must be negotiated according to the politics of the case. For example, tension exists between federal agencies such as the Federal Bureau of Investigation (FBI) and local law enforcement agencies. Depending on the circumstances of the case, investigators must decide whether federal or state laws have been violated and which agency has the primary responsibility for investigation. Although interagency cooperation is the stated norm, conflict does arise. (See Crosscurrents 1.2 to learn more about interagency cooperation.) Also, problems between different components of the criminal justice system might exist. The goals and missions of law enforcement are not always viewed as identical to those of the judicial system or the prison. Individual criminal justice practitioners might believe that other agencies are working against them. For example, the police sometimes believe that district attorneys and judges are working against them by procuring probation, plea bargains, and light sentences for offenders. Or prison officials might think that lawmakers who legislate tougher, longer sentencing are overcrowding the prisons.

Now let's examine how the criminal justice system is set up.

Levels of Government

One of the most perplexing features of the criminal justice system is that responsibilities are spread unevenly across different levels of government.[23] Law enforcement, courts, and corrections tasks are divided differently across the local, state, and federal branches of government. Additionally, an inherent overlap exists between jurisdictions in terms of appeal and oversight functions. This overlap is inevitable given the checks-and-balances aspect of the Constitution. Although this redundancy makes the criminal justice system inefficient, the goal is to protect citizens against overzealous police officers and prosecutors.[24]

The picture of the criminal justice system that emerges is complex, overlapping, and difficult to predict. Each level of government is responsible for some aspect of law enforcement, courts, and corrections and is authorized to enforce and apply the law within narrow, often vague, parameters. Also, criminal justice agencies at each level of government answer to the public through unequal voting pressures. For example, voting your local sheriff out of office is much easier than getting rid of an FBI director whose agency has blown a case in your community.

LOCAL-LEVEL CRIMINAL JUSTICE   Each state has a different configuration of political jurisdictions. Cities, counties (or parishes), and multijurisdictional agencies are vested with responsibility in varying ways depending on the state law. What is most striking about how the criminal justice system is organized is the fact that most of the authority for law enforcement lies at the local level. Many people misunderstand the relationship among the three levels of police, believing that local police answer to state police, who, in turn, answer to federal police. This is not true. Generally, police departments answer to themselves, their communities, and the courts.[25]

The chief law enforcement officer for each county is the locally elected **sheriff.** There are more than 3000 sheriff's departments in the United States.[26] The sheriff's office is responsible for a variety of functions that go beyond traditional law enforcement.

Serving **warrants,** providing **bailiffs** to the courts, and administering the local jail are all responsibilities of the sheriff's office. In addition, the sheriff provides law enforcement to unincorporated areas of the county or parish.

sheriff
From the English words shire and reeve ("king's agent"); an official of a county or parish who primarily carries out judicial duties.

warrant
A judicial writ that authorizes a law officer to perform a specified act required for the administration of justice, such as an arrest or search.

bailiff
An officer of the court responsible for executing writs and processes, making arrests, and keeping order in the court.

CrossCurrents

Why They Can't Just All Get Along: A Comparison of Federal, State, and Local Law Enforcement

One of the most intractable problems in U.S. law enforcement is getting agencies to work together. Although we call it a criminal justice "system," historic, structural, personal, and jurisdictional issues prevent or impede criminal justice agencies from conducting a seamless transfer of information and resources. The various law enforcement agencies—local, state, and federal—are all subject to individual agency cultures, rather than one national law enforcement culture affecting individual law enforcement agencies. This philosophy had an especially tragic effect after September 11, 2001, when investigators discovered that the major federal law enforcement and investigation agencies all held separate pieces of the terrorist plot but had not communicated them to one another. Later, National Security Adviser Condoleezza Rice told the 9/11 Commission, "Integrating our counterterrorism and regional strategies was the most difficult and the most important aspect of the new strategy to get right."[1]

The solution to this problem might be to create a large, federally mandated law enforcement agency, but this is unlikely to happen. Although other countries have this type of law enforcement structure, the United States has as one of its intrinsic values the idea that whenever possible, government control should be vested at the level that is closest to the people.

According to Sunil B. Desai, a U.S. Marine Corps major who served on the Council on Foreign Relations, four factors challenge the transition to greater interagency cooperation:

- There is no formal, comprehensive concept of coordination for either routine or crisis situations.
- There is no independent authority to develop and train personnel in interagency cooperation.
- Individual agencies organize their policies and operations differently.
- Personnel policies focus on developing personnel who are primarily dedicated to the individual agency rather than the community of agencies.[2]

Therefore, our law enforcement system will long be challenged to find ways to get federal, state, and local agencies to work together. The following table illustrates how the agencies are organized and funded and what they do.

Comparison of Law Enforcement Levels of Jurisdiction

	Federal	State	Local
Types of Agencies	FBI Immigration and Customs Enforcement Secret Service	State highway patrol State investigative agencies	Municipal police departments County sheriff's offices
Mandate for Enforcing Laws	Offenses on federal property and military reservations Interstate crime	Interstate highway systems Offenses of local and state government officials	State statutes within local jurisdictions
Funding	Federal income tax	State income tax Sales tax User taxes (driver's license, license plate fees, etc.)	Sales tax Property tax

As we can see from the preceding chart, law enforcement agencies at different levels of government have contrasting resources, funding authorities, and mandates. Cooperation between these agencies is always a goal, but their differences are grounded in legal mandates. Also, agency cultures dictate that there will always be some degree of conflict, competition, and distrust between law enforcement agencies operating from different levels of government.

Think About It

1. What would you do to encourage law enforcement agencies to work together?
2. Should there be a national police force?

[1]Sunil B. Desai, "Solving the Interagency Puzzle," *Policy Review* (February 1, 2005): 57–71.

[2]Ibid.

Incorporated cities usually have their own police departments. The city police are responsible only for the jurisdiction of the city and do not provide the range of services that the sheriff's office does. Because their jurisdictions overlap to a large degree, the municipal police and the sheriff's office cooperate at many levels. In some large metropolitan areas, the law enforcement functions of the city and county are combined to save the costs of duplicate services.

Some court functions are vested at the local level and vary widely according to how each state organizes its governmental functions. For the most part, the city and county deal with **misdemeanor** violations of the law. As opposed to **felony** cases that are punishable by more than one year in a state prison, misdemeanor cases are punishable by up to one year in a local jail.

JAILS   County jails serve an important and underappreciated function by holding two basic types of inmates.[27] The first consists of those who are awaiting trial and unable to make bond or get released on their own recognizance. These inmates include both those who have committed very minor offenses and some very dangerous individuals. This makes the job of the local jail extremely difficult. Jails seldom have the resources to protect both the public and all of the inmates. Many jails are overcrowded, dangerous places, even though most of the inmates are not violent people.[28] The second type of inmate consists of those who have been sentenced to a year or less of incarceration. Often these inmates are transferred to a **county stockade** to separate them from those awaiting trial. In many counties, these inmates can be seen on work crews picking up trash on the highways.

One distressing aspect of the local jail in many jurisdictions is the number of state inmates who serve all or part of their sentences in local jails. Because of overcrowding in many state prison systems, the flow of inmates backs up into the local jails, where inmates must serve their time while waiting for bed space in a state prison.[29] Although local jails are paid by the state for housing the sentenced inmates, this situation causes security problems for the jail and limits opportunities to provide any sort of rehabilitative programs at the local level.

STATE-LEVEL CRIMINAL JUSTICE   Law enforcement functions at the state level are usually confined to specialized missions. State highway patrol units maintain safety on the state roads and interstate highways and may also issue driver's licenses. Most states also have an agency responsible for investigating offenses that transcend the local level of jurisdiction. For example, the Georgia Bureau of Investigation (GBI) investigates accusations of political corruption and assists local law enforcement agencies with cross-jurisdictional issues. States also have crime laboratories that examine evidence from cases across the state. Each state has its own criminal code, and some states have special agencies that deal with violations of alcoholic beverage or fish and wildlife laws.

Although most law enforcement in the criminal justice system is done at the local level, most of the action for the courts is at the state level. Most states divide their courts into multicounty judicial circuits that rule on state law. Homicide, rape, robbery, and most other offenses, unless committed under special circumstances (for example, on federal land or when perpetrators cross state lines), are tried in the state court system.[30] The court function at the state level is an important part of the criminal justice process. Judges, prosecutors, and public defenders are paid by state budgets and answer to voters at the **circuit** level rather than at the city or county level. Some court officials, such as attorneys general and state supreme court judges, answer to voters in statewide elections.

States are also responsible for most prison inmates. Each state, depending on size, has an extended prison system that can house thousands of inmates. Still, overcrowding in many state prison systems has resulted in a backup of inmates into local facilities and also in pressure for parole boards to release more inmates to make room for more recent offenders.[31] States also have extensive probation and parole agencies to deal with many thousands more offenders.

FEDERAL-LEVEL CRIMINAL JUSTICE   Law enforcement functions at the federal level include a wide range of agencies responsible for enforcing federal laws and assisting state and local governments (see Figure 1-3 for the organization of the U.S. Department of Justice, the primary law enforcement arm of the federal government). The best-known federal agency is the FBI, followed closely by the U.S. Secret Service.

misdemeanor
A lesser offense punishable by a fine and/or jail time for up to one year.

felony
An offense punishable by a sentence of more than a year in state or federal prison and sometimes by death.

county stockade
A component of a county corrections system that usually holds offenders who have already been sentenced.

circuit
A judicial district established within a state judicial system or the federal judicial system.

Department of Justice

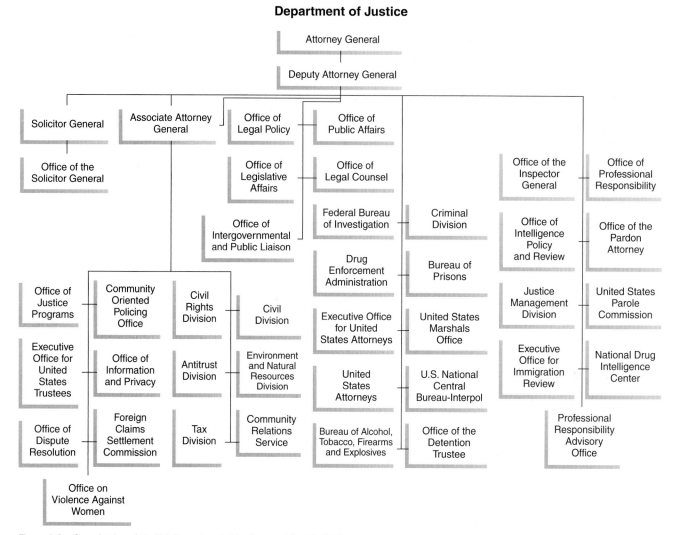

Figure 1-3   **Organization of the U.S. Department of Justice as of April 1, 2008.**

Source: U.S. Department of Justice Organization as of April 1, 2008 http://www.usdoj.gov/dojorg.gif.

However, the work of these agencies is often at odds with public perception. The romanticized popular conception of the FBI and the Secret Service leads many criminal justice students to desire a career in federal law enforcement. In truth, the work of these agencies is often not as exciting as that of local law enforcement agencies. Much of the work of federal law enforcement is concerned with white-collar crime. Thus the tasks of investigation are often more suited to the accountant than the detective. As part of the Department of the Treasury, the Secret Service spends more time and resources dealing with counterfeiting than protecting the president. For a brief description of the major federal law enforcement agencies, see Criminal Justice Reference 1.1.

The federal court system parallels the state system and processes offenders who break federal laws. In addition, there is a system of appellate courts at which cases from either the state or federal courts can be appealed. The U.S. Supreme Court is the final court of appeal, but it deals with only a few cases. The federal government has its own prison system for those convicted of federal offenses. In the past, federal prisons were considered safer than many state systems because they housed mainly white-collar offenders. However, with the war on drugs in recent decades, the federal prison system now receives many inmates with extensive histories of drug-related offenses, some of which are connected to the violent drug trade. The federal government

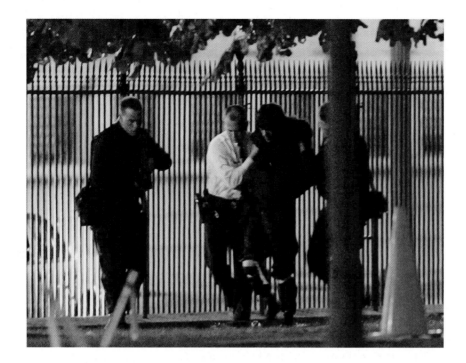

The Secret Service is responsible for protecting the White House, as well as the president and visiting officials. Here, the Secret Service arrests an intruder who jumped the White House fence.
Source: AP Wide World Photos

also has probation and parole agencies that supervise federal offenders in the community.

The Criminal Justice Process

With an appreciation of how complex the criminal justice system is, we now turn to a discussion of how cases are processed. It is clear to most observers that only a small percentage of offenses result in someone going to prison. The criminal justice system is frustrating not only for the general public, but also for those who work in the system, as well as for victims, offenders, and their respective families. By examining the process that cases undergo in the criminal justice system and identifying why cases exit the system before they reach what the public believes is the desired result, we can see why the system generates so much annoyance. The system is close to being overloaded. An even slightly larger percentage of cases would be nearly impossible for the system to process in a fair and legal manner given the resources currently available. Therefore, police officers, prosecutors, judges, and corrections officials use **discretion** to decide which cases are pushed further into the criminal justice system and which ones are kicked out.

It is useful to envision the criminal justice system as a large funnel in which cases move downward toward their final disposition (see Figure 1-4). The problem with the funnel is that it is too small to hold all the cases, and so a considerable amount of leakage occurs.

OFFENSES   At the wide mouth of the funnel are all of the offenses committed, both known and unknown. This includes every instance of murder, rape, burglary, insurance fraud, shoplifting, and car theft. It includes all of the harms done to society and individuals that are covered by the criminal law. It includes all of the acts that can be defined as crime whether they have been reported or not. We have no idea of the total number of criminal offenses. Many, maybe even most, crimes are never reported, or if they are, they are handled informally and never make it into the official crime reporting systems. Criminologists call these unreported acts the **dark figure of crime.** We know it is large but have no idea exactly how many or what percentage of criminal behavior it actually constitutes. We will discuss the dark figure of crime further in Chapter 2.

discretion
The power of a judge, public official, or law enforcement officer to make decisions on issues within legal guidelines.

dark figure of crime
A metaphor that describes crime that is unreported and never quantified.

1.1   CRIMINAL JUSTICE REFERENCE

Federal Law Enforcement Agencies

Bureau of Alcohol, Tobacco, Firearms, and Explosives (ATF)

The Bureau of Alcohol, Tobacco, Firearms, and Explosives is a principal law enforcement agency within the U.S. Department of Justice that enforces federal criminal laws, regulates the firearms and explosives industries, and investigates cases of arson and illegal trafficking of alcohol and tobacco products.

U.S. Customs and Border Protection (CBP)

U.S. Customs and Border Protection manages, controls, and protects the borders of the United States at and between official ports of entry. Located within the Department of Homeland Security, CBP combines the inspectional workforces and border authorities of U.S. Customs, U.S. Immigration, the Animal and Plant Health Inspection Service, and the U.S. Border Patrol.

Drug Enforcement Administration (DEA)

The Drug Enforcement Administration, which is organized within the Department of Justice, enforces the controlled-substance laws and regulations of the United States. The agency also manages a national drug intelligence program, seizes assets used in drug trafficking, and enforces laws pertaining to legally produced controlled substances.

Federal Bureau of Investigation (FBI)

The principal investigative arm of the Department of Justice, the FBI investigates major violent and financial crime and interstate crime and assists in terrorism investigations. Areas of investigation include computer-related crimes, cases of public corruption, hate crime, white-collar crime, and organized crime.

U.S. Immigration and Customs Enforcement (ICE)

Immigration and Customs Enforcement is the largest investigative branch of the Department of Homeland Security. The agency was created in March 2003 by combining the law enforcement arms of the former Immigration and Naturalization Service and the former U.S. Customs Service.

U.S. Marshals Service (Federal Marshals)

Created in 1789, the U.S. Marshals Service is a federal police agency that protects federal judges and courts and ensures the effective operation of the judicial system. The agency also carries out fugitive investigations, custody and transportation of federal prisoners, security for government witnesses, asset seizures, and serving court documents. There is one U.S. Marshal for each of the 94 federal judicial districts.

U.S. Secret Service

The U.S. Secret Service protects the president of the United States, as well as other U.S. government officials and visiting officials. The agency also investigates financial fraud and counterfeiting.

OFFENSES KNOWN TO THE POLICE   A bit lower and at a point narrower in the funnel are crimes known to the police. This is the first real, and somewhat imperfect, measure of crime. These are the behaviors that the police include in their reports and are officially measured. However, individual police officers or police administrators can exercise considerable discretion in determining just how a behavior will be categorized for reporting purposes. Because we have no idea what percentage of crime the police actually know about, this measure may be a better indication of what the police do with the offenses they know about than it is of the crime rate.

INVESTIGATION   In April 1983, the pelvic portion of a female torso was found on the banks of the Mississippi River near Davenport, Iowa. In an autopsy, the pathologist estimated that the victim was between 18 and 40 years old, had probably given birth, and likely had been dismembered with a chainsaw. A forensic anthropologist estimated the victim to be between 4 feet, 7 inches and 5 feet, 9 inches tall, 27 to 49 years old, and weighing between 125 and 145 pounds.[32] With the help of techniques considered cutting-edge

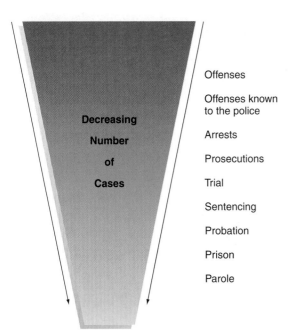

Figure 1-4 **The Funnel Effect**

This figure represents the pattern of how cases move through the criminal justice system. The actual number of cases varies by jurisdiction, severity, and annual occurrence. At each point along the way, cases drop out of the system. Only a small percentage of offenders ends up in prison.

Decreasing

Number

of

Cases

Offenses

Offenses known
to the police

Arrests

Prosecutions

Trial

Sentencing

Probation

Prison

Parole

at the time, including DNA evidence, investigators matched the woman's characteristics to those of Joyce Klindt, a Davenport woman who had gone missing the month before. Eventually, her husband admitted murdering her, cutting her up with a chainsaw, and dumping her remains in the river.[33] The case has been cited as a classic example of good investigation and set precedents for the use of scientific evidence in court.[34]

Although the police do their best to solve crimes, such success stories are not the norm. In probing the 1996 murder of JonBenet Ramsey, a local police detective was accused of making several crucial mistakes in the investigation.[35] To this day, no one has been charged with the child's murder. In other, less sensational cases, police investigate to the best of their abilities, but must deal with limited resources, poor physical evidence, a cold trail, or just bad luck.

Typically, police gather tissue samples and fingerprints, talk with witnesses and victims, and examine police records of potential suspects. In some cases, officers must first secure a warrant before performing a search (see Case in Point 1.1). Sometimes the evidence is gathered quickly, and a suspect is apprehended at once. A large number of cases, however, languish, only to be solved years later or not at all.

ARRESTS   Once the police become aware that a criminal offense has been committed, they look for the person(s) responsible, and if they have enough evidence, they make an arrest. It should come as no surprise that the police do not make an arrest for every offense they detect. In fact, **clearance rates** can vary widely depending on the type of offense and the priorities of the law enforcement agency. For instance, most driving under the influence (DUI) offenses go undetected, but proactive police practices such as sobriety checkpoints can greatly increase police arrest statistics. Arrests represent only a small picture of what the police do, but they are an important measure in our crime funnel because they provide a good indication of what will happen in the rest of the criminal justice system. Arrests provide the rest of the system with the cases it must handle. Police may continue to question a suspect after an arrest but must respect the suspect's constitutional rights (see Case in Point 1.2).

BOOKING   Booking occurs at the police station, where a suspect's name, age, and address are recorded, as well as information on the time, place, and reason for arrest. Usually, a photograph and fingerprints are taken, and the suspect's clothing and personal effects are stored. The suspect usually is placed in a holding cell until he or she can be questioned further.

clearance rate
The number of offenses that have been solved by the police.

1.1 CASE IN POINT

MAPP V. OHIO

THE CASE	THE POINT
Mapp v. Ohio, 367 U.S. 1081, 81 S.Ct. 1684 (1961)	*Illegally seized evidence is inadmissible in state criminal courts.*

In 1957, Cleveland, Ohio, police suspected that a person who was wanted for questioning in a bombing was at the home of a woman, Dollree Mapp. When police went to the home, Mapp would not let them in and requested that the officers get a warrant. While the officers were gone, Mapp called her attorney over. When the officers returned, they waved a piece of paper saying that it was a warrant, but would not show it to either Mapp or her attorney. Mapp grabbed the paper and shoved it into her clothing. It was retrieved by an officer who also handcuffed Mapp. The officers found no bomb materials in the house, but did find a trunk in the basement full of what the officers said were pornographic materials. Mapp was arrested and later convicted of possessing pornography and sentenced to seven years in prison. Mapp appealed to the Supreme Court, claiming that the police had no right to search her house because no warrant was ever issued. The decision established that the exclusionary rule, in which illegally seized evidence is inadmissible in court, is extended to state criminal cases.

CHARGES FILED BY THE PROSECUTOR   Of all the arrests made by the police, only a small percentage result in a person being charged with a crime by the prosecutor and funneled deeper into the criminal justice system. The discretion used by the prosecutor to decide which cases to eliminate from the criminal justice system depends on a number of factors. The first factor is resources. As at every other point in the criminal justice system, the decision to prosecute depends on personnel, budget, space, and agency priorities. The prosecutor might have too many other cases that are deemed more important and so will simply decline to pursue certain ones. The prosecutor might decide that the police have not presented sufficient evidence to ensure successful prosecution

1.2 CASE IN POINT

ESCOBEDO V. ILLINOIS

THE CASE	THE POINT
Escobedo v. Illinois, 378 U.S. 478, 84 S.Ct. 1758 (1964)	*Upon being accused of murder, a suspect is entitled to counsel and the right to remain silent.*

On the night of January 19, 1960, the brother-in-law of Michael Escobedo was shot and killed. Police arrested Escobedo at 2:30 A.M. without a warrant. Escobedo was interrogated but did not make a statement, and he was released that afternoon after his lawyer obtained a state court writ of *habeas corpus*. Eleven days later, Escobedo was arrested again after an acquaintance (who was also later indicted for the murder) told police that Escobedo had shot the man. At the police station, Escobedo asked several times to see his lawyer, who was in the building and was being refused access to his client. Escobedo was not advised of his right to remain silent and after a lengthy interrogation gave a damaging statement that was admitted at trial. Escobedo was convicted and appealed to the state supreme court, which affirmed the conviction. The U.S. Supreme Court reversed the decision on the grounds that Escobedo had been denied counsel after repeatedly requesting it. The court also distinguished between police investigation and police accusation. When Escobedo was arrested, police were merely investigating a murder. This later shifted to the police accusing Escobedo of committing the murder, a situation in which a suspect is entitled to counsel and the right to remain silent.

of the case. Additionally, the prosecutor might discover that the police made procedural errors in the arrest that would be brought out by the defense attorney and result in a dismissal. Finally, the prosecutor might have personal or agency priorities concerning what types of cases will be pressed. Political corruption cases might be encouraged or discouraged depending on the party affiliation of the state attorney versus the defendant.

GRAND JURY   Grand juries are formed to decide whether enough evidence exists to justify an indictment and trial. Grand jurors are usually selected from the same pool of people that provides trial jurors and are sworn in by a court. The prosecutor bringing the case presents the jurors with the charges or a **bill of indictment** and introduces the evidence. Grand jury proceedings are secret, and witnesses can be called to testify against the suspect without the suspect or the suspect's witnesses being present. Indicted suspects can sometimes later obtain transcripts of grand jury proceedings.

A grand jury returns a **true bill** if it decides to indict. If not, a **no-bill** is returned. A prosecutor may still file charges against a suspect in the event of a no-bill. Prosecutors can bring further evidence to the same jury or present the original evidence to a second jury. In some jurisdictions, prosecutors sometimes choose not to use a grand jury and instead file a criminal complaint.

Grand juries usually sit for longer than trial juries. Federal grand juries sit about 18 months, but can have their terms extended in six-month increments up to 36 months. State grand juries sit for shorter terms, from a month up to a year. Unlike trial jurors, grand jurors do not convene daily, but may meet once a week or once a month.

INITIAL APPEARANCE, PRELIMINARY HEARING, AND ARRAIGNMENT   After arrest, suspects must be brought before a judge within a reasonable time for an *initial appearance*. Here, the defendant is formally charged with a crime and responds by pleading guilty, not guilty, or *nolo contendere* (no contest). Defendants are also informed of their rights to bail and to an attorney. Those charged with a misdemeanor may enter a plea immediately. If the plea is *guilty*, the judge may impose the sentence. However, defendants charged with felonies, which are more serious, usually do not enter pleas at this time. Also, they probably have not been able to consult an attorney before the hearing. At this point, the defendant is scheduled for a *preliminary hearing*, also known as the *preliminary examination* or *probable cause hearing*. Here, the prosecutor presents enough evidence to establish probable cause, or a *prima facie* **case.** The exception is when defendants have been indicted by grand juries, in which probable cause has already been established. In this case, the defendant's first court appearance is at an **arraignment** similar to the initial appearance.

BAIL/BAIL BONDING   The word *bail* comes from the Old French word *bailler*, which means "to hand over" or "to entrust." Bail is money paid to the court to ensure that a defendant who is released from jail will appear in court. Usually, the amount of bail is based on the gravity of the offense and how likely the defendant is to flee. Sometimes, despite a high amount of bail, the defendant runs anyway. For example, in January 2003, Andrew Luster, age 39, was supposed to appear in court to defend himself on 87 criminal counts that included rape and poisoning. The primary charges against Luster were that he drugged women at his home, then raped them. Luster, who was heir to a massive cosmetics fortune, skipped his $1 million bail and fled the country.[36] A California jury convicted Luster *in absentia*, and he was sentenced to 124 years in prison.[37] Six months later, a bounty hunter caught Luster in Mexico.

One alternative to bail is release on one's own recognizance (ROR), in which the defendant pays no money and promises to appear in court when required. Defendants with strong community ties, such as a steady job and family, might qualify for such release. Defendants who do not qualify for release on their own recognizance or cannot pay the bail amount are held in jail. Other defendants who are believed to be serious threats to the community or to an individual (such as a witness) or are very likely to flee are held in **preventive detention.**

---

bill of indictment
A declaration of the charges against an accused person that is presented to a grand jury to determine whether enough evidence exists for an indictment.

true bill
The decision of a grand jury that sufficient evidence exists to indict an accused person.

no-bill
The decision of a grand jury not to indict an accused person as a result of insufficient evidence.

nolo contendere
Latin for "I do not wish to contend." The defendant neither admits nor denies committing the offense, but agrees to be punished as if guilty.

prima facie case
A case established by evidence sufficient enough to establish the fact in question unless it is rebutted.

arraignment
A court appearance in which the defendant is formally charged with a crime and asked to respond by pleading guilty, not guilty, or nolo contendere.

preventive detention
The jailing of a defendant awaiting trial, usually in order to protect an individual or the public.

In U.S. custody, Andrew Luster arrives in the United States to begin serving his 124-year prison sentence. Convicted of rape, Luster skipped his $1 million bail and fled to Mexico, where he remained on the run for five months.

Source: *Corbis/Reuters America LLC*

Bail bonding refers to the money posted by a bonding company for a defendant who cannot afford bail. The defendant pays a percentage of the bail amount to the bonding company as a fee, and the company agrees to be responsible to the court for the entire amount of the defendant's bail. If the defendant does not show up for court, the judge can issue a warrant for his or her arrest and threaten to keep the money. The bonding company then will track down the defendant and bring him or her back, by force if necessary.

PLEA BARGAINING   In 2002, one of the world's largest long-distance telephone companies, WorldCom, announced that its accounting practices had been fraudulent. The company declared bankruptcy, wiping out its shareholders' stocks and its employees'

Former WorldCom executive Bernard Ebbers (center) leaves the federal building in custody in March 2004 in New York City. Ebbers was later convicted of perpetrating an accounting fraud that led to one of the largest bankruptcies in U.S. history.

Source: *Stephen Chernin / Getty Images*

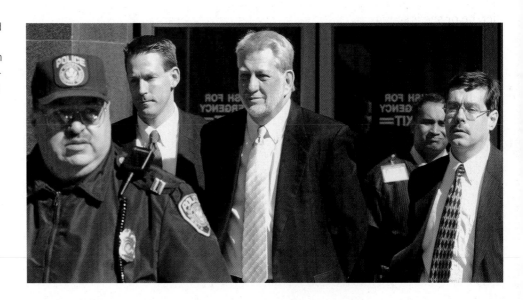

jobs, sparking an investigation. Two former company executives, David Myers and Scott Sullivan, were accused of hiding more than $7 billion in expenses by manipulating the company's books. Eventually, they struck plea bargains with prosecutors in order to help convict former company chairman Bernard Ebbers of even greater financial wrongdoing. In 2005, Sullivan was sentenced to five years in prison; Myers, a year and one day. Ebbers, then age 65, was sentenced to 25 years in prison. Sullivan and Myers received relatively light sentences because they cooperated with prosecutors to convict Ebbers.[38]

One point in the criminal justice system that results in the most attrition of cases is the plea-bargaining stage. There are many reasons for plea bargaining, and they are not all for the benefit of the defendant.[39] The state has a lot to gain by disposing of cases quickly and efficiently. Prosecutors might decide that the case is weak and, rather than risking dismissal, opt for a negotiated plea that results in some type of punishment. Plea bargaining is necessary and often desirable. Sometimes, as in the case of WorldCom, prosecutors accept a plea bargain from a lesser defendant who offers to help with the case to ensure conviction of a defendant accused of more serious offenses. If law enforcement is doing a good job, then most defendants are actually guilty, and the prosecutors have reliable evidence that is likely to stand up in court. Defense attorneys who see no realistic hope of having their clients acquitted are keenly interested in limiting the sentence imposed by the court. There is no need for a trial, and by plea bargaining, the defense can strike a deal for a less-than-maximum sentence. Although plea bargaining is not popular with the public, for the criminal justice system (and possibly less so for some defendants) it is a reasonable and inevitable practice.

TRIAL   Few cases actually make it to the trial phase of the criminal justice process. Of the cases that go to trial, only a small percentage end up in guilty verdicts that allow further processing of the case. Some defendants are acquitted or found not guilty. Sometimes the case is dismissed because the prosecution is unable to present a viable case against the defendant. Sometimes the case is dismissed because of prosecutorial misconduct in which the rights of the defendant were violated. However, the trial is what most people think about when they imagine justice in the United States. However, the media image of life in U.S. courtrooms is highly distorted. Last-minute confessions on the witness stand by distraught individuals who are pressured or tricked by a crafty lawyer do not represent what actually happens in the courtroom. Most of the decisions are made behind the scenes, and excitement and drama in the courtroom are actually quite rare.

SENTENCING   Once a defendant has been determined guilty either by plea or by verdict, he or she is sentenced by the judge at a sentencing hearing. When the judge has discretion, he or she considers the circumstances of the offense and the attitude of the offender, as well as the prosecutor's recommendation and the probation office's **presentence report.** Depending on the offense, a sentence can range from a fine and community service to several years in prison, life imprisonment, or death. Usually, the law limits the judge to a few options.

Sentencing guidelines are rules for deciding sentences and are set down by a commission. The guidelines classify offenses and offenders and prescribe punishments. According to the U.S. Sentencing Commission, the sentencing guidelines for federal offenses were created to ensure that "similar offenders of similar crimes would receive similar sentences."[40] *Determinate* or *fixed sentencing* limits the judge's discretion in much the same way and is also intended to limit sentencing disparity.

Indeterminate sentencing specifies a range of time that the offender must serve before parole can be granted (for example, a sentence of "10 years to life" for first-degree murder). This shifts the discretion for determining the offender's release from the judge to the parole board.

presentence report

An account prepared by a probation officer that assists the sentencing court in deciding an appropriate sentence for a convicted defendant.

In a capital case, in which the choice for the offender is either life in prison without parole or the death penalty, a jury chooses the sentence.

PROBATION   Probation is a common disposition for criminal cases. It occurs either after the trial as part of the sentence handed down by the judge to offenders who were found guilty by a jury, or instead of a trial as part of a plea-bargaining agreement. Probation is a form of community corrections and is appropriate for offenders who are not an immediate risk to the community. However, because of prison overcrowding, many offenders who might otherwise have been incarcerated are being placed on probation.[41]

The main advantage of probation is cost. Probationers live at home, go to work, support their families, and pay taxes. The state pays probation officers to supervise the offenders, but with caseloads of between 100 and 400 offenders per officer, depending on the jurisdiction and level of supervision, the cost is much less expensive than incarceration. Additionally, many communities now charge cost-of-supervision fees to the offenders to help pay for this expense. The actual level of supervision can vary widely, from reporting to the probation officer once a month all the way up to taking weekly drug tests, participating in **electronic monitoring,** and reporting on a daily basis. See Focus on Ethics 1.1 for a look at the decisions probation officers must sometimes make.

electronic monitoring

A form of intermediate punishment in which an offender is allowed to remain in the community but must wear an electronic device that allows the authorities to monitor his or her whereabouts.

APPEAL   A written request to a higher court to modify or reverse the judgment of a trial court or intermediate-level appellate court is called an *appeal*. The process begins when a defendant who loses a trial files a notice of appeal, which usually must be filed within 30 days from the judgment date. The appellate court does not retry the

---

FOCUS *on* ETHICS

1.1

A BALANCE OF INTERESTS

In your job as a probation officer you are assigned the case of a rich and successful accountant who is on probation for driving under the influence of alcohol. As part of her community service, the accountant has spent each Saturday morning at a local nursing home where she has been helping the residents fill out their tax forms. This accountant has secured thousands of dollars in tax refunds for these elderly citizens. In fact, one of the residents, who also happens to be your grandmother, reports that not only is this accountant helping the residents save money, but she also has been coming to the nursing home during the middle of the week, on her own time, to talk to lonely and depressed residents.

You feel a little guilty that this accountant has developed a close relationship with your grandmother and that you have not been to the nursing home in months. Being suspicious, you investigate to see whether the accountant knows that you have a relative in the home, and you discover that not only does she not know, but she has volunteered to serve as a member of the board of directors of the home and help the residents deal with confusing social service agencies such as Medicare and Social Security.

Late one night you get a call from the accountant. She is obviously drunk and informs you that she has just crashed her car into a tree and that she needs a ride home before the police come and arrest her. You know that if she gets another DUI, she not only will lose her license, but will also have to spend 90 days in jail and might lose her job. Although you have little sympathy for people who cannot control their drinking, this young woman has been turning her life around and doing good works, especially for the elderly. You see potential in this client.

What Do You Do?

1. Pick her up. You owe her for helping your grandmother, and this is one of the few things you can do to repay the help and kindness that she has shown.

2. Call the police and report her. You are an officer of the court, and you cannot ethically do anything else. Also, you might get in trouble if you do not call.

3. Help her but make a deal stipulating that she will check herself into a clinic and get help for her drinking problem. Use this last incident as leverage to force her to confront her drinking. She is too talented and accomplished to give up on now.

4. Call your supervisor and ask to be relieved of the case because you can no longer be objective.

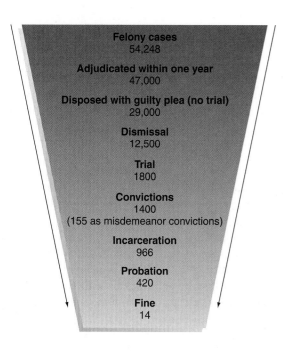

Figure 1-5   Decreasing Number of Cases

This figure illustrates how cases from the 75 largest counties move through the criminal justice system. Seventy-two percent of convicted defendants, by guilty plea and by trial, were sentenced to incarceration in a state prison or local jail. (All numbers are approximate.)

Source: Thomas H. Cohen and Brian A. Reaves, *Felony Defendants in Large Urban Counties, 2002* (Washington, DC: Bureau of Justice Statistics, 2006), 2, 28, 30, www.ojp.usdoj.gov/bjs/pub/pdf/fdluc02.pdf.

case. Rather, the defendant, now known as the *appellant,* and the trial's winner, or *appellee,* submit written arguments, or *briefs,* and sometimes make oral arguments addressing why the decision should be upheld or overturned. When appellate courts reverse lower-court judgments, it is usually because of **prejudicial error,** and the case is returned to a lower court for retrial. There is no constitutional right to appeal; however, some states have established the right to appeal by statute, whereas others have established it by custom.

PRISON   Relatively few of the people whom the police arrest end up in prison (see Figure 1-5 for an example of how felony cases move through the criminal justice system). Prison is an extremely costly option that, in theory, should be reserved for offenders who are a threat to the community. Many individuals are so dangerous that incarcerating them is the only way to ensure that they do not continue to kill, rob, and rape in the community. Other individuals have committed serious offenses such as embezzlement, and although they are not an immediate threat to the community, they are incarcerated to show the rest of us that serious offenses can lead to serious consequences. Ideally, prison should help change the individual and help him or her prepare for life as a free person. However, because of prison overcrowding, the rehabilitative function of the institution has been all but abandoned.[42] Many states are finding the cost of maintaining extensive prison systems prohibitive and are looking for new ways of dealing with offenders, including turning to prisons run by for-profit private corporations. Boot camp prisons for young offenders typically have 90-day programs that employ a paramilitary culture to emphasize order and discipline. These types of programs have their critics, but they are a good deal less expensive than traditional prisons.[43]

PAROLE   Parole is similar to, and sometimes confused with, probation. Probation occurs instead of prison, whereas parole occurs after prison. Inmates who adjust to prison life may get the opportunity for an early release on parole.[44] The idea behind parole is to aid the offender in returning to the community, such as providing help with finding a place to live, obtaining employment, and dealing with personal issues such as drug and alcohol abuse. Today, parole has evolved into a surveillance role in which parole officers act more as police officers than as social workers.[45] Some states

prejudicial error
An error affecting the outcome of a trial.

have abolished parole altogether in lieu of making the offender serve almost the entire sentence.

CAPITAL PUNISHMENT   Capital punishment is a relatively rare event and one for which only a small proportion of offenders are even eligible. Many states do not employ this sentence, and some that do, such as Illinois, have suspended it because of the appearance of discriminatory use and errors.[46] According to Amnesty International, the United States is one of only six stable, industrialized countries to use capital punishment (the others are China, Japan, Russia, Singapore, and Taiwan).[47] Although there is strong public support for it, there is also vocal opposition.[48] It is a controversial practice that is sure to be contested in the courts over the next decade. One clear trend is the move by many states to change their method of capital punishment from electrocution to lethal injection. However, critics contend that it is impossible to deliberately kill a person in a humane way.

WHY SOME OFFENSES ARE EXCLUDED   The criminal justice system is much more complex than suggested by the funnel analogy, and this complexity will be revealed in subsequent chapters that deal in greater detail with components of the system. The analogy's goal has been to indicate how the numbers dwindle drastically when we move down the funnel from offense to sentencing. This funnel analogy illustrates the low number of offenses that catch the full implications of the public's perception of justice. Many of the offenses that enter the system are systematically excluded for a variety of reasons. In review, these reasons include, but are not limited to, the following:

1. **Cost.**   As a society, we simply cannot afford to spend the money and resources necessary to have a totally crime-free society. Although crime is a serious social problem, many other worthy items compete for our tax dollars. Increased spending on crime means that health care, national defense, education, highways, and a host of other legitimate and desirable services do not get enough of the resources they require to function effectively. For example, decisions have to be made on which military aircraft are built because we cannot afford all of them. Similarly, most students must take out loans to pay for a college education because the government can fund only so many scholarships. The criminal justice system, by some estimates, could bankrupt the nation if funded for all its legitimate needs. This is especially true at the local level: local governments spend far more on criminal justice than state governments or the federal government (see Figure 1-6). Therefore, only a relatively small percentage of offenses ever receives what the public believes to be "full justice."

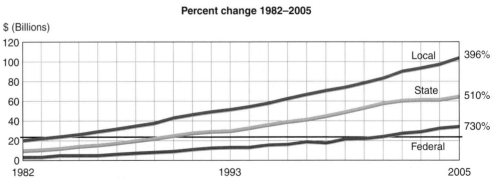

Figure 1-6   Direct Expenditures on Criminal Justice by Level of Government, 1982–2005.

Source: Bureau of Justice Statistics, www.ojp.usdoj.gov/bjs/glance/expgov.htm, using data from the Census Bureau's Annual Government Finance Survey and Annual Survey of Public Employment.

2. **Discretion.** Criminal justice practitioners exercise a considerable amount of discretion in deciding what happens to individual cases. Although this discretion is constrained by resources, a good amount of personal philosophy and judgment also goes into deciding what happens to cases. This discretion is sometimes deemed problematic, and the influence of individual decision makers is curbed. For example, there can be wide disparity in sentencing across jurisdictions or even between judges in the same city. In an effort to ensure that similar cases are treated more equally, legislatures have passed laws calling for fixed sentences. Mandatory-minimum statutes and three-strikes laws greatly limit the discretion judges have in sentencing offenders. Similarly, some law enforcement agencies are mandated to make arrests in domestic assault cases in which there is clear evidence of physical abuse. Some discretion is inherent in the criminal justice system, but its use is contested.

3. **Errors.** Sometimes cases simply fall through the cracks. Criminal justice practitioners are human and can make mistakes. They are often overworked and underpaid and experience a considerable amount of stress in doing a difficult job. Most jurisdictions do not have sophisticated computer systems that link all the components of the criminal justice system that would help ensure that cases are handled efficiently. Also, criminal justice practitioners might make errors in judgment. The police officer who gives a suspect a second chance or the judge who places the sex offender on probation can find himself or herself betrayed by offenders who do not or cannot appreciate the break they have been given.

Problem with the System Metaphor

Is the criminal justice system a system at all? On one hand, the components share an overall common goal of providing justice, but each agency may define that goal in a slightly different way. For example, a police chief may view his or her role as taking dangerous offenders off the street and locking them behind bars for a long time so they cannot further victimize citizens. The prison counselor may see his or her role as helping the inmate adjust to prison life and gain the necessary skills to achieve parole and live successfully in the outside world. These goals are not mutually exclusive. If the counselor is successful in rehabilitating the offender, then the police chief's goal of making the community safe is also realized. However, in the execution of their everyday jobs, the police chief and the counselor see their goals in a limited way and might feel as though they are working at cross purposes. To these individuals, the criminal justice system does not function as a system in which all the parts work in a coordinated manner toward a common goal. At times, it might seem to them, rather, as though they are competing with one another to find the best way of making society safer.

THE MULTIPLE GOALS OF THE CRIMINAL JUSTICE SYSTEM   The criminal justice system has five basic goals (see Figure 1-7). Different aspects of the system have different goals, and depending on one's relationship with the system, different concerns and values are emphasized. For instance, police officers are concerned with capturing suspects, whereas correctional officers and administrators are concerned with changing offenders' behavior through punishment or treatment. These different goals are manifested in vastly different policies and practices. The multiple and sometimes conflicting goals of the criminal justice system are as follows:

1. **Deterrence.** Two types of deterrence are important to the criminal justice system. Specific deterrence occurs when an offender is caught and punished and decides not to break the law in any significant way anymore because he or she now understands the consequences of that behavior. General

Figure 1-7   **Multiple Goals of the Criminal Justice System**

deterrence occurs when an offender is caught and punished, and the rest of us do not break the law because we saw what happened to the offender and understand that the same consequences would befall us if we were caught breaking the law. By far, general deterrence is the more important of these two types.[49] Imagine how chaotic society would be if each of us had to be caught and punished for each type of offense before deciding not to commit it anymore.

2. **Incapacitation.**   Incapacitation is a more limited goal than deterrence. This entails removing the offender's ability to break the law. These days, incapacitation usually means incarceration. An offender who is behind bars cannot harm citizens. Historically, incapacitation included exile and the use of such devices as the **pillory.** Today, some believe that **chemical castration** of sex offenders would prevent them from committing rape.[50]

3. **Retribution.**   Many people believe that justice prevails when an offender is punished. If people are going to cede to the criminal justice system the authority to capture, prosecute, and sentence offenders, then they need to feel that their values are taken into account. If offenders do not "get what they deserve" in the eyes of citizens, then the criminal justice system loses credibility, and citizens might take the law into their own hands.[51] Retribution is an ancient motive with religious connotations, and for many people it is one of the most important goals of the criminal justice system.

4. **Rehabilitation.**   One of the most controversial goals of the criminal justice system—and one that has fallen on hard times recently—is rehabilitation. This involves correcting the offender's behavior and giving him or her the skills and emotional strength to survive in society without violating the law. Some corrections practitioners say that *habilitation* would more accurately describe this goal because many offenders never had these social and emotional skills to begin with. The debate as to whether rehabilitation works and whether the criminal justice system allocates suitable resources toward this goal is ongoing.[52]

5. **Restoration.**   One of the most promising philosophies emerging in the criminal justice literature in recent years is that of restorative justice. The

pillory
A wooden frame with holes for securing the head and hands that was used to secure and expose an offender to public derision.

chemical castration
Anti-androgen drugs, usually administered by injection, that have the effect of lowering the testosterone level and blunting the sex drive in males.

goal of restorative justice is to repair the harm crime has done to the relationship between the offender and victim and between the offender and the community.[53] Because many criminal offenses involve relationships between individuals who will continue to interact after the criminal case has been settled, it is advisable to settle the case with the input of the participants so that they have a sense of commitment to the judgment. Empowering family members, neighbors, and co-workers to help solve disputes allows them to repair the harm done by the crime and to live and work with each other in the future. Restorative justice will be covered in greater detail in Chapter 16.

When considering these multiple goals, we can see why the criminal justice system does not always work as a smooth-functioning and well-coordinated mechanism. With criminal justice agencies spanning different levels of government and contrasting and overlapping jurisdictions, the responsibility for crime is not always clear and agreed on. With each level of government and each individual agency having its own goals and pressures, the overall accountability for crime is fragmented and disputed. Depending solely on the criminal justice system to maintain social control could lead to even bigger problems. Fortunately, other institutions help to maintain civil behavior and make the job of the criminal justice system easier.

CRIME: A SOCIAL RESPONSIBILITY

Controlling and preventing antisocial behavior is not just the responsibility of the criminal justice system; it is also the responsibility of the other major societal institutions: the family, religion, schools, and the media. These social institutions all have positive functions in society. Although their main job is not to exert social control, they all do to a certain extent. Only by recognizing that institutions besides the criminal justice system perform social control can we appreciate just how massive and difficult this job is. When these other institutions fail to fully socialize youth or do not satisfy citizens' needs, the criminal justice system must deal with the consequences.

The Family

The primary institution of socialization in society is the family. The tasks of families are great in terms of transmitting the expectations of behavior in society and providing an emotionally secure and supportive environment. Although we hear a lot about "family values" from politicians, this term is loaded with the political and social expectations of one way of thinking about the family. Although the ideal of the nuclear family is laudable and still the social norm, it is not the statistical norm. Other configurations of families and other worthy values also exist.

Whether the living arrangement of the family comprises an intact nuclear family with two parents and their children, or divorced and remarried parents with children from prior marriages, the task of the family is still the same. The intact nuclear family is not always the best arrangement for some children. If one parent is abusive or neglectful, or both parents are in conflict over money and family power, the best solution might be for the family to dissolve.[54] The important issues for the student of the criminal justice system are how the norms and rules of society are transmitted to the children and how well the children, in turn, transmit values to their children. See Focus on Ethics 1.2 to see how the role of families and communities affect a child's behavior.

An emerging feature of some families is the use of "tough love" discipline to try to make children conform. In an age when parents are too busy with careers, relationships, and recreation to spend time getting to know their children's friends and

| **1.2** | **FOCUS on ETHICS** |

A KID IN TROUBLE

While working at the big bookstore in the mall, you see the 12-year-old who lives across the street enter the store and head for the magazine section. As you approach the youth to say hello, you notice him slipping some magazines under his shirt. His mother is a good friend of your parents, and he is in the same classroom as your little sister, so you know he has a troubled life. His father, a police officer, was killed in the line of duty three years ago, and the boy has been in trouble ever since. When he realizes you saw him steal the magazines, he offers them back to you with the plea that you do not tell anyone because his mother's new boyfriend, also a police officer, will beat him. You suspect this is true because your parents have expressed concern about his mother's new relationship. You feel conflicted because your boss has been good to you and has allowed you to work many overtime hours while you go to college. Additionally, she has been accommodating to how your class schedule changes each semester and always finds a way to keep you on the job.

What Do You Do?

1. Help the boy. Put the magazines back on the shelf and do not tell anyone.

2. Follow store procedure and alert the security guard.

activities, some parents have turned to drug-testing their own children. This tough-love aspect of dealing with children is mirrored in the criminal justice system with its "war on crime" approach.

Religion

Religion is a powerful institution. Although many people do not attend any type of religious service, most people in the United States have been exposed to some sort of religious instruction that has influenced the way they think about dealing with others. Émile Durkheim detailed how religion provides important and positive functions in society by strengthening our sense of community, providing answers about the ultimate meaning of life, providing emotional comfort in times of loss and stress, providing guidelines for everyday life, exerting social control, and sometimes acting as a vehicle for social change.[55]

The part that religion plays in exerting social control is important to the study of crime. By providing rules to guide individuals in the practice of their faith, religion supports many of the laws of civil society. In many ways, societies enact laws that reinforce their citizens' religious beliefs. Rules about adultery, gambling, child rearing, and observance of religious holidays have all made the transition from religious rules to civil law or practice.

How much should we look to religion in developing secular laws to be enforced by the criminal justice system? The founders of the United States, in an effort to guard against religious persecution, made a clear distinction between church and state. Coming from countries that had national religions and persecuted those who believed differently, the founders established the United States as a country in which all people would be free to follow their own hearts in religious matters. This freedom to believe has been tested repeatedly over the last two centuries as people arrived from many other parts of the world to become U.S. citizens. Although a change has occurred in the overall pattern of religious practices in the United States (from European Protestantism to all the various religions found today), it is fair to say that religion has exerted a consistent, and for the most part positive, form of social control.[56]

Like the family, the institution of religion provides people with internal controls over their behavior, which allows them to interact with others without breaking the law. Civil society is possible only when people behave themselves without the supervision of the criminal justice system. If the criminal justice system had to socialize and supervise everyone, the United States would be a police state.

Schools

As institutions, schools do more than teach children how to read and write. They are also a powerful force in socializing them into the culturally approved ways of interacting with other people. In his 1975 article "Learning the Student Role: Kindergarten as Academic Boot Camp," Harry L. Gracey detailed how 5-year-olds are taught to take turns, be quiet, share, and raise their hands and be recognized before speaking.[57] These lessons are reinforced throughout their school years and, from the point of social control, make the job of the teacher much easier. As children internalize these behaviors and learn to conduct themselves in a law-abiding way, the job of the criminal justice system is made much easier also.

However, the job of the school as a socializing institution is sometimes difficult, and it is not always done well. At times, schools have overreacted to the activities of young people and have enacted overly punitive policies. Some of the zero-tolerance policies of recent years have been so draconian as to invite public ridicule.

The Media

The media are also agents of social control. There is a risk in thinking of the media as a single entity because it comprises so many aspects, and its components pursue different goals. It is easy to be critical of the media as socializing agents when we treat them as institutions that have an exact goal or purpose. It is useful for our purposes here to select aspects of the media that affect the criminal justice system and suggest how they exert a direct and/or indirect influence on social control.

- **The news**   The way crime is reported exerts a great influence on how we envision and react to it.[58] Although the media should give us an accurate and unbiased picture of the nature of crime, we are also aware that some news programs have as one of their primary goals an entertainment function to attract more viewers to their station. To a large degree, the same can be said of the print media. Even more problematic are some of the quasi news programs such as those shown on some cable news channels. These shows use the facts of some cases, but highlight the sensational aspects and fail to provide a balanced picture of crime.[59] Given the decreasing crime rates of the last decade, it would seem that the media would present an improving picture of the crime situation in the United States.

- **Hollywood**   How much is the crime and violence that is depicted on television a reflection of society, and how much distorts the problems and possibly even contributes to them? That is, do individuals filter the imaginary violence that is shown by Hollywood and recognize it for its entertainment value, or do some people go out into society and mimic what they have viewed?[60] Movies, television, and popular music all have come under attack by concerned citizens because of messages of sex and violence portrayed in a positive light.[61] What are realistic expectations of the entertainment industry in a country that values free speech and expression? We will not, and cannot, answer this question here. It is raised solely to emphasize how institutions other than the criminal justice system influence social control.

- **The Internet**   An emerging part of the media that affects social control is the Internet. The problems of sex offenders recruiting young people for illicit sexual purposes, online stalkers, and the proliferation of all types of pornography have been well documented and lamented by the media. The Internet is a wonderful communications tool that presents new challenges for the social control of citizens. Although the Internet has empowered all of us with access to unlimited sources of information, it has also allowed a variety of lawbreakers to communicate in pursuit of their criminal activities. Although some would allow the government to exert greater control over the Internet, this is not really a viable option. The genie is out of the bottle, and we must accept that with the empowerment of the Internet come new opportunities for lawbreakers and new ways for all of us to be victimized.

System of Last Resort

As we will see in later chapters, the causes of crime have many explanations. Many of the reasons why individuals violate the law are outside the scope and responsibility of the criminal justice system. The criminal justice system has a difficult mission for several reasons. These reasons include, but are not limited to, the following:

- **The offender**   Criminal offenders can be unpleasant. In fact, they are often under the influence of alcohol or drugs, armed and dangerous, and in a really bad mood. Regardless of the reasons, they have already committed acts that have hurt others either financially or physically and are resistant to the idea of being held accountable for their actions. Criminal offenders often have convinced themselves that they have legitimate reasons for their transgressions and picture themselves as victims of circumstance and an overzealous criminal justice system. They are arrested, prosecuted, and incarcerated involuntarily. Unlike the school or the church, the criminal justice system cannot expect much cooperation from its charges. In short, the criminal justice system must deal with some of the most disagreeable people in society, often at great risk to its practitioners.

- **Resources**   Despite the fact that crime consistently rates as one of society's major problems, the criminal justice system is not high on the list of things for which citizens want their tax money used. Schools, roads, parks, national defense, and health care all are more popular destinations for public resources. Within the criminal justice system, the law enforcement role is deemed more worthy than corrections, and within corrections, locking up offenders is viewed as a better use of resources than attempting to rehabilitate them. The criminal justice system will most likely always be underfunded, and those who work in it will do so for reasons of service, dedication, and excitement rather than money. Many good employees will move on to other, more lucrative professions, and the criminal justice system will struggle to attract the best and the brightest young people entering the workforce.

- **Structure**   As we have already discussed, the criminal justice system is not really a system. This is partly intentional and partly because of poor funding. It is intentional to the degree that checks and balances are built into our democracy. The inefficiencies built into the system ensure that in addition to being slow, the process allows for justice to be pursued through due process and oversight. Only in a police state could a criminal justice system give the appearance of abolishing crime. Along with our freedoms, a certain amount of crime and inefficiency in the criminal justice system is inherent in a free society.

Social control in a democratic society is complicated. The place of the criminal justice system in providing this social control is problematic. It is, for all intents and purposes, the institution of last resort. The family, religion, school, and the media exert a tremendous amount of influence over the behavior of individuals. When these institutions individually or collectively fail to develop law-abiding citizens, the criminal justice system must deal with the consequences. It is unrealistic to expect the criminal justice system to be fully successful where these other institutions have failed. Those who end up in prison are not randomly selected from a representative cross section of the population. Rather, a pronounced selection bias results in the most dangerous and disagreeable people tending to be the ones who enter the criminal justice system.

INDIVIDUAL VS. SOCIETAL RESPONSIBILITY FOR CRIME Most of our discussion up to this point has focused on the idea that crime is committed by individuals who have not been properly socialized into mainstream society. In keeping with the subtitle of this book, "Mainstream and Crosscurrents," we now introduce a competing idea that argues that crime is a natural result of a flawed cultural and economic system. A body of criminological theory (to be covered in detail in Chapter 3) contends that the individual offender is not solely to blame for crime. Critical criminology theories look at issues such as racism, sexism, ageism, and the vast disparities in wealth in the United States and suggest that this arrangement continues to be maintained because it works well for those in power.[62] In these critical theories, the criminal justice system is considered one of the tools that the wealthy and powerful use to enhance their privileged position in society. This is evidenced by the observations that the wealthy can hire private security firms to protect themselves and their property, by how the wealthy can hire private attorneys to represent them in court, and by how the powerful can get their concerns encoded into the law. Any balanced discussion of the discipline of criminal justice requires that this critical perspective be examined. It challenges our concept of what justice is in the United States and forces us to look at how individuals benefit or are victimized by such a criminal justice system.

In reviewing such critical issues, the intent of this book is not to denigrate capitalism or criminal justice system practitioners. Rather, these important and legitimate concerns are offered as opportunities for reflection and reform. As students and practitioners of criminal justice, we all have the responsibility to honestly and thoughtfully evaluate how justice is dispensed and to do whatever we can not only to prevent crime, but also to improve the criminal justice system.

SUMMARY

1. The distinguishing feature of the U.S. criminal justice system is the way that individual rights are protected as a part of the law enforcement function. The criminal justice system must balance the imposition of order and the preservation of individual rights. When the law is broken, the criminal justice system must respond in the name of society.

2. Crime is an action that violates the rules of society to the point of harming citizens or society. Crime is a difficult problem that does not respond to simple solutions.

3. The crime rate does not always accurately reflect the public's perception of the crime rate. Many crimes go undetected and their harm is not generally perceived. Other crimes are sensationalized and their cases given such vast resources the public's perception of the amount and seriousness of crime is distorted.

4. The public's fears are focused on street crime. Other types of crime that are just as damaging include corporate crime, white-collar crime, and organized crime.

5. Law enforcement, courts, and corrections tasks are divided across the local, state, and federal branches of government. Law enforcement functions at the state level are usually confined to specialized missions. At the federal level, law enforcement functions include a range of agencies that enforce federal laws and assist state and local governments. Police officers, prosecutors, judges, and corrections officials use discretion to decide which cases proceed further into the criminal justice system and which do not. Many of the cases that enter the system may be eventually excluded, as well.

6. The criminal justice system has multiple goals for cases that proceed further into the system, specifically deterrence, incapacitation, retribution, rehabilitation, and restoration.

7. Other means of social control besides the criminal justice system include the family, religion, schools, and the media. The criminal justice system is the institution of last resort.

KEY TERMS

arraignment 23	electronic monitoring 26	*prima facie* case 23
bailiff 15	felony 17	Prohibition 13
bill of indictment 23	misdemeanor 17	sheriff 15
chemical castration 30	no-bill 23	socialization 14
circuit 17	*nolo contendere* 23	sociological imagination 6
clearance rate 21	organized crime 13	street crime 10
corporate crime 11	pillory 30	true bill 23
county stockade 17	prejudicial error 27	war on drugs 13
dark figure of crime 19	presentence report 25	warrant 15
discretion 19	preventive detention 23	

REVIEW QUESTIONS

1. Why do we sometimes have a faulty idea of the nature of crime in the United States?

2. In addition to the criminal justice system, which institutions exert social control?

3. Could the criminal justice system be more efficient? What would the implications be?

4. In what way is the criminal justice process like a funnel?

5. What are the goals of the criminal justice system? Which of these goals is most important? What should be done when these goals conflict?

6. Why is the criminal justice system considered the system of last resort?

7. What is the difference between white-collar crime and corporate crime? Should the penalties for both types of crime be more harsh?

8. Why is sensationalized crime not representative of most crime?

9. What general type of crime does the public fear most?

10. Discuss the effect of socialization on social control.

SUGGESTED FURTHER READING

Arrigo, Bruce A, ed. *Social Justice/Criminal Justice: The Maturation of Critical Theory in Law, Crime, and Deviance.* Belmont, CA: Wadsworth, 1998.

Crank, John P. *Imagining Justice.* Cincinnati, OH: Anderson, 2003.

Fichtelberg, Aaron. *Crime without Borders: An Introduction to International Criminal Justice.* Upper Saddle River, New Jersey: Pearson, 2008.

Krisberg, Barry, Susan Marchionna, and S. Christopher Baird. *Continuing the Struggle for Justice: 100 Years of the National Council on Crime and Delinquency.* Los Angeles: Sage Publications, 2007.

Reiman, Jeffrey. *The Rich Get Richer and the Poor Get Prison*, 8th ed. Boston: Allyn & Bacon, 2006.

Wright, Lawrence. *The Looming Tower: Al-Qaeda and the Road to 9/11.* New York: Knopf, 2006.

ENDNOTES

1. Kenneth Pringle, "Inside the Mind of Jeffrey Dahmer," APBNews.com, August 10, 2000, www.apbnews.com/media/gfiles/dahmer/dahmer0814.html. At his 1992 trial, Jeffrey Dahmer was determined to be sane and sentenced to 16 consecutive life terms. Another inmate beat him to death in a prison gym in November 1994. In 1996 a man offered more than $400,000 for the tools he used to torture, kill, and dismember his victims, but the tools were secretly buried.

2. The Troy State University Montgomery Rosa Parks Library and Museum, www.tsum.edu/museum/parksbio.htm.

3. Infoplease, "Rosenberg Case," www.infoplease.com/ce6/history/A0842422.html. Several screenwriters and actors lost their careers and went to prison after being investigated by the House Un-American Activities Committee in 1947 and 1951. In 1950 Senator Joseph McCarthy announced his famous list of Communist

Party members and charged that the State Department had been infiltrated by Communists.

4. C. Wright Mills, *The Sociological Imagination* (New York: Oxford University Press, 1959).

5. Ray Surette, ed., *Media, Crime, and Criminal Justice: Images and Realities*, 2nd ed. (Belmont, CA: West/Wadsworth, 1998). See especially Chapter 3, "The Construction of Crime and Justice in the News Media," for an enlightening analysis of how news is socially constructed.

6. Randall G. Shelden, *Controlling the Dangerous Classes: A Critical Introduction to the History of Criminal Justice* (Boston: Allyn & Bacon, 2001).

7. Jeffrey Reiman, *The Rich Get Richer and the Poor Get Prison: Ideology, Class, and Criminal Justice*, 6th ed. (Boston: Allyn & Bacon, 2001).

8. Federal Bureau of Investigation, "Financial Crimes Report to the Public," 7, www.fbi.gov/publications/financial/fcs_report2006/publicrpt06.pdf.

9. See Reiman, *The Rich Get Richer*, for a discussion on how we treat street crime more seriously than corporate crime.

10. Each year the government publishes the *Uniform Crime Report*, which includes the Crime Clock.

11. William G. Doerner and Stephen P. Lab, *Victimology*, 5th ed. (Cincinnati, OH: Lexis-Nexis, 2008), 289–299.

12. Alfred Blumstein and Joel Wallman, *The Crime Drop in America* (New York: Cambridge University Press, 2005).

13. Ronald D. Hunter and Mark L. Dantzker, *Crime and Criminality: Causes and Consequences* (Upper Saddle River, NJ: Prentice Hall, 2002).

14. James Q. Wilson and George L. Kelling, "Broken Windows," in *Critical Issues in Policing: Contemporary Issues*, 2nd ed., eds. Roger G. Durham and Geoffrey P. Alpert (Prospect Heights, IL: Waveland Press, 1993).

15. Reiman, *The Rich Get Richer*.

16. Ibid.

17. Lewis R. Mizell, Jr., *Masters of Deception: The Worldwide White-Collar Crime Crisis and Ways to Protect Yourself* (New York: Wiley, 1997).

18. Jay S. Albanese, *Organized Crime in America*, 3rd ed. (Cincinnati, OH: Anderson, 1996).

19. ABC News, "Holloway Suspect: 'I Know What Happened,'" February 3, 2008, http://abcnews.go.com/International/story?id=4222253; Neil Websdale and Alexander Alvarez, "Forensic Journalism as Patriarchal Ideology: The Newspaper Constructions of Homicide-Suicide," in *Popular Culture, Crime, and Justice*, eds. Frankie Bailey and Donna Hale (Belmont, CA: West/Wadsworth, 1998), 123–141. This is an interesting study of how a newspaper in Arizona in its reporting of 153 homicide-suicide cases stresses sensational crime-scene minutiae over the social structural context.

20. For a fascinating explanation of how videos of crime not only extend the story, but also distort it, see Peter K. Manning, "Media Loops," in *Popular Culture, Crime, and Justice*, eds. Frankie Bailey and Donna Hale (Belmont, CA: West/Wadsworth, 1998), 25–39.

21. Stuart L. Hills, *Demystifying Social Deviance* (New York: McGraw-Hill, 1980). See Chapter 2, "The Politics of Social Deviance."

22. Diana Scully and Joseph Marolla, "Riding the Bull at Gilley's: Convicted Rapists Describe the Rewards of Rape," *Social Problems* (February 1985): 251–263.

23. Daniel L. Skoler, *Organizing the Non-System: Governmental Structuring of Criminal Justice Systems* (Lanham, MD: Lexington Books, 1977).

24. Abraham S. Blumberg, *Criminal Justice: Issues and Ironies*, 2nd ed. (New York: New Viewpoints, 1979).

25. Randy L. LaGrange, *Policing American Society* (Chicago: Nelson-Hall, 1993), 54.

26. Matthew J. Hickman and Brian A. Reaves, *Sheriffs' Offices, 2000* (Washington, DC: Bureau of Justice Statistics, 2003), 1, www.ojp.usdoj.gov/bjs/pub/pdf/s000.pdf.

27. Michael Welch, *Corrections: A Critical Approach* (New York: McGraw-Hill, 1996). Chapter 7 provides a good analysis of jails and detention.

28. John Irwin, *The Jail: Managing the Underclass in American Society* (Berkeley: University of California Press, 1985).

29. Bureau of Justice Statistics, *Prisoners in 1998* (Washington, DC: U.S. Department of Justice, 1999).

30. Patrick Langan, *State Felony Courts and Felony Laws 1987* (Washington, DC: Bureau of Justice Statistics).

31. James Austin and John Irwin, *It's About Time: America's Imprisonment Binge*, 3rd ed. (Belmont, CA: Wadsworth, 2001).

32. U.S. District Court for the Northern District of Iowa Central Division, "Report and Recommendation," No. C96–3011-MWB, Decision, Judge Zoss, April 29, 1998; state habeas, www.iand.uscourts.gov/iand/decisions.nsf/274509d70785a9eb8625693e005be79c/c68c627c75bbc256862569690052534f.

33. "Disposing of Body Was Desperate Act, Husband Recalls," *Omaha World-Herald*, July 15, 1992.

34. "Evidence in Case Set Precedent, Experts Say," *Des Moines Register*, June 1, 1999.

35. "Ramsey Detective 'Made Mistakes,' Chief Testifies," TheDenverChannel.com/Associated Press, June 12, 2001, www.thedenverchannel.com/den/news/stories/news81537020010612–060634.html.

36. Charlie LeDuff, "Cosmetics Heir Is Missing as His Rape Trial Proceeds," *New York Times*, late edition, January 8, 2003, A20.

37. Tim Weiner, "Fugitive and Heir to Cosmetics Fortune Is Captured in Mexico," *New York Times*, late edition, June 19, 2003, A20.

38. Greg Farrell, "Ebbers' Luck Runs Out in Sweeping Victory for Feds," *USA Today*, March 16, 2005, final edition, 1B.

39. Arthur Rosett and Donald R. Cressey, *Justice by Consent: Plea Bargains in the American Courthouse* (New York: Lippincott, 1976).

40. U.S. Sentencing Commission, "Overview of the Federal Sentencing Guidelines," November 1998, www.ussc.gov.

41. Welch, *Corrections*.

42. Austin and Irwin, *It's About Time*.

43. Doris Layton Mackenzie and Alex Piquero, "The Impact of Shock Incarceration Programs on Prison Overcrowding," *Crime and Delinquency* (April 1994): 222–249.

44. Richard McCleary, *Dangerous Men: The Sociology of Parole*, 2nd ed. (Albany, NY: Harrow & Heston, 1992).

45. Todd R. Clear and Edward E. Latessa, "Surveillance vs. Control: Probation Officers' Roles in Intensive Supervision," *Justice Quarterly* 10 (1993): 441–462.

46. Hugo Adam Bedau, *Death Is Different* (Boston: Northeastern University Press, 1987).

47. Amnesty International, "Website Against the Death Penalty, Abolitionist and Retentionist Countries," www.fpp.unilj.si/~fdimc/zanimivosti/Amnesty%20International%20Website%20Against%20the%20Death%20Penalty%20Abolitionist%20and%20Retentionist%20Countries.htm.

48. Hugo Adam Bedau, William Lofquist, and Michael L. Radelet, "Miscarriages of Justice in Potentially Capital Cases," *Stanford Law Review* (November 1987): 21–179.

49. Greg Pogarsky, "Deterrence, Context, and Crime Decision Making," *Criminology and Public Policy* 7 (2008): 508.

50. Douglas J. Besharov, "Sex Offenders: Is Castration an Acceptable Punishment?" *ABA Journal* 78, no. 7 (1992): 42–43.

51. Steven F. Messner, Eric P. Baumer, and Richard Rosenfeld, "Distrust of Government, the Vigilante Tradition, and Support for Capital Punishment," *Law and Society Review* 40 (2006): 559–590.

52. Francis T. Cullen, "Make Rehabilitation Corrections' Guiding Paradigm," *Criminology and Public Policy* 6, (2007): 717–727.

53. Daniel W. Van Ness and Karen Heetderks Strong, *Restoring Justice*, 2nd ed. (Cincinnati, OH: Anderson, 2002).

54. Murray A. Strauss, Richard J. Gelles, and Suzanne K. Steinmetz, *Behind Closed Doors: Violence in the American Family* (New York: Anchor/Doubleday, 1980).

55. Émile Durkheim, *The Elementary Forms of Religious Life* (New York: Free Press, 1965). First published in 1912.

56. Roger Finke and Roger Starke, *The Churching of America, 1776–1990: Winners and Losers in Our Religious Economy* (New Brunswick, NJ: Rutgers University Press, 1992).

57. Harry L. Gracey, "Learning the Student Role: Kindergarten as Academic Boot Camp," in *Down to Earth Sociology: Introductory Readings*, 9th ed., ed. James M. Henslin (New York: Free Press, 1997), 376–388.

58. Surette, *Media, Crime, and Criminal Justice*.

59. Kenneth D. Tunnell, "Reflections on Crime, Criminals, and Control in News Magazines and Television Programs," in *Popular Culture, Crime, and Justice*, eds. Frankie Bailey and Donna Hale (Belmont, CA: West/Wadsworth, 1998), 111–122.

60. Will Wright, *Six Guns and Society* (Berkeley: University of California Press, 1975).

61. National Research Council, *Understanding Violence* (Washington, DC: National Research Council, 1992).

62. Bruce A. Arrigo, *Social Justice/Criminal Justice: The Maturation of Critical Theory in Law, Crime, and Deviance* (Belmont, CA: West/Wadsworth, 1999).

CHAPTER 2

The Nature and Measurement of Crime

Objectives

1. Understand how crime is categorized and measured.

2. Be able to discuss some of the problems of measuring crime.

3. Understand the dark figure of crime.

4. Be able to compare and contrast the public's fear of crime with the amount of crime that is represented by crime statistics.

Measuring crime is a tricky business. Criminal justice scholars, government officials, and the public all have different motivations, vested interests, and ideologies that dictate why and how crime should be measured. There are economic and political reasons that these entities wish to have crime measured in different ways. For example, a police chief who wants to make the case that the department needs more resources could use a crime wave as a justification. Conversely, a police chief who is in political trouble might determine that a drop in the **crime rate** would be evidence that he or she is doing a good job. Even if there were no political or social reasons for criminal justice administrators to manipulate the measurement of crime, the logistical obstacles to effectively and efficiently measure crime are daunting. These logistical problems, which we will cover in greater detail later in the chapter, include the following:

crime rate

The number of Crime Index offenses divided by the population of an area, usually given as a rate of crimes per 100,000 people.

- **Problems of definition**   Although laws are written in a specific manner to remove ambiguity, the interpretation of behaviors that seem to be criminal offenses can be problematic. For the legislator who writes the law in the safety of his or her office, the circumstances might be clear-cut and easily defined. For the police officer on the street, the information needed to determine whether a criminal offense is committed might be conflicting, absent, or even false. For the corporate officer, activities that the legislator and the law enforcement officer believe to constitute a criminal offense might simply be a good business move.

- **Problems of resources**   Thousands of criminal justice jurisdictions report official criminal justice statistics. Some large metropolitan or state agencies have teams of well-trained personnel to keep track of crime; other smaller agencies do not have specially dedicated individuals to perform this task. Consequently, the priority of maintaining these types of records varies significantly across jurisdictions based on the resources available.

- **Problems of politics**   Public officials do not want their communities perceived as high-crime areas. The economic and social effects of the perception of crime can cause city officials to place undue pressure on law enforcement agencies to minimize the reporting of crime. For this reason, aggravated assaults might be reported as simple battery, or motor vehicle theft might be deemed joyriding, depending on political circumstances.

To understand crime's effect on individuals and society, we must understand how crime is conceptualized and measured. There is a big difference between a homicide and some children throwing rocks through the windows of an abandoned house. Similarly, there is a big difference between massive corporate fraud and the motorist whose license is suspended after three drunken-driving convictions. Crime can affect individuals or an entire society. Crime can be a minor irritant or a catastrophic blow from which one never recovers. In short, not all criminal offenses are the same.[1] The total numbers of criminal offenses, or even the crime rate, fails to capture the variability and deleterious effects of crime. Although crime measures are useful when attempting to compare the relative safety of cities, states, or regions, the way crime is measured can provide misleading and inaccurate pictures of how it is distributed and how it affects people.[2]

This chapter will review the various ways crime has been categorized and measured. By considering the problems of differentiating among different types and levels of crime and appreciating how crime statistics are gathered and reported, we will see how social, economic, and political factors shape the way we comprehend and respond to crime.

CATEGORIES OF OFFENSES AND OFFENDERS

The behaviors that offend our sensibilities can be categorized in many ways. We have rules, regulations, norms, folkways, and laws that dictate what is acceptable and what is punished. Laws attempt to define crime in a comprehensible manner, the most basic distinction being between misdemeanors and felonies. This distinction is a rather crude way to distinguish the seriousness of these actions, and it is not made until a law enforcement officer decides which law was violated by the action. The distinction between a misdemeanor and a felony may be blurred when the prosecutor decides what the formal charge will be, and the process becomes even more complicated when, as a result of plea negotiations, the judge passes sentence.[3] Therefore, a man who gets into a fistfight might believe he is acting in self-defense, but he may also find that because he severely hurt his opponent, a police officer charges him with misdemeanor assault. The prosecutor may decide to kick the charge up to a felony because of the use of a baseball bat, but after a plea negotiation, the charge might once again become a misdemeanor. The relationship between a behavior and the legal designations that are ultimately attached to it is sometimes difficult to justify. Therefore, the legal categorizations of offenses are not the best indicators of the nature of crime.[4]

Another way to understand crime is to consider the victimization. Focusing on the victim or object of harm instead of the charge can provide a better measure of the level of crime. The following three-group typology elucidates the similarities and differences among the general classes of crime:

1. **Offenses against the person.**   These offenses include the violent personal offenses of homicide, rape, sexual assault, robbery, and assault.
2. **Offenses against property.**   These offenses include burglary, arson, embezzlement, larceny/theft, and auto theft.
3. **Offenses against the public order.**   These offenses include drug use, disturbing the peace, drunkenness, prostitution, and sometimes gambling.

Considering crime in this manner gives us a better idea of the harm caused by unlawful actions than does the simple misdemeanor/felony dichotomy. Although each of these categories spans the range of seriousness from minor irritation to extreme disruption, they group offenses in terms of who or what is harmed. Exploring this typology in greater detail is useful because it reflects the type of harm done to victims. Each of these categories includes a continuum of offenses that differ in degree and may be either stringently punished or relatively neglected by the criminal justice system.

A riot is classified as an offense against the public order. Riots often occur after a sports team wins (or loses) a game. Destruction of property, drunkenness, and personal injury are often features of riots.

Source: Scott Olson/Corbis/ Reuters America LLC

Figure 2-1   Victimization Rates, 2005 and 2006.

Source: Michael Rand and Shannan Catalano, *Criminal Victimization, 2006* (Washington, DC: Bureau of Justice Statistics, 2007), 3, www.ohp.usdoj.gov/bjs/pub/pdf/cv06.pdf.

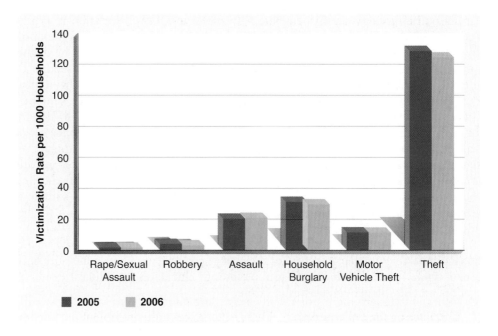

Offenses against the Person

The most severe penalties, including capital punishment, are reserved for those who commit offenses against the person. Personal violent offenses such as murder and rape are the most devastating and the most feared of all offenses and garner the most media coverage.[5] These serious offenses occur much less frequently than do offenses against property—and the most serious of these offenses occur less often than the least serious (see Figure 2-1)—but they are of the most concern to law enforcement and victims. When considering homicide and assault cases, we can discern certain motivations that apparently compel offenders to engage in this serious antisocial behavior.

- **Interpersonal disputes**   Violence is sometimes not the means of last resort to settle disputes. Some people use violence as a negotiating tool, and sometimes, when negotiations break down, they employ lethal violence. Sources of dispute can include disagreements over money, charges of infidelity, challenges to masculinity, or insults to moral character. Often the difference between offender and victim is who is fastest on the draw; that is, there is sometimes no clear relationship between who is responsible for starting the dispute and who emerges the winner.[6] Criminologists use the term **victim precipitation** to refer to instances when the victim plays an active role in initiating the conflict or escalating it to the point of violence.[7] In some segments of society, a subculture of violence emerges in which assault or murder is expected as a way of resolving conflict.[8]

- **Instrumental violence**   Violence is sometimes used as a means to another criminal end. Drug dealers sometimes kill competitors, robbers sometimes shoot convenience store clerks, and carjackers sometimes assault drivers to steal automobiles. The violence in these cases is used as a tool to accomplish another offense. Killing a witness or a prison guard during an escape is an unfortunate by-product of an offender's greater goal and might have been avoided under different circumstances.[9] Other forms of instrumental violence, however, are premeditated. Intimidating witnesses or "teaching a lesson" to an informant employs violence as an extreme form of communication when "a message" needs to be sent.[10] Often the motivation or message of instrumental violence is

victim precipitation

A situation in which a crime victim plays an active role in initiating a crime or escalating it.

difficult to discern, such as when a bank robber successfully takes the money, then shoots the clerk on the way out of the bank.

- **Group violence**   Another source of motivation to commit violence can be found in the dynamics of certain groups. Assaults or homicides often occur in situations in which groups of young people come into conflict. Violence is often used in instrumental ways when youth gangs clash over territory or symbolic concerns such as colors of clothing or other displays of gang affiliation.[11] Youths often feel a greater sense of bravado when surrounded by friends and might feel a greater need to demonstrate their courage and rebellion. Group dynamics may encourage and facilitate, and, in some cases even demand, members' use of violence to address some real or imagined insult. When alcohol or drugs enter the equation, violence is even more likely.[12]

- **Chronic violent offenders**   Some offenders commit numerous acts of violence for a variety of reasons. Sometimes the violence is instrumental as a part of a larger pattern of crime, and sometimes it is random and indiscriminate. Often, this type of offender is the hardest to understand because there is no apparent motivation. Although **serial murderers** are extremely rare, they usually have some underlying personal logic regarding their targets. Some might kill young women with a certain hair color, such as the case of Ted Bundy. Others might kill exclusively young men, as was the case with John Wayne Gacy.[13] Even though the motivation might be the result of a psychological problem, the serial murderer is often capable of committing many offenses and eluding detection and arrest. If the serial murderer moves from state to state, linking the cases to discern a pattern is often difficult.[14]

- **Political violence**   Some offenses are meant to send a message. This is the case with political violence, of which the most well-known type is terrorism. **Terrorism** can be domestic, as in the case of the 1995 bombing of the Murrah Federal Building in Oklahoma City, or it can be of the international variety, as in the suicide plane hijackings of September 11, 2001. The subject of terrorism will be covered in greater detail in Chapter 16, but it is important to stress here that the political nature of this type of violence sets it apart from other types of crime.[15] Terrorism is often committed by intelligent, sincere people who believe that violence is necessary to have their voices heard.[16]

- **Rape and sexual assault**   Because the motivations for committing **rape** and **sexual assault** are often different from the motivations for committing other types of personal violent offenses, and because the effect on the victims can be so devastating, these offenses will be considered unique forms of violence. Rape is just one of a number of sex offenses that has garnered more attention from criminologists in recent years.[17] Although rape has been a consistent occurrence

serial murder
Homicides of a sequence of victims committed in three or more separate events over a period of time.

terrorism
The use or threat of violence against a state or other political entity in order to coerce.

rape
Sexual activity, usually sexual intercourse, that is forced on another person without his or her consent, usually under threat of harm. Also sexual activity conducted with a person who is incapable of valid consent.

sexual assault
Sexual contact that is committed without the other party's consent or with a party who is not capable of giving consent.

Serial killer Dennis Rader, known by police as BTK (for *bind, torture, kill*), was active for 31 years. Rader was finally arrested in 2005. Rader pleaded guilty to 10 murders, the earliest dating to 1974. Rader was sentenced to 10 consecutive life sentences with no chance of parole for more than 40 years.

Source: AP Wide World Photos

Police approach a suspect after a shootout in the wake of a unsuccessful robbery of a Bank of America branch in Hollywood, California, in 1997. Both robbery suspects were killed, and 10 police officers and five civilians were injured.

Source: Handout/Reuters/KNBC-TV Corbis/Reuters America LLC

throughout recorded history, the past 40 years have seen an increased awareness of the definition of what types of behavior constitute sexual assault and greater legal protections for victims. Women and children, once considered as not having individual rights when the perpetrator was a husband or father, are now protected by the criminal justice system.[18] Child molestation, date rape, acquaintance rape, and sexual harassment are now recognized as serious types of antisocial behavior and are dealt with in a more humane and serious manner by law enforcement and the courts.[19]

robbery
The removal of property from a person by violence or by threat of violence.

- **Robbery**   Robbery varies by location, whether on the street (such as a mugging) or within an institution (such as a bank or a convenience store).[20] Sometimes robbery, such as a purse-snatching or pocket-picking, is classified as a felony when a certain level of force or fear is exerted on the victim.[21] Finally, even though carjackings involve theft of a motor vehicle, they are considered robberies because of the force involved.

Offenses against Property

Not all societies have the same attitude about property as modern Western-style democracies.[22] The accumulation of wealth and possessions is an important cornerstone of individual and group well-being in the United States, and laws have been constructed to protect the rights of those who own and control property. These laws range from prohibitions against theft to the copyright procedures that protect intellectual and creative endeavors. The types of property crime that are best measured by the criminal justice system are those in which the offender is a stranger to the victim. Although many laws address differences in opinion while transacting business, these conflicts are usually covered by tort law. Burglary, larceny/theft, and motor vehicle theft are dealt with by the criminal law. Following are several points of interest when considering the measurement of property crime.

larceny/theft
A form of theft in which an offender takes possessions that do not belong to him or her with the intent of keeping them.

burglary
Breaking into and entering a structure or vehicle with intent to commit a felony or a theft.

- **Burglary is different from larceny/theft**   When classifying the taking of another person's property, several distinctions determine whether the offense is **larceny/theft** or **burglary.** Burglary involves the unlawful entry of a structure to commit a felony. Larceny/theft involves the unlawful taking of another

In 2006, arsons involving structures accounted for 42.3 percent of the total number of arson offenses. Arsons of industrial and manufacturing structures result in the highest average dollar losses.

Source: © *Peter Turnley/CORBIS. All Rights Reserved*

person's property. Larceny/theft includes theft from a person by stealth such as pocket-picking, purse-snatching (when only minimal force is used), shoplifting, thefts of articles from motor vehicles, and thefts from coin-operated machines.

- **Motor vehicle theft involves only automobiles and trucks**   The theft of motorboats, construction equipment, airplanes, and farming equipment is classified as larceny rather than motor vehicle theft.

- **Arson involves fires that are purposely set**   It does not matter whether the fire was started with the intent to defraud, only that it was willfully or maliciously set. Fires of suspicious or unknown origin are not treated as **arson.**[23]

Offenses against the Public Order

Some criminal offenses involve no discernible victim. **Victimless crimes** involve consensual interactions or behaviors that offend the powerful groups of society who have succeeded in having their concerns and sensibilities elevated to the level of the criminal law. Although broad consensus exists on some of these behaviors, there is also a good deal of controversy about offenses that are a matter of values.[24] (Chapter 15 deals in greater detail with drug use, gambling, and sex work.) Behaviors that fit into the category of offenses against the public order include vagrancy, disorderly conduct, and liquor law violations. These are often considered nuisance offenses, reflecting quality-of-life concerns for many people. The laws concerning these offenses are vigorously enforced in some places and almost completely ignored in others.[25] For instance, when vagrants, street people, and the homeless are considered to be interfering with the tourism trade, shopkeepers, hotel owners, and restaurant managers might ask the police to clear the streets of the "riff-raff and rabble."[26] The police have broad discretion in deciding how to enforce public-order laws. They might overlook possession of small amounts of marijuana in one instance and decide to make an arrest in another if the offender does not show respect.[27]

arson
Any willful or malicious burning or attempt to burn a dwelling, public building, motor vehicle or aircraft, or personal property of another.

victimless crime
Activities such as gambling or prostitution that are deemed undesirable because they offend community standards rather than directly harm people or property.

MEASUREMENT OF CRIME

Now we will turn to identifying some of the issues and concerns raised by trying to measure the amount of crime in communities. Whenever crime rates vary, care must be taken to ensure that these variations are the result of actual changes in crime and

Figure 2-2   **The Dark Figure of Crime.**

Source: John Randolph Fuller, *Juvenile Delinquency: Mainstream and Crosscurrents* (Upper Saddle River, NJ: Pearson Prentice Hall, 2008), 67.

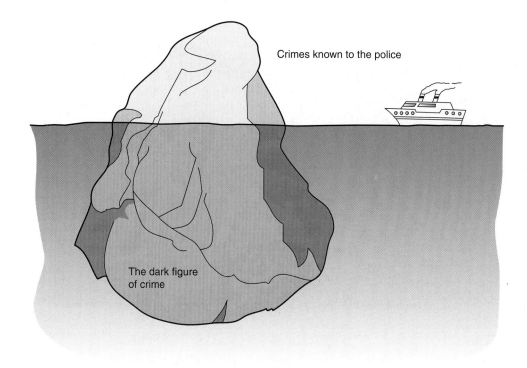

Crimes known to the police

The dark figure of crime

not measurement error. Besides definitional problems as to how to classify certain behaviors, there might also be perceptual problems about exactly when a behavior rises to the level of a criminal offense. To kids who are fist-fighting, their blows might mean they are "just horsing around," but to the parent of the child with the bloody nose, it looks like an assault. To be included in the measurement of crime, the incident must be reported to authorities or researchers who are concerned with determining the level and frequency of unlawful actions. This means that the offense must be reported to the police, who will enter it into the *Uniform Crime Reports* system and, in some circumstances, to the National Incident-Based Reporting System (NIBRS). This section will review other ways of measuring crime: victimization surveys and self-report studies.

One of the problems of attempting to measure crime is that not all offenses are reported. If an offense is not reported to the police, it will not be counted in the indexes that comprise the official measures of crime rates. The offenses that actually occur but do not get reported are known to criminologists as the "dark figure of crime" (see Figure 2-2). According to noted criminologists Paul and Patricia Brantingham, a victim might not want to report an offense to the police for several reasons.

- An offense might be so subtle that it is never known to have happened. Suppose that a person uses a passkey to break into an apartment with the intent to steal a television belonging to the resident, then changes his mind and leaves, disturbing nothing. This action constitutes breaking and entering, but no one save the offender would ever know it happened.

- An offense might not be perceived as such. Suppose that in the course of a championship playoff game, a defenseman for the Philadelphia Flyers were to slash a star center of the Montreal Canadiens with his hockey stick, opening a cut requiring six stitches to close. Such incidents do occur in the heat of competition and are defined as major penalties within the context of the game. The incident described, of course, also constitutes a criminal offense that may be classified as an aggravated assault under the U.S. *Uniform Crime Reports* or as a wounding in the *Canadian Crime Statistics*. However, the event is unlikely to be perceived as a criminal offense by either player, by either team, by the referees,

Fights that occur during professional sports are not typically considered assault and do not fall within the purview of the criminal justice system, unless the violence is extreme.

Source: Brian Snyder\Corbis/Reuters America LLC

or by the fans, and it is unlikely to be reported to the police. In the sport of boxing, a fighter who abides by the sport's rules might cause the death of the other fighter and face no sanctions from the criminal justice system, the referee, or the sport's ruling body.

- An offense might not be reported because the offender is a family member, a friend, or an acquaintance.
- An offense might not be reported because the victim believes that it was trivial, or that the potential penalty is too grave for the harm done.
- An offense might not be reported because the victim fears reprisal.
- An offense might not be reported because the victim feels antipathy toward the police.
- Sometimes the victim has broken the law as well, or is embarrassed by the circumstances under which the offense occurred.[28]

Given these reasons for not reporting crime, does it make any sense to try to measure crime and then base criminal justice system policy on these flawed numbers? The answer is yes, but with caution. Although the dark figure of crime will always be unknown, an idea of the extent of crime can be surmised with the development of precise definitions and uniform reporting standards. Because crime rates are calculated every year and show a pattern of stability, criminal justice experts can assume that unreported crime varies at about the same rates.[29] That is, an unknown but consistent ratio exists between reported and unreported crime. However, this assumption can be misleading when a change in reporting behavior is interpreted as a change in the level of crime. For example, suppose a community establishes a new rape crisis center. As part of their duties, the center's staff members begin an educational prevention and awareness project in which they visit schools and community groups and encourage women to report sexual assaults. The staff members also support victims in the ordeal of reporting their experiences to the police. Although the number of rapes in the community might remain constant, the rape crisis center has stimulated an increase in victim reporting that has resulted in more arrests, prosecutions, and incarcerations. Rape appears to be on the rise in the community, when in reality, more of the dark figure of crime is becoming known to the police, and the crime rate has become more accurate.[30]

TO REPORT OR NOT TO REPORT

You are a married man, and you have made your share of mistakes in life, but now you have placed yourself in a dilemma that threatens to ruin your reputation, your career, and your marriage. If you do nothing, all will be saved in your life, but it will be at the expense of public safety and might result in a life-or-death situation.

While your wife went to Des Moines to take care of her ailing grandmother, you strayed off the path of monogamy, fidelity, and loyalty. You met a young girl who was walking her dog in the park, and after some shameless flirting, you accepted her invitation to meet her at a downtown bar that night. Because this bar was a place you would never have gone to on your own, you were unconcerned that your friends might see you out with another woman. The time at the bar was a blur of drinking, flirting, and suggestive dancing. At 2:00 A.M. you drove her back to her apartment, and agreed to go inside with her. However, after much soul searching, you decided that you could not violate your marriage vows. Unfortunately, the girl was mad and demanded the $200 that she said you agreed to pay her at the bar. You were shocked by her accusation. When you tried to leave, her boyfriend jumped out of the closet with a baseball bat and beat you senseless. After waking up in the hospital, you claimed that you were mugged in the park and did not get a good look at your assailant. Your wife flew home to take care of you and as you began to heal, you renewed your determination to never again do anything that would hurt your wife.

As the months pass, your unfortunate experience has faded, and you believe that no one will ever discover your dalliance. One day, however, as you are watching the local news, you see an exposé about how a number of men have been beaten with a baseball bat and dumped in the park. One of these men was beaten so badly that he had permanent brain damage. The police chief tells the newscaster that it will be only a matter of time before someone is killed by the man with the bat.

You remember the exact location of the apartment and the name of the girl, and you can describe her boyfriend. You know you should tell the police what you know but realize that if you pursue this course, your unfaithful behavior will be revealed. Because you are the vice president of your father-in-law's construction company, you are afraid that you will lose your wife and your job. You are experiencing tremendous stress worrying that someone will be killed by this couple and that it is your moral responsibility to do something about it.

What Do You Do?

1. Tell your wife the truth and hope she does not demand a divorce.
2. Go to the police and tell them what you know and beg them not to drag you into the case.
3. Write an anonymous letter to the police telling them what you know but protecting your identity.
4. Keep your mouth shut and let others worry about themselves.

Uniform Crime Reports (UCR)

Uniform Crime Reports (UCR)
An annual publication by the Federal Bureau of Investigation that uses data from all participating law enforcement agencies in the United States to summarize the incidence and rate of reported crime.

The ***Uniform Crime Reports (UCR)*** are the most extensive and useful measure of crime available. Despite the numerous issues and concerns with how these records are compiled and used, they remain the best available picture of crime, even though that picture tends to be out of focus at times.[31] In 2006, more than 17,500 law enforcement agencies throughout the nation voluntarily participated in the Uniform Crime Reporting Program, representing 94 percent of the U.S. population.[32]

In the 1920s, the International Association of Chiefs of Police developed a system for gathering crime statistics. The association studied criminal codes and record-keeping procedures of a number of law enforcement agencies and came up with a model for categorizing and counting criminal offenses that became the foundation for the UCR Program. The FBI took over the program in 1930, and today more than 17,000 city, county, and state law enforcement agencies voluntarily report crime data to the FBI. By 2002, the program collected data on more than 93 percent of the U.S. population. The *UCR* is used by scholars, legislators, planners, and the media for research and decision making and to keep citizens informed about the level and seriousness of crime (for example, see Figure 2-3).

Although the *UCR* provides a useful picture of crime in the United States, it does have some sources of error.[33] The sources of error are of two types: unintentional and intentional.

- **Unintentional sources of error**   The *UCR* reporting system represents a massive collection effort. Tens of thousands of law enforcement officers and

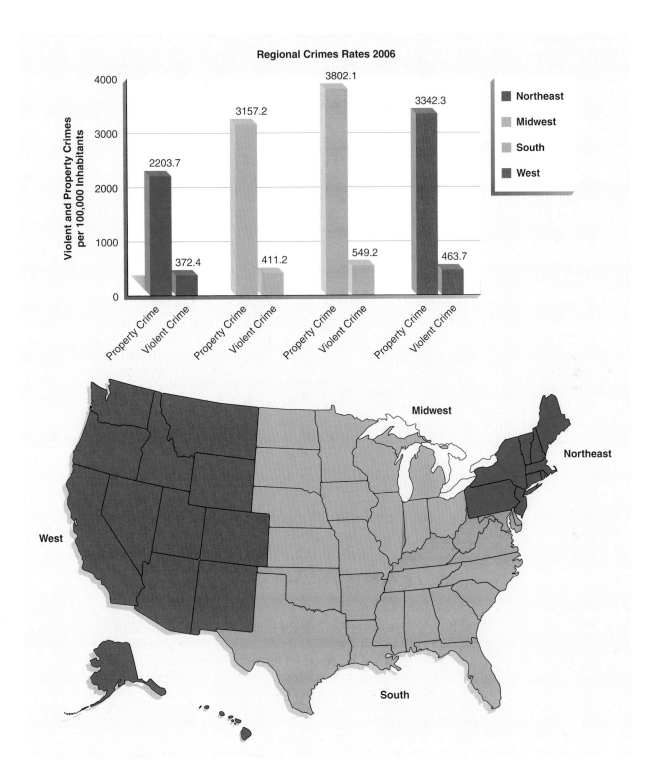

Figure 2-3   **Regional Crime Rates, 2007.**

Source: U.S. Department of Justice, Federal Bureau of Investigation, "Crime in the United States, 2007, Crime Map," September 2007, www.fbi.gov/ucr/cius2007/about/crime_map.html.

recording clerks enter data into the system, and each interpretation by each individual is an opportunity for errors to be made in good faith. For instance, homicide would seem to be the most unambiguous category of crime. Someone is dead, which means the offense will be reported and coded as such. Yet in some cases of assault, the victim dies in the hospital weeks after the case has been entered into the system. Some jurisdictions are better than others at follow-up reporting of the subsequent death and the new homicide charge.

Figure 2-4   *Uniform Crime Report* Part I and Part II Offenses.

Source: FBI.

Part I Offenses

Violent Crimes   **Property Crimes**

Murder and non-negligent manslaughter

Forcible rape

Robbery

Aggravated assault

Part II Offenses

Curfew and loitering laws (juveniles only)

Disorderly conduct

Driving under the influence

Drug abuse violations

Drunkenness

Embezzlement

Forgery and counterfeiting

Fraud

Gambling

Liquor law offenses

Offenses against the family and children

Prostitution and commercialized vice

Runaways (juveniles only)

Sex offenses (except rape and prostitution)

Simple assaults

Stolen property offenses

Vagrancy

Vandalism

Weapons offenses

All other offenses (except traffic)

Additionally, police officers might view certain offenses differently depending on their personal philosophies about gender roles. For example, variations exist within and across jurisdictions in the categorization of rape if the parties involved are spouses or intimate partners. Also, researchers found that few rapes are committed along with other offenses, such as a robbery and a rape. However, rapes that do co-occur with other offenses are more likely to be reported to police than rapes that occur as single offenses. This means that the source of error within rape statistics is probably higher than in statistics for other violent offenses.[34]

- **Intentional sources of error**   The *UCR* is an important social indicator that reflects the quality of life in a jurisdiction. Police chiefs, sheriffs, mayors, and other public officials are judged by the efficacy of their policies, and the *UCR* presents objective criteria on which to base pay raises, promotions, and firings. Because careers are based on these numbers, and the opportunity exists to influence these numbers, it is not surprising that sometimes "the books get cooked."[35] This can happen in two directions. For example, a sheriff who wants to modernize the fleet of squad cars may instruct deputies to change their crime-reporting behavior by counting every trivial infraction, inflating the level of crime and bringing in more money. By contrast, a police chief who is worried about reappointment may

$$\frac{Number\ of\ Crimes}{(Population\,/\,segment\ of\ population)}$$

or

$$\frac{number\ of\ crimes}{population} * number\ of\ people$$

For example, in the U.S. in 2002 . . .

$$\frac{11,877,218\ reported\ crimes}{288,368,698\ t} * 100,000 = 4118.8\ crimes\ per\ 100,000\ people$$

and

$$\frac{420,637\ reported\ robberies}{288,368,698\ total\ U.S.\ population} * 100,000 = 145.9\ robberies\ per\ 100,000\ people$$

Figure 2-5   How to Calculate a Crime Rate.

Source: Department of Justice, Federal Bureau of Investigation, *Uniform Crime Reports, 2006*, Table 1, www.fbi.gov/ucr/cius2006/data/table_01.html.

Violent Crimes	Property Crimes
Murder and non-negligent manslaughter	Burglary
Forcible rape	Larceny-theft
Robbery	Motor vehicle theft
Aggravated assault	Arson

Figure 2-6   FBI Classification of Offenses

instruct officers to overlook crime so that the reported crime rate seems to indicate that the chief's policies have been effective in reducing crime.

These examples should not be interpreted to suggest that law enforcement officials are corrupt or that their staffs are incompetent when assigned to participate in the *UCR* program. Rather, these examples are provided to demonstrate that many possible sources of error exist in the reporting of crime and that this error is unknowable.

CHANGES TO THE UNIFORM CRIME REPORTS   From 1960 to 2004, the *UCR* compiled the Crime Index, with eight serious violent and property offenses listed as *Part I offenses* and a group of lesser offenses listed as *Part II offenses* (see Figure 2-4). The Part I offenses were selected because they are serious, widely identified by victims and witnesses as criminal incidents, and most likely to be reported to the police. Reporting of the less-serious Part II offenses was not mandatory for participation in the UCR Program. The FBI would calculate a jurisdiction's crime rate using the total annual number of Part I offenses for that jurisdiction (see Figure 2-5).

In 2006, the FBI discontinued the Crime Index as it was found to be a poor indicator of the crime rate within jurisdictions. The reason for this was that the index tended to be driven upward by the most-committed offense, usually larceny/theft. This means that a jurisdiction with a high number of larceny/thefts, but a low number of more serious offenses such as murder and rape, would have a higher crime rate, and therefore appear more dangerous.[36] Now, the FBI simply classifies offenses into four violent crimes and four property crimes (see Figure 2-6).

The FBI still calculates crime rates for individual offenses, as well as rates for violent offenses and property offenses. Why not just compare the total numbers of offenses with jurisdictions? The *UCR* shows the actual number of criminal offenses in each jurisdiction, but jurisdictions with more people will always have more crime. Consequently, to compare the crime rates for a specific offense across jurisdictions, the crime rate is calculated.

When considering the categories the *UCR* uses to conceptualize types of crime, we must remember that these categories do not reflect the actual criminal statutes in each jurisdiction. For instance, a misdemeanor drug possession in Wabasha, Minnesota, might qualify as a felony possession in the *UCR*. The reporting system collects data from thousands of jurisdictions, and the categories of crime are

2.1   *CrossCurrents*

The Danger Zone

The FBI compiles and publishes *Uniform Crime Reports: Crime in the United States* so that the statistics can be used for administrative purposes, criminal justice research, and community planning.[1] However, because the statistics are public, the numbers can be quoted in a variety of ways to suit a variety of purposes.

City Crime Rankings: Crime in Metropolitan America, which has been published for about two decades, bases its findings on the *Uniform Crime Reports*. The report states that it provides "easy-to-understand crime comparisons for cities and metro areas throughout the United States," by listing the "safest" and "most dangerous" cities in which to live.[2] In 2007, the report considered the per-capita rates of homicide, rape, robbery, aggravated assault, burglary, and auto theft in 378 cities with populations of 75,000. Presumably, the purpose of *City Crime Rankings* is to help people choose the most crime-free places to live and inform established residents as to how their home cities stack up against other cities in terms of crime rate. In 2007, the report listed Detroit, Michigan, as the nation's most dangerous city. The nation's formerly top dangerous city, St. Louis, Missouri, dropped to number two.

City Crime Rankings has drawn a lot of criticism. Although it is based on government statistics, the report's compilers say they use a "proprietary weighting system" to establish its rankings.[3] That means the compilers interpret *UCR* statistics in ways known only to them to produce the report. *City Crime Rankings* and the way it is produced has criminologists, city boosters, and even the FBI up in arms about its methods. The American Society of Criminology called the report "an irresponsible misuse" of crime data. Michael Tonry, president of the American Society of Criminology, told the media that the rankings "do groundless harm to many communities."[4] On the UCR website, starting with the 2006 edition of *Crime in the United States*, the FBI now displays a warning before reports can be accessed:

> These rough rankings provide no insight into the numerous variables that mold crime in a particular town, city, county, state, or region. Consequently, they lead to simplistic and/or incomplete analyses that often create misleading perceptions adversely affecting communities and their residents. The data user is, therefore, cautioned against comparing statistical data of individual reporting units from cities, metropolitan areas, states, or colleges or universities solely on the basis of their population coverage or student enrollment.[5]

One of the problems with using the *UCR* to rank cities and states in this manner is the difference in each state's crime-reporting techniques. As discussed in the chapter, each state collects its own crime figures and reports them to the *UCR*. The fact that each state collects and reports statistics in a different way leaves room for variability in the numbers. In 2007, South Carolina ranked as the fourth-most dangerous state in the nation, and number one for assaults. However, a representative of the South Carolina Sheriff's Association said that South Carolina captures its statistics more thoroughly than other states, making the state appear more dangerous than it actually is.[6]

Such variability is possible in every state and within every law enforcement department. Some offenses, because of their nature, are reported more thoroughly than others. For instance, almost all homicides are reported and recorded, whereas relatively few rapes are. However, jurisdictions that have more confidence from victims and better relations with the public might actually record more rapes—because more rapes are reported—than jurisdictions with poorer relationships with the public in which more rapes might happen, but fewer are reported.

Think About It

1. Would *City Crime Rankings*, or a similar ranking, influence your decision on where to live or visit?
2. Do you agree with criminologists and the FBI that the *UCR* statistics should not be used to compile popular rankings? Do you disagree? Why?
3. Do you think your city is dangerous? If so, why?

[1]U.S. Department of Justice, Federal Bureau of Investigation, "Crime in the United States, 2006," www.fbi.gov/ucr/cius2006/about/index.html.

[2]CQ Press, "City Crime Rankings," www.cqpress.com/product/City-Crime-Rankings-14th-Edition.html.

[3]David N. Goodman, "Ranking the Safety of Nation's Cities," Associated Press/*Virginian-Pilot* (Norfolk, VA), November 19, 2007, A3.

[4]Ibid.

[5]U.S. Department of Justice, *Crime in the United States, 2006.*

[6]Noah Haglund, "Our State 4th-Most Dangerous?" *Post and Courier* (Charleston, SC), final edition, March 18, 2008, B1.

2.1   CRIMINAL JUSTICE REFERENCE

The Hierarchy Rule

The UCR program refers to the occurrence of several offenses committed at the same time and place as a "multiple-offense situation." In this situation, the law enforcement agency must determine which offense occurs highest in the violent crime/property crime hierarchy and record that offense. The offenses in order of hierarchy are as follows:

1. Criminal Homicide
   a. Murder and Nonnegligent Manslaughter
   b. Manslaughter by Negligence
2. Forcible Rape
   a. Rape by Force
   b. Attempts to Commit Forcible Rape
3. Robbery
   a. Firearm
   b. Knife or Cutting Instrument
   c. Other Dangerous Weapon
   d. Strong-Arm—Hands, Fists, Feet, etc.
4. Aggravated Assault
   a. Firearm
   b. Knife or Cutting Instrument
   c. Other Dangerous Weapon
   d. Aggravated Injury—Hands, Fists, Feet, etc.
5. Burglary
   a. Forcible Entry
   b. Unlawful Entry—No Force
   c. Attempted Forcible Entry
6. Larceny-Theft (Except Motor Vehicle Theft)
7. Motor Vehicle Theft
   a. Autos
   b. Trucks and Buses
   c. Other Vehicles
8. Arson
   a.–g.   Structural
   h.–i.   Mobile

Source: U.S. Department of Justice, Federal Bureau of Investigation, *Uniform Crime Reporting Handbook* (Washington, DC: U.S. Government Printing Office, 2004), 10, www.fbi.gov/ucr/handbook/ucrhandbook04.pdf.

---

designed to quantify the criminal behavior in each jurisdiction, not to reflect which actual criminal laws have been violated. Because the *UCR* represents a limited agenda of counting offenses and comparing crime rates, it distorts the crime picture in the way it defines wrongdoing. (See Crosscurrents 2.1 to learn why the FBI and criminologists are concerned about the public's use of *UCR* statistics.) This problem is most apparent when several offenses are committed in one incident.

Suppose someone breaks into your home, beats you up, steals your television set, kicks your dog, and smokes a marijuana cigarette while spray-painting obscene graffiti on your living room walls. You report the incident to the police, and after making the arrest, they charge the suspect with multiple offenses. What gets reported to the *UCR* system, however, is another matter. Because the *UCR* uses the *hierarchy rule* when dealing with multiple offenses, only the most serious offense is reported and the rest are ignored.[37] In this case, your assault would be entered into the system, and the vandalism, drug use, theft, and abuse of your dog would not be counted. The offender may be prosecuted for each of the offenses (well, maybe not for kicking the dog), but only the assault will be included in the official crime statistics. See Criminal Justice Reference 2.1 to understand how the hierarchy rule is applied.

Given the strengths and weaknesses of the *UCR* system, it should be evident that although the *UCR* provides a reasonably good picture of crime, it does not tell the whole crime story.[38] Fortunately, other measures supplement the *UCR*.

National Incident-Based Reporting System (NIBRS)

The *UCR* system is more than six decades old, and although it has been improved greatly, its basic structure still has some problems that make it deficient in providing the types of information necessary for a clear picture of crime in the United States.

**National Incident-Based
Reporting System (NIBRS)**

*A crime-reporting system in which
each separate offense in a crime is
described, including data describing
the offender(s), victim(s), and property.*

Therefore, the government has embarked on a new and more comprehensive crime-reporting system designed to rectify some of the *UCR*'s shortcomings. The **National Incident-Based Reporting System (NIBRS)** is constructed to gather data on each criminal offense even if several offenses are committed at one time. That is, an incident that includes several different offenses will have each one enumerated in the statistics rather than only the most serious one. This new system is an improvement over the *UCR* because it compensates for the hierarchy rule.[39]

Developed in 1985, the NIBRS collects data on each single incident and arrest for 22 offense categories comprising 46 specific offenses in its Group A offenses. Additionally, only arrest data are reported in 11 Group B offense categories (see Figure 2-7). The advantage of the NIBRS over the *UCR* is that it allows law enforcement officials to precisely identify when and where an offense takes place, its form, and the characteristics of victims and perpetrators. According to the FBI, "NIBRS has the capability of furnishing information on nearly every major criminal justice issue facing law enforcement today, including terrorism, white-collar crime, weapons offenses, missing children, where criminality is involved, drug/narcotic offenses,

Group A Offenses
Extensive crime data for these are collected in the National Incident-Based Reporting System.

Arson

Assault offenses (aggravated assault, simple assault, intimidation)

Bribery

Burglary/breaking and entering

Counterfeiting/forgery

Destruction/damage/vandalism of property

Drug/narcotic offenses (drug/narcotic violations, drug equipment violations)

Embezzlement

Extortion/blackmail

Fraud offenses (false pretenses/swindle/confidence game, credit card/automatic teller machine fraud, impersonation, welfare fraud, wire fraud)

Gambling offenses (betting/wagering, operating/promoting/assisting gambling, gambling equipment violations, sports tampering)

Homicide offenses (murder and nonnegligent manslaughter, negligent manslaughter, justifiable homicide)

Kidnapping/abduction

Larceny/theft offenses (pocket-picking, purse-snatching, shoplifting, theft from building, theft from coin-operated machine or device, theft from motor vehicle, theft of motor vehicle parts or accessories, all other larceny)

Motor vehicle theft

Pornography/obscene material

Prostitution offenses (prostitution, assisting or promoting prostitution)

Robbery

Sex offenses, forcible (rape, sodomy, sexual assault with an object, fondling)

Sex offenses, nonforcible (incest, statutory rape)

Stolen property offenses (receiving, etc.)

Weapons law violations

Group B Offenses
Only arrest data are reported.

Bad checks

Curfew/loitering/vagrancy violations

Disorderly conduct

Driving under the influence

Drunkenness

Family offenses, nonviolent

Liquor law violations

Peeping Tom

Runaway

Trespass of real property

All other offenses

Figure 2-7   **The National Incident-Based Reporting System (NIBRS).**

Source: FBI.

drug involvement in all offenses, hate crimes, spouse abuse, abuse of the elderly, child abuse, domestic violence, juvenile crime/gangs, parental kidnapping, organized crime, pornography/child pornography, driving under the influence, and alcohol-related offenses."[40]

Participation in the NIBRS system requires that a state overhaul how it collects and reports crime data.[41] As of December 2003, 23 states were NIBRS certified, 13 states were testing the NIBRS, and nine states were developing plans to test the NIBRS procedure.[42] It will be some years yet before the NIBRS system is used nationwide and can produce the detailed information required by law enforcement agencies in the 21st century.[43]

This new system of recording crime might produce some unintended consequences. One issue concerning NIBRS is the complexity of the reporting and coding procedures. Law enforcement agencies will be required to invest increased resources and personnel in crime-data collection efforts. In the past, the job of collecting and analyzing data has been done by police administrators, but the NIBRS may require skilled civilians to make the program work. Another issue of concern is the effect that NIBRS will have on the duties of street-level police officers. NIBRS requires a much greater level of detail in the reporting of offenses than does the *UCR*, and some critics are concerned that street-level officers will consider this as interfering with "real" police work. Street-level officers might believe that the NIBRS program is more useful to researchers than to themselves. Finally, law enforcement officials might be concerned with what appears to be an increase in crime because the NIBRS reports each offense separately, rather than reporting only one offense as does the *UCR*. The media and the public might not understand how changing the way crime is reported could result in the appearance of more crime. This could be a public relations problem for police executives who are evaluated on how well they control crime in their jurisdictions.[44]

NIBRS MEASURES OF WHITE-COLLAR AND CORPORATE CRIME   White-collar and corporate crime are a special case where the measurement of crime is concerned. This type of crime damages society in the long term possibly as much as street crime, but more of it is represented by the dark figure of crime than street crime. That is, more white-collar and corporate offenses go unnoticed and unrecorded than street offenses. This is important because it is impossible for the criminal justice system to address crime that goes unreported and remains unknown. On a large scale, the financial offenses that usually occur within the framework of white-collar and corporate crime can damage the nation's economy, and on an individual scale, they can hurt thousands of people, particularly those who are impoverished and are struggling to get by.[45] Therefore, it is important that white-collar and corporate crime be measured with the same rigor as street crime. The NIBRS is better equipped than the *UCR* to do this, but measuring white-collar and corporate crime remains a difficult task for several reasons:

- Like the *UCR*, the NIBRS primarily reflects street crime. This is because local and state agencies, not federal agencies, were originally surveyed during the development of the NIBRS. Because of their concern with immediate public safety, local and state agencies are more concerned with street crime and want street-crime statistics to improve policing.

- White-collar and corporate crime typically fall within federal jurisdiction, so offenses that are not fraud, embezzlement, counterfeiting, or bribery—which are already represented in the NIBRS—are not as thoroughly represented in the NIBRS as street offenses.

- Much of the investigation and regulation of corporate and white-collar crime is done by regulatory agencies and professional associations, not by law enforcement agencies and legislation. This means that corporate and white-collar offenses are reported to the *UCR* and NIBRS only if criminal charges are filed, which is not always the case in corporate crime. Corporate crime is usually handled by a regulatory agency or in the civil courts.

- Common corporate offenses are typically classified as "All Other Offenses" in the NIBRS Group B offenses (refer to Figure 2-7). Currently, there is no way to distinguish corporate offenses from the rest of the offenses in this category.

- Victims often do not know they have been deceived or are too ashamed of being swindled to report the offense. In the same vein, corporations tend not to report white-collar offenses perpetrated against them because to do so might harm the company's reputation. Finally, major corporate offenses are often too complicated and widespread for most people to understand that they have been victims of a corporate offense.

- Both the *UCR* and the NIBRS are voluntary, which means that white-collar and corporate offenses might go unreported to the system.

- The *UCR* was developed at about the same time, during the 1920s and 1930s, as the concept of white-collar crime. Therefore, many of the laws that criminalized white-collar and corporate offenses did not yet exist. Most white-collar crime laws were passed during three periods: antitrust laws were passed in the 1920s during the Progressive Era; social welfare laws were passed during the New Deal of the 1930s; and consumer protection laws came about in the 1960s.

WHAT IS MEASURED   The *UCR* provides little information on white-collar and corporate crime, with the related categories being fraud, forgery/counterfeiting, embezzlement, and "all other offenses." Because white-collar and corporate offenses are not Index Crimes, the only information available is arrest information, including age, sex, and race of arrestees. An interesting note is that arrest rates for embezzlement, fraud, and forgery/counterfeiting are much lower than the arrest rates for property crime or for total offenses. This could be related to problems in investigation and reporting.

The NIBRS classifies white-collar and corporate offenses in greater detail than the *UCR* (see Table 2-1). The categories include fraud, bad checks, bribery, sports tampering, counterfeiting/forgery, embezzlement, and all other offenses. Four elements in the NIBRS measures of white-collar crime include "offender(s) suspected of using . . . ," "location type," "property description," and "type of victim." The "offender(s) suspected of using . . ." category is especially useful for describing offenses committed with computers. Of all the offenses committed using computer equipment, 42 percent are white-collar offenses, the largest proportion of those being larceny-theft. Figure 2-8 describes the locations in which white-collar offenses most occur; for example, most embezzlement offenses occur within commercial establishments.

The FBI is working to improve the NIBRS system for reporting of all criminal offenses. Because the NIBRS is being directed to include more information on white-collar and corporate offenses, a type of crime that was once thought to be relatively rare might be discovered to be quite common and widespread. The measurement of white-collar and corporate crime is a good example of the collection of statistics shining a light on the dark figure of crime.

Victimization Surveys

Previous discussions of the *UCR* and the NIBRS have highlighted flaws and issues that each system has in developing an accurate picture of the nature and extent of crime in the United States. Because both reporting systems require citizens to report criminal offenses to law enforcement officials, they fail to account for the dark figure of crime. As suggested earlier, citizens might not report an offense to the police for several reasons, but to truly comprehend and respond to unlawful behavior, law enforcement personnel must find other ways to persuade people to assist in measuring the real level of criminal activity.

victimization survey

A survey that attempts to measure the extent of crime by interviewing crime victims.

One such method for trying to get at the level of unreported crime is **victimization surveys.** Victimization surveys differ from the previously mentioned ways of reporting crime in many important ways. As the name implies, victimization

Table 2-1 NIBRS Classifications of White-Collar Offenses

Offense	Type
Academic crime	Fraud
Adulterated food, drugs, or cosmetics	Fraud
Antitrust violations	All Other Offenses
ATM fraud	Fraud
Bad checks	Bad Checks
Bribery	Bribery
Check kiting	Fraud/Bad Checks
Confidence game	Fraud
Contract fraud	Fraud
Corrupt conduct by juror	Bribery
Counterfeiting	Counterfeiting/Forgery
Defense contract fraud	Fraud
Ecology law violations	All Other Offenses
Election law violations	All Other Offenses
Embezzlement	Embezzlement
Employment agency and education-related scams	Fraud
Environmental law violations	All Other Offenses
False advertising and misrepresentation of products	Fraud
False and fraudulent actions on loans, debts, and credits	Fraud
False report/statement	Fraud
Forgery	Counterfeiting/Forgery
Fraudulent checks	Bad Checks
Health and safety laws	Fraud
Health care provider fraud	Fraud
Home improvement fraud	Fraud
Impersonation	Fraud
Influence peddling	Bribery
Insider trading	Fraud
Insufficient-funds checks	Bad Checks
Insurance fraud	Fraud
Investment scams	Fraud
Jury tampering	Bribery
Kickback	Bribery
Land sale fraud	Fraud
Mail fraud	Fraud
Managerial fraud	Fraud
Misappropriation	Embezzlement
Ponzi schemes	Fraud
Religious fraud	Fraud
Sports bribery	Sports Tampering
Strategic bankruptcy	Fraud
Subornation of perjury	Bribery
Swindle	Fraud
Tax law violations	All Other Offenses
Telemarketing or boiler room scams	Fraud
Telephone fraud	Fraud
Travel scams	Fraud
Unauthorized use of a motor vehicle	Embezzlement
Welfare fraud	Fraud
Wire fraud	Fraud

Source: Cynthia Barnett, *The Measurement of White-Collar Crime Using Uniform Crime Reporting (UCR) Data* (Washington, DC: U.S. Department of Justice, Federal Bureau of Investigation, n.d.), Appendix A, 7, www.fbi.gov/ucr/whitecollarforweb.pdf.

Figure 2-8   **White-Collar Offenses by Location Type.**

Source: Cynthia Barnett, *The Measurement of White-Collar Crime Using Uniform Crime Reporting (UCR) Data* (Washington, DC: U.S. Department of Justice, Federal Bureau of Investigation, n.d.), 4, www.fbi.gov/ucr/whitecollarforweb.pdf.

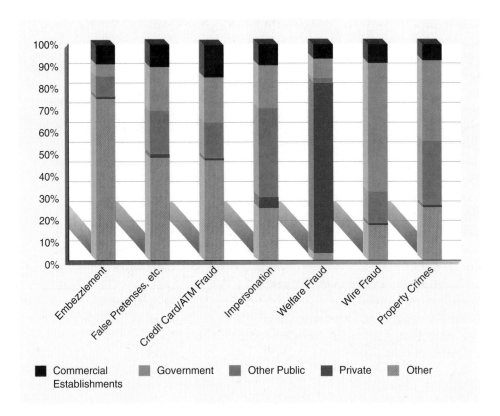

surveys ask crime victims about their experiences. They are essentially self-report studies that are done as part of survey research. As such, victimization surveys do not attempt to create a comprehensive account of criminal offenses, as in the *UCR* program, but rather, usually study random samples of the general public and focus on specific types of offending. Additionally, a number of offenses are not measured because the parties act in a consensual manner, and there is no reporting victim. For instance, whereas the *UCR* measures arrests for drug sales, victimization surveys miss successfully completed drug transactions because buyers consider themselves satisfied customers, not crime victims. The same could be said of gambling and prostitution.[46] Although these offenses might produce some indirect victims (such as the government not collecting taxes on these business transactions), the participants do not view themselves as victims and do not report these offenses in victimization surveys.

Other offenses are more accurately measured by the *UCR* than by victimization surveys. Perhaps the most obvious is homicide. Although nearly every homicide is reported by the *UCR*, homicide victims cannot respond to a victimization survey. Additionally, white-collar and corporate offenses are difficult to measure using victimization surveys because people are often unaware that they have been victims of subtle corruption or fraud. Because of these differences in the types of offenses that are measured, comparing the crime picture of the *UCR* with victimization surveys is problematic.[47] Rather than attempting to decide which method most accurately reports crime, it is more useful to think of them as measuring different aspects of crime. Used in conjunction, rather than in competition, these measures foster development of a deeper appreciation of the types of crime and how it affects the community.

Like other methods of measuring crime, victimization surveys have evolved from rather crude devices with glaring shortcomings to extremely sophisticated instruments that attempt to account for a variety of confounding variables. Therefore victimization surveys have earned a place in the kit of tools that criminologists use to measure crime. Victimization surveys have evolved in an interesting manner. There have been four generations of victimization surveys since their inception in the late 1960s.

- **First-Generation Victimization Surveys**   One of the concerns of the 1968 President's Crime Commission was the inaccurate and biased picture of crime derived from the *UCR*. As a result, the government attempted to get a clearer picture of crime by asking victims about their experiences. The first national victimization survey, from the National Opinion Research Center (NORC), collected information from 10,000 households across the United States. The most significant conclusion reached by the NORC survey was that the *UCR* underreported crime by about 50 percent. The way the NORC survey defined crime and gathered its data raised a number of methodological concerns. Still, this first generation of surveys demonstrated that victims were willing to talk about their experiences with researchers.

- **Second-Generation Victimization Surveys**   A second, and improved, generation of victimization surveys was created around 1970. These surveys attempted to gauge the amount of error in the first generation of studies. One way to measure this perceived error was to survey victims who had reported crime to the police to see whether they had problems with memory decay, *telescoping* (when victims mistakenly place the time of the offense within the study period, misjudging how long ago the incident took place), or miscategorizing the type of offense. Some of these studies attempted a forward records search to see whether information provided by the victim was also reported in the *UCR*. Also, commercial establishments were added to the survey to attempt to measure crime not connected to single households. One problem with comparing victimization surveys with the *UCR* is the difficulty of matching initial crime reports with victims after months or years. This is especially true for commercial establishments with a high staff turnover. For example, if a restaurant was robbed last year, the manager and employees surveyed in the victimization survey done this year might be new and thus unable to provide useful information about the robbery.

- **Third-Generation Victimization Surveys**   A third generation of victimization surveys was done in 1972, and although some of the components of the surveys were short-lived because of the exorbitant cost, these surveys provided an outline for ambitious data-gathering efforts that has informed future research efforts. The National Crime Survey (NCS) surveyed about 12,000 households a month on a rotating basis to correct for some of the concerns of the previous surveys. One improvement was that researchers interviewed more than just the head of the household. In addition to the survey of households, the NCS gathered data on commercial establishments and 26 cities in which both residences and businesses were contacted. Unfortunately, both the business victimization surveys and the city surveys were discontinued after a few years because they were deemed too expensive to conduct.

- **Fourth-Generation Victimization Surveys**   The fourth and current generation of surveys has continued to improve. Although not error-free, they are more sophisticated and have addressed somewhat successfully many of the problems of former surveys. The National Crime Victimization Survey (NCVS) gathers data on subgroups of victims, seeks to determine what can be done to aid victims, and attempts to provide empirical information that helps households and individuals avoid victimization. One of the most significant improvements of the NCVS is the use of better screening questions that allow researchers to identify victims of specific offenses and ask detailed follow-up questions of only those respondents. The surveys are also increasingly using technology, such as computer-assisted telephone interviews. These improvements have resulted in an increase in victimization reporting.[48]

What is the crime picture according to recent victimization studies? According to the NCVS, both violent and property victimizations have continued to decrease (see Figures 2-9 and 2-10). Since the 1990s, violent victimizations have significantly decreased

Figure 2-9 Rates of Violent Victimization per 1,000 Persons.

Source: Michael Rand and Shannan Catalano, *Criminal Victimization, 2006* (Washington, DC: Bureau of Justice Statistics, 2007), 2, www.ojp.usdoj.gov/bjs/pub/pdf/cv06.pdf.

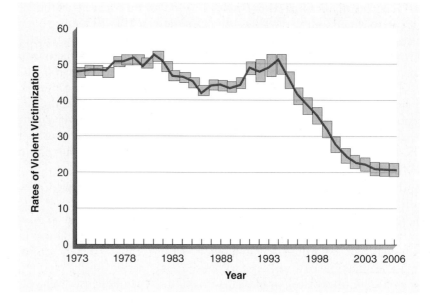

Figure 2-10 Property Crimes Rate per 1000 Households.

Source: Michael Rand and Shannan Catalano, *Criminal Victimization, 2006* (Washington, DC: Bureau of Justice Statistics, 2007), 2, www.ojp.usdoj.gov/bjs/pub/pdf/cv06.pdf.

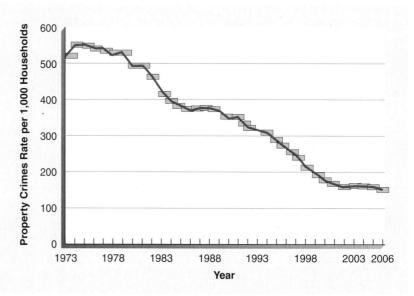

for both males and females, as well as for individuals of different races, although 2006 shows a slight rise in victimizations for blacks and females. (See Figure 2-11.)

Self-Report Studies

The third major technique for collecting data on unlawful behavior is self-report studies. In self-report studies, respondents are asked to identify the types of offenses they have committed over the study period. Although there are some significant concerns about veracity when individuals are asked to admit to criminal behavior, there are also reasons to believe that these data provide a different and important picture of crime that is not supplied in government studies.[49] Self-report studies are important because they are not filtered through criminal justice system agencies. The *UCR* provides better measures of what the police do than what the picture of crime actually looks like. Victimization surveys provide the perspective of those who have suffered some loss, but they fail to record offenses that have no direct victim. Self-report studies, however, provide an accurate picture of crime without having to view delinquency and criminal behavior through the lens of law enforcement agencies or victims, both of whom might introduce bias.

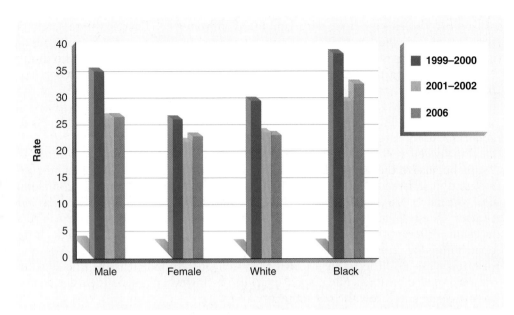

Figure 2-11   **Average Annual Rate of Violent Victimizations per 1000 Persons (Age 12 or Older).** *Source:* Michael Rand and Shannan Catalano, *Criminal Victimization, 2006* (Washington, DC: Bureau of Justice Statistics, 2007), 4, www.ojp.usdoj.gov/bjs/pub/pdf/cv06.pdf.

Researchers were initially concerned about the willingness of respondents to admit to delinquent or criminal behavior in self-report studies.[50] However, people were forthcoming in these studies about many behaviors they would not admit to publicly. Questions about the underreporting of criminal behavior were eventually matched with questions about overreporting. That is, although some people might lie and not admit to offenses they have committed, others might lie and claim they committed violations that they did not.

Because of the anonymity of many self-report studies, it is impossible to determine whether respondents are telling the truth and whether the studies are reliable.

Researchers typically give respondents one of two types of assurances to make them feel comfortable in answering questions. The first assurance is confidentiality. Here, the researcher tells respondents that no one else will see who answered the questions. Only the researcher knows which respondents answered which questions because this information can be used to acquire follow-up data. The other type of assurance that researchers give is anonymity. The research instrument is given to a group of respondents, and no names are recorded. This means that the researcher cannot link specific answers to specific respondents. Research projects that promise anonymity presumably will elicit more truthful answers because respondents can safely report their offenses without fear that anyone, researchers or police, will be able to connect specific offenses to them.

One may legitimately question the incentive for people to tell the truth in self-report studies. The answer is that there is no real incentive. However, over repeated surveys, the same approximate level of dishonesty can be expected, and researchers can thus assume that the measures are comparable and valid. For instance, if I give a self-report study to my students in Georgia and another professor gives the same survey in Texas or California, researchers would assume that there is a constant percentage of respondents who will over-self-report or under-self-report offenses. If responses are consistent over repeated surveys, researchers assume that any differences in self-reported crime measure actual offenses rather than signify errors that have been introduced by lying respondents. Critics question whether these assumptions are warranted.[51]

Researchers have attempted to determine whether respondents tell the truth in self-report studies. For example, in one study of drug use, researchers gave the subjects a urinalysis test to determine whether their answers to questions about drug use were accurate. More than two-thirds of those who used marijuana lied about it to the researchers, and more than 85 percent of those who used cocaine lied.[52]

Another concern about using self-report studies to examine the amount and degree of crime has to do with the issue of representativeness. Many of the early self-report studies were done with samples of convenience. That is, the researchers simply asked students in their classrooms to answer questionnaires. Generalizing to larger populations is difficult when the sample is constructed according to who shows up to class on a particular day. To correct for such a biased sample, researchers use probability theory to draw a sample that reflects the relevant characteristics of the population from which it is drawn. In this way, the researchers can be reasonably confident that the findings derived from their study of a small number of respondents are applicable to the larger population.[53]

Finally, self-reported crime can give an inaccurate picture of the overall crime situation because of the way studies are administered. Basically, two types of techniques are used in self-report studies. The first is a questionnaire that subjects complete. Questionnaires are relatively inexpensive, standardized, and do not require personal contact. Questionnaires can be mailed, so information can be collected from subjects in many different locations. The disadvantages of questionnaires include little opportunity for researchers to clarify questions that confuse respondents. Also, the researcher can do little to ensure that the intended respondent is the one actually answering the questions. The response rate can be low when respondents decide not to participate and throw the questionnaire away.[54]

Self-report studies and victimization surveys are powerful techniques for getting at the dark figure of crime, but these measures are not substitutes for the *UCR* or the NIBRS. They provide another view of the crime picture but are not as comprehensive as the *UCR* or the NIBRS, and each has its limitations.[55] Taken together, however, these methods of collecting crime data give us the best picture we have ever had of crime, but there are still issues that keep the picture of crime out of focus. Like the proverbial blind men trying to describe an elephant by touch, each of these measures of crime concentrates on a different aspect of the problem and none sees the whole picture. The logical question to ask at this point remains, What part of the crime picture do these measures miss or obscure?

1. **Corporate crime.**   As we discussed earlier, the three measures of crime are not very good at detecting the types of criminal offenses that corporations might commit in their business pursuits. Price fixing, insider stock trading, and bribery are all offenses that are unlikely to be detected by any of these measures.[56] The reasons for this are complicated and numerous. The line between shrewd business practices and corporate crime is vague, and accounting irregularities, collusion and price fixing, and corporate fraud are difficult to detect. Business executives often employ sophisticated accountants and lawyers to skirt the edges of the law and give themselves a competitive advantage. Sometimes, the wrongdoing is not labeled as such until an investigation is initiated.

2. **Organized crime.**   Those involved in organized criminal activities are unlikely to self-report their unlawful behaviors. Additionally, victims of threats and extortion are often afraid to identify their persecutors and are unlikely to respond truthfully to victimization surveys.[57] Furthermore, organized crime has occasionally been successful in bribing or intimidating law enforcement officials, ensuring that their offenses are not recorded. Additionally as previously mentioned, much organized-crime activity involves supplying the demand for illegal drugs, prostitution, and gambling, which means that those who participate in such activities deem themselves neither victims nor criminals.

3. **Drug sales.**   Although self-report studies have had some success in getting individuals to talk about their drug-taking behaviors, getting them to talk about their drug-selling behaviors has been less successful. The larger the drug dealer's business, the less likely the dealer is to self-identify as such for fear that a response could lead to arrest.[58] An additional problem in gathering information from drug dealers is that they are unlikely to be included in self-report or victimization studies of crime. These studies are unable to get at the subculture of drug dealers who maintain unlisted cell phone numbers, live in dwellings

registered to family members or friends, and are otherwise invisible to normal research techniques.

4. **Prostitution and gambling.**   Those who engage in prostitution and gambling do not always think a crime has been committed. When there is a satisfied service provider and a satisfied customer, both think of the behavior as a successful business transaction and do not consider themselves to be either criminal or victim.[59]

One may reasonably ask why we even bother trying to measure crime when the data-collection methods are so limited. The answer is that we have no choice. Legislators, criminal justice administrators, law enforcement officers, and the public all make decisions based on their perceptions of how much crime exists and how it affects victims. It is best that they base their decisions on as accurate a picture as possible. Although the crime picture that scholars and government officials provide is limited, the quality of this picture is constantly improving, and it is better than relying on the media or public opinion for the information on which public policy is made and criminal justice system budgets are based. By employing the systematically gathered *UCR* data with the snapshots provided by victimization surveys and self-report studies, we can get a reasonable idea of the scope and severity of the crime problem. Because crime is a socially constructed concept, some ambiguity will always exist about what behaviors constitute crime and whether particular incidents fit those definitions. Additionally, even when we agree on the definitions of crime, there will always be incentives and motivations for individuals not to report.

FEAR OF CRIME

Only the direct consumers of crime statistics are affected by the limitations of crime-measuring efforts. Government funding agencies, law enforcement departments, and the media are concerned with discovering the overall crime picture so they can decide where to allocate resources or how to enlighten the public. However, most of us know little about these elaborate and expensive ways to measure crime and make our daily decisions to prevent, avoid, or respond to crime based on our perceptions of danger and assumed likelihood of victimization. Despite our relative lack of knowledge of the actual level and seriousness of crime in our communities, we have a healthy respect for the potential effect of crime on our lives, and we take measures to reduce the chances of becoming crime victims.[60] In this way, a realistic fear of crime is useful. The questions to be addressed here concern where our fear of crime comes from and whether that fear is justified.

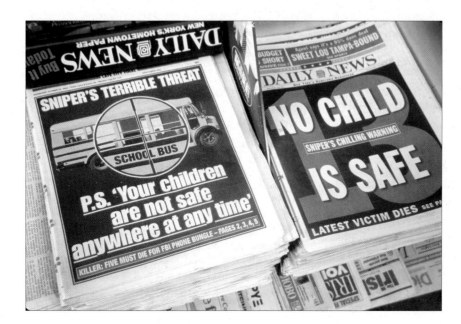

The news media can inflame the public's fear of crime, especially after particularly shocking incidents.

Source: Joel Gordon/Joel Gordon Photography

For many people, the fear of crime is a constant feature that dictates how they conduct their daily lives (see Crosscurrents 2.2).[61] While waxing poetically about the "good old days" when they could leave their homes for an afternoon of shopping and not bother to lock their doors, they spend considerable amounts of money on dead-bolt locks, security systems, cameras, and noise machines that sound like big, barking dogs. More generally, they isolate themselves in gated communities, are suspicious of delivery people, and to a large degree, surrender public spaces to street people at night. The fear of crime, although healthy to some degree, has also diminished our sense of community and has developed into a self-fulfilling prophecy that stimulates crime by reducing the interconnectedness of people. How justified is this fear?[62]

In his book *Random Violence*, sociologist Joel Best addressed the perception of many people that crime is a significant problem that will soon affect their lives unless they take steps to avoid it. Best contended that perceptions of violence are constructed not by official measures of crime, but by the media, which can distort and sensationalize particular incidents. Isolated violent events can appear to be a threat to everyone.[63] One of the first issues that Best confronted was the notion of random violence, pointing out problems with three popular conceptions that compose the idea of random violence.

1. **Patternlessness.**   The term *random violence* implies that anyone could be a victim at any time. In fact, crime is highly patterned. That is, certain people are more likely to be victims than are other people. When we examine homicide rates (for which we have the most reliable statistics), we see that age, race, and gender clearly affect the probability of victimization. For example, Best argued that homicide rates for white males peak for those between ages 20 and 24, then gradually decline as the men grow older. Crime can be examined for patterns, and according to Best, the patterns are so clear and distinct that the term *random violence* is inaccurate.

2.2 CrossCurrents

The Social Security Check Phenomenon

Could the fear of crime keep someone from going to the doctor? A 2008 study of the elderly in Baltimore suggested that they avoid going to the emergency room at the beginning of the month because they want to stay home and ensure that their Social Security checks are not stolen from their mail.

Study author Dr. David Jerrard, a professor of emergency medicine, noticed that elderly patients were less likely to visit the emergency room at the first of the month. After he mentioned to some of his elderly patients that he noticed that fewer of them came in at the first of the month, the patients told him the reason was that they were waiting at home for their Social Security checks so that no one would steal them.

Jerrard said that although waiting a couple of days to visit an emergency room would not hurt most elderly patients, it was worrisome to think that patients might be remaining at home with more serious problems while waiting for their checks to arrive. Dr. James S. Goodwin of the University of Texas Medical Branch calls it the "Social Security check

phenomenon," something that is well known to doctors who work with the low-income elderly. "Older people living in certain low-income neighborhoods have a realistic fear of crime," Goodwin said.[1]

Although the elderly might fear crime more than younger people, they actually experience less crime. Purse-snatching and pocket-picking are the only measured offenses for which the elderly are victimized at the same rates as other age groups.[2]

Think About It

1. Why would the elderly fear crime more than younger people?
2. Do you think the "Social Security check phenomenon" is real or just a coincidence?

[1]Randy Dotinga, "Seniors Avoid ER at Start of Month," HealthDay/*Washington Post*, April 4, 2008, www.washingtonpost.com/wp-dyn/content/article/2008/04/04/AR2008040402305.html.

[2]Patsy Klaus, *Crimes against Persons Age 65 or Older, 1993–2002* (Washington, DC: U.S. Department of Justice, Bureau of Justice Statistics, January 2005), 1, www.ojp.usdoj.gov/bjs/pub/pdf/cpa6502.pdf.

2. **Pointlessness.**   Sensational incidents of crime can appear to be pointless. When the car driven by Susan Smith in South Carolina was allegedly carjacked and found at the bottom of a lake with her two small children still strapped into their car seats, people were at a loss to explain such a senseless and pointless act of cruelty. It was later discovered that Smith drowned her children because she had had an affair with a man who did not want a long-term relationship with her because of her children. Smith then killed her children to get them out of the way of her quest to maintain her relationship with her boyfriend. Most criminal offenses have a motive. Violence can be instrumental, but even when it seems random, on further examination it is often found to have a purpose.

3. **Deterioration of society.**   When the media report a number of sensational offenses, random violence appears to be epidemic. Because of the national and international scope of the media, all news can be perceived as local news. Widely scattered occurrences of firearm violence in schools can appear to constitute a wave of school shootings that makes all teenagers seem violent.[64]

Violent crime is usually not random. Crime has clear patterns, and it almost always has a purpose despite initial appearances.[65] Unrelated offenses distributed over large geographic areas do not constitute an epidemic and do not signal the deterioration of the social order and a rapid descent into chaos. Yet the public's fear of crime suggests that crime is such a serious problem that society has lost its cohesion and that the old processes of social control are no longer effective.[66] It is enlightening to look at some of the offenses that have fueled the public's perception of random violence.

- **Wilding**   One evening in April 1989, a young woman was attacked in New York City's Central Park while she was jogging. A number of young men were accused and ultimately convicted of the sexual assault, and the term *wilding* entered the crime-news lexicon to refer to gangs of young men going on crime sprees in which they rob, assault, and rape at random in public spaces.[67] According to Best, the term *wilding*, essentially constructed by the media, finally fell out of favor after two years of heavy usage and dozens of stories in the *New York Times*. The term is used only sporadically today. Perhaps the most revealing aspect of this incident as it pertains to the fear of crime is the later confession to the attack by another man. The young men who were convicted of the offense turned out to be innocent, and the "wilding" might not even have occurred. Repairing the social fabric after such a high level of publicity is difficult. Even after the confession, which was corroborated by DNA evidence, some police officers continue to believe that the youths had been involved.

- **Freeway Violence**   According to Best, journalists have a rule of thumb that states that the third occurrence of a type of event constitutes a trend. For example, after some apparently unrelated acts of firearm violence on the Los Angeles freeways, the media began to report stories about the new freeway violence crisis.[68] Despite the fact that official data collections did not separate freeway violence from other types of violence, the media started listing all previous incidents of freeway violence to make it appear as though a new phenomenon were afoot.[69] Other jurisdictions began reporting incidents of freeway violence, but the term soon faded from the media even though it continues in the popular culture. It has taken on a life of its own to the point that many motorists keep firearms in their cars for self-defense. Although it can be argued that most of these weapons are never used, many motorists feel a sense of comfort from having a handgun within reach as they travel.

- **Stalking**   Stalking emerged as a social problem at about the same time as wilding and freeway violence, but took an entirely different trajectory as a media concern and became established as a distinct and important issue for the criminal justice system. *Stalking* refers to the activity in which someone is repeatedly followed, harassed, or physically threatened by another person.[70]

2.2   FOCUS *on* ETHICS

IF IT BLEEDS, IT LEADS

You are a new producer for a major network's local television news program in a large metropolitan city. This program has trailed its rivals for the past seven years and holds a paltry market share for its time slot. Your predecessor was fired because she failed to produce sensational, lurid, and sex-related news segments. Although you understand the need to be flashy, you trained at a good journalism school in which the professional ethic was deeply ingrained in the curriculum. After several newscasts, your segments have been nominated for regional awards, but the number of viewers has not increased significantly. Your network bosses are pressuring you to deliver the goods or get canned.

Your sports reporter has alerted you to several fights after football games at local high schools. After some initial investigation, you decide that the fights are unrelated and that it is not much of a story. However, with a bit of hyperbole and exaggeration, you could portray these fights as a youth gang problem. Never mind that your city has no history of youth gangs and that the police chief and head of the school board will not go on camera because they know the fights are not gang related. However, being under pressure, you instruct one of your news crews to selectively film graffiti, look for stereotypical gang symbols, and find some youths who will claim to be afraid of gang activity in the schools. After several stories about these "gangs," the ratings for your newscast skyrocket. Because of your newscasts, concerned parents have been meeting with school officials, tensions have increased among the city's high schools, and police officials are concerned that your stories about the nonexistent gang problem might inspire kids to actually start gangs. In an almost comical way, young people have started to adopt the accoutrements of gang culture: wearing red or blue bandanas, flashing gang signs, and even carrying weapons.

The police chief asks for an off-camera meeting with you. At the meeting she requests that your network stop doing stories about the gang problem. She is convinced that your stories about gangs are creating a problem rather than reflecting reality. Your bosses at the station take the opposite view. You are instructed to start laying the groundwork for a new series of programs about the gang problem that is set to air in two months during sweeps week, when the ratings for television advertising are pegged to the number of viewers for each program. Your bosses and the network promise you raises and promotions if you can produce a hard-hitting series that can link the high school fights to dangerous gangs, drug dealing, and violence. You know this would be a real stretch and that it would violate all the bounds of journalistic integrity. Recalling a Criminal Justice 101 class from college, you realize that your news programs about gang-related crime have caused people to become afraid of crime that does not really exist.

What Do You Do?

1. Hype the gang story and reap all the benefits.
2. Try to do a fair and balanced story about the high school fights, downplay the whole issue of gangs, and forfeit the raises, Emmy nominations, promotions, and possibly your job.
3. Get out of journalism.

The stalker might be a stranger with a romantic fixation on the victim or an ex-lover or estranged spouse who does not want to end the relationship. Because of the links that researchers and law enforcement officials have made between stalking and domestic violence, the issue has gained traction as a social problem. Most states, as well as the federal government, have established antistalking laws to protect victims. Although stalkers certainly existed before the recent interest in stalking, the efforts of the media reporting cases of celebrity stalking and the persistent problems of domestic violence have elevated this behavior to a category of crime in its own right.[71]

Each of these types of crime that the media has manufactured competes for a place in the public's collective imagination. Although the actual incidence of individual offenses might not be a legitimate cause for concern, the media have been successful in portraying the appearance of a crime trend for each. What is most interesting to the student of the criminal justice system, however, is the way that wilding and freeway shootings have almost disappeared as criminal justice concerns, whereas stalking has been institutionalized by states that have passed specific laws to protect victims. Once stalking was linked to domestic violence, women's groups were successful in forcing state and federal legislators to enact laws making stalking a new category of crime.[72]

Researchers have spent a good deal of time attempting to measure citizens' fear of crime. Government agencies and national polling firms have conducted surveys on issues such as neighborhood safety and whether citizens believe that crime rates are rising or falling. Until about 1965, fear of crime was not rated high on the list of citizens' concerns. Now, although it seldom ranks as high as the economy, taxes, or education, fear of crime is a consistent worry among many Americans.[73]

After a decade of declining crime rates, people still believe that crime has been consistently rising. Although crime has risen slightly for the past couple of years, the national homicide rate dropped 33 percent between 1990 and 1998. The news coverage on homicide, however, increased by 473 percent.[74] It is easy to appreciate why the fear of crime is a slippery concept to measure when the actual incidence of illegal behavior is so distorted.

SUMMARY

1. The measurement of crime, how crime is measured, and the level of crime all affect the criminal justice system and the public's fear of crime.

2. One useful typology of crime is offenses against the person, offenses against property, and offenses against the public order. Offenses against the person most disrupt the lives of citizens, so they carry the most severe penalties. Offenses against property, although disruptive, do not usually carry the same penalties. Offenses against the public order offend the sensibilities of some groups of people who have been successful in getting their values encoded into the criminal law.

3. Offenses against the person include homicide, rape, sexual assault, robbery, and assault. Offenses against property include burglary, arson, embezzlement, larceny/theft, and auto theft. Offenses against the public order include drug use, disturbing the peace, drunkenness, prostitution, and sometimes gambling.

4. One of the problems of attempting to measure crime is that not all offenses are reported. Offenses that are not reported and never known by the police constitute the dark figure of crime.

5. A victim might not want to report an offense for the following reasons: the offense is so subtle that it escapes the victim's attention; the offense is not perceived as such; the victim knows the offender; the victim believes that the offense was trivial; the victim fears reprisal; the victim feels antipathy toward the police; or the victim has broken the law as well.

6. Crime is measured in three major ways: the Federal Bureau of Investigation's *Uniform Crime Reports (UCR)*; the National Incident-Based Reporting System (NIBRS); and victimization surveys and self-report studies.

7. The *UCR* is the largest, most expensive, most comprehensive, and oldest method used to get an accurate picture of the incidence and seriousness of crime. The *UCR* does have some limitations, including intentional and unintentional sources of error and classification by the hierarchy rule. The *UCR* produces the statistics used to calculate the crime rate.

8. The National Incident-Based Reporting System, an improved method for gathering national crime statistics, is designed to correct some of the *UCR*'s flaws and is still under development. The NIBRS collects data on all criminal offenses that take place in an incident.

9. More white-collar and corporate offenses go unnoticed than street offenses. The NIBRS classifies white-collar and corporate offenses in greater detail than the *UCR*. Measuring white-collar and corporate crime remains a difficult task for several reasons.

10. Victimization surveys and self-report studies both represent attempts to shed some light on the dark figure of crime. Victimization surveys ask crime victims about their experiences. In self-report studies, respondents are asked to identify the types of offenses they have committed.

11. Corporate crime, organized crime, drug sales, prostitution, and gambling are categories of crime that the *UCR*, NIBRS, and victimization surveys and self-report studies typically miss.

12. The influence of the media on the public's fear of crime is of concern. A gap clearly exists between fear of crime and the actual danger posed by crime. Those who have the least to fear are often those who go to the greatest extremes to avoid dangerous situations, and groups who are victimized the most, such as young males, are the ones who engage in high-risk behavior.

13. According to Best, there are three problems with this popular conception of random violence: crime is actually highly patterned; most offenses have motivations; and national news coverage makes local criminal offenses seem more widespread.

14. The media tend to elevate isolated incidents to the level of crime trends and have facilitated the institutionalization of categories of offenses such as stalking.

15. The understanding of the level and frequency of crime is imperfect. Knowledge of criminal behavior and victimization should be used with caution because data-gathering instruments have their limitations and flaws.

KEY TERMS

arson 47
burglary 46
crime rate 42
larceny/theft 46
National Incident-Based Reporting System (NIBRS) 56

rape 45
robbery 46
serial murder 45
sexual assault 45
terrorism 45
Uniform Crime Reports (UCR) 50

victimization survey 58
victimless crime 47
victim precipitation 44

REVIEW QUESTIONS

1. Name the three major types of offenses.

2. What is the dark figure of crime?

3. List several reasons for a victim not to report a crime.

4. What are the *Uniform Crime Reports*?

5. What is the National Incident-Based Reporting System?

6. What is a crime rate? How is it calculated?

7. How did victimization surveys evolve?

8. What part of the crime picture do crime measures typically miss or obscure?

9. Which three popular conceptions compose the idea of random violence?

10. According to sociologist Joel Best, what institution constructs our perceptions of violence?

SUGGESTED FURTHER READING

Blumstein, Alfred, and Joel Wallman, eds. *The Crime Drop in America*, rev. ed. New York: Cambridge University Press, 2006.

Catalano, Shannan. *The Measurement of Crime: Victim Reporting and Police Recording.* New York: LFB Scholarly Publishing, 2006.

Ericson, Richard V. *Crime in an Insecure World.* Malden, MA: Polity, 2007.

Lee, Murray. *Inventing Fear of Crime: Criminology and the Politics of Anxiety.* Portland, OR: Willan, 2007.

Santana, Shannon. *Self-Protective Behavior and Violent Victimization.* New York: LFB Scholarly Publishing, 2007.

Simon, Jonathan. *Governing through Crime: How the War on Crime Transformed American Democracy and Created the Culture of Fear.* New York: Oxford University Press, 2007.

ENDNOTES

1. Scott H. Decker, "Deviant Homicide: A New Look at the Role of Motives and Victim-Offender Relationships," in *Victims and Victimization: Essential Readings*, eds. David Shichor and Stephen G. Tibbetts (Prospect Heights, IL: Waveland Press, 2002), 170–190.

2. Harvey Wallace, *Victimology: Legal, Psychological, and Social Perspectives* (Boston: Allyn & Bacon, 1998).

3. Ellen Hochstedler Steury and Nancy Frank, *Criminal Court Process* (Minneapolis/St. Paul: West, 1996).

4. Máximo Langer, "Rethinking Plea Bargaining: The Practice and Reform of Prosecutorial Adjudication in American Criminal Procedure," *American Journal of Criminal Law* 33 (2006): 223–299.

5. Chris McCormick, ed., *Constructing Danger: The Mis/Representation of Crime in the News* (Halifax, NS: Fernwood, 1995).

6. Lance Hannon, "Race, Victim Precipitated Homicide, and the Subculture of Violence Thesis," *Social Science Journal* 41 (2004): 115–121.

7. Marvin E. Wolfgang, *Patterns in Criminal Homicide* (Montclair, NJ: Patterson Smith, 1958/1975).

8. Albert K. Cohen, *Delinquent Boys: The Culture of the Gang* (New York: Free Press, 1955).

9. Mitch Stacy, "Details Sketchy in Killing of Charlotte County Prison Guard," *(Jacksonville) Florida Times-Union,* June 12, 2003.

10. Frederic G. Reamer, *Criminal Lessons: Case Studies and Commentary on Crime and Justice* (New York: Columbia University Press, 2003). See especially Chapter 5, "Crimes of Revenge and Retribution," 97–119.

11. Alix Pianin, "City Councilman Condemns Gang-Related Clothing," Columbia Spectator Online (Columbia University, New York), November 21, 2007, www.columbiaspectator.com/node/28267.

12. Malcolm Klein, *The American Street Gang: Its Nature, Prevalence, and Control* (New York: Oxford University Press, 1997).

13. Eric W. Hickey, *Serial Murderers and Their Victims,* 4th ed. (Belmont, CA: Wadsworth, 2006).

14. Steven A. Egger, *The Killers among Us: An Examination of Serial Murder and Its Investigation* (Upper Saddle River, NJ: Prentice Hall, 1998).

15. Jerrold M. Post, *The Mind of the Terrorist: The Psychology of Terrorism from the IRA to Al-Qaeda* (New York: Palgrave, 2007).

16. Alex Schmid and Janny de Graaf, *Violence as Communication: Insurgent Terrorism and the Western News Media* (Newbury Park, CA: Sage, 1982).

17. Eric W. Hickey, ed., *Sex Crimes and Paraphilia* (Upper Saddle River, NJ: Prentice Hall, 2006).

18. David Finkelhor and Kersti Yllo, *License to Rape: Sexual Abuse of Wives* (New York: Holt, Rinehart & Winston, 1985).

19. Dean G. Kilpatrick, David Beatty, and Susan Smith Hawley, "The Rights of Crime Victims: Does Legal Protection Make a Difference?" in *Victims and Victimization: Essential Readings,* eds. David Shichor and Stephen G. Tibbetts (Prospect Heights, IL: Waveland Press, 2002), 287–304.

20. *Uniform Crime Reports,* 1998, www.fbi.gov/UCR/UCR.htm.

21. Terance D. Miethe and Richard C. McCorkle, *Crime Profiles: The Anatomy of Dangerous Persons, Places, and Situations,* 2nd ed. (Los Angeles: Roxbury, 2001).

22. Colin M. Turnbull, *The Forest People: A Study of the Pygmies of the Congo* (New York: Simon & Schuster, 1961).

23. Miethe and McCorkle, *Crime Profiles.*

24. Robert F. Meier and Gilbert Geis, *Victimless Crime? Prostitution, Drugs, Homosexuality, Abortion* (Los Angeles: Roxbury, 1997).

25. William H. Daly, "Law Enforcement in Times Square, 1970s–1990s," in *Sex, Scams, and Street Life: The Sociology of New York City's Times Square,* ed. Robert P. McNamara (Westport, CT: Praeger, 1995), 97–106.

26. John A. Backstand, Don Gibbons, and Joseph F. Jones, "Who's in Jail? An Examination of the Rabble Hypothesis," *Crime and Delinquency* 38 (1992): 219–229.

27. Joseph Goldstein, "Police Discretion Not to Invoke the Criminal Process," in *The Invisible Justice System: Discretion and the Law,* eds. Burton Atkins and Mark Pogrebin (Cincinnati, OH: Anderson, 1978), 65–81.

28. Paul Brantingham and Patricia Brantingham, *Patterns in Crime* (New York: Macmillan, 1984), 49.

29. William A. Bonger, *Criminality and Economic Conditions* (Boston: Little, Brown, 1916).

30. Peggy Reeves Sanday, *Fraternity Gang Rape: Sex, Brotherhood, and Privilege on Campus* (New York: New York University Press, 2007).

31. J. Kitsuse and A. V. Cicourel, "A Note on the Uses of Official Statistics," *Social Problems* 11 (1963): 131–139.

32. U.S. Department of Justice, Federal Bureau of Investigation, "Crime in the United States, 2006," www.fbi.gov/UCR/cius2006/about/crime_summary.html.

33. Michael D. Maltz, "Crime Statistics: A Historical Perspective," *Crime and Delinquency* 23 (1977): 32–40.

34. Lynn A. Addington and Callie Marie Rennison, "Rape Co-Occurrence: Do Additional Crimes Affect Victim Reporting and Police Clearance of Rape?" *Journal of Quantitative Criminology* 24 (2008): 205–226.

35. Ron Martin, "Crime Stats: Questions Linger after Atlanta Audit," *Atlanta Journal-Constitution,* January 28, 1999.

36. U.S. Department of Justice, "Crime in the United States, 2006."

37. Clayton J. Mosher, Terance D. Miethe, and Dretha M. Phillips, *The Mismeasure of Crime* (Thousand Oaks, CA: Sage, 2002).

38. David Seidman and Michael Couzens, "Getting the Crime Rate Down: Political Pressure and Crime

Reporting," *Law and Society Review* 8 (1974): 457–493.

39. Michael Maxfield, "The National Incident-Based Reporting System: Research and Policy Applications," *Journal of Quantitative Criminology* 15 (1999): 119–149.

40. U.S. Department of Justice, Federal Bureau of Investigation, "National Incident-Based Reporting System," www.fbi.gov/UCR/faqs.htm.

41. Cynthia Barnett-Ryan and Gregory Swanson, "The Role of State Programs in NIBRS Data Quality," *Journal of Contemporary Criminal Justice* 24 (2008): 18–31.

42. U.S. Department of Justice, Office of Justice Programs, Bureau of Justice Statistics, "*UCR and NIBRS Participation*," www.ojp.usdoj.gov/bjs/nibrsstatus.htm.

43. David J. Roberts, *Implementing the National Incident-Based Reporting System: A Project Status Report* (Washington, DC: U.S. Department of Justice, 1977).

44. Mosher, Miethe, and Phillips, *The Mismeasure of Crime*, 72.

45. Jeffrey Reiman, *The Rich Get Richer and the Poor Get Prison: Ideology, Class, and Criminal Justice*, 8th ed. (Boston: Allyn & Bacon, 2006).

46. Meier and Geis, *Victimless Crime?*

47. Brantingham and Brantingham, *Patterns in Crime*, 76–79.

48. William G. Doerner and Steven P. Lab, *Victimology*, 2nd ed. (Cincinnati, OH: Anderson, 1998), 28–40.

49. Terence Thornberry and Marvin D. Krohn, "The Self-Report Method for Measuring Delinquency and Crime," in *Criminal Justice 2000: Measurement and Analysis of Crime and Justice* (Washington, DC: U.S. Department of Justice, 2000), 33–83.

50. Gordon Waldo and Theodore G. Chiricos, "Perceived Penal Sanction and Self-Reported Criminality: A Neglected Approach to Deterrence Research," *Social Problems* 19 (1972): 522–540.

51. Gary Kleck, "On the Use of Self-Report Data to Determine the Class Distribution of Criminal and Delinquent Behavior," *American Sociological Review* (1982): 427–433.

52. Thomas Gray and Eric Walsh, *Maryland Youth at Risk: A Study of Drug Use in Juvenile Detainees* (College Park, MD: Center for Substance Abuse Research, 1993).

53. Delbert Elliott, David Huizinga, and Barbara Morse, "Self-Reported Violent Offending: A Descriptive Analysis of Juvenile Violent Offenders and Their Offending Careers," *Journal of Interpersonal Violence* 1 (1986): 472–514.

54. William S. Aquilino, "Interview Mode Effects in Surveys of Drug and Alcohol Use," *Public Opinion Quarterly* 58 (1994): 210–240.

55. David Huizinga and Delbert S. Elliot, "Reassessing the Reliability and Validity of Self-Report Delinquency Measures," *Journal of Quantitative Criminology* 2 (1986): 293–327.

56. Elizabeth Moore and Michael Mills, "The Neglected Victims and Unexplained Costs of White-Collar Crime," in *Readings in White-Collar Crime*, eds. David Shichor, Larry Gaines, and Richard Ball (Prospect Heights, IL: Waveland Press, 2002), 49–59.

57. Gary Potter and Larry Gaines, "Underworlds and Upperworlds: The Convergence of Organized and White-Collar Crime," in *Readings in White-Collar Crime*, eds. David Shichor, Larry Gaines, and Richard Ball (Prospect Heights, IL: Waveland Press, 2002), 60–90.

58. Tom Mieczkowski, "Crack Dealing on the Street: Crew System and the Crack House," in *Drugs, Crime, and Justice: Contemporary Readings*, eds. Larry K. Gaines and Peter B. Kraska (Prospect Heights, IL: Waveland Press, 1997), 193–204.

59. Robert McNamara, *The Times Square Hustler: Male Prostitution in New York City* (Westport, CT: Praeger, 1994).

60. Ronald V. Clarke, *Situational Crime Prevention: Successful Case Studies* (New York: Harrow & Heston, 1992).

61. Barry Glassner, *The Culture of Fear: Why Americans Are Afraid of the Wrong Things* (New York: Perseus Books, 1999).

62. Paul J. Brantingham and Patricia L. Brantingham, "Understanding and Controlling Crime and the Fear of Crime: Conflicts and Trade-Offs in Crime Prevention Planning," in *Crime Prevention at a Crossroads*, ed. Steven Lab (Cincinnati, OH: Anderson, 1997), 43–60.

63. Joel Best, *Random Violence: How We Talk about New Crimes and New Victims* (Berkeley: University of California Press, 1999).

64. Ibid., 7–21.

65. Marc Riedel and Wayne Welsh, *Criminal Violence: Patterns, Causes, and Prevention* (Los Angeles: Roxbury, 2002).

66. Ray Surette, ed., *Media, Crime, and Criminal Justice: Images and Realities*, 2nd ed. (Belmont, CA: West/Wadsworth, 1998).

67. Charles Derber, *The Wilding of America: How Greed and Violence Are Eroding Our Nation's Character* (New York: St. Martin's Press, 1996).

68. Van Gordon Sauter, "No Shelter from Freeway Violence," *Los Angeles Times*, June 26, 1987, V-I.

69. Bill Billiter, "Traffic Dispute Results in Third Freeway Shooting," *Los Angeles Times*, July 20, 1987, I-3.

70. Matthew J. Gilligan, "Stalking the Stalker," *Georgia Law Review* 27 (1992): 285–342.

71. Valerie Jenness and Kendal Broad, *Hate Crimes: New Social Movements and the Politics of Violence* (Hawthorne, NY: Aldine de Gruyter, 1997).

72. T. K. Logan et al., "The Impact of Differential Patterns of Physical Violence and Stalking on Mental Health and Help-Seeking among Women with Protective Orders," *Violence against Women* 12 (September 2006): 866–888.

73. Bilan R. Wyant, "Multilevel Impacts of Perceived Incivilities and Perceptions of Risk on Fear of Crime," *Journal of Research in Crime and Delinquency* 45 (2008): 39–64.

74. "Scary News, Soothing Numbers," *U.S. News & World Report*, April 23, 2001.

CHAPTER 3

Theories of Crime

Objectives

1. Discuss the strengths and weaknesses of the classical school of criminology.

2. Discuss early biological theories of crime versus modern biological theories of crime.

3. Understand the differences among the biological, psychological, sociological, and critical sociological theories of crime.

If the job of the criminal justice system is to control crime and punish or treat the criminal offender, then those vested with these responsibilities should have some idea about why people break the law. And they do. We all do. Whether one is a law enforcement officer, a judge, a prison warden, or a citizen, we all have ideas and beliefs about why people rob, rape, embezzle, and kill. However, these ideas and beliefs might not be well formulated, and are typically the result of our parents' teachings, media influence, or biases developed from our personal experiences. Still, we not only believe in these ideas about the causes of crime, we also act on them. We lock our doors at night, warn our children about associating with certain friends, wage campaigns against drug and alcohol abuse, or condone the use of capital punishment, all based on our personal ideas about the causes of crime. Whether we realize it or not, each of us, to some extent, uses theories of crime in our everyday life.

One of the challenges that criminologists face is to develop ideas about why people break the law into systematic theories that clearly spell out perspectives and concepts in ways that can be tested and measured. As criminal justice grows as an academic discipline, its theories become more sophisticated and specific. By considering the various ways that criminologists have explained crime over the years, we can see not only the history of criminology, but also to some extent the history of intellectual thought. The beauty and utility of criminological theories is that they mirror the intellectual activities of their time. For instance, in this chapter we will learn how criminological theory changed from the Dark Ages through the Enlightenment to today's postmodern era.

This chapter will help us understand the variety and complexity of criminological theories. By looking at the explanations of crime that have guided the actions of people and the criminal justice system, we can better understand why and how crime remains a significant social problem and continues to demand serious study in the 21st century. By understanding the history of how our ideas about the causes of crime have evolved, we can learn to appreciate the fascinating complexity of the law, the criminal justice system, and other methods of social control.

DEMONOLOGY

The earliest explanations for deviant behavior attributed crime to supernatural forces. In an age in which religion was a powerful force for social control, the actions of wayward people were blamed on the influence of the devil. Powerful rulers invoked the church to legitimize their control of wealth and power, and the church answered by claiming that deviant behavior was not only unlawful, but also sinful. Minor transgressions were therefore violations of God's rules, as well as punishable by the law. The church and state worked together to control the populace.[1]

trial by ordeal

An ancient custom in which the accused was required to perform a test that appealed to divine authority to prove guilt or innocence.

One of the methods used to determine guilt or innocence in earlier times was **trial by ordeal,** in which it was believed that God would intervene and save the innocent. Representatives of the law placed heavy stones on suspects or threw them into deep water based on the idea that God would let only a guilty person die under such circumstances. People who were crushed by tons of stone or disappeared into the swirling waters of a river were "proven" guilty by their inability to summon aid from God.[2] Sometimes this supernatural explanation created an unwinnable situation. During the Salem witch trials, women were subjected to the dunking pond and held under water during trials of ordeal. Those who did not drown were considered witches who had invoked the aid of Satan and were killed anyway. Those who drowned were considered to have been innocent.[3]

Even today, some people claim that either God or the devil instructed them to commit crimes. Often we think that those who use such an argument are insane. For example, in Texas in 2002 Andrea Yates said she drowned her five small children because she believed it was the only way to save them from going to hell.[4] Although we are shocked by her offense, we also consider her mentally ill.[5] Yet others who "kill for God" are not viewed with the same compassion. Those who have assassinated

Trial by ordeal was one method of investigation. It depended on the supernatural to provide evidence of guilt or innocence.
Source: CORBIS-NY

abortion providers are viewed as rational and responsible people who possess the ability to control their behavior but choose to kill as a political and moral statement. Likewise, many acts of terrorism are attributed to religious or supernatural explanations, but the secular courts deem these acts of premeditated homicide.[6]

Some people still use supernatural explanations for crime, but the criminal justice system has moved on to other theories that lend themselves to empirical testing (see Table 3-1). It is impossible for the court to determine whether God or the devil instructed someone to break the law, and in a secular society such as the United States, such religious explanations cannot be considered by the criminal justice system.

CLASSICAL SCHOOL OF CRIMINOLOGY

The study of human behavior changed during the Enlightenment, an exciting time in human history when people looked to reason to explain the workings of the physical world and social activities of humans rather than relying solely on supernatural explanations. Many of the great thinkers of Western civilization such as Voltaire, Rousseau, and Hume helped usher in a new emphasis on independent thinking. The Enlightenment advanced the scientific method in the physical sciences and allowed philosophers, playwrights, and novelists new freedom to criticize powerful social institutions. One of the institutions that was most affected by the Enlightenment was government. Challenges to monarchies to make the rules by which society lived came under constant scrutiny and criticism, and the procedures for dispensing justice, such as it was, were fundamentally altered by the emergence of the classical school of criminology.

Unlike early theories of crime that used supernatural forces to explain criminal behavior, the **classical school of criminology** argues that people freely choose to

classical school of criminology
A set of criminological theories that uses the idea of free will to explain criminal behavior.

Table 3-1 **Criminological Theories**

Name/Class of Theory	Theory	Practice	Theorists
CLASSICAL SCHOOL			
Nine Principles	Free will and punishment based on humane principles.	Deterrence through social contract, public education, and legal clarity and equity. Punish proportionally. Eliminate systemic corruption.	Beccaria
Utilitarianism	People are guided by desire for pleasure and aversion to pain.		Bentham
POSITIVIST SCHOOL **Biological Theories**			
Phrenology	Criminality can be determined by the shape of the skull.	Alter, isolate, sterilize, or eliminate the body. Brain surgery, execution, imprisonment, medication. Also, improvements in diet and health care. These theories have fallen out of favor.	Gall
Atavisms	Criminals have measurable physical differences from non-criminals.		Lombroso
Body measurement			Hooton
Somatotyping			Sheldon, Kretschmer
XYY syndrome	Males born with an extra chromosome tend toward criminal behavior.		
Biochemistry	Hormones, brain structure, and/or brain chemistry may cause criminal behavior.	Medication, diet changes.	
Psychological Theories			
Psychoanalytic theory	Focused on unconscious forces and drives.	Counseling.	Freud
Behaviorism (operant conditioning)	Behavior is determined by rewards and punishments.	Reward reform, punish continued offensive behavior.	Skinner
Observational learning	Cognition, behavior, and environment mutually reinforce each other. Observers, especially children, imitate behavior they see.	Model good behavior.	Bandura
Moral development theory	Human moral development proceeds through stages of moral reasoning. Criminal offenders are stuck at the lower levels of development.	Attentive parenting, effective schools, and public programs for children, such as Head Start.	Kohlberg
Psychopathy	Psychopathy is a specific psychological condition that sometimes co-occurs with heinous criminal offending.	For serious offenders, lifelong incarceration or commission to a mental institution is common.	Hare
Antisocial personality disorder (APD)	APD has much in common with psychopathy except that its definition is marked by behavior, as well as aggression, violence, and irritability.	As those with APD continually break the law, incarceration is common, as are counseling and medication.	
Sociological Theories			
Chicago School	Social disorganization causes criminal behavior in individuals.	Social reform, ensure equal access to societal incentives and norms.	Shaw, McKay
Differential association theory	Crime is learned.		Sutherland
Strain theory	Unequal access to societal norms.		Merton
Social control theory	Questions why people do not commit crimes.		Hirschi
Neutralization theory	Offenders "neutralize" blame and feelings of shame.		Sykes, Matza
Labeling theory	Deviants conform to the "deviant" label.		Lemert
Critical Sociological Theories			
Marxism	Those in power make laws to favor themselves.	Social reform, providing minority groups access to more power and decision making, recognizing oppression, allocating group-specific research.	Marx
Feminism (gender)	Crime study and the criminal justice system is male-dominated, -oriented.		
Critical race theory	The criminal justice system targets and oppresses people of color		
Integrated Theories			
Integrated theory of delinquent behavior	Strain theory, social control, and social learning theories are combined to explain delinquency within the lower and middle classes.	Social reform, ensure equal access to societal incentives and norms	Elliott, Ageton, Canter

Table 3-1   **Criminological Theories (continued)**

Interactional theory of delinquency	Low social control and exposure to delinquent peers over the course of adolescent development contribute to delinquency and antisocial behavior.		Thornberry
Control balance theory	People seek to correct and balance power differentials in their relationships.		Tittle
Life Course Theories			
Pathway theory	Life-course-persistent offenders engage in antisocial behavior for long periods of time, possibly all their lives. Adolescence-limited offenders break the law in adolescence, but desist on reaching adulthood.	Social reform, ensure equal access to societal incentives and norms.	Moffitt
Persistent-offending and desistance-from-crime theory	As delinquents age, some continue to break the law well into adulthood; others experience turning points in which they bond to conventional society.		Laub, Sampson

break the law. The principle of "free will" allows us to consider various courses of action, then select the one we believe is most desirable. If we structure the criminal justice system in such a way that penalties for breaking the law are sufficiently severe, swift, and certain, then people will rationally choose not to break the law.[7]

The classical school of criminology is embodied primarily in the works of Cesare Beccaria and Jeremy Bentham. Both of these men were more concerned with reforming the criminal justice system than in finding the causes of crime. The philosophy behind the classical school had implications for how the criminal justice system was organized and how it responded to crime. In a time when many viewed criminal justice as arbitrary, cruel, and inefficient, leading scholars such as Beccaria and Bentham sought to inject rationality and humaneness.[8]

Cesare Beccaria (1738–1794)

Beccaria's ideas about reforming the way society dealt with crime are found in his seminal work *On Crimes and Punishments*, published in 1764.[9] In this work he presented nine principles that should guide our thinking about crime and the way society responds to lawbreakers (see Criminal Justice Reference 3.1). These and other ideas formulated by Beccaria have found their way into many of the principles that guide our criminal justice system today. Beccaria suggested that punishment should be only stringent enough to deter crime. He also advocated the abolition of physical punishment and the death penalty. The presumption of innocence, the right to confront accusers, the right to a speedy trial, and the right not to be required to testify against oneself are all traceable to this important thinker.

Jeremy Bentham (1748–1832)

Jeremy Bentham is the other major thinker associated with the classical school of criminology. According to Bentham's **utilitarianism** theory, people are guided by their desire for pleasure and aversion to pain. As he said so elegantly:

> Nature has placed mankind under the governance of two sovereign masters, pain and pleasure. It is for them alone to point out what we ought to do, as well as to determine what we shall do. On the one hand the standard of right and wrong, on the other the chain of causes and effects, are fastened to their throne. They govern us in all we do, in all we say, in all we think: every effort we can make to throw off our subjection, will serve but to demonstrate and confirm it.[10]

utilitarianism

A theory associated with Jeremy Bentham that states that people will choose not to break the law when the pain of punishment outweighs the benefits of the offense.

Cesare Beccaria's ideas about crime and punishment have provided inspiration for the values of the criminal justice system.
Source: Corbis/Bettmann

3.1   CRIMINAL JUSTICE REFERENCE

Cesare Beccaria's Nine Principles
from *On Crimes and Punishments*

1. Social action should be based on the utilitarian principle of "the greatest happiness for the greatest number."
2. The sovereign's right to punish is founded on the necessity of defending public liberty, and the punishments are to be just in proportion, and liberty is to be preserved by the sovereign and considered sacred and valuable.
3. Punishments are set by the legislator by the making of penal laws and the magistrate cannot increase the punishment already determined by law.
4. Obscurity in the law is evil. Crimes will be less frequent if the code of laws is more universally read and understood. A scale of crimes should be formed where the most serious consist of those which immediately tend to the dissolution of society, and the last of the smallest possible injustice done to a private member of that society.
5. The intent of punishment is to prevent the criminal from doing future injury to society and to prevent others from committing similar offenses. Punishments and the mode of inflicting them ought to make the strongest and most long lasting impressions on the minds of others while inflicting the least torment to the body of the criminal.
6. Secret accusations are a manifest abuse.
7. Torture during the criminal trial is a cruelty consecrated by custom in most nations and should be abolished. No man is judged a criminal until he has been found guilty and is entitled to the public protection. Torture is a flawed tool of investigation where the strong go free and the feeble are convicted.
8. There are advantages to immediate punishment. The smaller the interval of time between the punishment and the crime, the stronger and more lasting will be the association.
9. Crimes are more effectually prevented by certainty of punishment than by the severity. Furthermore, if punishments are very severe, men are likely to commit further crimes to avoid punishment.

Source: Cesare Beccaria, On Crimes and Punishments (Indianapolis, IN: Bobbs-Merrill, 1963).

To understand the actions of people, we need only understand how they comprehend pleasure and pain. According to Bentham, we perform a mental exercise he called the **hedonistic calculus** when we consider our behavior. We attempt to weigh the pleasures we would accrue from breaking the law and the pain that would result if we were caught. In considering pleasure or pain, we consider the following:

hedonistic calculus
An individual's mental calculation of the personal value of an activity by how much pleasure or pain it will incur.

1. Intensity
2. Duration
3. Certainty or uncertainty
4. Propinquity or remoteness

In this consideration of the balance between pleasure and pain, Bentham believed society could affect antisocial behavior.[11] Crime can be prevented by structuring the criminal justice system and the law in such a way that potential offenders can calculate that the pains of crime outweigh the pleasures. Bentham's idea is why modern sentencing patterns have a high degree of proportionality. Murder can get the offender the death penalty, but stealing a car will not. When Bentham lived, there were more than 200 offenses for which one could be put to death. His work focused on reforming the system by introducing some logic into how, and how much, punishment was meted out.[12]

Bentham's hedonistic calculus is also apparent in the attempt to increase the certainty of punishment. More police officers, better crime-fighting technology, more efficient court systems, and other reforms are aimed at influencing the calculations made by potential offenders. By making prison sentences of longer duration (such as life imprisonment), certain types of severe crime are discouraged. However, some people do not make rational decisions when calculating the rewards versus the risks of crime. Why do offenders rob convenience stores when the potential for reward is so small? Why not rob a bank, where there is so much more to gain? Bentham would answer that even though the potential gain is greater in robbing the bank, the potential pain is also greater when one factors in the uncertainty of success. Banks are more carefully guarded and have better technology (vaults, multiple cameras) than convenience stores. Additionally, the uncertainty of robbing a bank is increased when

Jeremy Bentham's ideas are part of the reasoning behind the classical school of criminology. He believed criminals do a mental calculus, weighing the benefits of committing a crime against the costs of getting caught.
Source: Corbis/Bettmann

one considers that this constitutes a federal offense and would involve such agencies as the FBI.

Neither Bentham nor Beccaria was concerned with why people broke the law. Motivation was assumed. Bentham particularly believed that lawbreakers acted to increase pleasure.[13] The work of these two theorists is relevant to the legal and administrative functions of the criminal justice system. Later, when we deal with some of the sociological and economic theories of crime, such as **rational choice theory,** we will see how the classical school provides insights.

rational choice theory
A theory that states that people consciously choose to break the law on realizing that the offense's benefits probably outweigh the negative consequences.

POSITIVIST SCHOOL OF CRIMINOLOGY

One of the reasons the classical school lost much of its influence is that it assumed motivation and treated all offenders equally. But not all offenders are equal. They break the law for different reasons and are not affected by punishment in the same way. The idea that free will determines when and how people break the law fails to account for the complex nature of crime and the vast differences among people. Although some of the neoclassical theories attempted to measure free will in a scientific way, one of the weaknesses of the classical theories was that, like demonology, they really were not subject to empirical analysis. There was no way to determine how one exercised free will in deciding to break the law.[14]

positivist school of criminology
A set of criminological theories that uses scientific techniques to study crime and criminal offenders.

The **positivist school of criminology** is a natural outgrowth of the rise of the scientific method, which began to develop during the Enlightenment in the 19th century. By applying the emerging scientific disciplines that built on the work of Charles Darwin, criminologists shifted the focus of criminology away from the law and the criminal justice system and toward the offender.[15] The question now became, What factors influence people to break the law? Even more interesting to later theorists was the possibility that social behavior is simply part of a biological imperative that can explain human interactions.[16] That is, do human beings behave according to some survival-of-the-fittest urge embedded in their genes? Can science help us understand the patterns of crime that affect society? The positivist school offers us a two-century adventure as we seek to understand criminal behavior.

Biological Theories of Crime

We are all familiar with how our moods and behaviors are influenced by how we feel. When we are tired, we get cranky. When we go to the supermarket hungry, we come home with cookies and ice cream. When we have the flu, we neglect our homework. To argue that the body affects behavior is easy. But does the body influence antisocial behavior? Additionally, can science shed light on how this might work? Wouldn't it be useful if we could examine the body for clues of a propensity toward criminality? Scientists have long attempted to find such a relationship.[17] Here we will briefly review some of the better-known theories that sought to cast light on heredity, hormones, blood chemistry, and environmental problems such as alcohol and drug use.

PHRENOLOGY   Franz Joseph Gall (1758–1828) is considered to have invented the "science" of phrenology. Phrenology was a technique in which a practitioner assessed a subject's personality by measuring the size and pattern of the bumps on a subject's skull. The term *science* is used with caution because phrenology is not a real science. However, it was once all the rage in medical science and, like many forms of quackery, had just enough scientific trappings to sound plausible. Physicians knew that certain parts of the brain were responsible for certain conditions, problems, and activities.[18] For example, they noticed that the location of a head injury could have much to do with how the patient acted or recovered. Phrenologists, however, believed that the shape, size, and features of the brain exerted pressures on the skull, which showed up as bumps that could be deciphered by someone with the proper training.[19]

Phrenology was accepted as reliable science. It was believed that a trained phrenologist could discern a person's character from bumps on the skull.

Source: CORBIS-NY

Phrenology was the beginning of a long and fascinating history of scientists' attempts to understand human behavior by looking for physical markers in or on the body. Phrenologists thought that proclivities for things such as destructiveness, secretiveness, and philoprogenitiveness (love of offspring) could be uncovered by massaging the skull. Although some relationship may exist between the body and behavior, phrenology did not prove to be a realistic method with which to assess this connection. It eventually fell into disrepute because of the political and religious differences among some of the major practitioners and because it was hijacked by outright charlatans. However, it is still possible, even today, to find adherents of this technique.[20]

ATAVISMS Cesare Lombroso (1835–1909), an Italian physician, believed that criminal offenders were physically different from the rest of the population. Lombroso looked closely at human anatomical features, measuring precisely several points on the face and body. Lombroso claimed that "born criminals" were not as physically evolved as people who obeyed the law, and he compared the born criminal to what he called "savage people."[21] The physical differences of the born criminal were called **atavisms.** These included low cranial capacity, retreating forehead, highly developed frontal sinuses, greater pigmentation of the skin, tufted and crispy hair, and large ears. Other atavisms included dullness of the sense of touch, great agility, relative insensitivity to pain, ability to recover quickly from wounds, precocity for sexual pleasures, laziness, absence of remorse, and impulsiveness. Clearly, it is easier to observe physical characteristics than behavioral characteristics, but regardless of the type of characteristic, all of Lombroso's atavisms were judged against the standard of what he considered the average law-abiding 19th-century Italian to look like.

atavisms

The appearance in a person of physical features thought to be from earlier stages of human evolution.

Lombroso's work is widely acknowledged because it was one of the first attempts to use the scientific method to examine criminal offenders. Although his method was greatly flawed and riddled with many of the prejudices and biases of his society, he laid the groundwork for using science to find differences between offenders and the general population.[22]

In some ways, variations of his work go on today as we deconstruct the human genetic code and gain a better understanding of how brain chemistry works. However, the tools used by Lombroso were so crude and so lacking in the requirements of good scientific method that we are amused today to see what passed for cutting-edge science more than a century ago. Lombroso's theory was dealt a major setback in 1913 when Sir Charles Goring published *The English Convict*, a study of 3000 English convicts who were compared with a large group of nonoffenders. Goring did not find significant differences between the groups in terms of physical measurements or the presence of Lombroso's atavisms. Goring concluded that there was no such thing as a "criminal type," severely damaging Lombroso's ideas that criminal offenders were physically different from law-abiding citizens.[23] However, Goring's work was also flawed in many respects. Piers Beirne, in his fascinating book *Inventing Criminology: Essays on the Rise of "Homo Criminalis,"* provides a complete and complicated analysis of the debate between the proponents of Lombroso and Goring, and concludes that although the methodology of both were flawed, they had much in common in the way they viewed the relationship between crime and the body. Beirne concluded:

> Ironically, *The English Convict*'s dubious merit was to have replaced Lombroso's criminal—an unfortunate genetically stamped with atavistic physical features—with a convict born with inferior weight, stature, and mental capacity. Despite its rhetorical asides to the contrary, within the psychologistic notion of "character," *The English Convict* allowed a definitive space for the intersection of rigidly determinist concepts of criminality and abnormality.[24]

PHYSIOLOGY   Earnest Hooton (1887–1954) was a Harvard anthropologist who studied the relationship between physiology and crime. He used many of the same concepts as Lombroso in studying 14,000 male inmates and a control group of more than 3000 civilians. Hooton claimed to have found differences between offenders and nonoffenders across a wide range of physical features. His findings were criticized by other scholars who objected to his sampling technique, his labeling of inmates as being certain types of offenders, and his racially prejudiced conclusions.[25]

Hooton believed that inmates were representative of all criminal offenders. Furthermore, he placed labels on the inmates, such as "murderer" or "robber," based on the offense for which they were incarcerated. Further examination revealed that many of these inmates had prior records for different types of offenses and therefore could have had different labels applied to them. Hooton's claimed relationship between physical characteristics and crime could not stand up under such nebulous labeling. An additional problem concerned the control group of ordinary citizens used by Hooton. A large number of them were firefighters or militiamen, occupations that required certain physical qualifications, and therefore were not representative of the general population.

One example of Hooton's cultural prejudices was that, like Lombroso, he believed that tattooing was the mark of an inferior person. Cultural prejudices against tattooing are now waning as we see a wide variety of people using tattooing as a means of self-expression. Tattooing has entered the mainstream culture to such an extent that it is ceasing to bring negative reactions from parents, employers, and university professors. To be sure, an age-based acceptance dynamic is also at work here. The younger the person, the more likely he or she is to understand the tattooing phenomenon. Also, tattooing is an important and respected part of many cultures throughout the world. So the argument can be made today that tattooing is not a sign of degeneracy or criminality, but simply a fashion statement or cultural rite of passage.

SOMATOTYPING   Another interesting idea that links behavior to physical differences is the concept of *body typing*. Developed first by the German psychiatrist Ernst Kretschmer, it was refined and popularized in the United States by William Sheldon (1898–1977). Sheldon used the term **somatotyping** to describe his three variations of the body: endomorph, mesomorph, and ectomorph. According to Sheldon, everyone's body has these components in some ratio, and they can be measured on a

somatotyping

The use of body types and physical characteristics to classify human personalities.

3.1 FOCUS *on* ETHICS

PHYSICAL GRAFFITI

Your roommate is a real trip. She has started to judge all your friends by the physical characteristics she has learned about in her introductory criminological theory class. First, she contends that your boyfriend has so many atavisms that he is a throwback to the Neanderthals. According to her, he has beady eyes, a sloping forehead, an insincere mouth, and deviant ears. Although she has never read the writings of Cesare Lombroso, she is convinced that she can judge a person's character by physical appearance. For instance, your little brother is tall and skinny. According to your roommate's interpretation of Sheldon's body types, he is an ectomorph and likely to become a check forger or counterfeiter. At a party you found your roommate running her hands through the hair of each young man who asked her to dance. You found out later that she thought she was practicing phrenology. You would not be surprised to find her asking for tissue samples from her dates to check for extra Y chromosomes.

After you confront her about the shallowness of her judgments of others and suggest that there is more to a person's character than can be revealed by his or her physical makeup, she starts reading pop psychology books and decides she can psychoanalyze everyone. She studies astrology, Chinese placemats, enneagrams, archetypes, tarot cards, and the *I Ching*. She understands none of them and misuses each as she tries to understand people's personalities and motivations.

Here is the problem. Your roommate is in love with the idea of theory. She is looking for a system or explanation that will help her appreciate how people develop character. She adopts every psychological and criminological theory she can lay her hands on, and after they fail to explain everything about everyone, she discards them and moves on to the next theory. She has no tolerance for ambiguity, gray areas, partial truths, or contrary facts. Her ideal theory must be mutually exclusive and exhaustive, and as each theory fails to neatly order her world, she goes off in search of another. You want to explain to her that there is no perfect theory and that searching for one is not only useless, but also counterproductive.

What Do You Do?

1. Tell her that theories are only tools to aid understanding.
2. Tell her that theories are social constructions and not objective realities.
3. Tell her that instead of demanding one theory, she would be better off trying to integrate several theories.
4. Get a new roommate.

Table 3-2 **Sheldon's Components of Somatotyping**

Body Type	Temperament
Endomorph: Soft, round, pudgy, possibly obese	Viscerotonic: Relaxed, sociable, loves physical comfort, food, affection, approval, and the company of others
Mesomorph: Muscular, strong	Somatic: Active, assertive, aggressive, noisy; loves power and to dominate others
Ectomorph: Thin, fragile	Cerebrotonic: Private, restrained, inhibited, and hyperattentive

Source: William H. Sheldon, *Varieties of Delinquent Youth: An Introduction to Constitutional Psychiatry* (New York: Harper & Row, 1949).

seven-point scale. For example, someone scoring a 1-7-1 would be considered an extreme mesomorph. Although it is easy to see how people could be given scores for how their bodies look, Sheldon claimed that body type was an indication of one's psychology. The argument that structure equaled behavior was a simple claim dressed up in the jargon of somatotyping science. Sheldon's characterization of the extreme types can be seen in Table 3-2.

Most interesting about Sheldon's work are the policy implications he advocated. If discerning behavior from body type is really possible, then why not control who can and cannot reproduce? If we could simply prevent "inferior" types from reproducing and encourage good stock, we could breed a better class of society. After all, selective breeding had produced beautiful roses and fast racehorses, so why not employ this method to improve society? Luckily, other criminologists, legislators, and the general public did not take Sheldon's ideas seriously. His terminology of *endomorph, mesomorph,* and *ectomorph* has remained in the literature, but for the most part, no one believes that body type determines behavior.[26]

XYY SYNDROME   In the search for physical differences between criminal offenders and the rest of the population, science has gotten a lot better at using sophisticated techniques. From the rather gross methods of atavisms and bumps on the head, researchers have moved to examining chromosomes.

Each of us is born with two sex chromosomes. Typically, females have two X chromosomes and males have an X and a Y chromosome. A small percentage of males are born with an extra Y chromosome. About one in 1000 to 2000 males is an XYY. Typically, these men are not much physically different from XY males besides being a bit above average in height and sometimes having severe acne. Some studies claim that XYY males tend to possess a slightly lower IQ, but this has been disputed. The theoretical link between **XYY syndrome** and crime is attributed to several studies that found that males with XYY syndrome were overrepresented in the populations of correctional institutions. But what could be the theoretical basis for this observation? What is it about the extra Y chromosome that could lead one to break the law? At first it was thought that the extra Y chromosome was responsible for more testosterone in the body, which led to more aggression. However, it has been conclusively shown that XYY males are actually somewhat less aggressive than XY males. Lacking a physical explanation for why the studies found more XYY males in prison populations, criminologists have suggested three social explanations:

XYY syndrome

A condition in which a male is born with an extra Y chromosome.

1. Because XYY offenders are tall, criminal justice system practitioners might arrest them, convict them, and sentence them to prison at a greater rate because they look more menacing.

2. The institutionalization rate of XYY males simply mirrors their percentage in lower-income populations.

3. Because they tend to be slightly less intelligent than the normal population, they are less able to compete in legitimate enterprises and therefore turn to crime more often.

The extra-Y-chromosome theory can account for only a small proportion of crime because XY males are still responsible for most crime.[27] The interesting policy implication of the XYY controversy is the idea that we could predict which men would be crime-prone by looking at their chromosomes. As with all the biological theories of crime, the policy implications suggest that by identifying crime-prone males early, we can intervene in the life of the individual and prevent crime. The potential for abuse here is significant, however.

BIOCHEMISTRY   As science allows us to better understand the relationship between the body and behavior, researchers are examining three areas to determine whether some people break the law for physical reasons. Hormones, brain structure, and brain chemistry all appear to affect behavior. However, isolating a single, identifiable physical influence on crime is problematic. At best, we hope to understand the interaction that physical factors might have with social and psychological influences and pressures related to criminal behavior.[28]

- **Hormones**   The body secretes hormones for a number of reasons, but one of the by-products of this activity appears to be alterations in mood and behavior. For instance, a relationship exists between the release of testosterone in males and aggression. However, the question that scientists and criminologists ask is, Which one comes first? Because testosterone levels respond to competitive challenges, the relationship between testosterone and aggression might be a by-product rather than the cause of aggression.[29] That is, as men engage in activities such as sports or crime, the level of testosterone rises as a result of the activity instead of causing it. Hormones affect women's behavior, as well. A popular conception is that premenstrual syndrome (PMS) causes women to act differently than they normally would.[30] Because of a few high-profile cases in which women have used PMS as a criminal defense, the woman with PMS has become a stereotype of a person who is depressed, hysterical, and out of control. A great deal of anecdotal evidence exists that PMS can affect a woman's behavior, but its relationship to crime remains uncertain at best. Although PMS has been used in some cases as a mitigating circumstance to reduce a woman's sentence, studies do not give us a clear and convincing picture of how this natural condition could cause or influence women to break the law.[31]

- **Brain structure and brain chemistry**   Since the heyday of phrenology, researchers have learned a great deal about the brain. The brain is a complex organ that we still know relatively little about. Especially humbling is the sparse knowledge about links between the brain and antisocial behavior. However, there are tools to examine how different parts of the brain are responsible for different activities. Techniques such as computed tomography (CT) scans, magnetic resonance imaging (MRI), position emission tomography (PET) scans, and single photon emission computed tomography (SPECT) scans allow researchers to observe how the brain is influenced by injury. There is no consensus about exactly how the brain influences behavior; however, this research is still in its early stages. Some critics would liken this research to phrenology, albeit with more sophisticated tools, but some evidence suggests that it might eventually prove to be fruitful. Brain chemistry is another area in which researchers are looking for causes of crime. Such hormones as norepinephrine, dopamine, and serotonin are of particular interest to criminologists because they regulate behaviors such as impulsivity, feelings of pleasure, and response to danger. Clearly, drug therapy is both promising and subject to abuse. Given the way people use recreational drugs, it is important to pursue research on the relationship between crime and brain chemistry.[32]

All of these biological theories of crime demonstrate a continuing search for the physical reasons for crime. Although some of the older theories may be amusing, they once represented conventional wisdom. These theories often had direct or indirect effects on who was arrested and convicted of crimes. Furthermore, these theories dictated the kinds of punishments or treatments that were applied. Although many criminologists and criminal justice practitioners find biological theories problematic, they may well ultimately provide us with not only a clear understanding of the motivations and causes of criminal behavior, but also effective methods of intervention. However, we should be aware that, as in the past, some severe ethical issues will have to be considered.

3.1 CASE IN POINT

ROBINSON V. CALIFORNIA

THE CASE	THE POINT
Robinson v. California, 370 U.S. 660, 82 S.Ct. 1417 (1962)	The Supreme Court holds that drug addiction is a disease, not a crime.

A Los Angeles police officer arrested Lawrence Robinson on noticing on Robinson's arm what appeared to be scars and scabs from narcotics use. At his trial four months later, Robinson was convicted under a California law that made it a misdemeanor to be addicted to narcotics. At the trial, the examining officer said Robinson was neither under the influence of narcotics nor experiencing withdrawal symptoms at the time of arrest, and that the scabs on Robinson's arms had been several days old.

On appeal, the Supreme Court held that narcotics addiction is a disease and that people afflicted with disease should not be treated as criminals and incarcerated. Therefore, incarcerating a narcotics addict "inflicts a cruel and unusual punishment in violation of the Fourteenth Amendment." The California law was declared unconstitutional, and Robinson's conviction was reversed.

Psychological Theories of Crime

Although it is inadvisable, and maybe impossible, to separate the influence of the body and brain on behavior, criminologists make a distinction between biological and psychological theories. With this in mind, we now turn to psychological explanations of criminal behavior. Sometimes when people commit irrational acts of crime and violence, we think of them as crazy. But what does "crazy" mean? The argument can easily loop back on itself. Crazy people do crazy things, so anyone whose behavior we cannot understand must be crazy. This line of thinking is a dead end in the understanding of criminal behavior. Therefore, notions such as "crazy" have been discarded in favor of more logical explanations of criminal behavior. Contemporary criminal psychology focuses on how antisocial individuals acquire, display, maintain, and (sometimes) modify their behavior, as well as considering the influence of societal, personality, and individual mental processes on behavior.[33]

3.1   CrossCurrents

The Criminal Profile

Most of us are familiar with how criminal profiling is performed in the movies or on television: an FBI profiler examines a crime scene or other evidence and from those materials alone comes up with a psychological profile of the killer or even the killer's identity. In *The Silence of the Lambs*, FBI rookie Clarice Starling brandishes a tattered, overstuffed file folder, exclaiming that "Lecter said everything we need to catch [the killer] is in these pages!"

Unfortunately, criminal profiling is neither that easy nor that exact. Criminal profiling, an aspect of the now set-aside trait approach of psychology, is about 90 percent art and 10 percent science.[1] Traits are personal characteristics that mark an individual's tendency to behave in a certain way and distinguish individuals from each other. Shyness is a trait, as is aggression. Early into the study of antisocial behavior, psychologists thought that the likelihood that people would break the law and the way in which they would break the law could be predicted to some degree by their traits. However, as discussed further in the chapter, criminal psychologists now look to cognitive or developmental approaches to understand antisocial behavior. Trait psychology, however, is still at work in the practice of criminal profiling.[2]

Criminal profiling, is, according to criminology scholars Curt and Anne Bartol, "the process of identifying personality traits, behavioral tendencies, and demographic variables of an offender based on characteristics of the crime."[3] The FBI began to use criminal profiling in 1970, based on the U.S. Office of Strategic Services' work constructing psychological profiles of Axis leaders during World War II.[4] Despite the current popularity of profiling, much of it, according to Bartol and Bartol, is "guesswork based on hunches and anecdotal information accumulated through years of experience, and it is full of error and misinterpretation." What profiling does achieve is to narrow investigations from an unwieldy, large pool of suspects to a relatively smaller one.[5] Although profiling can be used for any type of offender, such as shoplifters, it appears to be particularly useful in investigating cases of serial murder and serial sexual homicides, probably because there is more research into these offenses than other types of offenses, such as burglary and robbery.[6]

One of the first official uses of profiling to investigate a criminal suspect occurred in 1956 in New York City. During the 1940s and 1950s, New York City was plagued by the "Mad Bomber," a man who planted homemade bombs throughout the city while sending letters to the police complaining that the power company Con Edison "will pay for their dastardly deeds." The Mad Bomber planted six bombs throughout New York City in 1955, and the police still had no leads on the case. In 1956, the police turned to James Brussel, a psychiatrist in the tradition of Sigmund Freud. After thumbing through the case file, Brussel wrote later that he told the police the Mad Bomber was probably an eastern European immigrant, a never-married loner who lived with a mother figure in southeastern Connecticut and dressed neatly in very conservative, almost old-fashioned clothing. Brussel told the police, "When you catch him— and I have no doubt you will—he'll be wearing a double-breasted suit. And it will be buttoned."

Police arrested George Metesky a month later. Metesky was of eastern European extraction and unmarried, and he lived in Connecticut with his two unmarried sisters. He had worked for Con Edison from 1929 to

1931 and said he had been injured on the job. Extremely neat and concerned about his appearance, he was wearing a buttoned double-breasted suit when police escorted him from his home.[7]

This incident sounds like an incredible application of criminal profiling. The problem is that it is not entirely accurate. Psychology researchers state that profiling has two basic flaws:

- It assumes that humans behave consistently in a variety of situations.
- It assumes that the manner of the offense and the evidence are directly related to specific personality characteristics.[8]

As forensic scientist Brent Turvey told the *New Yorker*:

You've got a rapist who attacks a woman in the park and pulls her shirt up over her face. Why? What does that mean? There are ten different things it could mean. It could mean he doesn't want to see her. It could mean he doesn't want her to see him. It could mean he wants to see her breasts, he wants to imagine someone else, he wants to incapacitate her arms—all of those are possibilities. You can't just look at one behavior in isolation.[9]

When literary scholar Donald Foster studied James Brussel's work on the Mad Bomber, he saw that Brussel had greatly altered his original analysis when writing about it years later. Brussel had originally told police to look for the Mad Bomber in White Plains, New York, and that he would have a facial scar, be between ages 40 and 50, work a night job, and be skilled in handling weapons or ammunition. None of these identified Metesky, who was also over age 50 at the time of his arrest.[10]

In fact, the case was broken by old-fashioned investigative work. In 1957, a Con Edison clerk who had been assigned to search the company's personnel files discovered angry letters from an employee named George Metesky who claimed his illness had been caused by an accident at the company in the 1930s. In the letters was a phrase that also appeared in the Mad Bomber's letters: "to take justice in my own hands." Police arrested Metesky a short while later.

Think About It

1. Why is the idea of criminal profiling so popular?
2. What are the implications for mistakes made by profilers for those accused of serious offenses?
3. What are the scientific alternatives to this type of psychological profiling?

[1] Curt R. Bartol and Anne M. Bartol, *Criminal Behavior: A Psychosocial Approach*, 8th ed. (Upper Saddle River, NJ: Pearson Prentice Hall, 2008), 7–8.
[2] Ibid.
[3] Ibid.
[4] Richard L. Ault and James T. Reese, "A Psychological Assessment of Crime: Profiling," *FBI Law Enforcement Bulletin* 49, no. 3 (1980): 22–25.
[5] John E. Douglas et al., "Criminal Profiling from Crime Scene Analysis," *Behavioral Sciences and the Law* 4 (1986): 401–426.
[6] Anthony J. Pinizzotto and Norman J. Finkel, "Criminal Personality Profiling: An Outcome and Process Study," *Law and Human Behavior* 14, no. 3 (June 1990): 215–233.
[7] Malcolm Gladwell, "Dangerous Minds: Criminal Profiling Made Easy," *New Yorker*, November 12, 2007, 36.
[8] Laurence Alison et al., "The Personality Paradox in Offender Profiling: A Theoretical Review of the Processes Involved in Deriving Background Characteristics from Crime Scene Actions," *Psychology, Public Policy, and the Law* 8, no. 1 (2002): 115–135.
[9] Gladwell, "Dangerous Minds."
[10] Ibid. For the essay on Brussel and the Mad Bomber, see "A Professor's Whodunit," in Don Foster, *Author Unknown: Tales of a Literary Detective* (New York: Holt, 2001).

Early criminal psychology looked for individual "traits" that influenced behavior, such as extroversion or introversion (see Crosscurrents 3.1 for more about trait theories and their relationship to criminal profiling). People with certain types of personalities were thought to be more likely to break the law in ways that complemented their personalities. A simple example would be that a shy person might be more suited to burglary than robbery, because it is important for burglars not to be seen, whereas robbers accost their victims. Addressing the antisocial behavior meant first addressing the personality trait that caused the offender to behave in an antisocial fashion. Criminal psychology has moved on from this perspective, however, to embrace cognitive and developmental approaches. Cognition refers to the act of thinking, which includes attitudes, beliefs, and values that individuals hold about themselves, other people, and their surroundings. An approach that addresses the way an individual thinks, then, is a cognitive approach. Developmental approaches address individual human development from childhood to adulthood.[34]

This section provides a broad overview of the field of criminal psychology and its history by giving a brief description of major developmental and cognitive theories. We will begin with the work of Sigmund Freud and continue through the major contemporary psychological theories.

PSYCHOANALYTIC THEORY   Many scholars contend that all modern psychology began with Sigmund Freud (1859–1939). If a school of psychology is not descended from Freud's psychoanalytic theory, then it was developed in opposition to Freud's ideas. Freud's major contribution was to take the study of the mind from the medical paradigm of considering brain structure and chemistry and to develop a psychological paradigm that focuses on unconscious forces and drives. Freud was trained as a physician and neurologist, so this was a major break with his training and profession. He opened up entirely new ways to think about behavior, and although he is held in some disrepute now for many of his ideas, his terminology has worked its way into our language and, to a large extent, how we think about the mind as opposed to the brain.[35]

Freud contended that the personality is composed of three parts: the id, ego, and superego.

- **Id**   The id is like a small child. It comprises our instincts and unsocialized biological drives. It pursues what it wants and has to be controlled, or we cannot operate in society. At an early age, the ego and superego start controlling the id.
- **Ego**   The ego is the part of the personality that learns to solve problems and acts as a brake on the id. The ego deals with reality and analyzes situations so that the id does not cause trouble.
- **Superego**   The superego is the conscience. It can be likened to that little voice that tells us what is right and what is wrong.[36]

According to Freud, healthy people have the proper balance of these three components. (For example, an underdeveloped ego will let the id run amok and engage in all kinds of mischief in fulfilling its desires.) This coverage of Freud's ideas is greatly oversimplified. A true understanding of the many facets and nuances of his theory can take years of study.[37]

BEHAVIORISM   B. F. Skinner (1904–1990) was an interesting man who theorized that behavior is determined by rewards and punishments. His theory, known as **behaviorism,** is based on the psychological principle of **operant conditioning.** That is, behavior is more likely to occur when it is rewarded and less likely to occur when

behaviorism

The assessment of human psychology via the examination of objectively observable and quantifiable actions, as opposed to subjective mental states.

operant conditioning

The alteration of behavior by rewarding or punishing a subject for a specified action until the subject associates the action with pleasure or pain.

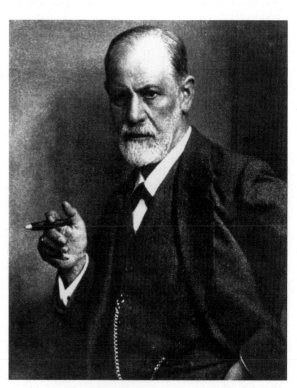

Sigmund Freud is considered the father of psychology. His ideas about personality and behavior influenced how we think about antisocial behavior.

Source: National Library of Medicine

it is punished or not rewarded. Operant conditioning is more complicated than it first appears. For example, slot machines are set up to pay on an intermittent schedule. They dispense just enough coins just often enough to keep gamblers pulling the lever. Slot machine designers calculate payoff intervals to encourage more gambling. If the schedule of reinforcement is too long—that is, if the machine does not pay off often enough—then gamblers will stop inserting coins. Like slot machine designers, behaviorists study how people deal with events of rewards and punishments to see how good behavior can be encouraged and bad behavior eliminated.[38] In the criminal justice system, behaviorism is used extensively in therapeutic communities in which residents are placed on token economies that reward appropriate behavior.[39]

Some issues of behaviorism concern criminologists. First, rewards and punishments in the real world are not given according to predictable or dependable schedules. That is, hard work does not guarantee rewards. Often, the real world favors the strong, the lucky, the well connected, and those who cheat. Behaviorism works best in the artificial environments of the laboratory, the classroom, and the therapeutic community. Offenders can get frustrated quickly when they experience the inequities of the real world. Behaviorism is undependable as a guide for criminological policy because rewards come in many forms. What the middle-class, middle-age criminologist might think is a deterrent to inappropriate behavior might be considered by the impoverished, immigrant, and/or young gang member as a reward. For instance, incarceration evokes fear in most of us, but for some gang members it is seen as a necessary step in the development of a gang identity.[40]

OBSERVATIONAL LEARNING Albert Bandura, a psychologist at Stanford University, has spent his career looking at modeling or **observational learning** as a form of social learning. Although modeling is an aspect of behaviorism, it also significantly involves the study of cognitive development. Bandura focuses on what he calls *reciprocal determinism*, which refers to how cognition (thought), behavior, and environment reinforce each other (see Figure 3-1). Basically, what we think affects how we behave and how we perceive our surroundings, including other people. In return, our surroundings reflect our behavior to some extent, which affects how we think. This has implications for the study of antisocial behavior, especially considering that much of Bandura's work concerns how aggressive and violent behavior is learned.[41]

Bandura's most famous experiments, the "Bobo doll experiments," used an inflated plastic toy called a *Bobo doll* that sits on the floor and pops back up when it is struck. Children of kindergarten age were shown a film of a woman punching the doll repeatedly as it popped up. When the children were led into the room with the doll, they immediately started punching and kicking the doll in imitation of what they had seen the woman do. This modeling behavior is not particularly surprising because the Bobo doll is designed to be used this way. However, Bandura conducted further experiments in which he showed the children a film of a woman punching and kicking a live clown. When the children were given the opportunity to punch and kick

observational learning
The process of learning by watching the behavior of others.

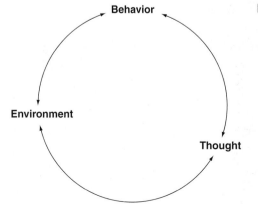

Figure 3-1 **Bandura's Reciprocal Determinism**

the clowns themselves, they did so. The model (the woman) reinforced the observers (the children), who then imitated the behavior.[42]

It is easy to see how this line of reasoning can be extended to antisocial behavior. When individuals routinely see others being abused or physically assaulted, they might imitate or model the behavior. Of course, there are many obstacles to overcome before this process takes place. Most adults have a certain level of self-regulation that prevents them from imitating everything they see. Also, the psychological processes involved in modeling behavior are complex and have certain limitations. Specifically, behaviorism considers external behavior and fails to consider individual cognitive processes.

COGNITIVE PSYCHOLOGICAL THEORY   In addition to psychoanalytic theory and behaviorism, cognitive psychological theory has promise for explaining antisocial behavior. Here, we will concentrate on the work of a psychologist whose work is relevant to the criminal justice system. According to Lawrence Kohlberg's *theory of moral development*, human moral development proceeds through clearly defined stages of moral reasoning. Children learn the higher stages of morality from older children, teenagers, and adults.

The level of an individual's moral reasoning is related to the decision to break the law.[43] The earlier stages are representative of egocentric behavior. In other words, the world revolves the individual, who then acts in his or her best interests all the time. Criminal offenders are stuck at the lower stages of moral development because those who wish to simply avoid punishment are more likely to engage in antisocial behavior than those who feel an obligation to the abstract principles of justice, equality, and respect for human life. Cognitive theory suggests that the teaching of problem-solving skills could be useful in helping offenders understand their motivations and actions, which in turn can prevent them from breaking the law again.

Moral development, according to Kohlberg, develops in three main stages, with six substages.[44] It is interesting that Kohlberg believed that most law-abiding adults never proceed beyond the Conventional level.[45]

- **Preconventional**   Children learn to avoid punishment by following simple rules. At this stage, children follow the rules because if they do not, they will be punished.

    Stage 1: Obedience and punishment orientation   The punishment defines the rules.

    Stage 2: Individualism and exchange   Children learn that it is in their self-interest to avoid punishment, so the rules must be followed. Adult and older adolescent criminal offenders are "stuck" at this level of reasoning.

- **Conventional**   At this point, usually during adolescence, people adopt and support their society's values.

    Stage 3: Good interpersonal relationships   Young teenagers believe that being "good" and maintaining personal relationships are important. "Good" and "bad" are usually clearly defined at this point.

    Stage 4: Maintaining the social order   Older teenagers and adults believe that the social order is of the utmost importance and that laws must be obeyed for the sake of the social order. Kohlberg found that most adolescents and adults function at this level.

- **Postconventional**   Adults who reach this stage compare rules and laws to universal moral laws and ethics. At this point, adults question exactly what is required for society to be "good." Justice demands that everyone be treated equally and impartially.

    Stage 5: Social contract and individual rights.
    Stage 6: Universal principles.

Kohlberg also theorized that the quality of our moral development is related to how we adapt to *cognitive disequilibrium*, which is the thinking that occurs when we realize that what we learn does not match what we know and that we must consciously, or unconsciously, change the way we think about things. Cognitive disequilibrium can result from confronting moral challenges and conflicts and from talking to peers.[46] Progression through the stages is also marked with the development of empathy, or the ability to put oneself in the place of others. Studies have found that juvenile delinquents also show strong signs of being developmentally delayed in their capacity for moral judgment.[47]

PSYCHOPATHY   In common usage, the term *psychopath* refers to criminal offenders who commit the most heinous crimes, apparently without remorse. Offenders who appear to kill indiscriminately are typically branded as "psychopaths" in public opinion. However, psychopathy actually refers to a specific condition which is only sometimes paired with heinous criminal offending. According to psychologist Robert Hare, the three categories of psychopath are the primary, the secondary, and the dyssocial.

- **Primary psychopath**   Primary psychopathy is a set of innate psychological, emotional, cognitive, and biological differences that distinguish primary psychopaths from the rest of society. These differences are manifested in pathological lying; a lack of remorse, empathy, or guilt; poor behavioral controls; irresponsibility; low empathy; and a grandiose sense of self-worth. These characteristics make for a person who maneuvers through society doing what he or she wants, and when, with little or no forethought, regardless of the consequences. Primary psychopaths are often in trouble with the law because of this behavior, but many manage never to break the law.
- **Secondary psychopath**   A person with this condition engages in antisocial and violent behavior because of severe emotional issues.
- **Dyssocial psychopath**   This offender is aggressive, violent, and antisocial because he or she has learned these behaviors, not because of any illness or inner conflict. A violent gang member is a good example of a dyssocial psychopath.[48]

Neither the secondary psychopath or the dyssocial psychopath is considered a true psychopath because their conditions are caused by external factors, such as mental illness or the individual's surroundings. There is some concern about the diagnosis of "psychopathy" because it is difficult to recognize before serious crime has occurred. When researchers interview offenders who have committed heinous offenses, it is usually after they have been convicted. The critical issue in identifying psychopathy is to identify psychopaths who might commit serious offenses and prevent their behavior.[49]

ANTISOCIAL PERSONALITY DISORDER (APD)   Another condition often confused with psychopathy is antisocial personality disorder. These two conditions have much in common, but clinicians distinguish them for diagnostic reasons. According to the American Psychiatric Association, APD is "a pervasive pattern of disregard for, and violation of, the rights of others that begins in childhood or early adolescence and continues into adulthood."[50] APD has much in common with psychopathy, but its definition is marked by behavior, whereas the definition of psychopathy includes cognitive and emotional characteristics. APD is also marked by aggression, violence, and irritability; psychopaths might not display any of these symptoms. Those with APD, which occurs more frequently in males than females, are almost certain to break the law repeatedly, whereas psychopaths might break the law only occasionally.[51]

Sociological Theories of Crime

The biological and psychological theories of crime focus on the mind and body to determine why people break the law. In short, these theories argue that something is wrong with the offender, either physically or mentally. Consequently, the policy implications of these types of theories revolve around incapacitating or treating the offender. However, another type of criminological theory finds problems not so much with the individual, but with the social situation or environment. A variety of sociological theories consider social structure and social processes as explanations for crime.

THE CHICAGO SCHOOL   The University of Chicago instituted the first sociology department in the United States. The scholars there developed not only several theories of crime, but also a method for examining crime. Basically, Chicago-school criminologists rejected the idea that crime is individual in nature, as the biological and psychological theories suggested, and turned to examining external factors. Two researchers connected to the **Chicago school,** Clifford Shaw and Henry McKay, studied the social disorganization of the neighborhoods of delinquent youths and concluded that something about bad neighborhoods caused crime.[52] Curran and Renzetti summarize this finding as follows:

> They concluded that in terms of such characteristics as personality, intelligence, and physical condition, delinquents, for the most part, were no different from nondelinquents. Of equal significance was their finding that crime and delinquency were not dominated by any particular ethnic or racial groups. This could be seen in the fact that while the racial and ethnic composition of certain neighborhoods changed over the years, the rates of delinquency remained fairly constant. . . . Shaw and McKay reported that neighborhoods with the worst delinquency problems also had the highest rates of other social problems, including deteriorated housing, infant mortality, and tuberculosis. The residents of these neighborhoods were the most economically disadvantaged in the city.[53]

What was it about these communities that contributed to crime? Poverty was not the only issue. Those unstable neighborhoods caused a breakdown in the traditional bonds of social control.[54] With families moving in and out of the neighborhood, children were exposed to many different influences. The normal social ties were weakened and new norms emerged. Without the traditional family and community life that immigrants had in the "old country," their children were forced to blend the old ways of doing things with the street culture of the new country. As families gained economic power and moved out of these socially disorganized neighborhoods, their children committed fewer delinquent acts. The policy implications of social disorganization theory suggests that efforts to improve the physical blight of the community and the social interaction and integration of all citizens can reduce crime. Although we are accustomed to seeing places change significantly throughout our lifetimes, some places require many generations to change. For example, many neighborhoods in Chicago are as disordered as they were at the turn of the century (see Crosscurrents 3.2).

DIFFERENTIAL ASSOCIATION THEORY   Edwin Sutherland (1883–1950) developed **differential association theory,** one of the most popular theories of delinquency. Sutherland's theory claims that antisocial behavior is learned and that young people learn antisocial behavior in intimate play groups (friends and family) rather than from the media.[55] Sutherland presented his theory in nine propositions (see Criminal Justice Reference 3.2). What Sutherland's theory does not explain is how this learning takes place. In fact, one could question whether learning is really taking place in these groups, or whether it is simply a case of "birds of a feather flock together." If we accept that one's chances of being a delinquent are greater when one's friends are also delinquent, this still does not prove that delinquency is learned in intimate groups. However, Sutherland's work has stimulated other theorists to pursue the idea that antisocial behavior is learned.[56]

DIFFERENTIAL ASSOCIATION-REINFORCEMENT THEORY AND BEHAVIORISM
Ronald Akers took Sutherland's differential association and incorporated it with behaviorism, contending that crime is learned according to the principles of operant

Chicago school
Criminological theories that rely, in part, on individuals' demographics and geographic location to explain criminal behavior.

differential association theory
A theory developed by Edwin Sutherland that states that crime is learned.

3.2   CrossCurrents

A History of Violence in Chicago

In April 2008, the city of Chicago experienced one of the worst periods of violence in recent history. According to unofficial statistics, at least 42 homicides occurred during the first three weeks of April, 12 more than the entire month of April 2007, and 545 people were injured in nonfatal shootings.[1]

Like most U.S. cities, Chicago is no stranger to violent crime, but the violence of April 2008—which has been blamed on causes such as unexpected warm weather and unemployment—shocked the city's leadership, citizens, and law enforcement into action. Chicago police sent SWAT teams and other special units on late-night patrols. Major Richard Daley met with community groups and clergy to discuss the situation.[2] Crime experts from the University of Chicago were set to work on a study of youth violence, as well as a "series of intervention policies" to augment the city's current antiviolence strategies, including city curfews, safety cameras in public schools, and additional police patrols near schools.[3] City officials, pointing to a report that connects child abuse to violent crime, asked Illinois lawmakers to increase funding for child-abuse prevention programs with the idea that children who are treated well at home will be less likely to become violent outside the home.[4]

Unfortunately, the story of crime and violence in Chicago is nearly as old as the city itself. The Chicago School of theorists developed their social disorganization theories in the first half of the 20th century surrounded by a ready-made laboratory of socially disorganized neighborhoods. Social change came rapidly to Chicago, which had a population of only 4000 when it was incorporated in 1833. By 1890, the population, drawn by employment opportunities in the city's factories and mills, had jumped to 1 million, and by 1910 to 2 million.[5] With thousands of immigrants from Europe and the American South, corruption and vice were rampant, as were the organized groups who controlled much of the criminal activity.

However, the 1920s and Prohibition introduced a whole new level of corruption and organized crime. As the number of homicides leaped in the years between 1918 and 1930, Chicago became infamous for its corrupt judiciary and police force. Many of the city's officials ran their own organized crime rings to take advantage of the trade in illegal liquor, prostitution, and gambling. Meanwhile, the working poor, many of whom were immigrants literate in neither English nor their native language, had no financial security of any sort. When Chicago's economy was good, these poor worked in low-wage jobs and relied on churches and charities to survive. In rough economic times, according to Bienen and Rottinchaus, "thousands of homeless men roamed the streets and slept in public buildings."[6]

Prohibition just made everything worse. Writing in 1960, John H. Lyle observed:

> During the Prohibition Era Chicago and many other major cities were swept by what may be called without exaggeration a typhoon of crime. There were two tidal waves and they traveled in tandem. The beer and booze barons, the new aristocracy, the nouveau riche of outlawry rode the first wave. Behind them were the common run of criminals, the journeymen in the trades of thievery. It is not surprising that the dry law years saw what was undoubtedly the greatest crime spree in the nation's history. Literally, the organized gangsters were getting away with murder.[7]

Recently, federal law enforcement arrested 28 people associated with a faction of one of the nation's largest gangs, the Gangster Disciples, which has traditionally has had a strong power base in Chicago. Two Gangster Disciples sets, the Damenville Gangster Disciples and the 5–4 Crew, had taken over part of a South Side neighborhood to sell drugs. Just the year before, federal agents moved on a similar Gangster Disciples operation in the West Pullman neighborhood. Federal agents say the structure of large gangs in Chicago, such as the Gangster Disciples, has changed, with most now acting as "umbrella" organizations for local sets. In announcing the arrests, U.S. Attorney Patrick Fitzgerald told the media, "Today, the residents of the South Side of Chicago got one of their blocks back."[8]

Think About It

1. Is Chicago any different from other large U.S. cities in its recent upsurge of violent crime?
2. Besides social disorganization, what other more contemporary theories may help explain crime in Chicago?
3. What types of community programs may best address violent crime?

[1]Angela Rozas and Rex Huppke, "City to Beef Up Police Patrols Over Weekend," *Chicago Tribune*, April 26, 2008.
[2]Ibid.
[3]Lesley R. Chinn, "Mayor Daley Calls for Citiwide Solutions," *Chicago Citizen*, April 30, 2008.
[4]Monique Garcia, "Curbing in Child Abuse in City May Have Future Dividend," *Chicago Tribune*, May 14, 2008.
[5]John J. Palen, *The Urban World*, 3rd ed. (New York: McGraw-Hill, 1981).
[6]Leigh Bienen and Brandon Rottinchaus, "Learning from the Past, Living in the Present: Understanding Homicide in Chicago, 1870–1930," *Journal of Criminal Law and Criminology* 92, nos. 3/4 (Spring/Summer 2002): 437.
[7]John H. Lyle, *The Dry and Lawless Years* (Englewood Cliffs, NJ: Prentice Hall, 1960).
[8]Jeff Coen, "Officials Charge 28 in Gang Sweep," *Chicago Tribune*, May 22, 2008.

3.2   CRIMINAL JUSTICE REFERENCE

Edwin Sutherland's Nine Principles of Differential Association

1. Criminal behavior is learned.
2. Criminal behavior is learned in interaction with other persons in a process of communication.
3. The principle part of the learning of criminal behavior occurs within intimate personal groups.
4. When criminal behavior is learned, the learning includes (a) techniques of committing crime, which are sometimes very complicated and sometimes very simple; and (b) the specific directions of motives, drives, rationalizations, and attitudes.
5. The specific direction of motives and drives is learned from definitions of legal codes as favorable and unfavorable.

6. A person becomes delinquent because of an excess of definitions favorable to violation of law over definitions unfavorable to violation of law.
7. Differential association may vary in frequency, duration, priority, and intensity.
8. The process of learning criminal behavior by association with criminal and anticriminal patterns incorporates all the mechanisms that are involved in any other learning.
9. Although criminal behavior is an expression of general needs and values, it is not explained by those general needs and values because noncriminal behavior is an expression of the same needs and values.

conditioning. Akers's social learning theory incorporates more than just modeling, however. Akers looks at differential association, definitions (how individuals justify their behavior), differential reinforcement, and imitation (modeling).[57]

According to differential association-reinforcement, behaviors are conditioned by environmental feedback and are likely to increase when they are given positive reinforcement (reward received) or negative reinforcement (punishment removed or avoided).[58] Behaviors are likely to decrease when they receive positive punishment (punishment received) or negative punishment (reward removed or lost). Akers also included the process of modeling in his theory. Modeling involves imitating the behavior of someone who is respected and admired, especially if that person's behavior is being rewarded. (Modeling is a complex process that is difficult to test, however, especially for more serious forms of behavior.)[59]

Basically, the social rewards and punishments that a person receives determine whether he or she continues to break the law or follow the law. Behaviors that receive more reward than punishment are likely to continue, and behaviors that receive more punishment than reward are not. However, the weight of these rewards and punishments determines how they affect the individual. Family and friends who are the most important to the individual provide the most meaningful rewards and punishments. So a punishment that comes from a less well-regarded person means less than a reward that comes from a highly regarded person. An adolescent whose friends' opinions mean more to her than her parents' will seek her friends' approval far more than her parents' approval, and her parents' punishments will mean less.

We can see another example of this in the attraction of gangs to impoverished young people. Adolescents who have grown up in poverty and fear might not feel rewarded by the society that tells them that they ought to follow the law. The gang, however, promises these teens respect, money, and a sense of belonging to something that matters. Several of the teenagers' relatives may already be in the gang, and their older relatives may still be affiliated with the gang, even if they are no longer active. The rewards and punishments that come from the gang mean far more to these teenagers than those offered by a greater society that does not appear to care about them.

Social learning theory has been exhaustively tested and, for the most part, provides a powerful explanation for why people break the criminal law. Akers and Jensen have extended their theory beyond the micro level and contend that it is useful as an integrated theory to explain a broad range of antisocial behaviors. Although this claim has not been empirically tested, it promises to be an exciting venue for future criminological thinking.[60]

Some overlap exists between psychological theories and social-psychological theories, such as behaviorism and learning theory. Such theories are not easily categorized as either psychological or sociological explanations, as they tend to bridge the gap between the two areas of thought.

STRAIN THEORY   Sociologist Robert Merton has made many contributions to the field of criminology, including the **strain theory** of delinquency. Merton was influenced by French sociologist Émile Durkheim's theory of **anomie** or "normlessness." In times of rapid social change, Durkheim contended that the old norms break down and people lack controls on their behavior. Before new norms can be established, people experience a sense of normlessness and are more likely to engage in antisocial behavior. Merton looked at norms and recognized that society holds out the same norms for everybody. The problem arises when there is unequal access to these norms. Those who share the goals promoted by society but find their means to attain these goals systematically blocked experience anomie. This anomie can be translated into antisocial behavior when the person attempts to adapt to the barriers to the goal.[61] For example, American society has a cultural goal of acquiring wealth. The goal of financial independence is pushed by our families, the schools, and the media. It is such a pervasive goal that we tend to take it for granted and assume that it is appropriate for everyone. As we attempt to reach this goal, some of us encounter obstacles. Sexism, racism, class bias, and age restrictions can frustrate our desires to become wealthy. For many people, simply working hard and saving money does not guarantee success. Does one disregard the goal when the means are lacking? According to Merton, the answer is no. One finds other ways of addressing the goal and adapts to the lack of means (see Table 3-3).

Merton's strain theory is easy to understand and seems to have positive policy implications. If people break the law because they find their means to compete in legitimate society blocked by poverty and inequality, then all that needs to be done is to remove those blockages. The theory has its critics, however. For instance, is it accurate to say that drug addicts withdraw from society? Many of those who use drugs maintain conventional lifestyles. Their drug use is not a retreat from society but an effort to engage in society in a more meaningful way. For some people, drugs enhance experiences of dancing, viewing concerts, and relating to others and do not cause them to become stereotypical, nonfunctioning drug addicts. Also, it may be unfair to claim that Americans are primarily materialistic. Other culturally approved, nonmaterialistic

strain theory
The theory that the causes of crime can be connected to the pressure on culturally or materially disadvantaged groups or individuals to achieve the goals held by society, even if the means to those goals require the breaking of laws.

anomie
A condition in which a people or society undergoes a breakdown of social norms and values.

Table 3-3   **Robert Merton's Strain Theory**

Adaptive Type	Goals	Means
Conformist: Most people fit this adaptation, accepting the goal of having money and adopting the culturally approved way to get it: hard work and deferred gratification. Most university students would be considered conformists. They work hard, defer gratification, and prepare for legitimate occupations.	Accepted +	Accepted +
Innovator: One accepts the goal of having money but rejects the culturally approved means to obtain it, finding alternative methods instead. Innovations can include crime or legal ways to make money, but the key is that this adaptation does not fall within societal norms. It is legal and possibly lucrative to work as a dancer in a strip club, but generally it is not a socially respected method of obtaining wealth.	Accepted +	Rejected or is blocked −
Ritualist: The goal is rejected, but the means are still accepted. Ritualists are not usually deviant, but they no longer have the goal of achieving wealth and success. Ritualists tend to go through the motions without really hoping to make an impact. For example, some professors deliver the same lecture term after term and seem not to care whether the lecture is current or the students learn.	Rejected −	Accepted +
Retreatist: Both the goals and the means are rejected (or blocked), and nothing is substituted. Examples of retreatists would be drug addicts, alcoholics, hermits, and outcasts. Many of these people end up as clients of the criminal justice system.	Rejected −	Rejected or is blocked −
Rebel: Rebellious people reject culturally approved means and goals and substitute new ones. Some domestic terrorist groups would fit into this category, as well as hippies of the 1960s who dropped out of conventional society and established communes based on shared resources and responsibilities. Although some of these communes violated the popular sense of appropriate living arrangements, they seemed to meet the residents' needs.	Rejected (substitute) −	Rejected (substitute) −

| 3.2 | FOCUS *on* ETHICS |

WITH FRIENDS LIKE THESE

You are a good parent. You love your kids, provide them with all that they need, and are constantly finding ways to give them new growth experiences. You have taken them to Europe, taught them to play chess, allowed them to drink your fine wines with dinner from the time they turned 12, and turned a blind eye to their occasional marijuana use when they went to college. You pride yourself on raising two wonderful, successful, and accomplished children, one a lawyer and the other now in dental school. However, your third child is somewhat different. Your 16-year-old daughter has not taken the same route as her siblings. Although your older children were A students, officers in their class, and star athletes, your youngest daughter has gone Goth. Her entire wardrobe is black; she wants to get a tattoo of a bat (the kind that flies), and she wears a safety pin in her ear and silver rings in her eyebrows. Recently, she has taken to wearing a dog collar and changes her hair color with her mood.

All these issues are of little concern to you because she is a bright girl with a good sense of values who is just going though her rebellion phase. What is troubling you are her friends. They are older, unambitious, parasitic, unclean, and uncouth high school dropouts who spend their time hanging out at the town's punk dive, the Corner Grill. Try as you might, you fail to detect any social redeeming qualities in them whatsoever. You are afraid your daughter's new friends will influence her in negative ways. You do not want her using drugs, experimenting with intimacy, or adopting the nihilistic philosophy that denigrates all that you hold precious about American culture.

Now you have a decision to make. Your daughter has announced that she is leaving home to live with her friends, dropping out of school, renouncing religion, and becoming a vegan.

What Do You Do?

1. Trust that your daughter will not make any disastrous decisions and allow her to work out her own relationships.
2. Forbid your daughter to move out, make her cease seeing her friends, and insist that she return to school.
3. Pack her off to a boarding school where she will be forced to make new friends, get an expensive but excellent education, and learn some social skills, such as ballroom dancing.

goals drive Americans, such as the quest to get an education, the desire to feel like part of a community, and the wish to help and serve family, church, and country. Merton's theory assumes that having money is the overriding cultural goal. For many people, this is not the case.[62]

Robert Agnew has greatly expanded the theoretical breadth of strain theory to encompass a variety of situations and conditions that might compel people to break the law. Although Merton viewed economic success as a strain that was the predominant factor in lawbreaking, Agnew and his general strain theory consider the following list equally important:

- Parental rejection
- Erratic, excessive, and/or harsh supervision\discipline
- Child abuse and neglect
- Negative secondary school experiences (e.g., low grades, negative relations with teachers, the experience of school as boring and a waste of time)
- Abusive peer relations (e.g., insults, threats, physical assaults)
- Work in the secondary labor market (e.g., "bad jobs" that pay little, have few benefits, little opportunity for advancement, and unpleasant working conditions)
- Chronic unemployment
- Failure to achieve selected goals, including thrills\excitement, high levels of autonomy, masculine status, and the desire for much money in a short period of time
- Criminal victimization
- Residence in economically deprived communities
- Homelessness
- Discrimination based on characteristics such as race/ethnicity and gender[63]

Agnew's general strain theory has several advantages over Merton's theory. In addition to considering more types of strain, he also considers the mechanisms that people use to cope with their strain. For instance, because males are more often exposed to strains conducive to crime, they are more likely to cope with strain through crime.[64] This theory also suggests ways of reducing crime. According to Agnew, strategies for reducing exposure to strain include the following:

- Eliminating strains conducive to crime
- Altering strains to make them less conducive to crime (e.g., reducing their magnitude or perceived injustice)
- Removing individuals from strains conducive to crime
- Equipping individuals with the traits and skills to avoid strains conducive to crime
- Altering perceptions and goals of individuals to reduce subjective strains

Strategies for reducing the likelihood that individuals will respond to strain with crime include (a) improving conventional coping skills and resources, (b) increasing social support, (c) increasing social control and (d) reducing association with delinquent peers and beliefs favorable to crime.[65]

SOCIAL CONTROL THEORY   Travis Hirschi's **social control theory** is interesting because it approaches crime from a different angle than other theories. Most theories assume that people are good and turn to crime only when something is wrong with them or their environment. Hirschi's social control theory, however, does not ask why some people break the criminal law. It questions why most people do not. Instead of seeking to explain the relatively infrequent event of crime, social control theory explores the pervasive conforming behavior that makes meaningful communities possible. Hirschi speculated that the mechanism that accomplishes this is a social bond that links us to conventional society.[66] Only when this social bond is weakened is crime likely to occur. Hirschi contended that this social bond has four elements:

social control theory
A theory that seeks not to explain why people break the law, but instead explores what keeps most people from breaking the law.

1. **Attachment.**   When people are concerned with the feelings of other people, they are less likely to do things that are wrong. Children who value their parents' approval and affection will engage in behavior designed to maintain that good relationship. Hirschi believed that one's attachments to parents, schools, and peers help form the social bond that keeps one from engaging in criminal behavior.
2. **Commitment.**   People are committed to a society when they are successful in it. There is an old saying, "When you ain't got nothing, you ain't got nothing to lose." People who have money, property, and good reputations are committed to the social system that allowed them the opportunities for that success. A frequent mistake in the study of criminal behavior is the assumption that most criminals are committed to conventional society when, in fact, they have not been able to realize their needs in that society. In a sense, then, most criminals have little or nothing to lose.
3. **Involvement.**   People involved in conventional activities have less time and energy to engage in crime. "Involvement" is the idea behind a vast array of programs designed to keep young people occupied. Although ballet lessons, Little League baseball, police athletic league programs, after-school day care, and parks and recreation areas for children may have a number of positive features, one of the primary benefits is that they keep children busy.
4. **Beliefs.**   Children who believe in the conventional value system of society are less likely to break the law. According to Hirschi, children who commit delinquent acts have weakened beliefs in the conventional moral code. Unlike other theories that speculate about deviant subcultures that supply contrasting codes of conduct, Hirschi's theory considers only the dominant culture and envisions

that everyone is bonded to it to some degree. The strength of that bond is what determines whether one will become delinquent.

neutralization theory

A perspective that states that juvenile delinquents have feelings of guilt when involved in illegal activities and search for explanations to diminish that guilt.

NEUTRALIZATION THEORY   Most people do not break the law most of the time. Just about everyone seems to be able to get through each day without causing harm to others or stealing property. Most people are committed to a law-abiding lifestyle and break the law only sporadically, and then only in nonserious ways, such as driving faster than the speed limit. How, then, do occasional criminal offenders and delinquents justify their behavior? How do they account for the harm they do to others and still think of themselves as essentially good and decent people? Gresham Sykes and David Matza developed **neutralization theory** to explain how delinquents drift between conventional lifestyles and delinquent lifestyles. Neutralization theory states that offenders use techniques of neutralization to deflect feelings of blame and shame.[67] These neutralization techniques are rationalizations, justifications, and accounts of how the offending behavior can be excused or explained away. Sykes and Matza identified five techniques of neutralization:

1. **Denial of responsibility.**   Offenders deny that the offense was their fault. They might blame the influence of drugs or alcohol for "not being myself." This way they can live with their deviant acts without thinking of themselves as bad people.
2. **Denial of injury.**   Offenders claim that no one actually got hurt. If a male batterer "just slaps his wife around a little," he might try to minimize his actions by saying, "If I really wanted to hurt her, I would have used my fist." Also, drug users say that drugs affect only themselves, so the law should not be concerned with their drug use.
3. **Denial of victim.**   Thieves contend that the property they steal is insured, so the victim is not really harmed at all. Steroid-using athletes claim that everyone does it, so using illegal performance-enhancing drugs is not bad. A rapist might contend that the victim was "asking for it."
4. **Condemnation of condemners.**   Here, offenders claim that the criminal justice system or society is corrupt and unfair. Illegal drug users point to the harm done by legal drugs, such as tobacco and alcohol, and claim that marijuana is illegal because the alcohol industry is afraid of competition. The offenders claim a morally superior position from which they reject the legitimacy of those judging them.
5. **Appeal to higher loyalty.**   Offenders take responsibility for their actions but claim they were acting to satisfy a higher calling. Those who get arrested for protesting at abortion clinics, and even those who kill abortion providers, contend that they are fully aware that they are violating laws but believe they are upholding a higher law. They view themselves as "following God's law" when they commit murder. In this way, these otherwise conforming people can commit acts of violence that they would never commit under other circumstances.

According to Curran and Renzetti, there are two major issues concerning neutralization techniques. First, even though these appear to be after-the-fact justifications, they can also occur before the misbehavior. One might facilitate one's behavior by loosening one's moral bonds. Second, these techniques of neutralization act as mitigating circumstances in the eyes of offenders. They understand that the law excuses self-defense, accident, and insanity, and they justify their own behavior by claiming that these neutralizations constitute extenuating circumstances.[68]

labeling theory

A perspective that considers recidivism to be a consequence, in part, of the negative labels applied to offenders.

LABELING THEORY   Edwin Lemert (1912–1996) is one of the sociologists responsible for the development of **labeling theory.** Labeling theory contends that people engage in deviant behavior because they see themselves as "outsiders" and therefore attempt to live up to that label. Society defines some actions as deviant or unlawful and contends that anyone who engages in these behaviors is a criminal, prostitute, drug addict, thief, sexual pervert, and so on. People who do not get caught escape these labels and find it much easier to exist in society. Therefore, according to labeling theorists such as Howard Becker, "deviance is not a quality of the act the person commits, but rather a consequence of the application by others of rules or sanctions to an 'offender.' The deviant is one to whom that label has been successfully applied; deviant behavior is behavior that people so label."[69]

Labeling does not happen accidentally. We go to great lengths to apply positive and negative labels that can greatly affect people's lives. On the positive side, consider the elaborate ceremonies surrounding graduations and weddings. People dress up in elaborate costumes suitable for only this type of occasion; invitations are sent out to friends and relatives; respected officials read sacred documents to legitimize the event, and finally there is often a party or "reception" so everyone can celebrate the labeled person's change in social status.

On the negative side, there are public status-degradation ceremonies in which people are stripped of their positive statuses and labeled with deviant tags. Think about the old movies in which a soldier is court-martialed and has his stripes and insignia ripped from his uniform in a public ceremony. The intent is to shame him and to send a signal to others that bad behavior has negative consequences. By doing this in such a public way, the system influences more than just the individual offender. The courtroom is just such a public stage where a predictable drama is played out so that an offender can be labeled for all to see. The judge sits in an elevated position and wears an imposing costume. The judge looks down on the defendant, who sits with the defense attorney at a table that is physically separated from the others in the courtroom. When the sentence is announced, the defendant is required to stand so that all can witness the reaction. This could all be done in a much less elaborate manner, but the ceremony is designed to accomplish two goals: to impress on the defendant the disapproval of society and to impress on the rest of us that unlawful behavior has consequences.[70]

In his theory, Lemert made a distinction between primary deviation and secondary deviation, which is important to appreciating just how powerful the labeling process is in shaping unlawful behavior. *Primary deviation* is the initial lawbreaking. This can occur for any number of reasons and is of little concern to the labeling perspective. Once someone is caught by the criminal justice system, processed through the court, and successfully labeled, *secondary deviation* sets in. The offender comes to

Status degradation includes the process of incarceration. The correctional systems of some states clothe prison inmates in old-fashioned black-and-white stripes to impress on the inmates and the public the inmates' reduced social status.

Source: A. Ramey\PhotoEdit Inc.

believe that the label is appropriate and starts to act according to what he or she perceives is the proper role. The offender thinks, "If they are going to treat me like a criminal, then I must be one, and I will act like one." The offender internalizes the criminal label and acts accordingly.[71] The policy implications of the labeling theory focus on keeping the offender from internalizing the secondary label. First-offender programs that divert offenders from the traditional criminal justice system are based, in part, on labeling theory. Allowing offenders to escape the criminal label encourages them, one hopes, to embrace a more conventional lifestyle.[72]

Labeling theory has implications for more than just the criminal justice system. Families and schools are also venues in which children can be affected by positive or negative labels.[73] For example, it is a heavy burden to go through school thinking that you are stupid, slow, ugly, a nerd, a geek, or unpopular. To the extent that secondary deviance sets in, this negative label can become a self-fulfilling prophecy. The child stops trying to succeed in school because he or she believes that he or she is not as smart as the others.

Critical Sociological Theories of Crime

We turn now to another set of theories of crime that, although sociological in nature, must be examined separately because they represent a distinct type of theory with far-reaching implications for understanding the causes of crime and for enacting policies to address crime. *Critical theory* is an umbrella term that encompasses a range of perspectives that critique the current manner in which justice is dispensed and consider social justice a legitimate end. The following theories examine how power is distributed in society and how the criminal justice system often is simply a reflection of power and sometimes a tool of power. Criminologists have developed a number of theories that can be considered critical. These theories are also called *conflict* or *radical* theories. Although there are major distinctions among these terms, we group all these theories under the term *critical* with the caveat that the interested student will find much to explore in researching the different types of theories that concern power.[74]

MARXISM   Karl Marx (1818–1883) is an important social theorist whose name is linked with communism. Although the idea of communism reflects his ideas, Marx died before the modern communist states in the former Soviet Union, China, North Korea, Vietnam, and Cuba were established. Because these countries and their economic systems have been historically viewed as problematic by the United States, Marx and the term *Marxism* are not popular. In academic circles, however, Marx is given credit for his unique perspective. It is possible to appreciate Marx's critique of capitalism and its effect on social justice without embracing communism. Therefore, we consider Marx and his ideas in the spirit that there is much here that is important to the understanding of crime.

Marx studied the 19th-century capitalist system in Europe and found it wanting. Specifically, he said the owners of the means of production (factories and such) paid their workers poorly and used the government to pass laws that prevented reform. Those with economic power, then, controlled the system, and they used that power to make sure things did not change. Churches, schools, the economy, and other institutions were all under the control of the owner class. Marx said that the workers put up with this inequitable arrangement because they suffered from **false consciousness**. Because the owners controlled the opinion makers (newspapers, churches, and schools), they could make the workers believe that they were lucky just to have a job and that they should be grateful. The solution to this state of affairs, according to Marx, was for the workers to rise up and grab the means of production for themselves, through violence if necessary.[75]

Could the workers develop a society that was better than the one they overthrew? Or were they just exchanging one set of exploitive masters for another? George Orwell wrote a scathing satire of Marx's ideas in his novel *Animal Farm*, in which the

false consciousness
The idea that the attitudes held by the lower class do not accurately reflect the reality of that class's existence.

3.2 CASE IN POINT

GIDEON V. WAINWRIGHT

THE CASE	THE POINT
Gideon v. Wainwright, 372 U.S. 335, 83 S.Ct. 792 (1963)	Indigent defendants have the right to court-appointed attorneys in felony cases.

Clarence Gideon, an impoverished drifter, was charged in 1961 with breaking and entering a poolroom, a felony under Florida law. Gideon went to court without money or a lawyer and asked the court to appoint counsel for him. The judge told him that counsel was appointed only if the punishment for the offense involved the death penalty. The case went to a jury trial in which Gideon defended himself. He was found guilty and sentenced to five years in prison. On appeal, the Supreme Court overturned his conviction and established that indigent defendants have the right to court-appointed attorneys in felony cases.

Justice Hugo Black wrote, "In our adversary system of criminal justice, any person hauled into court, who is too poor to hire a lawyer, cannot be assured a fair trial unless counsel is provided for him."

Karl Marx's ideas about the effect of class on society and justice continue to inform critical criminologists.

Source: Corbis/Bettmann

ruling pigs said, "All animals are equal, but some animals are more equal than others." This is, of course, the critical issue with communism.[76] How can power be evenly distributed across society? Is it just human nature for those with power to use that power to benefit themselves? In the end, pitting capitalism against communism is a false dichotomy. There are plenty of variations between these extremes, such as labor unions, employee stock ownership plans, Social Security, and owner-financed health plans that 19th-century capitalists would have rejected.

Although Marx said little about crime and the criminal justice system, the criminologists who study his tradition point out that those in power control the making and the enforcement of the law.[77] One need only look at how political campaigns are financed to see how big money influences the making of laws. There is a continuing struggle to balance the rights of people to talk to their legislative representatives on one hand, and to ensure that those representatives are not unduly influenced by gifts, favors, and money on the other hand. When we consider the disparities between how street crimes and corporate crimes are dealt with by the criminal justice system, we can appreciate why critical criminologists continue the tradition of studying Marx and considering the role of social class and power in society.[78]

GENDER AND JUSTICE   One of the historical defects of criminological theory has been the reliance on male subjects. Like research in education, health, and business, crime research has always assumed that women are just a subset of men and that research findings about men could be readily transferred to women. With the rise of the modern feminist movement in the 1960s, this problem in the research on crime has been addressed with productive results.[79]

Feminism examines how women are treated differently from men in a society dominated by male power structures. As a starting point in addressing the social condition of women, feminists employ the concept of gender, which argues that society has different expectations of females and males. In addition to the obvious physical differences between men and women, gender asserts that there are also different rules, opportunities, and consequences that are automatically distributed according to sex. Sexism is a way of valuing the contributions of males and females according to different standards. (For example, a sexually adventurous boy might be called a "stud" or a "player," whereas the same behavior in a girl elicits a less positive label.) Because men have historically dominated our social system, women have been excluded from many occupations, including roles of leadership in the criminal justice system. Consequently, much of what we think we know about female offenders and female criminal justice system practitioners has been based on the study of males. Feminist criminologists (both female and male) have begun to correct this gap in our knowledge about crime.[80]

Feminist theory has many variations. Each has its own perspective and critiques the way women are treated. Curran and Renzetti provided a valuable analysis of the state of feminist criminology in which they highlighted three ways crime can be appreciated from feminist perspectives:

1. **Liberal feminism and criminology.**   Liberal feminists consider two features of society as being in need of attention. First, women's opportunities are blocked by a social system controlled by men who reserve most of the power for themselves. Power should be distributed according to accomplishment rather than gender. The second issue for liberal feminists is the way girls are socialized differently from boys. Women are systematically taught to be passive, nurturing, and dependent, whereas men are taught to be assertive, competitive, and aggressive. By changing the way women are socialized and removing barriers to power, women will be able to fully realize their talents and not be limited by a patriarchal, sexist system. As these goals are accomplished, however, women also have opportunities to engage in deviant behavior. As women become more equal, they will also find more opportunities to engage in illegitimate activities and be treated more like males by the criminal justice system.

2. **Radical feminist criminology.**   The radical feminist contends that sexism is not so much a product of class relations as of the patriarchal structure that places all women at a severe disadvantage, regardless of their social class or race. Radical feminists point to how women are victims of stranger and acquaintance rape, pornography, and spousal abuse as evidence that the criminal justice system does not seriously address women's concerns. Traditional criminology has focused primarily on male street crime and neglected the types of personal violent crimes that affect women. This is true even for rape, in which stranger rape is considered easier to prosecute and more serious than acquaintance rape. Radical feminists call for a fundamental overhaul of patriarchal systems rather than the less ambitious legal changes advocated by the liberal feminists.

3. **Socialist feminist criminology.** Socialist feminists use the combined effects of social class and gender to explain women's disadvantaged status in society and the criminal justice system. Women's opportunities for crime are influenced by the greater controls they experience in society. They are more closely supervised by their parents, husbands, boyfriends, and authorities for what is believed to be "their own good." This greater surveillance both limits their opportunities and increases the chances that their deviant behavior will be detected. Additionally, women are underrepresented in official positions of power and responsibility. If the disadvantages of race are added to the disadvantages of social class and gender, the combined effects produce even greater marginalization.[81]

Feminist theories of criminology also have relevance for men. By looking at how power is concentrated in the privileged male sex role, we can begin to understand how race, sexual orientation, and gender are factors that determine how the criminal justice system treats practitioners, offenders, and victims. Feminist theories also have policy implications. Changes in the way rape victims are treated by police officers and prosecutors are one example of how a feminist perspective can introduce some social justice into legal proceedings. Feminism is more than just a theory. Its various forms also constitute a social movement that forces us to reexamine how people are treated by society's institutions.[82] In the criminal justice system, we can expect to see feminists continue to push for reforms in the treatment of women.

CRITICAL RACE THEORY   Critical theories of crime and justice also consider other aspects of both criminal behavior and the reaction of agencies of social control to explain why people break the law, how crime is defined, and how the criminal justice system operates. One theory that is attracting a good deal of attention is critical race theory.[83] This theory begins with the observation that people of color are overrepresented at every decision point of the criminal justice system and suggests that race is a crucial variable for scholars to examine when attempting to explain the dynamics of the justice system in the United States and, to varying degrees, in other countries.

In its starkest form, critical race theory asserts that the concept that "we are a nation of laws and not of men" masks the function of the criminal justice system to legitimize white supremacy and oppress people of color.[84] As a theoretical perspective, critical race theory focuses on inequality, discrimination, prejudice, and differential law enforcement and explains issues such as racial profiling, interracial crime, and racial hoaxes. For example, in the case of Susan Smith, who was found guilty of drowning her two children, the initial search was for a black man who Smith claimed hijacked her car. Smith provided a detailed description to the police and helped a police artist compose a sketch of the alleged perpetrator. As the case unfolded, it became clear that Smith was lying and that there was no black male suspect. Critical race theory would stipulate that white people were willing to believe that a black man was the likely suspect and that numerous similar miscarriages of justice have been accomplished because of the criminal justice system's racial bias. To understand the experiences of people of color and their treatment by the criminal justice system, we must conduct research based on personalized accounts of harm. Traditional criminal justice research methods do not uncover the types of injustices that are the focus of critical race theory.

Integrated Theories of Crime

A number of criminologists have attempted to develop integrated theories of crime. Recognizing that traditional biological, psychological, and sociological theories are of limited utility, integrationists have attempted to link theories either in an end-to-end approach to demonstrate where one theory's dependent variable may be used as another theory's independent variable, or by looking for central issues that run through several theories.[85] What the integrationists have not attempted to do is link the biological, psychological, and sociological families of theories. This monumental task of creating a grand theory might not be possible given our limitations in designing research methods, our lack of understanding of the human brain, and the ethical issues that apply to research on human subjects.

There is some question as to whether integrating theories is even desirable. Many theories have contrasting assumptions that make integration not only difficult, but in some cases impossible. For instance, control theories assume that the motivation to break the law is relatively constant, whereas strain theories consider the motivation to break the law as variable and as an issue that can be measured and tested. Furthermore, some theories are developed at a micro (individual) level, so combining them with theories developed at a macro (group or societal) level can violate the assumptions of both types of theories. Nevertheless, the integration of theories has produced a number of perspectives that are well worth investigating. Following are the most popular integrated theories.

INTEGRATED THEORY OF DELINQUENT BEHAVIOR   Delbert Elliott, Suzanne Ageton, and Rachel Canter combine strain theory, social control theory, and social learning theory to explain delinquency within the lower and middle classes. Elliott and his colleagues assert that all youths experience issues with strain, social control, and association with delinquent peer groups regardless of class; however, the types of issues differ slightly depending on social class depending on class expectations or aspirations.

For example, most youths want to achieve certain socially approved goals, want to have control over their environment and others' perceptions of them, and have the opportunity at some point during adolescence to associate with delinquent or near-delinquent peers. A lower-class youth may aspire to go to a community college, get a blue-collar job, and eventually leave the impoverished, socially disorganized neighborhood, while being pressured to join the local gang. A middle-class youth may aspire to major in pre-med at an Ivy League university and eventually buy a home with a pool, but in the meantime be tempted to construct a fake driver's license in order to buy beer and get drunk with friends before attending a keg party. The aspirations and expectations of each class are a matter of degree. Also, youths in each class can have equal amounts of difficulty in achieving their goals. In the preceding examples, both the lower- and middle-class youths might have poor grades, which would keep both from achieving their educational goals. Both youths could get into equally deep trouble by associating with their delinquent peers. This highlights the strain and social control aspect of the theory. According to the theory, youths who experience more strain and weak feelings of social control are more likely to seek out delinquent peers. In fact, Elliott and his colleagues found that the best predictor of future delinquency, other than prior delinquency, was association with delinquent peers.[86]

This theory is attractive to those who study delinquency because it greatly expands the range of variables under consideration and attempts to understand multiple paths to delinquency.[87] A critique of this theory, however, is that although strain and loss of social control might contribute to association with delinquent peers, those two factors were not found to have a direct effect on delinquency.[88]

INTERACTIONAL THEORY OF DELINQUENCY   Terence Thornberry has developed an integrated theory in which he looks at low social control and exposure to delinquent peers over the entire course of adolescent development. Thornberry does not include strain theory as part of his integrated perspective but rather looks at how parental attachment diminishes as youths grow older and how commitment to conventional values, such as employment and education, protects the youth from delinquent behavior. Furthermore, Thornberry employs life-course perspective to demonstrate how the effects of delinquent peers and self-control change as adolescents are exposed to changes in sets of peers. Life-course changes such as plans for marriage and family bond the youth to conventional society and inevitably result in a lower involvement in delinquency.

Perhaps the most interesting aspect of Thornberry's theory is that of reciprocity. According to Thornberry, association with delinquent peers increases the chances for individual delinquency, but individual delinquency also increases the chances for association with delinquent peers. In a sort of feedback loop, the group and individual aspects of delinquency feed one another until the youth is fully involved in delinquency, usually with a set of delinquent friends.[89] Thornberry's theory has much in common with the integrated theory of delinquent behavior in that it relies on the effect of delinquent peers for part of its explanation of delinquency. Thornberry's theory, however, does not include strain as a factor in delinquency, instead relying mostly on low social control for its explanations.[90]

CONTROL BALANCE THEORY   Charles Tittle has proposed a theory that is extremely involved and complicated but has great appeal to a number of criminologists who find value in integrated theories. According to Tittle, all relationships exhibit a power differential. Whether it is between parent and child, parole officer and parolee, or professor and student, this difference in power is an interesting and understudied variable, and manifests itself in any type of relationship involving any number of people. Tittle states that "the amount of control to which people are subject relative to the amount of control they can exercise affects their general probability of committing some deviant acts as well as the probability that they will commit specific types of deviance."[91] In other words, it is a balance between the amount of control one has and the amount that one is controlled that determines how or whether he or she will break the law. A person with too little social control or a powerful person who has too much are each at risk for breaking the law, in the first case to reduce the lack of control or in the second to even further extend control.

Tittle contends that those who have the subordinate power position attempt to balance their power through a variety of strategies. One of these strategies is antisocial behavior. For example, if an adolescent is doing poorly in school, he or she might employ a number of strategies to regain a sense of dignity. The adolescent might drop out of school as a way of escaping the feeling of failure, might claim that he or she is not interested and is not trying to succeed as a way of minimizing the feeling of failure, or might simply attempt to burn the school down or attack other students. Each strategy is aimed at reducing the humiliation of failure and restoring the sense of control the adolescent has over his or her life.[92]

These are but a few examples of how criminologists have attempted to integrate various theories of crime, which represent efforts to extend the range and explanatory power of criminological theories. These integrated theories are involved and complex, and students can appreciate their subtleties more on further study of criminological theory.

Life-Course and Developmental Theories

Life-course and developmental theories represent a major step in the advancement of ways to explain why individuals break the law. The theories we have considered so far have limited utility because they are *static*—that is, the researchers testing these theories examined their subjects at a single point in time. This "slice of life" perspective is a compromise made because of time and resources. Researchers have interviewed adolescents, looked at official records, and attempted to explain crime based on information gathered in a single research effort. Although many of these theories are appealing, the information on which they are based is simply a snapshot of one particular population captured at one point in time.[93] However, psychologists who examine adolescent behavior have long used a developmental perspective. By focusing on how infants and adolescents develop behavior patterns, they can predict and explain many of the consistent features of behavioral development. Until recently, criminologists have largely ignored this developmental perspective and have not accounted for the likelihood of growth and change in a subject's behavior over the life course.

Life-course theories greatly improve the quality of research presently employed by many criminologists. The life-course perspective is *dynamic* in that it uses longitudinal data to observe how subjects grow and mature over long periods of time. In this way, life-course theories provide a broader context to their explanations of crime and demonstrate how continuity and change are important. We will now examine two life-course theories that illustrate not only how the research is different from traditional criminological research, but also how the results generated are more robust and theoretically rich.

MOFFITT'S PATHWAY THEORY   British criminologist Terrie Moffitt has developed a life-course theory of crime that focuses on two types of adolescent that she calls *life-course-persistent* and *adolescence-limited* offenders. Although dividing delinquents into two mutually exclusive groups might have some limitations, it also allows Moffitt to specify how patterns in the life course are related to crime in a much more theoretically sophisticated manner. The differences between the two groups are significant and provide for clear explanations as to why some adolescents seem to break the law over their entire life course whereas others engage in antisocial behavior only during adolescence. By examining these two groups in greater detail, it is possible to appreciate Moffitt's pathway theory.[94]

LIFE-COURSE-PERSISTENT OFFENDERS   According to Moffitt, life-course-persistent offenders engage in antisocial behavior for long periods of time. Moffitt looks at biological, psychological, and sociological variables in an attempt to explain why some individuals are continually in trouble over their life course. There is a cumulative effect of problems that start in early childhood and escalate into serious crime as the subject grows older. Moffitt explains:

> Across the life course, these individuals exhibit changing manifestations of antisocial behavior: biting and hitting at age 4, shoplifting and truancy at age 10, selling drugs and stealing cars at age 16, robbery and rape at age 22, and fraud and child abuse at age 30; the underlying disposition remains the same, but its expression changes form as new social opportunities arise at different points in development. This pattern of continuity across age is matched also by cross-situational consistency: lifecourse-persistent antisocial persons lie at home, steal from shops, cheat at school, fight in bars, and embezzle at work.[95]

One strength of Moffitt's theory is the manner in which she integrates concepts from different perspectives. She considers personal traits and their interaction with the social environment that individuals pass through as they age. This allows Moffitt to speculate on how the life-course-persistent offenders get increasingly tangled into antisocial behavior.

ADOLESCENCE-LIMITED OFFENDERS   This type of offender can be contrasted with the life-course-persistent offenders by the absence of problems in childhood and the unlikely continuation of crime into adulthood. Although the offenses of adolescence-limited offenders might be serious, there is little continuity to the patterns of crime they engage in, and there are long periods during which they do not break the law at all. Rather than being a way of life, crime for the adolescent-limited offender is episodic and instrumental. By this, we mean that on the few occasions in which this type of offender breaks the law, it is usually to achieve a specific goal. Adolescence-Limited offenders comprise the vast majority of delinquents, but most of them age out of crime and develop into normal productive citizens. According to Moffitt, these offenders respond to shifting contingencies as they age:

> With the inevitable progression of chronological age, more legitimate and tangible adult roles become available to teens. Adolescence-limited delinquents gradually experience a loss of motivation for delinquency as they exit the maturity gap. Moreover, when aging delinquents attain some of the privileges they

coveted as teens, the consequences of illegal behavior shift from rewarding to punishing, *in their perception*. An adult arrest record will limit their job opportunities, drug abuse keeps them from getting to work on time, drunk driving is costly, and bar fights lead to accusations of unfit parenthood. Adolescence-limited delinquents have something to lose by persisting in their antisocial behavior beyond the teen years.[96]

Moffitt's theory details these two pathways in which adolescents are drawn to crime. For the purposes of theoretical distinction she treats these pathways as mutually exclusive. However, in real life, there are probably several other types of crime-related pathways that could be fruitfully explored. Nevertheless, the reason Moffitt's theory is so appealing is because she clearly specifies how developmental factors can be used to explain crime and delinquency.

LAUB AND SAMPSON'S PERSISTENT-OFFENDING AND DESISTANCE-FROM-CRIME THEORY

Criminologists John Laub and Robert Sampson have developed one of the more elaborate and productive life-course theories. After finding a rich dataset collected between 1949 and 1963 by Sheldon and Eleanor Glueck in the basement of the Harvard Law Library, Laub and Sampson followed up on this longitudinal data and detailed how those delinquents either persisted in their antisocial orientation or desisted from crime over their life course. On tracing some of the subjects' lives until age 70, Laub and Sampson found that some of the subjects continued in a trajectory of crime while others experienced *turning points* in which they became more involved in society and adopted conventional behaviors.

Perhaps the most interesting aspect of this theory is that Laub and Sampson were compelled to revise their theory as a follow-up to the life course development of these delinquents. In 1993, they published *Crime in the Making: Pathways and Turning Points through Life*, in which they looked at the Gluecks' data on the subjects into early adulthood and concluded that crime was relatively stable throughout the life course even though some delinquents developed more conventional behaviors in adulthood.[97] However, after following up on the Gluecks' data and tracking some of the subjects down in late adulthood and old age, they revised their theory in 2003 and published *Shared Beginnings, Divergent Lives: Delinquent Boys to Age 70*, in which they concluded that almost all of the delinquent boys eventually stopped breaking the law.[98] They found that desisting from crime is typically the result of youths experiencing a turning point in life in which they become connected to conventional society. This change can be summarized as follows:

1. **The offenders experienced a structural turning point.**   This might have been in the form of marriage, getting a new job, or joining the military. As the delinquents aged, they had increased opportunities to engage in conventional behavior and become bonded to a law-abiding lifestyle.

2. **Conventional lifestyles resulted in greater social control over their lives.**   When one gets married, it is more difficult to go out "drinking with the boys" or engage in other activities that may present opportunities for crime. One's spouse has expectations that must be dealt with, which inevitably curtails any antisocial behavior that took place during bachelorhood. Similarly, when one enters the military, the rules and regulations that must be followed limit one's exposure to crime-producing situations. Many of the delinquents in the study became bonded to conventional lifestyles in this way.

3. **The new lifestyle provided opportunities for prosocial activities.**   The ex-delinquents had fewer opportunities to hang out with deviant peers, but more opportunities to engage in prosocial activities, such as going on family outings, going to church, and becoming involved in the community.

4. **The new lifestyle required commitment.**   As one becomes successful in conventional behavior, it is no longer acceptable to participate in activities that put

the new lifestyle at risk. Additionally, the new lifestyle provides benefits that replace the social and emotional needs that were addressed by the antisocial lifestyle. For example, for many of the ex-delinquents, holding down a well-paying job meant that they were less willing to do anything that jeopardized that job.

Although this change to conventional activities simply happened to some of the offenders, Laub and Sampson also accounted for the *agency* of the individual. By this, they meant that some of the subjects made conscious choices to change their lifestyle. Other subjects made similar conscious decisions to continue breaking the law. This idea of agency is particularly important because it suggests that an antisocial lifestyle begun in childhood does not always continue through the life course.

In discussing the future of developmental criminology, Cullen and Agnew state:

> Developmental theories are now at the center stage in criminology. Even if one takes issue with the main theories that have been set forth, the fundamental point underlying these perspectives is indisputable: crime is a dynamic process that potentially begins in childhood and occurs across the life course. Accordingly, the challenge for all theoretical criminology is to explain continuity and/or change in criminal involvement. For many years, however, traditional theories remained largely silent on these key issues. This does not mean that traditional perspectives have no value. But it does mean that their credibility will be judged, in large part, by how well they're able to address the key life-course issues of continuity and change in offending.[99]

What we have provided here are but two examples of life-course theories of crime. Because longitudinal data is so difficult to develop, the challenge for life-course criminology is to find ways of examining criminal careers.[100] Although it is relatively easy to check official crime statistics to pinpoint every instance when an offender breaks the law, it is much more difficult to observe when delinquents and offenders become attached to society and desist from antisocial behavior. Part of the problem of following this activity is that it requires following what an offender, or ex-offender, does *not* do. Researchers cannot look into an alternate universe and see crimes the offender would have committed had he or she not begun to follow a conventional lifestyle. Nevertheless, life-course theories demonstrate great promise that criminologists are destined to pursue.

SUMMARY

1. The earliest explanations for antisocial behavior attributed crime to supernatural forces; however, the criminal justice system has moved on to other theories that lend themselves to empirical testing.

2. The classical school of criminology argues that people choose to break the law. The principle of "free will" allows us to consider various courses of action, then select the one we believe is most desirable. The classical school assumes motivation and treats all offenders equally.

3. The classical school of criminology is embodied primarily in the works of Cesare Beccaria and Jeremy Bentham. Beccaria's nine principles guide

our criminal justice system today. Bentham's utilitarianism theory states that people are guided by their desire for pleasure and aversion to pain.

4. The positivist school of criminology is based on the scientific method. The positivist school takes into account biological, psychological, and sociological influences on criminal offenders, as well as how external factors affect individuals' decisions to break the law.

5. Biological theories of crime look for physical reasons that individuals break the law, including heredity, hormones, blood chemistry, and environmental factors such as alcohol and drug use.

6. Psychological theories of crime look for behavioral, cognitive, and developmental reasons that offenders break the law, considering the influence of society and personality as well as individual mental processes on behavior. Approaches include behaviorism, observational learning, moral development theory, psychopathy, and antisocial personality disorder.

7. Sociological theories consider social structure and social processes as explanations for crime. Approaches include differential association theory, strain theory, social control theory, neutralization theory, and labeling theory.

8. Critical sociological theories are a set of perspectives that critique how justice is dispensed. These theories consider problems with society and the criminal justice system, not with individuals. These include Marxism, feminist criminology, and critical race theory.

9. Integrated theories of crime are an attempt to either link theories or identify similar issues that run through several theories. The integrated theory of delinquent behavior combines strain theory, social control theory, and social learning theory to explain delinquency within the lower and middle classes. Interactional theory of delinquency considers low social control and exposure to delinquent peers throughout adolescent development.

10. Life-course theories consider the behavior of offenders and what affects them throughout their entire lives. Moffitt's pathway theory focuses on life-course-persistent and adolescence-limited offenders. Laub and Sampson's persistent-offending and desistance-from-crime theory considers how some delinquents eventually become bonded to society through turning points as they age.

KEY TERMS

anomie 97
atavisms 83
behaviorism 90
Chicago school 94
classical school of
  criminology 77
differential association theory 94
false consciousness 102

hedonistic calculus 81
labeling theory 100
neutralization theory 100
observational learning 91
operant conditioning 90
positivist school of
  criminology 82
rational choice theory 82

social control theory 99
somatotyping 84
strain theory 97
trial by ordeal 76
utilitarianism 79
XYY syndrome 86

REVIEW QUESTIONS

1. Why are supernatural explanations for crime not considered by the criminal justice system?

2. What is the classical school of criminology's main argument?

3. What modern rights can be traced to Cesare Beccaria?

4. How are individuals guided, according to Jeremy Bentham?

5. What factors gave rise to the positivist school of criminology?

6. Why are critical theories called *critical*?

7. What is strain theory?

8. How do integrated theories use other theories of crime?

9. What is behaviorism?

10. Compare and contrast observational learning with moral development theory.

11. What advantages do life-course theories have over other criminological theories?

SUGGESTED FURTHER READING

Agnew, Robert. *Why Do Criminals Offend: A General Theory of Crime and Delinquency.* Los Angeles: Roxbury, 2005.

Cullen, Francis T., John Paul Wright, and Kristie R. Blevins, eds. *Taking Stock: The Status of Criminological Theory.* New Brunswick, NJ: Transaction, 2006.

Messner, Stephen F., and Richard Rosenfeld. *Crime and the American Dream.* Belmont, CA: Wadsworth, 2001.

Miller, Jody. *One of the Guys: Girls, Gangs and Gender.* New York: Oxford University Press, 2001.

Thornberry, Terence P., and Marvin D. Krohn, eds. *Taking Stock of Delinquency: An Overview of Findings from Contemporary Longitudinal Studies.* New York: Kluwer Academic/Plenum, 2003.

Wilson, William Julius. *The Truly Disadvantaged: The Inner City, the Underclass, and Public Policy.* Chicago: University of Chicago Press, 1990.

ENDNOTES

1. Israel Drapkin, *Crime and Punishment in the Ancient World* (Lexington, MA: Heath, 1989).

2. Randall McGowan, "The Changing Face of God's Justice: The Debates over Divine and Human Punishment in Eighteenth-Century England," *Criminal Justice History* 9 (1988): 63–98.

3. Frances Hill, *A Delusion of Satan: The Full Story of the Salem Witch Trials* (New York: Doubleday, 1995).

4. Frederica Mathewes-Green, "Did the Devil Make Her Do It?" Beliefnet, www.beliefnet.com/story/101/story_10163_1.html.

5. Peggy O'Hare et al., "The Andrea Yates Case; Not Guilty, But Not Free," *Houston Chronicle*, 3-star edition, July 27, 2006, 1A.

6. Associated Press, "Minister Who Killed Abortion Doctor Awaits Execution," *USA Today*, September 3, 2003, www.usatoday.com/news/nation/2003–09–03-hill_x.htm.

7. Erling Eide, *Economics of Crime: Deterrence and the Rational Offender* (North Holland, Netherlands: Elsevier, 1994).

8. Philip Jenkins, "Varieties of Enlightenment Criminology," *British Journal of Criminology* 24 (1984): 112–130.

9. Cesare Beccaria, *On Crimes and Punishments*, trans. Henry Paolucci (Indianapolis, IN: Bobbs-Merrill, 1963). First published in 1764.

10. Jeremy Bentham, "An Introduction to the Principles of Morals and Legislation," in *Classics of Criminology*, 2nd ed., ed. Joseph E. Jacoby (Prospect Heights, IL: Waveland Press, 1994), 80.

11. Frank P. Williams III and Marilyn D. McShane, *Criminological Theory*, 4th ed. (Upper Saddle River, NJ: Prentice Hall, 2004), 15–32.

12. Imogene L. Moyer, *Criminological Theories: Traditional and Nontraditional Voices and Themes* (Thousand Oaks, CA: Sage, 2001).

13. José Brunner, "Modern Times: Law, Temporality and Happiness in Hobbes, Locke and Bentham," *Theoretical Inquiries in Law* 8, no. 1 (January 1, 2007): 21.

14. Derek B. Cornish and Ronald V. Clarke, *The Reasoning Criminal: Rational Choice Perspectives on Offending* (New York: Springer, 1986).

15. Charles Darwin, *The Origin of the Species* (Cambridge, MA: Harvard University Press, 1964). First published in 1859.

16. Deborah W. Denno, "Human Biology and Criminal Responsibility: Free Will or Free Ride," *University of Pennsylvania Law Review* 137 (1988): 615–671.

17. Hans-Ludwig Kroeber, "The Historical Debate on Brain and Legal Responsibility—Revisited," *Behavioral Sciences and the Law* 25, no. 2 (March 1, 2007): 251.

18. Nicole Rafter, "The Murderous Dutch Fiddler: Criminology, History and the Problem of Phrenology," *Theoretical Criminology* 9, no. 1 (February 1, 2005): 65–96.

19. John van Wyhe, The History of Phrenology on the Web, http://pages.britishlibrary.net/phrenology/.

20. The Phrenology Page, http://134.184.33.110/phreno/.

21. Cesare Lombroso, "The Criminal Man," in *Criminological Theory: Past to Present*, 2nd ed., eds. Francis T. Cullen and Robert Agnew (Los Angeles: Roxbury, 2003), 23–25.

22. J. Robert Lilly, Francis T. Cullen, and Richard A. Ball, *Criminological Theory: Context and Consequences*, 3rd ed. (Thousand Oaks, CA: Sage, 2002).

23. Moyer, *Criminological Theories*, 39.

24. Piers Beirne, *Inventing Criminology: Essays on the Rise of "Homo Criminalis"* (New York: State University of New York Press, 1993), 213.

25. Lilly, Cullen, and Ball, *Criminological Theory*, 23.

26. Daniel J. Curran and Claire M. Renzetti, *Theories of Crime*, 2nd ed. (Boston: Allyn & Bacon, 2001), 33–35.

27. Patricia Jacobs et al., "Aggressive Behavior, Mental Subnormality, and the XYY Male," *Nature* 208 (1965): 1351–1352.

28. Ty A. Ridenour, "Genetic Epidemiology of Antisocial Behavior," in *Theories of Crime: A Reader*, eds. Claire M. Renzetti, Daniel J. Curran, and Patrick J. Carr (Boston: Allyn & Bacon, 2003), 4–24.

29. Alan Booth and D. Wayne Osgood, "The Influence of Testosterone on Deviance in Adulthood: Assessing and Explaining the Relationship," *Criminology* 31, no. 1 (February 1, 1993): 93.

30. Katharina Dalton, "Menstruation and Crime," *British Medical Journal* 2 (1961): 1752–1753.

31. James W. Lewis, "Premenstrual Syndrome as a Criminal Defense," *Archives of Sexual Behavior* 19, no. 5 (October 1, 1990): 425.

32. Debra Niehoff, "The Biology of Violence," in *Theories of Crime: A Reader*, eds. Claire M. Renzetti, Daniel J. Curran, and Patrick J. Carr (Boston: Allyn & Bacon, 2003), 26–31.

33. Curt R. Bartol and Anne M. Bartol, *Criminal Behavior: A Psychosocial Approach*, 8th ed. (Upper Saddle River, NJ: Pearson Prentice Hall, 2008), 6–8.

34. Ibid.

35. Ibid., 9–10.

36. Sigmund Freud, *The Ego and the Id* (London: Hogarth, 1927).

37. Sigmund Freud, *A General Introduction to Psychoanalysis* (New York: Boni & Liveright, 1920).

38. G. Terence Wilson, "Behavior Therapy," in *Current Psychotherapies*, 4th ed., eds. Raymond J. Corsini and Danny Wedding (Itasca, IL: Peacock, 1989), 241–282.

39. Michael J. Lillyquist, *Understanding and Changing Criminal Behavior* (Englewood Cliffs, NJ: Prentice Hall, 1980).

40. G. David Curry and Scott H. Decker, *Confronting Gangs: Crime and Community* (Los Angeles: Roxbury, 1988).

41. Bartol and Bartol, *Criminal Behavior*, 121–123.

42. C. George Boeree, http://webspace.ship.edu/cgboer/bandura.html.

43. Carol Veneziano and Louis Veneziano, "The Relationship between Deterrence and Moral Reasoning," *Criminal Justice Review* 17, no. 2 (1992): 209–216.

44. William Crain, *Theories of Development*, 5th ed. (Upper Saddle River, NJ: Prentice Hall, 2005), 154–158.

45. Eric K. Klein, "Dennis the Menace or Billy the Kid: An Analysis of the Role of Transfer to Criminal Court in Juvenile Justice," *American Criminal Law Review* 35, no. 2 (January 1, 1998): 371–410.

46. Ibid.

47. Geert Jan Stams et al., "The Moral Judgment of Juvenile Delinquents: A Meta-Analysis," *Journal of Abnormal Child Psychology* 34, no. 5 (October 1, 2006): 697–713.

48. Robert D. Hare, *Psychopathy: Theory and Research* (New York: Wiley, 1970); Bartol and Bartol, *Criminal Behavior*, 188.

49. John Randolph Fuller, *Juvenile Delinquency: Mainstream and Crosscurrents* (Upper Saddle River, NJ: Pearson Prentice Hall, 2008), 188.

50. American Psychiatric Association, *Diagnostic and Statistical Manual of Mental Disorders* (Washington, DC: American Psychiatric Association, 1994), 645–650.

51. Bartol and Bartol, *Criminal Behavior*, 235.

52. Clifford R. Shaw and Henry D. McKay, *Juvenile Delinquency and Urban Areas* (Chicago: University of Chicago Press, 1942).

53. Curran and Renzetti, *Theories of Crime*, 101–102.

54. Douglas S. Massey and Nancy A. Denton, *American Apartheid: Segregation and the Making of the Underclass* (Cambridge, MA: Harvard University Press, 1993).

55. Edwin H. Sutherland, Donald R. Cressey, and David F. Luckenbill, *Principles of Criminology* (Dix Hills, NJ: General Hall, 1992).

56. Ross Matsueda, "The Current State of Differential Association Theory," *Crime and Delinquency* 34 (1988): 277–306.

57. Ronald L. Akers and Christine S. Sellers, *Criminological Theories: Introduction, Evaluation, and Application*, 4th ed. (Los Angeles: Roxbury, 2004).

58. Robert L. Burgess and Ronald L. Akers, "A Differential Association-Reinforcement Theory of Criminal Behavior," *Social Problems* 14 (1966): 128–147.

59. Ronald L. Akers, *Social Learning and Social Structure: A General Theory of Crime and Deviance* (Boston: Northeastern University Press, 1998).

60. Ronald L. Akers and Gary F. Jensen, "The Empirical Status of Social Learning Theory of Crime and Deviance: The Past, Present, and Future," in *Taking Stock: The Status of Criminological Theory*, eds. Francis T. Cullen, John Paul Wright, and Kristie R. Blevins (New Brunswick, NJ: Transaction, 2006), 37–100.

61. Robert K. Merton, "Social Structure and Anomie," *American Sociological Review* 3 (1938): 672–682.

62. Robert Agnew, "The Nature and Determinants of Strain: Another Look at Durkheim and Merton," in *The Future of Anomie Theory*, eds. Nikos Passas and Robert Agnew (Boston: Northeastern University Press, 1997), 27–51.

63. Robert Agnew, *Pressured into Crime: An Overview of General Strain Theory* (Los Angeles: Roxbury, 2006).

64. Lisa Broidy and Robert Agnew, "Gender and Crime: A General Strain Theory Perspective," *Journal of Research in Crime and Delinquency* 34 (1997): 275–306.

65. Robert Agnew, "Pressured into Crime: General Strain Theory," in *Criminological Theory: Past to Present*, 3rd ed., eds. Francis T. Cullen and Robert Agnew (New York: Oxford University Press, 2006), 201–209.

66. Travis Hirschi, *Causes of Delinquency* (Berkeley: University of California Press, 1969).

67. Gresham M. Sykes and David Matza, "Techniques of Neutralization," *Sociological Review* 22 (1957): 644–670.

68. Curran and Renzetti, *Theories of Crime*, 167.

69. Howard Becker, *Outsiders: Studies in the Sociobiology of Deviance* (New York: Free Press, 1963).

70. Harold Garfinkel, "Successful Degradation Ceremonies," *American Sociological Review* 61 (1956): 420–424.

71. Edwin M. Lemert, *Human Deviance, Social Problems, and Social Control*, 2nd ed. (Upper Saddle River, NJ: Prentice Hall, 1972).

72. Edwin Schur, "Reactions to Deviance: A Critical Assessment," *American Journal of Sociology* 75 (1969): 309–322.

73. Ross L. Matsueda, "Reflected Appraisals, Parental Labeling, and Delinquency: Specifying a Symbolic Interactionist Theory," *American Journal of Sociology* 6 (1992): 1577–1611.

74. Bruce A. Arrigo, ed., *Social Justice/Criminal Justice: The Maturation of Critical Theory in Law, Crime, and Deviance* (Belmont, CA: West/Wadsworth, 1999).

75. Karl Marx, *Capital* (New York: International, 1974). First published in 1867.

76. George Orwell, *Animal Farm* (New York: Harcourt Brace, 1946).

77. Michael J. Lynch and Paul Stretesky, "Marxism and Social Justice: Thinking about Social Justice Eclipsing Criminal Justice," in *Social Justice/Criminal Justice: The Maturation of Critical Theory in Law, Crime, and Deviance*, ed. Bruce A. Arrigo (Belmont, CA: West/Wadsworth, 1999), 14–29.

78. Francis T. Cullen, William J. Maakestad, and Gray Cavender, *Corporate Crime under Attack: The Ford Pinto Case and Beyond* (Cincinnati, OH: Anderson, 1987).

79. Kathleen Daly and Meda Chesney-Lind, "Feminism and Criminology," *Justice Quarterly* 5 (1988): 497–535.

80. Sally Simpson, "Feminist Theory, Crime, and Justice," *Criminology* 27 (1989): 605–631.

81. Curran and Renzetti, *Theories of Crime*, 209–228.

82. Gregg Barak, Jeanne M. Flavin, and Paul S. Leighton, *Class, Race, Gender, and Crime: Social Realities of Justice in America* (Los Angeles: Roxbury, 2001).

83. Katheryn K. Russell, "Critical Race Theory and Social Justice," in *Social Justice/Criminal Justice: The Maturation of Critical Theory in Law, Crime, and Deviance*, ed. Bruce A. Arrigo (Belmont, CA: West/Wadsworth, 1999), 178–188.

84. The phrase "We are a nation of laws and not of men" originates from John Adams.

85. Francis T. Cullen, John Paul Wright, and Mitchell B. Chamlin, "Social Support and Social Reform: A Progressive Crime Control Agenda," *Crime and Delinquency* 45 (1999): 188–207.

86. Delbert S. Elliott, David Huizinga, and Suzanne S. Ageton, *Explaining Delinquency and Drug Use* (Beverly Hills, CA: Sage, 1985); Delbert S. Elliott, David Huizinga, and Scott Menard, *Multiple Problem Youth: Delinquency, Substance Use, and Mental Health Problems* (New York: Springer-Verlag, 1989).

87. Delbert S. Elliott, Suzanne S. Ageton, and Rachel J. Canter, "An Integrated Theoretical Perspective on Delinquent Behavior," *Journal of Research in Crime and Delinquency* 16, no. 1 (1979): 3–27.

88. Francis T. Cullen and Robert Agnew, eds., *Criminological Theory: Past to Present*, 3rd ed. (New York: Oxford University Press, 2006), 537.

89. Terence P. Thornberry, "Toward an Interactional Theory of Delinquency," *Criminology* 25, no. 4 (November 1987): 863–892.

90. Terence P. Thornberry, "Toward an Interactional Theory of Delinquency," in *Criminological Theory: Past to Present*, 3rd ed., eds. Francis T. Cullen and Robert Agnew (New York: Oxford University Press, 2006), 551.

91. Charles R. Tittle, *Control Balance: Toward a General Theory of Deviance* (Boulder, CO: Westview, 1995), 142.

92. Ibid.

93. The terms "life course" and "developmental" are used interchangeably here. For a good overview of these theories, see Francis T. Cullen and Robert Agnew, *Criminological Theory: Past to Present*, 3rd ed., eds. Francis T. Cullen and Robert Agnew (New York: Oxford University Press, 2006), 482–494.

94. Terrie Moffitt, "Adolescent-Limited and Life-Course Persistent Antisocial Behavior: A Developmental Taxonomy," *Psychological Review* 100 (1993): 674–701.

95. Terrie E. Moffitt, "Pathways in the Life-Course to Crime," in *Criminological Theory: Past to Present*, 3rd

ed., eds. Francis T. Cullen and Robert Agnew (New York: Oxford University Press, 2006), 504.

96. Ibid., 519.

97. Robert J. Sampson and John H. Laub, *Crime in the Making: Pathways and Turning Points through Life* (Cambridge, MA: Harvard University Press, 1993).

98. John H. Laub and Robert J. Sampson, *Shared Beginnings, Divergent Lives: Delinquent Boys to Age 70* (Cambridge, MA: Harvard University Press, 2003).

99. Francis T. Cullen and Robert Agnew, "Developmental Theories: Crime and the Life Course," in

Criminological Theory: Past to Present, 3rd ed., eds. Francis T. Cullen and Robert Agnew (New York: Oxford University Press, 2006), 492.

100. For a review of research studies on Moffitt's theory, see Terrie E. Moffitt, "A Review of Research on the Taxonomy of Life-Course Persistent versus Adolescence Limited Antisocial Behavior," in *Taking Stock: The Status of Criminological Theory*, eds. Francis T. Cullen, John Paul Wright, and Kristie R. Blevins (New Brunswick, NJ: Transaction, 2006), 277–311.

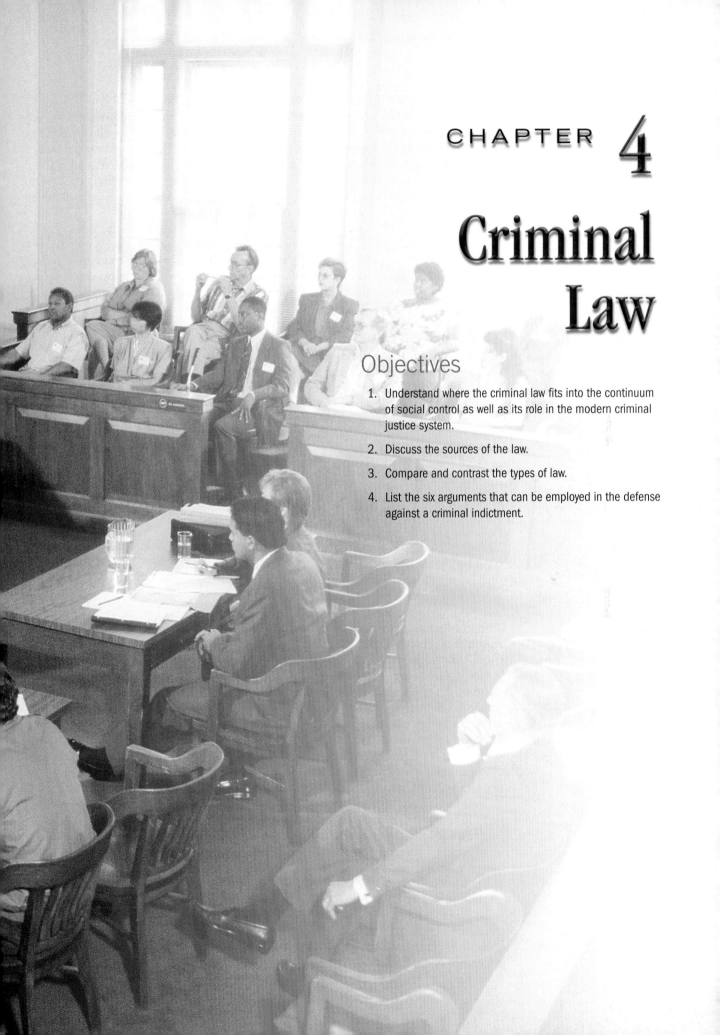

CHAPTER 4

Criminal Law

Objectives

1. Understand where the criminal law fits into the continuum of social control as well as its role in the modern criminal justice system.

2. Discuss the sources of the law.

3. Compare and contrast the types of law.

4. List the six arguments that can be employed in the defense against a criminal indictment.

The foundation for the criminal justice system is the criminal law. It protects society from predators and suspects from the whims of prosecutors and judges, as well as giving victims redress against those who have harmed them. The rule of law is an important differentiating feature between democratic societies and authoritarian ones. In a democratic society, this idea is captured by the Latin phrase *nullen crimen, nulla poena, sine lege*, which means "there is no crime, there is no punishment, without law." However, this philosophy does not apply to authoritarian societies, where crime and punishment can exist without law.

In *The Gulag Archipelago*, Aleksandr Solzhenitsyn recounted life in the former Soviet Union, where the police basically operated without laws, arresting whomever they wished, often for no reason. For example, a man was with his wife at a train station when an unidentified man asked to speak to him in private. The two men stepped into an adjoining room. The woman did not hear from her husband again for a decade. In another incident, a woman went to the police station to inquire what she should do about her neighbor's daughter, a young girl who was left alone after the arrest of her parents. The police told her to wait, then arrested her a couple of hours later solely to meet their arrest quota. According to Solzhenitsyn, the Soviet police and courts were ruthless, and operated with absolute authority and no oversight.[1] Without the checks and balances found in democracies, a government could easily turn a country into a police state.

Laws must be enacted by the legislature, published in the criminal code, and enforced in a fair and evenhanded manner by the authorities. Laws cannot be applied retroactively, and they are subject to review by appellate courts for their constitutionality. The criminal law specifies and clarifies the relationship between citizens and the government.

The criminal law performs many functions in society. It details what behaviors are to be punished, as well as dictating just how governments can go about doing the punishing. The criminal law supports citizens' strongly held values, and also, by omission, allows some people to engage in acts that many others may find objectionable. Therefore, we must remember that the criminal law is not a simple set of rules but a complex, ever-changing, and highly politicized tool of government. As a form of social control, the criminal law occupies one end of a continuum.

folkways → mores → norms → laws

This continuum ranges from mild controls, such as the table etiquette and polite manners taught to us by our parents, violations of which result in "that look from Mom" or a literal slap on the wrist, to the law that has the full force of the criminal justice system behind it and can result in incarceration or even death. The continuum of proscribed behaviors is loosely matched by ever-increasing sanctions. One of the principles behind social control, therefore, is *proportionality*: The more serious the infraction of society's rules and sensibilities, the more severe the sanction.[2] However, as we will see throughout this chapter, one of the main crosscurrents of the criminal justice system is the variation in how similar cases are treated according to wealth, skin color, culture, gender, and a number of other factors that demonstrate that justice is not always blind.[3]

We must keep in mind that the imperfections of the criminal justice system are less the result of the criminal law and more the result of its application. We can distinguish between the impartial law as it is written in the criminal code and the way it is enforced by human beings. Law enforcement officers, prosecutors, judges, and probation officers might be sincere in their application of the law but flawed in other ways. They might have personal biases; they might make mistakes, and some of them might be corrupt, all of which results in discrepancies between how the law is meant to be applied and how it is actually applied.

A democratic society has the opportunity to ensure that the criminal law reflects the values of all citizens. This is relatively easy to do when a consensus exists about which behaviors need to be outlawed. Certainly homicide, rape, embezzlement, and carjacking are behaviors we all wish to be protected from by the criminal law. We all agree that some dangerous individuals are best kept behind bars because of the harm they do. However, there are other behaviors for which there is no consensus and for which the criminal law is constantly in flux depending on which political groups can get their values addressed by the legislature and the courts.[4]

Gambling laws are a good example of how economic and social values compete in the criminal law. In the not-too-distant past, Las Vegas and Atlantic City were the only places in the United States where legal gambling was available. Now, many states allow various forms of gambling, and, in an interesting twist of the criminal law that illustrates the distinctions among jurisdictions, must allow casinos on federal lands controlled by American Indians. Citizens in many states have voted to allow lotteries that produce revenue to offset taxes. It is easy to see, then, that all laws are not equally grounded in the values of all citizens. Although most of us agree on laws concerning assault and rape, no such agreement exists on laws covering gambling, drug use, abortion, or pornography. However, all of these issues are settled by the criminal law, and that law changes depending on which groups are best able to get their concerns heard by the legislature.[5] For example, several states prohibit those who have been convicted of felonies from voting. The individuals who would most like to see the legislature reverse this type of law are former felons. However, because ex-felons cannot vote in many states, they are unable to support candidates who might be sympathetic to their desires. Those who have been convicted of felony drug offenses—even offenses that did not involve violence—are ineligible to vote for candidates who might legalize or decriminalize drugs. These are just a couple of examples of how those who have influence and power can best ensure that their values are encoded into the law.

As covered in Chapter 3, some critical theories contend that those in power will use the criminal law to maintain and enhance their power. As the crimes of the powerful differ in kind and degree from the crimes of the powerless, we can expect the penalties to be more severe for the latter. For example, crack cocaine use has been concentrated in minority communities, and the penalties are harsh. According to some critical theories, if crack cocaine moves into middle-class neighborhoods and schools, the penalties for its use might be relaxed.[6]

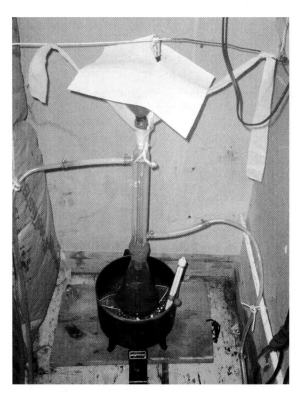

Law enforcement constantly faces new challenges in the war on drugs. As with crack cocaine in the 1980s, the steep rise in the usage and manufacture of methamphetamine is causing headaches for police. Here, a device for making methamphetamine is shown during a bust in a rural Tennessee home.
Source: C. E. Jones/The Grundy County Herald\.AP Wide World Photos

DEVELOPMENT OF CRIMINAL LAW

The history of the development of the criminal law is interesting because the process was episodic, uneven, and political. Societies did not systematically build on the laws of previous cultures, but instead chose elements consistent with their own values, religions, and economic structures, and discarded elements that were not. Therefore, our own system is a hodgepodge of other societies' attempts to govern conduct through the criminal law.[7] A brief look at some of the previous systems of law provides insights into how our laws came to be structured as they are.

Code of Hammurabi

In 1901 a stone tablet was discovered that bore the laws of ancient Babylonia as written by its king, Hammurabi. These laws are the earliest known written laws. The 8-meter tablet, chiseled in the Akkadian language, dates to about 1780 B.C.E. and includes laws relating to a wide range of behaviors. The laws followed, literally, the "eye for an eye" or *lex talionis* philosophy, an indication that severe penalties have always been part of legal codes. However, Hammurabi used this philosophy as a way of introducing some type of proportionality into the law.

> In the criminal law the ruling principle was the *lex talionis*. Eye for eye, tooth for tooth, limb for limb was the penalty for assault upon an *amelu* [a free citizen]. A sort of symbolic retaliation was the punishment of the offending member, seen in the cutting off the hand that struck a father or stole a trust; in cutting off the breast of a wet-nurse who substituted a changeling for the child entrusted to her; in the loss of the tongue that denied father or mother (in the Elamite contracts the same penalty was inflicted for perjury); in the loss of the eye that pried into forbidden secrets. The loss of the surgeon's hand that caused loss of life or limb or the brander's hand that obliterated a slave's identification mark, are very similar. The slave, who struck a freeman or denied his master, lost an ear, the organ of hearing and symbol of obedience. To bring another into danger of death by false accusation was punished by death. To cause loss of liberty or property by false witness was punished by the penalty the perjurer sought to bring upon another.[8]

The **Code of Hammurabi** contained more than 250 laws that covered a wide range of economic, social, and criminal issues that reflect the values of the times. (For a sample of these laws, see Criminal Justice Reference 4.1.) For instance, some of the laws make the penalties for the death or injury of slaves less severe than those for the death and injury of free people. Perhaps the most significant message to be learned from this code has nothing to do with the actual laws—which, after all, apply to a society much different from ours—but rather, that a code of laws even existed more than 3000 years ago. This tells us not only that the criminal law has a long and fascinating history, but that all complex human societies are likely to have some form of criminal law.[9] The Code of Hammurabi is just one example of the various codes of law that were drawn up over the centuries. Figure 4-1 provides a partial list of historical documents that have influenced the development of modern laws.

The Magna Carta

The English **Magna Carta,** a major document that contributed to U.S. law, limited the king's power and provided for the rights of citizens. King John signed the Magna Carta at Runnymede, England, on June 15, 1215, conceding a number of legal rights to the barons and the people. To finance his foreign wars, King John had taxed abusively. His barons threatened rebellion and coerced the king into committing to rudimentary judicial guarantees, such as freedom of the church, fair taxation, controls over imprisonment (***habeas corpus***), and the rights of all merchants to come and go freely, except in times of war. The Magna Carta has 61 clauses, the most important of which

Code of Hammurabi
An ancient code instituted by Hammurabi, a ruler of Babylonia, dealing with criminal and civil matters.

Magna Carta
"Great Charter"; a guarantee of liberties signed by King John of England in 1215 that influenced many modern legal and constitutional principles.

habeas corpus
A writ issued to bring a party before the court.

This 7-foot, black basalt stele depicts Hammurabi receiving his power to administer the law from the sun god Shamash. Hammurabi's laws are carved underneath.

Source: *From the Louvre, Paris, France, courtesy of SuperStock, Inc.*

4.1 CRIMINAL JUSTICE REFERENCE

A Few Laws from the Code of Hammurabi

3. If any one bring an accusation of any crime before the elders, and does not prove what he has charged, he shall, if it be a capital offense charged, be put to death.

7. If any one buy from the son or the slave of another man, without witnesses or a contract, silver or gold, a male or female slave, an ox or a sheep, an ass or anything, or if he take it in charge, he is considered a thief and shall be put to death.

53. If any one be too lazy to keep his dam in proper condition, and does not so keep it; if then the dam break and all the fields be flooded, then shall he in whose dam the break occurred be sold for money, and the money shall replace the corn which he has caused to be ruined.

109. If conspirators meet in the house of a tavern-keeper, and these conspirators are not captured and delivered to the court, the tavern-keeper shall be put to death.

137. If a man wish to separate from a woman who has borne him children, or from his wife who has borne him children: then he shall give that wife her dowry, and a part of the usufruct of field, garden, and property, so that she can rear her children. When she has brought up her children, a portion of all that is given to the children, equal as that of one son, shall be given to her. She may then marry the man of her heart.

for our purposes is number 39: "No freeman shall be captured or imprisoned . . . except by lawful judgement of his peers or by the law of the land." This was the first time a king admitted that even he could be compelled to observe a law, with the barons allowed to "distrain and distress him in every possible way," which was just short of a legal right to rebellion. Once sworn to the document, letters were sent to all sheriffs ordering them to read the charter aloud in public. It was the first "bill of rights" that attempted to levy some kind of controls over the powers of English kings.[10]

Figure 4-1   Important Dates in Legal History

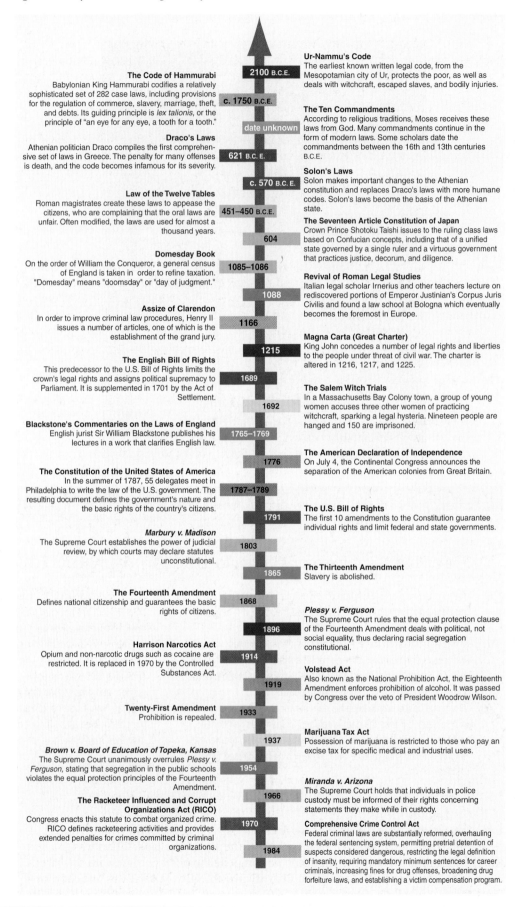

The Code of Hammurabi
Babylonian King Hammurabi codifies a relatively sophisticated set of 282 case laws, including provisions for the regulation of commerce, slavery, marriage, theft, and debts. Its guiding principle is *lex talionis*, or the principle of "an eye for any eye, a tooth for a tooth."

Draco's Laws
Athenian politician Draco compiles the first comprehensive set of laws in Greece. The penalty for many offenses is death, and the code becomes infamous for its severity.

Law of the Twelve Tables
Roman magistrates create these laws to appease the citizens, who are complaining that the oral laws are unfair. Often modified, the laws are used for almost a thousand years.

Domesday Book
On the order of William the Conqueror, a general census of England is taken in order to refine taxation. "Domesday" means "doomsday" or "day of judgment."

Assize of Clarendon
In order to improve criminal law procedures, Henry II issues a number of articles, one of which is the establishment of the grand jury.

The English Bill of Rights
This predecessor to the U.S. Bill of Rights limits the crown's legal rights and assigns political supremacy to Parliament. It is supplemented in 1701 by the Act of Settlement.

Blackstone's Commentaries on the Laws of England
English jurist Sir William Blackstone publishes his lectures in a work that clarifies English law.

The Constitution of the United States of America
In the summer of 1787, 55 delegates meet in Philadelphia to write the law of the U.S. government. The resulting document defines the government's nature and the basic rights of the country's citizens.

Marbury v. Madison
The Supreme Court establishes the power of judicial review, by which courts may declare statutes unconstitutional.

The Fourteenth Amendment
Defines national citizenship and guarantees the basic rights of citizens.

Harrison Narcotics Act
Opium and non-narcotic drugs such as cocaine are restricted. It is replaced in 1970 by the Controlled Substances Act.

Twenty-First Amendment
Prohibition is repealed.

Brown v. Board of Education of Topeka, Kansas
The Supreme Court unanimously overrules *Plessy v. Ferguson*, stating that segregation in the public schools violates the equal protection principles of the Fourteenth Amendment.

The Racketeer Influenced and Corrupt Organizations Act (RICO)
Congress enacts this statute to combat organized crime. RICO defines racketeering activities and provides extended penalties for crimes committed by criminal organizations.

2100 B.C.E.
c. 1750 B.C.E.
date unknown
621 B.C. E.
c. 570 B.C. E.
451–450 B.C.E.
604
1085–1086
1088
1166
1215
1689
1692
1765–1769
1776
1787–1789
1791
1803
1865
1868
1896
1914
1919
1933
1937
1954
1966
1970
1984

Ur-Nammu's Code
The earliest known written legal code, from the Mesopotamian city of Ur, protects the poor, as well as deals with witchcraft, escaped slaves, and bodily injuries.

The Ten Commandments
According to religious traditions, Moses receives these laws from God. Many commandments continue in the form of modern laws. Some scholars date the commandments between the 16th and 13th centuries B.C.E.

Solon's Laws
Solon makes important changes to the Athenian constitution and replaces Draco's laws with more humane codes. Solon's laws become the basis of the Athenian state.

The Seventeen Article Constitution of Japan
Crown Prince Shotoku Taishi issues to the ruling class laws based on Confucian concepts, including that of a unified state governed by a single ruler and a virtuous government that practices justice, decorum, and diligence.

Revival of Roman Legal Studies
Italian legal scholar Irnerius and other teachers lecture on rediscovered portions of Emperor Justinian's Corpus Juris Civilis and found a law school at Bologna which eventually becomes the foremost in Europe.

Magna Carta (Great Charter)
King John concedes a number of legal rights and liberties to the people under threat of civil war. The charter is altered in 1216, 1217, and 1225.

The Salem Witch Trials
In a Massachusetts Bay Colony town, a group of young women accuses three other women of practicing witchcraft, sparking a legal hysteria. Nineteen people are hanged and 150 are imprisoned.

The American Declaration of Independence
On July 4, the Continental Congress announces the separation of the American colonies from Great Britain.

The U.S. Bill of Rights
The first 10 amendments to the Constitution guarantee individual rights and limit federal and state governments.

The Thirteenth Amendment
Slavery is abolished.

Plessy v. Ferguson
The Supreme Court rules that the equal protection clause of the Fourteenth Amendment deals with political, not social equality, thus declaring racial segregation constitutional.

Volstead Act
Also known as the National Prohibition Act, the Eighteenth Amendment enforces prohibition of alcohol. It was passed by Congress over the veto of President Woodrow Wilson.

Marijuana Tax Act
Possession of marijuana is restricted to those who pay an excise tax for specific medical and industrial uses.

Miranda v. Arizona
The Supreme Court holds that individuals in police custody must be informed of their rights concerning statements they make while in custody.

Comprehensive Crime Control Act
Federal criminal laws are substantially reformed, overhauling the federal sentencing system, permitting pretrial detention of suspects considered dangerous, restricting the legal definition of insanity, requiring mandatory minimum sentences for career criminals, increasing fines for drug offenses, broadening drug forfeiture laws, and establishing a victim compensation program.

As the law developed over the centuries, it specified not only what rulers may do, but also what they may not do. The law limited the capricious decision-making powers of kings and dictated that people had certain protections from the government. Law thus became a double-edged sword. On one hand, it set forth numerous behaviors that citizens were told not to engage in, while on the other hand granting them rights and protections.

These dual functions of the law became extremely important in the modern criminal justice system. A major factor in this system is the **common law,** which was first developed in England and brought to the North American colonies, where it was modified to fit the new culture.

Common Law

Common law is different from **statutory law.** Instead of being expressly specified by a constitution or a legislature, the common law is based on the past decisions of the judiciary. Sometimes called case law, judiciary law, judge-made law, customary law, or unwritten law, common law is based on the doctrine of **precedent.** This means that judges look to previous cases with similar circumstances to see how justice was meted out. The idea behind common law is that similar cases should be treated in a similar manner. Over the decades, thousands of cases came to form the foundation of common law. As precedents were set, lawyers and judges had to consider those precedents in the administration of cases. Today, four issues guide precedent:

1. **Predictability.**   Predictability provides the concept of precedent with a certain level of order. By being consistent with the reasoning of previous cases and providing an outcome that fits with that reasoning, the common law gains legitimacy among people because they can understand how judgments are determined.

2. **Reliability.**   Participants in the legal system expect the court to follow precedent. Even if some facts of the case are disputed, the court is obliged to consider how previous cases were decided. Reliability means that the court is using precedent as a guide.

3. **Efficiency.**   Participants expect cases to be resolved in a reasonable time. Common law has created an expectation of how long cases should take to resolve. Of course, there will be some extreme exceptions to the time it takes to try a sensational case, but precedent defines when the time is becoming excessive.

4. **Equality.**   Similar cases are expected to be treated in similar fashion. This is the most important function of the concept of precedent. The concept of justice depends on the perception that the court treats individuals fairly. To have vast differences in outcomes of similar cases violates the concept of equality.[11]

Courts are generally bound by the decisions of previous courts by this doctrine of precedent. This legal principle is know as *stare decisis,* whereby the precedent of a previous case becomes the standard by which subsequent cases are considered.[12] Part of the art of the practice of law is the attorney's skill in finding similar cases and convincing the court that the circumstances are so close to the present case that a similar decision should be imposed. The opposing attorney will dispute the similarity of the circumstances and find other similar cases with different outcomes to support a given position. Consequently, the law is not as cut-and-dried as sometimes believed. The law is open to interpretation, and the legal reasoning, persuasive arguments, and reputation of one's attorney may play an important role in how a case is decided.

Common law is important not only for the doctrine of precedent, but also because it has informed the development of other sources of law. As legislatures developed constitutions and statutes, they used the common law as a guide. In most areas, however, common law has been superseded by more formal and explicit sources of

common law
Laws that are based on customs and general principles and that may be used as precedent or for matters not addressed by statute.

statutory law
The type of law that is enacted by legislatures, as opposed to common law.

precedent
A prior legal decision used as a basis for deciding a later, similar case.

stare decisis
The doctrine under which courts adhere to legal precedent.

law. It is worth considering these in greater detail to gain a fuller understanding on how the criminal law operates.

SOURCES OF LAW

The law is derived from no single source. Consequently, inconsistent principles, overlapping jurisdictions, and unclear nuances often appear in the criminal justice system. Considering the sources of the law can shed some light on this confusion. These sources of law are constitutions, statutes, and administrative rules.

Constitutions

In democracies, constitutions play a central and critical role in the development of criminal law. Constitutions express the will of the people. In a representative democracy, such as the United States, the Constitution binds elected legislators, the institutions of society, and the citizens to a system of government and laws. In the United States, the federal Constitution governs the country. Each state also has a constitution that pertains to the citizens and businesses of that state. State constitutions supplement but do not supersede the federal Constitution. This means that states cannot take away freedoms granted by the federal Constitution. Although the U.S. Constitution does not proscribe many behaviors, it sets out some broad values that cannot be abridged by the criminal law. The Constitution specifies how the government is structured and the roles played by the various branches of government. One of the first issues the framers of the Constitution dealt with almost immediately after the Constitution was completed was specifying how citizens were to be protected from the government. The first 10 amendments to the Constitution, also known as the **Bill of Rights,** dictate the basic freedoms enjoyed by U.S. citizens (see Criminal Justice Reference 4.2). Later legislators did not stop there. The Constitution has been amended 27 times. Emendation is a cumbersome process, requiring the ratification of state legislatures, but the important point to remember is that the Constitution is a living and changing document, not an absolute one.

Bill of Rights
The first 10 amendments to the U.S. Constitution, which guarantees fundamental rights and privileges to citizens.

Statutes

Federal and state legislative bodies have developed the common law into specific **statutes** that proscribe criminal behavior. These laws are debated and voted on by the legislative bodies and presumably represent the will of the people. For many behaviors, such as rape or homicide, a consensus exists as to what the law should cover. However, there are other offenses, such as drug use or gambling, that many citizens contend should not be illegal. Regardless of personal beliefs, however, all citizens are expected to obey the law or risk entering the criminal justice system. The advantage of statutes over the common law is that statutes are published in **penal codes** and therefore fit the principles of predictability, reliability, efficiency, and equality better than the doctrine of precedent. Statutes are easier to change than the Constitution, but new laws cannot violate rights given in the Constitution.[13] Consequently, new laws are often challenged on constitutional grounds. There are two ways in which laws may be challenged for constitutionality. The first is *unconstitutional per se*. In these cases it is claimed that the law is unconstitutional under any and all circumstances. The other challenge is called *unconstitutional as applied*, which is to claim that although the law may be valid, it is applied in a way that restricts or punishes the exercise of constitutional rights. This is an important distinction because a law that is found to be unconstitutional per se must be removed from the criminal code, whereas a law that is unconstitutional as applied requires only changes in the procedures of a criminal justice agency.

statute
A law enacted by a legislature.

penal code
A code of laws that deals with crimes and the punishments for them.

The Bill of Rights

Amendment I

Congress shall make no law respecting an establishment of religion, or prohibiting the free exercise thereof; or abridging the freedom of speech, or of the press; or the right of the people peaceably to assemble, and to petition the government for a redress of grievances.

Amendment II

A well regulated militia, being necessary to the security of a free state, the right of the people to keep and bear arms, shall not be infringed.

Amendment III

No soldier shall, in time of peace be quartered in any house, without the consent of the owner, nor in time of war, but in a manner to be prescribed by law.

Amendment IV

The right of the people to be secure in their persons, houses, papers, and effects, against unreasonable searches and seizures, shall not be violated, and no warrants shall issue, but upon probable cause, supported by oath or affirmation, and particularly describing the place to be searched, and the persons or things to be seized.

Amendment V

No person shall be held to answer for a capital, or otherwise infamous crime, unless on a presentment or indictment of a grand jury, except in cases arising in the land or naval forces, or in the militia, when in actual service in time of war or public danger; nor shall any person be subject for the same offense to be twice put in jeopardy of life or limb; nor shall be compelled in any criminal case to be a witness against himself, nor be deprived of life, liberty, or property, without due process of law; nor shall private property be taken for public use, without just compensation.

Amendment VI

In all criminal prosecutions, the accused shall enjoy the right to a speedy and public trial, by an impartial jury of the state and district wherein the crime shall have been committed, which district shall have been previously ascertained by law, and to be informed of the nature and cause of the accusation; to be confronted with the witnesses against him; to have compulsory process for obtaining witnesses in his favor, and to have the assistance of counsel for his defense.

Amendment VII

In suits at common law, where the value in controversy shall exceed twenty dollars, the right of trial by jury shall be preserved, and no fact tried by a jury, shall be otherwise reexamined in any court of the United States, than according to the rules of the common law.

Amendment VIII

Excessive bail shall not be required, nor excessive fines imposed, nor cruel and unusual punishments inflicted.

Amendment IX

The enumeration in the Constitution, of certain rights, shall not be construed to deny or disparage others retained by the people.

Amendment X

The powers not delegated to the United States by the Constitution, nor prohibited by it to the states, are reserved to the states respectively, or to the people.

During Prohibition, law enforcement was responsible for hunting down liquor operations and literally breaking up the stills.

Source: Brown Brothers

Administrative Rules

A number of agencies have developed rules consistent with their responsibilities to oversee aspects of commerce and public protection. Health, environment, customs, and parole agencies all have the authority to enact rules that limit the freedoms of individuals operating within their spheres of influence. Sometimes, these administrative rules overlap with criminal statutes or constitutional rights and end up being contested in court.[14] For instance, administrative rules about minority hiring practices or university admission policies have been found to be at odds with constitutional guarantees. In another example, parolees are subject to a host of conditions that require approval from one's parole officer, such as changing residences, traveling out of state, getting married, or drinking alcohol. These are all rules considered by the parole agency to be necessary to aid the parolee in the transition from incarceration to the free world. Violation of these conditions can result in the parolee returning to prison. Because these issues are administrative rules rather than legal statutes, the parolee is not accorded the full range of constitutional rights, as is the criminal defendant.

TYPES OF LAW

As a form of social control, the law is required to perform many functions. In addition to defining socially unacceptable behaviors, it also regulates the rules of social conflict, dictates how authorities control behavior and maintain public order, and regulates how behavior is punished. Different types of laws accomplish these multiple functions. The main distinction discussed here is the one between criminal law and civil law.

Criminal Law

What criteria are used to determine that a behavior is so serious that it be made a criminal offense and specified in the criminal law? Many objectionable behaviors are not covered by criminal law. Conversely, the criminal law covers some behaviors that many people believe it should not cover. Ideally, the criminal law is a mechanism of social control used only when other mechanisms (family, church, community) have failed, and is used only on serious transgressions. Three criteria determine what behaviors are made criminal:

1. **The enforceability of the law.** Laws that cannot be enforced do little good. The prohibition of alcohol in the 1920s showed what happens when the law cannot be enforced. People continued to drink alcohol, but the government received no revenue from alcohol sales that could be used to combat the negative effects of drinking. Many critics believe that the war on drugs is another example of laws that cannot be effectively enforced. Even as prison systems are overflowing with those convicted of drug-related offenses, illegal drugs continue to be bought and sold.

2. **The effects of the law.** Sometimes the cure is worse than the disease. During Prohibition, the consequences of attempting to enforce alcohol laws had a deleterious effect on society. Although alcohol was illegal, a great demand for it remained, bringing some unintended consequences in the form of organized crime and violence. Additionally, many otherwise law-abiding citizens were drawn into the criminal enterprise of alcohol production, transportation, and sales because of the lucrative alcohol trade. Perhaps even more harmful to society was the effect on the criminal justice system. Widespread corruption of judges and law enforcement officers seriously damaged the faith of citizens in the efficacy and fairness of government officials.

3. **The existence of other means to protect society against undesirable behavior.** Many people argue that even though drug and alcohol use have some unattractive features, the criminal justice system is not the most efficient and effective institution to control this behavior. Instead of attempting to discourage addictive behavior by punishment and deterrence, some experts contend that medical and psychological treatment would be more effective and not cause the harmful side effects of the war on drugs. Instead of using the criminal law as a weapon against drugs, the medical and mental health community could be better funded and expanded to address the problem. The repeal of Prohibition did not eliminate the problems of alcohol, but most would agree that by legalizing alcohol, the United States dealt more effectively with its health and social problems and spared the criminal justice system the temptations of corruption.[15]

The criteria for deciding which behaviors should be made criminal are not always heeded by legislators. The making of criminal law is as much a political enterprise as it is a legal one. Most citizens try to obey the law, but all of us are guilty of choosing to disregard some laws. Think about the last time you exceeded the legal speed limit. Was it on your way to class today? Because of people like you, the government decided to repeal the once-universal 55-miles-per-hour speed limit on the interstate highway system. The trucking industry and those who traveled routinely broke the speeding laws, and ultimately, the federal and state governments were lobbied for a higher speed limit. From a safety perspective, the 55-miles-per-hour limit was useful, but it was ignored by too many citizens and eventually modified.

Criminal versus Civil Law

There is an important difference between the criminal law and another type of law called **civil law.** Both types of law try to control the behavior of people, and both can impose sanctions. Also, there is some considerable overlap in the types of behavior they address, such as personal assault or environmental pollution. The important difference between them, however, concerns the identity of the aggrieved party. In civil law, the case is between two individuals. In criminal law, the case concerns the defendant and the government. When someone is charged with assault, the dispute is taken

civil law

The law that governs private rights as opposed to the law that governs criminal issues.

4.1 CrossCurrents

Liable, but Not Guilty

Perhaps one of the most interesting demonstrations of the difference between criminal and civil law was connected to the O. J. Simpson murder case. In June 1994 Simpson was charged with murdering his former wife, Nicole Brown Simpson, and her friend, Ronald Goldman, at her Brentwood, California, home. O. J. Simpson was tried for the murders in 1995 and acquitted that October. A year later the families of Nicole Brown Simpson and Ronald Goldman sued O. J. Simpson for the victims' wrongful deaths and won an $8.5 million judgment against him. How could O. J. Simpson be acquitted of murder, yet liable for wrongful death?[1]

The major difference between civil trials and criminal trials is the threshold of guilt. To find a defendant guilty in a criminal trial, a jury must determine whether there is proof of guilt beyond a reasonable doubt. In Simpson's criminal trial, then, doubt was all that was needed to acquit, and Simpson's attorneys were successful in introducing this doubt. However, a finding of liability in a civil trial requires a much lower threshold. A jury needs only a preponderance of evidence—not proof beyond a reasonable doubt—to find a defendant liable for a given action. The evidence that failed to bring a guilty finding in the criminal trial was enough for a liability finding in the civil trial.

Another important difference is the number of jurors who must agree on a verdict. In a criminal trial, unanimity is required, and the jurors in Simpson's civil trial were unanimous. But in a civil trial, only nine of 12 jurors are required to agree that a defendant is responsible. Also,

damages are not awarded in criminal trials. The plaintiff in criminal trials is the state, not the aggrieved party. Therefore, civil trials can be a way for those who believe they have been harmed by a defendant's action to recoup damages.

In another example, David Westerfield was found guilty of the kidnapping and murder of his 7-year-old neighbor, Danielle van Dam, and sentenced to death in August 2002. In May 2003 Danielle's parents settled a wrongful-death suit against Westerfield, who is currently on California's death row. Westerfield, who liquidated his assets to pay for his defense, did not agree to the settlement and paid no money to the van Dams. Instead, Westerfield's automotive and homeowners' insurance companies paid the van Dams an amount the family's attorney said ranged from $400,000 to $1 million.[2]

Think About It

1. Do situations such as the one in the Simpson case—with a defendant being found liable, but not guilty—make a mockery of the justice system, or is it merely a curiosity and a necessary part of the justice system?
2. In the case of the van Dams, should Westerfield's insurance company have had to pay the van Dams?

[1]CNN, "Simpson Civil Trial Special Section," www.cnn.com/US/OJ/simpson.civil.trial/.
[2]Harriet Ryan, "Van Dams Settle Civil Suit against Daughter's Killer," Court TV.com, May 15, 2003, www.courttv.com/trials/westerfield/051403_ctv.html.

---

tort law

An area of the law that deals with civil acts that cause harm and injury, including libel, slander, assault, trespass, and negligence.

double jeopardy

Prosecution in the same jurisdiction of a defendant for an offense for which the defendant has already been prosecuted and convicted or acquitted.

away from the victim and the assailant by the court and becomes the property of the government. The victim's role is greatly reduced by the government, which prosecutes the case in the name of the state.[16] This aspect of the criminal law confuses and frustrates many victims who still consider the case a problem between themselves and the accused. The court, meanwhile, disposes of the case and inflicts the sentence on the convicted offender without substantial input from the victim or often any personal restitution or satisfaction.[17]

At this point, the victim can invoke the civil law for redress. The victim can sue the offender for compensation for damages. Private attorneys, as opposed to the state prosecutor, represent the victim and offender. The sentence of the court is concerned with monetary damages, not with the prospect of incarceration. Civil law covers contracts, personal property, maritime law, and commercial law. **Tort law,** a form of civil law, covers personal wrongs and damage and includes libel, slander, assault, trespass, and negligence.[18]

A well-known but misunderstood principle of law known as **double jeopardy** states that a person cannot be tried for the same offense twice.[19] This concept applies to the criminal law but does not preclude the victim of a crime from suing for private damages after the criminal trial has concluded. For example, it was because of this distinction between the criminal law and civil law that the families of Nicole Brown

Simpson and Ronald Goldman were awarded monetary damages from O. J. Simpson after he was acquitted of criminal charges. The standards of proof in a civil trial (preponderance of evidence) are not as stringent as those in a criminal trial (beyond a reasonable doubt), which explains how two juries can consider the same case and produce such different verdicts.[20] (See Crosscurrents 4.1.) In addition to the distinction between criminal law and civil law, an important difference within the criminal law must be appreciated. This distinction concerns **substantive law** and **procedural law.**

Substantive Law

Substantive law tells us which behaviors have been defined as criminal offenses. The "thou shall nots" of the criminal law, substantive laws are found in the criminal codes of the state and federal governments and are the result of generations of political and social development (see Focus on Ethics 4.1). Homicide, rape, assault, money laundering, and all the other behaviors that are against the law are proscribed in the substantive law. The substantive law also sets the parameters on the punishment for each type of offense. Once a suspect has been convicted, the judge does not have unlimited discretion in imposing sentence. Few offenses are eligible for the death penalty. In the case of minor offenses, the judge can choose a short period of incarceration or decide that society is better served by placing the offender on probation.

Procedural Law

Whereas the substantive law specifies what individuals are allowed to do, the procedural law specifies how the criminal justice system is allowed to deal with those who break the law (see Figure 4-2). The procedural law sets the rules by which the

substantive law
The law that defines rights and proscribes certain actions (crimes).

procedural law
Laws that prescribe the methods for their enforcement and use.

4.1 FOCUS *on* ETHICS

CHANGING THE SUBSTANTIVE LAW

Laws are made by elected legislators to reflect the wishes of their constituents. In an ideal situation, communities enjoy a broad consensus as to what behaviors should be considered illegal and what the punishments should be for violating the law. However, there are many laws that citizens do not support. These are broken regularly and sometimes enforced selectively.

Imagine that you are a state senator and that the majority party leader has told you that because of your hard work and your casting of several key votes, she can fix it with the rest of the party for you to have any law you want added to your state's criminal code. What behavior that is now legal in your state would you choose to make against the law? Does your new law address a significant social problem, or does it simply expose the rest of us to your personal aesthetic tastes, your religious sensitivities, or your individual pet peeves? For example, some people think that anyone smoking in public, even outdoors, should be arrested because of the danger of secondhand smoke.

On the other hand, what law that is currently on the books would you like to see removed? Why do you think this is a bad law, and what would be the social consequences of legalizing this behavior? For instance, if you are concerned with the right of people to choose to use drugs and decide to repeal the marijuana laws, some unanticipated consequences might accompany this change. More people might use marijuana in unsafe situations, such as while driving. Marijuana might become more easily available to children, and many people could develop health problems from long-term use.

Think through the possible ramifications of adding or deleting substantive laws. Even though no one would suggest that our system of laws is perfect, we do need to be cautious when we change the law. One of the foundations of a democracy is the confidence of the people in the wisdom and fairness of the law. The criminal justice system cannot maintain the order of society without widespread voluntary social control. Consider how the laws that you would add to the legal code and the laws that you would delete would affect the relationship between citizens and the government.

What Do You Do?

1. What laws would you add?

2. What laws would you delete?

3. Should all new laws be subject to public vote? Why or why not?

Figure 4-2   **The Difference Between Procedural Law and Substantive Law**

PROCEDURAL LAW
HOW

The procedural law specifies *how* the criminal justice system is allowed to deal with crimes and sets the rules by which police and courts process cases. Procedural law protects citizens from arbitrary decision making of criminal justice professionals by dictating how cases are handled. Procedural law specifies rules of arrest, search and seizure, rights to attorneys, and attorney/client privilege.

SUBSTANTIVE LAW
WHAT

Substantive law tells us *what* behaviors are defined as crime. The substantive laws are found in the criminal codes of the state and federal governments and are the result of generations of political and social development. The substantive law also sets the parameters on the punishment for each type of crime.

police and courts process cases. Based to a large degree on the rights granted to accused individuals by the Constitution, procedural law protects citizens from arbitrary decision-making of criminal justice professionals by dictating how cases are to be handled.[21] Procedural law specifies rules of arrest, search and seizure, rights to attorneys, and attorney/client privilege, as well as other "rules of the game." Procedural laws change with the creation of new case precedents, new laws, or new court opinions. For instance, in the wake of the terrorist attacks on New York and Washington, D.C., on September 11, 2001, the federal government decided that attorney–client privilege is not absolute and that the police may monitor conversations to prevent future terrorist acts. Whether this evidence could be used against an accused terrorist in court is not clear at this time. This question will have to be decided by the courts.

Case Law

case law
See *common law (page 123).*

Case law comes from judicial decisions and requires judges to consider how previous cases have dealt with similar issues. Case law enables the courts to prevent a vast disparity in judicial outcomes and ensure that a degree of uniformity exists across courts. Like common law, case law depends on the principle of precedent to ensure that cases are in line with how past cases have been decided and also serves as a guide for future cases. However, the past is not destiny. That means that case law evolves as new decisions are applied to new circumstances in each case. The legal reasoning of case law changes as appellate courts review the decisions of trial courts and note the reasons for their decisions that consequently guide future cases. The issue of jurisdiction also heavily influences case law. Cases decided in one judicial circuit might not be as influential in other circuits. Although the decisions of the U.S. Supreme Court are important to every court, a decision of a court in Omaha might be less influential on a court in New York than on another court in Nebraska.[22] See Criminal Justice Reference 4.3 for a look at how cases, statutes, regulations, and law review articles are cited.

TYPES OF CRIME

The criminal law has categorized crime according to a number of different features. For instance, the difference in the seriousness of criminal offenses is captured by the felony versus misdemeanor distinction. Also, criminal offenses are differentiated by who commits the behavior, as in the distinction of juvenile status offenses (underage drinking, for instance). Also, some statutes recognize criminal history in classifications for first-time offenders, career criminals, or sex offenders.

How to Read Legal Citations

Many students are perplexed by the seemingly complicated system of citations for legal cases. This figure decodes the numbers and abbreviations that go into the making of a legal citation.

CASES

United States Supreme Court

Brown v. Board of Education, 347 U.S. 483, 490 (1954).

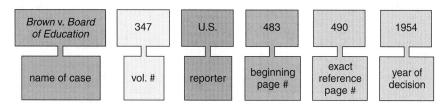

Lower Federal Court

Brown v. Board of Education, 98 F. Supp. 797 (D. Kan. 1951).

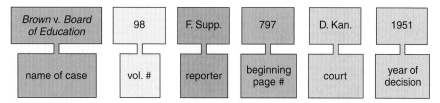

"Universal" or "Vendor-Neutral" Case Citation as adopted by the Wisconsin State Bar

Jones v. Smith, 1996 Wis 47 ¶ 15.

STATUTES

Session Law

Civil Rights Act of 1964, P.L. 88-353, 78 Stat. 241 (1964).

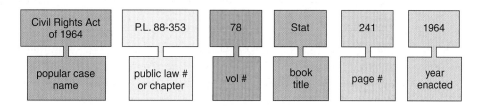

Code

Civil Rights Act of 1964, 42 U.S.C. §1971 et seq. (1988).

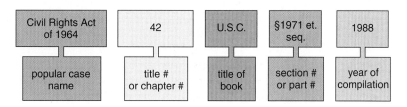

4.3   CRIMINAL JUSTICE REFERENCE

How to Read Legal Citations (*continued*)

REGULATIONS
As Promulgated
44 Fed. Reg. 29375 (May 18, 1979).

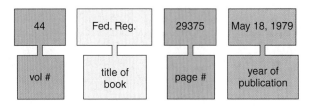

As Codified
42 C.F.R. §124.501 (1991).

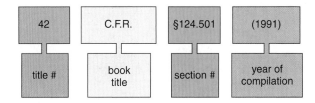

LAW REVIEW ARTICLES
Zygmunt J.B. Plater, *Environmental Law as a Mirror of the Future: Civic Values Confronting Market Forces Dynamics in a Time of Counter-Revolution*, 23 B.C. Envtl. Aff. L. Rev. 739 (1996).

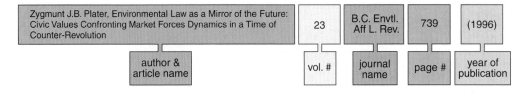

Source: Courtesy of Reading Legal Citations. Boston College of Law Library. http://www.bc.edu/schools/law/library/research/researchguides/citations/.

Felonies

Felonies are considered the most serious type of criminal offense. Felonies include murder, rape, assault, larceny, arson, and a host of other offenses at the state and federal level (see Tables 4-1 and 4-2). The felony distinction is important because many agencies and corporations deny employment to those convicted of this type of crime. Felons are not allowed to run for public office, own a firearm, or enter certain professions, such as law enforcement or medicine. Also, the penalties for felonies are often more severe than for other types of offenses. Incarceration for felonies is usually more than one year, and life imprisonment or capital punishment is specified for some felonies.

Misdemeanors

Misdemeanors are less serious offenses than felonies and are subject to lighter penalties. Usually, the maximum incarceration for a misdemeanor is up to one year in jail.

Table 4-1 **Elements of Crimes against Persons**

Charge	Criminal Act	Criminal Intent	Circumstances (or Extenuation)	Causation
Premeditated first-degree murder	Unlawful killing of a person	Specific intent preceded by premeditation and deliberation		Factual and legal causation
Second-degree murder	Unlawful killing of a person not amounting to first-degree murder	Specific intent (without premeditation and deliberation)		Factual and proximate causation
Felony murder	Unlawful killing of a person during the commission of a felony	Intent to commit felony	Victim died in conjunction with commission of felony or flight	Victim's death is causally related to the committed felony
Voluntary manslaughter	Unlawful killing of a person	Intent to kill	Extenuation: Reasonable provocation and sudden passion or self-defense	Factual and proximate causation
Involuntary manslaughter	Unlawful killing of a person	Occurs as a result of the commission of a misdemeanor or a negligent act	Reckless or gross negligence	Factual and proximate causation
Battery	Unlawful, harmful, or offensive touching of a person	General intent		Factual and proximate causation
Attempted battery assault	Unsuccessful attempt to batter	Specific intent to batter		
Threatened battery assault	Making a person reasonably fear imminent battery	Specific intent to make a person fear imminent battery		Factual and proximate causation
Rape	Sexual penetration without consent and with use or threat of force	General intent		
Kidnapping	Seizing, detention, and hiding	Specific intent		
False imprisonment	Unlawful confinement and/or hiding of a person	Specific intent		

Source: Compiled and adapted from Frank A. Schubert, *Criminal Law: The Basics* (Los Angeles: Roxbury, 2004). Used by permission.

Misdemeanants spend their time in county jails or stockades as opposed to state prisons. More often than not, misdemeanor offenders are placed on probation, fined, or required to do some type of community service rather than be incarcerated.

The distinction between felonies and misdemeanors can be confusing. An offense could be categorized as either, depending on the circumstances. Additionally, the prosecutor has wide discretion in deciding which type of offense to charge the offender with and may, as a result of plea bargaining, reduce the indictment from felony to misdemeanor. In some ways, this distinction gives the prosecutor immense power to coerce plea bargains from a defendant who is afraid of the vast consequences of being convicted as a felon as opposed to a misdemeanant.

Another important issue to remember about the difference between felonies and misdemeanors is that a specific behavior may be a felony in one jurisdiction and a misdemeanor in another (or maybe not even a criminal offense at all). Gambling is a good example. Nevada has many types of legal gambling, whereas in other states many types of gambling are outlawed. For example, Georgia had no legalized gambling at all until the state decided that the revenue was so attractive that it instituted its own lottery system while continuing to prohibit other types of gambling. Additionally, the differences between felonies and misdemeanors can be observed in drug laws in which the amount of drug in possession necessary to be a felony varies widely from state to

Table 4-2   **Elements of Property Crime**

Charge	Criminal Act	Criminal Intent	Circumstances (or Extenuation)	Causation
Common larceny	Unlawful taking (caption) and carrying away	Specific intent to permanently deprive possessor of personal property	Personal property of another	
Embezzlement	Entrustment, conversion	Specific intent to defraud		
Larceny by false pretenses (theft by deceit)	Accused person has misrepresented material facts	Intent to defraud, knowledge that material facts were misrepresented	Victim relied on misrepresented facts to transfer title	
Robbery	Larceny by means of force or intimidation	Specific intent to permanently deprive possessor of property	Taken from the victim or from the victim's presence	
Extortion	Offender intimidates victim by threatening harm to victim's person, family, reputation, or property	Specific intent to permanently deprive possessor of property	Some jurisdictions require the offender to obtain the demanded property from the victim	
Forgery	Making, altering, falsifying, signing, or reproducing writing	Specific intent to defraud		
Burglary	Use of force that facilitates entry; unconsented entry (trespass)	Specific intent during trespass to commit a felony within the structure	A structure (originally a dwelling house or outbuildings) of another at night	
Arson	Burning or charring	General intent: accused person intends to commit the criminal act	A protected dwelling or structure	Factual and proximate causation
Trespass to land/premises	Entry/remaining on land or premises of another person	General intent	Entry/remaining is not without consent but after receiving written or oral notice not to enter/remain	

Source: Compiled and adapted from Frank A. Schubert, *Criminal Law: The Basics* (Los Angeles: Roxbury, 2004). Used by permission.

state. So although the distinction between a felony and misdemeanor is important, the actual practice in the application of the label by the criminal justice system is sometimes inconsistent and problematic.

Inchoate Offenses

A crime does not always have to be completed for the offender to be arrested, charged, and punished. To limit the harm caused by crime and to deter individuals from planning and attempting wrongdoing, a category of crimes was created termed **inchoate offenses.** One example of this type of offense is conspiracy. Although it is often difficult to prove, conspiracy to commit a criminal offense is a behavior that legislators have deemed to be so serious that it needs to be discouraged and punished. For example, if Timothy McVeigh had been apprehended while collecting the materials and making the plans to bomb the Murrah Federal Building in Oklahoma City in 1995, then he could have been charged with inchoate offenses. With the focus on terrorism, we can appreciate the need to have conspiracy laws available to incapacitate and deter individuals and groups intent on causing the type of mass destruction witnessed in the Oklahoma City bombing and the terrorist attacks on September 11, 2001.

inchoate offense

An offense comprising acts necessary to commit another offense.

Another type of inchoate offense involves attempt. An attempted rape (sexual assault) can distress a victim as much as one that is completed. Although the offender could be charged with assault, the concept of sexual assault comes closer to capturing the type of trauma done to the victim, so the punishment is more severe. The idea behind inchoate offenses is that the offender should not have to be successful in completing the crime before the criminal justice system can successfully and severely respond. For instance, if law enforcement agents are aware of a plan to kill the president of the United States, they do not have to wait until it is successfully completed before they arrest the conspirators.

FEATURES OF CRIME

Not all harmful acts are considered criminal offenses. Certainly, many automobile accidents have serious consequences for the victims, but unless the features necessary for the legal definition of a crime are present, then the accident, no matter how serious, will not be considered by the criminal court. Three elements must be present in order for an act to be labeled a criminal offense:

1. The criminal act (***actus reus***)
2. The criminal intent (***mens rea***)
3. The relationship between *actus reus* and *mens rea* (**concurrence**)

Together, these three elements constitute ***corpus delicti*** or the "body of the crime." This does not mean an actual dead human body, as is found at the scene of a homicide, but rather, the aforementioned elements of the crime relevant to the case at hand.

Actus Reus

Actus reus or "guilty deed" occurs when an individual (whether as a principal, accessory, or accomplice) engages in a behavior prohibited by the criminal law. This can involve either doing something wrong (commission) or failing to do something that is legally obligated (omission). The law requires that this commission or omission be an actual behavior as opposed to a thought. The criminal law does not punish thoughts. Those thoughts must be translated into some type of action or intentional inaction. This is unlike inchoate offenses, which must involve something more than thoughts, even if it is only speech. For example, a bank teller is not criminally liable for considering embezzling money. However, when false accounts are created into which money is diverted, or when customers' deposited money is not recorded, then the requirements of the criminal act are met. Likewise, merely thinking about suicide is not against the law. Attempting to commit suicide by, say, taking an overdose of drugs or jumping off a tall building is a physical act that meets the definition of *actus reus*.

Actus reus does not refer to someone's status. A person who is addicted to drugs or alcohol is not considered to have met the standard of *actus reus*. However, if a person carries illegal drugs around, sells drugs, or conspires with others to sell drugs, then it is reasoned that actual criminal acts have occurred, and the person could be arrested. Additionally, drunken drivers are not punished for their consumption of alcohol, but because they committed the act of driving while impaired. To meet the test of *actus reus*, the behavior must also be voluntary. A person under the suggestion of hypnosis or some form of brainwashing is not aware of committing a criminal offense. Similarly, liability does not extend to one who is unconscious or is having a convulsion or other reflexive reaction that causes harm.

Actus reus is sometimes more difficult to prove when it involves the act of criminal omission. Failing to act when one is legally required to report child abuse is one example. People are also expected to take steps to save the life of a victim of some trauma. Allowing someone to die—even if for logical reasons and with the consent of the person, as in cases involving the terminally ill—can sometimes be considered the basis for *actus reus*.

actus reus
"Guilty deed"; the physical action of a criminal offense.

mens rea
"Guilty mind"; intent or knowledge to break the law.

concurrence
The coexistence of actus reus and mens rea.

corpus delicti
"Body of the crime"; the criminal offense.

Mens Rea

In addition to considering the criminal act, the offender's state of mind is taken into consideration when deciding whether a behavior is a criminal offense. *Mens rea* or a "guilty mind" is considered present when a person acts purposefully, knowingly, recklessly, or negligently. The law distinguishes between general intent and specific intent when considering *mens rea*. General intent is present when the prosecution can prove that the defendant intended to do what the law forbids. Specific intent involves the intention of the defendant to accomplish a specific goal. In the case of murder, the prosecution often says that the defendant shot the victim with the *intent* to kill. It is possible that the defendant was shooting to wound the victim or shooting warning shots into the air and struck the victim by mistake, but these conditions would need to be buttressed by other evidence to circumvent specific intent. For instance, if witnesses hear me say, "Stop or I'll shoot you in the kneecap," and then I shoot you in the kneecap and the bullet ricochets into your head and kills you, my intent might not have been "to kill" but simply to do "great bodily harm." Whereas shooting someone in the head allows the court to infer a specific intent to kill, shooting a person in the kneecap allows the court to infer intent to injure.[23]

Concurrence

Both *actus reus* and *mens rea* must be present at the same time for a behavior to be considered a crime. If a person is killed in an automobile accident that involves another car, the driver of the other car is not charged with murder or manslaughter, because the driver did not intend to cause the accident or a death.

Strict Liability

strict liability
Responsibility for a criminal offense without intention to break the law.

Mens rea is not required for some statutory offenses; those that involve **strict liability** are the primary exception to the requirement of the presence of both *mens rea* and *actus reus*. Strict-liability offenses tend to be offenses in which the public's welfare is at issue, such as narcotics violations, health and safety violations, traffic violations, or sanitation violations. The offender need not have a guilty mind when breaking strict-liability laws. For example, many bars and restaurants have a sign that reads, "We Card Everyone, Every Time." If the bartender or waiter serves alcohol to an underage person, even if that person appears to be of legal drinking age, then the bartender is guilty of a criminal offense. Because a liquor license can be crucial to a restaurant, the owners cannot afford to depend on the discretion of a bartender who works only on weekends and has no real investment in keeping the restaurant within the law. Requiring proof of age for every customer requesting an alcoholic beverage is the only way the establishment's owners can ensure that their employees do not put the business at risk of violating the strict-liability rules.

Laws to protect children may also fall under the strict-liability doctrine. Whereas sex between consenting adults is not considered criminal, sex between an adult and a child, even a consenting child, is a criminal offense. Sometimes it is difficult to tell when a person is old enough to legally consent to sex, but it makes no difference to the court if an adult makes a mistake. The law is designed to protect children from predatory adults, and ignorance of a child's age is not a valid excuse.

CRIMINAL RESPONSIBILITY AND CRIMINAL DEFENSE

The law recognizes that not all people are completely aware of the effect their behaviors have on others. Even though great physical harm or property damage might result from criminal behavior, the capacity of the offender to understand the ramifications of his or her behavior can produce mitigating reasoning that can excuse the individual from the full force of the criminal law. The defense attorney will look for reasons to justify or excuse the criminal behavior. Essentially, six arguments can be employed in the defense against a criminal indictment:

1. My client did not do it.
2. My client did it, but my client is not responsible because he or she is insane.
3. My client did it but has a good excuse.
4. My client did it but has a good reason.
5. My client did it but should be acquitted because the police or the prosecutor cheated.
6. My client did it but was influenced by outside forces.

MY CLIENT DID NOT DO IT   The best way to defend a client from a criminal charge is to show that the defendant did not do it. Unlike the rest of the defenses discussed in this section, this one claims that the defendant is completely innocent of the charges. An **alibi** can be an essential part of maintaining one's innocence, demonstrating that one was not at the scene of the crime. An alibi may be established in many ways, all of which hinge on credible evidence. If other people claim you were 200 miles away in another city at the time of the offense, it is important that your witnesses be believable. Your spouse could say you were watching television together, but the court may wonder whether your spouse is telling the truth. However, if your witness is the sheriff from a neighboring county who testifies that you were locked up in jail for two weeks before and after the crime, then the court is much more likely to believe the alibi. Often, dated documents such as hotel receipts, credit card purchases, and cash withdrawals from ATM machines can be used to help establish an alibi. With so many cameras around to protect establishments against robbery or other offenses, you might be able to show that you were in a store buying milk and ice cream at the time the offense took place many miles away. These cameras record the date and time of the pictures, and this evidence can be compelling in convincing the court that you have a valid alibi.

alibi
A defense that involves the defendant(s) claiming not to have been at the scene of a criminal offense when it was committed.

MY CLIENT DID IT, BUT MY CLIENT IS NOT RESPONSIBLE BECAUSE HE OR SHE IS INSANE   The **insanity defense** is based on the concept that although the defendant did commit the criminal act, he or she is not criminally responsible because of insanity

insanity defense
A defense that attempts to give physical or psychological reasons that a defendant cannot comprehend his or her criminal actions, their harm(s), or their punishment.

4.1   **CASE IN POINT**

DURHAM V. UNITED STATES

THE CASE	**THE POINT**
Durham v. United States, 214 F.2d 862 (D.C. Cir. 1954)	*The Supreme Court created a new test for insanity.*

Monte Durham was convicted, by way of a trial without a jury, of breaking into a house. Durham's defense at the trial was that he was of unsound mind at the time of the offense. Before this conviction, Durham had spent years in and out of prisons and mental institutions. In 1945 at age 17, Durham had been discharged from the navy because he had "a profound personality disorder." In 1953, after the housebreaking incident, he was subjected to "subshock insulin therapy," released, and appraised by the hospital superintendent as "mentally competent to stand trial" on the housebreaking charge.

Given Durham's history, the D.C. Court of Appeals reversed the decision and remanded the case for a new trial. In setting forth a landmark new test for insanity, the court wrote that "an accused is not criminally responsible if his unlawful act was the product of mental disease or mental defect."

(see Case in Point 4.1). The defendant did not appreciate that the behavior was wrong, that the behavior could hurt others, or that he or she was even committing the behavior. Because insanity is a legal term and not a medical one, this type of criminal offense sometimes elicits much confusion and bitterness.[24] Often, the public believes that the defendant is faking insanity to escape the brunt of the criminal law. Some believe that spending time in a hospital for the criminally insane would be preferable to spending time in prison and that it is easier to be released from the hospital. Obviously, defendants facing the death penalty would see the value in being considered insane and therefore innocent of the guilty mind (*mens rea*) required for the state to invoke capital punishment.

How is someone determined to be insane? This question is difficult because the legal and medical professions have different agendas. The medical profession is concerned with understanding the cause of mental illness and the best methods for treating it. The legal profession needs only to determine whether the defendant had the requisite mental capacity to have a guilty mind, so it uses its own standards to determine insanity (see Table 4-3).

MY CLIENT DID IT BUT HAS A GOOD EXCUSE   In addition to the insanity plea, a defense may use a number of other reasons or excuses to attempt to explain away a defendant's culpability. These include duress, age, mistake, and intoxication. An excuse contends that the defendant should not be held legally responsible for the offense because of one of these personal disabilities.

- **Duress**   Sometimes, according to the law, a person commits a criminal offense out of fear for his or her own life or fear of bodily injury. Although not an excuse for homicide, duress or compulsion might help mitigate other types of criminal offenses as long as the defendant can show that he or she did not voluntarily join in or continue in engaging in the criminal activity. The Patty Hearst case from the 1970s is a good example of duress. Hearst was kidnapped by a group called the Symbionese Liberation Army and subjected to months of abuse, isolation, and rape. She was required to participate in a robbery of a bank

In June 2001, Andrea Yates drowned her five children in a bathtub, later telling authorities that she was trying to save them from hell. Although Yates was found guilty of murder in her first trial, that verdict was later overturned because of erroneous testimony from a forensic psychiatrist. In a second trial in 2006, a jury found Yates not guilty by reason of insanity, and she was committed to a state mental hospital.

Source: *Steve Ueckert\AP Wide World Photos*

Table 4-3   **Some Legal Standards Used to Determine Insanity**

M'Naghten Rule	Irresistible Impulse Rule
In 1843 Daniel M'Naghten was charged with murder after he shot and killed Edward Drummond, the assistant to the prime minister of Great Britain, Sir Robert Peel. M'Naghten believed he was being persecuted by Peel, and, unfortunately for Drummond, mistook him for the prime minister. At the trial, evidence showed that M'Naghten was incapable of determining right from wrong at the time of the incident, and the jury found him not guilty. The House of Lords then produced a doctrine that the jury should acquit the defendant if it found that the accused "was laboring under such a defect of reason, from disease of the mind, as not to know the nature and quality of the act he was doing, or, if he did know it, that he did not know it was wrong." This test spread throughout the world where the British legal system had influence and became the foundation for the insanity defense. Many jurisdictions still use the M'Naghten rule. It is up to the defense to prove that the defendant is insane.	In some states, an additional feature has been added to the M'Naghten standards. The irresistible-impulse rule states that although a defendant understands the nature and quality of the criminal act and understands that it is wrong, if a defendant experiences as a result of a mental disease an irresistible impulse that makes the person incapable of preventing himself or herself from doing the act, this is grounds for acquittal. But what constitutes an irresistible impulse? Just because the defendant failed to resist, does that make an impulse irresistible? Many of us are tempted by chocolate, beer, or pizza. Most of us can control our impulses and consume these products in moderation. Could a rapist use the irresistible-impulse defense by claiming the victim was especially good-looking? The burden of proof for the irresistible impulse defense rests with the prosecution and is at the level of beyond a reasonable doubt.
Durham Rule	**Guilty but Mentally Ill**
This is sometimes called the "products test." Based on a rule created in New Hampshire in 1871, it was revived in 1954 in the case *Durham* v. *United States*. The rule asks the jury to decide whether the unlawful act was a product of the defendant's insanity. Unfortunately, little guidance is given to the jury in making this determination, and the Durham rule is used relatively infrequently. The Durham rule is a legal construct, and without any clear criteria for making this determination, juries must depend on intuition rather than medical evidence or legal reasoning. The burden of proof for the Durham rule defense rests with the prosecution and is at the level of beyond a reasonable doubt.	This verdict says the defendant is factually guilty of the crime but was incompetent to control his or her behavior. This finding is not really a justification or an excuse for the crime, but merely reflects society's frustrations with the line of legal versus medical reasoning that underlie the insanity defense. Under the guilty-but-mentally-ill concept, the judge can sentence the defendant to any sentence specified by the law. However, the judge is required to address three criteria in imposing the sentence: the protection of society, holding offenders accountable for their offenses, and making treatment available to those with mental illness.
Appreciation Test	**Modern Penal Code Test**
The federal government has adopted a test that in some ways is similar to the M'Naghten rule in that it requires the defendant to be unaware of what he or she was doing or unaware that what he or she was doing was wrong. However, the defendant must show that he or she had a lack of control. The main feature of the appreciation test is that it shifts the burden of proof back to the defense, and that burden of proof need not be beyond a reasonable doubt but merely constitute "clear and convincing evidence."	The Modern Penal Code provides another criterion for determining whether the defendant is mentally ill. Sometimes called the "substantial capacity test," the code is not used by many states. It attempts to determine whether the defendant, as a result of mental disease or defect, lacks the substantial capacity either to appreciate the criminality of his or her conduct or to conform his or her conduct to the requirements of the law. The burden of proof rests with the prosecution at the level of beyond a reasonable doubt.

and was photographed by bank cameras holding a gun. Her attorneys claimed she was acting under duress in that she had been conditioned to fear her assailants. Although she could have thrown down her gun and run away from her captors during the robbery, she did not recognize this course of action as realistic. More recently, cases using the duress defense have concerned the subjugation of women. Known as the battered women's syndrome defense, this reasoning recasts the defendant into the role of a victim of a man whose power compels her to break the law. This defense is sometimes used with a claim of self-defense or defense of others to mitigate a homicide charge.

infancy

In legal terminology, the state of a child who has not yet reached a specific age; almost all states end infancy at age 18.

- **Age**   At what age should a person be held accountable for breaking the law? Can a 5-year-old child understand the ramifications of harmful acts? Can a 15-year-old? Common law has long established that children under age 7 are presumed incapable of having the necessary criminal intent for their unlawful acts to be considered crimes. For children between ages 7 and 14, however, this presumption can be challenged, and the prosecution can present evidence that the child had the capacity to form criminal intent.[25] This excuse of age, called **infancy,** is the foundation of the juvenile court system. With a few exceptions, young offenders are handled in the juvenile court, where the emphasis is on treatment rather than on punishment. Those age 16 or older may have their cases waived to criminal (adult) court if their offenses are serious. In fact, as we will see in Chapter 14, trying juveniles in criminal court is becoming more frequent. However, a hearing in juvenile court is required before this jurisdiction can be changed.

- **Mistake**   There is an old saying, "Ignorance of the law is no excuse." This is reasonable because it would be impossible to prove that someone knew or should have known what the law is. For example, if you claim deductions on your taxes that are not allowed by the law, even if you do so not understanding that the deductions are not allowed, the government can punish you. Part of participating in a democracy is knowing and obeying the law. Although ignorance of the law is seldom an effective excuse, ignorance of facts is. For example, suppose someone sells you a car and you have good reason to believe that the seller actually owned the car. If after a traffic stop you discover the car is stolen, then you might have a valid excuse. However, if the price you paid for the car was a fraction of what it was worth, then you are considered responsible for suspecting deviance and investigating further. People can make honest mistakes, and the court will consider the possibility that the defendant acted honestly and in good faith.

- **Intoxication**   People who are drunk or under the influence of drugs might do things they would not normally do. Should this excuse shield them from the law? The answer is generally no. Those who use intoxicants are responsible for their behaviors. However, what if the use of intoxicants is involuntary? What if someone spikes a drink or serves marijuana brownies without the guests' knowledge? Under these circumstances, the defendant is unable to appreciate or control his or her behavior and is not responsible for the circumstances that cause the offense. Involuntary intoxication is more likely to involve drugs than alcohol. (Most people can detect the smell and taste of alcohol.) Sometimes voluntary intoxication can be used to reduce the level of the offense. For instance, an intoxicated person could claim that he or she did not have the capacity to establish *mens rea* and ask that a murder charge be reduced to manslaughter.

MY CLIENT DID IT BUT HAS A GOOD REASON   Sometimes bad must be done in order for good to prevail. Justifications as criminal defenses contend that the harm caused by committing an offense was more desirable than the harm that would have been caused if one had done nothing. The justifications discussed here are self-defense, consent, and necessity.

- **Self-defense**   Law enforcement officers cannot be everywhere all the time to protect everyone. Sometimes a person faced with imminent danger is not in a position to call the police. Self-defense has long been established to be a legitimate justification for violating the law. However, to be successful, the claim of self-defense is limited to certain conditions. First, the defendant must believe that physical force is necessary for self-protection or the protection of others. Second, this belief that physical force is necessary must be based on reasonable grounds. Third, the defendant must believe that the force used is necessary to avoid imminent danger. Finally, the force used cannot be in excess of that believed necessary to repel the unlawful attack. One of the key issues in the self-defense claim is the amount of force used. The defendant is allowed to use only reasonable force for self-defense. That means that if a 250-pound linebacker is attacked by his 105-pound girlfriend, he is not justified in pulling out a gun and shooting her. The requirement of reasonable force would assume that he could protect himself without resorting to deadly force. However, if the roles were reversed, and the linebacker were beating the woman, then her use of deadly force to defend herself might be a legitimate justification. Individuals must consider other solutions before using deadly force. State laws differ on the requirement that the defendant first attempt to retreat or escape before employing deadly force. In Kentucky a person is allowed to stand his or her ground and meet the attack with deadly force. The court contends that "it is tradition that a Kentuckian never runs. He does not have to." In Florida, however, a person must use every reasonable means, including escape, before resorting to deadly force.[26] Cases involving the defense of others must follow similar criteria as cases of self-defense. Only reasonable force can be used unless there is a threat of imminent death. Likewise, a third party cannot be an aggressor in the incident. If your friend starts a barroom fight and is getting the worst of it, you are not justified in rushing to his defense. Deadly force could be used in the same circumstances as self-defense. If someone were strangling your child, you would be justified in shooting the attacker.

- **Consent**   The consent defense is often used in rape cases. For instance, the defendant claims the victim agreed to sex, whereas the victim claims there was either no consent or consent was under duress or intoxication. For the consent to be legitimate, it must be given knowingly and freely. Persuading an intoxicated person to have sex can result in a charge of rape when the intoxication wears off. Some defendants claim they were confused when they consented, and retract their consent after the fact. In such cases the court will consider closely the circumstances to decide the verdict. Many years ago, in cases of female victims, the sexual history of the victim was examined to determine her character; however, the court now protects women from being doubly victimized.[27] If the woman is a prostitute, she still has the right to withhold consent. In cases of an adult having sex with a minor, consent is not a justification. Children are not deemed capable of giving informed consent, and such actions will invoke a charge of **statutory rape.**

- **Necessity**   Defense based on the principle of necessity must show that the harm that would have resulted from compliance with the law would have exceeded that from its violation. For example, a man rushing his pregnant wife

statutory rape
Sexual activity conducted with a person who is younger than a specified age or incapable of valid consent because of mental illness, mental handicap, intoxication, unconsciousness, or deception.

Consent is not an acceptable justification in the case of an adult having sexual relations with a minor. In 2005, former Florida school teacher Debra Lafave (right) was accused of having sex with a 14-year-old student. She later pleaded guilty to lewd and lascivious behavior with the student as part of a plea deal.
Source: *Victor Junco\AP Wide World Photos*

to the hospital is justified in exceeding the speed limit as long as he takes certain precautions such as flashing his lights and honking his horn to warn others. Campers trapped in a mountain snowstorm might use the necessity defense to justify breaking into a cabin to keep warm as long as they later notify the owner and pay for the repairs. However, a juvenile cannot claim necessity as a defense for carrying a gun to school because he or she is afraid of other students. There are other means of protecting oneself, such as informing parents, school officials, or police about the perceived dangers posed by other students. The necessity defense involves choosing the lesser of evils. For example, it is permissible to burn some land to check a larger fire threatening a nearby town.[28]

MY CLIENT DID IT BUT SHOULD BE ACQUITTED BECAUSE THE POLICE OR THE PROSECUTOR CHEATED   A number of criminal defenses concentrate on the conduct of law enforcement authorities (see Focus on Ethics 4.2). Failure to follow procedural law, engaging in fraud or other misconduct, and treating defendants in a selective and discriminatory manner can all be reasons to challenge a criminal indictment. Examples of these include the following:

- **Statute of limitations**   A statute of limitations is a law applying to civil and criminal cases that specifies that prosecution must take place within a specified period. If a police officer knocked on your door and informed you that you were being arrested for an offense that happened 10 years ago, you would be hard pressed to reconstruct where you were and what you were doing at the time of the offense. Developing an alibi would be impossible because most people, unless they kept detailed diaries, would not be able to remember whether they were anywhere near the scene of the crime. Depending on the jurisdiction, many offenses have statutes of limitations. Murder, however, usually does not have a statute of limitations, and suspects can be charged decades after the crime if sufficient evidence can be developed.

- **Entrapment**   Many offenses are difficult for law enforcement agencies to react to. Prostitution, in which consenting adults exchange sex for money, is not something the police are going to be aware of if no one complains. The police must be proactive in developing prostitution cases, and in doing so, they run the risk of entrapping defendants. By posing as customers seeking the services of prostitutes, the police give the prostitute an opportunity to commit the

Murder typically has no statute of limitations. In June 2005, Edgar Ray Killen, age 79, was found guilty of felony manslaughter in the killings of three civil rights workers in Mississippi in 1964. Killen, who was a 38-year-old Ku Klux Klan official at the time of the killings, was sentenced to 60 years in prison.

Source: Lori Waselchuk/The New York Times

offense in their presence. The issue is complex. Would the prostitute engage in this behavior without the inducement of the police? What has developed is an elaborate verbal dance in which the prostitute must be the first party to mention the cost of sex. Otherwise, the police cannot arrest the prostitute without risking entrapment. Entrapment has also been the defense of politicians caught accepting bribes or engaging in other illegal behavior. In the famous Abscam case, federal agents posing as rich Middle Eastern sheiks offered public officials, including members of Congress, money for influencing legislation. The defendants were videotaped stuffing large amounts of cash into their pockets and were subsequently prosecuted. The defendants were unable to convince the court that they were victims of entrapment.[29] Another case of a public official who claimed entrapment is former Washington, D.C., mayor Marion Barry. Federal agents used a friend of Barry's to lure him to a hotel room, where she gave him crack cocaine to smoke. Barry turned down the drug several times before he decided to smoke it. He was videotaped ingesting the cocaine and immediately arrested. Given that the federal agents supplied the woman and the cocaine, Barry tried to claim entrapment, but was unsuccessful.[30]

- **Double jeopardy** According to this defense, a defendant cannot be tried or punished twice for the same offense. Based on common law and the Fifth Amendment of the Constitution, the double jeopardy defense is designed to protect the defendant from repeated trials and excessive punishments. In a few circumstances, however, the same behavior may be considered for different purposes without violating the right against double jeopardy. In 1993, four Los Angeles police officers who were acquitted in the beating of motorist Rodney King were later tried in federal court on the charge of violating King's civil rights.[31] Two of the officers were found guilty. Another exception is found when a case is tried both in criminal court and in civil court. In criminal court, the defendant's guilt must be proved beyond a reasonable doubt, and he or she may face incarceration. In civil court, only a preponderance of evidence is required for a ruling against the defendant, and the penalty will not include prison but only monetary damages.

- **Police fraud or prosecutor misconduct** Law enforcement officials must play by the rules established by procedural law. Withholding evidence, making false statements, and putting forth evidence that they know is false can be grounds for a defense claim of police fraud or prosecutor misconduct.

MY CLIENT DID IT BUT WAS INFLUENCED BY OUTSIDE FORCES   Some defenses for criminal acts attempt to shift the blame from the defendant to something outside his or her control. The best example of this is the alleged "Twinkie defense." The word *alleged* is used because this case did not happen the way it was reported in the press and has become something of an urban legend (see Crosscurrents 4.2). Although this case did not develop as many people assume, the principle is important and is used to justify a wide variety of behaviors. The central question remains: Can the diet alter body chemistry in such a way as to contribute to, or cause, someone to engage in unlawful behavior? Ask any parents who have seen their kids bouncing off the walls after consuming too much sugar, and you will get an affirmative response. However, in court this is a tough defense to put forth successfully. The prevalence of sugar in American diets would surely demonstrate a great deal more deviant behavior and crime if it were as influential as those who support the Twinkie defense claim. The fact that most of us consume large quantities of sugar and do not break the law makes this defense problematic.

Another defense that has garnered its share of publicity involves premenstrual syndrome (PMS). Here, the theory is that hormonal changes within the female body during menstruation might induce some women to break the law. We will not deal with the scientific evidence of PMS here, but courts in England do recognize PMS as a legitimate defense, and the issue has been addressed in U.S. courts. The difficulty with mounting such a defense rests with the task of convincing a judge

4.2 FOCUS on ETHICS

A CHANGE OF HEART

You have been a judge for a long time and have established a reputation for strictness and fairness. You plan to retire soon, but something has happened recently that has given you a new interest in your job and a new sense of the complexities of the criminal justice process.

Your 18-year-old granddaughter has been convicted of selling cocaine in a neighboring state. Although you do not condone her behavior, you are concerned with the way her case was handled by the police. You learn that your granddaughter is technically guilty, but that the police came close to using entrapment to entice her to commit the offense. An undercover officer asked her several times to help him find some cocaine, and she repeatedly told him she did not know any dealers. The officer then promised her that if she would simply introduce him to some people at her sorority party, he would leave her alone. She did know one young woman whose boyfriend had a brother who used cocaine, and a week after she made the introduction, she accompanied an undercover officer to a restaurant where the buy was made. She was arrested and charged with cocaine sales even though she did not know the boyfriend's brother, received no money from the transaction, did not use any drugs, and did not even know that the undercover officer had set up the drug buy. The police contend that she was instrumental in arranging the introduction and was present at the transaction.

As a judge you are appalled by the conduct of this police officer, but because the case took place in another state, you cannot help your granddaughter. However, you are now taking a hard look at the conduct of the police officers who come before your court, and you are discovering that undercover officers who buy drugs are creative people. You begin to see each case in a different light, and you do not like what you see. In your opinion, some police officers are getting a bit too proactive in developing their drug cases. They are skirting the limits of entrapment, which, although questionable from an ethical standpoint, is still legal. What concerns you most is that the officers are not using their borderline tactics to sniff out big-time drug dealers, but are instead targeting basically decent young people who are on the periphery of the drug scene. In your opinion, the problem is so acute that you are throwing some cases out of court. Although you cannot prove entrapment, you are so suspicious that you now give the benefit of the doubt to the defendant rather than the police officer in nearly every case.

The chief judge has asked you if there is a problem because the word in the courthouse is that you are the judge preferred by defense attorneys in drug cases.

What Do You Do?

1. Tell the chief judge that it is your court and you will do as you please.
2. Tell the chief judge about your granddaughter's experience. Say that you are discovering the same entrapment issues in your courtroom and that it is probably the same in every courtroom in the county.
3. Resign because you have lost your perspective.
4. Resign and run for governor and try to get laws passed that will correct this problem statewide.

and/or a jury that the client's PMS is so severe that it would cause her to commit a criminal offense. When one considers the millions of women who deal with this normal human condition, it is difficult for a defense attorney to make a case that a client suffered diminished capacity to the extent that PMS contributed to, or caused, her commission of the offense.

A related defense against criminal prosecution is battered women's syndrome (BWS). The reason for criminal behavior rests on the extensive literature and experiences of women caught in domestic-violence relationships. It is often difficult for women to disengage from such relationships because of economic and safety reasons. Therefore, the defense contends, the women are forced to commit what at first glance might appear to be premeditated acts of violence against their spouses or partners. These acts might include homicide in which the woman strikes at the man when he is most vulnerable, such as when he is sleeping. Because of the power imbalance (the man is physically stronger, controls the money, and is psychologically domineering), battered women act in a way that seems unfair by striking in a deliberate, but not immediately provoked, manner. The BWS defense argues that she is temporarily insane from the years of abuse and that killing her partner is an act of self-defense.[32] On the other hand, the defense could claim that the woman was sane and that she believed she was in imminent danger of bodily harm or death and that she acted in reasonable self-defense.

After the Vietnam War, a number of veterans engaged in criminal offenses and deviant behavior as well as some rather bizarre activities that caused psychologists to

Just Deserts: the "Twinkie Defense"

If enough people believe in something that never happened, does that make it real?

Yes and no.

Putting aside arguments about exactly what constitutes "reality," if enough people believe in an incident that did not happen and then base their opinions and behaviors on that belief, the myth can indeed affect reality because its believers use its lessons to construct their lives and opinions. However, this does nothing to improve the myth itself. Although certain myths may be useful or instructive, they can also cause trouble.

This is the case in the infamous Twinkie defense. Here is what most people believe: a long time ago a man killed some people and blamed the dessert cake Twinkies for his behavior and escaped serious punishment. Although this nutshell version of the story might or might not be harmless, many people have come to base their low opinions of the "unfair" legal system, at least in part, on this story. The problem is, it never happened.

On November 10, 1978, Dan White resigned from his position as a San Francisco city supervisor, but several days later asked Mayor George Moscone to reinstate him. Moscone refused. For this, White blamed another supervisor, Harvey Milk, as well as Moscone. On November 26, White entered City Hall through a basement window to avoid the metal detectors and shot Mayor George Moscone twice in the body and twice in the head. He then reloaded, went to a different part of the building, and shot Supervisor Harvey Milk three times in the body and twice in the head. White then turned himself over to police.

At the trial, White's attorneys used a diminished-capacity defense to explain White's actions, claiming that White had experienced severe depression in the days before the shooting. Four psychiatrists and a psychologist testified that White's decision-making ability was impaired by depression. The prosecution offered only the testimony of a psychiatrist, who found White to be "moderately depressed," but retaining the "capacity to deliberate and premeditate."

During the trial, one defense psychiatrist, Dr. Martin Blinder, mentioned that White, who was normally health conscious, had been eating large amounts of junk food during his depression. Blinder said that this radical change of behavior was a symptom of White's depression and that eating so much junk food probably made him more depressed. Years later, Blinder said that the mention of junk food took about two minutes of the hours he spent on the stand. It is telling that in White's appeal, in which the doctors' testimony was reviewed, there is no mention of Twinkies or sugar or of any food whatsoever.[1]

Dan White's defense, then, was that he was too depressed to make rational decisions, not that a sugar high from a Twinkie made him go nuts. In the end, a jury found White guilty of two counts of voluntary manslaughter, and White was sentenced to less than eight years in prison.[2]

This is how a small, relatively insignificant mention of a dessert became inflated to the point that it escaped reams of expert testimony, shrugged off almost all relationship to the truth, and was transformed into an indictment of the legal system. Not only does one find the Twinkie defense still kicking around in popular opinion, but it is also proffered as truth by pundits, journalists, and scholars. What happened?

In any other trial, a brief mention of junk food may have gone unnoticed. However, the White shootings were extremely violent and unprecedented, and the victims were politically controversial. Harvey Milk was possibly the first openly homosexual elected public official. Milk, who was politically liberal, had persuaded Mayor Moscone to replace the conservative White with another liberal. After the verdict, rioters set fire to police cars and marched on City Hall. San Francisco's volatile political situation plus the sensational murders ensured that every word said during the trial would be scrutinized. Apparently, *Twinkie* especially stood out. In a column about the situation, *San Francisco Chronicle* writer Herb Caen mentioned that an attorney had called White's plea "the Twinkie insanity defense." Weeks later, the Twinkie defense was everywhere, and the truth was rarely to be seen again.

However, the plea of "diminished capacity," which had truly spared White more serious punishment, did not escape unharmed. In 1982 California voters approved a proposition to eliminate the defense.

Think About It

1. What do you think of White's sentence? If he had committed the murders in 1998, what would his sentence have been?
2. Were California voters right to eliminate the diminished-capacity defense?
3. Does the fact that the Twinkie defense is a myth make you think differently about this case?

[1]Carol Pogash, "Myth of the 'Twinkie Defense,'" *San Francisco Chronicle*, November 23, 2003, www.sfgate.com/cgi-bin/article.cgi?f=/c/a/2003/11/23/INGRE343501.DTL; *People* v. *White*, 117 Cal. App. 3d 270, 172 Cal. Rptr. (1981)

[2]White appealed and lost. He served a little more than five years, leaving prison in January 1985. He committed suicide that October.

wonder how their war experiences influenced their adjustment to civilian life. Post-traumatic stress syndrome was developed as an explanation, and before long this justification for crime was introduced into the criminal courts as a defense.

Finally, a related defense against criminal prosecution centers on the conflict of cultures experienced by many immigrants (see Case in Point 4.2). In some societies, it is a matter of family honor when a woman is seduced or raped. Brothers or fathers are honor bound to avenge the insult to the family by killing the man responsible, and in some extreme cases by also killing the woman involved. Although this behavior is clearly outside the criminal law in the United States, a defense attorney can argue that the defendant was not purposely breaking the law, but was rather upholding the traditional norms of his homeland. This defense seldom works because it is unreasonable to expect the U.S. criminal justice system to grant exception for every custom that someone may bring to this country. U.S. citizens and residents are protected by U.S. law but also subject to it. However, in at least one case, *People* v. *Aphaylath*, a client had his homicide conviction reversed by the court of appeals and got a new trial.

4.2 CASE IN POINT

PEOPLE V. APHAYLATH

THE CASE	THE POINT
People v. Aphaylath, 68 N.Y.2d 945; 502 N.E.2d 998; 510 N.Y.S.2d 83 (1986)	The value of expert testimony that provides evidence of a pertinent issue does not depend on whether the witness personally knows a defendant or a defendant's particular characteristics.

May Aphaylath, a Laotian refugee who had been living in the United States for about two years, had been married for one month when he killed his wife. According to Aphaylath, she had displayed affection for an unmarried ex-boyfriend and had received telephone calls from him. Aphaylath's attorney attempted to establish that the homicide was mitigated because Aphaylath was experiencing undue pressure in trying to assimilate to American culture and had been shamed by his wife's behavior. According to the defense, in Laotian tradition, a man is shamed when his wife displays affection for another man. The combination of these factors, Aphaylath stated, caused him to "snap" and kill his wife. The defense presented evidence about Laotian culture and refugee stress by cross-examining two prosecution witnesses. The trial judge excluded this evidence because the witnesses did not personally know Aphaylath or his personal characteristics.

Later, an appeals court stated that expert witnesses do not have to personally know a defendant for their testimony to be relevant. The court ruled that Aphaylath had been denied the chance to present evidence of Laotian culture that might have been relevant to his defense and ordered a new trial.

SUMMARY

1. The foundation for the criminal justice system is the criminal law. The rule of law is an important differentiating feature between democratic societies and authoritarian ones. There is a fairly consistent pattern of laws across the nation.

2. The U.S. criminal law developed in a sporadic and uneven fashion. It can trace its influences back to the Code of Hammurabi, which represents one of the first known attempts to put the law in writing.

3. The early North American colonies adopted the principles of English common law that called for cases to be decided on precedent. Common-law ideals are based on predictability, reliability, efficiency, and equality.

4. In addition to the common law, the inspirations for U.S. criminal law can be found in other sources. The federal and state constitutions provide one foundation for criminal law. The first 10

amendments, the Bill of Rights, are an especially important cornerstone of the criminal law. The U.S. Congress and state legislatures also provide statutes. The last source of the criminal law is administrative rules. A number of agencies that govern health, customs, the environment, and parole promulgate rules that are enforceable by the criminal law.

5. The criminal law represents the state against individuals, whereas the civil law is concerned with disputes between individuals. Civil law deals with contracts, personal property, maritime law, and commercial law.

6. Substantive law is concerned with the criminal acts committed by citizens and prescribes penalties. Procedural law is concerned with how criminal justice system officials enforce substantive law.

7. Case law comes from judicial decisions and requires judges to consider how previous cases have dealt with similar issues.

8. Felonies are considered the most serious type of criminal offense. Felonies include murder, rape, assault, larceny, and arson, as well as other offenses at the state and federal level. Misdemeanors are less serious than felonies and are subject to lighter penalties. Usually, the maximum incarceration for a misdemeanor is up to one year in jail.

9. The purpose of inchoate offenses is to deter individuals from planning and attempting wrongdoing. Conspiracy is an example of inchoate offenses.

10. Three elements must be present in order for an act to be labeled a criminal offense: the criminal act (*actus reus*); criminal intent (*mens rea*); and the relationship between *actus reus* and *mens rea* (concurrence). Together, these three elements constitute *corpus delicti*, or the "body of the crime."

11. Six arguments can be employed in the defense against a criminal indictment: my client did not do it; my client did it, but my client is not responsible because he or she is insane; my client did it but has a good excuse; my client did it but has a good reason; my client did it but should be acquitted because the police or the prosecutor cheated; my client did it but was influenced by outside forces.

KEY TERMS

actus reus 135
alibi 137
Bill of Rights 124
case law 130
civil law 127
Code of Hammurabi 120
common law 123
concurrence 135
corpus delicti 135

double jeopardy 128
habeas corpus 120
inchoate offense 134
infancy 140
insanity defense 137
Magna Carta 120
mens rea 135
penal code 124
precedent 123

procedural law 129
stare decisis 123
statute 124
statutory law 123
statutory rape 141
strict liability 136
substantive law 129
tort law 128

REVIEW QUESTIONS

1. What is the Code of Hammurabi? What is the Magna Carta?

2. How is common law different from statutory law?

3. What four issues guide precedent?

4. What are the three sources of law?

5. What are the first 10 amendments to the Constitution called?

6. What three criteria determine what behaviors are made criminal?

7. What effect does dual sovereignty have on the double jeopardy prohibition?

8. What is the difference between substantive law and procedural law? What is case law?

9. What three elements must be present for most acts to considered criminal offenses?

10. What six arguments can be employed in the defense against a criminal indictment?

SUGGESTED FURTHER READING

Bazelon, David L. *Questioning Authority: Justice and Criminal Law*. New York: Knopf, 1989.

Dershowitz, Alan M. *The Abuse Excuse and Other Cop-Outs, Sob Stories, and Evasions of Responsibility*. Boston: Little Brown, 1994.

Gardner, Thomas J., and Terry M. Anderson. *Criminal Law*. Belmont, CA: Wadsworth, 2006.

Johnson, Herbert A., and Nancy Travis Wolfe. *History of Criminal Justice*, 3rd ed. Cincinnati, OH: Anderson, 2003.

Nolan, Joseph R., and Jacqueline M. Nolan-Haley. *Black's Law Dictionary: Definitions of the Terms and Phrases of American and English Jurisprudence, Ancient and Modern*, 8th ed. St. Paul, MN: West, 2004.

Scheb, John M., and John M. Scheb II. *Criminal Law*. Belmont, CA: Wadsworth, 2006.

ENDNOTES

1. Aleksandr I. Solzhenitsyn, *The Gulag Archipelago 1918–1956* (New York: HarperCollins, 2002).

2. James Austin and John Irwin, *It's About Time: America's Imprisonment Binge*, 3rd ed. (Belmont, CA: Wadsworth, 2001).

3. Jeffrey Reiman, *The Rich Get Richer and the Poor Get Prison: Ideology, Class, and Criminal Justice*, 6th ed. (Boston: Allyn & Bacon, 2001).

4. Samuel Walker, *Sense and Nonsense about Crime and Drugs: A Policy Guide*, 4th ed. (Belmont, CA: West/Wadsworth, 1998).

5. Robert F. Meier and Gilbert Geis, *Victimless Crime? Prostitution, Drugs, Homosexuality, Abortion* (Los Angeles: Roxbury, 1997).

6. Samuel Walker, Cassia Spohn, and Miriam DeLone, *The Color of Justice: Race, Ethnicity, and Crime in America* (Belmont, CA: Wadsworth, 1996).

7. Herbert A. Johnson and Nancy Travis Wolfe, *History of Criminal Justice*, 3rd ed. (Cincinnati, OH: Anderson, 2003).

8. Claude Hermann and Walter Johns, "Babylonian Law: The Code of Hammurabi," *Encyclopedia Britannica*, 11th ed. (1910–1911), quoted www.fordham.edu/halsall/ancient]/hamcode.html.

9. L. W. King, trans., "The Code of Hammurabi," The Avalon Project at Yale Law School, www.yale.edu/lawweb/avalon/medieval/hammenu.htm.

10. Magna Carta, British Library, www.bl.uk/collections/treasures/magna.html.

11. Richard A. Wasserstrom, *The Judicial Decision: Toward a Theory of Legal Justification* (Stanford, CA: Stanford University Press, 1961).

12. Lief H. Carter, *Reason in Law*, 4th ed. (New York: HarperCollins, 1994).

13. Kermit Hall, *The Magic Mirror: Law in American History* (New York: Oxford University Press, 1991).

14. Richard J. Pierce Jr., Sidney A. Shapiro, and Paul R. Verkuil, *Administrative Law and Process*, 3rd ed. (New York: Foundation Press, 1999).

15. John C. Klotter, *Criminal Law*, 6th ed. (Cincinnati, OH: Anderson, 2001), 6.

16. Nils Christie, "Conflicts as Property," *British Journal of Criminology* 17 (1977): 1–15.

17. Jennifer Eastman, "A Constitutional Amendment for Victims: The Unexplored Possibility," in *Victimology: A Study of Crime Victims and Their Roles*, eds. Judith M. Sgarzi and Jack McDevitt (Upper Saddle River, NJ: Prentice Hall, 2003), 333–346.

18. Raymond J. Michalowski, *Order, Law, and Crime: An Introduction to Criminology* (New York: Random House, 1985), 139–141.

19. Frank A. Schubert, *Criminal Law: The Basics* (Los Angeles: Roxbury, 2004), 101–103.

20. Ibid., 10–13.

21. James R. Acker and David C. Brody, *Criminal Procedure: A Contemporary Perspective* (Gaithersburg, MD: Aspen, 1999).

22. Charles Rembar, *The Law of the Land: The Evolution of Our Legal System* (New York: Simon & Schuster, 1980).

23. Schubert, *Criminal Law*.

24. Eric Hickey, *Serial Murderers and Their Victims* (Belmont, CA: Wadsworth, 1991), 37–45.

25. Klotter, *Criminal Law*, 514.

26. Ibid., 547.

27. William G. Doerner and Steven P. Lab, *Victimology*, 2nd ed. (Cincinnati, OH: Anderson, 1998), 118–119.

28. Klotter, *Criminal Law*, 540–542.

29. "Abscam," *Columbia Encyclopedia*, 6th ed., quoted at Bartleby.com, www.bartleby.com/65/e-/E-Abscam .html.

30. Sharon LaFraniere, "Barry Arrested on Cocaine Charges in Undercover FBI, Police Operation," *Washington Post*, January 19, 1990.

31. Jim Newton, "Koon, Powell Get 2½ Years in Prison," *Los Angeles Times*, August 5, 1993.

32. Lenore E. Walker, *The Battered Woman* (New York: HarperCollins, 1979).

PART TWO
Enforcing the Law

CHAPTER 5

History and Organization of Law Enforcement

Objectives

1. Discuss how the English heritage of policing produced three enduring features of American policing: limited police authority, local control, and a fragmented system.

2. Discuss the problem of jurisdiction.

3. Compare and contrast the federal, state, and local levels of law enforcement.

4. Discuss the pros and cons of technological and social changes on U.S. law enforcement.

5. Discuss the effects of research and new ideas on U.S. law enforcement.

The institution of the police is a relatively new phenomenon. Having an agency devoted solely to maintaining order and apprehending violators of the law entails a degree of occupational specialization that is available only in highly developed societies. However, like physicians, teachers, and farmers, law enforcement officers are needed for communities to function effectively. As long as human beings have lived in large groups, there has been a need for social control. Much of this control was exerted through informal means, such as censure from families, friends, and other social institutions. However, as social groups became larger and less personally interconnected, formal means became required to deal with situations that did not respond to informal means, such as legal disputes and the control of violent people.

Although we commonly think of policing as a stable institution built on unchanging tradition, the police are, in fact, subject to rapid social change and constant challenges.[1] The way policing is done in the 21st century is the result of a long, uneven development that continues even today.

A BRIEF HISTORY OF THE POLICE

One function of society is the maintenance of social control. Those who break the law are subject to judgment and penalties. The police are vested with the responsibility of detecting crime and bringing lawbreakers to justice. By studying how the police have evolved through the centuries, we can fully appreciate the necessary but delicate function of law enforcement.

Police in Ancient Times

The law enforcement function has existed in one form or another for thousands of years. Police in early history usually derived from a military connected with a government or ruler, or from the community when citizens joined in informal groups to protect themselves.

In the seventh century B.C.E., the Roman emperor Augustus created one of the earliest recorded organized police forces. There were three groups of police, who were part of the army and were commanded by the urban prefect. The city was divided into 14 *regiones* or wards, which in turn were divided into *vici* or precincts. Police also developed in other cultures independent of Rome. In 17th-century Japan, for example, each town had a military official, the samurai warrior, whose duties included acting as judge and chief of police. In Russia from 1881 to the revolution in 1917, the tsars' *Okhranka* was a police force that dealt with political terrorism and revolutionary matters.

Policing in Early England

The nascent form of policing that most directly led to that of modern U.S. policing was the **frankpledge system.** The frankpledge system began in Anglo-Saxon England and continued after the Norman conquest in 1066, enduring until the 19th century. This system divided a community into *tithings*, or groups of 10 men who were responsible for the conduct of the group and ensured that a member charged with breaking the law would show up in court. The tithing was supervised by a *tithingman*. The tithings were collected into groups of 10, or a hundred, which was headed by a **hundred-man.** The hundred-man served as an administrator and judge. The Normans updated the frankpledge system by adding the ***comes stabuli***, or **constable**. Originally part of the royal court, the constable became, by the late 13th century, an officer attached to manors and parishes. Constables oversaw the **watch-and-ward system** that guarded the city's or town's gates at night.

An office that existed before the Norman conquest was that of the **shire reeve** or **sheriff.** The person holding this office led the shire's (or county's) military forces and judged criminal and civil cases. Later, the sheriff's duties became more restricted, and

frankpledge system
An early form of English government that divided communities into groups of 10 men who were responsible for the group's conduct and ensured that a member charged with breaking the law appeared in court.

hundred-man
The head of a group of 10 men who served as an administrator and judge.

constable (comes stabuli)
The head of law enforcement for large districts in early England. In the modern United States, a constable serves areas such as rural townships and is usually elected.

watch-and-ward system
An early English system overseen by the constable in which a watchman guarded a city's or town's gates at night.

sheriff (shire reeve)
The shire reeve led the English shire's military forces and judged cases.

his job included trying minor criminal offenses, investigating offenses within the shire, and questioning suspects. (The office of sheriff in England continues until this day.) As for the actual nitty-gritty job of law enforcement, this was up to the citizens, who were expected to raise the alarm, or **hue and cry,** and catch the person accused of breaking the law. If there were no witnesses to an offense, the victim alone was responsible for identifying the perpetrator.

In 1285 these efforts were fortified and set to record by the *Statute of Winchester*. The statute set forth, in part, that anyone could make an arrest; that it was every citizen's duty, especially the constable's, to keep the peace; that a hue and cry must be raised to apprehend an offender and that every citizen was expected to participate; and that it was the constable's job to present the suspect in court.

Although this system lasted for hundreds of years, it had serious problems. For example, many citizens resented watchman duty, and many were not good at it. Some were too elderly to be effective; some were drunk when standing night watch, and some were lawbreakers themselves. In some ways, it was like asking the fox to guard the henhouse. This type of policing was riddled with inefficiencies and corruption. Likewise, it did little or nothing to prevent crime.[2] Watchmen also spent a great deal of time hiding, as it had become a common sport of rich young men to taunt and terrorize them. Consequently, the streets were dark and unsafe, and only the rich who had armed themselves or had bodyguards had any degree of safety. Those who had money hired substitutes to perform their watchman duties and private guards to protect their property. Those who could not recover their stolen property often hired "thieftakers," a sort of bounty hunter who went after the suspected thief and attempted to recover the stolen property.

THE GIN EFFECT   A pivotal factor that advanced the development of law enforcement was the invention of gin.[3] Before that time, most citizens drank beer, ale, or wine. Because of a grain surplus, the agricultural interests saw the mass consumption of gin as a way to profit from their excess grain. Hard liquor had been expensive and was consumed mainly by the rich, who engaged in habits of brawling and killing.[4] Gin democratized drunkenness and brought all kinds of new problems to London.

> Public drunkenness became a commonplace sight, and drink-crazed mobs often roamed the city. The streets of London, never safe, were now filled with people whose behavior was unpredictable and occasionally quite violent. Not surprisingly, the gin craze was accompanied by a great rise in violent crimes and theft.[5]

The government responded to these problems by hiring more watchmen. Unfortunately, this just fed conditions for greater corruption. As the government proceeded to get tough on lawbreakers, the rich continued to hire *linkmen* or bodyguards, arm themselves with pistols, and move to new parts of the city, which resulted in the type of residential segregation that we see in our major cities today.[6] The government attempted to deal with these problems by licensing the gin outlets, which proved largely ineffective because of the further corruption it encouraged. Only after taxes made gin expensive did its consumption fall.

RISE OF ORGANIZED POLICING   Another tactic to combat the increase in crime was developed around 1748 by magistrates Henry Fielding and his brother Sir John Fielding. The **Bow Street Runners** represented a more centralized system than the watch-and-ward arrangement, and members were required to patrol their areas rather than just sit in their watch boxes. Fielding, for a brief time, even organized a mounted patrol of the highways. The Bow Street Runners did not last long after Henry Fielding died, but his innovations were the first time that the police were mobile.[7]

In 1798 the West India Trading Company created the first professional, salaried police force in London, the **Thames River Police.** This private police force, formed to prevent thefts from the port, was different from the frankpledge system in two major ways. First, its officers patrolled to prevent crime, and second, they were salaried

hue and cry
In early England, the alarm that citizens were required to raise on the witness or discovery of a criminal offense.

Bow Street Runners
A police organization created circa 1748 by magistrates Henry Fielding and his brother Sir John Fielding whose members went on patrol, rather than sitting at a designated post.

Thames River Police
A private police force created by the West India Trading Company in 1798 that represented the first professional, salaried police force in London.

This 18th-century illustration, "Gin Lane," represents the liquor's harmful effects on society. Alcohol was popular in part because the drinking water was not safe.

Source: Getty Images, Inc./Hulton Archive Photos.

BEER STREET AND GIN LANE.

Metropolitan Police Act
Created in 1829 by Sir Robert Peel, the first successful bill to create a permanent, public police force.

and not allowed to accept any other payments. The police force worked so well that two years later the government added it to the public payroll.

Citizens accustomed to a system in which they were basically responsible for themselves were suspicious of a standing police force. However, London's social problems were mounting as a result of poverty and a burgeoning population. Finally, in 1829 Sir Robert Peel sponsored the **Metropolitan Police Act,** the first successful bill to create a permanent, public police force. Like the Thames River Police, these "new police" carried out preventive patrols and were paid regular salaries. They were also uniformed, and like the watchmen of old, kept a lookout for fires, called out the time, and lighted public lamps.

bobbies
A slang term for the police force created in 1829 by Sir Robert Peel's Metropolitan Police Act, derived from Bob, the short form of Robert.

These police were viewed as a civilizing instrument whose effort and example would make for better civil relations in society. The police, who were nicknamed **bobbies** after their founder's nickname of "Bob," were expected to adhere to a strict military-type discipline based on Peel's nine principles of policing (see Criminal Justice Reference 5.1). The bobbies set a new standard of police professionalism; however, their jurisdiction was limited to the city of London. It was not until 1856 that the rural provinces were required to establish police forces.

Policing in the United States

Like many aspects of American culture, policing has its roots in English tradition. Although the police have developed differently in England than they have here, some commonalities are worth examining. According to Samuel Walker and Charles Katz, "the English heritage contributed three enduring features to American policing":[8]

1. **Limited police authority.** As opposed to other countries in Europe, the Anglo-American tradition of policing places a good deal of emphasis on the rights and liberties of the individual.

5.1   CRIMINAL JUSTICE REFERENCE

The Nine Principles of Policing

The following principles appear in the appendix of Charles Reith's *A New Study of Police History* (1956). Although popularly attributed to Sir Robert Peel, the principles were probably written by Charles Rowan and Richard Mayne, whom Peel appointed to direct and organize the newly created Metropolitan Police.

1. To prevent crime and disorder, as an alternative to their repression by military force and severity of legal punishment.
2. To recognize always that the power of the police to fulfill their functions and duties is dependent on public approval of their existence, actions, and behavior and on their ability to secure and maintain public respect.
3. To recognize always that to secure and maintain the respect and approval of the public means also the securing of the willing co-operation of the public in the task of securing observance of laws.
4. To recognize always that the extent to which the co-operation of the public can be secured diminishes proportionately the necessity of the use of physical force and compulsion for achieving police objectives.
5. To seek and preserve public favor, not by pandering to public opinion; but by constantly demonstrating absolutely impartial service to law, in complete independence of policy, and without regard to the justice or injustice of the substance of individual laws, by ready offering of individual service and friendship to all members of the public without regard to their wealth or social standing, by ready exercise of courtesy and friendly good humor; and by ready offering of individual sacrifice in protecting and preserving life.
6. To use physical force only when the exercise of persuasion, advice, and warning is found to be insufficient to obtain public co-operation to an extent necessary to secure observance of law or to restore order; and to use only the minimum degree of physical force which is necessary on any particular occasion for achieving a police objective.
7. To maintain at all times a relationship with the public that gives reality to the historic tradition that the police are the public and that the public are the police; the police being only members of the public who are paid to give full time attention to duties which are incumbent on every citizen in the interests of community welfare and existence.
8. To recognize always the need for strict adherence to police-executive functions, and to refrain from even seeming to usurp the powers of the judiciary of avenging individuals or the State, and of authoritatively judging guilt and punishing the guilty.
9. To recognize always that the test of police efficiency is the absence of crime and disorder, and not the visible evidence of police action in dealing with them.

Source: Charles Reith, *A New Study of Police History* (Edinburgh: Oliver & Boyd, 1956), 121–142, 287–288; Civitas: The Institute for the Study of Civil Society, "Principles of Good Policing," www.civitas.org.uk/pubs/policeNine.php.

2. **Local control.** Law enforcement agencies are, for the most part, local, city, or county institutions. The United States does not have a national police force. We do have many state and federal law enforcement agencies, but they are not like the national police forces found in many parts of the world where control is highly centralized in the federal government.

3. **Fragmented system.** There are more than 18,000 separate law enforcement agencies in the United States, ranging from federal (FBI, Secret Service) to state (highway patrol) to local (city police, county sheriff). These agencies are loosely coordinated, and the state and local agencies have little oversight from the federal level.[9]

Many differences between the United States and England affected the development of their respective policing styles. One was the lack of a single, coherent philosophy. Whereas the English police were unified under the vision of Sir Robert Peel, local police organizations in the United States formed their own policies and procedures. Another factor was the large and ever-expanding political geography of the United States. As stakes were claimed and territories formed, government and law enforcement followed slowly. This led to the phenomenon of the "Wild West." The further the country developed from the cities and seats of government on the East Coast, the less controllable it became. A third factor was immigration. The constituency of the United States was—and is—in constant flux, resulting in cities, states, and territories filled with people representing a vast array of cultures and languages. Conversely, the English police of the day were responsible for a static political and physical geography that had a homogeneous culture and language.

"Peel Fights Night Watchmen."
A satirical English cartoon
depicts Sir Robert Peel
fighting a group of night
watchmen.

Source: CORBIS-NY

THE 19TH CENTURY   Jurisdictional difficulties and labor troubles gave rise to some of the nation's most famous private police. Laws were passed that allowed companies to maintain or contract with their own police forces and agencies. Pennsylvania's Coal and Iron Police became famous for its strong-arm antilabor activities. The Pinkerton National Detective Agency, founded in 1850 by Scottish political refugee Allan Pinkerton, was used by railroad and coal companies for protection against thieves and labor activists.

As the century waned, urban police became an integral part of their communities—so integral, in fact, that many police officers began to work for the political bosses of their communities. For example, officers would, through various measures, help ensure the election of "their" candidates. Or they would accept money in return for not enforcing certain laws. Two of the most important cities in which this type of activity—and its reform—occurred were New York and Chicago.

NEW YORK CITY INFLUENCE   Informal policing began in New York City in 1625 when the Dutch settlement was called New Amsterdam. There, a "schout fiscal" or "sheriff attorney" had such duties as settling disputes and warning the colonists of fire. From 1609 to 1664 a group of men called the "Rattle Watch" patrolled at night, carrying loud rattles to raise an alarm if anything was amiss. The city's first professional police force of 800 men was organized in 1845. Their copper badges of eight-pointed stars were so distinctive that civilians nicknamed the officers "coppers," which was later shortened to "cops."

LONDON VERSUS NEW YORK   Although the English police systems and those in the United States share a common heritage, some distinct differences arose from the social and political cultures of the two countries. In an article titled "Cops and Bobbies, 1830–1870," Wilber Miller discussed how policing developed along different lines in London and New York.[10] Miller argued that a major distinction between the two systems of law enforcement lay in the individual patrolman's authority. The London officer had an impersonal authority that rested on the limited discretion granted by the government. The New York patrolman, by contrast, had a much broader latitude of discretion, giving him a personal basis for his authority. For instance, by 1860 New York officers were allowed to carry revolvers to protect themselves from heavily armed offenders, making New York patrolmen a powerful force to be reckoned with. The power of the London bobby resided in the citizens' belief that the officer represented a collective power rather than an individual one.

THE CHICAGO INFLUENCE   The law enforcement environment in Chicago at the beginning of the 20th century is closely related to the differences in the supervision styles of the London police and the New York police. Chicago's official police force was created around 1855 and reorganized several times over the next six decades until 1913. The city's police officers were not trained in the law, and the criminal justice system did not emphasize legal procedure. Chicago police had four particular orientations to the law:

1. Police and courts were highly decentralized and often reflected, in important ways, the values of local communities. Democratic sensitivities rather than legal norms were expected to guide police behavior and check abuses.
2. The police, as part of a larger political system, were a significant resource at the command of local organizations. Police, courts, and prosecutors provided political leaders with patronage jobs, were a source of favors for constituents, and were important agencies for collecting money that lubricated political campaigns.
3. Criminal justice institutions operated as rackets, providing the means by which police officers and other officials earned extra income.
4. Police officers and other criminal justice system personnel developed informal systems of operation that reflected their own subcultures and organizational needs. These informal methods of operation bore, at best, only an indirect relationship to the formal legal system.[11]

The political nature of the Chicago police in the early 20th century resulted in a system in which the police took bribes, solicited votes, harassed the homeless, beat suspects, and assisted gamblers. They also performed many duties now normally considered outside the responsibilities of crime control, such as taking injured people to the hospital, mediating family quarrels, rounding up stray dogs, returning lost children to their parents, and removing dead horses from city streets. One of the hallmarks of the professionalization of law enforcement that emerged over the past hundred years is the degree to which the police mission has become less informal and more legally constrained.

VIGILANTE POLICING   The development of professional police departments in large metropolitan areas is important, but it is by no means the only heritage that contributed to the development of the police in the United States. In rural areas and small towns across the nation, particularly in the South and West, the vigilante tradition was part of American life. In the newly developed areas of the frontier, the normal mechanisms of social control emerged slowly. The normal constraints on deviant behavior exercised by churches, schools, and cohesive community life were absent, and the formal system of law enforcement was inadequate. As citizens struggled to maintain order in newly settled areas, they took the law into their own hands by engaging in vigilante actions. (See Focus on Ethics 5.1 for a modern vigilante scenario.)

Vigilante committees were usually established by the elites of society to protect property and social order from rogues and criminals.[12] The justice meted out by the vigilantes was a rough one that included, but was not limited to, flogging, expulsion, and killing. These actions served not only as punishments, but also as a warning to others that a system of social order existed that everyone was expected to obey.[13]

Vigilantism had its advantages and disadvantages. It was socially constructive in that it established order in the community and prevented anarchy and lawlessness whereby

5.1 FOCUS *on* ETHICS

RIGHTEOUS VENGEANCE?

As a police officer you have been on the trail of a serial child molester who frequents the city's parks. You have a good idea of who it is, but this suspect has been smart enough to elude arrest and conviction for more than 10 years. This morning you found your suspect dead, lying in a pool of blood with his skull crushed. Close to the body you discover a baseball bat with the name of the son of a prominent politician printed on the bat handle.

You know that this 17-year-old boy was a victim of molestation 10 years ago when this problem first surfaced in the community. Your suspicion is that the boy killed the molester, but you also believe that the suspect needed killing and that the boy did the community a great service. If you hide the bat, there will be no way to trace the offense to this young man, who you think had a good reason to commit this act. If you enter the bat into evidence, the boy could be convicted of murder and sent to prison for a long time.

Because you have twin 8-year-old sons, you are happy this perpetrator will no longer prowl the city parks. Can you turn a blind eye to this offense? Should you protect this otherwise good boy? If you do hide the bat, should you tell his father so that he can protect you if you are found out, or maybe because you think he can help get you promoted? You know that the correct procedure would be to arrest the boy, but a little voice inside your head is whispering something about a "greater justice," and you are tempted to hide the bat.

What Do You Do?

1. Arrest the boy and let the criminal justice system take its course.
2. Hide the bat and protect the boy.
3. Hide the bat, protect the boy, and tell his father the truth.

---

thieves, gamblers, drunkards, and rapists were free to break the law. Social order benefited everyone, both the wealthy and impoverished, but it should be noted that the vigilante movements were concerned mostly with the interests of the wealthy.[14] In some places, antivigilante movements emerged as rival local political parties or extended families vied for control of the government. Respectable men joined in fighting vigilantes, not because they had any sympathy for rogues and outlaws, but because they saw certain elements of society using the vigilantes to promote their own economic advantage rather than maintain order. Additionally, some of these vigilante movements were to become outright terrorist organizations, such as the Ku Klux Klan. Even though these types of organizations had broad support in some segments of the community, they promoted judicial, racial, and religious injustice in the South and West.[15]

As some of these vigilante movements were transformed into actual police agencies, a double standard arose that was applied to the disenfranchised in society. The Texas Rangers, organized in 1835, were among the first advanced police agencies in the United States. However, the Mexican and American Indian citizens of Texas were subject to laws that were enforced to benefit the Anglo cattle barons. Members of these minority groups were killed with impunity because the Rangers tended to "shoot first and ask questions later."[16]

This discussion of law enforcement in U.S. history goes against many of our ideas of life on the frontier. Television and film have provided us with a highly romanticized view of law and order during this period, and the idea that the good guys always wore white hats and had to battle the "bad" American Indians and Mexicans ignores the reality of the power politics of the past. Of course, there were outlaws, criminals, and threats to the public order that required citizens to band together to protect themselves and others. What should be remembered here, however, is that vigilante groups almost always served the needs of those who had power, high positions in the social structure, and property (see Crosscurrents 5.1).

Introduction of Police Professionalism

At the start of the 20th century, law enforcement in the United States was caught in a web of inefficiency, corruption, and special-interest politics.[17] The police were an arm of the interests that used the resources, budgets, labor, and authority of the city to control the lower classes and to amass power and wealth. City after city could be seen using local government institutions, such as the police, in favor of the elites.[18] Spurred by muckraking journalists, the cities began to correct some of the most obvious inequities in how citizens were treated by government and business. Politicians and heads of industry realized that maintaining popular support for the existing political and economic system required some changes. Some scholars contend that the resulting progressive movement simply stabilized the grip of the elites on the institutions of society rather than producing fundamental changes, but it is fair to say that this period saw a surge of useful reform efforts.[19] One such effort was the Pendleton Civil Service Act of 1883. A response to public frustration with incompetence and corruption within the federal government, the purpose of the act, according to its text, was to "regulate and improve the civil service of the United States." The act basically formed a civil service system that did away with patronage and administered employment and promotions based on merit rather than political connections. This legislation shook much of the corruption out of the U.S. civil service bureaucracy, including the nation's budding police forces.

THE WICKERSHAM COMMISSION AND AUGUST VOLLMER   The work of August Vollmer, a police chief of Berkeley, California, is a highlight of the reform movement. In 1931 he wrote the Wickersham Commission report, which set the police reform agenda for the rest of the century. Vollmer is important to the police professionalization movement because he instituted many policies and practices that still influence law enforcement today. He was among the first police chiefs to recruit college graduates, and he organized the first police-science courses at the University of California. Many of his students went on to become police chiefs in other cities, where they extended his reform policies.

According to Samuel Walker and Charles M. Katz, Vollmer's police reform movement, which dominated the law enforcement agenda through the 1960s, focused on six issues:

1. Policing is defined as a profession in which the police serve the entire community on a nonpartisan basis.

2. Policing should be free of political influence.

3. Qualified executives should lead the police. This means that the chiefs of large cities should have some experience running large organizations.

4. The standards for being a policeman should be raised. Law enforcement personnel should be screened for intelligence, health, and moral character. (Although slow in developing, this increase in the quality of personnel resulted in specialized police academies where professional training is required.)

5. Modern principles of scientific management should be introduced that involve centralizing command structures so the chief can better control officers.

6. Specialized units such as traffic, juvenile, and vice should be developed to increase the size and complexity of police agencies and allow officers to focus on particular types of crime. (This increase in complexity had the benefit of opening up law enforcement to women, who were originally hired only for juvenile units.)[20]

Other features of the progressive movement in policing included an emphasis on technology to help the police do their job. Of particular importance was the introduction of the patrol car, or as Vollmer called it, "the swift angel of death."[21] Improved communications, advanced record-keeping techniques, and the creation of crime analysis laboratories were all new uses of technology that were introduced to law enforcement during this move toward professionalism.

Police professionalization also introduced preventive strategies that dealt with high-risk individuals such as juveniles and the unemployed before they had a chance to become career criminals. The police also engaged in public relations activities to

CrossCurrents

Frontier Justice

The American West presented an unusual chapter in the history of U.S. law enforcement. Unlike the Old World, where people had divided lands and developed societies and laws over thousands of years, North America was largely a blank slate, with only a relatively vulnerable population of American Indians. As pioneers flooded into the "wide open spaces" of the West seeking land, economic opportunities, or distance from government, the frontier outgrew the ability of the young country to formally police it.

Apprehending offenders, or even awareness of crime, was much easier in the tight-knit urban East than in the expanses of the West, where settlements were miles apart and those who had broken the law could simply disappear into the wilderness. Many lawless types were attracted to the frontier for its weak law enforcement, feeble and sometimes corrupt governments, and vast spaces. Compounding law enforcement troubles were the new offenses that came with Western settlement: pilfered livestock; illegally grazed ranch lands; and racial stress among Anglos, Mexicans, and American Indians. The transportation of goods also provided new opportunities for crime. Stagecoaches and, later, trains were easy targets for outlaws, and the need for protecting these vehicles gave rise to new forms of private policing. In the end, the challenge of enforcing the law on the frontier gave the United States some of its enduring law enforcement institutions.

Private Citizens and Vigilance Committees

The first official Anglo police agency was formed in 1831 in the town of San Felipe de Austin, Texas, with the establishment of a community patrol that, much like the old English watch-and-ward system, alerted citizens to danger.[1] In the beginning, these patrols sometimes employed men who were not far from being lawbreakers themselves, but they were rough, tough, and the only ones willing to volunteer for the job. Later, more modern-type police organizations were formed, complete with well-paid officers and responsibilities to local governments and citizens. Still, official police often allowed ordinary citizens to expedite their own policing duties. In some areas, one private person could arrest another or might be deputized if there was a shortage of regular officers.

Vigilante groups became common, springing up in response to social undesirables as varied as lawbreakers and labor organizers. These groups usually operated with the approval of local law enforcement, or instead of it, if no official agency existed. In Colorado, vigilantism was made law, with citizens who were appointed to "examine into . . . all criminal violations of the laws. . . ."[2] Other vigilante groups included Arizona's "Outlaw Exterminators" and Texas's "Partizan Rangers."[3] Violence in Dodge City in 1873 led to the formation of a vigilance committee that, although at first it brought peace to the town, later caused even more trouble. (The sheriffs elected in response to the vigilance committee fiasco included Bat Masterson and Wyatt Earp.)

Rangers

Although the frontier eventually became more settled, there was still the problem of keeping the peace and ensuring some kind of justice among populations that were scattered across hundreds of miles of territory. To address this problem, several states created early forms of state police known as "rangers." Arizona, Nevada, and New Mexico all had rangers, but the most famous of these organizations is the Texas Rangers, the oldest statewide law enforcement organization in North America.[4]

The first Rangers were assembled in 1823 by Stephen F. Austin to protect Anglo Texas colonists. In 1835 a resolution made the Rangers official. For the next 180 years, the state of Texas depended, to varying degrees, on bands of men called "rangers" for law enforcement and public safety. The first Rangers protected settlers and tracked stolen horses, cattle, and escaped slaves.[5] After 1848 the U.S. Army took over protection of the Texas frontier, and a brief resurgence of the Rangers before the Civil War was drained by that conflict as Rangers became soldiers. Not until 1874, after the Rangers had driven off the last of the American Indians and the conflict with the Mexicans had quieted, did the Rangers become a statewide police force.[6]

Hired Guns

Doing business in the Wild West was often dangerous. Merchants and corporations could not trust the uneven, sometimes corrupt, law enforcement organizations to provide adequate protection, so they hired their own police. These police were not confined to railroads and stagecoaches; ranchers employed range inspectors, and mining and oil companies hired their own security. In towns and villages, business owners would form special "merchants' police."[7] Later, Allan Pinkerton's private force was hired to protect railroads and conduct criminal investigations, and even guarded Buffalo Bill's Wild West Show.[8] Another famous organization, Wells Fargo, protected stagecoaches, steamboats, and railroads. Some of the agencies, through violence and corruption, eventually wore out their welcome. Pinkerton, for example, was accused of bribing juries, employing assassins, and violently breaking strikes.[9] Several improve their image in the community. Such programs as "junior police" were instituted to give boys positive interactions with law enforcement and to provide role models.

Finally, the move toward police professionalism involved removing functions not normally concerned with crime control. The police had been sort of a "catch-all" agency that, along with catching lawbreakers, chased stray dogs, licensed various enterprises, and enforced minor morals laws such as those against kissing in public. These functions did little to protect society, and they offered too many opportunities for selective enforcement and corruption.[22] Enforcing dress codes or purely administrative regulations became considered an inefficient use of police resources, so these activities were shifted to other means of social control, leaving the police with the sole job of maintaining public order and controlling crime.

OTHER REFORMERS   August Vollmer was not the only notable police reformer. One of his students, Orlando W. Wilson, became the police chief of Wichita, Kansas, dean of the School of Criminology at the University of California, and later the superintendent of the Chicago Police Department. Wilson made the police more efficient by using a workload formula that assigned officers based on the amount of reported crime and calls for service. He is credited with accelerating the shift from foot patrol to automobile patrol.

Perhaps the most famous of the law enforcement administrators who championed professionalism was the Federal Bureau of Investigation's J. Edgar Hoover. Hoover built the FBI into one of the premier law enforcement agencies in the world with his skillful political maneuvering, masterful public relations efforts, and surveillance of not only lawbreakers, but also political rivals, politicians, and U.S. presidents. His reputation is a mixed bag of progressive reformer and repressive tyrant. There is little doubt that the agency he created is a cornerstone of law enforcement in the United States, but the abuses of the constitutional rights of citizens that he authorized and used as leverage to keep himself in power are as disturbing as they are legendary. Under Hoover's direction, FBI agents harassed civil rights and antiwar activists, ignored white-collar crime, and intimidated politicians.[23] Nevertheless, the FBI's crime labs, National Training Academy, Behavioral Analysis Unit (made famous by the movie *The Silence of the Lambs*), and administration of the *Uniform Crime Reports* all attest to its mission to bring coordination and professionalism to U.S. law enforcement.

Attempts to professionalize both police practices and police ethics have been a long-term concern for police reformers. (See Case in Point 5.1 for *Miranda* v. *Arizona*,

5.1 CASE IN POINT

MIRANDA V. ARIZONA

THE CASE	THE POINT
Miranda v. Arizona, 384 U.S. 436, 86 S.Ct. 1602 (1966)	*This decision set forth that confessions made by suspects who have not been advised of their due process rights cannot be used as evidence.*

Ernesto Miranda was arrested in 1963 on suspicion of rape and kidnapping. Police interrogated Miranda, a Mexican immigrant, for several hours without advising him of his right to an attorney or permitting him to speak with one. Miranda signed a written confession and was later convicted and sentenced to 60 years. Miranda's case, and several others like it, were appealed, and the Supreme Court agreed with their contention that the suspects' right to due process had been violated because they had not been advised of their rights to an attorney or to remain silent. The 1966 decision set forth that confessions made by suspects who have not been advised of their due process rights cannot be used as evidence. *Miranda* was upheld by the Supreme Court in June 2000, in *Dickerson* v. *United States*. In that case, one of the questions considered by the court was the constitutionality of a statute enacted by Congress in 1968 that states that confessions are admissible if "voluntarily given." The court held that its constitutional decisions may not be overruled by Acts of Congress.

The Miranda warning is as follows:

1. You have the right to remain silent and refuse to answer any questions.
2. Anything you say may be used against you in a court of law.
3. As we discuss this matter, you have a right to stop answering my questions at any time you desire.
4. You have a right to a lawyer before speaking to me, to remain silent until you can talk to him or her, and to have him or her present when you are being questioned.
5. If you want a lawyer but cannot afford one, one will be provided to you without cost.
6. Do you understand each of these rights I have explained to you?
7. Now that I have advised you of your rights, are you willing to answer my questions without an attorney present?

an important step in police professionalization.) These commissions and reports demonstrate that, as an institution, law enforcement has been historically plagued by political interference, corruption, and lack of resources. Nevertheless, police and elected officials continue in their efforts to modernize, professionalize, and humanize law enforcement agencies. There have been flagrant abuses in the past, and there will always be individual officers who exceed their authority or even behave in a criminal fashion, but most law enforcement officers are honest public servants who do a difficult and demanding job.

MODERN POLICE ORGANIZATION

Law enforcement agencies are influenced by their structural components. By this we mean that the organization of police departments in terms of command structure, degree of centralized decision making, the expressed focus of their mission, and how success is measured all determine what type of occupational culture will exist. The potential exists for a wide range of organizational differences among police departments. However, police departments vary little in how they are organized. With the exception of some small departments, most law enforcement agencies hearken back to Peel's model with a structure based on a quasi-military template complete with uniforms, ranks, hierarchical chains of command, and centralized decision making. For examples of the organization of modern police departments in small and large cities, see Figures 5-1 and 5-2.

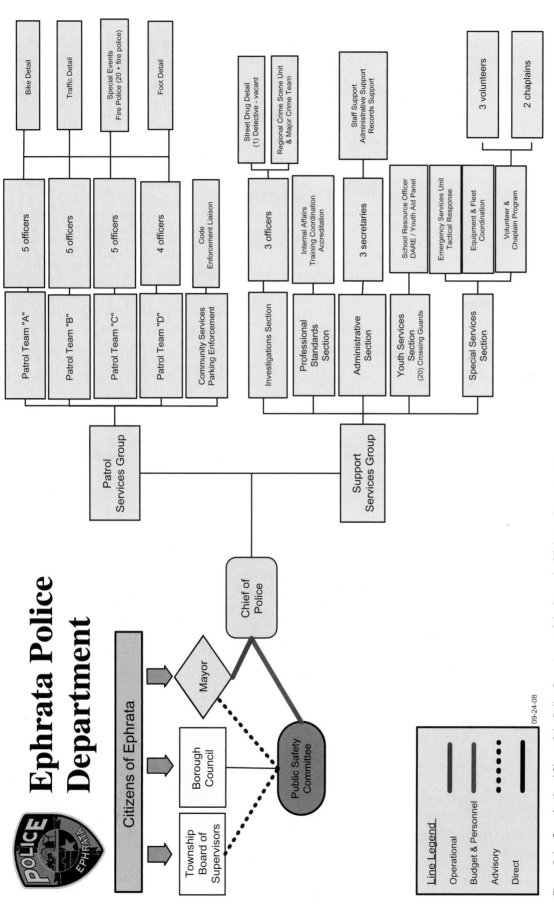

Figure 5-1 Organizational Chart of the Police Department of the Borough of Ephrata, Pennsylvania

Source: Courtesy of Borough of Ephrata, www.ephrataboro.org/ephrataboro/cwp/view.asp?A=6&Q=536483.

Figure 5-2 **Organization of the Los Angeles, California, Police Department as of April 1, 2008**

Source: Courtesy of Los Angeles Police Department.

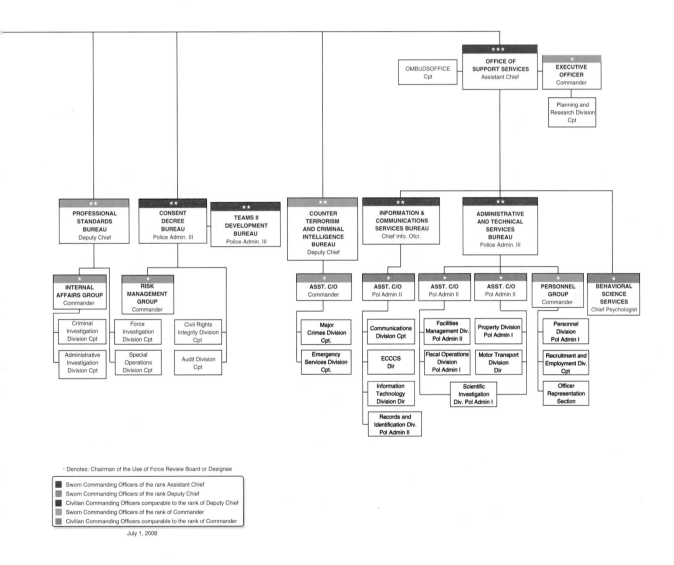

OMBUDSOFFICE
Cpt

★★★
OFFICE OF
SUPPORT SERVICES
Assistant Chief

★
EXECUTIVE
OFFICER
Commander

Planning and
Research Division
Cpt

★★
PROFESSIONAL
STANDARDS
BUREAU
Deputy Chief

★★
CONSENT
DECREE
BUREAU
Police Admin. III

★★
TEAMS II
DEVELOPMENT
BUREAU
Police Admin. III

★★
COUNTER
TERRORISM
AND CRIMINAL
INTELLIGENCE
BUREAU
Deputy Chief

★★
INFORMATION &
COMMUNICATIONS
SERVICES BUREAU
Chief Info. Ofcr.

★★
ADMINISTRATIVE
AND TECHNICAL
SERVICES
BUREAU
Police Admin. III

★
INTERNAL
AFFAIRS GROUP
Commander

★
RISK
MANAGEMENT
GROUP
Commander

★
ASST. C/O
Commander

★
ASST. C/O
Pol Admin II

★
ASST. C/O
Pol Admin II

★
ASST. C/O
Pol Admin II

★
PERSONNEL
GROUP
Commander

★
BEHAVIORAL
SCIENCE
SERVICES
Chief Psychologist

Criminal
Investigation
Division Cpt

Force
Investigation
Division Cpt

Civil Rights
Integrity Division
Cpt

Major
Crimes Division
Cpt.

Communications
Division Cpt

Facilities
Management Div.
Pol Admin II

Property Division
Pol Admin I

Personnel
Division
Pol Admin I

Administrative
Investigation
Division Cpt

Special
Operations
Division Cpt

Audit Division
Cpt

Emergency
Services Division
Cpt.

ECCCS
Dir

Fiscal Operations
Division
Pol Admin I

Motor Transport
Division
Dir

Recruitment and
Employment Div.
Cpt

Information
Technology
Division Dir

Scientific
Investigation
Div. Pol Admin I

Officer
Representation
Section

Records and
Identification Div.
Pol Admin II

· Denotes: Chairman of the Use of Force Review Board or Designee

Sworn Commanding Officers of the rank Assistant Chief
Sworn Commanding Officers of the rank Deputy Chief
Civilian Commanding Officers comparable to the rank of Deputy Chief
Sworn Commanding Officers of the rank of Commander
Civilian Commanding Officers comparable to the rank of Commander

July 1, 2008

authority

The right and the power to commit an act or order others to commit an act.

However, to think of police organizations simply in terms of their military style would be a mistake. Some crucial differences between the police and the military make supervising the police a different, and in many ways more difficult, job than supervising the military. These problems can be briefly summarized as discretion, visibility, and **authority.**

1. **Discretion.**   Perhaps the most fundamental difference between law enforcement and the military is the locus where discretion is exercised. In typical military units, the allowance for discretion is highest at the top, and the individual soldier makes few decisions. There is a consistent and simple pattern of supervision in which the generals choose the battlefield strategy. The officers choose which units to commit to battle; the sergeants choose which soldiers will rush the machine-gun nest; and the soldiers do their duty, follow orders, and either succeed, retreat, or die. By contrast, in law enforcement organizations, most discretion is in the hands of the individual police officer. The chief can set some broad policies, and the supervisors can require the officers to keep them apprised of situations via radio, but the individual police officer makes the important decisions. Determining whether a law has been broken, deciding to make an arrest, and giving advice to citizens are activities that are difficult for the command structure of law enforcement organizations to control. In effect, each police officer exercises a great deal of decision-making authority. That is one reason many individuals find police work rewarding.

2. **Visibility.**   Police work is seen by the public on a daily basis. Officers must interact with citizens, have their decisions second-guessed by the media, and answer to the chief for any violations of procedure and laws. The military is not quite as exposed to the spotlight of public scrutiny. Battlefields are in other countries; the press is given extremely limited access (especially since the Vietnam War), and anonymity protects soldiers from having their actions judged by the public in all but the most egregious cases.

3. **Authority.**   Military commanders have a great deal more authority over soldiers than police administrators have over police officers. If an officer fails to follow orders, he or she may be disciplined or dismissed. If a soldier fails to follow orders, he or she may be court-martialed. Additionally, many police departments are under collective-bargaining agreements that specify the terms of employment and disciplinary procedures. These collective-bargaining agreements are much more "worker friendly" than the Uniform Code of Military Justice, which spells out the rights of military personnel.

Police organizations are, first and foremost, bureaucracies. This means that they have rigid rules and procedures that work both to make policies more equitable and predictable and to stifle quick changes and innovation. The bureaucratic nature of police organizations protects officers from a capricious and arbitrary chief, while limiting officers' ability to respond to what they might determine to be preventable problems. Robert Regoli and John Hewitt suggested that the bureaucratic model inhibits police organizations in several ways:

1. Restricts personal growth and development
2. Fosters a groupthink mentality
3. Underestimates the power of the informal organization
4. Does not provide adequate due process
5. Discourages communication[24]

It is worth exploring a couple of these ways bureaucracies do not work as well in police practice as they appear to in theory. For instance, Peter Manning argued that patrol officers do not trust their supervisors because in police organizations the rules are often vague and are applied after the fact. According to Manning, some officers

Illustration depicting shortcomings of the police court.

Source: CORBIS-NY.

remedy this by keeping information to themselves, competing with other officers for credit and prestige, and sometimes lying to escape supervision.[25]

As Regoli and Hewitt suggest, another reason the formal police organization does not reflect the realities of police work is that there is a big difference between the organizational chart and how power is really distributed within the force. Informal power structures that rival formal authority exist in all organizations. Peer pressure can exert a tremendous influence on individuals, causing them to violate rules and procedures. In law enforcement, a subculture might encourage an individual officer to engage in corrupt activities. Thomas Barker argued:

> The police occupation per se provides its members with numerous opportunities for corrupt acts and other forms of deviance. In some police departments there is a social setting where this inherent occupational structure is combined with peer group support and tolerance for certain patterns of corruption. The peer group indoctrinates and socializes the rookie into patterns of acceptable corrupt activities, sanctions deviations outside these boundaries, and sanctions officers who do not engage in any corrupt acts. The peer group can also discipline officers who report or attempt to report fellow officers.[26]

Police organizations suffer from many of the same problems as other types of agencies that use a bureaucratic structure, and the patterning of police departments after military units may be troublesome. Police departments and military units are vastly different because of the nature of their missions, the exercise of discretion, and the visibility of their actions.

We turn now to an examination of the many types of law enforcement agencies. Our goal is not to be exhaustive, but simply to demonstrate the range and complexity with which policing is organized at the federal, state, and local levels.

Problem of Jurisdiction

The development of law enforcement agencies has been contentious. There has been no centralized planning, and the pattern of federal, state, local, specialized, and private law enforcement agencies has developed according to historical accident, politics, special interests, and public welfare. However, what has been sacrificed in coordination and efficiency has been gained in responsiveness and accountability. One of the founding principles of the United States is that control of government should be as close to the people as possible. For that reason, local governments have been allowed to enact laws that speak to the unique needs of their citizens, and overall, an unorganized patchwork of ordinances reflects diversity instead of uniformity.

This phenomenon is extremely visible in the development of law enforcement agencies. There are more than 18,000 agencies nationwide. Policing is a fragmented industry that provides differing levels of protection to citizens depending not only on geographic location, but also on social economic class, race, and gender. We will talk in greater detail about these sociological variables in Chapter 7, but we note them here because they cannot be entirely divorced from the structure and authority of law enforcement.

LEVELS OF LAW ENFORCEMENT

There are three distinct levels of law enforcement in the United States: federal, state, and local. Federal law enforcement can be seem quite complicated, with a multitude of agencies and jurisdictions. The Federal Bureau of Investigation is the nation's foremost law enforcement agency and the one that deals with most criminal offenses that occur on a nationwide basis (rather than within a single state); however, many federal agencies that seem to have nothing to do with law enforcement actually have their own police forces (see Criminal Justice Reference 5.2) that deal with offenses within those agencies' jurisdictions. State law enforcement agencies typically consist of state police, state highway patrols (except for Hawaii) and, sometimes, a state investigative agency. Local law enforcement comprise city and urban police departments, as well as county police forces (sheriff's offices).

Police officers who patrol beats and deal directly with offenses in progress wear uniforms, whereas investigative officers and detectives do not (see Criminal Justice Reference 5.3). Most law enforcement officers are required to be armed while on duty, as law enforcement work at all levels can be dangerous. Officers, especially those on patrol, must meet specific levels of physical fitness and maintain those fitness levels, as well as maintaining proficiency with firearms. Speaking languages other than English is an asset, and, regardless of the level of service, law enforcement officers must know how to write reports.

The duty of all law enforcement officers is to keep the peace, maintain order, ensure adherence to the law, and investigate when those laws appear to have been broken. This is as true of the patrol officer who is trying to find out who is throwing rocks through shop windows as it is of the federal agent who is investigating a large, complicated financial offense. Much of local police work is especially concerned with order maintenance and problem-solving, such as resolving disputes, finding missing persons and runaways, and even dealing with small quality-of-life violations, such as telling the neighbors to turn the music down.[27]

Now, let us take a look at each level of law enforcement.

Federal Level

Federal law enforcement agencies have nationwide jurisdiction but concentrate on specific offenses. They are not general-service agencies that respond to 911 calls or

5.2   CRIMINAL JUSTICE REFERENCE

Partial List of Federal Law Enforcement Agencies

Department of Agriculture
  Forest Service
  Office of the Inspector General
Department of the Air Force
  Office of Special Investigations
Department of the Army
  Armed Forces Police
  Criminal Investigation Command
  Provost Marshal
Department of Commerce
  Bureau of Industry and Security (Formerly Bureau of Export Administration)
  National Institute of Standards and Technology Office of Security
  National Marine Fisheries Service
Department of Defense
  Defense Criminal Investigative Service
  National Security Agency (NSA)
  Naval Criminal Investigative Service
Department of Homeland Security
  Border and Transportation Security
    Animal and Plant Health Inspection Service
    Federal Law Enforcement Training Center
    Federal Protective Service
    Office for Domestic Preparedness
    Transportation Security Administration
    U.S. Citizenship and Immigration Services
    U.S. Customs and Border Protection
    Office of Border Patrol
  Information Analysis and Infrastructure Protection
    Federal Computer Incident Response Center
    National Communications System
    National Infrastructure Protection Center
    Energy Security and Assurance Program
  U.S. Coast Guard
  U.S. Secret Service
Department of the Interior
  Bureau of Indian Affairs
    Division of Law Enforcement
  Bureau of Land Management
    National Law Enforcement Security and Investigations Team
    National Office of Fire and Aviation
  National Park Service
    U.S. Park Police

Department of Justice
  Bureau of Prisons
  Drug Enforcement Administration (DEA)
  Federal Bureau of Investigation (FBI)
  U.S. Marshals
Department of State
  Bureau of Diplomatic Security
    Diplomatic Security Service (United Nations)
    Protective Liaison Division
Department of the Treasury
  Bureau of Alcohol, Tobacco, Firearms, and Explosives (BATF)
  Financial Crimes Enforcement Network
  Internal Revenue Service
    Criminal Investigation Division
    Office of the Regional Inspector (internal investigations)
  U.S. Mint Police
Supreme Court Police
Independent Agencies
  Amtrak Police
  Central Intelligence Agency
    Office of Security
  Environmental Protection Agency
    Office of Criminal Investigations
  Federal Emergency Management Administration
    Security Division
  General Services Administration (GSA)
    Office of the Inspector General
  Nuclear Regulatory Commission
    Office of Enforcement
  Securities and Exchange Commission
    Division of Enforcement
  Smithsonian
    National Zoological Park Police
    Office of Protection Services
  Tennessee Valley Authority (TVA)
    Office of the Inspector General
    Police
  U.S. Capitol Police
  U.S. Postal Service
    Postal Inspection Service
    Postal Security Force

engage in order-maintenance policing. Instead, they are special-purpose agencies that concentrate on a limited set of offenses. For instance, an FBI agent will not arrest a person in connection with a traffic violation unless it somehow relates to a case he or she is working on. Similarly, the customs officer is not concerned with prostitution activities unless they involve transnational trade.

5.3   CRIMINAL JUSTICE REFERENCE

Why Detectives Don't Wear Uniforms

Many criminal justice students want to become detectives. When pressed for the reason, it is often because the student wants to be a law enforcement officer but does not want to wear a uniform. Uniforms seem to be equated with blue-collar occupations, whereas the suits and blazers worn by detectives are equated with white-collar management. Additionally, uniforms not only identify you as a public servant of whom there are expectations, but also reveal your rank and exact status to the public.

Why do some police officers wear uniforms whereas detectives do not? Uniforms identify police officers immediately and instantly establish their authority. This is useful for patrol officers who are the first to respond to a crime in progress or a traffic accident. The officers do not have to negotiate their identity with suspects or the public. When people are running around firing guns, it is useful to know friend from foe. From

time to time, mistakes are made, such as when a vice officer in civilian clothes is mistaken for a drug dealer during a gunfight. Many departments have a "code" such as a blue baseball hat that plainclothes officers can wear when situations are dangerous and they want to be sure that other police officers recognize them as officers.

Detectives usually do not respond immediately to a crime. They appear afterward and gather evidence, interview witnesses, and testify in court. They generally interact with the public in ways that do not require them to be immediately recognizable as law enforcement. This can be advantageous when looking for suspects or dealing with the public.

A note of caution: Police uniforms are easy to obtain. Many military-supply stores carry a wide variety of police uniforms and gear. Badges can be bought over the Internet. Occasionally, offenders or police-wannabes impersonate a police officer. This is a criminal offense.

Although there are about 60 federal law enforcement agencies, the main ones are organized under just three departments: the Department of Justice, the Department of the Treasury, and the Department of Homeland Security.

- Founded in 1870, the Department of Justice is responsible for enforcing federal laws. Its primary agencies are the Drug Enforcement Administration (DEA), the Federal Bureau of Investigation (FBI), the Border Patrol and Immigration and Naturalization Service (INS), and the U.S. Marshals.

- The Department of the Treasury, established in 1789, primarily enforces the collection of revenue. Its main agencies are the Bureau of Alcohol, Tobacco, Firearms, and Explosives (ATF); the U.S. Customs Service; and the Internal Revenue Service (IRS).

- The Department of Homeland Security, created after September 11, 2001, is the newest cabinet-level department. Under its auspices are a number of agencies that have been transferred in whole or in part to Homeland Security because their duties are related to controlling terrorism. An organizational chart of the Department of Homeland Security appears in Chapter 16.

As of 2004, more than 105,000 full-time federal agents were authorized to make arrests and carry firearms.[28] The duties of most federal officers involve criminal investigation (see Figure 5-3). In terms of citizens' constitutional rights, federal law enforcement is held to the same standards as state and local law enforcement (see Case in Point 5.2 for an example). Federal officers are among the best-paid law enforcement personnel, and competition for these jobs is stiff. Most federal officers train at the Federal Law Enforcement Training Center, which is headquartered in Glynco, Georgia. FBI and DEA agents also take some of their training at their respective academies in Quantico, Virginia. Many young people who go into law enforcement hope to advance to the federal level. One aspect of this level of law enforcement is the likelihood that employees will be transferred around the country as they advance along the career path. For this reason, some individuals who want to stay in one region will opt for jobs at the local level.

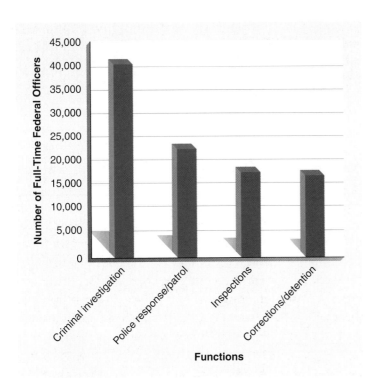

Figure 5-3   **Functions of Full-Time Federal Officers with Arrest and Firearm Authority, September 2004**
Source: Brian A. Reaves, *Federal Law Enforcement Officers, 2004* (Washington, DC: U.S. Department of Justice, Office of Justice Programs, 2006), 2, www.ojp.usdoj.gov/bjs/pub/pdf/fle004.pdf.

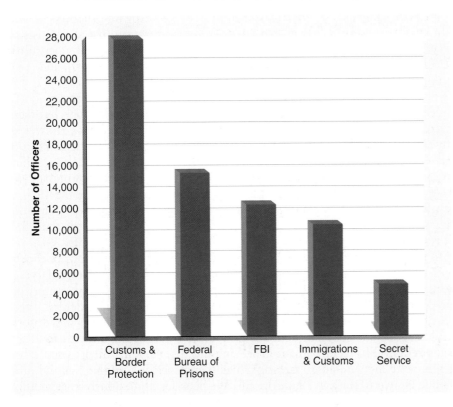

Figure 5-4   **Federal Law Enforcement Agencies with the Most Officers, 2004**
Source: Brian A. Reaves, *Federal Law Enforcement Officers, 2004* (Washington, DC: U.S. Department of Justice, Office of Justice Programs, 2006), 2, www.ojp.usdoj.gov/bjs/pub/pdf/fle004.pdf.

Although there are many federal police agencies, the Federal Bureau of Investigation and Secret Service are the ones that most people associate with federal law enforcement, so we will take a closer look at these agencies. Keep in mind, however, that neither of these two agencies employs the most officers (see Figure 5-4).

FEDERAL BUREAU OF INVESTIGATION   The FBI has nationwide jurisdiction to investigate federal offenses. The emphasis on which offenses get the most attention has shifted over the years as a result of political considerations and the leadership style of

5.2 CASE IN POINT

WEEKS V. UNITED STATES

THE CASE	THE POINT
Weeks v. United States, 232 U.S. 383, 34 S.Ct. 351 (1914)	*The exclusionary rule, which holds that illegally seized evidence is inadmissible in court, is applicable to federal criminal proceedings.*

Kansas City police suspected that Fremont Weeks, who was employed by an express company, was sending lottery tickets through the mail, which was illegal. Without benefit of a warrant, police entered Weeks' home, searched it, and took possession of "various papers and articles," which were given to a U.S. marshal. The police returned later with the marshal and, still without a warrant, took more papers. Among these items were lottery tickets.

At his trial, Weeks was convicted of unlawful use of the mail. He appealed on grounds that the officers should not have searched his house because they had no warrant. The Supreme Court concurred. This case established that the exclusionary rule, which states that illegally seized evidence is inadmissible in court, is applicable to federal criminal proceedings.

its directors. The FBI began in 1908 when President Theodore Roosevelt sent eight Secret Service agents to the Department of Justice to investigate violations of federal law. In the past century it has grown into a large organization that also assists state and local agencies with expert help in training (National FBI Academy), criminalistics (FBI Crime Laboratory), measuring crime (*Uniform Crime Reports*), and consultation on difficult cases (Behavior Analysis Unit).

The directorship of the FBI is one of the most prestigious positions in all of law enforcement, and a number of highly qualified and competent individuals have served in this capacity. By far the most famous and most influential is J. Edgar Hoover, who was appointed in 1924 and served until his death in 1972. The legacy of Hoover is mixed. His shadow hangs over the agency like the imposing headquarters building that bears his name. He is credited with transforming the FBI into a professional organization that has great influence in law enforcement circles. During the 1920s and 1930s, his agents pursued notorious bank robbers such as John Dillinger, Bonnie Parker, and Clyde Barrow. Hoover was a master at public relations, and the FBI became revered for its reputation of employing clean-cut, efficient agents.

Hoover built a personal empire at the FBI and survived numerous presidential administrations. He is rumored to have kept records on politicians' personal lives that protected his tenure.[29] Additionally, his agents kept records on private citizens such as Dr. Martin Luther King Jr., John Lennon, Marilyn Monroe, and Elvis Presley. (Parts of many of these records have been declassified by the Freedom of Information Act and make for fascinating reading.)[30] It can be argued that the turmoil of the era required the FBI to be vigilant in seeking out threats, but FBI agents also broke laws in conducting wiretaps, watching citizens, and breaking into homes and offices.

Since Hoover's death in 1972, the FBI has been trying to polish its reputation.[31] Although most of its agents have performed in stellar fashion, a few high-profile cases have tarnished its image. Following the incident at Ruby Ridge (discussed in Chapter 7) and the revelation that agent Robert Hanssen was a spy for the Soviets and the Russians, the agency struggled to regain its credibility. Also, since the events of September 11, 2001, the agency has shifted some of its focus to national security.

SECRET SERVICE   After September 11, 2001, the Secret Service was moved from the Department of Treasury and placed under the Department of Homeland Security. Its duties remain essentially the same but have been expanded somewhat to provide for defense against terrorism.

Mug shots of the FBI's "most wanted" circa 1934. Top row, left to right: John Dillinger, Arthur Barker (son of "Ma" Barker), Charles "Pretty Boy" Floyd. Bottom row, left to right: George "Baby Face" Nelson, Alvin Karpis, Homer Van Meter.
Source: Corbis/Bettmann

The Secret Service's original commission when it was created in 1865 was not to protect the president, but to control the proliferation of counterfeit money. Only in 1894 with President Grover Cleveland did the agency begin casual protection services. A year after the assassination of President William McKinley in 1901, the Secret Service began full-time executive protection, designating two agents to the job. However, it was not until 1913 that Congress authorized permanent protection of the president, and it was 1917 before the president's family received protection. Security was gradually stepped up over the years, owing partly to the 1951 assassination attempt on President Harry Truman and the 1963 assassination of President John F. Kennedy. Gradually, the list of protectees came to include major presidential and vice presidential candidates, presidential widows, and visiting heads of state. Former presidents and their spouses received lifetime protection in 1965, although Congress abbreviated this in 1994, giving presidents elected after 1997 protection for 10 years after leaving office.

The agency's Treasury Department mission came to the fore again in 1984 when Congress authorized it to investigate credit card fraud, some types of computer fraud, and fake IDs. Most agents employed by the Secret Service spend most of their time on duties other than executive protection.

State Level

In many ways, state law enforcement agencies are overshadowed by local and federal agencies. State agencies do not have the numbers of officers that local agencies have, nor the visibility of federal agencies. There are as many variations in how state law enforcement agencies are organized as there are states. Each state law enforcement system must be understood on its own terms because no two are exactly alike. This reflects the fact that the United States is a collection of united sovereign governments, with the elected government of each state deciding how that state is to be administered. State police forces were developed to keep the peace in rural areas that lay outside the jurisdictions of cities and towns. State highway patrols became necessary as automobile usage increased and the state and interstate highway systems were developed.[32]

Generally, there are two broad models of state law enforcement: the centralized model and the decentralized model. The centralized model combines investigative and highway patrol functions into one agency. The decentralized model separates these two functions. For example, the state of Georgia has a state highway patrol and an investigative agency, the Georgia Bureau of Investigation.[33] About half of the states have state highway patrols, and half have state police, with the exception of Hawaii, which has no state law enforcement agency.[34] Historically, three western states, Texas, Colorado, and Arizona, have police agencies called "rangers" that are more than a century old and are among the first professional state/territorial law enforcement organizations in the United States. However, the Pennsylvania State Police, created in 1905, is recognized as the first uniformed, professional state police department.

State investigative bureaus have statewide jurisdiction for investigating criminal offenses—such as political corruption—in which local police might not be in a position to investigate their local bosses. State law enforcement agencies also provide a number of services to local law enforcement agencies such as the coordination of multijurisdictional task forces, crime laboratory services, and when requested, help in investigating offenses. Additionally, most state law enforcement agencies have police training academies that provide the basic instruction that is beyond the capabilities of all but the largest local police forces.

Factors that may determine the simplicity or intricacy of a state police system include geography, population density, financial resources, and crime issues. Wealthy states with big cities may have state police agencies with special investigation units, community programs, and task forces. States with fewer resources might not have as many programs. A state's industry or culture can also dictate the type of programs it requires. For example, New Jersey's Department of Law and Public Safety has a gaming enforcement division to regulate the casino industry, and the Alaska Department of Public Safety has its Fish and Wildlife Protection division. Some states have placed all law enforcement divisions under one organizational umbrella, such as a department of public safety, whereas other states may separate these programs or lodge them within different bureaus of state government.

Law enforcement at the state level consists of a wide variety of activities. Those interested in a career in law enforcement should investigate opportunities in state agencies.

Local Level

Most of the nation's crime is handled by local law enforcement agencies. In many ways, local policing is where the action is. Each jurisdiction, whether big-city police department, county sheriff's office, or small-town police department, is the first responder to most criminal offenses. Additionally, these agencies have patrol and investigative duties in which they are often the only law enforcement agency involved in the case. Because local law enforcement officers handle most serious street-level crime, they are whom we call when we "call the cops."

Most local police forces are operated by municipalities, with a few run by tribal and county governments. There are about 13,000 local police departments in the United States. The largest local police force in the country is the New York Police Department. With more than 39,000 full-time officers, it is about three times the size of the next largest organization, the Chicago Police Department, which has just over 13,000 sworn officers. (See Figure 5-5 for the 10 largest police departments as of 2003.) At the other end of the spectrum, about 800 departments have just a single officer.

Full-service local law enforcement agencies perform a wide range of duties. The most labor intensive is routine patrol, in which officers travel around their assigned beats, respond to calls for service, and look for ways to keep the community safe. Some of the time that officers spend on patrol is used to interact with citizens who are not suspected of breaking any law. Officers talk to shopkeepers, watch for

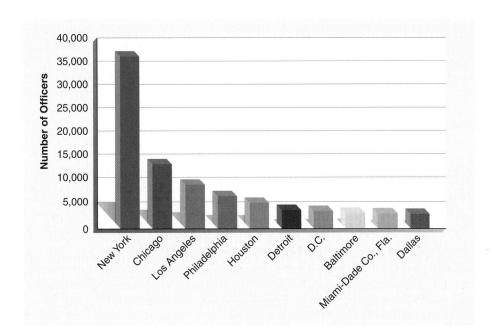

Figure 5-5   The 10 Largest Local Police Departments by Total Number of Full-Time Sworn Personnel, 2003
Source: Matthew J. Hickman and Brian A. Reaves, *Local Police Departments 2003* (Washington, DC: Bureau of Justice Statistics, 2003), 2, www.ojp.usdoj.gov/bjs/pub/pdf/lpd03.pdf.

traffic infractions, cruise neighborhoods to show citizens they are being served, and investigate anything that looks suspicious or out of place. The business of apprehending suspects constitutes a small fraction of the officers' time. Local law enforcement agencies also devote resources and personnel to investigative duties, including homicide, burglary, auto theft, sex offenses, and juveniles. To a lesser degree, their duties may also include animal control, emergency medical service, and civil defense.

Larger departments operate SWAT and bomb disposal teams. As of 2003, only 9 percent of all departments operated a jail.[35] Along with traditional car patrols, there has been a steady increase in bicycle and foot patrols. Community policing is also on the upswing, with most departments having a formal plan. Also, not all local police officers are sworn.[36] Nonsworn department employees may work in technical support, administration, and the jail. Some police officers specialize in specific areas, such as forensic analysis or in physical or firearms training and instruction. Large departments may assign officers to special units, such as horseback, bicycle, motorcycle, or boat patrols. Some departments may ameliorate officer shortages with supplemental and part-time personnel such as sworn reserve officers, as well as nonsworn auxiliary officers, community service officers, police aides, and other types of volunteers. Each agency organizes its investigative duties and personnel according to its problems, resources, and needs, but each of them in some way must ensure that there is an investigative follow-up to reported crime.

Sometimes law enforcement jurisdictions overlap. A person driving a car too fast within a city's limits may be pulled over and ticketed by a state patrol officer, a sheriff's deputy, or a city police officer. However, a homicide committed within a specific jurisdiction would likely be dealt with by the police agency responsible for that jurisdiction, with rare exceptions in special cases. The state patrol or the county sheriff would be unlikely to get involved in investigating a homicide committed within a city's limits. An example of such an exception would be the Atlanta child murders. From July 1979 to May 1981, 29 young black males were murdered in or near Atlanta, Georgia. Although the murders occurred mainly in the city of Atlanta and Fulton County, several agencies became involved in the investigation, including the local police, the sheriff's office, the Georgia Bureau of Investigation (GBI), and ultimately the FBI. (The federal agency, having no jurisdiction, became involved only by invitation from the local agencies.)

SHERIFF'S OFFICES   Sheriff's offices are the most common form of county law enforcement in the United States, with about 3100 offices.[37] Most sheriffs are elected officials and serve counties and municipalities without a police department. Their duties include routine patrols, crime investigation (some are responsible for crime lab services such as fingerprint and ballistics testing), executing arrest warrants, serving papers, and providing court security. Most offices operate at least one jail, and about half provide search and rescue services, as well as SWAT (special weapons and tactics) teams. Other services may include bomb disposal, animal control, emergency medical services, and civil defense. The number of sheriff's offices exceeds the number of counties (3066) in the United States. This is because a few counties have two sheriff's offices (one for criminal matters and one for civil matters), whereas others have no sheriff's office. In cases in which a city occupies the entire county, city and county law enforcement might be combined into one department.

REQUIREMENTS TO BECOME A POLICE OFFICER   Once upon a time, the requirements to become a police officer were simple and rather narrow: big, strong, young, healthy, brave, and male. Although some of the requirements still apply, they have been tempered in recent decades by the fact that the most important personal aspect an officer brings to the job is intelligence.[38] Each department, be it statewide, urban, or rural, has its own set of requirements for applicants, but these tend to follow similar lines for physical conditioning and ability, age, education, and personal legal history.

- **Education**   Applicants usually must have at least a high school diploma, and some departments require at least two years of college. Some departments require a college degree.

- **Training**   Recruits usually attend police academy for 12 to 14 weeks. State and large urban agencies may have their own academies; recruits at small departments may attend a state or regional academy. Recruits learn constitutional and state law as well as local ordinances. They also train in accident investigation, patrol, traffic control, firearms, self-defense, first aid, and emergency response.

- **Age, citizenship, physical, and residential qualifications**   Applicants must be U.S. citizens and usually must be at least 20 years old. Departments typically have basic requirements for vision, hearing, strength, and agility. For example, a department may require that uncorrected eyesight cannot be weaker than 20/100 in each eye and must be corrected to 20/20 with glasses, contact lens, or surgery. Some urban departments require officers to live in or near the city limits. For example, the Tallahassee (Florida) Police Department states that "Employees hired after October 1, 1978, must reside in Florida, within a 35-mile radius of the intersection of North Monroe and Tennessee Streets, Tallahassee."[39] This intersection is in downtown Tallahassee and represents the center of the city.

- **Personal history**   Departments may also extensively investigate their applicants' personal histories. Some agencies have a mental health professional interview candidates, and candidates usually must take lie detector and/or drug tests.

- **Disqualifications**   An applicant may be automatically disqualified by any of the following: a felony conviction, misdemeanor convictions within the past few years, a specified number of moving violations within the past few years, a dishonorable discharge from the armed forces, convictions for certain offenses (such as domestic violence), or refusal to submit to polygraph, psychological, or drug testing.

Not mentioned in this list are a number of criteria that were once used to prevent individuals from entering law enforcement employment. Most prominent among these criteria are the requirements that applicants be male, white, and heterosexual. Like all agencies in federal, state, and local governments today, law enforcement agencies are prohibited from discriminating against applicants based on these criteria.

INNOVATIONS IN POLICING

Innovations in policing come from three sources: innovations from technological and social changes, innovations from research, and innovations from the development of new ideas. Innovations from technological and social changes include the use of non-lethal weaponry to control individuals and crowds; the use of information technology to gather, store, and access information on citizens; and the innovations spurred by the terrorist events of September 11, 2001. Innovations can also stem from research such as the Kansas City Preventive Patrol experiment and the RAND Study of Detectives. Finally, innovations from the development of new ideas include the practices of community policing, problem-oriented policing, and zero-tolerance policing, as well as the school anti–drug abuse program DARE and broken-windows theory. We will discuss DARE further in this chapter. However, broken-windows theory, community policing, problem-oriented policing, and zero-tolerance policing require more discussion, so we will cover them in detail in Chapter 7.

Innovations from Social and Technological Changes

Many of the recent innovations to law enforcement are related to the increased need for national security, the desire for the safety of citizens, and the ability to acquire, store, and access information about law-abiding people, suspects, and offenders. Often these three concerns are closely related. For example, the need for increased security and desire for citizen safety has led to more active acquisition of information about U.S. residents, some of whom are suspected of terrorist activities. The desire for citizen safety is related to the control of violent individuals and crowds, which has led to the development of less-than-lethal weapons, some of which have been tested on the battlefield.

HOMELAND SECURITY   The events of September 11, 2001, brought fundamental change to the criminal justice system. September 11 especially affected law enforcement, whose mission has been radically altered by demands to meet the threat of terrorism. Samuel Walker and Charles M. Katz described four ways in which law enforcement changed because of these new demands:

- **Role expansion**   Federal, state, and local law enforcement agencies have been charged with responding to the terrorist threat. In addition to their normal duties, they must be on the lookout for suspected terrorists, design contingency plans for catastrophic terrorist events, and be prepared to deal with weapons of mass destruction. This greatly expands the training necessary for officers at all levels and requires a new level of coordination between agencies.

- **Racial and ethnic profiling**   In responding to possible terrorist activities, there is the ever-present problem of racial and ethnic profiling. Because the September 11 terrorists were of Middle Eastern background, there is a tendency to pay special attention to citizens and visitors who appear to come from that part of the world. Law enforcement agencies must ensure that while protecting citizens against terrorism, they do not engage in activities that violate individuals' legal and civil rights.

- **Immigration enforcement**   Law enforcement agencies at all levels are charged with the responsibility to enforce U.S. immigration law. The federal government has fundamentally changed its security structure by instituting the Department of Homeland Security, which now is primarily responsible for immigration enforcement. Although many local law enforcement agencies do not wish to expend resources on enforcing federal immigration laws, they are periodically charged with investigating the immigration status of suspects and offenders.

- **Personnel shortages**   Many law enforcement agencies are finding that their officers who are also members of the National Guard or who are military reservists are being called to active duty in Iraq or Afghanistan. This has caused acute shortages of trained police officers, which is especially damaging to small agencies. Creative and innovative ways of maintaining adequate personnel have had to be employed to maintain public safety.[40]

Although the events of September 11 have been problematic for many of concerns, this problem has been balanced somewhat by additional funding that has been made available to all levels of law enforcement. It is still too soon to tell how the threat of terrorism will change the nature and mission of many law enforcement agencies, but it appears that this will be an ongoing concern. One of the dangers of such a historic upheaval in law enforcement activities is that if the time comes when terrorism is no longer such a serious threat, law enforcement agencies will continue to expend resources on terrorism and ordinary citizens will become targets. When a bureaucracy builds up its infrastructure to deal with a specific threat, the infrastructure remains even after the threat is gone. For instance, the repeal of Prohibition in 1933 left many federal agents with no alcohol laws to enforce. With the relaxation of privacy afforded by the USA Patriot Act, the danger exists that these laws will be used to undermine the constitutional protections provided to U.S. citizens long after the terrorist threat has waned.

TECHNOLOGICAL CHANGE: LESS-THAN-LETHAL WEAPONS   For several decades, law enforcement has been looking for, developing, and testing weapons that immobilize human beings but do not kill them. Although these types of weapons are popularly known as "nonlethal" weapons, several of them have killed people. Therefore, the correct term for these weapons is "less-than-lethal" (LTL) because although they might cause fatalities, they are not intended to kill. The ideal LTL weapon, one that never causes fatalities and is perfectly safe and easy to use in all situations, has not yet been developed.[41] However, governments and private industry are still working with a variety of tactics and substances to produce an effective LTL weapon. See Table 5-1 for a brief history of the various types of LTL weapons.

The arguments supporting LTL weapons point to the fact that they are not intended to cause fatalities while also protecting police. In many instances throughout the world, police have been outnumbered by rioting crowds and barely able to protect themselves, much less the property or the lives of others. Crowd control is a critical issue, especially in urban areas and public events. For example, it is not uncommon in the United States for a crowd to riot at the results of a sports championship.

The primary critique of LTL weapons is that although their use does result in fewer fatalities than the use of firearms, there is the potential for misuse and their adoption as substitutes for "intelligent and professional policing and soldiering."[42] Instead of addressing the root of social problems, governments will simply rely on the use of reduced force through police departments and militaries—which are increasingly becoming involved in police-style actions—to control populaces.[43]

TECHNOLOGICAL CHANGE: INFORMATION TECHNOLOGY   One of the most important technological innovations in criminal justice has been the computerized database. A database, as you know, is an organized, searchable collection of related information. A phone book would qualify as a database. A computerized database is kept on and searched from a computer. What makes a database so useful is the volume of detailed information it can hold, the ability to cross-index and search that information, and the ease of sharing that information. A database containing the physical characteristics of all individuals who have ever been convicted of an offense is immensely useful to a law enforcement agency.

Table 5-1   **Less-Than-Lethal Weaponry**

	Weapon	Era	Usage and Effects
Kinetic impact munitions	Guard rounds	World War II	Copper-clad bullets used by sentries that had fluted cartridges to lessen their impact. Shot with conventional guns, guard rounds were designed not to inflict injury in case a sentry accidentally shot a friendly soldier.[1]
	Rock salt	1930s	During the Great Depression, train guards loaded shotguns with rock salt to keep unauthorized riders off freight trains.[2]
	Teakwood batons	1960s	In Hong Kong, British soldiers fired teakwood batons from flare guns to disperse crowds. The batons were fired at the ground and skipped up to hit targets at the knees. However, a baton was known to have killed at least one person.[3]
	Rubber and plastic bullets, chemical-filled "paintballs," and beanbags	1970s–present	Fired from low-velocity shot guns and flare guns. Intended to cause pain and bruising with no permanent injury. Some projectiles may contain chemicals that cause stinging and burning on contact. At least one person has died from being struck with a beanbag in the chest. Some projectiles can penetrate the body.[4]
Chemical	CN gas (Mace)	1960s, with limited current use	Both are forms of tear gas. The newer CS gas is more potent and less toxic than CN. Both types of gas canisters are thrown by hand or fired from a special gun. CN and CS affect primarily the eyes and skin.
	CS gas	Present	
	Pepper spray (oleoresin capsicum)	Present	Causes a burning sensation in the mucous membranes, eyes, and skin. Usually safe, with few side effects. Originally made with a substance from chili peppers.[5]
	Superlubricants and superadhesives	Present	"Goo" that is usually extremely sticky or extremely slippery.
Electroshock and microwave	Taser	Present	Uses a compressed-gas cartridge to launch two probes up to 35 feet. The probes have wires that attach to skin and clothing. The Taser can deliver 3000 volts through about two inches of clothing.[6] The shock affects the voluntary nervous system and prevents coordinated activity.[7]
	Stun gun	1980s	The stun gun resembled an electric razor and had to touch the body to deliver a shock. In New York City, several officers and sergeants were charged with using stun guns on suspects during interrogations.[8]
	Active denial technology	Developing	Generates and emits microwaves that cause a burning sensation in the skin in both crowds and targeted individuals.[9]
Audio and visual	Flash-bang grenades, the Long Range Acoustic Device, laser blinding devices	Present and developing	These "light-sound" devices divert or confuse targets. The Long Range Acoustic Device can make a sound that can inflict an instant headache on anyone within about 1,000 feet.[10] Laser blinding devices use light to temporarily blind or disorient targets.
Mechanical	Entanglements	Present	Nets, usually launched by a low-velocity gun or other launch device.
	Water	Present	High-pressure streams of water launched from cannons or hoses.

[1]Alan Dobrowolski and Sue Moore, "Less Lethal Weapons and Their Impact on Patient Care," *Topics in Emergency Medicine* 27, no. 1 (January–March 2005):45.
[2]Ibid.
[3]Ibid.
[4]Ibid.
[5]Ibid.
[6]Al Baker, "Tasers Getting More Prominent Role in Crime Fighting in City," *New York Times*, late edition, June 15, 2008, A25.
[7]Dobrowolski and Moore, "Less Lethal Weapons."
[8]Ibid.
[9]"The Future of Crowd Control," *Economist*, December 4, 2004, 11.
[10]Ibid.

Databases can contain physical and personality characteristics, legal histories, employment histories, addresses, Social Security numbers, phone numbers, license plates, fingerprints, arrest records, criminal investigations, and outstanding warrants. Large police departments have their own computer networks. Small departments with lower budgets might hire a private, third-party company to maintain their databases. Some jurisdictions combine their databases or allow other jurisdictions access.[44]

DNA DATABASES   A particularly useful and controversial type of database is the DNA database. DNA, or deoxyribonucleic acid, is the material in living organisms that determines heredity, and nearly every cell in a person's body has the same DNA. This makes DNA especially useful for identifying individuals. Currently, the military keeps DNA records of all in service; at least 43 states collect DNA from all felons, and some collect DNA from felony suspects.[45]

The National DNA Index System (NDIS) grew out of the FBI's Combined DNA Index System (CODIS), a project begun in 1990. Currently, more than 170 public law enforcement laboratories participate in NDIS, and more than 40 law enforcement laboratories in more than 25 countries use the CODIS software. CODIS has indexes for convicted offenders, forensic evidence, arrestees, missing persons, and unidentified human remains. CODIS generates leads in cases in which biological evidence is recovered from a crime scene. For example, a profile that has matches in both the forensic evidence and convicted offender indexes can provide the identity of a suspect.[46]

Biologically related people share some DNA, so one person's DNA can provide information about his or her sibling, parent, or other biological relative. For instance, in Houston, Texas, in 2006, a man was convicted of rape with the help of DNA collected from his twin brother.[47] The FBI has used the process to match DNA from the parent of a missing child to unidentified remains. Critics of this technique say that profiling DNA in this manner can target innocent people by placing them under police surveillance and violating their Fourth Amendment protection against unreasonable search and seizure.[48] However, DNA used in just this manner ended the 30-year killing spree of Dennis Rader (the BTK killer). The police, who suspected Rader, were allowed to collect his daughter's DNA without her knowledge by acquiring a Pap smear specimen she had given five years earlier at a university medical clinic. The woman's DNA closely matched the DNA collected from Rader's crime scenes, suggesting that the woman was the killer's child and giving the police enough evidence to arrest Rader.[49]

CRIME MAPPING   Making geographic maps of where criminal offenses occur and where suspects and offenders live is not a particularly new technique. However, the use of computer technology, as well as the ready availability of computerized geographic information, has made crime mapping a much easier task for police. In 2007, for example, the FBI used a program called Pinpoint that referenced city, state, and federal data from existing records. Color-coded dots on a map marked the homes of people wanted for probation violations, people wanted on bench warrants, known sexual offenders, and violent-offense suspects, as well as the locations of homicides, shootings, the homes of community leaders, places of worship, and police informants.[50] Of course, the hardware and software used to run crime-mapping programs is updated at the rapid pace of computer technology. However, the idea remains the same: to plot on a geographic map details about the individuals who live at specific points on the map.

A critique of crime mapping is that, like databases, they can be used to gather information on people who have not broken the law. In 2007, Muslims in Los Angeles protested a proposed counterterrorism mapping project that would have collected information on the city's Muslim communities. The idea was to track possible radicalization among the city's Muslims. Critics of the plan said that such mapping made law-abiding Muslims feel like suspects and that mapping should be reserved for communities in which crime was already occurring.[51]

Innovations from Research

How do we know whether the changes made in police practices actually work? From an occupational perspective, law enforcement agencies will embrace any innovation that provides the resources to hire new personnel or buy new equipment. The real test of successful innovations, however, is controlled research that not only looks at the desired effect of a new policy or tactic, but also attempts to uncover and measure any unintended consequences. In this section we review three of the better-known studies of police practices to illustrate how rigorous research can improve law enforcement strategies.

KANSAS CITY PREVENTIVE PATROL EXPERIMENT   Police patrol, in which officers walk the beat or ride around specified areas in patrol cars, is a stable feature of police activity. The idea that officers are responsible for specified geographic areas is one of the cornerstones of law enforcement supervision. As officers have shifted away from foot patrol and into police cars, a recurring question has been how the police, citizens, and criminals have perceived the success of police patrol. In 1972 the Kansas City Police Department and the Police Foundation designed an experiment to measure the efficacy of police patrol in terms of its effect on crime, the delivery of police services, and citizens' feelings of security. The experiment divided the city into 15 beat areas and assigned each of them one of three types of police patrol: reactive beats, control beats, or proactive beats.

1. Reactive beats did not receive regular police patrol. The police patrol cars would respond to calls for service but would otherwise stay out of the area.
2. Control beats experienced the same level of police patrol as they normally would have if there were no research experiment. For the most part, this meant a level of one car per beat.
3. Proactive beats experienced an intensified level of patrol with two to three times the number of cars passing through.

The Kansas City Preventive Patrol Experiment collected a large amount of information from official police records, surveys of citizens and businesses, interviews with officers, and the observations of participant-observer researchers. The bottom line from the summary report is as follows:

> Given the large amount of data collected and the extremely diverse sources used, the overwhelming evidence is that decreasing or increasing routine preventive patrol within the range tested in this experiment had no effect on crime, citizen fear of crime, community attitudes toward the police on the delivery of police service, police response time or traffic accidents.[52]

Does this mean that preventive patrol is a waste of time? Not really. This study found that the level of patrol made little difference. Even though the reactive beats, in which there was no patrol, had the same level of crime and citizens felt the same level of security as the beats that had patrol, we should not be misled about the advisability of having the police on the streets. Because the beats were randomly assigned, the citizens and offenders might not have perceived any difference in the level of patrol because they could not tell where one beat ended and another began.

Does this experiment suggest that the police should simply respond when an offense is reported or they are called for service? Again the answer is no. The response time it takes to get from the station house would surely be greater than it is when the police are routinely out on the street. This experiment, done in the early 1970s, has not ended the preventive-patrol concept, but it has forced police departments to assess how they can better serve their citizens. For example, focusing on "hot spots" where criminal offenses are concentrated can be a more effective way to prevent crime.[53]

RAND STUDY OF DETECTIVES   Many students who plan to go into law enforcement would just as soon skip the years of being a street officer doing patrol, traffic, and other routine duties. They would like to skip having to wear a uniform and go immediately to becoming a detective, where they believe the work will be more rewarding. These students might be disappointed. Aside from the fact that experience in patrol and other uniformed duties is a requirement for becoming a detective, "detective work is neither glamorous nor exciting," according to Samuel Walker, one of the nation's leading law enforcement scholars.[54] In fact, some officers who become detectives return to patrol because detective work simply is not exciting enough.

In 1977 the RAND Corporation, a research institution, conducted a study for the National Institute of Law Enforcement and Criminal Justice in which it attempted to determine just how effective detectives are in solving crimes. The results questioned the efficacy of devoting vast resources to detective work. The RAND study found detective work to be superficial, routine, and nonproductive. The findings can be summarized as follows:

1. **Arrest and clearance rates.**   Only 2.7 percent of the cases that are cleared can be attributed to investigative techniques. These tend to be high-profile cases such as homicide, robbery, and commercial theft. For the remaining 97.3 percent of the cases cleared, the contribution of victims, witnesses, and patrol officers is more important than that of investigators.

2. **How the investigator's time is spent.**   Investigators spend 93 percent of their time on activities that do not lead directly to solving previously reported offenses. They do paperwork, survey pawnshops or junkyards, give speeches, and prepare cases for court.

3. **Collecting and processing physical evidence.**   The study focused on fingerprint identification and concluded that only 4 to 9 percent of all retrieved fingerprints from four cities eventually matched those of a known suspect. They added, however, that some departments' cold searches produced more case solutions than investigators did. (Note that this study was published in 1977; with advancements in computer technology, fingerprint analysis has greatly improved.)

4. **Proactive investigation methods.**   Police investigation is essentially reactive. Once an offense has been committed, the patrol officer responds and calls in the detectives. An alternative method of detective work is to go into the community and question informants about offenses committed but not yet known to the police, conducting surveillance activities, or setting up sting operations in which the detectives pose as fences to buy stolen property. The RAND study looked at such activity in two police departments and concluded that although many of their arrests were attributable to the work of other police officers, such units can be effective for burglary and fencing arrests.[55]

The RAND study questioned the role of detectives in modern police departments and made several policy recommendations, including the following:

1. Place most postarrest investigations in the prosecutor's office.

2. Let patrol officers, not detectives, arrest known suspects.

3. Let clerks do most of the routine investigative tasks such as tracing ownership of weapons, showing mug shots to victims, and filing reports.

4. Create investigative teams that handle offenses without suspects. These teams would include clerical workers who are supervised by a detective. These teams could handle most of these cases more efficiently than individual officers could.

5. For proactive investigations, develop special strike forces as unique needs arise. These strike forces would be disbanded after the problem has been addressed and created again if the problem recurs.

6. Reallocate investigative duties to other parts of the police force.[56]

The RAND study did not recommend reducing total police resources. Instead, it suggested that a rethinking about detectives' duties justifies new ways of doing this work. By creating a role of generalist-investigator whose training and experience is less than that of the detective, the study argued, much of the routine and boring work of investigations could be done at less cost and more efficiently.

Innovations from New Ideas

We have looked at studies that deal with the major police functions of patrol and investigation, and now we turn our attention to other features of police work: drug abuse prevention and the control of gang violence.

DARE   The Drug Abuse Resistance Education (DARE) program began in 1983 in Los Angeles as a cooperative effort between the Los Angeles Police Department and the Los Angeles schools. The idea behind the program was to give children information about illegal drugs, an idea about what happens when people use or sell illegal drugs, and coping mechanisms to help them avoid illegal drugs.

From its modest beginnings, the DARE program has spread across the nation and to at least 44 other countries. By 1997 it was operating in at least three-quarters of the school districts in the United States and had an annual budget of $750 million.[57] DARE programs are a fixture in many schools. Police cars with bumper stickers state, "DARE to keep kids off drugs." This program has enjoyed widespread popularity until recently, when some evaluations of its effectiveness were published.[58] The evaluations say that despite widespread support for the program among schools, the public, and law enforcement agencies, the effect on preventing children from future drug use is absent (see Focus on Ethics 5.2). The studies contend that no measurable difference exists between students who participated in the program and those who did not.[59]

In looking at this research concerning police patrol, the use of detectives, and drug prevention activities by law enforcement officers, we have seen that controversy continues regarding how best to deploy police personnel. Clearly, these issues are only suggestive of the types of research done on police organization. Scores of other issues and hundreds of legitimate studies are conducted on police practices. What we

---

5.2   FOCUS *on* ETHICS

DO YOU DARE DUMP DARE?

As the police chief of a large city, you instituted the DARE drug education and prevention program 15 years ago. The popular program has been adopted by 90 percent of the city's schools, and many of your best officers have rotated through the assignment and are enthusiastic about their experience. The program has become a high-profile public relations success that has earned the department a reputation for community involvement.

When a team of researchers from the nearby university volunteered to evaluate the program, you eagerly accepted their offer because you were confident their report would confirm your belief that the DARE program was an unqualified success. Now the report has been completed, and it is devastating. It finds not only that students who were exposed to the DARE program fared no better in avoiding drug use later in life than those who were not exposed to the program, but also that the students, even young ones, think DARE is a joke. After meeting with the researchers, you are convinced that not only is the study methodologically sound, but it is consistent with the results of evaluations of other DARE programs from around the country.

What Do You Do?

1. Suppress the results by telling the researchers they no longer have permission to use the data they have collected from your records.
2. Close down the program and reassign your officers to other duties.
3. Continue the program because even though it doesn't work, it generates good publicity and everyone (except the kids) seems to like it.

have tried to do here is focus on three problems that illustrate the way research can inform us about how long-cherished police practices are not always as successful as we might assume.

PROJECT CEASEFIRE   Project Ceasefire is a component of the Boston Gun Project, a initiative created in 1995 by Boston public agencies as an effort to stem the violence among the city's youth. Some of the project's innovations came from new ideas; some came from research.

In Boston, homicides among those age 24 and younger had increased from 22 victims in 1987 to 73 victims in 1990, leveling off to about 44 youth homicides per year between 1991 and 1995.[60] Research indicated that gang-involved, young, chronic offenders committed the most homicides; 1200 youths, about 1 percent of Boston's youth population, had committed about 60 percent of the city's youth homicides.[61]

Project Ceasefire held meetings with these youths that included law enforcement, community activists, probation officers, and other agencies. At these "offender notification" meetings, the youths were informed that further violence would not be tolerated and would result in a particularly strict police response. The meetings were then followed by the use of all sanctions possible against further offenders, as well as crackdowns on gangs that continued to commit gun-related offenses. Analyses of these efforts showed that youth homicide later fell by two-thirds, with significant reductions in several types of gun offenses.[62] The project was later repeated with similar success in Minneapolis, Minnesota.[63]

SUMMARY

1. Maintenance of social control is a function of society. Early police usually derived from a military connected with a government, or from the community when citizens joined in informal groups to protect themselves.

2. U.S. law enforcement is based on the English system. American policing was greatly modified to fit the demands of the U.S. political structure and American emphasis on individualism and less government. Police in the United States had much broader latitude in the exercise of discretion than English police.

3. According to Walker and Katz, English policing contributed three characteristics to American policing: limited police authority, local control, and a fragmented system.

4. Informal policing in the United States began in New Amsterdam (New York City) in 1625. In the early American South and West, vigilante movements were created where established and effective law enforcement agencies were lacking.

5. During the early 20th century, developments in professional law enforcement were initiated by reformers such as August Vollmer in Berkeley, California.

Vollmer advocated that the police become nonpartisan, use scientific principles, become more specialized, and be led by qualified executives.

6. In 1966, the case *Miranda* v. *Arizona* set forth that confessions made by suspects who have not been advised of their due process rights cannot be used as evidence.

7. The primary differences between the supervision of police officers and the supervision of military soldiers are discretion, visibility, and authority.

8. There are law enforcement agencies at the federal, state, and local levels of administration. These agencies have developed according to historical accident, politics, special interests, and public welfare. Because of this, sometimes questions of jurisdiction develop.

9. Federal police forces typically serve federal agencies and their jurisdictions. The FBI's jurisdiction is nationwide. State law enforcement agencies typically comprise some combination of state police, state highway patrols, and state investigative agencies. Local law enforcement consists of city and urban police departments and county police forces (sheriff's offices).

10. State and local police departments each have their own set of requirements for applicants. However, these tend to follow similar lines for physical conditioning and ability, age, education, and personal legal history.

11. Innovations in policing come from three sources: innovations from technological and social changes, innovations from research, and innovations from the development of new ideas.

KEY TERMS

authority 168
bobbies 156
Bow Street Runners 155
constable (*comes stabuli*) 154

frankpledge system 154
hue and cry 155
hundred-man 154
Metropolitan Police Act 156

sheriff (shire reeve) 154
Thames River Police 155
watch-and-ward system 154

REVIEW QUESTIONS

1. How was law enforcement accomplished before the development of the first modern police force in London?

2. The Chicago Police Department of the early 20th century was considered political. Why?

3. What is vigilante policing?

4. Why is August Vollmer important to police professionalization?

5. Why is *Miranda* v. *Arizona* important?

6. The police are often compared to the military. Discuss how they are different in terms of discretion, visibility, and authority.

7. Name three federal law enforcement agencies besides the Federal Bureau of Investigation and the Secret Service.

8. Which level of law enforcement agency handles most of the nation's crime?

9. What is the most common form of county law enforcement in the United States?

10. How has the focus on terrorism changed U.S. law enforcement?

SUGGESTED FURTHER READING

Bayley, David H., and Clifford D. Shearing. *The New Structure of Policing: Description, Conceptualization and Research Agenda*. Washington, DC: National Institute of Justice, 2001.

Center for Research on Criminal Justice. *The Iron Fist and the Velvet Glove: An Analysis of the US Police*. Berkeley, CA: Author, 1977.

Poveda, Tony. *Lawlessness and Reform: The FBI in Transition*. Pacific Grove, CA: Brooks/Cole, 1990.

Wadman, Robert C., and William Thomas Allison. *To Protect and to Serve: A History of Police in America*. Upper Saddle River, NJ: Pearson Prentice Hall, 2004.

Walker, David M. *Homeland Security: Responsibility and Accountability for Achieving National Goals*. Washington, DC: U.S. General Accounting Office, 2002.

Zedner, Lucia. "Policing Before and After the Police: The Historical Antecedents of Contemporary Crime Control." *British Journal of Criminology* 46, no. 1 (2006): 78–96.

ENDNOTES

1. Jonathan Rubinstein, *City Police* (New York: Farrar, Straus, & Giroux, 1973).

2. Center for Research on Criminal Justice, *The Iron Fist and the Velvet Glove: An Analysis of the U.S. Police* (Berkeley, CA: Center for Research on Criminal Justice, 1977), 20.

3. Rubinstein, *City Police*, 5.

4. Ibid., 6.

5. Ibid.

6. Mark Abrahamson, *Urban Enclaves: Identity and Place in America* (New York: St. Martin's Press, 1996), 11–13.

7. Rubinstein, *City Police*, 6.

8. Samuel Walker and Charles M. Katz, *The Police in America: An Introduction*, 4th ed. (Boston: McGraw-Hill, 2002), 25.

9. Ibid., 25. Walker and Katz provided a nice discussion of why history is relevant to the understanding of the development of the police. They traced the political and social forces that were behind the major reforms of law enforcement.

10. Wilber R. Miller, "Cops and Bobbies, 1830–1870," in *Thinking about Police: Contemporary Readings*, ed. Carl B. Klockars (New York: McGraw-Hill, 1983), 72–87.

11. Mark H. Haller, "Chicago Cops, 1890–1925," in *Thinking about Police: Contemporary Readings*, ed. Carl B. Klockars (New York: McGraw-Hill, 1983), 87–99.

12. Richard Maxwell Brown, "Vigilante Policing," in *Thinking about Police: Contemporary Readings*, ed. Carl B. Klockars (New York: McGraw-Hill, 1983), 58.

13. Ibid., 57–71.

14. Ibid., 69.

15. Ibid., 70–71.

16. Center for Research on Criminal Justice, *Iron Fist*, 26.

17. Samuel Walker, *A Critical History of Police Reform* (Lexington, MA: Lexington Books, 1977).

18. Lincoln Steffens, *The Autobiography of Lincoln Steffens* (New York: Harcourt Brace Jovanovich, 1931). Lincoln Steffens was a leading muckraking journalist, and his autobiography is a fascinating and accessible account of how he exposed corruption in city and state governments across the nation.

19. Center For Research on Criminal Justice, *Iron Fist*, 32.

20. Walker and Katz, *Police in America*, 34.

21. Center for Research on Criminal Justice, *Iron Fist*, 37.

22. Ibid., 39.

23. Thomas Barker, Ronald D. Hunter, and Jeffery P. Rush, *Police Systems and Practices: An Introduction* (Englewood Cliffs, NJ: Prentice Hall, 1994), 77.

24. Robert M. Regoli and John D. Hewitt, *Criminal Justice* (New York: Prentice Hall, 1996), 259.

25. Peter K. Manning, "Lying, Secrecy, and Social Control," in *Police Deviance*, eds. Thomas Barker and David L. Carter (Cincinnati, OH: Pilgrimage, 1986), 96–119.

26. Thomas Barker, "Peer Group Support for Police Occupational Deviance," in *Police Deviance*, eds. Thomas Barker and David L. Carter (Cincinnati, OH: Pilgrimage, 1986), 7–19.

27. Samuel Walker and Charles M. Katz, *The Police in America: An Introduction*, 5th ed. (New York: McGraw Hill, 2005), 231.

28. Brian A. Reaves, *Federal Law Enforcement Officers, 2004* (Washington, DC: U.S. Department of Justice, Office of Justice Programs, July 2006), 1, www.ojp.usdoj.gov/bjs/pub/pdf/fle004.pdf.

29. Curt Gentry, *J. Edgar Hoover: The Man and His Secrets* (New York: Norton, 1991).

30. A long list of these files can be found at the FBI online Reading Room at http://foia.fbi.gov/foiaindex.htm.

31. Tony Poveda, *Lawlessness and Reform: The FBI in Transition* (Pacific Grove, CA: Brooks/Cole, 1990).

32. John S. Dempsey and Linda S. Forst, *An Introduction to Policing*, 4th ed. (Belmont, Calif.: Thomson/Wadsworth, 2008), 49.

33. Ibid.

34. Walker and Katz, *Police in America*, 71.

35. Matthew J. Hickman and Brian A. Reaves, *Local Police Departments 2003* (Washington, DC: Bureau of Justice Statistics, 2003), 17. Online at www.ojp.usdoj.gov/bjs/pub/pdf/lpd03.pdf.

36. Sworn officers are "police employees who have taken an oath and been given powers by the state to make arrests, use force, and transverse property, in accordance with their duties." Dean J. Champion, *The American Dictionary of Criminal Justice* (Los Angeles: Roxbury, 2001), 132.

37. Bureau of Justice Law Enforcement Statistics, www.ojp.usdoj.gov/bjs/abstract/s099.htm.

38. Dempsey and Forst, *An Introduction to Policing*, 49.

39. www.talgov.com/hr/specs/387pdf/.

40. Walker and Katz, *Police in America*, 527–528.

41. William P. Bozeman and James E. Winslow, "Medical Aspects of Less Lethal Weapons," *Internet Journal of Rescue and Disaster Medicine* 5, no. 1 (2005).

42. Brian Rappert, "A Framework for the Assessment of Non-Lethal Weapons," *Medicine, Conflict and Survival* 20 (2004): 51.

43. Ibid.

44. Sharon Gaudin, "Pennsylvania Police Use Database as Crime-Fighting Tool," *InformationWeek*, January 19, 2007, www.informationweek.com/news/security/showArticle.jhtml?articleID=196902236.

45. Diane Cardwell, "New York State Draws Nearer to Collecting DNA in All Crimes," *New York Times*, May 4, 2006, www.nytimes.com/2006/05/04/nyregion/04dna.html; David H. Holtzman, "The Dangers of DNA Testing," *Business Week Online*, March 5, 2007, www.businessweek.com/technology/content/mar2007/tc20070305_747605.htm.

46. Federal Bureau of Investigation, www.fbi.gov/hq/lab/pdf/codisbrochure.pdf.

47. Holtzman, "Dangers of DNA Testing."

48. Richard Willing, "DNA 'Near Matches' Spur Privacy Fight," *USA Today*, August 3, 2007, 3A.

49. Ellen Nakashima, "From DNA of Family, a Tool to Make Arrests," *Washington Post*, Met 2 edition, April 21, 2008, A1, www.washingtonpost.com/wp-dyn/content/article/2008/04/20/AR2008042002388_pf.html.

50. John Shiffman, "A Nifty Little Crimebuster," *Philadelphia Inquirer*, City-D edition, August 6, 2007, A1.

51. Neil Macfarquhar, "Los Angeles Police Scrap Mapping Plan, Elating Muslims," *New York Times*, late edition, November 16, 2007, A31.

52. George L. Kelling, Tony Pate, Duane Dieckman, and Charles E. Brown, "The Kansas City Preventive Patrol Experiment," in *Thinking about Police: Contemporary Readings*, eds. Carl B. Klockars and Stephen D. Mastrofski (New York: McGraw-Hill, 1991), 163.

53. Lawrence W. Sherman and David Weisburd, "General Deterrent Effects of Police Patrol in Crime 'Hot Spots': A Randomized, Controlled Trial," *Justice Quarterly* 12, no. 4 (December 1995): 625–648.

54. Walker and Katz, *Police in America*, 168.

55. Jan Chaiken, Peter Greenwood, and Joan Petersilla, "The Rand Study of Detectives," in *Thinking about Police: Contemporary Readings*, eds. Carl B. Klockars and Stephen D. Mastrofski (New York: McGraw-Hill, 1991), 170–187.

56. Ibid.

57. Walker and Katz, *Police in America*, 179.

58. Maia Szalavitz, "DARE Doesn't Work," *Gotham Gazette* (March 2001), www.gothamgazette.com/health/mar.01.shtml.

59. Susan T. Emmett et al., "How Effective Is Drug Abuse Resistance Education? A Meta-Analysis of Project DARE Outcome Evaluations," *American Journal of Public Health* (September 1994): 1394–1401.

60. Harvard University, Kennedy School of Government, Boston Gun Project, www.hks.harvard.edu/criminaljustice/research/bgp.htm.

61. Edmund F. McGarrell et al., "Reducing Homicide through a 'Lever-Pulling' Strategy," *Justice Quarterly* 23, no. 2 (June 2006): 214–231.

62. David Kennedy, "Pulling Levers: Getting Deterrence Right," *National Institute of Justice Journal*, no. 236 (July 1998): 3, www.ncjrs.gov/pdffiles/jr000236.pdf; McGarrell et al., "Reducing Homicide."

63. McGarrell et al., Reducing Homicide."

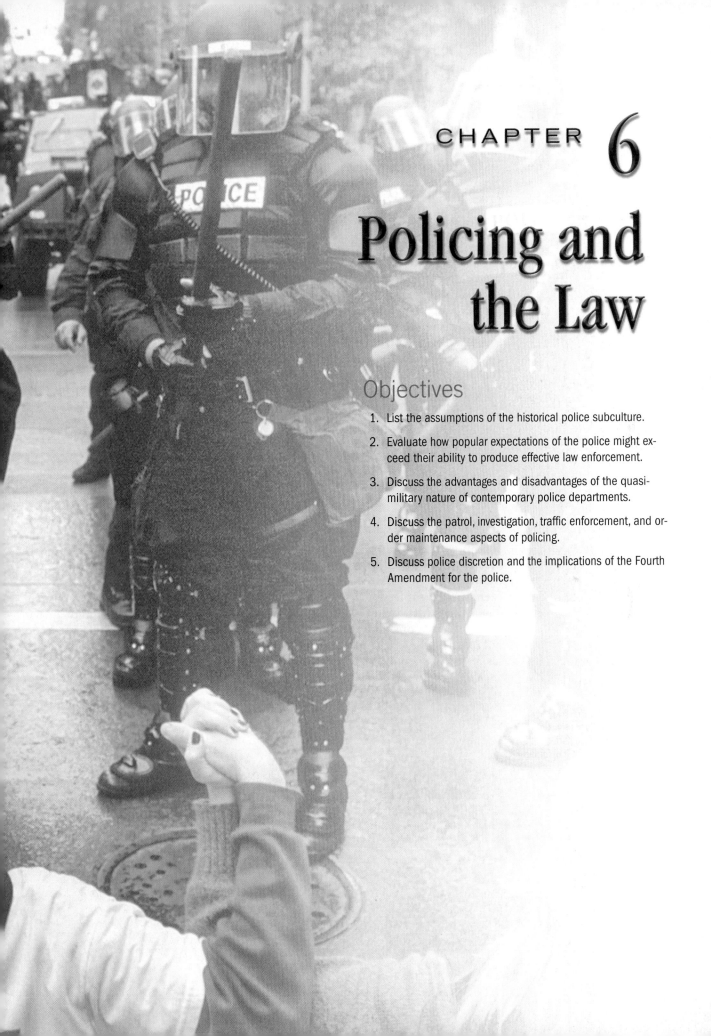

CHAPTER 6

Policing and the Law

Objectives

1. List the assumptions of the historical police subculture.

2. Evaluate how popular expectations of the police might exceed their ability to produce effective law enforcement.

3. Discuss the advantages and disadvantages of the quasi-military nature of contemporary police departments.

4. Discuss the patrol, investigation, traffic enforcement, and order maintenance aspects of policing.

5. Discuss police discretion and the implications of the Fourth Amendment for the police.

Law enforcement in a democratic society is accomplished with the greatest care and attention paid to how much authority is granted to the police. Although it may seem that the police simply enforce the legal statutes passed by the legislature, the reality of law enforcement in the United States is much more complicated, and for the student of criminal justice, far more interesting.

In this chapter we look at how the police are constrained in their efforts to keep order on the streets, provide services to citizens, and control crime. These constraints include legislative mandates that limit the power of the police, court opinions that police officers must consider in their duties, and an informal subculture of policing that exerts a powerful influence on how the police conceptualize their role. By appreciating how the police are controlled by forces both inside and outside their agencies, we can begin to understand why policing is often as much an art as a science.

The individual police officer makes dozens of decisions each day that consider the rights of offenders, the opinions of citizens, the demands of supervisors, peer pressure from fellow officers, legal statutes, and the officer's own good judgment as he or she decides how to act in what is a highly visible occupation. The first issue we will consider is police discretion. Discretion is mentioned in other chapters, but we will consider it here in more detail because it is at the core of the police officer's occupation.[1] Without the recognition of the problems and issues surrounding the exercise of discretion, a precise understanding of policing is impossible.

WHAT WE EXPECT OF THE POLICE

We expect a lot from our police, maybe too much. However, the police have claimed broad powers in staking out the mandate of their occupation.[2] As in other occupations, such as physicians, lawyers, and architects, the police have established a semi-monopoly on the core concerns of their profession. As the lawyer must possess certain education and training to be certified to practice law, and the physician must be qualified to practice medicine and prescribe drugs, so too the police officer has the authority to use legal force. When situations get out of hand, we "call the cops" to exercise their professional skills and judgment to maintain order and ensure justice. The alternative would be anarchy in which everyone decided for themselves what constituted reasonable force and appropriate justice. In fact, most police contacts do not require the use of force (see Figure 6-1). So, for the most part, law enforcement's mandate to use force seems reasonable. Some scholars, such as Peter Manning, however,

Figure 6-1   Of the 43.5 million people age 16 or older reporting contact with the police during 2005, about 1.6 percent had force used against them.
Source: Matthew R. Durose, Erica L. Smith, and Patrick A. Langan, *Contacts between Police and the Public, 2005* (Washington, DC: U.S. Department of Justice, Bureau of Justice Statistics, 2007), 7, www.ojp.usdoj.gov/bjs/pub/pdf/cpp05.pdf.

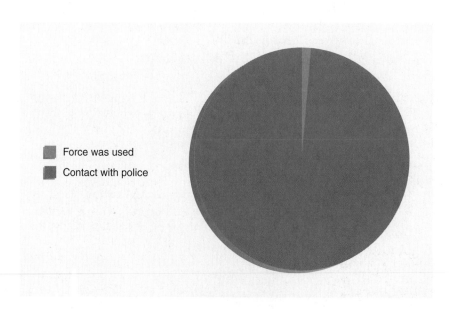

Force was used

Contact with police

contend that when we look at what the police claim as their legitimate domain, we can appreciate how their mandate is just too broad.[3]

According to Manning, the police have been assigned the tasks of crime prevention, crime detection, and the apprehension of criminal suspects in an efficient, apolitical, and professional manner. To respond to such an encompassing mandate, the police must develop an occupational culture that shapes their response to crime, lawbreakers, and the criminal justice system. Manning argued that this mandate requires the police to make assumptions about everyday life that give them an occupational perspective to guide their strategies and tactics in enforcing the law. These assumptions, created historically by American non-college-educated patrol officers, define the police subculture.[4]

1. People cannot be trusted; they are dangerous.
2. Experience is better than abstract rules.
3. You must make people respect you.
4. Everyone hates a cop.
5. The legal system is untrustworthy; police officers make the best decisions about guilt or innocence.
6. People who are not controlled will break laws.
7. Police officers must appear respectful and be efficient.
8. Police officers can most accurately identify crime and criminals.
9. The major jobs of the policeman are to prevent crime and to enforce laws.
10. Stronger punishment will deter criminals from repeating their errors.[5]

Given this occupational perspective, it is hardly surprising that police might view their role in a highly romanticized and idealistic way that portrays them as fighting dangerous lawbreakers and performing heroic acts. Yet the reality of law enforcement is quite different and much more routine.

> In an effort to gain the public's confidence in their ability, and to insure thereby the solidity of their mandate, the police have encouraged the public to continue thinking of them and their work in idealized terms, terms, that is, which grossly exaggerate the actual work done by the police. They do engage in chases, in gunfights, in careful sleuthing. But these are rare events. Most police work resembles any other kind of work: it is boring, tiresome, sometimes dirty, sometimes technically demanding, but it is rarely dangerous. Yet the occasional chase, the occasional shootout, the occasional triumph of some extraordinary detective work have been seized upon by the police and played up to the public.[6]

The problem of projecting this unrealistic image of the nature of law enforcement to the public is that this flawed portrayal of policing becomes the standard by which the police are evaluated. Unable to live up to this idealized image, the police are forced to construct what Manning referred to as "appearances." These appearances result in what can be called "goal displacement," in which the police concentrate on presenting themselves as crime fighters as opposed to public servants.[7] Because of this occupational culture of the police and the distorted view of the nature of law enforcement that the police project to the public, maintaining control of the police is a difficult issue.[8] The violent aspects of the use of force will be covered in Chapter 7, but it is useful here to consider how the military analogy affects how the police see and project themselves.

HOW THE POLICE WORK

Not all police officers adopt the same style of interacting with the public, other members of the criminal justice system, and offenders. Each individual brings different personality traits, motivations, training, and objectives to the job. Additionally, not all

Police officers must document their actions in order to effectively prosecute cases. Officers complain about excessive paperwork, but it is a necessary part of the law enforcement mission. Computer technology is beginning to make the paperwork less burdensome.

Source: Bob Daemmrich, Bob Daemmrich Photography, Inc.

law enforcement agencies are the same. The size of the community, the racial and ethnic diversity of the local population, the effects of local economic trends, and the history and political structure of the agency exert an influence on policing styles.[9] It is easy to see the differences between big-city departments and those of rural areas.[10] The nature of the crime problems is different, and citizens have varying expectations as to what constitutes optimal policing.

First we will discuss James Q. Wilson's classic typology from his book *Varieties of Police Behavior*. Wilson's three styles of policing illustrate important differences in how the police approach their tasks of maintaining order, controlling crime, and being of service to citizens.[11] These styles of policing are the **watchman style, legalistic style,** and **service style.** These styles are important because they set the tone of civility between the police and the public. By looking at what the police consider their primary mandates, we can begin to appreciate the distinct differences among departments. Finally, we will examine the quasi-military nature of police organizations, with a discussion of why police agencies are structured much like military units.

Watchman Style

The watchman style of policing distinguishes between two mandates of policing: order maintenance and law enforcement. Law enforcement is concerned with discovering who has violated the law and either arresting or otherwise sanctioning that person. This mandate is the one that we usually associate with policing. There is little need to exercise discretion in the law enforcement mandate: the person either broke the law or did not break the law. If he or she broke the law or is suspected of breaking the law, then an arrest is made or the person is otherwise sanctioned (such as being issued a ticket for driving too fast).

The other mandate, order maintenance, is also a primary concern of some departments.[12] Order maintenance involves discretion. Wilson recognized that arrests are not always made, even when the police discover a violation of the law and can identify the suspect. Often the police do not invoke the criminal sanction but instead release the offender with a warning or make an arrangement in which the suspect agrees to inform on other suspects in exchange for freedom. Thus, a police officer using the watchman style may tolerate a certain amount of gambling and vice, may let suspects in minor offenses go without arrest, or may simply tell unruly people (such as teenagers) to leave an area even when law violations are suspected. The key is to preserve the social order in an effort to keep citizens happy (especially powerful citizens, for whom the police officer will overlook some infractions).[13]

watchman style

A mode of policing that emphasizes the maintenance of order and informal intervention on the part of the police officer rather than strict enforcement of the law.

legalistic style

A mode of policing that emphasizes enforcement of the letter of the law.

service style

A mode of policing that is concerned primarily with serving the community and citizens.

The watchman style is a reminder of the past when the police worked for private agencies, and the interests of those private concerns took precedence over law enforcement. Under the watchman style, certain extralegal factors such as age, race, appearance, or personal demeanor are used in deciding when to arrest and when to release lawbreakers.

Legalistic Style

Unlike the watchman style of policing, the legalistic style requires little discretion. In many ways, this is a positive feature of policing, but it can be problematic. The legalistic style of policing concentrates on enforcing the law by writing more tickets, making more arrests, and encouraging victims to sign complaints. Whereas the watchman style of police officer may attempt to work out disputes informally, the legalistic style of officer will determine who is culpable, make the arrest, and allow the courts to resolve the incident.[14] The legalistic style is impersonal and disinterested. The focus is on treating all citizens alike and not requiring the officer to exercise discretion. The extralegal factors of age, race, social status, and appearance are much less influential in this style of policing than in the watchman style. The legalistic type of police officer is more likely to give the mayor a speeding ticket. Although this might be an oversimplification, we can think of the watchman style of police officer as walking a beat and the legalistic style of police officer as riding in a patrol car.

Service Style

The service style of policing shares characteristics with the other two styles but is concerned primarily with service to the community and the citizens. Like the legalistic style, it treats all law violations seriously, but the frequent result, as with the watchman style, is not to arrest. Instead, the department employs alternative strategies, such as official warnings or diversion programs. The discretion in these decisions is not used by the individual officer, but instead is part of the department's policy.[15] The key to the service style of policing is that discretion is widely used, but it is visible, is subject to formal review and evaluation, and can be altered when circumstances require.

Wilson's typology of policing is informative, but as with all typologies, it is not mutually exclusive and exhaustive. Other types of policing may be found in some departments, and a mixture of styles may occur within a department. A department might provide officers with little discretion in dealing with domestic assault cases and grant wide latitude in handling drug cases. Wilson's typology, therefore, is simply a guide, and in reality we may find considerable overlap or significant gaps.

Wilson's typology is more than three decades old, but the use and control of discretion remains a core issue for law enforcement scholars. What has changed is the ability of supervisors to consider the discretion of individual police officers. Primarily because of advances in technology, the work of the officer on the street has become more ascertainable.

The Quasi-Military Nature of Police Organizations

The structure of law enforcement agencies is similar to that of military units. A strict hierarchical chain of command accords status and responsibility according to rank, and uniforms display insignia that identify to both insiders and the public the exact social location of the officers. This quasi-military nature has some qualities that make it attractive to police organizations. Egon Bittner identified three reasons why the military model is attractive to police planners:[16]

1. **Controlling the use of force through discipline.**   Both the military and the police are in the business of using force, and the occasions for employing physical force are, as Bittner put it, "unpredictably distributed." Personnel must be

kept in a highly disciplined state of alert and preparedness, with reliance on "spit and polish" and obedience to superiors.

2. **Professionalization.**   The introduction of military-like discipline into police agencies in the 1950s and 1960s greatly professionalized departments that had been historically plagued by corruption and political favoritism and influence.

3. **An effective model of organization.**   The police lacked other models of organization. The military model, as primitive as it is, was easy to comprehend. Given that many officers had some sort of military background, it was easy to implement. Bittner argues that the police are the only large-scale institution that has not benefited from advances in management science.[17]

Although it is easy to understand how law enforcement organizations have evolved in this quasi-military manner, the military structure and culture result in some unintended and undesirable consequences. By having such a vast array of rules and regulations, law enforcement organizations ignore the reality that individual officers must exert a substantial amount of discretion in the everyday performance of their duties. To meet the expectations of the department, a good deal of energy is spent conforming to regulations, and creative and effective decision making is discouraged. According to Bittner, the police are beset with competing demands to stay out of trouble as far as internal regulations are concerned, while at the same time making arrests that "contain, or can be managed to contain, elements of physical danger."[18]

An important difference between law enforcement agencies and military units hampers the effectiveness of the military model in law enforcement. In the military, the superiors are expected to lead soldiers into battle. In police work, supervisory officers seldom have the chance to exert this kind of leadership and control, and are often viewed with contempt by officers on the line.[19] This is because the supervisors are unable to share the risks of policing but must hold the line officers accountable for decisions and behavior that are sometimes demanded by dangerous circumstances without the luxury of a great deal of time to contemplate.[20]

POLICE AS SOLDIERS   As we have previously discussed, the police and the military have a lot in common. Uniforms, classification of status by rank, the use of weapons, and chains of command are features of both organizations. The military model for

The police have adopted many features of the military. Here, a SWAT team in Saline County, Nebraska, moves in formation toward a house to serve a search warrant.

Source: Mikael Karlsson / Arresting Images

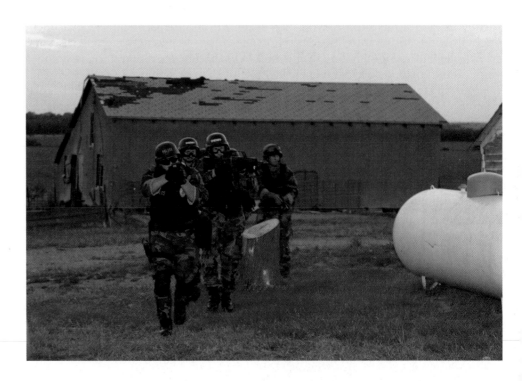

the police mission, however, is problematic.[21] The analogy of the police as soldiers is inexact and faulty and creates problems when the use of force is at issue. According to police scholars Jerome Skolnick and James Fyfe:

> [In responding to a comparison of policing to the Gulf War] . . . it relies upon an inexact analogy and is far more likely to produce unnecessary violence and antagonism than to result in effective policing. The lines between friend and foe were clear in the Arabian desert, but police officers on American streets too often rely on ambiguous clues and stereotypes in trying to identify the enemies in their war. When officers act on such signals and roust people who turn out to be guilty of no more than being in what officers view as the wrong place at the wrong time—young black men on inner-city streets late at night, for example—the police may create enemies where none had previously existed.[22]

There is a fundamental difference between how military organizations and police agencies deal with the issue of decision making.[23] In military organizations, important decisions are made at the top of the chain of command and flow downward. In policing, essential discretion is vested in the judgment of the individual police officer, who determines when an offense has been committed and whether to make an arrest. Even though the police agency has a hierarchical structure that, on the surface, resembles a military organization, the nature of discretion and the authority for decision making is actually reversed. Although police administrators can make broad policy and direct their officers' activities to some degree, police officers are dispersed widely, and each officer must decide individually when to invoke the criminal sanction. Modern communication has made the oversight of officers more efficient, but improved communications cannot mimic the type of organizational oversight that is available in the military. This is one reason that the selection and training of police officers is so important. They must be able to reason for themselves and interpret a given situation within a timeframe that often precludes getting input from superiors.

The military overtones of police departments have become entrenched in the war-on-crime philosophy promoted by politicians and the media.[24] In many ways, the idea of waging war on crime is an attractive way to think about a serious social problem. Much like President Lyndon Johnson's war on poverty, the war on crime implies that, finally, we are going to allocate the resources and mobilize the troops necessary to rid ourselves of the problem once and for all.[25] The war metaphor implies that sacrifices are going to be made and that a final victory over the enemy is possible. However, as Skolnick and Fyfe have already said, "police officer as soldier" is not a realistic or productive way to envision how the police do their job.

WHAT THE POLICE DO

The job of police officer involves a wide variety of activities. Many of these activities are well known and highly visible, such as patrol, whereas others are less obvious but equally vital, such as providing services to crime victims, helping individuals in distress, and answering calls for assistance about real and imagined problems. Police officers are among the first responders to natural disasters, accidents, emergencies, and criminal offenses.[26] In order to appreciate the complexity and range of activities performed by the police, it is useful to review the major functions of a typical police department.

Patrol

The most visible function of the police is patrol. The police patrol in squad cars or aircraft and on foot, bicycles, horseback, or motorcycle. Police patrol has three primary goals:

- **To deter crime**   When potential lawbreakers see police officers in the community, they are less likely to break the law. Because potential lawbreakers do not know how close the police are and because they fear that a patrol car could show up at any moment, they can be deterred from spontaneously breaking the law. Although people often break laws without thoughts of getting apprehended by police officers, many other offenses are deterred because of the ever-present threat of an immediate police response. When individuals see police officers patrolling the community, they are more likely to desist from breaking the law or move to another location.

- **To enhance feelings of public safety** Not only potential lawbreakers are affected by police patrol, but also ordinary citizens who are more confident if they can go about their daily routines without fear of being attacked or robbed or having their homes burglarized. Citizens who have confidence that the police are nearby are more likely to participate in recreational and civic activities and more likely to take advantage of public spaces such as parks and shopping malls. Feelings of security and public safety are essential for the development of meaningful communities where citizens interact with one another based on trust and courtesy rather than on the basis of suspicion and fear.

- **To make officers available for service** Think how inefficient and ineffective it would be if the police had to respond to calls for service in outlying areas of the community from a downtown police station. A good deal of time would be lost by traveling to crime scenes or other incidents, which would result in suspects leaving the scene, disagreements escalating into serious fights, and even people dying because the police took too long to arrive. By having the officers patrolling assigned beats or sectors of the city, they can be dispatched more quickly to calls for service.[27] Some large cities even have district police stations and storefront precincts that decentralize law enforcement resources. Police patrol not only reduces response time, but also allows officers to become more familiar with a particular section of the city, where they get to know shopkeepers, street people, and local residents. This knowledge enhances the ability of the police to gather intelligence about troublemakers, gangs, and neighborhood bullies, and puts a human face on the police agency because citizens recognize individual police officers.[28]

One of the duties of law enforcement is to secure government buildings. Although it might be unexciting and uncomfortable (especially in cold weather), this function is a vital part of our collective security.

Source: CORBIS-NY

Patrol officers enjoy facing new and different challenges each day. They are constantly bombarded with requests for services that can be either frivolous or serious. Because the police are first responders, it is their duty to assess situations and determine what type of resource should be committed to their resolution. Patrol officers are the public face of government and must deal with a host of situations that many would not consider serious police work. John Dempsey and Linda Forst provide the following list of activities the police are asked to perform:

> Patrol officers respond to calls about overflowing sewers and light being out, reports of attempted suicides, domestic disputes, neighborhood disputes, dogs running loose, reports of Martians trying to enter people's homes, reports of people banging their heads against brick walls, requests to check on the welfare of elderly people who have not been seen for a few days, requests to check out strange smells, requests to "do something about" the aggressive person on the street corner, and requests for information and help with almost anything you can think of. When citizens do not know whom to call, or other businesses or services are not available, they call the police.[29]

The police employ a number of strategies for patrol that vary according to administrative policies, urban geography, and the availability of officers in patrol cars. It is probably safe to say that no police chief believes that there are enough resources to provide comprehensive police patrol in his or her city, so police chiefs constantly struggle to convince city managers that police forces are inadequately staffed. Given this environment of limited resources, police administrators have developed a number of strategies designed to best maximize their patrol functions within a given jurisdiction.

- **Single-officer patrol cars**   The advantage of single-officer patrol cars is that more officers can be dispersed over a wider area. Many calls for service, such as responding to traffic accidents, involve mundane and routine activities for which only one officer is normally required.

- **Two-officer patrol cars**   Many departments staff a patrol car with two officers because of safety concerns. When the police must respond to offenses in progress, gang activity, or domestic disputes, it is advisable to have two officers so that they can protect each other. This show of force not only deters people from challenging the police presence, but it also makes catching and subduing suspects easier. The downside of a two-person patrol car is that they can patrol only half the area of two one-person patrol cars.

Experts debate the wisdom of single- versus two-officer patrol cars.[30] On one hand, officers are concerned about their safety, and on the other hand, police administrators are concerned about allocating resources efficiently. However, the Police Foundation found that officers in single-officer units were assaulted less often than when they had a partner.[31] Additionally, single officers made more arrests and wrote more crime reports than officers with partners.[32]

A major reason why police patrol is so popular is that the time it takes the police officer to get to the scene is assumed to be greatly reduced. However, research has not shown that a quick response time has any effect on clearance rates. This is because response time is a more complicated matter than generally thought. In fact, at least four aspects to response time must be considered:

1. **Discovery time.**   Not all offenses are immediately detected. A great time gap can exist between when the offense is committed and when someone notices it. This is especially true in burglaries in which the homeowner is away and returns only to discover that his or her house has been burglarized. In such cases, it makes little difference how quickly the police were notified because the perpetrator might be miles away by then.

2. **Reporting time.**   People often delay calling the police after discovering an offense. This can occur for many reasons, including fear or embarrassment on

the part of a victim, poor telephone service in rural areas, or the victim's thinking that he or she can solve the problem without police assistance. When such delays occur, the crime scene can go cold, perpetrators can escape, and witnesses can wander away.

3. **Processing time.**   Once the police are notified, it might take some time for a car to be dispatched. Reasons for this are an inadequate number of dispatchers, antiquated dispatch equipment, and lack of available officers in patrol cars.

4. **Travel time.**   Depending on how patrol cars are dispersed throughout the community, it may take a while for them to get to the crime scene. Often patrol officers are already engaged in incidents in neighboring sections of the city, where they may be doing such things as supporting other police officers in making arrests, quelling domestic disturbances, or simply taking a break for lunch. Travel time can vary greatly depending on the officers' distance from the crime scene or difficulty in reaching the crime scene, such as heavy traffic or other delays.[33]

Although we might commonly think that patrol cars are ready and poised to descend immediately on a crime scene, there are many reasons to worry that the police are not as close as one would hope. However, patrol strategy may be useful for other reasons besides response time. In proactive policing, officers take the initiative to detect and respond to crime rather than reacting to calls for service. In these incidents, a patrol officer may stop suspicious individuals or cars and detect lawbreaking. Furthermore, proactive policing allows officers to keep an eye on areas that historically have a high crime rate and intervene when they see someone breaking the law.[34] For all these reasons, police patrol is the most commonly used tactic for the allocation of law enforcement resources.

Are patrol cars the best way for police agencies to ensure quality service to their communities? Single-officer versus two-officer patrol cars are a constant debate in law enforcement circles, as is the rationale that the police should be in cars at all. Alternative forms of patrol are encouraged in some situations and environments. In fact, some experts say that officers patrolling on foot can be more effective in connecting with the community. Foot patrols have several advantages.[35] Officers can form a more intimate relationship with citizens and become sensitized to the ebb and flow of community life. They can enhance the quality of police–community relations while also acting as a deterrent on their beat. The obvious downside of foot patrol is the limited geographic area that one officer can physically patrol. Foot patrol is highly inefficient in cities that are spread out over many miles. However, for certain areas, such as shopping malls, parks that restrict motor vehicles, housing projects, and certain "hot spots," foot patrol can be more effective than patrol cars.

Police agencies are constantly looking for techniques to solve the inherent tension between patrol cars and foot patrol. How can officers patrol a large geographic area while also maintaining close contact with citizens? One solution that many police agencies have adopted is bicycle patrol. Bicycle patrol has the advantages of expanding the range that police officers can cover, allowing police officers to patrol areas where motor vehicles are prohibited, and keeping officers in close touch with the community. In many ways, the patrol car acts as a barrier between the police and citizens, whereas a bicycle requires officers to interact with people on a more personal basis. An obvious disadvantage that bicycle patrol shares with foot patrol is that should a suspect jump into an automobile, the police officer is unable to pursue.

Investigation

Deterring crime and responding to citizen complaints are only some of the aspects of police work. Another common function of the police is to investigate offenses. Detectives go to a crime scene after the patrol car has responded and take over the evidence gathering so that the patrol car can be released to resume patrol. Although detectives are often glamorized in the media and movies, their work is really not as exciting as that of a patrol officer. A great deal of their time is spent questioning victims and witnesses and trying to re-create what happened.[36] Often many days, weeks, or months go by before the full picture can be put together and an arrest made. Unfortunately, all too often the detectives are unable to find out who committed the offense. At other times, the patrol officer has done everything necessary to make the case against the suspect, and the detective simply fills out the paperwork and ensures that the case is presentable to the prosecutor.

A host of other individuals, including photographers, crime-scene technicians, and representatives of the coroner's office, help detectives investigate the case and put together the evidence. The coordination between patrol officers and detectives is handled by police administrators with the overall goal of ensuring that crimes are solved and that patrol officers are not unduly hampered in their primary duties.

Traffic Enforcement

Local police agencies and state highway patrols are responsible for ensuring safety on the roadways, including streets, roads, rural routes, interstate highways, and anywhere that automobiles are allowed. The activities of these agencies include responding to accidents, setting up roadblocks to detect drunk drivers or apprehend suspects, and enforcing traffic laws. Although not as glamorous as police patrol or investigation work, traffic duties most often bring police officers into close contact with citizens (see Figure 6-2).

However, enforcing traffic laws can be among the most dangerous aspects of police work. An officer never knows who he or she is stopping, and citizens can resent being pulled over. One study shows that 13 percent of police deaths have occurred during traffic stops.[37] When making routine traffic stops, the officer might be tempted to let down his or her guard. However, the driver might be fleeing a crime scene, an escaped felon, impaired by drugs or alcohol, or all three. Additionally, many traffic stops are made at night when it is more difficult for an officer to accurately assess a dangerous situation.

Traffic enforcement policy can vary greatly by jurisdiction. For some agencies, traffic enforcement is a major source of revenue, whereas for others enforcing traffic laws is a low priority because they are busy with more serious offenses. At times, police agencies make major initiatives to crack down on drunk driving.[38] On holiday weekends, when more people are expected on the highways, local agencies and state

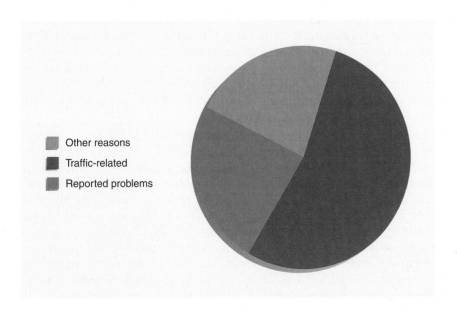

Figure 6-2   **Just over half of reasons for contact with police in 2005 involved traffic-related incidents.**
Source: Matthew R. Durose, Erica L. Smith, and Patrick A. Langan, *Contacts between Police and the Public, 2005* (Washington, DC: U.S. Department of Justice, Bureau of Justice Statistics, 2007), 1, www.ojp.usdoj.gov/bjs/pub/pdf/cpp05.pdf.

Other reasons
Traffic-related
Reported problems

patrols step up efforts to enforce speeding and driving-under-the-influence laws to try to reduce the number of automotive fatalities.[39]

Peacemaking and Order Maintenance

Although traffic enforcement, patrolling the streets, and investigating offenses constitute the heart of police work, they do not encompass the varied and subtle duties that the police must perform. A major function of being a police officer is solving problems. A number of issues routinely arise that might be better addressed by other agencies, but these often fall to the police because of the time of day or a lack of resources, or because the police are assumed to be the appropriate agency because of their authority. The following is a partial list of these extraordinary police duties:

- **Domestic disputes** Police officers are often called to domestic disputes between married couples, family members, roommates, and neighbors. When people cannot reasonably solve an interpersonal dispute, sometimes the police are called to mediate. Sometimes the mere presence of an officer is enough to quell the disturbance, and sometimes the arrival of police escalates the problem. Domestic disputes can be especially dangerous incidents for the police because emotions run high and, all too often, drugs or alcohol are involved. However, police officers are trained to lessen the tension and negotiate solutions. Often a police officer can defuse the situation through a combination of reason, understanding, or threat of arrest.[40]

- **Crowd control** Sociologists have long observed that large groups of people engage in collective behavior when they will do something as part of a group that they would not do by themselves. This "mob mentality" can be witnessed at social protests, sporting events, and public celebrations. Police officers are dispatched to contain crowds and ensure that laws are not broken and people are not injured. This type of policing presents special challenges for police agencies because it requires the coordination of a large number of officers. Normally, officers work alone or in pairs and are expected to use a great deal of discretion. In crowd-control situations, officers are required to act more as a military unit in which a commander makes a judgment and individual officers work as a team to implement it. These types of situations require special training, coordination between numerous law enforcement agencies, and advanced communications technology.[41]

- **Vice** Gambling, recreational drug use, and prostitution are just a few "victimless crimes" that police officers must deal with.[42] Vice laws vary by jurisdiction: for example, casino gambling is legal in Nevada but not in other states. Vice offenses, many of which are a response to supply and demand forces in the marketplace, are extremely difficult for police officers to deter, investigate, and prosecute. Nevertheless, police agencies do not get to select which behaviors are going to be illegal. They are obligated to enforce every law. However, police agencies can decide that certain offenses are less of a priority than others and simply spend less time on them.

- **Mental illness** One of the most perplexing problems that police officers must face is dealing with the mentally ill. The police are responsible for keeping the mentally ill from harming themselves and others while at the same time preserving their constitutional rights. Often mentally ill people are unable to understand and accept reason and must be physically restrained. Although police officers may have sympathy for a mentally ill individual who is causing problems, the possibility of violence means that the officer must always be prepared. Part of the problem is that many communities provide few alternatives for dealing with the mentally ill. Experts agree that, for the most part, the mentally ill are better treated in the community than in secure institutions, so the laws have specified that many people with mental health problems cannot be locked up. Therefore, it falls to the police to deal with the mentally ill, who are often poor, homeless, or hostile. Police require special training in the laws of dealing with the mentally ill, techniques for defusing individuals with a tenuous grasp of reality, and maintaining their own sanity when dealing with dangerous and unreasonable people.[43]

- **Juveniles**   In addition to enforcing the law, police officers must deal with juveniles who break the law and engage in behaviors that are prohibited because of their age, such as drinking alcohol, skipping school, and running away from home. Additionally juveniles can commit serious offenses that the police must respond to without knowing the suspect's age. Dealing with juvenile suspects presents a host of legal, social, and moral dilemmas for police officers. Larger police agencies have officers specially dedicated to dealing with juvenile offenders.[44]

- **First response**   In times of crisis such as natural disasters, terrorist attacks, and other types of emergencies, the police not only are among the first officials to arrive on the scene, but are also responsible for maintaining order, limiting damage and injury, and ensuring that the situation does not become completely chaotic. This duty as a first responder is taken for granted by society until something drastically goes wrong. In recent years, the role of the police as first responders has been emphasized by the terrorist attacks of September 11, as well as the Hurricane Katrina disaster in the Gulf Coast states. When Hurricane Katrina struck New Orleans, the social order broke down as the levees failed to hold back floodwaters. Police officers did not have the necessary equipment, communications, and command structure to act effectively as first responders, and nearly 300 officers did not report for duty after the storm.[45] In an assessment of the New York Police Department's response to the September 11 attack, an independent consultant for the department found that the NYPD effectively rescued civilians, evacuated Lower Manhattan, and managed traffic. However, lapses in leadership, communication, coordination, and training were evident, with officers and senior leadership unsure of who was in charge.[46] Unfortunately, real-life disasters such as September 11 and Hurricane Katrina test police departments and expose any weaknesses. However, such tests give police departments the information to improve their first-response capabilities. The intent here is not to criticize the decisions made by these police officers, which were made under great duress, but to study these examples in order to understand how crucial the police are in times of emergency.

THE RULES THE POLICE FOLLOW

In Chapter 4, we studied the distinction between substantive law and procedural law. As you recall, substantive law delineates which behaviors are proscribed by criminal statute. Homicide, rape, larceny, arson, and a wide range of other activities are defined in the substantive law, as are the penalties for committing them.

By contrast, the procedural law dictates how the government can go about discovering and prosecuting violations of the substantive law. One way to consider procedural law is to think of it as the rules by which the government must play. Some people may think of procedural law as "tying the hands of the police" or "letting criminals go free because of technicalities," but the positive aspects of this control of government actions are extremely valuable in providing for a free and democratic state. Aspects of the procedural law were placed in the Constitution because its framers wanted to protect us from government abuses such as those found in the European monarchies of the time. For instance, in England, the crown used the device of general warrants to allow the king's agents to search shops and homes for whatever they wished.[47] In a famous speech before the House of Commons,

William Pitt articulated the value that a person's home is private, and that the government ought not intrude:

> The poorest may in his cottage bid defiance to all forces of the crown. It may be frail—its roof may shake—the wind may blow through it—the storm may enter—but the King of England cannot enter—all his force dares not cross the threshold of the ruined tenement.[48]

Those who work in the criminal justice system sometimes get frustrated by the scope and complexities of the procedural laws and often test the interpretation with aggressive crime fighting. The law is forever in flux as new cases are brought before the courts for rulings concerning new technologies, changing community standards, evolving political pressures, and the widening of constitutional protections to more and more groups of people. Consequently, the law is a living, breathing, changing set of rules that is adjusted to the demands of society. However, the law is based on long-held principles that limit just how far it can be stretched, and it dictates that either the underlying values incorporated by the Constitution must be met or the Constitution amended.

Police Discretion

The police do not make an arrest every time they are legally authorized to do so. Police officers turn a blind eye to many violations and never engage in full enforcement of the law. If the police attempted to enforce all the laws, at least two bad things would happen. First, the criminal justice system would be swamped by the workload. The wheels of justice would simply grind to a halt under the weight of a system clogged by many times the number of cases it can reasonably process.[49]

The second problem with enforcing every law would be that the most serious offenders would be obscured by the sheer mass of cases. The police would not have the time and resources to address the cases that represent the greatest dangers to society. Therefore, it is important to appreciate that the police, both as an organization and as individual officers, decide which laws to enforce, how much to enforce them, when to let some offenses slide, and when to devote attention to truly significant offenses.[50] These decisions on differential law enforcement are called *discretion*. Decisions to investigate, arrest, charge, and incarcerate are all made by the police in the legitimate performance of their duties. It is important to understand the dynamics that structure these decisions.

Kenneth Culp Davis, in his book *Police Discretion*, argued that the fact that the police do not engage in the full enforcement of the law is positive:

> Even though the police insist on interpreting the full enforcement legislation literally, they also insist on following what they regard as their own common sense. This means that they violate their own interpretation of the full enforcement legislation. And I regard that as an accomplishment. *The police wisdom has on a wide scale overridden the legislative unwisdom embodied in the literal terms of the full enforcement legislation.* The police are properly lenient to many offenders. They do adapt their enforcement practices to the dominant community attitudes they are able to perceive. They do often refuse to make arrests for offenses committed in their presence. They have even established many patterns of nonenforcement.[51]

For example, consider an interstate highway on which the posted speed limit is 55 miles per hour, but where traffic generally moves at 70 miles per hour. The police do not enforce the posted limit because to do so would mean ticketing about 90 percent of the drivers. There is an unstated understanding between the police and the public that a pattern of nonenforcement is permissible.

In some incidents the police use their discretion to engage in nonenforcement of the law. It might be fair to argue that the more trivial the offense is, the more likely the police will be not to practice full enforcement.[52] For instance, laws involving the possession of marijuana have long been subject to less enforcement than those involving heroin or cocaine. Additionally, the police are less likely to arrest two teenagers who fight at school than they are two adults who fight after a traffic accident. The context in which the violation occurs has a great deal to do with whether the police decide to invoke the criminal sanction.[53]

Although we might agree that the use of police discretion in deciding against full enforcement of the law is desirable, another side of police discretion is troubling. Police discretion also provides an opportunity for selective enforcement.[54] When the police use their judgment in deciding which infractions to pursue, prejudice, bias, discrimination, and individual values may factor into how the law is enforced. When accusations of **racial profiling** (discussed in greater detail in Chapter 7), favoritism, corruption, or laziness accompany selective enforcement, the community begins to lose faith in the fairness of the criminal justice system.[55] Yet the police might feel the need to enforce the law selectively as a result of the inconsistencies and unpredictability of the criminal justice system.[56] Kenneth Culp Davis listed four questions regarding selective enforcement:

racial profiling
Suspicion of illegal activity based on a person's race, ethnicity, or national origin rather than on actual illegal activity or evidence of illegal activity.

1. Should the police make arrests when they know the prosecutors will not prosecute the defendants or that the court will dismiss the case?

2. Do the police violate full-enforcement legislation when a law is broken in their presence but an arrest is (a) physically impossible, (b) less important than some other urgent duty, or (c) impossible because of limited resources?

3. Does insufficiency of police resources for full enforcement justify a system of enforcement priorities that takes into account all relevant reasons for enforcing or not enforcing? Or must the police indiscriminately try to enforce on any and all occasions, so that what remains unenforced will be so because of limited resources and not policy requirements?

4. Are the police always forbidden to make enforcement decisions on individual grounds?[57]

There are good reasons both for and against selective enforcement of the law. On one hand, it violates the idea of fair play: that everyone who breaks the law should be treated equally. When the police use discretion to decide whom to arrest, it can appear discriminatory. On the other hand, there might be legitimate reasons to engage in selective enforcement, reasons that result in a community with less overall crime and less damage to citizens and property.[58]

Take the hypothetical case of the vice officer who arrests a drug user and finds out that the offender is responsible for a number of burglaries to get money to support drug purchases. Although we might reasonably expect that the vice officer would charge the drug user with the burglaries, the officer also has an interest in discovering the user's source of the drugs. By arresting the user, some offenses are cleared, but the vice officer is more interested in drying up the source of the drugs with the reasoning that many more drug-related burglaries will be prevented if there are fewer or no sellers to satisfy the demand for drugs. By encouraging the user to provide information on the seller in exchange for dropping the burglary charges, the vice officer can attempt to clean up the drug trade in that neighborhood. It becomes, then, a value judgment on whether this selective enforcement is a justifiable action. Certainly the owner of a home that is burglarized would want the thief arrested and prosecuted. However, if drugs were being sold to the homeowner's children, the homeowner might consider it a reasonable compromise to let the burglar go if that person could help eliminate drug sales in the homeowner's community. See Focus on Ethics 6.1 for another selective enforcement scenario.

Faced with these mixed messages sent by legislators, police administrators, and citizens, police officers must exercise a great deal of discretion in deciding which laws to enforce and how fully to enforce them.[59] Certainly we do not want to give full rein to the police to completely decide how to enforce the law. Law enforcement without boundaries is a frightening prospect that the Constitution protects us from. Later in

6.1

FOCUS *on* ETHICS

IT'S ONLY MARIJUANA

As a city police officer, you are constantly called on to use your discretion in deciding when to invoke the criminal law. To be honest, you do not make an arrest every time you have the opportunity because you do not want to spend all your time processing petty cases.

One evening you and your partner are called to a fraternity house on the local university campus after neighbors complained of loud partying at 2 A.M. You are admitted into the house by an obviously intoxicated fraternity president, who says, "Come on in, officers. Look around all you want. There's nobody here but us chickens." As he giggles hysterically at his joke, you realize two things. First, he has given you permission to conduct a legal search of the house, and second, there is the unmistakable smell of marijuana emanating from both the fraternity house and its president.

As you and your partner conduct a cursory search, you easily find a water pipe, several half-full bags of high-grade marijuana, and about a dozen marijuana cigarettes that were tossed behind the couch, under chairs, and under the rug. You are about to cobble together all the marijuana to determine whether

a felony case can be made when your partner takes you aside and informs you that his wife's little sister, a high school junior, is present but passed out cold in one of the bedrooms. Your partner says his wife would kill him if her sister gets arrested, and he begs you to let everyone go with just a warning. You are concerned about the number of youths who are engaged in underage drinking and drug use, but your partner is insistent and says, "Hey, it's only marijuana."

What Do You Do?

1. Tell your partner that "the law's the law" and arrest everyone in the house on whom you think you can make a good case, including his wife's little sister.

2. Warn everyone in the house to keep the noise down and that if the neighbors complain again and you have to come back, you will institute option 1.

3. Gather up all the marijuana and alcohol and flush them down the toilet while sending everyone home, thus ending the party.

this chapter we review how the law constrains the police. However, although the law limits the actions of the police, it also allows them to exercise discretion on when to apply specific laws to certain situations. Consequently, even though we try to control discretion, it will always be a contested area of law enforcement.[60]

The Fourth Amendment

The procedural law that controls the activities of law enforcement is derived from the Fourth Amendment of the Constitution. Although a number of state laws, court cases, and departmental regulations specify how the police can go about investigation, interrogation, and arrest, all of these rules and regulations must be consistent with the Supreme Court's interpretation of the Fourth Amendment (see Criminal Justice Reference 6.1).

Although it constitutes only one sentence, the Fourth Amendment covers a lot of territory. It specifies a wide range of protections from police activity and essentially ensures that citizens are not subject to the arbitrary actions of overzealous police officers (see Crosscurrents). However, the Fourth Amendment does not completely tie the hands of the police. It is subject to interpretation by the courts, and its wording allows justices to include in their rulings their judgment about what the framers of the Constitution intended and what contemporary society demands. For instance, the

6.1

CRIMINAL JUSTICE REFERENCE

The Fourth Amendment

The right of the people to be secure in their persons, houses, papers, and effects, against unreasonable searches and seizures, shall not be violated, and no Warrants shall issue, but upon probable cause, supported by oath or affirmation, and particularly describing the place to be searched, and the persons or things to be seized.

6.1 CrossCurrents

The Fourth Amendment: A Constitutional Hurdle

The Fourth Amendment makes the job of police officers more challenging. It strictly limits the discretion they have in searching for and seizing evidence, and it requires the oversight of a judge to determine whether **probable cause** exists to obtain a search warrant. Because the police can become frustrated by procedural law, they sometimes attempt to circumvent it in fulfilling their duties.

Criminologist L. Paul Sutton examined how the Fourth Amendment actually is implemented in several cities. Sutton found that the process most often appeared to operate as intended, but he also found that police officers attempt to get around the Fourth Amendment in several ways. Listed here are several strategies that are problematic:

- *Consent.* Conducting a search with the consent of the subject is legal. However, that consent should be given voluntarily and intelligently. There is sometimes a question of whether a suspect knows that consent for a search can be denied. Police officers are not required to advise a suspect that he or she is allowed to deny consent.

- *Timing.* The police might time their arrest of the subject so that they can, for example, impound a car and conduct a legal inventory search of the contents for safekeeping. Even though the facts of the arrest might not be sufficient for a formal charge, the results of the search can be allowed. Thus, arrest can be used as a ruse to legally search the car.

- *Harassment.* Even when the police know they do not have probable cause to seek a legal search warrant, they might attempt to harass the suspects. Sutton reported some officers saying they would knock on a door and shout, "This is the police. Open up." As they listened to the toilets being repeatedly flushed, they speculated that expensive illegal drugs were being destroyed. The intent of the police was not to conduct a search but to simply scare the suspects into destroying their drugs.

- *Judge shopping.* Some judges are more sympathetic to the concerns of law enforcement than others are. Thus, in almost every jurisdiction there are preferred judges for the police to approach with a request for a search warrant. Although Sutton did not interview any judges who admitted to being "easy," he did talk to judges who claimed that some of their brethren did not sufficiently consider the specifics of the case.

- *Falsification or misrepresentation.* Sometimes the police simply lie to the judge to obtain a search warrant. The lie might sometimes be a little "fudging" of the actual circumstances, but could occasionally involve intentional perjury.

Although police officers may circumvent the Fourth Amendment to be more effective in controlling crime, it is problematic for society. Violating the procedural law means not only that a case may be thrown out of court on a technicality, but more important, it denies citizens the full protection of the law.

Think About It

1. Should police try to circumvent the Fourth Amendment in order to search suspects they believe are guilty or dangerous?
2. Should search-and-seizure rules be relaxed in favor of the police? Should they be tightened in favor of citizens?

Source: L. Paul Sutton, "Getting around the Fourth Amendment," in *Thinking about Police: Contemporary Readings*, 2nd ed., eds. Carl B. Klockars and Stephen D. Mastrofski (New York: McGraw-Hill, 1991), 433–446.

---

interpretation of the word *unreasonable* is fraught with difficulty. What is reasonable to one individual is unreasonable to another. Yet the police must be given guidelines to ensure that the cases they present to the prosecutor are not considered unreasonable by the court. To appreciate the intricacies of the Fourth Amendment as a guide for procedural law, we must examine its language in greater detail.

SEARCH   Prosecuting criminal cases depends on information. Many times, the required information is readily available to police officers, but more often they have to work hard at assembling the evidence necessary to secure a conviction. Suspects, especially the guilty ones, do not always cooperate fully with the officers who are investigating them. Suspects might hide, alter, or destroy evidence in their efforts to avoid detection and arrest. The police may search the suspect in a reasonable manner,

probable cause
A reason based on known facts to think that a law has been broken or that a property is connected to a criminal offense.

but the court draws a line at the fuzzy concept of unreasonable searches, and the police must be trained in procedural law to judge which is which. A review of some of the concerns of the court is instructive.

1. **Trespass doctrine.**   The trespass doctrine defines what constitutes a search. The court says that a search requires physical intrusion into a constitutionally protected area. The Fourth Amendment specifies these areas as persons, houses, papers, and effects. Thus, any search of these areas must meet the requirements of the Fourth Amendment as being reasonable. Asking for a handwriting sample is not considered physically intrusive and is not deemed a search protected by the Fourth Amendment. However, most of us believe the government has no right to demand our bodily fluids in its search for evidence. After all, doesn't the Fourth Amendment protect our person? The courts have ruled that under some circumstances, such as when you drive an automobile, participate in high school sports (or more recently, in any high school extracurricular activities), the safety of others makes taking blood or urine tests reasonable searches.[61]

2. **Privacy doctrine.**   In 1967 the privacy doctrine essentially replaced the trespass doctrine in *Katz* v. *United States*. This case held that people, not places, are protected from government intrusion whenever they have an expectation of privacy that society recognizes as reasonable. The police are given quite a bit of latitude in dealing with citizens on the street and in public places where privacy is usually not expected.[62] Deciding between the needs of law enforcement to maintain safety and the citizens' rights to privacy is a delicate balancing act.[63]

3. **Plain-view doctrine.**   The plain-view doctrine is actually not an accurate name for the principle that officers have a lawful right to use all their senses (sight, smell, hearing, and touch) to detect evidence of unlawful action. The plain-view doctrine also stipulates that such detection of evidence does not constitute a search because the police are not searching when they merely observe what is around them. Thus, the plain-view doctrine holds that the Fourth Amendment does not protect such gathering of evidence because no search has actually occurred.[64] Three criteria must be met for the discovery of evidence to fall outside the Fourth Amendment's definition of a search: (a) officers are lawfully present when and where they discover the evidence; (b) detection occurs without advanced technology enhancing the ordinary senses; and (c) detection is inadvertent. Thus, when a police officer pulls a car over for speeding and sees a bag of marijuana on the passenger seat in plain view, the officer can arrest the driver for possession without the Fourth Amendment becoming an issue because no search was conducted.[65] Conversely, if the officer stopped the car because the driver simply looked suspicious and, without asking the driver's permission, felt under the seat and found a bag that contained marijuana, the actions of the officer would be deemed an illegal search according to the Fourth Amendment.[66] The court does not allow law enforcement to use sophisticated technology to enhance their natural senses in discovering evidence in plain view. This does not mean that absolutely no technology can be used, only technology that is not available to most people. Thus, the police may use flashlights, binoculars, and even airplanes to look for unlawful activity. In a recent case, the court drew the line at the use of thermal-imaging devices. The police used such a device to measure the heat emitted by special lights used to grow marijuana in a house as probable cause to secure a search warrant. The court ruled against the government, contending that such a device was beyond the plain-view doctrine.[67]

4. **Open-fields doctrine.**   The right to privacy does not extend to open fields even if the property is privately owned. The police can arrest landowners for cultivating marijuana on private land even if the police were trespassing on that land. The line at which the Fourth Amendment protections apply is drawn at where someone has a reasonable expectation of privacy.[68] Thus, the open-fields doctrine does not include the curtilage (surrounding area of land) of a home.

One's yard, pool or patio area, and attached garage are covered by the Fourth Amendment, whereas a barn far out in a field that is not used for family purposes would fall under the open-fields doctrine.[69]

5. **Public places.**   The Fourth Amendment does not protect individuals from being observed by the police using ordinary senses in public places. The street, parks, private businesses that are open to the public, and the public areas of restrooms are all outside the protection of the plain-view doctrine of the Fourth Amendment. However, employee areas of a business are protected, as are the stalls of a restroom where one could reasonably expect privacy. If, however, the police officer saw smoke rising over the top of the stall and that smoke gave off the distinctive odor of marijuana, the protections of the Fourth Amendment would not apply.[70]

6. **Abandoned property.**   The Fourth Amendment does not extend to abandoned property. Again, the expectation of privacy is important in concluding whether the Fourth Amendment covers the property. Abandonment requires the individual to intend to permanently discard the property. For example, turning your car over to a valet parking attendant would not constitute abandonment because you expect to get your car back, and you also expect that your rights of privacy will remain intact. Putting your household trash on the curb to be picked up by the garbage collector is another matter. Because we cannot expect that our trash will be free from the prying eyes of others, we are careful (or should be) to make sure credit card numbers and other sensitive information are destroyed before they go into the trash.[71]

We are left then with a complex pattern of the legality of law enforcement searches (see Case in Point 6.1). The Constitution does not say the government cannot search, only that it cannot conduct unreasonable searches. Police officers must understand the parameters of lawful searching to ensure that their cases can withstand constitutional scrutiny.

We recognize the necessity of police officers to search for evidence, but we also understand that unreasonable searches are one of the most intrusive features of the criminal justice system. No one likes to have his or her person, home, or "stuff"

6.1   CASE IN POINT

ILLINOIS V. GATES

THE CASE	THE POINT
Illinois v. Gates, 462 U.S. 213, 103 S.Ct. 2317 (1983)	Probable cause for a search does not demand proof beyond a reasonable doubt.

A married couple, Lance and Sue Gates of Illinois, were accused in an anonymous letter to police of buying and selling large amounts of illegal drugs. The letter contained explicit details about a complicated operation in which Mrs. Gates would drive a car down to Florida to be loaded with drugs, and then Mr. Gates would fly down and drive the laden car back to Illinois, leaving Mrs. Gates to fly back alone. The letter stated that the couple had bragged about their drug-selling business. Following the details in the letter, police tracked the Gateses' movements and found them consistent with the letter. The police obtained a warrant and searched the Gateses' home, where large quantities of drugs were found. The Gateses were arrested and convicted.

The couple appealed to the Supreme Court, stating that because the police could not assess the reliability of the letter's anonymous writer, no basis existed for the search warrant of their home. The court disagreed, citing that the "totality of circumstances"—meaning, in this case, how precisely the letter's specifics matched the Gateses' actions—and not the letter itself justified the search warrant. As for the informant, according to the court, "probable cause does not demand the certainty we associate with formal trials." The Gateses' convictions were upheld.

searched, and the court has tried to balance the rights of privacy of citizens with the needs of law enforcement to collect evidence of crime. The police are restrained in their searches by the requirement that they have a warrant. A valid warrant requires probable cause, a specific description of the persons and places that are going to be searched, and a description of the items that are to be seized. Furthermore, the warrant must be approved by a judge. Additionally, the officers must knock and announce their presence and give the occupants a brief time to answer before they enter the house to search.[72]

Two considerations exempt law enforcement from these Fourth Amendment provisions. The first is the problem of officer safety. If the police believe that an armed and dangerous subject is inside a home, should they be required to knock and announce their presence? To do so might invite a hail of gunfire. Second, by knocking and announcing their presence, the police may give suspects an opportunity to destroy evidence. Drugs can be flushed down the toilet or documents burned before the police have time to secure the scene. The court does not recognize any blanket exception such as a search of a dwelling where drugs might be used and sold, but it does recognize that, on a case-by-case basis, the knock-and-announce rule can be abbreviated. Anyone who has ever watched the television program *COPS* can see how the knock-and-announce rule is abbreviated in actual law enforcement practice.

A police officer must obtain a judge's approval to get a search warrant. As a practical concern, this requirement presents difficulties that can greatly hinder the case. It can take a long time to get the warrant, time in which suspects can escape or destroy evidence. Consequently, far more searches are conducted without warrants than with legally secured warrants. The court has recognized the following four major exceptions to the requirement that officers obtain warrants before conducting a search:

1. **Searches incident to arrest.**   When the police arrest a suspect, it is reasonable, according to the court, for them to search that suspect for weapons and incriminating evidence (see Case in Point 6.2). Additionally, the police may search the immediate area under control of the suspect to further ensure their safety and prevent destruction of evidence. The legal issue of what constitutes "under immediate control" of the suspect does not allow the police to extend the search to the whole house. To do this, the police would need to secure a warrant. In the case of an arrest of an individual in an automobile, the area under the control of the offender is deemed to be the **grabbable area**, which constitutes the inside of the passenger compartment but not under the hood or in the trunk. Again, the immediate safety of the police officers at the time of arrest and the danger of escape or the destruction of evidence allow this type of warrantless search.[73]

grabbable area
The area under the control of an individual during an arrest in an automobile.

6.2	CASE IN POINT

CHIMEL V. CALIFORNIA

THE CASE	THE POINT
Chimel v. California, 395 U.S. 752, 89 S.Ct. 2034 (1969)	*An arrest warrant allows only the search of a suspect's person and the immediate vicinity. Any further searches require a search warrant.*

Police officers suspected Ted Chimel of burglarizing a coin company in California. They went to his house with an arrest warrant, but not a search warrant, and Chimel's wife let them in. The police waited for Chimel and served him with the warrant when he returned home from work. Chimel denied the officers' request to search the house. The officers searched anyway and found some of the stolen coins in Chimel's attic. The evidence was used against him in court, and he was convicted of burglary. The Supreme Court overturned the conviction on Chimel's appeal because it said the officers' search of Chimel's house went far beyond what the arrest warrant allowed.

2. **Consent searches.**   Police officers may conduct a search without a warrant if they obtain the suspect's consent. Individuals may waive their right against a search as long as the police advise them that they have the right to refuse consent and that if the officers find incriminating evidence, it will be seized and used against them. This advisement regarding the waiver of consent is like the Miranda warning regarding self-incrimination. For a waiver of consent to be considered voluntary, it must be given by a suspect who feels free of coercion, promise, or deception.[74]

3. **Exigent-circumstances searches or emergency searches.**   Sometimes events happen so quickly that it is unreasonable to expect the police to stop and get a search warrant to determine whether there is a danger to their safety, a chance of suspect escape, or the likelihood of the destruction of evidence (see Case in Point 6.3). For instance, if the police chase a suspect into a house, they are not required to get a warrant to search the immediate area, but the search would be limited to the room in which the suspect was caught. The police could not go on a fishing expedition and search the whole house.[75]

4. **Vehicle searches.**   Historically, vehicles are exempt from the requirement of a search warrant. In short, a person in a vehicle has a reduced expectation of privacy as compared to someone at home. This does not mean that the police are free to search a vehicle arbitrarily.[76] Probable cause would still be needed, but one's car is not considered as sacred as one's home. Additionally, objects in a car that could conceal items the police have probable cause to suspect, such as a purse, are also subject to a warrantless search.[77]

The procedural law attempts to strike a delicate balance between the rights of individuals to be protected from overzealous police officers and the needs of society to provide those officers with the flexibility and discretion to protect society. Although the Fourth Amendment requirement of a search warrant is highly desirable, it is not practical in all situations in which the safety of an officer or evidence preservation is at issue. Therefore, the court has allowed a number of exceptions. Other types of searches pose legal issues that result in procedural law continuing to be contested. These are special-needs searches.

6.3 CASE IN POINT

TERRY V. OHIO

THE CASE	THE POINT
Terry v. Ohio, 392 U.S. 1, 88 S.Ct. 1868 (1968)	*Police have the right to search suspects to ensure their own safety if they think that the suspects are armed.*

A Cleveland police officer who was in an area that he had patrolled for many years saw two men, John Terry and a man surnamed Chilton, walking back and forth repeatedly in front of a store and pausing to stare in the window. The officer reported that they did this about 24 times. After each pass, they met and talked on a nearby street corner. They were joined by a third man, who left the group, but met up with them again a few blocks away from the store. The officer suspected the three men of inspecting the store in order to rob it later. The officer went up to the men and identified himself as a policeman. Suspicious, he checked Terry for weapons and felt a gun concealed in his coat pocket, and, in a further search, a gun in Chilton's pocket. Terry and Chilton were charged with and convicted of carrying concealed weapons. Terry appealed, the central argument in the case being whether police have the right to search people acting suspiciously if they believe a criminal offense is being planned. The Supreme Court upheld Terry's conviction.

SPECIAL-NEEDS SEARCHES   So far, our review of Fourth Amendment issues has dealt with how police officers must handle cases in which a law is believed to have been broken. In some circumstances searches are allowed in an attempt to prevent crime rather than to catch suspects. This discussion of special-needs searches will demonstrate how individuals other than criminal suspects are protected from unreasonable searches by the Fourth Amendment. Although these searches can result in criminal prosecution and imprisonment and do not require warrants of probable cause, they must meet a standard of reasonableness that balances the needs of the government against the invasion of individual privacy. For instance, the government cannot require all citizens to submit to drug testing even though many consider the drug problem in American society to be extreme. In certain situations, however, individuals who are not suspected of breaking the law are subject to special-needs searches because of a special status such as student, prison inmate, or pilot. Examples of special-needs searches include the following:

1. **Inventory searches.**   When the police impound property, they carefully inspect it and give the owner a receipt. This process protects the police from accusations of theft and ensures that drugs, guns, or explosives are not unknowingly handled in a dangerous manner while in police custody. If in conducting these searches, illegal drugs, weapons, or incriminating evidence are found, the police are allowed to use this information to prosecute cases without having to meet Fourth Amendment requirements of probable cause or search warrants. For example, if your car is seized and you have stashed drugs in a backpack in the trunk, the police may inspect the backpack and charge you with illegal possession.[78]

2. **Border searches.**   The right to control what comes into or goes out of the country allows law enforcement to conduct searches at the border without probable cause or a warrant.[79] There are some limitations, however. **Reasonable suspicion** is necessary for strip searches, and probable cause is required for body-cavity searches.[80] In addition to the problems of drug smuggling, increased concerns about terrorist attacks can be expected to make searches at borders more common and more rigorous.

3. **Airport searches.**   Because of a wave of airplane hijackings in the 1960s, the government instituted a process of inspecting all passengers with metal detectors before allowing them to fly. After the hijacking and terrorist attacks of September 11, 2001, the security at airports has become even more stringent. Now, in addition to carry-on baggage, all checked baggage is inspected by powerful X-ray equipment. The searches apply to all passengers, so the court does not consider these searches discriminatory. Also, advance notice is posted advising everyone that they will be searched, so individuals are free to not fly and not subject themselves and their luggage to intrusive inspections.[81]

4. **Searches of inmates.**   Do those who violate the law and are sentenced to prison lose all their rights? Does the Constitution stop at the prison door? For the most part, the answer is yes. The need to maintain a safe institution where weapons and contraband are constant threats allows the prison administration to extend only a "diminished scope" of Fourth Amendment rights to prisoners. The issues of prisoner rights will be discussed in more detail in Chapter 12, but it is sufficient to say that the court allows special-needs searches in prisons and jails to circumvent the protections of the Fourth Amendment in order to ensure safe, secure, and orderly institutions.[82]

5. **Searches of probationers and parolees.**   Those on probation and parole do not enjoy the same rights as those who are not under the supervision of the court or corrections department. One reason why probationers and parolees cannot expect full Fourth Amendment protections is that to secure their release from prison, they have signed a document waiving many of their freedoms. The court, therefore, considers any searches of probationers and parolees by a

reasonable suspicion

A suspicion based on facts or circumstances that justifies stopping and sometimes searching an individual thought to be involved in illegal activity.

Correctional officers must constantly search prison inmates for drugs, weapons, and contraband. Although inmates do not lose all their rights, rights against searches are greatly diminished.
Source: CORBIS-NY

probation or parole officer to be reasonable because they have consented to their restricted liberty.

6. **Searches of students.**   What level of privacy can students expect at school? Clearly, school administrators are responsible for ensuring a safe and secure learning environment, but where is the line drawn when considering the students' Fourth Amendment rights?[83] School officials do not need probable cause or a search warrant to search students. Reasonable suspicion is enough.[84] Additionally, some students, such as athletes and those engaged in extracurricular activities, may be subjected to random drug testing.[85]

7. **Employee drug testing.**   Although not strictly a law enforcement matter, the illegal use of drugs is of concern to society for a number of reasons. Drug use and abuse will be covered in greater detail in Chapter 15, but it is necessary here to point out how drug testing of employees is related to the other search-type issues that have been discussed in this chapter. With employee drug testing, the privacy of the individual from intrusion by the government must be balanced with the safety needs of society.[86] Those who are engaged in occupations that affect the safety of others, such as pilots, bus drivers, and train engineers, can be routinely and randomly tested for drug use to ensure that they are physically competent to operate their vehicles. Additionally, those charged with maintaining order, such as police and correctional officers, are also tested.[87] A wide range of other employees not engaged in public safety tasks are tested by private companies. These searches do not fall under the purview of the Fourth Amendment because the government does not conduct them.

SEIZURES   **Seizures** are an interesting and complex issue. The Fourth Amendment does not allow evidence that the police have acquired in illegal seizures to be presented in court. The police have the right to **stop** individuals and ask questions, and those individuals have the right to decline to answer the questions and walk away. If citizens exercise this right, the police cannot use the refusal to talk to them as probable cause that something is amiss and search the citizen. The police must have some other objective evidence in order to seize an individual. Citizens may feel a moral obligation or a civic duty to talk to the police, and the Fourth Amendment does not cover this. However, if the police intimidate the suspect to the point that he or she does not feel free to leave, then an illegal seizure may be deemed under the Fourth Amendment

seizure
The collecting by police officers of potential evidence in a criminal case.

stop
A temporary detention that legally is a seizure of an individual and must be based on reasonable suspicion.

6.4

CASE IN POINT

FLORIDA V. BOSTICK

THE CASE	THE POINT
Florida v. Bostick, 501 U.S. 429, 111 S.Ct. 2382 (1991)	The test of what constitutes seizure is whether the suspect is free to decline an officer's request for a search and terminate the encounter.

In Broward County, Florida, sheriff's department officers boarded a bus at a scheduled stop and asked passengers for permission to search their luggage for drugs. Two officers asked Terrance Bostick if they could search his luggage and advised him of his right to refuse. Bostick gave his permission, and the officers found cocaine in his luggage. Bostick was arrested and later convicted of cocaine possession. The Supreme Court upheld his conviction because he had allowed his luggage to be searched. The officers' actions did not constitute seizure under the Fourth Amendment because, according to the court, "taking into account all of the circumstances surrounding the encounter, a reasonable passenger would feel free to decline the officers' requests or otherwise terminate the encounter."

(see Case in Point 6.4). Surrounding the suspect with several officers, display of a weapon by an officer, physical touching of the citizen, or the use of language or tone of voice indicating that compliance with the officers' request may be compelled are the types of circumstances that could invoke a Fourth Amendment defense.[88]

stop-and-frisk
A term that describes two distinct behaviors on the part of law enforcement officers in dealing with suspects. To conduct a lawful frisk, the stop itself must meet the legal conditions of a seizure. A frisk constitutes a search.

STOP-AND-FRISK   From a procedural standpoint, the term **stop-and-frisk** encompasses two distinct behaviors on the part of police officers, and they must be considered separately before we can appreciate how they are related. The most basic way to think about them is to consider stops to be seizures and frisks to be searches. To conduct a lawful frisk, the stop must meet the conditions of a lawful seizure. It is useful to consider these actions individually:

1. Two types of situations in which police officers stop suspects are of concern to the student of the Fourth Amendment. These two situations are **actual-seizure stops** and **show-of-authority stops.** Actual-seizure stops involve police officers physically grabbing a person and restricting his or her freedom. Show-of-authority stops involve the officers showing their authority (such as flashing a badge) and the suspects submitting to it. The Supreme Court uses a **reasonable stop standard** that considers whether a reasonable person would feel free to terminate the encounter in deciding whether the stop is constitutional. The courts have ruled on the admissibility of stops in a wide range of circumstances. Some of the issues that have been considered by the courts are as follows:

actual-seizure stop
An incident in which police officers physically restrain a person and restrict his or her freedom.

show-of-authority stop
An incident in which police show a sign of authority (such as flashing a badge), and the suspect submits.

reasonable stop standard
A Supreme Court measure that considers constitutionality on whether a reasonable person would feel free to terminate an encounter with law enforcement personnel.

   - The role of reasonable suspicion in an officer's decision to stop a suspect
   - The use of an anonymous tip as a sufficient reason to make a stop
   - Race as an indicator for reasonable suspicion
   - The use of preestablished profiles as valid reasons to make a stop
   - The stopping of individuals at international borders
   - The constitutionality of roadblocks

   The legality of a stop, then, is highly contextualized and has been codified into procedural law by decisions made on a wide range of cases.[89]

2. Stops are seizures; frisks are searches. Although these two actions are closely linked, they are also quite different procedures that the law considers in great detail. Police officers may conduct a legal stop but engage in an illegal search

6.2   FOCUS *on* ETHICS

IMPROBABLE CAUSE

As a probationary rookie police officer, you are riding with your training officer, whom you have grown to respect and like. One night he tells you that it is time to learn how to do real police work. He spots a carload of young black males cruising the local strip mall and turns his blue lights on and pulls them over to the side of the street. He cautiously approaches the car when one of the passengers says, "Hey, cop. I'm a criminal justice major in college and I want to know what your probable cause is for pulling us over. This looks like a typical case of Driving While Black. We didn't do nothing."

Your training officer, himself a black man, walks to the back of the car. Using his large flashlight, he smashes the left taillight and says, "You have a broken taillight with an inoperative turn signal. That's my probable cause. Now I want each of you to exit the car slowly and lie facedown on the street. We'll start with you, Mr. Criminal Justice Major."

A search of the youth and the car results in the discovery of nine marijuana cigarettes and an unloaded .22-caliber pistol under the front seat. Despite the protests of the youths, your training officer tells you to arrest the subjects and says, "I'm giving you the credit for this one, rookie. You get the collar and you will get to go to court and testify. It will be great experience for you."

You know you are being tested here, but you are not sure exactly what the right answer is. On one hand, your training officer might be trying to determine whether you will go along with the illegal stop and bow to his pressure. He could be testing whether you will back a fellow police officer. On the other hand, the youth with the big mouth looks uncannily like your training officer and could even pass for his son. You wonder if you have been set up, in which case the right answer would be to challenge your training officer and refuse to make the arrest, thus showing that your first loyalty is to the law.

What Do You Do?

1. Challenge your training officer. Insist that you do what the law requires.
2. Support your training officer. You understand that in order to be an effective police officer, you must be trusted by fellow officers even if they want you to commit minor violations.

(see Focus on Ethics 6.2). A frisk involves a light patting of a suspect's outer clothing with the intent to determine whether a weapon is present. However, if the officer detects contraband (such as drugs) during the frisk, then even though the frisk was initiated to detect weapons, an arrest can be made for drug possession or even intent to sell. At issue is the extent of the frisk. Frisks are considered the least invasive type of search; full body-cavity searches are the most invasive. The court will consider evidence obtained in a frisk only if it is confident that the evidence was discovered by officers conducting the frisk with the intention of detecting weapons to ensure their own safety.[90]

ARRESTS   An arrest is more invasive than a stop. It involves being taken into custody, photographed, fingerprinted, interrogated, and booked (or formally charged with a criminal offense). A suspect who is stopped and frisked may be released, but if the case proceeds to the arrest phase, then a temporary loss of liberty results. Because this loss of liberty can last anywhere from a few hours to a few days, a higher standard of suspicion of guilt is required. Although reasonable suspicion is sufficient for a stop-and-frisk, arrest requires the police officers to have probable cause that the suspect broke the law.[91]

The way the police arrest suspects is also important. The amount of force used in the arrest should be consistent with maintaining the dignity of the suspects as much as circumstances allow. The court has ruled that deadly force is constitutionally unreasonable if it is used simply because the felony suspect is fleeing. In order to use deadly force, the officer must believe the suspect to be a threat to others. The court also has spoken to the need to have a warrant to arrest someone at home.[92] Although a multitude of circumstances and situations complicate the sanctity-of-the-home concept (such as when the police are chasing a suspect who runs into a residence), these exceptions must be considered in light of the language and intention of the

In *Terry* v. *Ohio*, the Supreme Court found that police have the right to search suspects to ensure their own safety if they think that the suspects are armed. Here, police officers remove a handgun from a suspect's person.

Source: *Mikael Karlsson / Arresting Images*

Fourth Amendment's guarantee that people should be secure in their homes. To arrest someone at home, the court recommends four restrictions:

1. **The offense should be a felony.**   This guards against arbitrary and abusive arrests and ensures that homes are invaded only for serious offenses.

2. **The police must knock and announce.**   This allows the individuals to get dressed and open the front door, thus assuring them of some degree of dignity.

3. **The arrest should be made in daylight.**   The fear produced by someone pounding on the door in the middle of the night should be avoided.

4. **The police must meet a stringent probable-cause requirement that the suspect is at home.**   This guards against the police entering the home and frightening others who live there or ransacking the home in their search for the suspect.[93]

Bear in mind that the four criteria listed here refer to arrests in homes, not searches. If these requirements were applied to drug busts, then the suspects would have opportunities to dispose of evidence.

INTERROGATION, CONFESSIONS, AND THE EXCLUSIONARY RULE   One of the primary ways that law enforcement officials gather information about criminal offenses is from the suspects themselves. By questioning suspects, the police can develop the required evidence to charge, prosecute, and convict lawbreakers. Although this interrogation of possible lawbreakers is exactly what we expect of the police, there are limits on exactly what methods can be used and on what types of help the suspects are entitled to. Even though the police might have good reason to suspect that an individual has broken the law, that person has constitutional rights that must be respected in the questioning process.[94] These rights stem from the Fifth, Sixth, and Fourteenth Amendments of the Constitution (see Criminal Justice Reference 6.2).

1. **Fifth Amendment self-incrimination clause.**   "No person . . . shall be compelled in any criminal case to be a witness against himself."

2. **Sixth Amendment right-to-counsel clause.**   "In all criminal prosecutions, the accused shall . . . have the assistance of counsel for his defense."

3. **Fourteenth Amendment due process clause.**   "No state shall . . . deprive any person of life, liberty, or property without due process of law."

6.2   CRIMINAL JUSTICE REFERENCE

Constitutional Amendments Related to Interrogation

Amendment	Text
Fifth Amendment	No person shall be held to answer for a capital, or otherwise infamous crime, unless on a presentment or indictment of a Grand Jury, except in cases arising in the land or naval forces, or in the Militia, when in actual service in time of War or public danger; nor shall any person be subject for the same offence to be twice put in jeopardy of life or limb; nor shall be compelled in any criminal case to be a witness against himself, nor be deprived of life, liberty, or property, without due process of law; nor shall private property be taken for public use, without just compensation.
Sixth Amendment	In all criminal prosecutions, the accused shall enjoy the right to a speedy and public trial, by an impartial jury of the State and district wherein the crime shall have been committed, which district shall have been previously ascertained by law, and to be informed of the nature and cause of the accusation; to be confronted with the witnesses against him; to have compulsory process for obtaining witnesses in his favor, and to have the Assistance of Counsel for his defence.
Fourteenth Amendment	Section 1. All persons born or naturalized in the United States and subject to the jurisdiction thereof, are citizens of the United States and of the State wherein they reside. No State shall make or enforce any law which shall abridge the privileges or immunities of citizens of the United States; nor shall any State deprive any person of life, liberty, or property, without due process of law; nor deny to any person within its jurisdiction the equal protection of the laws.

These amendments are used by defense attorneys and the court to oversee how the police conduct interrogations, elicit confessions, and seize evidence. In some cases, law enforcement officials might violate the law in conducting these activities, and the evidence gathered can be disallowed in court. We will deal with these issues in greater detail in Chapter 10, where we will examine them in the context of all the legal rights given to suspects. They are highlighted here to remind us that mistakes made at this stage by police officials will be ruled on at a later stage of the criminal justice process.[95]

SUMMARY

1. The police have the authority to use legal force. According to Manning, the police have the tasks of crime prevention, crime detection, and the apprehension of criminal suspects in an efficient, apolitical, and professional manner.

2. The individual officer, the size of the community, the diversity of the local population, local economic trends, and the history and political structure of the law enforcement agency influence policing styles.

3. Wilson's three styles of policing are the watchman style, legalistic style, and service style. The watchman style of policing is most concerned with order maintenance. The legalistic style focuses on enforcing the letter of the law. The service style is concerned primarily with service to the community and the citizens.

4. The structure of law enforcement agencies is similar to that of military units. According to Bittner, the military model is attractive to police planners for three reasons: it controls the use of force through discipline, it is an aid to professionalization, and it is an effective model of organization.

5. The job of police officer involves a wide variety of activities such as patrol, investigation, traffic enforcement, peacemaking, and order maintenance.

6. Police patrol has three primary goals: to deter crime, to enhance feelings of public safety, and to make officers available for service.

7. Another function of the police is to investigate offenses. Detectives go to a crime scene after the patrol officers have responded and take over the evidence gathering so that the patrol officers can be released to resume patrol.

8. Local police agencies and state highway patrols are responsible for ensuring safety on the roadways. Traffic duties most often bring police officers into close contact with citizens.

9. A final major function of being a police officer is solving problems such as domestic disputes, crowd control, investigating vice offenses, dealing with mentally ill suspects and juvenile delinquents, and acting as first responders to disasters and emergencies.

10. The procedural law, which dictates how the government can discover and prosecute violations of the substantive law, also governs how the police do their work. The procedural law that governs the activities of law enforcement is derived from the Fourth Amendment.

11. The police do not make an arrest every time they are legally authorized to do so because the workload would overwhelm the criminal justice system and the most serious offenders would be obscured by the large number of cases. The police, both as an organization and as individual officers, decide which laws to enforce, how much to enforce them, when not to enforce them, and when to devote attention to truly significant offenses.

12. State laws, court cases, and departmental regulations specify how the police can go about investigation, interrogation, and arrest. However, all rules and regulations must be consistent with the Supreme Court's interpretation of the Fourth Amendment, which concerns searches, seizures, and stop-and-frisks.

13. Suspects have constitutional rights that must be respected in the questioning process. These rights stem from the Fifth, Sixth, and Fourteenth Amendments.

KEY TERMS

actual-seizure stop 214	reasonable stop standard 214	stop 213
grabbable area 210	reasonable suspicion 212	stop-and-frisk 214
legalistic style 194	seizure 213	watchman style 194
probable cause 207	service style 194	
racial profiling 205	show-of-authority stop 214	

REVIEW QUESTIONS

1. Can discretion ever be removed from the role of the street-level police officer? What would be the likely consequences of such a change in the way laws are enforced?

2. Do we expect too much of our police officers?

3. Why are the police patterned after the military style of organization? What are the advantages and disadvantages of this structure?

4. James Q. Wilson presented three types of policing styles. Compare and contrast these styles and tell which one you think is the most effective.

5. What is the police subculture? In what ways might it be problematic for the fair and impartial application of the law?

6. Why is traffic enforcement the most common type of personal contact that police have with citizens?

7. What type of duties comprise the peacemaking and order-maintenance role of the police?

8. Compare the role of detectives and patrol officers in investigation.

9. What do we mean by the term *procedural law*? Where in the U.S. Constitution do we find the authority for our laws concerning searches?

10. What is a stop-and-frisk? How does this activity relate to search and seizure?

SUGGESTED FURTHER READING

Dempsey, John S., and Linda S. Forst. *An Introduction to Policing*, 4th ed. Belmont, CA: Thomson Wadsworth, 2008.

Oliver, Willard M. *Homeland Security for Policing*. Upper Saddle River, NJ: Pearson Prentice Hall, 2007.

Peak, Kenneth J. *Policing America: Methods, Issues, Challenges*. Upper Saddle River, NJ: Pearson Prentice Hall, 2006.

Skolnick, Jerome H. *Justice without Trial: Law Enforcement in Democratic Society*. New York: Wiley, 1966.

Travis, Lawrence F., and Robert H. Langworthy. *Policing in America: A Balance of Forces*. Upper Saddle River, NJ: Pearson Prentice Hall, 2008.

Walker, Samuel, and Charles M. Katz, *The Police in America: An Introduction*, 5th ed. New York: McGraw-Hill, 2005.

ENDNOTES

1. Kenneth Culp Davis, *Police Discretion* (St. Paul, MN: West, 1975).

2. The police claim the right to use force to resolve societal problems as part of their mandate. The rest of us are mostly happy to let the police do this "dirty work" on our behalf. This relationship has been sanctioned by legislatures that pass laws giving the police their powers. As in most occupations, law enforcement officials guard their powers by forming unions, lobbying lawmakers, maintaining the image they present to the public, and ensuring that rival groups, such as the private security industry, are given only limited authority. For an excellent discussion of how occupations, especially the police, establish their mandates, see Peter K. Manning, "The Police: Mandate, Strategies, and Appearances," in *The Police and Society: Touchstone Readings*, 2nd ed., ed. Victor E. Kappeler (Prospect Heights, IL: Waveland Press, 1999)

3. Peter K. Manning, "The Police: Mandate, Strategies and Appearances," in *The Police and Society: Touchstone Readings*, 2nd ed., ed. Victor E. Kappeler (Prospect Heights, IL: Waveland Press, 1999), 94–122.

4. Manning qualified these assumptions, which he drew from a number of studies conducted mainly in the 1960s, with the following paragraph: "Some qualifications about these postulates are in order. They apply primarily to the American non college-educated patrolman. They are less applicable to administrators of urban police departments and to members of minority groups within these departments. Nor do they apply accurately to non-urban, state, and federal policemen" ("Police and Society," 99).

5. Ibid.

6. Ibid., 100–101.

7. Jack R. Greene and Carl B. Klockars, "What Police Do," in *Thinking about Police: Contemporary Readings*, 2nd ed., eds. Carl B. Klockars and Stephen D. Mastrofski (New York: McGraw-Hill, 1991), 273–284. Greene and Klockars contended that the police spend more time on crime-related work than previous studies have indicated.

8. Thomas Barker, Ronald D. Hunter, and Jeffery P. Rush, *Police Systems and Practices: An Introduction* (Englewood Cliffs, NJ: Prentice Hall, 1994). These authors identified three primary roles for law enforcement: crime fighting, order maintenance, and service. They discussed the consequences of the crime-fighter image that they contended is promoted by the public, the media, and the police themselves. These authors said of the crime-fighter image, "in addition to creating unrealistic expectations about the police's ability to reduce crime, this narrow view prevents an informed analysis of the use of police resources" (p. 102).

9. Phillip B. Taft Jr., "Policing the New Immigrant Ghettos," in *Thinking about Police: Contemporary Readings*, 2nd ed., eds. Carl B. Klockars and Stephen D. Mastrofski (New York: McGraw-Hill, 1991), 307–315.

10. William V. Pelfrey Jr., "Style of Policing Adopted by Rural Police and Deputies: An Analysis of Job Satisfaction and Community Policing," *Policing* 30 (October 1, 2007): 620–636.

11. James Q. Wilson, *Varieties of Police Behavior: The Management of Law and Order in Eight Communities* (New York: Atheneum, 1968).

12. Ibid., 17–34.

13. Ibid., 140–171.

14. Ibid., 172–199.

15. Ibid., 200–226.

16. Samuel Walker and Charles M. Katz, *The Police in America: An Introduction*, 4th ed. (Boston: McGraw-Hill, 2002), 464.

17. Egon Bittner, "The Quasi-Military Organization of the Police," in *The Police and Society: Touchstone Readings*, 2nd ed., ed. Victor E. Kappeler (Prospect Heights, IL: Waveland Press, 1999), 171.

18. Ibid., 174–175.

19. Louis A. Campanozzi, "The Challenge of Interactive Management—Moving Gracefully from the Outdated Quasi-Military Police Management Style," *Law Enforcement News* (October 13, 1987): 6.

20. Bittner, "Quasi-Military Organization," 176.

21. Peter B. Kraska and Victor E. Kappeler, "Militarizing American Police: The Rise and Normalization of Paramilitary Units," *Social Problems* (February 1997): 1–17.

22. Jerome H. Skolnick and James J. Fyfe, *Above the Law: Police and the Excessive Use of Force* (New York: Free Press, 1993), 114.

23. Peter B. Kraska and Louise J. Cubellis, "Militarizing Mayberry and Beyond: Making Sense of American Paramilitary Policing," *Justice Quarterly* (December 1997): 607–629.

24. Peter B. Kraska and Larry K. Gaines, "Tactical Operations Units: A National Study," *Police Chief* (March 1977): 34–38.

25. In May 1964, while running for presidential office, Johnson called for a nationwide war against poverty and presented economic and social welfare legislation designed to create what he called the "Great Society." Infoplease, "Lyndon Baines Johnson," www.infoplease.com/ce6/people/A0859055.html.

26. Willard M. Oliver, *Homeland Security for Policing* (Upper Saddle River, NJ: Pearson Prentice Hall, 2007), 114–116.

27. Larry K. Gaines and Victor E. Kappeler, *Policing in America* (Cincinnati, OH: LexisNexis, 2008), 183–185.

28. Samuel Walker and Charles M. Katz, *The Police in America: An Introduction*, 5th ed. (New York: McGraw-Hill, 2005), 195–196.

29. John S. Dempsey and Linda S. Forst, *An Introduction to Policing*, 4th ed. (Belmont, CA: Thomson Wadsworth, 2008), 230.

30. Larry D. Nichols, *Law Enforcement Patrol Operations: Police Systems and Practices* (Berkeley, CA: McCutchan, 1995), 27–28.

31. John E. Boydstun, Michael E. Sherry, and Nicholas P. Moelter, *Patrol Staffing in San Diego: One- or Two-Officer Units* (Washington, DC: Police Foundation, 1977).

32. Walker and Katz, *Police in America*, 200.

33. Ibid., 213.

34. Lawrence Sherman, Patrick Gartin, and Michael Buerger, "Hot Spots of Predatory Crime: Routine Activities and the Criminology of Place," *Criminology* 27 (1989): 27–55.

35. George Kelling, *Foot Patrol* (Washington, DC: National Institute of Justice, 1987).

36. William B. Sanders, *Detective Work: A Study of Criminal Investigations* (New York: Free Press, 1977).

37. Illya Lichtenberg and Alisa Smith, "How Dangerous Are Routine Police-Citizen Traffic Stops?" *Journal of Criminal Justice* 29 (2001): 419–428.

38. H. Laurence Ross, *Confronting Drunk Driving: Social Policy for Saving Lives* (New Haven, CT: Yale University Press, 1992).

39. James B. Jacobs, *Drunk Driving: An American Dilemma* (Chicago: University of Chicago Press, 1989).

40. Franklyn W. Dunford, David Huizinga, and Delbert S. Elliott, "The Role of Arrest in Domestic Assault: The Omaha Police Experiment," *Criminology* 28 (1990): 183–206.

41. Bittner, "Quasi-Military Organization," 171.

42. Robert F. Meier and Gilbert Geis, *Victimless Crime? Prostitution, Drugs, Homosexuality, Abortion* (Los Angeles: Roxbury, 1997).

43. Judy Hails and Randy Borum, "Police Training and Specialized Approaches to Respond to People with Mental Illness," *Crime and Delinquency* 49 (2003): 52–61.

44. John Randolph Fuller, *Juvenile Delinquency: Mainstream and Crosscurrents* (Upper Saddle River, NJ: Pearson Prentice Hall, 2009), 395–429.

45. Alan Levin, "12 Officers under Investigation," *USA Today*, final edition, September 30, 2005, A3; Jere Longman, "New Orleans Police Superintendent Quits Amid Criticism," *New York Times*, late edition, September 28, 2005, A1.

46. William K. Rashbaum, "Report on 9/11 Finds Flaws in Response of Police Dept.," *New York Times*, late edition, July 27, 2002, A1.

47. Joel Samaha, *Criminal Procedure*, 5th ed. (Belmont, CA: Wadsworth, 2002), 88.

48. Quoted in Samaha, *Criminal Procedure*, 88.

49. Arthur Rosett, "Discretion, Severity and Legality in Criminal Justice," in *The Invisible Justice System: Discretion and the Law*, eds. Burton Atkins and Mark Pogrebin (Cincinnati, OH: Anderson, 1978), 24–33.

50. Ibid., 25.

51. Davis, *Police Discretion*, 65–66. Chapter 3 is titled "The Pervasive False Pretense of Full Enforcement."

52. Albert Reiss Jr., "Discretionary Justice in the United States," in *The Invisible Justice System: Discretion and the Law*, eds. Burton Atkins and Mark Pogrebin (Cincinnati, OH: Anderson, 1978), 41–58.

53. Melissa Schaefer Morabito, "Horizons of Context: Understanding the Police Decision to Arrest People with Mental Illness," *Psychiatric Services* 58 (December 1, 2007): 1582–1587.

54. Raymond Goldberg, *Drugs across the Spectrum* (Englewood, CO: Morton, 1997), 80.

55. Jerome H. Skolnick and Elliott Currie, *Crisis in American Institutions* (Boston: Little, Brown, 1973). See especially the sections on police and criminal law and corrections.

56. Aleksandar Tomic and Jahn K. Hakes, "Case Dismissed: Police Discretion and Racial Differences in Dismissals of Felony Charges," *American Law and Economics Review* 10 (April 1, 2008): 110–141.

57. Davis, *Police Discretion*, 83.

58. Clearly, the police develop strategies that target high-crime areas or events where crime is likely to appear. The difference between the police presence at a symphony orchestra performance and at a basketball tournament is likely to be significant even though the size of the crowd is the same.

59. Igor Areh, Bojan Dobovsek, and Peter Umek, "Citizens' Opinions of Police Procedures," *Policing* 30 (October 1, 2007): 637–650.

60. American Friends Service Committee, "Discretion," in *The Invisible Justice System: Discretion and the Law*, eds. Burton Atkins and Mark Pogrebin (Cincinnati, OH: Anderson, 1978), 35–40. This report argues that discretion should be removed from the criminal justice

system so that constitutional protections of due process and equal application of the law will apply to everyone.

61. *Silverman* v. *United States*, 365 U.S. 505, 81 S.Ct. 679 (1961).

62. "Vehicle Search after Arrest Violated Driver's Rights, Rules Wyoming Supreme Court," *Lawyers USA*, June 2, 2008.

63. *Katz* v. *United States*, 389 U.S. 347, 88 S.Ct. 507 (1967).

64. "A Bullet Box Observed in Plain View on a Person Gives Probable Cause for Arrest," *Narcotics Law Bulletin*, November 1, 2005, 4.

65. "After Approaching Robbery Suspect, Police Spot Marijuana and Search Car," *Narcotics Law Bulletin*, May 1, 2003, 7–8.

66. Roadblocks used during DUI crackdowns are not illegal according to the Fourth Amendment because all cars are stopped. Probable cause is not an issue because no one is singled out for special treatment.

67. *California* v. *Ciraolo*, 476 U.S. 207, 106 S.Ct. 1809 (1986); *United States* v. *White*, 401 U.S. 745, 91 S.Ct. 1122 (1971).

68. "After Approaching Robbery Suspect."

69. *United States* v. *Dunn*, 480 U.S. 294, 107 S.Ct. 1134 (1987).

70. Samaha, *Criminal Procedure*, 112.

71. *Payton* v. *New York*, 445 U.S. 573, 100 S.Ct. 1371 (1980). White, Burger, and Rehnquist filed the dissenting opinion.

72. *Stanford* v. *Texas*, 379 U.S. 476, 85 S.Ct. 506 (1965); *Maryland* v. *Garrison*, 480 U.S. 79, 107 S.Ct. 1013 (1987); *Wilson* v. *Arkansas*, 514 U.S. 927, 115 S.Ct. 1914 (1995); *Richards* v. *Wisconsin*, 520 U.S. 385, 117 S.Ct. 1416 (1997).

73. *Chimel* v. *California*, 395 U.S. 752, 89 S.Ct. 2034 (1969); *New York* v. *Belton*, 453 U.S. 454, 101 S.Ct. 2860 (1981).

74. *Schneckloth* v. *Bustamonte*, 412 U.S. 218, 93 S.Ct. 2041, (1973); *United States* v. *Rodney*, 956 F.2d 295, 297 (D.C. Cir. 1992); *Illinois* v. *Rodriguez*, 497 U.S. 177, 110 S.Ct. 2793 (1990).

75. *United States* v. *Santana*, 427 U.S. 38, 96 S.Ct. 2406 (1976); *Cupp* v. *Murphy*, 412 U.S. 291, 93 S.Ct. 2000 (1973); *Ker* v. *California*, 374 U.S. 23, 83 S.Ct. 1623 (1963).

76. Nicola Persico and Petra E. Todd, "The Hit Rates Test for Racial Bias in Motor-Vehicle Searches," *Justice Quarterly* 25 (March 1, 2008): 37.

77. *Carroll* v. *United States*, 267 U.S. 132, 45 S.Ct. 280 (1925); *Wyoming* v. *Houghton*, 526 U.S. 295, 119 S.Ct. 1297 (1999).

78. *South Dakota* v. *Opperman*, 428 U.S. 364, 96 S.Ct. 3092 (1976).

79. "Constitutional Law—Fourth Amendment—Ninth Circuit Holds That Destructive Search of Spare Tire at Border Is Constitutional.—*United States v. Cortez-Rocha*, 394 F.3d 1115 (9th Cir. 2005)," *Harvard Law Review* 118 (June 1, 2005): 2921–2928.

80. *United States* v. *Ramsey*, 431 U.S. 606, 97 S.Ct. 1972 (1977).

81. Michael G. Lenett, "Implied Consent in Airport Searches: A Response to Terrorism, *United States v. Pulido-Baquerizo*, 800 F.2D 899 (9th Cir. 1986)," *American Criminal Law Review* 25 (January 1, 1988): 549–575.

82. *Hudson* v. *Palmer*, 468 U.S. 517, 104 S.Ct. 3194, (1984); *Bell* v. *Wolfish*, 441 U.S. 520, 99 S.Ct. 1861 (1979); *Mary Beth G.* v. *City of Chicago*, 723 F.2d, 1263 (7th Cir., 1983).

83. Lucy Ann Hoover, "Getting Schooled in the Fourth Amendment," *FBI Law Enforcement Bulletin*, March 1, 2007, 22–32.

84. *State* v. *Hunter*, 831 P.2d, 1033 (Utah Ct. App. 1992); *New Jersey* v. *T.L.O.*, 469 U.S. 325, 105 S.Ct. 733 (1985).

85. "Search and Seizure—Suspicionless Drug Testing," *Harvard Law Review* 103 (December 1, 1989): 591.

86. Michael F. Rosenblum, "Security vs. Privacy: An Emerging Employment Dilemma," *Employee Relations Law Journal*, July 1, 1991, 81.

87. *Hester* v. *United States*, 265 U.S. 57, 44 S.Ct. 445 (1924); *Abel* v. *United States*, 362 U.S. 217, 80 S.Ct. 683 (1960); *California* v. *Greenwood*, 486 U.S. 35, 108 S.Ct. 1625 (1988).

88. Samaha, *Criminal Procedure*, 123; *California* v. *Hodari D.*, 499 U.S. 621, 111 S.Ct. 1547 (1991).

89. *Terry* v. *Ohio*, 392 U.S. 1, 99 S.Ct. 1868 (1968).

90. *State* v. *Morrison*, Ohio App. 8 Dist. (1999).

91. *Illinois* v. *Gates*, 462 U.S. 213, 103 S.Ct. 2317 (1983).

92. *Payton* v. *New York*, 445 U.S. 573, 100 S.Ct. 1371 (1980).

93. *National Treasury Employees Union* v. *Von Raab*, 489 U.S. 656, 109 S.Ct. 1384 (1989).

94. Craig M. Bradley, "Mixed Messages on the Exclusionary Rule," *Trial*, December 1, 2006, 56–59.

95. Samaha, *Criminal Procedure*, 355.

CHAPTER 7

Issues in Policing

Objectives

1. Explain why, and under what circumstances, the use of force is legitimate.

2. Discuss the advantages and issues of using special weapons and tactics (SWAT) teams.

3. Appreciate the special issues that face female police officers.

4. Appreciate the special issues faced by minority police officers.

5. Understand how racial profiling is an old practice but a new concern for law enforcement.

6. Describe how community policing differs from traditional police practices.

7. Describe how problem-oriented policing differs from traditional police practices.

8. Explain broken-windows theory and discuss why it is problematic.

9. Discuss the special police problems that cause stress.

10. Appreciate how the police subculture affects the personalities of police officers.

11. Describe the types of police corruption and suggest ways that it can be addressed.

C hapters 5 and 6 illustrated how important and difficult the law enforcement mission has become. This chapter will focus on some additional issues that police agencies continue to grapple with, although many of these issues have been at the core of policing for a long time.

1. How can the police be further integrated into the community? Are strategies such as community policing and problem-oriented policing effective?

2. How can we ensure that police organizations recruit and promote minorities and women? How much progress has been made in diversifying policing over the past 40 years?

3. How do we determine the correct use of force by the police? Can policies be developed that will help the police make these split-second decisions?

4. What are the sources and results of police stress? What reasonable policies can be enacted to reduce the social and human costs of police work?

5. How does the danger of corruption affect the police?

By studying these issues, we can develop a greater appreciation for the role of the police in society. The public will better understand and support the work of the police to the extent that these problems can be addressed. However, one thing the public must always keep in mind is that these issues will never be fully resolved and must constantly be addressed by law enforcement for the foreseeable future. Because the police are vested with the responsibility to maintain the law and are given the authority to use force, there will always be questions and criticisms of how the police apply force in specific situations.

In this chapter, we will first look at the challenges to traditional policing, such as community policing, problem-oriented policing, and zero-tolerance policing. Next, we will discuss gender and race, and the effect that the hiring of women and minorities has had on policing. The next major issue is police use of force. This is a controversial issue, as law enforcement is the primary institution in civil society that is authorized to use force against citizens. We will then study the causes and effects of stress and burnout among police officers, and finally the police subculture and instances of corruption.

CHALLENGES TO TRADITIONAL POLICING

In the past 30 years, new theoretical foundations concerning how police are organized have begun to appear. In this section we will review and compare three challenges to the traditional policing model: community policing, problem-oriented policing, and zero-tolerance policing (see Table 7-1). Each of these forms of policing suggests different levels of interaction between the police and the public, and each is subject to criticism for what it fails to address as much as for what it successfully addresses.

Table 7-1   **Community Policing in Perspective**

	Community Policing	**Problem-Oriented Policing**	**Zero-Tolerance Policing**
Goal	Strengthen bond between police and community	Address specific problem areas	Address specific types of offenders
Tactics	Place officers back on foot patrol or bicycles	Target situations in which crime occurs: crack houses, bars that serve minors, etc.	Make arrests for all minor violations (e.g., loitering, drinking in public, fare jumping)
Style	Watchman style	Legalistic/service style	Legalistic style
Criticisms	Not much different from regular policing; token public relations	Discriminatory	Violates rights of those without power

Community Policing

One of the major new ways of thinking about how to organize the police is the concept of **community policing.** During 2003, 58 percent of all police departments used full-time community policing officers.[1] Community policing recalls the watchman style discussed in Chapter 6, in which the police officer is integrated into the community and has the advantage of being trusted by those being policed. The concept of community policing, however, is also different from the watchman style because both the police and the community have changed over the years. The watchman style of policing had its limitations, especially in affording equal justice to all citizens. In many cases, the watchman style simply reinforced the privileges of those in power while controlling the young and minorities. Community policing also has elements in common with the legalistic style of policing in that it strives to treat all citizens equally according to their orientation with the law. However, as you will recall from Chapter 6, the legalistic model emphasizes efficiency and exclusivity in the mandate for crime control. This exclusivity comes at a price, however, in terms of distancing the police from the communities they serve. Community policing is viewed as a reform that breaks the monopoly of the police over crime-control activities and brings the citizen back into the equation as an active participant. Community policing is different from both the watchman and legalistic styles in content and scope, and it is worthwhile to consider its history and potential.[2]

The term *community policing* covers a wide range of police activities and programs. Not all of the practices considered to be community policing are really legitimate features of it. An exact definition is difficult to provide, but it is fair to say that community policing involves enlisting citizens to help solve law-and-order problems in their own communities (see Criminal Justice Reference 7.1).[3] Good policing requires citizen cooperation. If people do not report offenses, do not provide information to the police, and are unwilling to testify in court, then the police cannot effectively control crime. During the civil unrest of the 1960s, the police were forced to do a difficult job in controlling large groups of people. This violence revealed a deep fissure between old and young, workers and hippies, minorities and whites, and also between the police and the communities they served. Many people believed that the police were out of touch with those they served. For this and other reasons, the community policing approach was proposed.[4]

community policing
A policing strategy that attempts to harness the resources and residents of a given community in stopping crime and maintaining order.

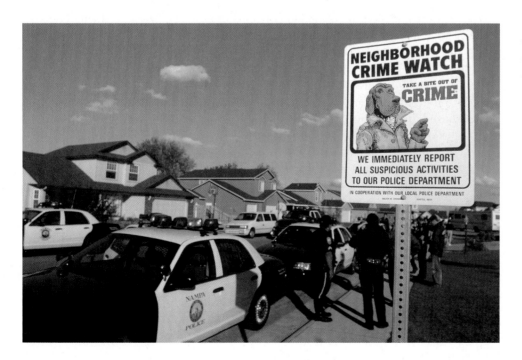

Neighborhood Watch programs enlist the support of citizens in keeping the community safe.
Source: Joe Rowley / AP Wide World Photos

7.1   CRIMINAL JUSTICE REFERENCE

What Is Community Oriented Policing?

The Department of Justice's Community-Oriented Policing Services (COPS) Web site defines community policing as follows:

Community policing is a philosophy that promotes organizational strategies, which support the systematic use of partnerships and problem-solving techniques, to proactively address the immediate conditions that give rise to public safety issues such as crime, social disorder, and fear of crime.

Source: COPS Office: Grants and Resources for Community Policing, www.cops.usdoj.gov/default.asp?Item=36.

According to Walker and Katz, community policing represents a major change in the role of the police: "While the police have traditionally defined their primary mission in terms of crime control, community policing seeks to broaden the police role to include such issues as fear of crime, order maintenance, conflict resolution, neighborhood decay, and social and physical disorder as basic responsibilities of the police."[5] By taking an active part in improving the quality of life in the community, the police would strive not only to control crime, but also to make other positive contributions to the everyday activities of citizens that will result in a more cohesive neighborhood and better police–community relations.[6]

The goal of community policing is ambitious. It involves not only bridging the gap between the police and the citizens, but also strengthening the bond among the citizens themselves. With the realization that the police cannot be everywhere, programs such as **Neighborhood Watch** organize citizens to watch over each other's safety and property. In an article published in the *American Journal of Police*, Gordon Bazemore and Allen Cole illustrated how diverse community policing actions can be:[7]

Neighborhood Watch

A community policing program that encourages residents to cooperate in providing security for the neighborhood.

1. On one street, drug dealers were escaping arrest because they hid their drugs under garbage barrels, inside fence post caps, and in mailboxes. Residents were armed with beepers and signaled police where the drugs were hidden. The police were able to find the drugs consistently, and asked if anyone wanted to claim them. No one did. The drug dealers were suspicious that there was a snitch, but because so many residents were participating in the programs, the dealers could not determine who was cooperating with the police.

2. On another street, gangs opened fire hydrants on the pretext of keeping cool and used the diversion to rob passing motorists and sell drugs. The community police officers closed the street to all traffic except those who could prove they were residents and issued $35 citations to those with no apparent reason to be on the street. In so doing, they effectively shut down the drug trade.

3. At another location, several neighborhood dealers sold drugs to individuals from outside the area. The police put up large signs reading, "Warning—area under surveillance due to illegal sale of drugs—motor vehicle registration numbers being recorded by the police." Letters were then sent to the owners of these cars informing them of the cars' presence in that location. (Presumably, many youths used their parents' cars.) According to Bazemore and Cole, the traffic reduced to a trickle in three weeks.

4. After extensively patrolling a drug-infested area, community police officers wanted to ensure that the neighborhood did not revert to its old patterns after the visible patrols ended. They invested $42 to disguise an old police special

operations truck that was headed to the junkyard to look like a surveillance van (tinting the windows and installing mirrors that were thought to be two-way mirrors). They then had uniformed officers deliver empty coffee cups and pizza boxes to give the impression that the van was continuously occupied.

5. In one parking lot, youths would congregate to play loud music and handball. Although most of the problems were nuisances such as littering and graffiti, some of the youths were gang members and would rob passing motorists. The community police officers got the youths to agree to behave in order to be allowed to congregate and play handball. Residents of a nearby apartment building agreed to tolerate a certain level of noise in exchange for the elimination of the robbery, graffiti, and car break-ins.

In addition to these small successes, these community policing efforts had other positive outcomes. Residents cleaned up parks, boarded up old buildings, and participated in a variety of community programs that engendered a sense of togetherness and responsibility for each other and the community's youths.

One strategy of community policing is to return the police to a close relationship with the public by having them patrol on foot or on bicycles.[8] The patrol car is considered a barrier to communication between police and citizens. Taking the officers out of the cars and placing them in more direct contact with people makes meaningful relationships more likely. Another method of community policing is the development of Neighborhood Watch programs. By encouraging citizens to work together and cooperate with police, these programs "put more eyes on the street" to help prevent and report crime. These programs have the added feature of developing stronger community ties that can help address other neighborhood problems. When neighbors feel responsible for each others' children, property, and well-being, the job of the police becomes much easier.[9]

One problem with community policing is that all communities are not created equal. Great variation persists among neighborhoods in terms of the socioeconomic, racial and ethnic, and age compositions of the citizens. For example, a suburb with $400,000 houses inhabited by the middle-aged and elderly faces few crime problems compared to a neighborhood populated with transients and drug dealers. It is much easier to institute a Neighborhood Watch program in affluent suburbs where the residents' comings and goings are less frequent and easier to identify than in poor neighborhoods where the pattern of social organization and movement is less obvious. Therefore, community policing can be said to work best in the communities that need it least. Nevertheless, studies have suggested that well-planned community policing efforts can achieve at least some of their goals.[10]

A final issue in community policing is that it covers such a vast array of activities. It is hard to say (1) whether it is really any different from traditional policing and (2) whether we can declare it a success based on the limited research done on such different types of activities. Although the goal of involving communities as partners in addressing the problems of crime is laudable, getting the police to be concerned with order maintenance and community building is problematic when many officers view themselves solely as crime fighters. The inherent tension between the roles of "criminal catcher" and "social worker" limits the potential for community policing. Changing the basic orientation and occupational perspective of the police is difficult. It is like trying to get an orthopedic surgeon to "treat the whole person," when all the doctor sees is a broken leg or dislocated shoulder.

Problem-Oriented Policing

A related strategy to community policing is **problem-oriented policing.** In many ways, problem-oriented policing can be thought of as simply one aspect of community policing, but it is important enough to be treated as its own topic. The reason we give special attention to problem-oriented policing is that it is designed to make more

problem-oriented policing
A style of policing that attempts to address the underlying social problems that contribute to crime.

fundamental changes than community policing does. Additionally, problem-oriented policing greatly expands the role of the police officer from one of reaction to one of proactive problem-solving. It allows police agencies to address crime on a more systemic level than traditional policing.[11]

By way of illustration, envision a downtown business district that is experiencing a spate of robberies and muggings. In addition to responding to these offenses, a problem-oriented law enforcement agency would analyze the causative factors. Included in this analysis might be a crime-mapping effort, which would reveal that the muggings are all in close proximity to a cluster of bars. On surveillance of these bars, the agency discovers that the bars are staying open well past the legal closing time and serving underage patrons. Going into these bars and enforcing the existing liquor laws could affect the robbery and mugging problem. Problem-oriented policing, then, is concerned with identifying and addressing the underlying issues that contribute to crime.[12] Within the scope of the law enforcement mission are many such opportunities that allow the police to do more than simply respond to crime. Of course, it is unrealistic to expect the police to solve all of the problems brought about by poverty, homelessness, and economic blight, but the police are in a position to understand the limitations in the structure of the community and design strategies to help.

Problem-oriented policing has different goals and techniques than community policing. In the long run, both types of policing may incur some of the same results, such as less crime and greater community support, but there are still important distinctions between these two styles. Problem-oriented policing is a more proactive process than community policing, and for this reason, it is more likely to appeal to police officers. Instead of responding to calls for service, the problem-oriented officer analyzes the specific trouble areas of the community and designs specific tactics to address those problems.[13] A couple of examples help illustrate the potential for problem-oriented policing.

1. **The Specialized Multi-Agency Response Team in Oakland, California.**
   The police identified a particular neighborhood that demonstrated a high level of crime and called for police service. This particular "hot spot" had a large amount of substandard housing. To address the problem, the police invited the cooperation of other city agencies to help improve the housing. Landlords were pressured to bring the houses up to housing code and fire code standards. As the housing improved, so did the overall quality of life in the neighborhood. The state government passed a law that made it a violation to maintain a dwelling where drugs were manufactured and sold. By solving the underlying problems of neighborhood neglect, the police were able to affect the crime problem. What is important to understand about this problem-oriented policing example is that the police were not authorized to deal with all of the problems they identified, so they enlisted the help of other local government agencies that did have the authority to target specific issues, such as housing code violations.[14]

2. **The Boston Gun Project: Project Ceasefire (also discussed in Chapter 5).** Because of a high rate of youth homicides, the Boston Police Department teamed with other agencies, including the Bureau of Alcohol, Tobacco, Firearms, and Explosives; the probation department; schools; and prosecutors to crack down on youth gangs. The project put out the word to gang members that unless the gun violence stopped, full enforcement of the law for every offense, even the smallest, would be used against them. Probationers were subject to bed checks and prosecution of minor alcohol violations. Any infraction of the law was to be met with full punishment. After two years, the homicide rate had dropped by 70 percent. The program was so successful that the federal government funded similar projects in other cities.[15]

Other problem-oriented policing measures include strict enforcement of drinking ordinances in areas with a high degree of assault. By arresting store clerks for selling alcohol to minors or bartenders for continuing to serve obviously drunk patrons, the police can reduce the incidence of fighting and drunk driving. The police can work with state and city officials to terminate the liquor licenses of establishments that violate the law. By strictly enforcing the liquor laws, the police can remedy the underlying problems, such as unruly and violent behavior.

Problem-oriented policing allows police agencies broad latitude in addressing the contributing factors that cause crime. Police officers are not simply reactive, but can go into the community and enlist the support of other agencies to target problems and "hot spots" before offenses occur. In this way, problem-oriented policing has a crime-prevention mission as well as a crime-responding mission. Perhaps the most important feature of problem-oriented policing is its capacity to prevent crime. By intervening early and effectively when patterns begin to emerge, problem-oriented policing can address the causes of crime.[16]

The ways the police can engage in problem-oriented policing varies widely and includes increased patrol efforts and helping communities remove abandoned cars and clean up trash-strewn vacant lots. Additionally, the police may establish substations in housing developments and assign officers on a permanent basis with the goal of creating a relationship with the residents.

As promising as problem-oriented policing appears to be, some of its implementations have been criticized. These critics are concerned with how problem-oriented policing has evolved from the controversial **broken-windows theory**, which is also an element of zero-tolerance policing.

Zero-Tolerance Policing

Zero-tolerance policing is a refinement of problem-oriented policing. **Zero-tolerance policing** is based on the idea that if every little infraction of the law is met with an arrest, fine, or other punishment, offenders will refrain from more grievous activities. James Q. Wilson and George L. Kelling developed the broken-windows theory, which provides the theoretical perspective behind zero-tolerance policing.[17] The broken-windows perspective is discussed in greater detail in the next section, but a brief review of it here will provide some background on zero-tolerance policing.

The central idea to the broken-windows theory is that when people see a dwelling with a broken window, they are tempted to throw rocks and break the other windows. According to this theory, a broken window signals that the property is not valued. Because it has been abandoned and the owners pay little or no attention to it, it is all right to vandalize it. Property with intact windows, fresh paint, and a clean environment sends a different signal. It says that the owners care about the property and will protect it. According to Wilson and Kelling, the broken-windows theory also applies to the community and to social behavior on the streets. If the community is well kept both physically and socially, then lawbreakers are less likely to disrupt the social order.[18]

But what do we mean by *socially well-kept*? According to Wilson and Kelling, it means keeping teenagers from hanging out in parking lots, shooing vagrants and homeless people, and chasing beggars and street people away from businesses and tourist locations. This sends a signal that the city, the police, and the citizens care about their community and are making the streets safe. When the people of the community reclaim the streets, then a safe community is more likely. With more law-abiding people on the street, people will be less likely to break the law, and vandals will be less likely to destroy property.

The broken-windows theory was the perspective behind the efforts of Mayor Rudy Giuliani's zero-tolerance policy in New York City during the early 1990s. By making misdemeanor arrests for panhandling, public drunkenness, prostitution, jumping subway turnstiles, and public urination, the New York Police Department aggressively sought to bring order and safety to the streets. In fact, serious crime did decrease, but critics point out that this was a nationwide trend and could not be attributed solely to the police department's zero-tolerance policies.[19]

broken-windows theory
The idea that untended property or deviant behavior will attract crime. This theory is used as a justification for clearing the streets of homeless people, drunks, and unruly teens, even when no law has been broken.

zero-tolerance policing
This form of policing punishes every infraction of the law, however minor, with an arrest, fine, or other penalty so that offenders will refrain from committing more serious offenses.

Although the zero-tolerance policies suggested by the broken-windows perspective are attractive to many politicians, law enforcement officials, and citizens, some important consequences remain to be considered.[20] The main targets of zero-tolerance policies tend to be poor people. Those who are young, live on the street, look uncouth and shabby, and are drunk or mentally ill find that their minor transgressions of the law are treated much more severely than are the transgressions of others. Zero-tolerance policies aimed at reducing crime result in the unequal treatment of those without power. The civil and human rights of the least powerful in society are easy to abridge when the expressed goal is crime control. Given the problems of increased legal judgments against police departments for the behavior of their officers, zero-tolerance policing might be more problematic than beneficial.[21]

Perhaps the most fundamental problem with zero-tolerance policing is the adversarial relationship it seems to set up between the police and the public. By treating citizens with such a heavy hand, the police alienate the very people who could help them solve more serious offenses. The marginalized street person is just as concerned with public safety as the homeowner, maybe even more so because she or he is more vulnerable.[22] When the police harass individuals for petty infractions, they cannot expect those people to help them investigate more serious offenses. Furthermore, zero-tolerance policies might deprive people of opportunities to eke out a living panhandling on the street and lead them to break more serious laws such as larceny, burglary, or robbery to survive. When people become angry and defiant, they are more likely to break major laws and be less likely to be of assistance to the police.[23]

BROKEN WINDOWS   Community policing and its variant, problem-oriented policing, are influenced by the broken-windows theory. Law enforcement scholars James Q. Wilson and George L. Kelling introduced the idea in a 1982 article in *Atlantic Monthly*. Based on the work of Stanford psychology professor Philip Zimbardo, Wilson and Kelling argued that crime follows community neglect. Zimbardo conducted a fascinating experiment in which he abandoned two cars, one in Palo Alto, California, and the other in the Bronx, New York City. Within 10 minutes, the car in the Bronx was attacked, and within a few hours it was totally destroyed. Everything of value was taken from the car, and the windows were smashed (according to Zimbardo, by well-dressed and clean-cut white vandals). The car in Palo Alto sat for more than a week untouched until Zimbardo smashed it with a sledgehammer. Again, within a few hours the car was destroyed. Wilson and Kelling concluded:

> Untended property becomes fair game for people out for fun or plunder, and even for people who ordinarily would not dream of doing such things, and who probably consider themselves law-abiding. Because of the nature of community life in the Bronx—its anonymity, the frequency with which cars are abandoned and things stolen or broken, the past experience of "no one caring"—vandalism begins much more quickly than it does in Palo Alto, where people have come to believe that private possessions are cared for, and that mischievous behavior is costly. But vandalism can occur anywhere once communal barriers—the sense of mutual regard and obligations of civility—are lowered by actions that seem to signal, "no one cares."[24]

It is difficult to argue with Wilson and Kelling that untended property can draw vandals, especially when it is already damaged. We have all seen the results of such acts of vandalism (and may even have engaged in some ourselves). But Wilson and Kelling took this analogy a step further. They suggested that "untended" behavior also leads to the breakdown of community controls.

When teenagers loiter in front of a convenience store, or a drunk sleeps on the sidewalk, Wilson and Kelling believe that this signals that "no one cares," much as a broken window does. Citizens feel unsafe in their neighborhoods, and instead of being outside and involved in community activities, they hide in their homes. These actions leave the streets empty of many citizens engaged in the type of everyday

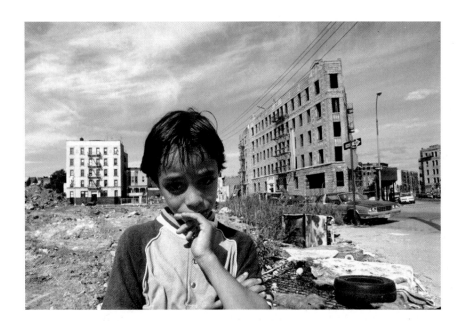

According to the broken-windows theory, vandalism and criminal activity occur when it appears that no one cares about a neighborhood. Such neighborhoods are also stressful places to live.

Source: *Susan Ragan / AP Wide World Photos*

pursuits that signify a healthy and involved community. People are not out walking their dogs, washing their cars, talking to neighbors, or otherwise being out in the community, which suggests that the neighborhood is filled with residents who are not concerned with property or public safety. According to Wilson and Kelling, this neglect of behavior is as damaging as leaving a broken window unfixed in terms of inviting crime into the community.[25]

The solution to this problem of the decline of the community is, according to the broken-windows theory, to "fix" the "untended" behavior just as one would fix a broken window. This means arresting the public drunk, chasing the teenagers away from the store or out of the mall, and otherwise "cleaning up" the riffraff of society. This becomes problematic when we consider that these individuals have not broken any laws and have not harmed anyone. Wilson and Kelling contend, however, that to maintain meaningful communities, police officers must address the issue of street people: "Arresting a single drunk or single vagrant who has harmed no identifiable person seems unjust, and in a sense it is. But failing to do anything about a score of drunks or a hundred vagrants may destroy an entire community."[26]

In trying to balance the rights of the individual against the rights of the community, Wilson and Kelling came down solidly on the side of the community. They argued that we have let our communities slip away from the watchman style of policing, in which police officers maintained order by enforcing community standards of civil behavior on the street. The broken-windows theory argues that arresting or chasing away undesirable individuals will reclaim the neighborhood for citizens engaged in normal, productive activities.[27]

Is there anything wrong with this prescription for social change? Many critics believe so. Following are three reasons to be cautious about adopting the broken-windows theory:

1. **Misreading of how communities were policed in the past.**   Criminologist Samuel Walker critiqued the broken-windows theory in his article "Broken Windows and Fractured History: The Use and Misuse of History in Recent Patrol Analysis." Walker contended that Wilson and Kelling misread the history of policing and that their call for an earlier model of the watchman style was misguided. In short, Walker said that there was no older tradition of policing that encompassed the principles of the broken-windows theory, and that if Wilson and Kelling wanted to implement these ideas, they would have to start anew. Walker did say that the community-oriented policing concept is a worthy and feasible goal, but that it must be developed slowly.[28]

2. **Concern for the rights of all citizens.**   Fixing a window or cleaning up a vacant lot can signal that people care about their neighborhood. Dealing with teenagers, drunks, the mentally ill, or the homeless presents a different set of problems. Wilson and Kelling erred in comparing this "untended" behavior to a broken window. They may have been right in thinking that street people affect a number of quality of life issues, such as creating excessive noise and feelings of discomfort in citizens walking the street. They were mistaken, however, in asserting that this issue can be solved by the police in a democratic country that values individual rights. The answer to the social problems presented by street people is not to arrest them or chase them to other parts of the city, but to marshal the resources of the entire community to solve the underlying problems. If the deinstitutionalization of the mentally ill means that they are in the street, then housing programs, drug treatment facilities, and a host of other social services are needed.[29]

3. **Problem of crime displacement.**   Removing undesirable people from a community does not mean that the problems associated with them will disappear.[30] These people could reappear in an adjoining community with all the negative and "untended" behaviors the first community was trying to suppress. Additionally, by threatening to arrest street people and otherwise devaluing any positive contribution they might make to the community, we might actually accelerate their undesirable behaviors from nuisances to crime. Our streets might be safer by sweeping away what we consider to be riffraff, but other communities will have to deal with these human beings who feel alienated from society and are not bound to conventional behavior.[31]

The process of involving the police in the community is a complex task. The term *community policing* does not have a definition that is shared by everyone who advocates its use. Community policing includes a wide variety of strategies and can mean anything from a simple slogan to a definite set of programs designed to effect significant social change in how policing is done. It is important to understand how the police are connected to the community because this bond can greatly influence how the police understand their job and deal with its pressures and dangers.

GENDER AND RACE

One of the basic principles advanced by critical criminologists is that social status can have a major effect on one's opportunities for pursuing a conventional lifestyle. Gender, race, and social class are considered powerful influences in determining who has access to the "American dream" and how one is treated by the institutions of society, including (and maybe especially) the criminal justice system.[32]

Gender and race are important issues in the study of law enforcement.[33] The quality of justice and the efficiency of police work are both dependent on, and a factor in, how well the police agency can win the confidence of the community. When the police are viewed as promoting and protecting only the interests of certain races, genders, or social groups, the criminal justice system is considered an instrument of the powerful and an oppressor of the weak.

It would be a mistake, however, to view the inclusion of women and minorities in police work as being a simple matter of politics. Diversity in criminal justice personnel adds more than the appearance of sexual or racial equity. Including women and minorities in the criminal justice system provides a broader array of tools to control crime and develop meaningful communities. It is useful, then, to examine both gender and race as factors of both police officers and offenders.

Women as Police Officers

One of the main objectives of the move to create social and economic equality for women has been to allow them access to previously all-male occupations. In the past 50 years, women have overcome barriers to employment in private professions, the military, and the criminal justice system. Female judges, prosecutors, and corrections administrators are so commonplace in the 21st century that remarks are seldom made about their suitability for their jobs. The same is becoming true of female police officers. Women are seen on virtually every large or medium-size police force, and they have moved into positions of leadership in many of them.

This road to equality for female police officers has been a rocky one, and for the most part, it is not yet complete.[34] Although the number of female officers continues to increase, the culture of the police force is still grounded in what many consider male values. The progress women are making in breaking down the barriers of sexism is incremental, sporadic, sometimes costly, and fraught with ambiguity. The resistance to female police officers from the public, male-dominated police administrations, fellow police officers, and even their own family members has caused many women to abandon their police careers.[35]

Before the integration of women into police forces, police officers saw their jobs as involving danger, violence, aggression, isolation, and authority.[36] These concerns were considered exclusive to men and legitimate reasons to keep women off the force. Women were stereotyped as being physically weak and emotionally fragile, and thus ill suited for police work. The entries they did gain into police departments were as ancillary and support personnel, working as dispatchers or with juveniles.[37] The idea of women in uniform and on patrol was not seriously considered. Job qualifications for police officers stated that the applicant had to be male, or referred to police officers as "him" and "he." The concept of female police officers was not seriously considered in almost all jurisdictions.

Of course, singling out policing for being reluctant to accord women full occupational equity is unfair because this form of sexism was the norm in society until relatively recently. It is interesting, however, to look at how police have responded to the demand for women's rights because police work had been considered one of the occupations that most justified that exclusion.[38] Arguments against women in policing included the following:

1. **Women are not physically strong enough to be police officers.** Police work can sometimes require the officer to fight a large, young, strapping, intoxicated, angry male offender. This is a dangerous task that often results in physical injury to the officer. Critics of this objection point out that only a few police officers can win a street fight with young, athletically gifted males. Police officers are required to use their powers of persuasion to make arrests without fighting, to use their weapons when their safety or the safety of others is at risk, and to depend on other officers to help subdue the suspects, tasks of which women are capable. Female recruits must pass the same physical testing that male recruits do, so winning a fight really depends on which police officers maintain their readiness.

2. **Women bring different psychological attributes to police work.** Critics of women in policing contend that "women, because they are more compassionate, less aggressive, and less competitive, see their job from a different perspective and hence adopt different policing styles than do men."[39] Advocates for women in policing agree, adding that the aggressive and competitive perspective brought to the street by male police officers is appropriate for only part of the police mission, and a small part at that. The emphasis on crime control must coexist with an emphasis on order maintenance and social support. The mind-set brought by women who have been socialized into roles of caregiving and nurturing significantly expands the nature of the police role.

In summary, the increased participation of women in policing has provided some important sociological lessons. There is more than one way to be a good police officer. According to some studies, the historically male-dominated police culture has been enriched by the infusion of women, who bring different perspectives to the job. At one time, it was believed that the police subculture shaped recruits into a **policeman's working personality** that was determined by danger, violence, aggression, isolation, and authority. Now the culture appears to be changing as women introduce other values into the culture of policing.[40]

Minorities as Police

As with the section on women as police, it is unfortunate that a textbook on criminal justice in the United States has to have a section on minorities as police. This country has a checkered past in its treatment of minorities, and the criminal justice system has experienced its own stresses in accommodating the inevitable progress of opening occupations to people who have experienced prejudice and discrimination.[41] It would be nice to say that law enforcement has led the way in providing equality to disenfranchised groups, but that has not been the case. However, some progress has been made, and the rate of improvement increases with each decade.[42]

At times in the distant past, black people worked as law enforcement officers, although these times have been rare and discontinuous. The first time black people appeared as police officers was in New Orleans in 1805. As slaves who had won their freedom because they served with the French or Spanish militia, they acted primarily to keep slaves under control and to catch runaways. The black police gradually lost their jobs to whites and did not engage in law enforcement activities again until after the Civil War. During Reconstruction, former slaves enjoyed a brief period during which they performed the same type of law enforcement duties as whites. This period of occupational equality was also quite brief, and soon, as in other aspects of politics, law enforcement was completely dominated by whites. With the exception of tokenism brought on by political patronage in northern cities, black police officers had few opportunities. Even when they were allowed into the occupation, their roles were greatly limited. Black people were responsible for policing their neighborhoods and were not allowed the full range of duties and certainly not allowed to advance into administration.[43]

A new era of opportunity for black people in all aspects of society was won during the civil rights movement in the 1950s and continues into the present day. Led by influential individuals such as Dr. Martin Luther King Jr., the civil rights movement called attention to the problems of peoples of color in the social, economic, legal, and educational arenas. Although far from complete, the civil rights movement has been successful in eliminating much of the institutional racism that had comprised the social fabric of American society. The Jim Crow laws of the South that prevented black people from going to the same schools, eating at the same lunch counters, and drinking from the same water fountains as whites are now just an ugly remembrance of the past.[44]

Today, black officers can be found on virtually every large police force in the country. Some medium-size and small departments do not have minorities, but this has more to do with location and population than with discrimination. The law no longer allows police agencies to exclude job candidates based on race. This march toward equality has not been easy. Many black police officers met with hostility when they sought to serve their communities. As police agencies began to be integrated, black officers faced what Nicholas Alex called **double marginality,** which means that not only were they treated differently by their fellow police officers, but they were also looked on with suspicion by the black people in their communities.[45] In larger cities, with more and more black officers, the double marginality issue has decreased. However, when we look at black female police officers, we can see a different type of

policeman's working personality

A term coined by Jerome Skolnick to refer to the mind-set of police who must deal with danger, authority, isolation, and suspicion while appearing to be efficient.

double marginality

A term that refers to the multiple outsider status of female and minority police officers.

Actor Clint Eastwood made the character "Dirty Harry" a symbol of the determined law enforcement officer. In reality, the attitude and tactics of Dirty Harry would get an officer fired and possibly prosecuted.

Source: © *Cinema Photo / CORBIS. All Rights Reserved*

marginality. These officers feel the dual prejudices against women and minorities as they attempt to develop a place for themselves in the law enforcement occupation.[46]

Blacks are not the only minority group in the United States that has been historically excluded from law enforcement. Hispanics, Asians, and American Indians have all experienced prejudice and discrimination.[47] The effects of this racism are sometimes difficult to overcome because both whites and minorities must adjust to new ways of thinking about what police officers look like. In policing, the contributions of all Americans make the community not only more tolerant of others but also more supportive of our institutions.

USE OF FORCE

According to Egon Bittner, civilized society has been developing mechanisms to eliminate the legitimacy of all forms of force. From international diplomacy to the internal workings of the criminal justice system, the **use of force** has been relegated to last-resort status. Bittner contrasted this movement of the modern state with the Roman Empire, which employed "*debellare superbos*, i.e., to subdue the haughty by force."[48] Today, physical force is considered legitimate only under the following conditions:

1. **Self-defense.** Self-defense laws vary from state to state, but the generally accepted principle is that after exhausting all other means of avoiding harm, including retreat, force may be used to protect oneself or others. This means that in court proceedings, one may be required to show how other options were ineffectively used or were unavailable when the force was employed in the name of self-defense.

use of force
The legal police use of violence to enforce the law. Excessive use of force is considered police brutality.

2. **Specifically deputized people against some specifically named people.**   In this case, Bittner was referring to agents such as mental hospital attendants and corrections officers. Here, the right to use force is given to those whose jobs may require them to deal with dangerous people in a special context. What is important to remember is that the right to use force does not extend beyond the confines of the job. Their jurisdiction is limited to the hospital or the prison; the law does not recognize their actions in other parts of society.

3. **Police force.**   This last legitimate use of force is much broader than the previous two. Comparatively, it appears to be almost unrestricted, but as we examine it more closely, we can see how it is circumscribed quite severely. According to Bittner, the restrictions of police use of force are as follows:

    a. Use of force is limited to certain types of situations. In some jurisdictions, the police may shoot to kill dangerous fleeing felons, but not those who have committed misdemeanors.

    b. The police may use force only in the performance of official duties and not to advance their personal interests or the private interests of others.

    c. The police may not use force maliciously or frivolously.[49]

Although these guidelines appear to limit the use of force by police and other agents of society, Bittner said they are essentially meaningless. No one really knows what is meant by the "lawful use of force" because each incident is different, and it is impossible to cover all the circumstances in which police may use force. It is curious how society places the police in such a precarious position when it comes to using force. On one hand, we expect them to use reasonable force when our interests are at stake; on the other hand, we decide what is reasonable force only after the fact. Situations in which police use force are highly contextual. This means that each situation is different, and it is difficult to decide later what pressures police officers were under when they decided that force was necessary. We know that the police use force in making arrests and keeping order. The problem is that we know little about how

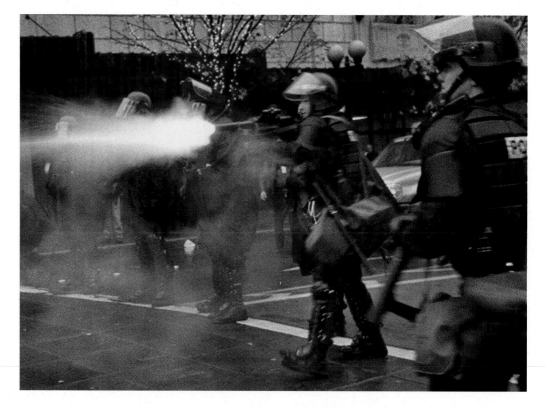

Law enforcement officers are mandated to use force in the name of society. The police are the institution that is trained and equipped to use legitimate force against those who break the law.

Source: CORBIS-NY

7.2   CRIMINAL JUSTICE REFERENCE

Police Use of Force

What we know with substantial confidence:

- Police use force infrequently.
- Use of force typically occurs at the lower end of the physical spectrum, involving grabbing, pushing, or shoving.
- Use of force typically occurs when a suspect resists arrest.

What we know with modest confidence:

- Use of force appears to be unrelated to an officer's personal characteristics, such as age, gender, and ethnicity.
- Use of force is more likely to occur when police are dealing with people who are under the influence of alcohol or drugs or are mentally ill.
- A small proportion of officers are disproportionately involved in use-of-force incidents.

What we do not know:

- The incidence of wrongful use of force.
- The effect of differences in police organizations, including administrative policies, hiring, training, discipline, and use of technology on excessive and illegal force.
- Influences of situational characteristics on police use of force and the transactional nature of these events.

Source: Kenneth Adams, "What We Know about Police Use of Force," in *Use of Force by Police: Overview of National and Local Data*, NCJ 176330 (Washington, DC: National Institute of Justice, October 1999).

this force is used and how often the police decide to use force. In a review of studies about police force, Kenneth Adams summarized what we know about police use of force and where studies are still needed (see Criminal Justice Reference 7.2).

Someone who considers calling the police into a situation spends much of that time considering the possibility that the situation might require an outside party to mediate it and possibly use force. For instance, we might be ready to use force ourselves but do not want to deal with the possibilities of lawsuits, retaliation, and the chance that someone could instead call the police on us. We call the police to use force on our behalf because they have been trained and are armed and authorized to do so. However, because the legitimate use of police force is so dependent on the context of the situation, and because the police must make decisions in the heat of the moment and often under dangerous conditions, the lawfulness of the use of force becomes problematic when considered after the fact.[50] This puts the police in a no-win situation. Failure to use appropriate force might risk injury or death to themselves or others (see Focus on Ethics 7.1). The use of too much force could result in disciplinary action. According to Bittner, we ask police to make a decision requiring the exercise of two conflicting parts of the nature of police work: the police must simultaneously balance their physical prowess with professional acumen.[51]

The expectation of how much and what type of force an officer will use in any given situation will vary according to a number of factors; the time of day, whether the officer is alone or working with a partner, the size and sex of the suspect, and the area of the city can all influence whether, and how much, force is used. A guide for police officers is to use only the force required to bring order to a situation and no more (see Case in Point 7.1). This is a highly contingent judgment and one for which considerable variation can be expected. Additionally, if force is applied appropriately, we would expect to see relatively low levels of force used more often than deadly force (see Figure 7-1). In fact, most force used by the police is relatively minor. Given that the police are allowed and expected to use force, it should be of some comfort to realize that they use extreme force rarely. The cases of extreme use of force that can be labeled police brutality result in the negative picture that many have of contemporary police work. However, we must keep in mind that the media can distort the amount of level of force used by police in their quest to develop stories.

FOCUS *on* ETHICS

MY BEST COP, BUT . . .

As a new police chief of a medium-size city, you have a variety of problems keeping up the morale in your department because of low pay, antiquated equipment, and the general resistance of the older officers to the city hiring an "outsider" to run the department. However, you have found one officer who seems to support all the improvements you are trying to make in the department. This guy is a real "hot shot." He has the highest arrest rate in the force, was cited for bravery when he rescued a baby from a burning car, and has just completed a master's degree in criminal justice at the local university. This officer is clearly "on the fast track," and you are anxious to promote him before some other department or the FBI can lure him away. Additionally, you are under pressure from the city to diversify the force, and this star happens to be black.

One morning you get a call from the deputy sheriff who runs the jail, and he tells you that your officer has brought in a youth who has been severely beaten. The deputy says that no formal complaints have been filed, but he thinks you should know what is going on because this is not the first time prisoners have complained that this officer uses excessive force.

What Do You Do?

1. Launch an investigation into all of this officer's previous controversial arrests.
2. Informally counsel the officer on the appropriate use of force.
3. Threaten the officer with suspension if you hear of any more complaints of excessive force.
4. Tell him he is doing a great job but that he needs to be more careful in covering up his use of force.

Figure 7-1   The Types of Force Used by Police, When Force Was Used, in 2005 Note that the type of force used the most (pushed/grabbed) is relatively low.
Source: Matthew R. Durose, Erica L. Smith, and Patrick A. Langan, *Contacts between Police and the Public, 2005* (Washington, DC: U.S. Department of Justice, Bureau of Justice Statistics, 2007), 10, www.ojp.usdoj.gov/bjs/pub/pdf/cpp05.pdf.

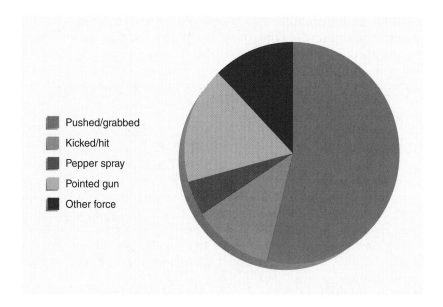

- Pushed/grabbed
- Kicked/hit
- Pepper spray
- Pointed gun
- Other force

SWAT Teams

The militarization of the police and the war-on-crime analogy are most apparent in the special weapons and tactics (SWAT) divisions of police agencies. The public has a love–hate view of these units.[52] On one hand, they are portrayed as jackbooted thugs who kick down homeowners' doors and employ police-state tactics to oppress people. On the other hand, they are sometimes viewed as professionals who must do a delicate and unpleasant job to protect the rest of us from terrorists, hostage takers, bank robbers, and mentally ill people who are violent.[53] The latter of these two characterizations is undoubtedly the more accurate portrayal of the work done by SWAT teams. In many ways, they are the elite of the police force. These officers are highly trained volunteers willing to do the more risk-laden tasks while employing the police mandate to use force. The types of situations in which a SWAT team may be used include, but are not limited to, the following:

1. Protecting police officers engaged in crowd control from sniper attack
2. Providing high-ground and perimeter security for visiting dignitaries
3. Rescuing hostages
4. Providing for the nonviolent apprehension of desperate barricaded suspects
5. Providing control-assault firepower in certain nonriot situations
6. Rescuing officers or citizens endangered by gunfire
7. Neutralizing guerrilla or terrorist operations against government personnel, property, or the general populace

---

7.1

CASE IN POINT

TENNESSEE V. GARNER

THE CASE	THE POINT
Tennessee v. Garner, 471 U.S. 1, 105 S.Ct. 1694 (1985)	*Deadly force now may be used only if the suspect poses a threat to the lives of police officers or bystanders.*

In 1974, Edward Garner, age 15, and a friend were in a house at night at which the owners were not present. A neighbor reported to police that someone had broken into the home. When the officers arrived, they saw someone running away, shouted warnings to stop, then shot at Garner, who was climbing a fence. The officer said that he was "reasonably sure" that Garner was unarmed, but thought that once he got over the fence, he would elude capture. One of the bullets struck Garner in the back of the head, and he died later on the operating table. Because the officers suspected the boys of a felony, burglarizing the house, they believed they were justified in shooting at the boys to stop them. Garner's father filed suit, claiming that his son's constitutional rights were violated. By 1985, the Supreme Court decided that the use of deadly force was not warranted. Justice Byron White wrote, "It is no doubt unfortunate when a suspect who is in sight escapes, but the fact that the police arrive a little late or are a little slower afoot does not always justify killing the suspect. A police officer may not seize an unarmed, non-dangerous suspect by shooting him dead."

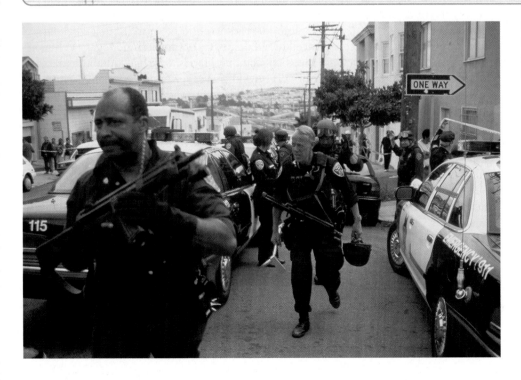

SWAT teams are part of every major law enforcement agency. They respond to hostage situations, terrorist attacks, and other situations that may require force.

Source: *Dwayne Newton / PhotoEdit Inc.*

Clearly, there are legitimate reasons to have SWAT teams. Police agencies are occasionally required to perform unpleasant and dangerous tasks. It makes sense to have some specially trained officers to respond to unusual situations. However, some critics are concerned that merely having a SWAT team means that it will be employed in situations that can be handled in more routine ways.[54] A SWAT team can reduce the danger to officers and civilians during a crisis, but it can also use force to resolve a situation with a quick decision. The Center for Research on Criminal Justice concluded in 1977 that, "The actual behavior of SWAT seems to contradict its avowed purpose of employing restraint in curbing incidents of urban violence. Quite the contrary, the net effect of SWAT's police-state tactics is to produce fear and outrage on the part of the community it purports to protect."[55]

It is a controversial judgment, then, on the part of law enforcement officials as to when a SWAT response is appropriate and likely to be effective. From time to time, that judgment appears to be in error when viewed in hindsight. The federal government received a lot of criticism for its handling of incidents in Ruby Ridge, Idaho, and Waco, Texas.[56] In addition to the loss of life from these two incidents, they were public relations disasters for the government. Even though the agencies' use of force was upheld by the courts in both incidents, one can only wonder whether better resolutions were possible. Clearly, the actions of Randy Weaver and David Koresh were precipitating, and in some ways causative, factors. However, lessons have been learned about how and when to use deadly force.[57] Let's take a closer look at the Ruby Ridge and Waco incidents as compared to a similar, more recent incident in New Hampshire in which a couple who had promised to die in a violent standoff with U.S. law enforcement officials were instead arrested without incident.

RUBY RIDGE, IDAHO   In August 1992, six federal marshals embarked on a "reconnaissance mission" to follow up on white separatist Randy Weaver in Ruby Ridge, Idaho. Federal law enforcement officers had been watching Weaver's cabin for a year, preparing to arrest him in connection with his indictment on the illegal sale of two sawed-off shotguns. Three of the marshals, who were in the woods near the family's mountain cabin, came across Weaver, his 14-year-old son Sammy, family friend Kevin Harris, and their dog. Everyone, both the marshals and the Weavers, was armed. The shootout began when one of the marshals shot the dog. Less than a minute later, Sammy Weaver and U.S. Marshal William Degan were dead as well. The next day, an FBI sniper wounded Weaver and Harris and shot and killed Randy's wife, Vicki, while she was holding her infant. Weaver and Harris surrendered more than a week later.

Weaver and Harris were acquitted by a federal jury of murdering Degan. When interviewed, most of the jurors said they believed that Harris, who had killed the marshal, had returned fire to defend Sammy Weaver. The Weaver family later filed wrongful death claims against the government, which settled with the family for $3.1 million.[58]

WACO, TEXAS   On February 28, 1993, ATF agents sustained gunfire while attempting to execute search and arrest warrants against David Koresh in his Branch Davidian compound in Waco, Texas. Four agents were killed, and 16 were wounded. Some sect members were also killed and injured. The FBI was called in, and agents were stationed in armored vehicles around the compound. Negotiations continued with Koresh by phone for several days and included tactical moves by the FBI such as the playing of loud music at night to disrupt sleep. Several of the cult members left the compound during the negotiations. At one point, Koresh said he and his followers would exit the compound after their observance of Passover on April 5. However, on April 7 Koresh would not give a firm date of surrender and said he would not leave until God told him to.

The FBI then planned to force out the cult members with tear gas. As the FBI prepared the attack, cult members held children up in the windows, as well as a sign reading, "Flames Await." On April 19 the FBI began using its armored vehicles to insert tear gas canisters into the building and knock holes in the walls. Fires broke out. Nine cult members were arrested while fleeing as the compound burned. In the end,

Local police and the FBI often work together in situations that require the use of force.

Source: CORBIS-NY

more than 80 cult members, including 22 children, died in the fire or were found shot to death. Arson investigators concluded that the cult members started the fire.

Probes into law enforcement's handling of the siege led to the firing of two ATF supervisors who were later reinstated at a lower rank. No FBI agents were officially disciplined. Seven of the surviving Branch Davidians received 40-year prison terms; one received five years, and one received three years after testifying for the government.[59]

PLAINFIELD, NEW HAMPSHIRE   In January 2007, Ed and Elaine Brown were convicted of withholding $1.9 million from federal tax authorities between 1996 and 2003. The courts rejected their argument that the federal income tax is illegal and that the 1913 constitutional amendment permitting it was improperly ratified. The couple retreated to their heavily fortified 103-acre New Hampshire compound, and in April 2007 they were sentenced in absentia to 63 months in prison and a $215,890 fine.

In June, when federal agents cut off the utilities to the Plainfield compound, the Browns switched to a wind turbine generator and solar panels for power and used satellite dishes to connect to the Internet. Supporters of the Browns' protest, including Randy Weaver, continued to bring supplies to the couple. In October 2007, federal agents posing as supporters who wanted to visit the couple arrested them on their front porch. On searching the compound, agents found homemade explosive devices, ammunition, and booby traps in the house.[60] Ed and Elaine Brown were sentenced to serve 63 months in federal prison.[61]

In summary, the police do not use extreme force as a matter of routine. Only on rare occasions is force used, and most of the time it is minimal. Most police officers are not required to use any force at all in their everyday duties. However, when force is required, it is law enforcement's responsibility to decide when and how much.[62] One can imagine how police officers might overreact in times of fear and stress and engage in inappropriate use of force, but for the most part we are willing to allow them to make some mistakes as long as those mistakes are made in good faith.[63] The risk that the police run is that they might not use enough force to protect themselves and others and that serious injury and lawsuits will result. In many ways, the police are in a no-win situation when deciding to use force, so we must appreciate that from time to time they will err on the side of using too much force.

Proactive Policing and Force

Do the police sometimes go looking for trouble? Yes, sometimes. Rather than waiting for laws to be broken and then reacting, sometimes police structure situations in which people might break the law. A prostitution sting, in which police officers pose as sex workers and then arrest those who proposition them, is one example.[64] Police units also raid illegal gambling establishments, homes where drugs are consumed or sold, and businesses that are suspected of violating liquor laws.[65] The police cannot always predict the level of risk they will encounter when conducting proactive raids, so they must be prepared for any eventuality. Gear that includes bulletproof vests, helmets with face masks, special camouflage uniforms, and automatic weapons are precautionary measures designed to protect the police and to exceed any possible use of force by the suspects. In some incidents, the police have been overzealous in their use of force and have caused injury or death to unarmed suspects.[66] Additionally, the police have also made mistakes, such as breaking into the wrong house and using force on innocent civilians.

The overzealous use of force has been termed the "Dirty Harry problem" by criminologist Carl Klockars.[67] In the film series, actor Clint Eastwood depicts a character named Harry Callahan who fights "psycho killers," corrupt police officers, and incompetent supervisors and politicians. Dirty Harry Callahan is not above bending a few procedural laws to catch the one-dimensional bad guys. Although these movies may be entertaining, they do not present the type of role model we want for our police. The Dirty Harry problem, according to Klockars, can be stated as, "When and to what extent does the morally good end warrant or justify an ethically, politically, or legally dangerous mean for its achievement?" Skolnick and Fyfe offered a further caution:

> The Dirty Harry dilemma faces every cop in the course of his or her career, and its ultimate resolution is always problematic and subject to hindsight criticism. Extralegal resolution of the Dirty Harry dilemma is difficult enough when the "bad guy" is an identifiable and factually guilty individual. It is most problematic when the criminal is not an individual but a loosely defined gang or criminal organization, where the consequences of a mistake can be tragic for innocent individuals or bystanders, and where gut-level racism can be imputed to the officers involved.[68]

This brings us to other issues of policing that have become increasingly problematic over the years. Police stress comes in many forms and can exert many different types of strain on officers, their families, and the police agency.[69]

STRESS AND BURNOUT

In May 1792, Deputy Sheriff Isaac Smith was trying to arrest John Ryer at an inn in what is now the Bronx, New York City. Ryer, who was drunk, shot and killed Smith, and fled. Arrested in Canada, Ryer was tried and hanged for the murder in New York in October 1793. Smith is believed to be the first law enforcement officer feloniously killed in the line of duty in the United States.[70]

Law enforcement can be a stressful career. Unlike many occupations, the threat of physical injury or death is a daily possibility (see Figure 7-2). According to the FBI, 57 law enforcement officers were feloniously killed in the line of duty during 2007 (see Figure 7-3 for the situations in which the officers were killed), nine more than in 2006.[71] Because the police are the ones called when force must be used, they have the most to fear from violence. At one time in our history, there was an unwritten rule among lawbreakers (probably a myth) that police officers should not be killed because the consequences would be severe. If that attitude ever saved a police officer's life in the past, there is little evidence that it persists today. In fact, with the vast sums of money and long prison sentences associated with some types of offenses (such as drug sales), human life, even that of a police officer, is often considered expendable and treated as simply part of doing business. Additionally, as the September 11 tragedy demonstrated, the police are often called to respond to situations in which their experience and training can do little to prevent harm (see Crosscurrents 7.1).

Stress for the police officer can come in many forms. It can be physical, emotional, social, marital, chemical, or occupational. At times, several types of stress can be experienced simultaneously. The job of police officer invites stress, and the way police agencies structure assignments, shifts, support, and discipline contributes to the anxiety and strain of the job.[72]

This section will review the literature on police stress and offer some suggestions on how it can be alleviated. This is done with the knowledge that stress is an inevitable part of the occupation and even the reason why some people select policing as a career. Not everyone wants to sit behind a desk staring at a computer screen. Some people want to be out working with people in jobs that offer something different every day and have a degree of excitement. However, along with this excitement comes stress. Not everyone handles stress in the same way, and sometimes the stress level can become so pronounced that it can overwhelm even the strongest person.

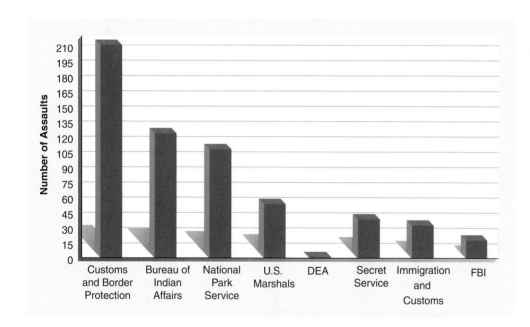

Figure 7-2   **Number of Assaults on Federal Officers 2007**

Source: Federal Bureau of Investigation, *Uniform Crime Reports*, Law Enforcement Officers Killed and Assaulted, 2007, www.fbi.gov/ucr/killed/2007/summary_doj.html.

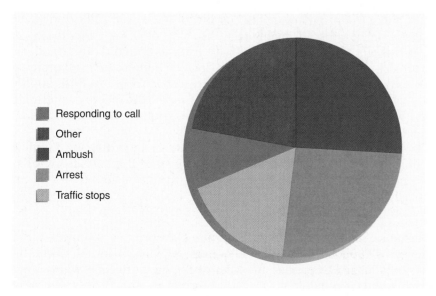

Figure 7-3   **Situations in Which Law Enforcement Officers Were Feloniously Killed in 2007**

Source: Federal Bureau of Investigation, "FBI Releases Preliminary Statistics for Law Enforcement Officers Killed in 2007," www.fbi.gov/pressrel/pressre108/leoka051208.htm.

CrossCurrents

Suicide by Cop

Like *road rage* and *going postal*, a new term has entered the media lexicon. *Suicide by cop* refers to suspects attempting to be killed by police officers. Most of these cases involve men who are estranged from wives or girlfriends and have a history of drug or alcohol use. Feeling lost and hopeless, these suspects orchestrate events so that the police must respond to their dangerous behavior. With no real effort to resolve the conflict or escape, the suspect threatens violence, and the police are forced to kill the suspect to protect themselves and innocent civilians. It can be a traumatic event for the police officer who seeks a peaceful means to end the case but is left with no alternative than to end the life of a distraught and troubled individual. Los Angeles County Sheriff's Homicide Department Sergeant Jack Yarbrough does not like the term *suicide by cop* because it connotes that the police officer is at fault. In reality, the police officer is a victim of a purposeful act by the suspect. Yarbrough prefers the term *police-assisted suicide*.

These incidents leave the police in a no-win situation. If they kill the suspect, they can experience stress even though they had no choice. If they simply wound the suspect, then others might get hurt, and the suspect might sue the police officer. Even the incident commanders who order the shooting might experience psychological or legal fallout.

Think About It

1. What do you think of the term *suicide by cop*? Is it appropriate?
2. Do you believe there are ways for police officers to avoid shooting suspects they think might be suicidal, or are such situations unavoidable in law enforcement?

Source: Dean Scoville, "Suicide by Cop," *Police Magazine*, November 1988, 36–44.

Police and Alcohol

In his 1975 novel *The Choirboys*, former Los Angeles policeman Joseph Wambaugh portrayed the police as consuming excessive amounts of alcohol to cope with the stresses of the job.[73] After their shift ended in the early-morning hours, the squad would go to what is euphemistically called "choir practice" at Los Angeles's MacArthur Park, where they would get drunk and tell each other stories about their night on patrol. Although the book can be funny at times, there is an undercurrent of tension caused, in part, by the excessive consumption of alcohol that Wambaugh links to the stress of policing.

This theme of policing and alcohol abuse can also be studied in the academic literature on policing. For example, one study looked at psychological stress, the demands of police work, and how police coped with these issues. The study found that the stress of police work was highly related to alcohol abuse. Other coping mechanisms such as emotional distancing (officers learn to objectify their emotions when faced with dead or injured people, victims, abused children, etc.) and cynicism were found to be related either directly or indirectly to alcohol use. What is important to learn from this study is that alcohol was used as a method to relieve the inherent stress of police work 20 times as often as cynicism or emotional distancing. In fact, when those methods failed, alcohol use became more likely.[74]

The stress of police work might not be the only factor, however, in influencing police officers to turn to alcohol. The police subculture also tends to exert a powerful influence on drinking patterns as it tests trustworthiness, loyalty, and masculinity. Additionally, it might act as an obstacle to the reporting of a fellow officer with a drinking problem. Consider the following:

1. The police subculture might socialize new officers into accepting a pattern of after-shift alcohol consumption. New employees are anxious to fit into the group. In many occupations, the older workers want to know whether the new person can be trusted. In police work, in which the officer must depend on his

or her partner, there is pressure to judge each other's reliability quickly. Learning what "makes the other person tick" through after-hours socializing is an important part of this judgment process. New officers are judged by their peers to "fit in" to the extent that they can hold their liquor; articulate the occupational worldview of the police subculture; and accept and participate in complaining about citizens, politicians, and superiors.

2. Socialization in the police subculture establishes that drinking alcohol is not deviant. Because "everyone drinks after work," the consumption of alcohol is soon viewed as normal behavior. Whereas in other circumstances, consistent and excessive alcohol consumption may be viewed as a problem, in police work it just means that an officer is "one of the guys." When embarrassing incidents happen or problems with family emerge because of alcohol, these issues are turned into amusing stories that are told over and over in future drinking bouts as evidence that "civilians don't understand police work."

3. This normalization of alcohol consumption may preclude treatment because "every one of my friends drinks." One of the issues that can lead people to seek treatment for their drug or alcohol addiction is the embarrassment it can cause in the workplace. To the extent that alcohol use is the norm among one's contemporaries, its abuse is not a cause for concern and its treatment may be viewed as a weakness or even a betrayal of the work group. When a fellow officer is forced to admit that alcohol is a problem, other officers might feel uncomfortable in examining their own drinking patterns. A reformed drinker can sometimes help his or her friends, but often the friends continue to maintain their lifestyle, and an unspoken barrier is erected.

The effect of alcohol on the police has not been lost on police administrators.[75] As with many other agencies and corporations, personnel policies are geared toward ensuring that the police maintain good health and do not put the force at risk of lawsuits because of unfitness for duty. In the past several years, many public safety organizations have instituted drug and alcohol testing to ensure that police officers are capable of performing their assignments.[76] Assistance is offered to those who need help, and continued failures to meet departmental standards can be cause for dismissal. This extreme remedy is more likely for those found to be using illegal drugs than it is for those who abuse alcohol, but police agencies are more attuned to the effects of intoxication now than they have been in the past. The police subculture that celebrates drinking as part of the job, as Joseph Wambaugh did in his novel, is coming under attack as a by-product of the war on drugs.

Family Problems and the Police

The individual police officer is not the only one affected by the stress of police work. Often, family members experience a variety of stressful concerns.[77] The first of these is the change in the personality of the police officer and his or her relationship with spouse and/or children. Jerome Skolnick coined the term *policeman's working personality* to explain how the police must cope with danger, isolation, authority, and suspicion.[78] Police families experience stress when the police officer brings the job home and starts to treat his or her spouse and children like potential suspects. The simple question, "Where are you going?" might be viewed as an interrogation rather than a normal concern. Children of police officers might be held to a higher standard of etiquette as the officer demands that they show proper respect and deference.[79]

The issue of isolation can take on two forms. The officer might not express the stress that comes from the job to the family, and he or she could appear withdrawn and disinterested in the family's concerns. Additionally, the family members might be treated with hostility by neighbors who believe they are being watched by the police officer. On one hand, integrating into the community is desirable; on the other hand, it might become problematic when the members of the community see the police as a threat.

The dangers associated with police work can also be a source of stress for officers' family members.[80] Knowing that one's spouse or parent is potentially just one radio call away from a deranged person with a gun can keep one in an uneasy state of mind. If each phone call could be the police commissioner calling to say there has been a shooting, it is only natural that some family members would suggest the police officer find less dangerous work. Having a spouse or parent as a police officer can be a source of pride, but it can also be a source of worry and concern.[81] Family members' pressure on the police officer about the job can create a dilemma. Feeling a loyalty to the job and responsibility to the family can result in the officer internalizing stress and, as a result, doing a bad job at both family life and policing.[82]

Finally, the nature of police work can cause hardships in the family because of rotating shifts. Depending on the department, the nature of shift work can exert an extreme hardship on both the police officer and the family. Scheduling day care, vacations, children's after-school activities, and a host of other domestic duties is difficult when the officer's shift is always in flux.[83] Most people work best when they have a routine to which their bodies can adjust. In police work, the routine is lost with constant changes in shifts.[84] People become irritable when their sleeping patterns are altered, and by the time an officer adjusts to a shift, the shift changes again. Some occupations that require 24/7 coverage keep stable shifts for their workers by paying a differential for the least desirable times. For example, in the medical profession, nurses who work the midnight shift are paid more than those who work the traditional 8 A.M. to 5 P.M. shift. Both develop a routine that allows them to balance the demands of work and home. The costs of illness, burnout, and stress might be higher than the cost of extra pay to individuals who are willing to work the least desirable shifts.

Police and Suicide

Suicide is an occupational hazard for police officers.[85] A number of studies have shown that law enforcement has one of the highest suicide rates of any occupation. Given the preceding discussion about the stress of policing and its contributions to alcohol abuse and family problems, it should not be too surprising to learn that suicide also concerns the police and their families. The question is, Why would police officers resort to suicide at rates higher than those in other occupations? The answer lies in the types of stress we have already discussed and in the access the police have to handguns.

Firearms are a constant feature in the lives of police officers. About 97 percent of officer suicides involve the officer's own service gun.[86] Police officers are trained in the use of guns, carry them on a daily basis, are prepared emotionally to use guns in the pursuit of lawbreakers, and have been sufficiently desensitized to the effects of guns.

It is hard to think of any other occupation, including the military, in which guns are such a constant part of the job. It should come as no surprise, then, that when faced with the high levels of stress that are part of policing, some officers use firearms to take their lives. In fact, the phrase "he ate his gun" is part of the police lexicon. It is unfair, however, to argue that the gun is solely responsible for police suicide rates. Although firearms are an efficient way to kill oneself (as opposed to a drug overdose), a determined person will find a way whether there is a convenient gun or not. It just so happens that for police officers, there is always a convenient gun. However, according to Robert Douglas Jr., a retired Baltimore, Maryland, police officer and executive director of the National P.O.L.I.C.E. Suicide Foundation, an officer's gun also has personal significance: "It has an identity. It picks up the personality of a best friend. It becomes 'someone' who is trustworthy, reliable and 'someone' with a solution."[87]

A final source of stress might contribute not only to the high suicide rate among police officers, but also to their problems with alcohol and family issues: dealing with the results of violent crime and other tragedies.[88] Seeing human beings dead days or weeks after they are first reported missing can be very stressful. Watching families fall apart because of poverty, drugs, or marital abuse can cause some officers to become depressed. Dealing with the mentally ill offender who is armed with a gun and having to

7.2 CrossCurrents

Another Look at Police Suicide

Law enforcement can be a stressful occupation, and the perception that police officers are at risk for suicide, alcoholism, and divorce is deeply rooted in the popular culture. Some studies and much anecdotal evidence support the impression of policing as an unhealthy occupation, but it is worthwhile to look more closely at what the research reveals.

Studies that show high rates of suicide for police officers include Nelson and Smith's finding of a rate of 203 suicides per 100,000 officers in Wyoming, Friedman's finding of 80 suicides per 100,000 officers in New York City, and Richard and Fell's finding of 69 suicides per 100,000 officers in Tennessee. According to Robert Loo, there are three problems with the way police suicide rates are calculated:

1. These studies use short time frames. One year of a high number of police suicides can give an impression of a higher rate. Loo contended that rates of police suicide should be calculated for at least 10-year time frames.

2. Agencies that reported no suicides were not always included in the analysis. Had this been done, the base number would have increased, and the rate would be lower.

3. Many studies fail to control for age, gender, and race. To the extent that police officers tend to be young, white males, they demonstrated higher rates than the general population. In a study conducted by Aamodt and Stalnaker, these variables were statistically controlled for, and police officers were found to commit suicide 26 percent less than those of similar age, race, and gender.

Police officers endure the same pressures and limitations as those who share their social position. Young men are more likely to engage in suicide and alcoholism than the general population. To the extent that police forces have always had an overrepresentation of males and those between ages 20 and 40, their rates of social problems can be expected to be at least as high. However, according to Stephen Curran, police officers are likely to be psychologically healthy, engage in exercise programs, and refrain from using tobacco or alcohol to excess. When comparing police officers to others who share their demographic characteristics, we do not necessarily find that police officers are victims of elevated occupational stress.

Think About It

1. Do you think police officers are more likely to commit suicide? Why or why not?

2. Do you believe that the research on police suicide is accurate?

Sources: Michael G. Aamodt and Nicole A. Stalnaker, "Police Officer Suicide: Frequency and Officer Profiles," in *Suicide and Law Enforcement*, eds. D. C. Shehan and J. I. Warren (Washington, DC: Federal Bureau of Investigation, 2001), www.radford.edu/~maamodt/Police%20Research/police%20suicide.pdf; Stephen Curran, "Separating Fact from Fiction about Police Stress," *Behavioral Health Management* 23, no. 1 (2003): 38–40; Paul Friedman, "Suicide among Police: A Study of Ninety-Three Suicides among New York Policemen, 1934–1940," in *Essays in Self-Destruction*, ed. E. Shneidman (New York: Science House, 1968), 414–419; Robert Loo, "A Meta-Analysis of Police Suicide Rates: Findings and Issues," *Suicide and Life-Threatening Behavior* 33, no. 3 (2003): 313–325; W. C. Richard and R. D. Fell, "Health Factors in Police Job Stress," in *Job Stress and the Police: Identifying Stress Reduction Techniques: Proceedings of a Symposium*, eds. W. H. Kroes and J. J. Hurrell Jr. (Washington, DC: U.S. Government Printing Office, 1975); Z. Nelson and W. Smith, "Law Enforcement Profession: An Incident of Suicide," *Omega* 1 (1970): 293–299.

shoot to protect other people can deeply affect police officers. Finally, as demonstrated in other chapters, the very nature of the criminal justice system can cause officers to become frustrated when they do their jobs well only to find the offender set free to victimize others. The police must deal with the underside of society, and after a time, unless officers can cope with the stress, the job can get so overwhelming that suicide, retirement, quitting, or engaging in deviant behavior can be considered the only ways to cope.[89] For a different interpretation of police suicide figures, see Crosscurrents 7.2.

Dealing with the Stress of Policing

Although many occupations can stress their practitioners, policing seems to have some special features that, although recognized in the literature on policing, have been neglected by police agencies. Certainly, police departments' human resources divisions have implemented policies aimed at helping individual officers, and community programs that are available to all citizens are also available to the police, but police officers often shun these resources.[90] Within the police subculture an attitude exists that to admit stress to the administration or to outsiders is a sign of weakness.

To successfully reduce police stress to manageable levels, police agencies, city or county administrations, and police officers themselves can use a variety of strategies. Bruce Arrigo and Karyn Garsky make three suggestions:[91]

1. **Stress management and stress reduction techniques.**   According to Arrigo and Garsky, police academies do not provide classes on how to cope with stress. They suggested that, in addition to physical exercise, officers be given information on nutrition and dieting practices; physical health, fitness, and exercise routines; mental wellness, imaging, and relaxation techniques; recreational, leisure, and outdoor activities; and humor, play, and amusement strategies.

2. **Group "rap" or process sessions.**   Arrigo and Garsky argued that although police agencies may have therapeutic assistance available to officers, using this counseling is perceived as an admission of weakness, troubled conscience, or ineffectiveness. What is needed is exposure to group sessions early in the training process and regularly throughout officers' careers as a way of sharing with contemporaries the inevitable stress present in policing. Important issues can be discussed away from the local bar and insights gained without the stimulus of alcohol that can aid individual officers in dealing with stress. Peer support is an effective and important counseling technique that is particularly relevant to policing, and if done under the right circumstances (while not drinking), it promises to be helpful.

3. **Police mentoring.**   Once out of the academy, the rookie police officer learns the job from experienced police officers. As a logical extension of the group sessions provided to new police officers, there is potential for ongoing programs in which skilled mentoring can reinforce the lessons of how to deal with stress.

Revisiting the effect of changing officers' shifts is a first step in reforming policing. Officers have family responsibilities that suffer when the officer has no control over his or her working hours. The problems of sleep deprivation are known, but sometimes appear to be ignored by police administrators. Making unattractive shifts more desirable for officers can be accomplished by paying more to those who are willing to assume the hardships. In the long run, the community will be safer, officers will be healthier, and the city will save money with a stable and alert police force.[92]

Another method of addressing the stress of police work is reducing the paramilitary focus that some departments have adopted. As was previously discussed, the military is a poor model on which to pattern a police department. Additionally, the police mission is considerably broader than the military mission, which concentrates on the use of force.

Finally, the move toward more community policing activities seems like a promising strategy to make police work less stressful. To the extent that the police become integrated into the community, it can be expected that their work will be not only more effective, but also more socially rewarding. When the police interact with citizens on a routine and constructive basis, they can form relationships that will engender trust and reciprocal goodwill, which can make policing a more positive experience.

POLICE SUBCULTURE AND CORRUPTION

The style of policing adopted by the officer is influenced by that officer's personal characteristics in coping with the demands of the job and with family members and friends. Like many occupations, policing imposes a lifestyle that might set the police officer apart from civilians in terms of sociability, social integration, and social acceptance.[93] Sometimes police officers are not invited to parties because people fear their reaction to rowdy behavior. The police often do not want to interact socially with others because their occupations tag them with a master status that causes others to treat them as a "cop."[94] Also, the police develop the *policeman's working personality*, which explains how police officers are drawn into a subculture that emphasizes a different set of values from those held by mainstream society.[95] Skolnick also pointed out that the particular occupational style will vary according to the demands of certain assignments:

> A conception of "working personality" of police should be understood to suggest an analytic breadth similar to that of "style of life." That is, just as the professional behavior of military officers with similar "styles of life" may differ drastically depending upon whether they command an infantry battalion or participate in the work of an intelligence unit, so too does the professional behavior of police officers with similar "working personalities" vary with their assignments.[96]

However, Skolnick went on to point out that all police officers begin their careers on the street in the constabulary role and that this experience tends to shape an occupational police perspective that socially isolates the officer and makes him or her suspicious of others. Therefore, it is useful to consider Skolnick's concept of the policeman's working personality in some detail by examining some of its key elements.

1. **The symbolic assailant.** Police officers must always be on guard. They are systematically trained and culturally reinforced to consider everyone a potential assailant until they can size up the situation and determine that an individual poses no threat. This is easy to do when confronted with a large, drunk, belligerent man wielding a knife. It is less easy when interacting with a gray-haired grandmother who seems lost and disoriented. Police officers will not relax until they are confident that the grandmother poses no harm to herself or others. They cannot assume that she is of no threat until they can independently establish that she is what she seems to be. In the grandmother's case, this is accomplished based on behavioral and contextual clues. The situation of the knife-wielding man, on the other hand, alerts officers to keep their guard up. According to Skolnick, the officer "develops a perceptual shorthand to identify certain kinds of people as symbolic assailants, that is, persons whose gestures, language, and attire may constitute a prelude to violence."[97]

2. **Danger.** Police work can be dangerous (see Figure 7-4). Although death in the line of duty and serious physical injury are not frequent, the possibility of confrontation is always there, and according to Skolnick, is part of the makeup of the policeman's working personality. In fact, police are drawn to the more dangerous assignments, as a function of both job prestige and excitement.[98]

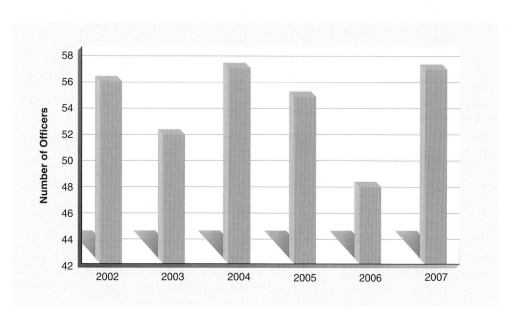

Figure 7-4 Number of Law Enforcement Officers Killed during the Commission of Felonies, 2002–2007

Source: Federal Bureau of Investigation, *Uniform Crime Reports*, Law Enforcement Officers Killed and Assaulted, 2002–2007, www.fbi.gov/ucr/ucr.htm#leoka.

3. **Social isolation.** The public treats police officers differently. Whereas police officers may perceive an individual as a symbolic assailant, the public sees the police officer as a symbolic authority figure. Thus, even when an individual has done nothing wrong, he or she might be wary of an officer because of the perceived power the officer has to detain, question, search, and arrest. Skolnick quoted a police officer who was at a party with his wife when someone threw a firecracker that exploded and slightly injured his wife. When the police officer confronted the man and told him to be careful, someone identified him as a police officer. What would have been a simple exchange between individuals was transformed into a situation in which a crowd of people sided against the police officer, and the officer felt unwelcome and left. Subsequently, he and his wife stopped associating with those people because his occupation of police officer was a barrier to open and honest interaction. Skolnick reported that this social isolation causes many officers to limit their social interactions to situations in which other officers are around.

4. **Solidarity.** The combination of danger and social isolation creates a sense of solidarity in the police subculture (see Focus on Ethics 7.2). An "us against them" mentality is developed to cope not only with law violators, but also with the public in general. The police, according to Skolnick, resent the lack of support they perceive coming from those whom they protect and serve. The police feel as though they are taken for granted by the public and that the public does not take enough responsibility for helping to fight the war against lawbreakers.[99]

The occupational culture of the police, like many other occupational cultures, fosters certain personality characteristics in its practitioners.[100] Danger, authority, potential symbolic assailants, and social isolation are features of the occupation that encourage the construction of the policeman's working personality. This process might have far-reaching implications for the recruitment, training, and control of police officers.[101] For example, how much money and resources should be spent on the selection and training of officers if the very nature of law enforcement occupations instills those individuals with an occupational perspective that dictates how they view the job and respond to suspects and the public? How should society address the negative features of the policeman's working personality?

FOCUS on ETHICS

7.2

TO TRUST A PARTNER

As a new female police officer, you have sailed through the police academy and in-service training with high marks, and you are excited to be teamed with one of the most popular and respected officers on the force. You find that the two of you work well together. He treats you with respect and increasingly gives you more authority in doing your job. You are developing mutual trust in each other, and you could not be happier with your assignment. However, in the last few weeks you have begun to become concerned about your partner's emotional stability.

When the squad goes out for a drink after the shift, you notice that your partner has been getting quite drunk. One Saturday night after a particularly stressful shift that included a high-speed chase, shots fired, and the wrestling of a suspect to the ground, your partner confides in you that he has been chronically depressed. After several beers, he admits that he and his wife are separating and that his children are the only passion he still has in life. Then the shocker comes. He looks around to make sure no other officers are listening, then tells you he has been having fantasies of "eating his gun." In the academy they told you to take all talk of suicide seriously, but you are committed to maintaining the trust you have developed with your partner.

What Do You Do?

1. Seek advice about your partner's depression from the police psychologist.

2. Try to counsel your partner, and tell no one about his depression.

3. Ask for a new partner.

Police Corruption

Although police corruption has been a significant problem for some agencies at particular times, we do not suggest that it is as pervasive as the issues of the policeman's working personality. However, the nature and extent of police corruption are worth our attention because of the constant temptations placed before police officers and because trust in the criminal justice system is one of the cornerstones of a democratic society.[102] Additionally, the history of policing is replete with examples not only of corruption of individual officers, but also of the widespread, systemic corruption of entire departments and the municipal governments they serve.[103]

Knapp Commission   In 1972, the Knapp Commission issued its report on police corruption in New York City. Based on the revelations made by undercover detective Frank Serpico, 19 officers were indicted for accepting payoffs. Subsequent investigations revealed even more violators. In examining this systematic corruption, the Knapp Commission made a distinction between **meat-eaters** and **grass-eaters**.

> Corrupt policemen have been informally described as being either "grass-eaters" or "meat-eaters." The overwhelming majority of those who do take payoffs are grass-eaters, who accept gratuities and solicit five- and ten- and twenty dollar payments from contractors, tow-truck operators, gamblers, and the like, but do not aggressively pursue corruption payments. "Meat-eaters," probably only a small percentage of the force, spend a good deal of their working hours aggressively seeking out situations they can exploit for financial gain, including gambling, narcotics, and other serious offenses which can yield payments of thousands of dollars.[104]

Not all police officers have equal opportunities to engage in corruption. The nature of the department, the community, and the particular assignment all influence how much temptation is placed in the officers' paths or how fertile the situation is for the meat-eater who aggressively seeks situations to exploit. Historically, illegal gambling, prostitution, substance prohibition, and other organized-crime activities have been major sources of police corruption. Presently, because of the war on drugs, tremendous amounts of money are changing hands, putting narcotics officers in positions to engage in a variety of corrupt acts. According to Peter K. Manning and Lawrence John Redlinger, narcotics law enforcement can invite police corruption in at least seven ways.

1. **Bribes.**   Officers can take bribes in a number of ways. They can provide advance warning of police raids or take bribes not to arrest those caught using or selling drugs. Additionally, police officers are reported to have testified badly in a case in exchange for a bribe. For instance, Manning and Redlinger cited the Knapp Commission's finding that an officer can admit while being questioned on the witness stand that he "lost sight" of the drugs as they fell to the ground, thus providing the defense attorney with an argument that the chain of custody was compromised.

2. **Using drugs.**   On occasion, police officers might use the very drugs they are mandated to suppress. Additionally, they might use other drugs without prescription to stay awake. The incidence of police officers using illegal drugs is probably not as serious a problem today as it might have been a generation ago. Many police agencies require random drug tests of employees that deters illegal drug use.

3. **Buying and selling narcotics.**   It may seem incredible that narcotics officers would deal in drugs, but in some circumstances, this type of corruption might seem reasonable to an officer. The testimony of addicts can be acquired by giving them drugs. Likewise, informers can be paid off by giving them a small amount of the seized drugs. Given limited budgets for operating expenditures

meat-eaters
A slang term from the 1971 Knapp Commission report on police corruption in New York City describing officers who actively seek out situations that can produce financial gain.

grass-eaters
A slang term from the 1971 Knapp Commission report on police corruption in New York City, describing officers who accept bribes but do not actively pursue them.

such as "buy money," enterprising narcotics agents might use drugs to finance operations the department cannot afford. However, these activities are still considered a form of corruption and are not sanctioned by police administrators. Finally, "meat-eating" officers have been known to sell narcotics and use the money for personal gain.[105]

4. **Arrogation of seized property.**   Property relevant to a criminal offense must be seized by the police department and held until the case is concluded, at which point the department determines whether to return it to its rightful owner, destroy it, or convert it to government use. The police must scrupulously account for all seized cash, drugs, guns, and automobiles. Although cash used by police to buy drugs is marked and the serial numbers recorded, the cash seized from drug dealers is subject to theft by the arresting officers. Some of the cash and drugs seized at a crime scene might be diverted before they are officially logged into the evidence room at the police station.

5. **Illegal searches and seizures.**   Police can engage in corrupt misconduct in several ways when initiating searches and seizures on drug suspects. Lying about smelling marijuana or seeing drugs in "plain sight" is one method officers can use to claim probable cause to conduct a search. The planting of evidence on a suspect can happen in any of three ways. *Flaking* consists of finding evidence the officer planted on the suspect. Some officers carry a "sure-bust kit" that contains a variety of drugs that can be planted on suspects to support the type of arrest the officers desire. *Dropsey* is a variation of flaking in which the officer claims to have seen the suspect drop something and then finds drugs at the offender's feet. *Padding* refers to the practice of adding drugs to a seizure to justify a raise in the charge from misdemeanor to felony. The police can use these practices to entice drug dealers and users to offer bribes of cash or sexual favors for lenient treatment.

6. **Protection of informants.**   Sometimes the police are willing to tolerate a certain level of crime to battle more serious infractions. This becomes a judgment call that can lead to substantial harm to victims, the community, and the reputation of the law enforcement agencies. Both within and between criminal justice agencies there are rivalries, competition, and distrust. The narcotics division might overlook the burglaries of a confidential informant if it is receiving good information that may facilitate the bust of a big drug dealer. A federal agency might hide the offenses of a snitch from a local police department if doing so furthers its agenda. Informants might coax all kinds of rewards, such as money, drugs, or reduced charges, from several agencies at the same time based on the promise of the same information.

7. **Violence.**   Finally, narcotics officers might use unwarranted violence to cope with drug dealers. They might claim the suspect "went for his gun" and then kill the suspect. They might threaten to tell others in the drug trade that the suspect is an informant, ensuring that person's violent death at the hands of others. The police might use illegal force in a number of ways that enables them to prosecute or extort lawbreakers.[106]

These forms of police behavior all represent some type of corruption. They might sometimes be used to advance the cause of legitimate police work, but because they are illegal, they are of concern to police administrators and police scholars. A police department that allows its officers to operate in devious ways inevitably exposes itself to the scandal of corruption and the problems of litigation.[107] Therefore, it seems prudent to consider these types of corruption as pressing issues within law enforcement.

SUMMARY

1. Three challenges to the traditional policing model are community policing, problem-oriented policing, and zero-tolerance policing.

2. Community policing recalls the watchman style and legalistic styles of policing.

3. Problem-oriented policing allows police agencies to address crime on a more systemic level than traditional policing.

4. Zero-tolerance policing is based on the idea that if every infraction of the law is punished, offenders will refrain from more destructive activities.

5. According to broken-windows theory, there is less crime in socially ordered communities because the residents appear to care about their surroundings.

6. Gender and race are important issues in the study of law enforcement. When the police are viewed as promoting and protecting only the interests of certain races, genders, or social groups, then the criminal justice system is considered to be oppressive.

7. Physical force is considered legitimate only under the following conditions: self-defense; specifically deputized people against some specifically named people, and police force.

8. The police use force in making arrests and keeping order, and situations in which the police use force are highly contextual. The expectation of how much and what type of force an officer will use in a situation varies according to a number of factors.

9. The militarization of the police and the war-on-crime analogy are the most apparent in the special weapons and tactics (SWAT) divisions of police agencies.

10. Unlike many occupations, the threat of physical injury or death in policing is a daily possibility. Because the police are the ones called when force must be used, they have the most to fear from violence.

11. Police stress can come in many forms: physical, emotional, social, marital, chemical, or occupational.

12. The job of police officer invites stress, and the way police agencies structure assignments, shifts, support, and discipline contributes to anxiety and strain.

13. Police officers often use alcohol to deal with the stresses of the job.

14. Police officers' families also experience a variety of stressful concerns. Police families often experience stress when the officer brings the job home and starts to treat his or her spouse and children like potential suspects.

15. Suicide is an occupational hazard for police officers. A number of studies have shown that law enforcement has one of the highest suicide rates of any occupation.

16. Like many occupations, policing imposes a lifestyle that might set the police officer apart from civilians in terms of sociability, social integration, and social acceptance. Police departments' human resources divisions have implemented policies aimed at helping individual officers.

17. The key elements of the policeman's working personality concept are the symbolic assailant, danger, social isolation, and solidarity.

18. According to Manning and Redlinger, narcotics law enforcement can invite police corruption in at least seven ways: bribery, using drugs, buying/selling narcotics, arrogation of seized property, illegal searches and seizures, protection of informants, and violence.

KEY TERMS

broken-windows theory 229
community policing 225
double marginality 234
grass-eaters 251

meat-eaters 251
Neighborhood Watch 226
policeman's working
  personality 234

problem-oriented policing 227
use of force 235
zero-tolerance policing 229

REVIEW QUESTIONS

1. The use of force is considered legitimate in only a few circumstances. What are they?

2. When is the use of police SWAT teams appropriate? When is their use inappropriate?

3. Have female police officers been fully integrated into the nation's law enforcement agencies? What about minorities?

4. What is community policing, and how does it differ from traditional models of law enforcement?

5. What is problem-oriented policing and how is it related to community policing?

6. What is broken-windows theory? What are this theory's implications for law enforcement? Why do some scholars see this theory as problematic?

7. Is policing more stressful than other occupations? What are the sources of police stress?

8. What problems are caused by stress in police work? What can police administrators do to make the job of policing less stressful?

9. What is the "policeman's working personality" and how can police agencies counteract this danger?

10. What are the major sources and types of police corruption?

SUGGESTED FURTHER READING

Alex, Nicholas. *Black in Blue: A Study of the Negro Policeman.* New York: Appleton-Century-Crofts, 1969.

Bayley, David. *Police for the Future.* New York: Oxford University Press, 1994.

Bittner, Egon. *The Functions of the Police in Modern Society.* Cambridge, MA: Oelgeschlager, Gunn, & Hain, 1980.

Fletcher, Connie. *Breaking and Entering: Women Cops Talk about Life in the Ultimate Men's Club.* New York: Harper-Collins, 1995.

Gaines, Larry K., and Victor E. Kappeler. *Policing in America*, 6th ed. Cincinnati, OH: LexisNexis, 2008).

Travis, Lawrence F. III. *Policing in America: A Balance of Forces*, 4th ed. (Upper Saddle River, NJ: Pearson Prentice Hall, 2008).

ENDNOTES

1. Matthew J. Hickman and Brian A. Reaves, *Law Enforcement Management and Administrative Statistics: Local Police Departments, 2003* (Washington, DC: U.S. Department of Justice, Bureau of Justice Statistics, 2006), www.ojp.usdoj.gov/bjs/pub/ascii/lpd03.txt.

2. David Alan Sklansky, "Police and Community in Chicago: A Tale of Three Cities," *Law and Society Review* 42 (March 1, 2008): 233–235.

3. Robert Trojanowicz, Victor E. Kappeler, Larry K. Gaines, and Bonnie Bucqueroux, *Community Policing: A Contemporary Perspective*, 2nd ed. (Cincinnati, OH: Anderson, 1998).

4. Samuel Walker and Charles M. Katz, *The Police in America: An Introduction*, 4th ed. (Boston: McGraw-Hill, 2002), 202–203. Walker and Katz also stated three other reasons for this change: the police car patrol, the existing use of detectives, and the emphasis on response time. All were found wanting. Additionally, policing was recognized as a complex job that involved more than crime fighting and that citizens were coproducers of police services. Our discussion here of these alternative forms of policing is heavily influenced by their ideas in Chapter 7 of their book.

5. Ibid., 205.

6. Byongook Moon and Laren J. Zager, "Police Officers' Attitudes toward Citizen Support: Focus on Individual, Organizational and Neighborhood Characteristic Factors," *Policing* 30 (July 1, 2007): 484–497.

7. Gordon Bazemore and Allen W. Cole, "Police in the 'Laboratory' of the Neighborhood: Evaluating Problem-Oriented Strategies in a Medium-Sized City," *American Journal of Police* 13, no. 3 (1994): 119–147.

8. Chris Menton "Bicycle Patrols: An Underutilized Resource," *Policing* 31 (January 1, 2008): 93–108.

9. April Pattavina, James M. Byrne, and Luis Garcia, "An Examination of Citizen Involvement in Crime Prevention in High-Risk versus Low- to Moderate-Risk Neighborhoods," *Crime and Delinquency* 52 (April 1, 2006): 203–231.

10. Wesley Skogan and Susan M. Hartnett, *Community Policing: Chicago Style* (New York: Oxford University Press, 1997).

11. Herman Goldstein, *Problem-Oriented Policing* (New York: McGraw-Hill, 1990).

12. Anthony A. Braga et al., "The Strategic Prevention of Gun Violence among Gang-Involved Offenders," *Justice Quarterly* 25 (March 1, 2008): 132.

13. Michael D. White et al., "The Police Role in Preventing Homicide: Considering the Impact of Problem-Oriented Policing on the Prevalence of Murder," *Journal of Research in Crime and Delinquency* 40 (May 1, 2003): 194–225.

14. Lorraine Green, "Cleaning Up Drug Hot Spots in Oakland, California: The Displacement and Diffusion Effects," *Justice Quarterly* 12 (December 1995): 737–754.

15. Walker and Katz, *Police in America*, 226–227.

16. David Weisburd and John E. Eck, "What Can Police Do to Reduce Crime, Disorder, and Fear?" *Annals of the American Academy of Political and Social Science* 593 (May 1, 2004): 42–65.

17. James Q. Wilson and George L. Kelling, "Broken Windows: Police and Neighborhood Safety," *Atlantic Monthly*, March 1982, 29–38.

18. Bernard E. Harcourt and Jens Ludwig, "Broken Windows: New Evidence from New York City and a Five-City Social Experiment," *University of Chicago Law Review* 73 (January 1, 2006): 271–320.

19. Samuel Walker, "Broken Windows and Fractured History: The Use and Misuse of History in Recent Patrol Analysis," in *Critical Issues in Policing: Contemporary Readings*, eds. Roger G. Dunham and Geoffrey P. Alpert (Prospect Heights, IL: Waveland Press, 2001), 480–492.

20. Ralph B. Taylor, "Illusion of Order: The False Promise of Broken Windows Policing," *American Journal of Sociology* 111 (March 1, 2006): 1625–1628.

21. Amnesty International, *United States of America: Police Brutality and Excessive Use of Force in the New York City Police Department* (New York: Author, 1996).

22. Hannah Cooper et al., "The Impact of a Police Drug Crackdown on Drug Injectors' Ability to Practice Harm Reduction: A Qualitative Study," *Social Science and Medicine* 61 (August 1, 2005): 673–684.

23. Lawrence Sherman, "Policing for Crime Prevention," *Preventing Crime: What Works, What Doesn't, What's Promising* (Washington, DC: National Institute of Justice, 1998), www.ncjrs.org/works/chapter8.htm.

24. Wilson and Kelling, "Broken Windows," 29–38.

25. Benjamin Chesluk, "'Visible Signs of a City Out of Control: Community Policing in New York City," *Cultural Anthropology* 19 (May 1, 2004): 250–275.

26. Ibid.

27. David Thacher, "Order Maintenance Reconsidered: Moving Beyond Strong Causal Reasoning," *Journal of Criminal Law and Criminology* 94 (January 1, 2004): 381–414.

28. Walker, "Broken Windows," 480–492.

29. D. W. Mills, "Poking Holes in the Theory of 'Broken Windows,'" *Chronicle of Higher Education* (February 9, 2001): A14.

30. Ronald V. Clarke, "Situational Crime Prevention: Its Theoretical Basis and Practical Scope," in *Crime Displacement: The Other Side of Prevention*, ed. Robert P. McNamara (East Rockaway, NY: Cummings & Hathaway, 1994), 38–70.

31. NPR, "Drug Crime Displacement," *All Things Considered*, September 16, 1998.

32. Gregg Barak, Jeanne M. Flavin, and Paul S. Leighton, *Class, Race, Gender, and Crime: Social Realities of Justice in America* (Los Angeles: Roxbury, 2001).

33. Suman Kakar, "Race and Police Officers' Perceptions of Their Job Performance: An Analysis of the Relationship between Police Officers' Race, Education Level, and Job Performance," *Journal of Police and Criminal Psychology* 18 (April 1, 2003): 45.

34. National Center for Women and Policing, "Equality Denied: The Status of Women in Policing: 2000," National Center for Women and Policing, Feminist Majority Foundation, April 2001, www.womenandpolicing.org/PDF/2000%20Status%20Report.pdf.

35. Jody Kasper, "Proven Steps for Recruiting Women," *Law and Order*, December 1, 2006, 63–67.

36. Jerome H. Skolnick, *Justice without Trial: Law Enforcement in Democratic Society*, 3rd ed. (New York: Macmillan, 1994), 41–68.

37. Susan E. Martin, "Women Officers on the Move: An Update on Women in Policing," *Critical Issues in Policing: Contemporary Readings*, 4th ed., eds. Roger G. Dunham and Geoffrey P. Alpert (Prospect Heights, IL: Waveland Press, 2001), 401–422.

38. John R. Lott Jr., "Does a Helping Hand Put Others at Risk? Affirmative Action, Police Departments, and Crime," *Economic Inquiry* 38 (April 1, 2000): 239–277.

39. Alissa Pollitz Worden, "The Attitudes of Women and Men in Policing: Testing Conventional and Contemporary Wisdom," *Criminology* 31, no. 2 (1993): 203–240.

40. Larry A. Gould and Marie Volbrecht, "Personality Differences between Women Police Recruits, Their Male Counterparts, and the General Female Population," *Journal of Police and Criminal Psychology* 14 (April 1, 1999): 1–18.

41. J. J. Donohue III and Steven D. Levitt, "The Impact of Race on Policing and Arrests," *Journal of Law and Economics* 44 (October 1, 2001): 367–394.

42. Clemens Bartollas and Larry D. Hahn, *Policing in America* (Boston: Allyn & Bacon, 1999). See especially Chapter 12, "The Minority Police Officer," for a discussion of black, Hispanic, American Indian, and homosexual police officers.

43. Ibid.

44. Melton McLaurin, "Growing Up Jim Crow: How Black and White Southern Children Learned Race," *Journal of Southern History* 73 (August 1, 2007): 735–737.

45. Nicholas Alex, *Black in Blue: A Study of the Negro Policeman* (New York: Appleton-Century-Crofts, 1969).

46. Susan E. Martin, "Outsider within the Station House: The Impact of Race and Gender on Black Women Police," *Social Problems* (August 1994): 389.

47. Bartollas and Hahn, *Policing in America*, 322–330.

48. Egon Bittner, *The Functions of the Police in Modern Society* (Cambridge, MA: Oelgeschlager, Gunn, & Hain, 1980), 36.

49. Ibid., 36–37.

50. James J. Fyfe, "The Split-Second Syndrome and Other Determinants of Police Violence," in *Critical Issues in Policing: Contemporary Readings*, 4th ed., eds. Roger G. Dunham and Geoffrey P. Alpert (Prospect Heights, IL: Waveland Press, 2001), 583–598.

51. Bittner, *Functions of the Police.*

52. Ed Sanow, "One-Trick Pony," *Law and Order*, November 1, 2006, 6.

53. Center for Research on Criminal Justice, *The Iron Fist and the Velvet Glove: An Analysis of the U.S. Police* (Berkeley, CA: Center for Research on Criminal Justice, 1977).

54. "Cape Coral Police Department's VIN Unit, SWAT Team, Street Crimes Unit Execute Search Warrants on Suspected Marijuana Grow Houses," U.S. Federal News Service, including U.S. State News, October 22, 2007.

55. Ibid., 97.

56. Betty A. Dobratz, Stephanie L. Shanks-Meile, and Danelle Hallenbeck, "What Happened on Ruby Ridge: Terrorism or Tyranny?" *Symbolic Interaction* 26 (May 1, 2003): 315–342.

57. "A Year after WACO, FBI Seeks to Avoid a Repeat Performance," *Law Enforcement News*, April 30, 1994, 7.

58. George Lardner Jr. and Richard Leiby, "Standoff at Ruby Ridge," *Washington Post*, September 3, 1995, www.washingtonpost.com/ac2/wp-dyn?pagename=article&node=digest&contentId=A99817–1995Sep3.

59. PBS, "Waco: The Inside Story," *Frontline*, www.pbs.org/wgbh/pages/frontline/waco/.

60. Anna Badkhen, "Marshals' Ploy Ended Standoff Peacefully," *Boston Globe*, third edition, October 6, 2007, B1.

61. Margot Sanger-Katz, "When Time Came, Ed Brown Folded," *Concord (NH) Monitor*, October 19, 2007, www.concordmonitor.com/apps/pbcs.dll/article?AID=/20071019/FRONTPAGE/710190306.

62. Michael R. Smith, Matthew Petrocelli, and Charlie Scheer, "Excessive Force, Civil Liability, and the Taser in the Nation's Courts: Implications for Law Enforcement Policy and Practice," *Policing* 30 (July 1, 2007): 398–422.

63. Bittner, *Functions of the Police.*

64. Thomas W. Nolan, "Galateas in Blue: Women Police as Decoy Sex Workers," *Criminal Justice Ethics* 20 (July 1, 2001): 63-67.

65. Peter B. Kraska and Louise J. Cubellis, "Militarizing Mayberry and Beyond: Making Sense of American Paramilitary Policing," *Justice Quarterly* (December 1997): 607–629.

66. "Colorado: Denver Pays $1.35m to Settle Shooting Case," *Crime Control Digest*, October 8, 2004, 5.

67. Carl Klockars, "The Dirty Harry Problem," *Annals of the American Academy of Political and Social Science* (November 1980).

68. Jerome H. Skolnick and James J. Fyfe, *Above the Law: Police and the Excessive Use of Force* (New York: The Free Press, 1993), 107.

69. "Justice Department Settles Employment Discrimination Lawsuit against the City of Virginia Beach, Virginia Police Department," U.S. Federal News Service, including U.S. State News, April 4, 2006.

70. Federal Bureau of Investigation, *Law Enforcement Officers Killed and Assaulted, 2003* (Washington, DC: Author, 2004), I, www.fbi.gov/ucr/killed/leoka03.pdf.

71. Federal Bureau of Investigation, "FBI Releases Preliminary Statistics for Law Enforcement Officers Killed in 2007," www.fbi.gov/pressrel/pressre108/leoka051208.htm.

72. Judith A. Waters and William Ussery, "Police Stress: History, Contributing Factors, Symptoms, and Interventions," *Policing* 30 (April 1, 2007): 169–188.

73. Joseph Wambaugh, *The Choirboys* (New York: Dell, 1975).

74. John M. Violanti, James R. Marshall, and Barbara Howe, "Stress, Coping, and Alcohol Use: The Police Connection," *Journal of Police Science and Administration* 13, no. 2 (1985): 106–110.

75. Charles Unkovic and William Brown, "The Drunken Cop," *Police Chief* (April 1978): 29–20.

76. Max T. Raterman, "Substance Abuse and Police Discipline," *Police Department Disciplinary Bulletin* (December 2000): 2–4.

77. Laurence Miller, "Police Families: Stresses, Syndromes, and Solutions," *American Journal of Family Therapy* 35 (January 1, 2007): 21.

78. Skolnick and Fyfe, *Above the Law.*

79. Bartollas and Hahn, *Policing in America*, 199.

80. Peter E. Maynard and Nancy E. Maynard, "Stress in Police Families: Some Policy Implications," *Journal of Police Science and Administration* 10 (1982): 302–314.

81. Mary J. C. Hageman, "Occupational Stress and Marital Relationships," *Journal of Police Science and Administration* 6, no. 4 (1978): 402–412.

82. Robert Henley Woody, "Family Interventions with Law Enforcement Officers," *American Journal of Family Therapy* 34 (March 1, 2006): 95–103.

83. Glory Cochrane, "The Effects of Sleep Deprivation," *FBI Law Enforcement Bulletin*, July 2001, 22–25.

84. Luenda E. Charles et al., "Shift Work and Sleep: The Buffalo Police Health Study," *Policing* 30 (April 1, 2007): 215–227.

85. Julia McKinnell, "Don't Let Their Only Friend Be a Gun," *Maclean's*, June 30, 2008, 59.

86. Michelle Perin, "Police Suicide," *Law Enforcement Technology* 34, no. 9 (September 2007): 8.

87. Ibid.

88. John M. Violanti, *Police Suicide: Epidemic in Blue* (Springfield, IL: Thomas, 2007).

89. John M. Violanti, "Predictors of Police Suicide Ideation," *Suicide and Life-Threatening Behavior* 34 (October 1, 2004): 277–283.

90. Laurence Miller, *Practical Police Psychology: Stress Management and Crisis Intervention for Law Enforcement* (Springfield, IL: Thomas, 2006).

91. Bruce A. Arrigo and Karyn Garsky, "Police Suicide: A Glimpse Behind the Badge," in *Critical Issues in Policing: Contemporary Readings*, 4th ed., eds. Roger G. Dunham and Geoffrey P. Alpert, (Prospect Heights, IL: Waveland Press, 2001), 664–680.

92. Göran Kecklund, Claire Anne Eriksen, and Torbjörn Åkerstedt, "Police Officers Attitude to Different Shift Systems: Association with Age, Present Shift Schedule, Health and Sleep/Wake Complaints," *Applied Ergonomics* 39 (September 2008): 565.

93. John Von Maanen, "Kinsmen in Repose: Occupational Perspectives of Patrolmen," in *The Police and Society: Touchstone Readings*, 2nd ed., ed. Victor E. Kappeler (Prospect Heights, IL: Waveland Press, 1999), 221. See also Victor E. Kappeler, Richard D. Sluder, and Geoffrey P. Alpert, "Breeding Deviant Conformity: Police Ideology and Culture," in *The Police and Society: Touchstone Readings*, 239.

94. *Master status* is a sociological term that refers to a status or a label that dominates over all other positive or negative labels. For instance, if you introduced your boyfriend to your parents and mentioned that he had served time in prison for rape, nothing else you could say could earn their trust of him. Conversely, a label such as "Medal of Honor winner" will supercede just about any other label.

95. Jerome H. Skolnick, *Justice without Trial: Law Enforcement in Democratic Society* (New York: Wiley, 1966).

96. Ibid., 43.

97. Ibid., 45.

98. Ibid., 47.

99. Ibid., 42–70.

100. Holly Bannish and Jim Ruiz, "The Antisocial Police Personality: A View from the Inside," *International Journal of Public Administration* 26 (June 1, 2003): 831–881.

101. Michael D. Lymon, *The Police: An Introduction* (Upper Saddle River, NJ: Prentice Hall, 2002). Lyman provided an excellent discussion on the topic in Chapter 8, "Personal Administration."

102. Sanja Kutnjak Ivkovic, "Police (Mis)behavior: A Cross-Cultural Study of Corruption Seriousness," *Policing* 28 (July 1, 2005): 546–566.

103. Lawrence W. Sherman, *Police Corruption: A Sociological Perspective* (Garden City, NY: Anchor Books, 1974). See particularly Sherman's introductory chapter with its important typology of police corruption.

104. Knapp Commission, "An Example of Police Corruption: Knapp Commission Report in New York City," in *Police Deviance*, eds. Thomas Barker and David L. Carter (Cincinnati, OH: Pilgrimage, 1986), 28.

105. "Ringleader in Boston Police Corruption Case Sentenced to 26 Years in Prison," U.S. Federal News Service, including U.S. State News, May 16, 2008.

106. Peter K. Manning and Lawrence John Redlinger, "Invitational Edges," in *Thinking about Police: Contemporary Readings*, 2nd ed., eds. Carl B. Klockars and Stephen D. Mastrofski (New York: McGraw-Hill, 1991), 398–413.

107. Lee Sullivan, "Drug Unit Corruption: Stopping the Scandal Before It Starts," *Sheriff*, January 1, 2008, 27–29.

PART THREE
The Role of the Courts

CHAPTER 8

History and Organization of Courts

Objectives

1. Discuss how courts are subject to outside influences.

2. Outline the development of the jury.

3. Discuss the beginnings of the jury trial.

4. Explain state and federal court organization.

5. Discuss the role of the courts of last resort.

Courts are a central feature in the U.S. criminal justice system. Typically, students of criminal justice are not as interested in courts as in law enforcement and corrections because working in the court requires legal knowledge. Many students go on to law school and successful careers as attorneys and judges, but that seems to be a long way in the future. However, students should seriously think about careers in the legal system because the quality of justice in the United States is determined by the technical expertise, professional acumen, and ethical demeanor of those who work in the courts.

Courts play a pivotal role in the U.S. criminal justice system. They are responsible for determining whether a defendant is guilty and deciding on the disposition or sentence for defendants who are. This all must be done according to a complex and ever-changing network of laws, personnel, and political pressures. The courts are besieged on all sides by those who observe an institution in crisis, such as the following:

- Police officers, who complain that offenders are treated too leniently[1]
- Corrections officials, who have no room in their prisons for new inmates and are concerned about the severe sentences that keep inmates incarcerated for many years[2]
- The public, which sees the court as an unfathomable machine that fails to provide justice when lawbreakers are released because of technicalities[3]
- Legislatures, which cannot provide the necessary resources to handle the huge caseloads because tax dollars must be shared with many other government functions, including law enforcement and corrections[4]
- Offenders and defendants, guilty or innocent, as well as victims, who do not believe that the court is dispensing justice in an evenhanded and fair manner[5]

The court seems to be in a powerful position within the criminal justice system because it makes the important determinations of what happens to suspects and offenders. However, the court is actually at the mercy of outside forces. It does not control how it is financed; it does not control how many cases are sent to it; it cannot ensure adequate resources to carry out its sentences; and because its work is done in a courtroom open to the press, it cannot control its public image. In many ways, then, the court is an institution that takes the blame for deficiencies not of its making.[6] For instance, when a police officer fails to read a suspect his or her Miranda rights or makes a mistake in the chain of custody of crucial evidence, the courts have no choice but to dismiss the case. This can result in the public's believing that the court released the offender on a technicality when, in fact, the court is obligated to interpret and implement the law. If citizens are dissatisfied with the work of the court, they perhaps would get better results by doing a more thorough job of educating the police or by changing the law.

Another concern of the U.S. court system also complicates its mission. The professional orientation of those who practice law affects the image and the functioning of the court. The problem is twofold:

1. The U.S. criminal court system is an adversarial process. The adversarial process uses defense attorneys and prosecutors to represent the positions of two opposing parties. The process places the burden on the prosecutor, who must prove to a jury (or a judge, in the case of a bench trial) that the defendant is guilty beyond a reasonable doubt. The defense attorney argues for the innocence, as well as the legal protections, of the accused. The judge, a disinterested party, ensures that the two sides play by the rules. The adversarial process can sometimes seem to result in defense attorneys and prosecutors advocating for one side at the expense of the truth. The process requires lawyers to strike the most advantageous deal they can for their clients, even if they realize that other outcomes may better reflect the goals of justice.[7]

2. Outsiders have difficulty understanding what is happening in the court. Because our legal system evolved over a long period of time and because it draws its inspiration and procedures from so many sources, the process and the language of the court seem foreign to outside observers, especially to defendants. Cynical individuals might believe that the reason the courts are so unfathomable is to ensure that only those with a legal education can successfully negotiate the corridors of the courthouse.

Because of the issues of professional orientation and lack of control over funding and image, the courts seem shrouded in mystery. The result is that a rather romantic view of the courts has emerged whereby the justice that is (or is not) dispensed is more a product of the courageous attorney and less a function of the criminal justice system process. The popular image of how the courts work is informed by television programs. A realistic image of the court is further compromised by law-as-entertainment programs such as *The People's Court*, *Judge Mills Lane*, *Judge Judy*, and *Judge Hackett*. Thus, the image of our courts is either one of the good-looking defense attorney fighting valiantly against a corrupt and inefficient system or one of a short-tempered judge humiliating confused or naive people. These are both distorted and confused images that have little relevance to the actual practice of law. This television presentation of justice as entertainment can give individuals a cynical and inaccurate vision of what courts actually do.

On the bright side, however, are the real court cases broadcast by truTV, formerly known as Court TV (see Crosscurrents 8.1). Here, much of the romanticism of the courts can be dispelled when the viewer sees the ponderous, methodical, and rule-bound

---

8.1   ***CrossCurrents***

Notes of a truTV Junkie

My name is John, and I'm a professor and a truTV junkie. I admit that I have a deep and perverse fascination with watching how conflicts are resolved (or not) in our courts. I admit that some afternoons I slip out of school and come home to watch the latest live trial of some celebrity, child molester, or abusive husband. I like summers, when my teaching duties allow me to watch hours of courtroom action with my cat in my lap while I eat ice cream out of the carton. I tell my wife I'm doing research for my books. She knows better. She knows I'm feeding my people-watching addiction.

Court junkies are found in courtrooms across the country. Voyeurs who like to watch people in distress, busybodies who want to know other people's business, and law geeks who like to watch the criminal justice system in action flock to truTV to watch high-profile trials featuring powerful judges, expensive lawyers, nationally known technical experts, and best of all, real people in real conflict. Programs like *Boston Legal, The Practice,* and *Law & Order* are sensationalized imitations of what really happens in a trial. For those of us who like the real thing, including the tedious and boring hours of routine examination, truTV offers access for our inquiring minds.

Personally, I like to watch the attorneys conduct their opening and closing arguments. Safe in my big leather chair, I critique their performances. I usually find their efforts wanting. "If that were me," I tell myself, "I would impeach that witness cold." As I shove yet another spoonful of ice cream into my mouth, I fantasize about how I would have the jury eating out of my hand. Being an armchair lawyer is easy, but it is also informative. A good bit of how the courts operate can be learned from truTV. However, what is not seen, such as plea bargaining, may be even more important.

Think About It

1. Do you watch television court and crime shows? Do you believe they are realistic? Why or why not?

2. Are reality court and crime television shows educational or are they pure entertainment?

process of the court. Rather than achieving justice in a fast-paced hour (including commercials), truTV reveals how cases are delayed, continued, interrupted, and even canceled by the motions made by lawyers. The public gets to see real victims, witnesses, offenders, attorneys, and judges, not Hollywood actors. TruTV, however, does not capture the whole truth. Only the most sensational cases are selected. Most of the real work of the court, such as plea negotiations and witness preparations, is done outside the eye of the camera.

Much of the picture we have of the court is therefore an imperfect one. Like an impressionist painting, our picture is fuzzy and idealized, rather than being a clear, accurate portrait of how the court functions. Our goal in these next three chapters on the criminal courts is to paint a more realistic picture of how the courts are structured and how they operate. Our picture will reveal that courts are less sensational than the image we get from television, but they are also more fascinating. By putting courts into the larger context of how they fit into the overall governmental structure, and how they interact with the other components of the criminal justice system, we can appreciate how they have evolved to the critical position they hold today in the lives of so many individuals who either work as practitioners within the courts or are the victims, witnesses, and offenders circulating within the criminal justice system.

COURTS IN HISTORY

Our concept of the court has been affected by religion, tradition, and the media. The idea that one day we will be held accountable for our sins, transgressions of the law, and insults to others is often a worry. As the saying goes, "What goes around comes around." Each of us needs to be careful about our behavior lest we find ourselves having to explain it to the judge. Some religions evoke a Judgment Day in which a higher power will tally our good deeds and compare them to our mistakes and then make a decision about the ultimate sentence.

Courts of some type have been consistent features of many societies.[8] Although it is impossible to know for certain whether ancient peoples resolved their conflicts with processes that resemble our courts, explorers and anthropologists have found similarities between the functions of modern courts and societies that were not yet influenced by European systems of government.[9] This leads us to believe that the duties of the court satisfy universal needs in one manner or another. According to E. A. Hoebel:

> Given such variability, we cannot assume that humans have any universal understanding of what specifically constitutes justice. We can only conclude that there appears to be a desire for some form of satisfaction, variously construed, that is felt to restore the balance that was disrupted by the offender's troublemaking.[10]

Before There Were Courts: The Blood Feud

Courts are a result of the increasing sophistication of societies in which a division of labor was necessary.[11] As societies became more complex, individuals could not be the doctor, farmer, hunter, religious leader, and stockbroker all at the same time.[12] Modern courts are mechanisms for resolving disputes that have evolved from a long and uneven history of feuds, duels, wars, and other types of conflicts that often caused more problems than they solved. A peaceful way to resolve contested issues between individuals and groups was required because of the disruption to society caused by primitive methods. The **blood feud** is an example of why courts had to be invented. An example of the blood feud in primitive cultures can be found in that of the Nuer people in what is now southern Sudan:

blood feud

A disagreement whose settlement is based on personal vengeance and physical violence.

> Disputes can often be settled on account of close kinship and other social ties, but between tribesmen as such they are either settled by the aggrieved party using force, and this may result in homicide and bloodshed, or by the debtor giving way in the knowledge that force may be used and a blood feud will result. It is the

8.1   FOCUS *on* ETHICS

MODERN-DAY BLOOD FEUD

Your little brother has been dating a girl from another school for several months. Recently, while arguing with her, he got carried away and struck her. The next night he was shot in a drive-by shooting on the front steps of your parents' home. You are certain your brother's killers are the girl's cousins, but the police have no solid evidence and are not close to making an arrest. Although you know your brother was no saint and that striking another person deserves some punishment, his death has devastated your family, and you believe that, in part, it was racially motivated. The girl's cousins are part of a white-supremacy group that has continually hassled people of color in your county. Being of Hispanic origin, your family has pleaded with the sheriff's office to investigate your brother's murder again. However, the sheriff himself has commented to reporters that your brother probably deserved what he got and that his office is too busy to expend more resources on this offense unless there is further evidence.

You have lost faith in the local criminal justice system's ability and motivation to solve your brother's murder and bring his killers to justice. Meanwhile, your grandfather is mumbling that in his day the family would have avenged this death themselves. He looks at you in disgust and implies that you are a coward and a disgrace to the family. As a criminal justice major at a local university, you have hopes of one day becoming an FBI agent, but the pull of family honor has you thinking that you should make sure the killers do not get away with this.

What Do You Do?

1. Do nothing. Even though you think the local criminal justice system has failed to properly investigate your brother's murder, there is little you can do that is within the law. Besides, you have your own career to think about. Even though your family expects you to seek justice, you are unwilling to continue the cycle of violence started by your hotheaded brother.

2. Uphold your family's honor and retaliate against the cousins of your brother's girlfriend. If the local criminal justice system does not care about your community, it is your duty to seek justice through revenge. If you don't, then the Hispanic community will continue to be victimized by the powerful white majority. It is time to show the community that there will be justice for your people, one way or another.

3. Go to the FBI and make a complaint charging that this was a hate crime and that your brother's constitutional rights were violated. If the local criminal justice system refuses to act, make a federal case out of your brother's murder.

knowledge that a Nuer is brave and will stand up against aggression and enforce his rights by club and spear that ensures respect for person and property.[13]

The blood feud is based on vengeance (see Focus on Ethics 8.1). If an individual is killed, then it is the right, indeed the obligation, of members of the family to exact justice by killing the murderer, or lacking that, a blood member of the murderer's family. Of course, this sets off another round of violence in which the original killer's family feels entitled to seek their own revenge. The result could be a long history of reciprocal killings based on family blood ties. In times of economic hardship, in which the labor of everyone is required for group subsistence, a blood feud could be devastating for a society. In lieu of violence, a payment could be made to the deceased's family to compensate for their loss and achieve a sense of justice. In the Germanic tribes of Europe this was known as a *wergeld* (which can be translated as "manprice").[14] The amount was determined by the status of the victim.[15]

Courts in England

In England, the payment to the victim's family was called a *bot* instead of a *wergeld*. An additional payment called a *wite* was also assessed against the perpetrator as compensation for the king or the noble holding court and as a penalty for breaking the king's peace.[16] Because the royalty found these fees a convenient way to raise revenue, and one that the people did not object to, they gradually increased the fees, instituted more fines, and generally institutionalized the practice of holding court as a way of resolving conflicts in a more peaceful manner.

The court did more than resolve conflicts, however. The court was usually convened to mark some celebration such as a royal birth, wedding, or religious festival.

Nobles used these occasions to meet and discuss war, taxes, and other matters of government, including the establishment of new laws. In many ways, the medieval court acted as both a court and a congress where a multitude of activities were accomplished. The lines between criminal and civil cases were not yet established, and the rights of the accused were absent. One important aspect of the court that needs to be emphasized is that this practice offered the king and other nobles an excellent way to raise revenues. Gradually, more and more behaviors were criminalized and made subject to fines and fees that swelled the king's coffers. This is important because offenses were gradually redefined not so much as disputes between individuals but as "crimes against the state" in which the king's peace represented public order.[17]

Trial By Compurgation

compurgation

In medieval German and English law, a practice by which a defendant could establish innocence by taking an oath and having a required number of people swear that they believed the oath.

Compurgation involved the practice of taking an oath that one was telling the truth. Both the defense and the prosecution would present oath takers who would swear they were telling the truth. However, many of the oath takers could not speak to the actual offense as a witness because they had no direct knowledge. They could only swear that the defendant or victim was telling the truth. In a sense, they were character witnesses. Not all oaths were equal. The value of one's oath was pegged to one's *wergeld*, or the price that the court deemed to be the value of the person's life.[18] Consequently, the oath of a noble, whose *wergeld* was 1000 shillings, would need to be countered by five freemen who were worth 200 shillings each. Those who had no established value under the law, such as women or slaves, could not offer their oath and had to have others swear for them. The accuser was required to offer more oaths than the defendant, which, in a way, echoes our current notion that one is innocent until proven guilty.

Finding others to take an oath swearing to one's trustworthiness was not easy. People placed a high value on the veracity of their oaths and would not swear for those whom they could not completely trust because of the prospect of eternal damnation. Consequently, thieves, pickpockets, and con artists could not persuade others to stand up for them and swear an oath to their honesty. Individuals were also required to take their oaths without making mistakes. Lifting your hand off the Bible or neglecting to kiss it afterward were considered acts against God and invalidated the oath's value.[19]

Trial By Ordeal

trial by ordeal

An ancient custom found in many cultures in which the accused was required to perform a test to prove guilt.

When someone could not get enough people to take an oath to support him or her, or when there were enough oath takers but the evidence was strong against the accused, **trial by ordeal** was required.[20] There were essentially three types of trial by ordeal: trial by cold water, trial by hot water, and trial by hot iron, or as it was sometimes called, trial by fire.[21] These ordeals were, by today's scientific standards, unlikely to find the truth and obviously biased against the accused. For instance, in a trial by hot water the accused was supposed to plunge a hand into a cauldron of boiling water and pick a large stone off the bottom. Not being able to pick up the stone was evidence of guilt. If the stone was plucked from the bottom, the accused's wounded hand was bound with bandages. When examined three days later, the accused was declared innocent if the wounds were healing naturally with no signs of infection. However, if the wounds were festering and full of pus, the accused was declared guilty, and a sentence was imposed.

These trials by ordeal depended on divine intervention to demonstrate the innocence of the accused and resulted in death or extreme pain for those whose bodies were simply following the laws of nature. Consequently, many individuals confessed to offenses they had not committed to escape the painful and unreliable trial by ordeal. The role of the judge in trial by ordeal was limited to declaring whether the accused passed the test and to imposing a sentence that was prescribed by the law.[22]

Trial By Battle

Trial by battle was another way to solve disputes that did not rely on religious concepts such as divine intervention. Although trial by battle could result in the same prospects of being determined guilty when in fact one was innocent, it did offer the accused a bit more control over the outcome.[23] Although originally reserved for knights to resolve their disputes, peasants also used trial by battle. The most interesting aspect of trial by battle was that litigants could select someone else to fight their battle for them. Thus, the rich, women, and those who were physically unable to fight could have someone "champion" their cause who could stand a reasonable chance of winning the trial by battle.[24]

DEVELOPMENT OF THE JURY

The **inquest** can be considered to be the first type of jury. After a war, the English crown needed to determine which lands it had conquered and so conducted an inquest in which men were summoned before the court to attest to the ownership of the land in the surrounding area. Gradually, the inquest was broadened to concerns other than land ownership, and the rudiments of a grand jury were developed whereby the crown would convene a court and suspect individuals would be charged with breaking the law.

inquest
In archaic usage, considered the first type of jury that determined the ownership of land. Currently, a type of investigation.

Grand Jury

In 1166, a law called the **Assize of Clarendon** was enacted to correct some of the problems and inefficiencies of the judicial process.[25] When the prosecution was simply an individual matter, the accuser would often fail to follow through on the complaint because of the time, expense, and difficulty of achieving a guilty verdict against the accused. This was problematic not only because the guilty would go free and the community would be left unprotected, but also because the king could not collect a court fee.

Assize of Clarendon
A 12th-century English law that established judicial procedure and the grand jury system.

The Assize of Clarendon was a series of ordinances that established the beginnings of the grand jury system. The jury, comprising 12 men from each jurisdiction, was given the duty of informing the king's judges of the most serious offenses committed in each jurisdiction. In this way, the charging decision was taken from the individual accuser and given to civic-minded citizens who performed this duty as a service to the community. Offenses, therefore, started their journey to being regarded as public problems rather than as private wrongs. The criminal justice system continued to become more a servant of the state than simply a mechanism in which individuals settled disputes. The Assize of Clarendon gradually developed from a process of simply identifying and charging wrongdoers to a body that determined whether the evidence was sufficient to detain the accused before trial.[26] Today, the successor of the Assize of Clarendon, the grand jury, is primarily a check on the power of the prosecutor. The grand jury determines whether the evidence is powerful enough to charge the accused with a criminal offense. Consequently, the grand jury has evolved into a body that protects the citizens from overzealous prosecutors.

Jury Trial

The jury trial was created to fill a vacuum in the criminal justice process. In 1215, the Fourth Lateran Council of the Roman Catholic Church forbade priests to participate in trials by ordeal. Because the trial by ordeal was determined by the divine intervention of God, and because priests not only blessed the instrument of trial by ordeal but also judged whether God did in fact provide a miracle to save the accused, the practice had to be stopped.[27] The priests had too many roles to play, creating a conflict of interest. Trial by ordeal, then, could no longer be ordained by the church.

Into this void stepped the jury trial. People had a difficult time accepting the judgment of mere men, especially when the sentence could be death. They were more comfortable letting God decide such issues with signs, such as miracles. However, with the church no longer sanctioning such spectacles, the judgment of 12 "good" men was gradually accepted. At first, individuals were given the choice between being held in a dungeon indefinitely and a jury trial.[28] This choice posed an interesting dilemma, however. If the jury convicted a person, the offender's lands were forfeited to the king. If the offender died in prison, however, his lands were passed to his heirs. The type of imprisonment the accused was subjected to was called *la peine forte et dure* (strong and hard punishment). This entailed a diet of bread and water, heavy chains, and generally the worst conditions that dungeons could offer.[29] Consequently, only the most stubborn decided to perish in prison in order to bequeath their property to their heirs.[30]

For the most part, the trial jury comprised the same men who sat on the grand jury that brought the charge against the defendant. These jurors were expected to know the facts of the case, so little testimony was required. Guilt or innocence was determined by the accused's reputation and the intimate knowledge about the facts of the case that the jurors had when they first charged the accused. This process was gradually determined to be flawed, and eventually the two juries were separated. In many places, this required the use of jurors from outside the community, which resulted in the need for testimony to educate all the jurors about the facts of the case.[31]

It took the jury 250 years to develop into the powerful institution it became at the end of the 15th century. Its authority to determine the guilt or innocence of the accused was paramount, and angry judges could not change its verdict. The concept of an independent jury became firmly established in the English system and provides for us today a key check against the power of the state to prosecute citizens.

A 15th-century English jury and court officials.
Source: CORBIS-NY

The Magna Carta

In 1215, about the same time as the jury began to develop, the Magna Carta was signed by King John (1199–1216). He was under pressure to sign this document, which limited the power of the king and recognized the rights of nobles. Many of these rights had long been in effect, but King John was a particularly arbitrary and power-hungry ruler who had been encroaching on centuries-old legal and political customs. The Magna Carta placed the king under the rule of law. This document did little at the time for the common man because it was the nobles who forced the king to recognize their rights. However, it did set a precedent of encoding in the law limitations on the state's power. In a sense, then, it is a conservative document rather than a revolutionary one.[32] Its effects were felt not so much immediately as over a longer period of time when the divine rights of the king were attenuated in favor of written legal rights of nobles and clergy and, eventually, through future documents patterned after the Magna Carta that called for rights for all citizens.[33]

Court of the Star Chamber

As a result of the religious strife and the power of the crown to use the courts as a tool of repression, the common law that protected the rights of the accused came under strain in the 15th century. Political offenses and treason were especially problematic, and a special judicial body, the **Court of the Star Chamber,** was established to deal with offenses such as riots, unlawful assembly, perjury, criminal libel, and conspiracy. The court, comprising the king of England's councilors, met in the palace of Westminster in London in a room in which stars were painted on the ceiling. Although the court's sentences included corporal punishments, convicts were never sentenced to death. Jurors of cases could be brought before the Star Chamber if judges felt they had violated their duties to convict the guilty.[34] The Court of the Star Chamber was notable for its abuses, such as the following:

Court of the Star Chamber
An old English court comprising the king's councilors that was separate from common-law courts.

- Interrogation of suspects in secret
- The use of torture as a fact-finding tool
- No right to a trial by jury
- Accusation brought without evidence
- The accused not informed of the identity of people making accusations[35]

The Court of the Star Chamber was important because it demonstrated how a court without any sort of due process could violate the human rights of citizens. Also, it showed how unfettered power could be used to subvert the law and cause findings of guilt when in fact the suspect was innocent. Consequently, the Court of the Star Chamber had the effect of reaffirming the protections of the common law and caused citizens to become even more wary of the power of the criminal justice system. It was abolished in 1641.

By the 18th century, because of the intense reactions to the abuses of the Court of the Star Chamber, many of the essential elements of modern criminal procedure were found in some form in the courts of England. Features were added to the process, such as a preliminary hearing, a grand jury, the opportunity for the defendant to challenge jurors who might be prejudiced against the case, and the idea that the verdict of the jury is the final decision when the defendant is acquitted.

Some aspects of modern due process that began to find their way into the 18th-century court, however, were applied in a haphazard and inconsistent fashion. Sometimes, but not always, defendants were allowed to have their own counsel. The juries were composed of "respectable" citizens who were usually of a different social class than the defendants. And finally, the concepts of probable cause and presumption of innocence were not yet fully ingrained into the criminal justice process. Nevertheless, the development of the English courts between the 11th and 18th centuries provided

This 18th-century painting depicts the Fleet, a debtors' prison.

Source: Courtesy of the Trustees of Sir John Soane's Museum, London/The Bridgeman Art Library

the foundation for the courts of the early North American colonies and eventually what became the United States.

COURTS IN COLONIAL AMERICA

The migration of courts from England to the North American colonies was an imperfect one. Because each of the 13 colonies was established under different motivations and conditions (for instance, Pennsylvania was founded by religious dissenters, whereas Virginia was founded by English gentry), the systems of government tended to vary widely. England made no concerted effort to develop standardized practices among the colonies, so the courts developed in response to the local economic, political, and social concerns of each colony.[36] Because many colonies were established by grants to individuals or corporations, the early governors would hold court as they saw fit, and many of the protections of the law that existed for defendants in England were absent in colonial America. Complaints about the courts were frequent, and individuals often appealed to England to send trained judges to administer the law.[37]

Slavery and the Law

The early adoption of slavery in the American colonies caused problems for the justice system. An alternative system of laws had to be created to control the slaves. Whereas England passed a tradition to the colonies on how to deal with freemen and indentured servants, the United States had to develop its own slavery laws to protect the interests of owners of large tracts of land.[38] Slave courts put a gloss of legitimacy on the abominable practices of slave control practiced by slave owners:

> The master himself was law, judge, and jury over most aspects of slave life: this was inherent in the system. But in North Carolina, at least as early as 1715, there were special courts for slaves who disobeyed the law. Whipping was the common mode of punishment. Serious crimes called for the death penalty; but a dead slave injured his owner's pocketbook; hence owners were repaid out of

The Boston Tea Party is an example of the early colonists' dissatisfaction with the English government. In response to an increased tax on tea, the colonists dressed as Indians, boarded English ships, and tossed the tea into the Boston Harbor.

Source: Corbis/Bettmann

public funds. Castration was an alternative punishment for serious crimes. Happily, this punishment was eliminated in 1764.[39]

In spite of the setbacks for legal rights of citizens that occurred during the transition of law from England to the North American colonies, progress did begin to develop (except for the slaves) because of the motivations of many individuals who deemed the New World a fresh start. The works of philosophers such as John Locke and Immanuel Kant inspired the Enlightenment with its values of liberty, limited government, and equality.[40]

Our Heritage of Due Process

One of the primary social forces that led to the American Revolution of 1776 was the colonists' belief that the English crown was treating them unfairly. The repressive measures used by England violated the understandings many had about the rights of English subjects. These abuses of what many considered the common law included the practice of searching houses under general warrants to find untaxed items that were smuggled into the colonies, and the use of admiralty courts in which trial by jury, right to counsel, and indictment by grand jury were absent. The colonists had their own interpretations about what common law, the Magna Carta, and the principles of the Enlightenment said about natural human rights. Not surprisingly, the English crown had a different interpretation about these rights, especially concerning matters of taxes and economics. Given the second-class citizenship felt by many colonists, therefore, a move for independence seemed inevitable.[41]

One of the enduring consequences of independence from England is the documents that were created to specify the relationship between the people and the state. For our study of the courts, these documents of importance include the U.S. Constitution, particularly the first 10 amendments, called the Bill of Rights.[42] The framers of the Constitution recognized that conditions and situations change, and the process for amending the Constitution has allowed for expansion and a further delineation of rights. The courts were left to interpret how specific behaviors should be viewed. This has resulted in an important balance between the laws enacted by the legislature and how those laws

8.1   CASE IN POINT

DUNCAN V. LOUISIANA

THE CASE	THE POINT
Duncan v. Louisiana, *391 U.S. 145, 88 S.Ct. 1444 (1968)*	*Under the Sixth Amendment, defendants charged with serious offenses are entitled to a jury trial.*

Gary Duncan was convicted of simple battery, which in Louisiana is punishable by a maximum of two years in prison and a $300 fine. Duncan requested a jury trial, but was denied one because Louisiana granted jury trials only when there was the potential of capital punishment or hard labor. At his bench trial, Duncan received 60 days in jail and a fine of $150. Duncan's appeal eventually reached the Supreme Court, which stated that any offense that carries a potential punishment of two years in prison is not a petty offense. The Court deemed Duncan deserving of a jury trial under the Sixth Amendment.

The judgment against Duncan was reversed and remanded.

are applied.[43] In fact, although the Bill of Rights lists numerous rights concerning criminal procedure, the only one that is also included in all the state constitutions is the right to a jury trial (see Case in Point 8.1). The other rights, such as the right against self-incrimination, were all derived from precedents established by courts. Informed by the Constitution, the courts can determine what constitutes cruel and unusual punishment and what is sufficient for probable cause for a defendant to be bound over for trial.

THE CHANGING NATURE OF THE COURT

Our discussion of the development of courts in England and the United States has demonstrated how this relatively recent institution has evolved to fit the changing social, political, and economic needs of a particular time and circumstance. Underlying the role of the court is the idea that justice should be blind to wealth, power, and social class. This idea took a long time to develop in courts in which special interests were paramount. Gradually, however, the rights given to nobles by the Magna Carta were extended to more categories of people.

A complete history of the evolution of the courts in the United States would take too much space to adequately cover here and would divert our attention from our limited concerns of the development of the criminal courts. However, some cases, historical events, and individuals profoundly affected the way the courts have evolved, which requires a brief acknowledgment.

- ***Marbury v. Madison***[44]   The 1803 Supreme Court case of *Marbury* v. *Madison* is notable because it established the judiciary as equal to the executive and legislative branches of government. The issue in the case was a rather minor decision concerning whether William Marbury should be given a commission as a justice of the peace as President John Adams had ordered. Because of an error, Marbury did not receive his commission, and the new president, Thomas Jefferson, ordered that the commission not be delivered.[45] Marbury did not get his commission, but the case is famous because Chief Justice John Marshall established the principle of judicial review, whereby the Supreme Court scrutinizes state and federal legislation and the acts of state and federal executive officers and courts to determine whether they conflict with the Constitution.[46] Marshall also initiated the practice of presenting the justices' decisions as collective rather than separate opinions and providing written statements of the reasons why the court reached its decision.[47]

- *McCulloch v. Maryland*[48]   The 1819 case of *McCulloch* v. *Maryland* established that the court could find that the Constitution included implied powers that could be deduced from its nature and language. This decision is the basis for the expansion of the power of the federal government into areas such as banking and social programs aimed at the welfare of the people.[49]

- **Supremacy clause**   In cases in 1816 and 1821, the Marshall court upheld the supremacy clause in Article VI of the Constitution and reaffirmed the superiority of federal law over state law. The cases concerned the sale of land and the right to conduct a lottery. The Court's decision established its power as the "final word" on all cases. The Supreme Court then became the court of last resort.[50]

- **Reconstruction and the expansion of federal authority**   The progress of the courts in granting the protections of due process to everyone was not a smooth and consistent path. The social and political issues of various places and decades influenced how courts ruled. This was especially evident in the South with its long history of support for slavery and the adjustment to post–Civil War reconstruction. Although Congress passed laws that enfranchised the newly freed former slaves (Civil Rights Act of 1866), the Supreme Court supported the Southern courts, which had eroded the constitutional status of black people in the areas of voting, jury service, and public accommodations.[51]

- **Business, unions, and civil liberties**   The courts also used the Fourteenth Amendment, which was adopted after the Civil War to protect the rights of liberated slaves, to protect the interests of business. The courts interpreted the substantive due-process language of the amendment to protect *any person* to include any corporate body or association, and *property* to mean business or the profits of business. Thus, the court's conservative interpretation of the law served the interests of the wealthy and made suing businesses difficult in state courts. Furthermore, the issues of the workers such as safety regulations, hours, and taxation were decided in favor of corporate interests.[52]

- *Plessy v. Ferguson*[53]   The 1896 Supreme Court decision of *Plessy* v. *Ferguson* held that a Louisiana law that mandated "equal but separate accommodations for the white and colored races" on all railroad cars was reasonable. This decision formed the basis for the Jim Crow laws of the South that treated people of color as second-class citizens and enforced a system of apartheid that did not began to change until 1954, when the Court ruled that the "equal but separate" doctrine in the public schools was unconstitutional.

- **The Warren Court**   In 1953, President Dwight Eisenhower nominated the former governor of California, Earl Warren, to be chief justice of the Supreme Court. As a Republican, Warren was expected to steer the court toward the conservative values and issues popular with the majority in the Republican Party. The Warren Court disappointed conservatives with several decisions that expanded the rights of due process for those accused of breaking the law.[54] Additionally, in decisions that ruled that religious ceremonies in public schools were unconstitutional, that the right of privacy is implied in the Constitution, and that public officials must prove actual malice when suing reporters writing about public affairs, the Warren Court earned a reputation for championing the causes of the unpopular and the marginalized classes of society.[55]

As we can see from this brief review of some of the cases and issues that have confronted our courts, progress in developing protections for all citizens has not been consistent. First and foremost, we must remember that the courts are political institutions and that those with the power to influence government will use the courts to advance their own agendas. Although some justices, such as Earl Warren, surprise observers by issuing rulings that are contrary to expectations, justices may also vote in strict accordance with perceived party affiliations.[56]

Chief Justice Earl Warren led the Supreme Court when it ruled on several cases that expanded the rights of those accused of criminal offenses.

Source: © Bettmann/CORBIS. All Rights Reserved

Many of the decisions of the Warren Court were politically unpopular. This billboard calls for Warren's impeachment.

Source: AP Wide World Photos

For example, in 2000 seven of the nine Supreme Court justices had been appointed by Republican presidents. In the controversial case *Bush* v. *Gore*, in which the Court had to decide which votes should be counted in the dead-heat presidential election in Florida, the court voted 5 to 4 in favor of Republican George W. Bush. Even though two of the four dissenting justices had been appointed by Republican presidents, the vote reflected the conservative leaning of the Supreme Court (even though the judiciary is supposed to be independent). With such a narrow margin between the numbers of conservative and moderate justices, the power of the president to nominate candidates for vacancies in the court is of special importance. In a sense, then, presidential politics becomes more entwined with Supreme Court politics with each passing election. This observation might alarm some of us, but we should keep in mind that, as we have seen from our selected history here, courts are, and are meant to be, political institutions.[57]

ORGANIZATION OF THE COURTS

The U.S. court system is a confusing array of organizational structures that defies quick description. Unlike other countries, the United States has no centralized court system that uses equivalent terminology, jurisdictions, and personnel. U.S. courts are the result of different developmental processes that have spawned a complex organizational structure that makes it difficult to understand how justice is meted out. Additionally, this hodgepodge structure has the unintended consequence of subtly changing not only the style of justice, but also the quality of justice. This means that the structure of the courts plays a large part in how the courts function, which makes for an uneven system of justice and a challenge for the observer of the courts to grasp the big picture. Therefore, we will examine the organization of the courts from several different angles with the intent of demonstrating its complexity.

First, we must establish the difference between civil courts and criminal courts, which lies in the types of laws they deal with: civil laws and criminal laws. Perhaps the major distinction between criminal law and civil law is that violations of criminal law are punishable by imprisonment. *Criminal law* concerns the major violations against society: homicide, rape, robbery, theft, and so on. *Civil law* is often employed as a general term for anything not covered by criminal law. Civil laws govern private issues, such as breach of contract, probate, divorce, and negligence. Violations of civil law are not punishable by a prison term.

Nature of Jurisdiction

A good starting point to our understanding of the courts is the concept of jurisdiction. *Jurisdiction* simply refers to the authority of the court to hear certain cases. The jurisdiction of any court depends on three features: the seriousness of the case, the location of the offense, and whether the case is being heard for the first time or is on appeal. The three types of jurisdiction can be labeled **subject-matter jurisdiction, geographic jurisdiction,** and **hierarchical jurisdiction.**[58]

SUBJECT-MATTER JURISDICTION   The nature of the case can determine which court will have jurisdiction. Sometimes the distinction between felonies and misdemeanors will dictate the court to which a case is sent. Courts of limited jurisdiction tend to handle preliminary hearings and misdemeanors, whereas courts of general jurisdiction deal with more serious felonies. Depending on the state, tasks such as issuing warrants, establishing bail, advising defendants of their rights, and setting a date for a preliminary hearing are all handled by the limited-jurisdiction court; felony criminal proceedings, including trials, are dealt with by the general-jurisdiction court. A number of specialized courts handle only specific types of cases. Drug courts, traffic courts, and juvenile or family courts can be classified by subject-matter jurisdiction. See Figure 8-1 for an example of the number of total incoming cases to state courts by subject-matter jurisdiction.

GEOGRAPHIC JURISDICTION   The political boundaries of cities, counties, and states can determine the geographic jurisdiction of a court. The location of a offense dictates which court will hear the case. Depending on the state, jurisdictions may include courts in several counties that operate under the term **circuit court.** Aimed at balancing the caseload according to population, a circuit might have one densely populated county or several less populated counties. Geographic jurisdiction can also include features such as military installations, American Indian reservations, or national parks. Offenses committed in these locations can be dealt with by courts established especially for the special needs of these political structures. For instance, although a homicide on a military installation may have happened within the jurisdiction of a state circuit court, it also occurred on federal land and would be handled by the federal court. Furthermore, if the defendant was military personnel, the case may be handled according to the Uniform Code of Military Justice rather than the federal court system.

subject-matter jurisdiction
The authority of a court to hear a case based on the nature of the case.

geographic jurisdiction
The authority of a court to hear a case based on the location of the offense.

hierarchical jurisdiction
The authority of a court to hear a case based on where the case is located in the system.

circuit court
A court that holds sessions at intervals within different areas of a judicial district.

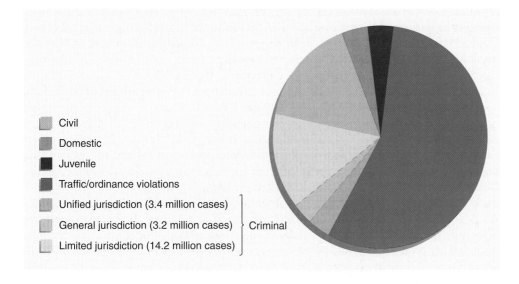

Figure 8-1   Total Incoming Cases to State Courts, by Subject-Matter Jurisdiction, 2005.

Incoming criminal cases make up the second-largest category of trial court caseloads, with about 21 percent of the 100.6 million cases entering state courts in 2005. Two-thirds of those cases entered came from courts of limited jurisdiction, although 10 states, including California, do not have courts of limited jurisdiction.

Source: R. LaFountain, R. Schauffler, S. Strickland, W. Raftery & C. Bromage, "Examining the Work of State Courts, 2006: A National Perspective from the Court Statistics Project" (National Center for State Courts, 2007).

Civil
Domestic
Juvenile
Traffic/ordinance violations
Unified jurisdiction (3.4 million cases)
General jurisdiction (3.2 million cases)   } Criminal
Limited jurisdiction (14.2 million cases)

HIERARCHICAL JURISDICTION   An important difference between trial courts and appellate courts has to do with their placement in the court structure. Trial courts hear the facts of the case, determine guilt, and impose a sentence. Appellate courts review the work of the trial court judge and determine whether the case was handled within the constraints of the Constitution. If the trial judge allowed evidence that was illegally gathered by the police, allowed testimony of a perjured witness, or allowed the court to miss important procedural deadlines, the appellate court can overrule the verdict and set aside the sentence. Trial courts are responsible for implementing the substantive law, whereas appellate courts are responsible for ensuring that the procedural law is followed.

These three ways of classifying the jurisdictions of courts alert us to the various organizational structures that compose our fragmented system of courts in the United States. As we delve deeper into the nature and structure of federal and state courts and get confused by the complex and overlapping terminology used to identify courts, it will be useful to remember that each court is somehow classified according to each of these three measures of jurisdiction. Each court is responsible for handling certain types of cases, according to the geographic location of the offense, and according to whether the case is being heard for the first time or is under appeal.

The Structure of the Federal Courts

The court system of the United States is divided into two entities: federal courts and state courts. We can think of this as a dual court system in which each part is further subdivided according to subject matter, geographic, and hierarchical jurisdiction. Federal courts comprise four levels: magistrate courts, U.S. district courts, U.S. circuit courts of appeals, and the U.S. Supreme Court. Federal courts hear cases involving the following issues:

1. Cases in which the U.S. government or one of its officers is being sued
2. Cases between two or more states
3. Cases involving counsels, ambassadors, and other public ministers
4. Cases involving laws enacted by Congress, treaties and laws related to maritime jurisdiction, and commerce on the high seas

Additionally, state and federal courts might sometimes have *concurrent jurisdiction*. These cases typically involve circumstances in which a resident of one state sues a resident of another state. For the most part, however, the lines between federal and state court jurisdiction are clear except in cases in which the offense violates both federal and state laws, such as bank robbery or drug dealing. Another high-profile example is the D.C. sniper case, in which the defendants killed a federal agent and committed murders in both the District of Columbia and other states (for more on this case, see Chapter 10, Focus on Ethics 10.3: Where to Try a Sniper?). For a look at how the caseloads within the federal system have risen since 1998, see Figure 8-2.

magistrate court

The lowest level of the federal court system, created in 1968 to ease the caseload of the U.S. district courts.

U.S. MAGISTRATE COURTS   The **magistrate court** is the lowest level of the federal court system. Congress created these in 1968 to ease the burdensome caseload of the U.S. district courts. The magistrate court judges are chosen by the district court judges and serve either as full-time judges (appointed to eight-year terms) or as part-time judges (appointed to four-year terms). The powers of federal magistrates are limited because their authority and independence are not explicitly delineated in the Constitution as are the roles of other federal judges. For instance, they do not serve for life and are not selected by the president and confirmed by the Senate.

Magistrate courts operate as courts of limited jurisdiction in that they perform many of the essential but routine tasks of the court system. For more serious felony cases that are typically handled by the district court, the magistrate court assists by dealing with the preliminary work of sitting for initial appearances, conducting preliminary hearings, appointing counsel for those who cannot afford their own lawyer, setting bail,

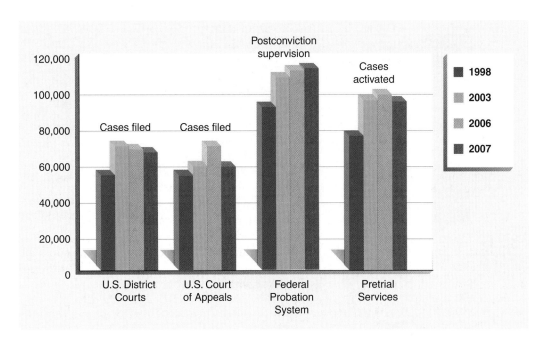

Figure 8-2   **Federal Judicial Caseloads, 1998, 2003, 2006, 2007**
Source: Judicial Caseload Indicators, www.uscourts.gov/caseload2007/front/IndicatorsMar07.pdf.

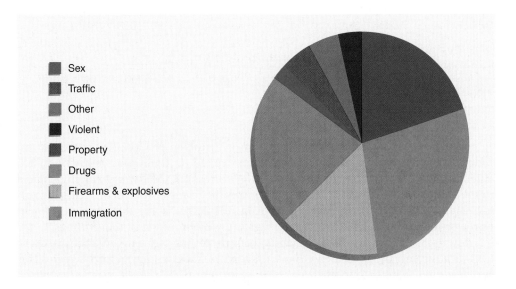

Figure 8-3   **U.S. District Courts, Criminal Cases by Offense, 2007**
Source: Table D-2, Cases: U.S. District Courts—Criminal Cases Commenced, by Major Offense (Excluding Transfers), During the 12-Month Periods Ending March 31, 2003 through 2007, www.uscourts.gov/caseload2007/tables/D02CMar07.pdf.

and issuing search warrants. This range of duties greatly relieves the workload of the district courts. Additionally, the magistrate court handles misdemeanor cases by presiding over trials, accepting pleas, and passing sentence. In addition to its criminal case duties, the magistrate court performs a comparable set of duties for civil cases.

U.S. DISTRICT COURTS   The U.S. **district courts** are courts of general jurisdiction that handle cases that are more serious and involve more money than the magistrate courts. The U.S. district courts try felony cases involving federal laws and civil cases in which the amount of money in controversy exceeds $75,000. Although civil cases constitute most of the district courts' workload, since 1980 drug prosecutions have gone up significantly and now represent a significant portion of all federal criminal cases (see Figure 8-3).[59]

Of the 94 U.S. district courts, 89 are located within the 50 states; the rest are in U.S. territories such as Puerto Rico and Guam, as well as in the District of Columbia (see Figure 8-4). Each state has at least one district court, and some states, such as New York and Texas, have as many as four. No district court crosses state lines. The 94 districts have 646 district court judgeships that are distributed according

district courts

Courts of general jurisdiction that try felony cases involving federal laws and civil cases involving amounts of money over $75,000.

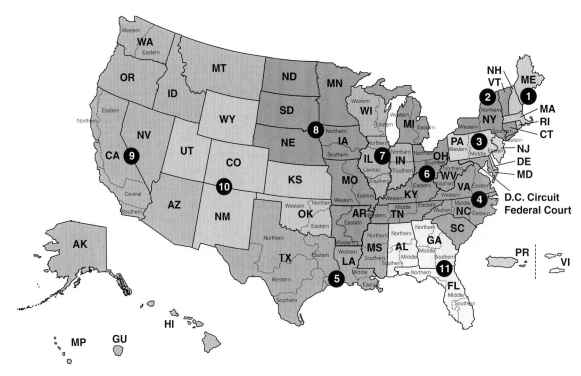

Figure 8-4 U.S. District Courts by District and Jurisdiction.

For example, the state of California is in the ninth circuit and has four districts: Northern, Eastern, Central, and Southern. Some states, such as Alaska, have no districts. Note also that there are district courts in Puerto Rico, the Virgin Islands, Guam, and the Northern Mariana Islands.

Source: Courtesy of uscourts.gov.

to population served and the political clout of members of Congress and senators. Judges are appointed to indefinite terms that depend on their good behavior, which amounts to a lifelong job unless they are caught breaking the law or bringing scandal to the court. The reason they are not given specific terms of four or six years is to allow them to be independent and objective. If they had to worry about reappointment or reelection, they might be concerned with the political effect of their rulings.

The U.S. district courts also handle bankruptcy cases, using adjunct judges to deal with the enormous caseload. Bankruptcy judges are appointed for 14-year terms and hear cases from both individuals and corporations. U.S. district courts are responsible for only a few of the types of cases that typically go to court. Most often, these are cases involving a federal question, an issue of diversity of jurisdiction, or a prisoner petition. The types of cases are as follows:

- **Federal questions** Federal-question cases involve laws that are passed by the federal government, have constitutional implications, or involve treaties with other nations. Issues such as Social Security, antitrust, and civil rights fall within the purview of the U.S. district courts.

- **Diversity of jurisdiction** Diversity of jurisdiction involves cases between citizens of different states or with someone from another country. Although the individual has the option of suing in a state court, the opportunity to use the federal court system is attractive because of the presumed objectivity and the possibility of a greater reward. For this reason, the amount of money in dispute must exceed \$75,000.[60]

- **Prisoner petitions** Prisoners in either federal or state prisons can file petitions in the U.S. district courts if they believe that their rights under federal law are being violated. Typically, these cases allege violations of due process (such as lack of an effective attorney), cruel and unusual punishment (such as prison overcrowding or bad food), or inadequate medical care. Many of these cases are heard in the magistrate court, which then makes a recommendation to the U.S. district judge.

U.S. COURTS OF APPEALS   The U.S. **courts of appeals** consist of 11 district courts, each of which encompasses several states, as well the District of Columbia Circuit. The 179 judges are nominated by the president, are confirmed by the Senate, and serve life terms as long as their behavior is not called into question. The U.S. courts of appeals serve as intermediate courts of appeals and can dispose of a vast number of appeals before they reach the Supreme Court. Only a few cases are heard each year by the Supreme Court, so for all practical purposes the U.S. court of appeals is the "court of last resort" for almost all federal cases.

In addition to criminal cases, the bulk of the U.S. courts of appeals caseload is taken up with cases dealing with civil rights violations, sex discrimination, and discrimination cases against the disabled. This requires each of the 11 circuits to have a vast staff of lawyers and clerks and for each judge to have three law clerks. The process of screening and reviewing all the cases presented on appeal involves a substantial investment of resources and time to ensure that the U.S. district courts did not make procedural errors.

U.S. SUPREME COURT   The **U.S. Supreme Court** is at the top of the hierarchical jurisdiction for both the federal and state court systems. (For an ethical scenario concerning how U.S. Supreme Court justices are chosen, see Focus on Ethics 8.2.) Even when a case has gone through the entire state court process, including the state supreme court, appeal to the U.S. Supreme Court might still be a possibility, although a remote one. The U.S. Supreme Court hears only about 80 cases a year, and these cases must involve a "substantial federal question" that concerns the Constitution or a federal law. The court does not attempt to serve as a court of last resort for all federal and state cases but instead marshals its few resources to decide cases that have broad policy implications for the important questions of the day (see Case in Point 8.2).[61]

The U.S. Supreme Court issues a **writ of *certiorari*** to the lower court that orders the records of a case to be sent to the justices so that they can decide whether the case presents the type of questions that need to be decided by the Supreme Court.

courts of appeals
Intermediate courts that dispose of many appeals before they reach the Supreme Court.

U.S. Supreme Court
The "court of last resort." The highest court in the United States, established by Article III of the Constitution, hears only appeals, with some exceptions.

writ of certiorari
An order from a superior court calling up for review the record of a case from a lower court.

The number of justices on the U.S. Supreme Court changed frequently before arriving at the present total of nine in 1869. The sitting justices of the Supreme Court of the United States are (clockwise from the rear left): Justice Stephen Breyer, Justice Clarence Thomas, Justice Ruth Bader Ginsburg, Justice Samuel Alito, Justice David Souter, Justice Antonin Scalia, Chief Justice John Roberts, Justice John Paul Stevens, and Justice Anthony Kennedy.

Source: © Matthew Cavanaugh/CORBIS. All Rights Reserved

CASE IN POINT

8.2

POWELL V. STATE OF ALABAMA

THE CASE	THE POINT
Powell *v.* State of Alabama, *287 U.S. 45, 53 S.Ct. 55 (1932)*	*This is the first case in which the U.S. Supreme Court applied the constitutional right to counsel to a specific prosecution. Powell also provides a historic look at racism within the criminal justice system.*

In March 1931 nine black men were accused of raping two white women during a train trip in Alabama. The men, who became known as the Scottsboro Boys, received no legal representation until their trial dates. Their trials lasted one day each, and all were sentenced to death. The state supreme court affirmed the convictions. However, the U.S. Supreme Court overturned their convictions on appeal because of the violation of their rights to counsel.

The Supreme Court was asked to consider three specific violations of the defendants' rights. Of the following, the court only considered the second: "(1) [The defendants] were not given a fair, impartial, and deliberate trial; (2) they were denied the right of counsel, with the accustomed incidents of consultation and opportunity of preparation for trial; and (3) they were tried before juries from which qualified members of their own race were systematically excluded."

Although the judgment was eventually reversed, two justices, Mr. Butler and Mr. McReynolds, dissented.

---

rule of four

A rule that states that at least four of the nine Supreme Court justices must vote to hear a case.

amicus curiae

A brief in which someone who is not a part of a case gives advice or testimony.

A **rule of four** exists whereby at least four of the nine Supreme Court justices must vote to hear a case before it is put on the docket.[62] Cases that are heard by the U.S. Supreme Court are heard by all nine justices, as opposed to the court of appeals in which a panel of three justices hears a case. When a case is scheduled to be heard, the attorneys file written arguments, as well as briefs on behalf of other parties that are called *amicus curiae* ("friend of the court") briefs.[63] For instance, an organization such as the American Civil Liberties Union or Amnesty International may file an *amicus curiae* brief in a case involving the death penalty for someone who is mentally retarded.

SPECIALIZED FEDERAL COURTS   A number of specialized federal courts handle primarily civil cases. These include the Tax Court, the Court of Federal Claims, the Court of Appeals for Veterans, the Court of International Trade, and the Court of Appeals for the federal circuit. These courts handle cases involving issues such as monetary claims against the federal government, tax disputes, trademarks, patents, and other issues in which the federal government is a party to a suit.[64] In terms of criminal cases, the federal court system has the Alien Terrorist Removal Court and the Foreign Intelligence Surveillance Court. These courts have been of greater interest to Americans since the terrorist events of September 11, 2001.[65]

Two other specialized federal courts decide a substantial number of criminal cases. The U.S. Court of Appeals for the Armed Forces handles cases of military law in which questions of due process are raised in the implementation of the Uniform Code of Military Justice. Military justice imposes a broad set of rules and laws on military personnel to which civilians are not subject. Failure to follow orders or showing disrespect for an officer are violations of the Uniform Code of Military Justice and can result in punishments that include incarceration or discharge from the armed services. Armed forces personnel are not entitled to all the protections of the Constitution, and the due process afforded to violators of military law is not as extensive as that afforded by civilian courts.[66]

The other specialized federal court that sees a good number of criminal cases is the tribal court. Indian tribes enjoy a certain level of self-determination and sovereignty on

8.2   FOCUS on ETHICS

JUDICIAL SELECTION

As president of the United States, you have a rare opportunity to nominate a replacement for a retiring Supreme Court justice. There are many qualified candidates to choose from, but members of your political party are pressuring you to make a historic selection and pick a minority female. The individual who is being proposed is someone you believe is a person of impeccable character and unquestioned integrity. She has the backing of the American Bar Association and seems to be a candidate that even the opposing political party would not object to.

Here is the problem: The present court is divided evenly over the constitutionality of the death penalty. The person you select will become the swing vote that will decide whether the United States continues to execute murderers. You are a staunch believer in the death penalty. When you were the governor of a large southern state, you signed more than 100 death warrants. The female candidate whom you are being pressured to select has stated on the record that she believes the death penalty is barbaric, cruel,

and unconstitutional. The two of you are like-minded on other important issues, and your party would gain a great deal of political capital from this nomination, but you are torn. Do you select this worthy candidate for this important position, or do you look for someone who shares your views on capital punishment?

What Do You Do?

1. Should a president's personal philosophy influence the court nomination process?

2. Is a difference of opinion on a single issue enough to pass over this candidate?

3. What other single issues may be used by a president to bypass a candidate for a judicial appointment?

4. Sometimes single issues such as this are called a litmus test. What does *litmus test* mean, and where does this term come from?

---

federal reservations. In many states, American Indians can establish gambling casinos on reservations regardless of the approval of state governments. Tribal law is administered by American Indians and can be imposed in lieu of state law in some circumstances.[67] Especially for issues dealing with traditional American Indian concerns, such as hunting and fishing rights, tribal law can take precedence over state or federal law. That is why, from time to time, the media covers a story about a tribe in Alaska that is allowed to harvest a protected whale as part of its traditional subsistence lifestyle.[68]

The Structure of State Courts

Like federal courts, **state courts** are generally divided according to a three-tier hierarchy.[69] At the lowest level are the courts of "first instance," state trial courts of limited and general jurisdiction. Some courts, especially those of limited jurisdiction and those with high caseloads, employ part-time judges or have staff hear cases as referees, commissioners, or hearing officers. These courts decide a case by examining the facts.[70] Further on, state intermediate courts of appeals review the trial court's application of the law to those facts.[71] Usually, an intermediate court of appeals reviews the cases of the lower courts before the opportunity of last resort, the state supreme court, makes its final ruling. However, we use the phrase *final ruling* with caution because for a few cases, such as those with a *substantial federal question*, there is always a chance that they could be selected for review by the U.S. Supreme Court.

According to the Court Statistics Project, there are probably about 16,000 courts within the United States, the District of Columbia, and Puerto Rico. The reason this number is not exact is that each jurisdiction has different criteria for deciding what constitutes a court. For example, Texas considers each judgeship to be a court and so reports more than 3300 trial courts. On the other hand, California counts 58 superior courts in its trial court system (see Crosscurrents 8.2 for a look at the effect of California courts on the rest of the country). Both states are among the largest in the

state courts
General courts and special courts funded and run by each state.

8.2

CrossCurrents

California Rules

The nation's courts follow California, at least according to a recent study by two legal experts. Jake Dear and Edward Jessen counted the number of times that state high courts followed the decisions made in the high courts of other states, and found that California was the state that most influenced the high courts of the other 49 states.

California has 1260 followed decisions, Washington 942, and Colorado 848. The state of New York has half as many followed decisions as California, with 627 cases. According to the study, one reason for California's legal prowess is the size and diversity of its population, culture, and economy. Basically, a large number of interesting cases is bound to bubble up out of such a large and diverse population.[1]

The following table presents California's most cited civil and criminal cases[2]:

Case	Year	Finding	Times Followed
Dillon v. *Legg*	1968	A woman sued for damages from the defendant who, through negligence, struck and killed her daughter with a car.	20
		Allows relatives to recover damages for emotional distress caused by witnessing the negligently caused death of a close family member.	*Dillon* has been followed more than any state opinion since 1940. The most recent following was in 2006.
Tarasoff v. *Regents of the University of California*	1976	Therapists did not warn a person of a patient's expressed intentions to kill that person. The patient later killed that person. The victim's parents alleged failure to warn of impending danger from the patient.	17
		Mental health professionals have a duty to warn others who may be in serious danger from a patient.	*Tarasoff* was relied on in two 2004 decisions.
People v. *Wheeler*	1978	Two black defendants were convicted by an all-white jury of murdering a white grocery store owner during a robbery. The prosecutor used peremptory challenges during *voir dire* to remove all the black jurors.	10
		Prohibits the use of peremptory challenges to use race as a reason to exclude prospective jurors.	This case was used substantially by the U.S. Supreme Court in 1986.
In re Alvernaz	1992	Alvernaz was convicted of robbery and kidnapping and sentenced to life with chance of parole. Alvernaz, who had rejected a plea bargain involving a lesser sentence, claimed that he rejected the deal because of ineffective counsel. Petitioners must prove that ineffective counsel affected a guilty plea.	7

Think About It

1. In your opinion, why is California so influential?
2. Do you believe these cases set good precedents for the rest of the country?

[1]Adam Liptak, "Around the Country, High Courts Follow California's Lead," *New York Times*, late edition, March 11, 2008, A12.

[2]These works, copyright 2007 and 2008 by Jake Dear and Edward W. Jessen, were originally published in the UC Davis Law Review, vol. 41, p. 683–711 and 1665–1670, copyright 2007 and 2008 by The Regents of the University of California. All rights reserved. Reprinted with permission.

union; however, they count courts differently.[72] For an example of how a state court works, see Figure 8-5.

JUVENILE COURTS   Although juvenile courts are part of the state court system, they differ in their goals and in the way they operate. Whereas courts that try adults follow criminal law, juvenile courts follow civil law because the primary goal of juvenile courts is rehabilitation, not punishment. The relationship between state courts and their juvenile counterparts differs from state to state. However, only a few states operate completely separate juvenile courts. Most juvenile courts are attached to family courts or trial courts. Juvenile courts will be discussed in greater detail in Chapter 14.

Appellate level

Court of Appeals: 7 judges, court of last resort
- Mandatory jurisdiction in civil, capital criminal, administrative agency, juvenile, original proceedings cases.
- Discretionary jurisdiction in civil, criminal, administrative agency, juvenile, disciplinary, original proceedings cases.

Appellate Divisions of Supreme Court
60 justices
- Mandatory jurisdiction in civil, criminal, administrative agency, juvenile, lawyer disciplinary, original proceedings, interlocutory decision cases.
- Discretionary jurisdiction in civil, criminal, juvenile, original proceedings, interlocutory decision cases.

Appellate Terms of Supreme Court
14 justices
- Mandatory jurisdiction in civil, criminal, juvenile, interlocutory decision cases.
- Discretionary jurisdiction in criminal, juvenile, interlocutory decision cases.

Intermediate appellate court

Supreme Court (12 districts)
326 justices with 59 judges from the Court of Claims
- Jury trials
- Tort, contract, real property, civil
- Exclusive marriage dissolution
- Felonies, misdemeanors

County Court (57 counties outside NYC)
129 judges
- Jury trials
- Tort, contract, real property ($0–$25,000), civil appeals, miscellaneous civil
- Criminal

Courts of general jurisdiction

Trial level

Court of Claims
86 judges
- No jury trials
- Tort, contract, real property involving the state

Surrogates' Court (62 counties)
31 surrogates with 51 judges from the county court
- Jury trials in probate/estate
- Probate/estate
- Adoption

City Court (61 courts)
158 judges
- Jury trials for highest level misdemeanor
- Tort, contract, real property ($0–$15,000), small claims (up to $5,000)
- Felony, misdemeanor, preliminary hearings
- Traffic infractions, ordinance violations

Family Court (62 counties)
127 judges
- No jury trials
- Guardianship
- Domestic relations
- Exclusive domestic violence
- Exclusive juvenile

District Court (Nassau & Suffolk counties) 50 judges
- Jury trials except traffic
- Tort, contract, real property ($0–$15,000), small claims (up to $5,000)
- Felony, misdemeanor, preliminary hearings
- Traffic, ordinance violations

Town and Village Justice Court (1,487 courts)
2,300 justices
- Jury trials in most cases
- Tort, contract, real property ($0–$3,000), small claims (up to $3,000)
- Misdemeanor or preliminary hearings
- Traffic/other violations

Courts of limited jurisdiction

Civil Court of the City of New York
120 judges
- Jury trials
- Tort, contract, real property ($0–$25,000), small claims (up to $5,000), miscellaneous civil

Criminal Court of the City of New York
107 judges
- Jury trials for highest misdemeanors
- Misdemeanor preliminary hearings
- Traffic infractions, ordinance violations

Figure 8-5   Court Structure of the State of New York

Source: Courtesy of National Center for State Courts, Court Statistics Project, http://www.ncsconline.org/D_Research/Ct_Struct/state_inc.asp?STATE=NY.

Figure 8-6 **Estimated Proportion of Felony Convictions in State Courts by Offense Type, 2004**

Source: Matthew R. Durose and Patrick A. Langan, *State Court Sentencing of Convicted Felons, 2004* (Washington, DC: U.S. Department of Justice, Bureau of Justice Statistics, 2005), Table 1.1, www.ojp.usdoj.gov/bjs/pub/html/scscf04/tables/scs04101tab.htm.

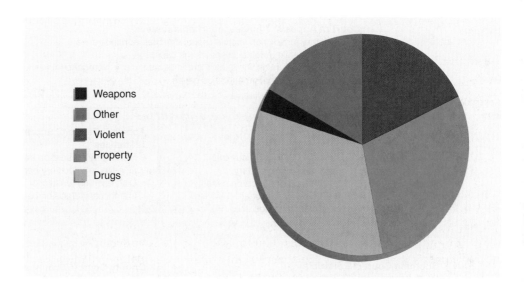

- ■ Weapons
- ▨ Other
- ■ Violent
- ▨ Property
- ▨ Drugs

lower courts

Sometimes called inferior courts, in reference to their hierarchy. These courts receive their authority and resources from local county or municipal governments.

STATE TRIAL COURTS   The trial courts of limited jurisdiction are called **lower courts** or inferior courts. This refers simply to their place on the hierarchical ladder and not to the quality of justice they dispense. Technically, they are not part of the state court system because, in most states, the lower courts of limited jurisdiction are not funded by the state but instead receive their authority and resources from local county or municipal governments. There are close to 14,000 trial courts of limited jurisdiction in the United States. They handle most cases by either passing sentence or holding preliminary hearings and motions.[73]

The trial courts of limited jurisdiction have a variety of names depending on the state in which they operate. They are called city magistrates, justices of the peace, county courts, or city courts. They handle more than 67 million matters a year, mostly traffic cases, but also misdemeanors, small claims, and the preliminary stages of felony cases. These courts of limited jurisdiction are where most citizens come into contact with the court system. The geographic jurisdictions of limited-jurisdiction courts vary by state, having either county jurisdiction or jurisdiction limited to a city or town.[74]

Trial courts of general jurisdiction are referred to as "major trial courts" and are variously named circuit courts, district courts, superior courts, or courts of common pleas. These courts handle the major cases in both the civil and criminal arenas. State trial courts of general jurisdiction hear most of the serious street-crime cases. Whereas the federal courts deal with major white-collar offenders and large-scale drug dealers, the state courts handle most cases involving rape, murder, theft, and small-scale drug dealing and drug possession (see Figure 8-6).

Although this is the court that is popularly portrayed on television and in the media when there is a jury trial, the bulk of the work of the state trial court of general jurisdiction is conducted in hallways, judges' chambers, and over the telephone and via e-mail as prosecutors and defense attorneys arrange plea bargains that eliminate the need for a trial.[75] These courts handle a wide variety of civil cases including those involving domestic relations, estate, and personal injury. General-jurisdiction trial courts are subdivided into circuits or districts. In some states, a single county serves as the judicial district, but most states have judicial districts comprising several counties.[76]

Finally, state attorneys general are the primary legal authorities of the states, commonwealths, and territories of the United States. Among other duties, they serve as legal counsel to government agencies and legislatures. The authorities of the attorneys general include the following:

- Prosecuting corporations that violate antitrust laws
- Representing state agencies and addressing issues of legislative or administrative constitutionality
- Enforcing air, water, and hazardous waste laws in most states
- Conducting criminal appeals and state criminal prosecutions
- Interceding in cases involving public utility rates
- Bringing civil suits[77]

STATE INTERMEDIATE COURTS OF APPEALS   Intermediate appellate courts are a relatively recent addition to the U.S. state court system. In 1957, only 13 states had permanent intermediate appellate courts. Currently, 39 states have such courts, which hear all appeals from the lower state courts. Only states with small populations, such as Wyoming, do not have this level of courts. Intermediate appellate courts often have rotating panels of three or more judges review cases, rather than the full complement of judges.[78] Typically, these courts must accept all criminal cases, but not necessarily all civil cases. Also, appellate courts often review the decisions made by administrative agencies.[79]

In most cases, the decision at the intermediate court of appeal level is the final decision because the state supreme courts, as does the U.S. Supreme Court, select only a small percentage of cases to consider each year. The exception to this rule is death-penalty cases. In states with capital punishment, the filing of death-penalty appeals in the court of last resort is usually mandatory.[80] There are no jury trials at the appeal level because guilt is not the overriding issue. These courts are more concerned with the conduct of the lower court in providing the protections of due process for the defendant and ensuring that the judge followed proper procedures.[81]

STATE SUPREME COURTS   Because court systems vary across the states, making many general statements about state supreme courts is difficult. In states that have an intermediate level of courts of appeals, the state supreme court has a *discretionary docket*, which means it can select the cases it wishes to consider. For sparsely populated states with no intermediate court of appeals, the state supreme court hears appeals from the lower courts. Like the U.S. Supreme Court, the state supreme courts have all the justices hear each case instead of having rotating three-judge panels. All courts of last resort have an odd number of judges, with the most typical arrangement being a seven-judge court, as found in 28 states and Puerto Rico. Sixteen states have five-judge panels, and five have nine-judge panels.

The state supreme court is the court of last resort for all but a few cases that involve issues of constitutional or federal law that the U.S. Supreme Court decides are significant. The state supreme courts also have some authority to discipline lawyers and judges and often serve as a venue for judicial training.[82]

LOCAL COURTS AND COMMUNITY COURTS   There is a wide range of variation in the nature and organization of local courts across the United States. Although it is impossible to describe every type of community court here because of space considerations, we will highlight a few of these types of courts to show how they specialize in justice for specific problems.

One of the primary features of U.S. government is that it should be close to the people. Therefore, each state has developed its own jurisdictional pattern to allow municipalities, counties, and neighborhoods to structure their local legal systems in a way that is most responsive to citizens' needs. The jurisdictional pattern of each state reflects different geographic features (urban versus rural), types of crime, and resources available to local governments.[83] Here are some of the types of local community courts.

- **Drug courts**   Many local jurisdictions have adopted the philosophy that minor drug offenses, especially possession, clog the courts with trivial cases and take resources away from more serious offenses. Because drug users who are otherwise respectable citizens and do not pose a threat of violence to the community are usually handled by the imposition of a fine or sent to a treatment program, it is deemed unnecessary to employ the traditional criminal court. Drug courts are specialized courts that can siphon off many cases that are routinely treated more leniently than more serious cases. Drug courts allow the criminal justice system to accomplish several goals. First, the vast numbers of drug offenders can be treated more consistently. Having a court that specializes in low-level drug offenders ensures that cases with similar conditions are assigned similar sanctions. Second, drug-court personnel are more aware of treatment options available in the community.[84] This means that someone who would benefit from counseling or drug treatment is more likely to receive it.[85] Third, it is less expensive and more efficient to deal with low-level drug offenders in the specialized court, thus freeing up the criminal courts for handling more serious offenses.[86]

- **Conflict resolution programs**   Many low-level offenses such as burglaries or street fights can be more efficiently dealt with by allowing offenders and victims to work out their disputes between themselves and not engage the formal legal system.[87] Often all that is required to satisfy victims is an apology, some restitution, and the feeling that offenders are being dealt with seriously. Because many offenders and victims have an ongoing relationship after the settlement of the case, conflict resolution programs are useful because they can deal with some of the underlying issues that resulted in the offense.[88] Conflict resolution programs represent an alternative to the traditional court process and not only are less expensive, but in many ways are more effective in satisfying offenders and victims that justice has been done.[89] In the future, we are likely to see more types of conflict resolution programs in attempts to lessen the burden on the court system.

- **Family courts**   Many jurisdictions have established family courts that deal with domestic assault, child abuse, and custody issues. Often family courts are incorporated into the juvenile court, although in some jurisdictions they are freestanding. The advantage of family courts is that court personnel, including judges, can be more specialized in their knowledge of family dynamics and resources available to solve family problems. Family court judges are better able to supervise personnel responsible for investigating child-abuse cases and ensure that all of the children in a family are being adequately addressed.

- **Magistrate courts**   Magistrate courts handle a number of minor offenses and preliminary court proceedings. These courts handle many pretrial intervention programs and establish bail. In many jurisdictions, the initial arraignment is now before the magistrate court. The magistrate court acts as a gatekeeper that keeps minor cases out of the criminal justice system and often diverts them to alternative treatment programs designed to solve the underlying problems that resulted in the offense. By establishing bail, permitting release on recognizance, and considering cases for dismissal, the magistrate court can relieve the local jail of the costly pretrial incarceration for those suspected of minor offenses.[90]

SUMMARY

1. Courts of some type have been consistent features of many societies. Courts are a central feature in the U.S. criminal justice system.

2. Courts were created as a peaceful way to resolve contested issues between individuals and groups because of the disruption to society caused by primitive methods.

3. To curtail the destruction of blood feuds, some early European courts developed a system of payment for a victim's family. In the Germanic tribes this was called a *wergeld* and in England a *bot*.

4. Compurgation involved the practice of character witnesses taking an oath that a plaintiff or defendant was telling the truth. If compurgation was not satisfactory, trial by ordeal was required. The three types of trial by ordeal were trial by cold water, trial by hot water, and trial by hot iron or fire; trial by battle was also used.

5. The inquest was the first type of jury. The Assize of Clarendon (1166) was a series of ordinances that established the beginnings of the grand jury system.

6. The jury trial was created to fill a vacuum in the criminal justice process left by priests who were no longer allowed to participate in trials by ordeal.

7. The Magna Carta (1215) placed the king under the rule of law. The Court of the Star Chamber was established to deal with offenses such as riots, unlawful assembly, perjury, criminal libel, and conspiracy.

8. The migration of courts from England to the North American colonies was imperfect. Because the 13 colonies that founded the United States were established under different motivations and conditions, their courts developed in response to the local economic, political, and social concerns of each colony.

9. The United States developed its own slavery laws to protect the interests of landowners. Slave courts sought to legitimize the abominable practices of slave control.

10. The U.S. Constitution, particularly the first 10 amendments, called the Bill of Rights, were written to specify the relationship between the people and the state.

11. Historical events and individuals that profoundly affected the way the U.S. courts evolved include *Marbury* v. *Madison*; *McCulloch* v. *Maryland*; the supremacy clause; Reconstruction and the expansion of federal authority; business, unions, and civil liberties; *Plessy* v. *Ferguson*; and the Warren Court.

12. Unlike other countries, the United States has no centralized court system. U.S. courts are the result of different developmental processes.

13. The court system of the United States is divided into two entities: federal courts and state courts. U.S. courts deal with civil issues and criminal issues. Violations of criminal law are punishable by imprisonment; violations of civil law are not and are usually punished by a fine.

14. Jurisdiction refers to the authority of the court to hear certain cases. The jurisdiction of any court depends on the seriousness of the case, the location of the offense, and whether the case is being heard for the first time or is on appeal. The three types of jurisdiction are subject-matter jurisdiction, geographic jurisdiction, and hierarchical jurisdiction.

15. Federal courts comprise four levels: magistrate courts, U.S. district courts, U.S. circuit courts of appeals, and the U.S. Supreme Court.

16. State courts are generally divided into a three-tier hierarchy: state trial courts of limited and general jurisdiction (including local and community courts); intermediate courts of appeals; and courts of last resort.

KEY TERMS

amicus curiae 280
Assize of Clarendon 267
blood feud 264
circuit court 275
compurgation 266
Court of the Star Chamber 269
courts of appeals 279

district courts 277
geographic jurisdiction 275
hierarchical jurisdiction 275
inquest 267
lower courts 284
magistrate court 276
rule of four 280

state courts 281
subject-matter jurisdiction 275
trial by ordeal 266
U.S. Supreme Court 279
writ of *certiorari* 279

REVIEW QUESTIONS

1. What two problems affect the image and functioning of the court?

2. Are courts purely a feature of European societies?

3. What system did Europeans use in lieu of violence to settle wrongs and disputes?

4. What was the first type of jury?

5. Why were the first grand juries and trial juries flawed?

6. What was the Court of the Star Chamber?

7. What served as the foundation for U.S. courts?

8. What is the only Bill of Rights item that is also included in all the state constitutions?

9. Name the three types of court jurisdiction.

10. What types of cases do federal courts hear? What levels constitute federal courts?

11. What is an inferior court?

12. Discuss the differences between trial courts of limited jurisdiction and trial courts of general jurisdiction.

13. What is the purpose of state intermediate courts of appeals? Do all states have them? Why or why not?

14. What do local and community courts do?

SUGGESTED FURTHER READING

Banks, Christopher. *Judicial Politics in the D.C. Circuit Court.* Baltimore: John Hopkins University Press, 1999.

Baum, Lawrence. *The Supreme Court,* 8th ed. Washington, DC: CQ Press, 2004.

Calvi, James V., and Susan Coleman. *American Law and Legal Systems.* Upper Saddle River, NJ: Prentice Hall, 2003.

Carp, Robert A., Ronald Stidham, and Kenneth L. Manning. *Judicial Process in America.* Washington, DC: CQ Press, 2007.

Friedman, Lawrence M. *A History of American Law,* 3rd ed. New York: Simon & Schuster, 2005.

Stojkovic, Stan, John Klofas, and David Kalinich. *The Administration and Management of Criminal Justice Organizations: A Book of Readings,* 2nd ed. Prospect Heights, IL: Waveland Press, 1994.

ENDNOTES

1. Samuel Walker and Charles M. Katz, *The Police in America: An Introduction,* 4th ed. (Boston: McGraw-Hill, 2002), 41.

2. James Austin and John Irwin, *It's about Time: America's Imprisonment Binge,* 3rd ed. (Belmont, CA: Wadsworth, 2001).

3. Frances Kahn Zemans, "In the Eye of the Beholder: The Relationship between the Public and the Courts," in *Courts and Justice: A Reader,* 2nd ed., eds. G. Larry Mays and Peter Gregware (Prospect Heights, IL: Waveland Press, 2000), 7–24.

4. David Orrick, "Court Administration in the United States: The On-Going Problems," in *Courts and Justice: A Reader,* 2nd ed., eds. G. Larry Mays and Peter Gregware (Prospect Heights, IL: Waveland Press, 2000), 207–227.

5. Stuart Nagel, "The Tipped Scales of American Justice," in *The Scales of Justice,* ed. Abraham Blumberg (New York: Transaction, 1970), 31–50.

6. Christopher Smith, *Courts, Politics, and the Judicial Process,* 2nd ed. (Chicago: Nelson-Hall, 1997), 4–7.

7. Pamela A. MacLean, "Mixed Signals on Plea Bargains," *National Law Journal,* December 17, 2007, 7.

8. Max Gluckman, *Politics, Law, and Ritual in Tribal Society* (Oxford, England: Blackwell, 1965).

9. Bronislaw Malinowski, *Crime and Custom in Savage Society* (London: Routledge & Kegan Paul, 1926).

10. E. A. Hoebel, *The Law of Primitive Man* (Cambridge, MA: Harvard University Press, 1964).

11. Raymond J. Michalowski, *Order, Law, and Crime: An Introduction to Criminology* (New York: Random House, 1985), 56.

12. Emile Durkheim, *The Division of Labor in Society* (New York: Free Press, 1933).

13. E. E. Evans-Pritchard, *The Nuer: A Description of the Modes of Livelihood and Political Institutions of a Nilotic People* (London: Oxford University Press, 1968), 171.

14. Bryce Lyon, *A Constitutional and Legal History of Medieval England*, 2nd ed. (New York: Norton, 1980).

15. See Janelle Brown, "The Impossible Calculus of Loss," *Salon*, January 2, 2002, http://archive.salon.com/mwt/feature/2002/01/02/fund_fairness/index.html. A victim's social status is still a factor in determining his or her monetary value. The government fund set up to compensate the families of the September 11, 2001, terrorist attacks took into account the victims' ages and future earning capacities. This caused many families anguish at the perceived unfairness of the compensation program.

16. Ellen Hochstedler Steury and Nancy Frank, *Criminal Court Process* (Minneapolis/St. Paul, MN: West, 1996), 66.

17. Lyon, *Constitutional and Legal History*, 84.

18. Ibid.

19. John S. Beckerman, "Procedural Innovation and Institutional Change in Medieval English Manorial Courts," *Law and History Review* 10 (Fall 1992): 203–204.

20. Margaret H. Kerr, Richard D. Forsyth, and Michael J. Plyley, "Cold Water and Hot Iron: Trial by Ordeal in England," *Journal of Interdisciplinary History* 22 (1992): 573.

21. Robert Bartlett, *Trial by Fire and Water: The Medieval Judicial Ordeal* (Oxford, England: Clarendon Press, 1986).

22. Hochstedler Steury and Frank, *Criminal Court Process*, 70–71.

23. Lorraine Attreed, "The Duel in Early Modern England: Civility, Politeness and Honour," *Canadian Journal of History* 40, no. 1 (2005): 100–102.

24. J. H. Baker, *An Introduction to English Legal History*, 3rd ed. (Boston: Butterworths, 1990).

25. Lyon, *Constitutional and Legal History*, 295.

26. Barbara J. Shapiro, *"Beyond Reasonable Doubt" and "Probable Cause": Historical Perspectives on the Anglo-American Laws of Evidence* (Berkeley: University of California Press, 1991), 47.

27. Hochstedler Steury and Frank, *Criminal Court Process*, 73.

28. Roger D. Groot, "The Early Thirteenth-Century Criminal Trial," in *Twelve Men Good and True: The Criminal Jury in England 1200–1800*, eds. J. S. Cockburn and Thomas A. Green (Princeton, NJ: Princeton University Press, 1988), 19–20.

29. Lyon, *Constitutional and Legal History*, 451.

30. Baker, *Introduction to English Legal History*, 581.

31. Thomas Andrew Green, *Verdict According to Conscience: Perspectives on the English Criminal Jury Trial* (Chicago: University of Chicago Press, 1985).

32. James Landman, "You Should Have the Body: Understanding Habeas Corpus," *Social Education*, March 1, 2008, 99.

33. Lyon, *Constitutional and Legal History*, 312–321.

34. Baker, *Introduction to English Legal History*, 591.

35. Hochstedler Steury and Frank, *Criminal Court Process*, 77.

36. Edwin C. Surrency, "The Courts in the American Colonies," *American Journal of Legal History* 11 (July 1967): 252–276.

37. Ibid., 256.

38. Donna J. Spindel, *Crime and Society in North Carolina, 1663–1776* (Baton Rouge: Louisiana State University Press, 1989), 20.

39. Lawrence M. Friedman, *A History of American Law* (New York: Simon & Schuster, 1985), 75.

40. Hochstedler Steury and Frank, *Criminal Court Process*, 84–85.

41. John Ferling, *A Leap in the Dark: The Struggle to Create the American Republic* (New York: Oxford University Press, 2003).

42. Robert Allen Rutland, *The Birth of the Bill of Rights* (Chapel Hill: University of North Carolina Press, 1955).

43. Bruce Ackerman, "The Living Constitution," *Harvard Law Review* 120 (May 1, 2007): 1737–1812.

44. *Marbury* v. *Madison*, 1 Cranch 137 (1803), 55, 56–57, 61.

45. Mary Ann Harrell and Burnett Anderson, *Equal Justice under the Law: The Supreme Court in American Life* (Washington, DC: Supreme Court Historical Society, 1982).

46. Mark Tushnet, "*Marbury v. Madison* and the Theory of Judicial Supremacy," in *Greatest Cases in Constitutional Law*, ed. Robert P. George (Princeton, NJ: Princeton University Press, 2000), 17–54.

47. Laurence H. Tribe, *God Save This Honorable Court: How the Choice of Supreme Court Justices Shapes Our History* (New York: Random House, 1985).

48. *McCulloch* v. *Maryland*, 4 Wheat. 316 (1819), 57–59, 194.

49. Harold J. Spaeth, *Supreme Court Policy Making: Explanation and Prediction* (San Francisco: Freeman, 1979).

50. Bernard Schwartz, *A History of the Supreme Court* (New York: Oxford University Press, 1993).

51. William M. Wiecek, *Liberty under Law: The Supreme Court in American Life* (Baltimore: Johns Hopkins University Press).

52. Christopher Wolfe, *The Rise of Modern Judicial Review: From Constitutional Interpretation to Judge-Made Law*

(New York: Basic Books, 1986). See also Anthony Woodiwiss, *Rights v. Conspiracy: A Sociological Essay on the History of Labor Law in the United States* (New York: Berg, 1990).

53. *Plessy* v. *Ferguson*, 163 U.S. 537 (1896), 68, 76, 175.

54. Robert Justin Goldstein, "*Mapp v. Ohio*: Guarding against Unreasonable Searches and Seizures," *Perspectives on Political Science* 36 (July 1, 2007): 171–172.

55. Howard Abadinsky, *Law and Justice: An Introduction to the American Legal System* (Upper Saddle River, NJ: Prentice Hall, 2003).

56. Howard Gillman, *The Votes That Counted: How the Supreme Court Decided the 2000 Presidential Election* (Chicago: University of Chicago Press, 2001).

57. Alan M. Dershowitz, *Supreme Injustice: How the High Court Hijacked Election 2000* (New York: Oxford University Press, 2001).

58. Gary A. Rabe and Dean J. Champion, *Criminal Courts: Structure, Process, and Issues* (Upper Saddle River, NJ: Prentice Hall, 2002).

59. David W. Neubauer, *America's Courts and the Criminal Justice System*, 7th ed. (Belmont, CA: Wadsworth, 2002), 68.

60. Larry Kramer, "Diversity Jurisdiction," *Brigham Young University Law Review*, 1990, pp. 3–66.

61. Robert A. Carp, Ronald Stidham, and Kenneth L. Manning, *Judicial Process in America* (Washington, DC: CQ Press, 2007). See pp. 28–30, "The Supreme Court as Policymaker."

62. Eric M. Freedman, "Can Justice Be Served by Appeals of the Dead?" *National Law Journal*, October 19, 1992, 13.

63. Aaron S. Bayer, "Amicus Briefs," *National Law Journal*, February 25, 2008, 15.

64. Lawrence Baum, "Specializing the Federal Courts: Neutral Reforms or Efforts to Shape Judicial Policy?" *Judicature* 74 (1991): 217–224.

65. "Federal Courts—Standing—Sixth Circuit Denies Standing to Challenge Terrorist Surveillance Program.—*ACLU v. NSA*, 493 F. 3d 644 (6th Cir. 2007)," *Harvard Law Review* 121 (January 1, 2008): 922–929.

66. John R. Crook, "UCMJ Proceedings against U.S. Personnel Accused of Offenses against Civilians in Afghanistan and Iraq," *American Journal of International Law* 101 (July 1, 2007): 663–664.

67. Judith Resnik, "Multiple Sovereignties: Indian Tribes, States, and the Federal Government," *Judicature* 79 (1995): 118–125.

68. Jon M. Conrad, "Bioeconomics and the Bowhead Whale," *Journal of Political Economy* 97 (August 1, 1989): 974.

69. National Center for State Courts, www.ncsconline.org/D_Research/Ct_Struct/Index.html. Click on this map to find the structure of your state court.

70. David B. Rottman and Shauna M. Strickland, *State Court Organization, 2004* (Washington, DC: U.S. Department of Justice, Bureau of Justice Statistics, 2006), 7, www.ojp.usdoj.gov/bjs/pub/pdf/sc004.pdf.

71. Ibid.

72. Robert C. LaFountain et al., *Examining the Work of State Courts, 2006* (Washington, DC: National Center for State Courts, 2007), 9, www.ncsconline.org/D_Research/csp/2006_files/EWSC-2007WholeDocument.pdf.

73. Kathleen Maguire and Ann Pastore, *Sourcebook of Criminal Justice Statistics, 1999* (Albany, NY: Hindelang Criminal Justice Research Center, 2000).

74. Rottman and Strickland, *State Court Organization, 2004*, 7.

75. David Bjerk, "Guilt Shall Not Escape or Innocence Suffer? The Limits of Plea Bargaining When Defendant Guilt is Uncertain," American Law and Economics Review 9, no. 2 (October 1, 2007): 305–329.

76. Ibid.

77. The National Association of Attorneys General, 2003, www.naag.org/ag/duties.php.

78. Ibid.

79. Rottman and Strickland, *State Court Organization, 2004*, 131.

80. Ibid.

81. Kevin M. Scott, "Understanding Judicial Hierarchy: Reversals and the Behavior of Intermediate Appellate Judges," *Law and Society Review* 40 (March 1, 2006): 163–191.

82. Hope Viner Samborn, "Disbarred—But Not Barred from Work," *ABA Journal* 93 (June 1, 2007): 57.

83. Scott Henson, interview by Eileen Smith, "The Gritty Truth," *Texas Monthly* (February 2008).

84. Patricia Marinelli-Casey et al., "Drug Court Treatment for Methamphetamine Dependence: Treatment Response and Posttreatment Outcomes," *Journal of Substance Abuse Treatment* 34 (March 1, 2008): 242.

85. "Utah Initiative for Offenders Links Treatment, Probation," *Alcoholism and Drug Abuse Weekly*, January 14, 2008, 1.

86. Sharon M Boles et al., "The Sacramento Dependency Drug Court: Development and Outcomes," *Child Maltreatment* 12 (May 1, 2007): 161–171.

87. Lorig Charkoudian and Carrie Wilson, "Factors Affecting Individuals' Decisions to Use Community Mediation," *Review of Policy Research*, July 1, 2006, 865–886.

88. Jon'a F. Meyer, "'It Is a Gift from the Creator to Keep Us in Harmony': Original (vs. alternative) Dispute Resolution in the Navajo Nation," *International Journal of Public Administration* 25 (November 1, 2002): 1379–1401.

89. Eileen Pruett and Cynthia Savage, "Statewide Initiatives to Encourage Alternative Dispute Resolution and Enhance Collaborative Approaches to Resolving Family Issues," *Family Court Review* 42 (April 1, 2004): 232–245.

90. Stewart J. D'Alessio and Lisa Stolzenberg, "Unemployment and the Incarceration of Pretrial Defendants," *American Sociological Review* 60 (June 1, 1995): 350.

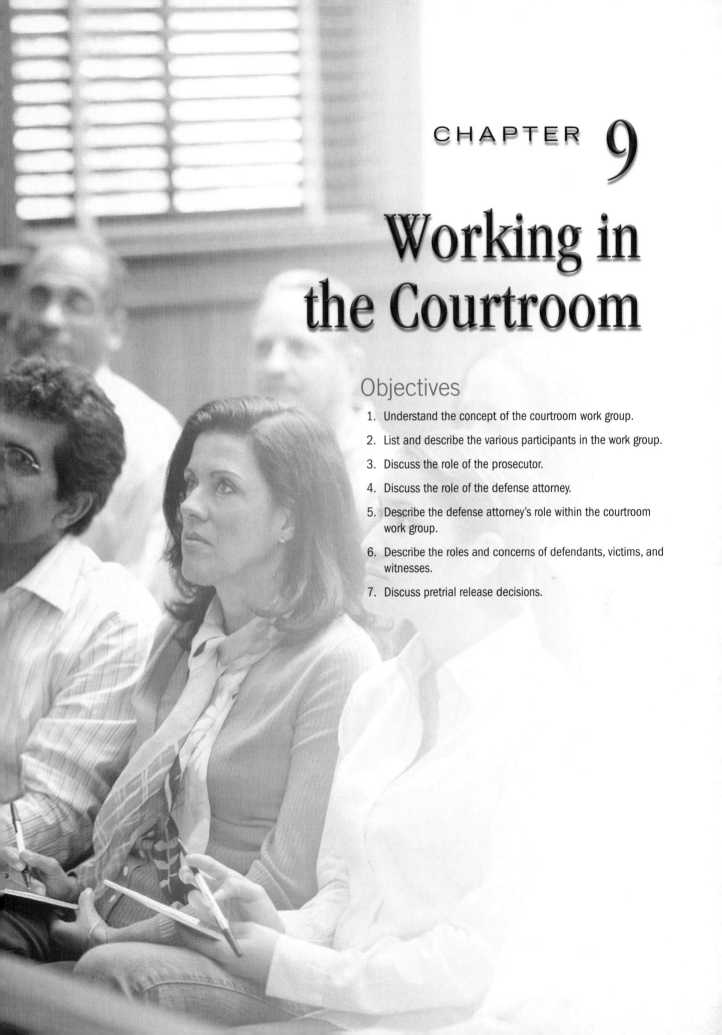

CHAPTER 9

Working in the Courtroom

Objectives

1. Understand the concept of the courtroom work group.

2. List and describe the various participants in the work group.

3. Discuss the role of the prosecutor.

4. Discuss the role of the defense attorney.

5. Describe the defense attorney's role within the courtroom work group.

6. Describe the roles and concerns of defendants, victims, and witnesses.

7. Discuss pretrial release decisions.

There is a tendency to think of the courts as an institution where justice is served in an assembly line fashion. Individual defendants are reduced to cases and are acted on by court officials who are simply court actors who do not display individual judgment but rather follow the prescribed procedures of the legal system. The aim in this chapter is to humanize the court by illustrating that those who work in the courthouse pursue various personal and institutional agendas. Furthermore, in working together, they display a form of individualized justice that is peculiar to each court. Only by understanding how the courtroom work group is constrained by legal, social, and institutional factors can we fully appreciate how the court interacts with other components of the criminal justice system.

The people who work in the courtroom form a complex and fascinating set of actors who work together at a variety of levels to fashion a product that is defined as "justice." On one hand, the processing of cases may look like a smoothly functioning system in which all people "get their day in court" and are assured the full range of constitutional protections, as well as the guarantee that their voices will be heard and seriously considered. On the other hand, below the surface of public scrutiny, the courtroom can be considered a chaotic place where attorneys and judges sometimes play fast and loose with the truth, individuals' rights, and justice itself. In an effort to move the docket—that is, to settle cases—justice is negotiated and bargained.[1] (See Criminal Justice Reference 9.1 for an example of the oath of attorney.)

Some people are alarmed by the dynamics of the courthouse, which differ vastly from the ideal of impartial justice being dispensed by wise judges. The notion of attorneys working deals with the prosecutor to garner more lenient sentences for obviously guilty defendants violates our image of the courthouse as a place where truth prevails, the guilty get their just deserts, victims receive justice, and the innocent go free.[2] However, understanding courtroom politics is vital to comprehending the activities of those who make up the courtroom work group. In this chapter, we will identify the roles and responsibilities of those whose job it is to handle the vast caseload that passes through the modern courthouse. We will start with the support personnel, then turn to the prosecutor's office and the various types of defense attorneys.

Serving on a jury is a serious endeavor because so much is at stake. Here, a deputy court administrator swears in potential jurors in a court.

Source: AP Wide World Photos

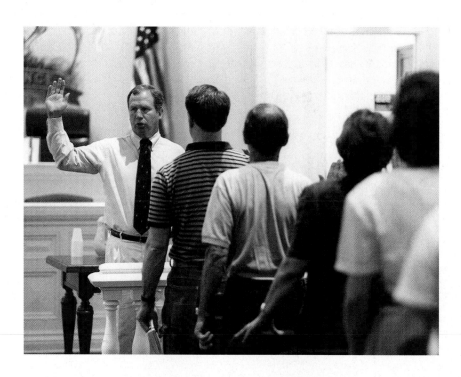

9.1   CRIMINAL JUSTICE REFERENCE

Oath of Attorney

Attorneys in each state must take an oath of attorney in order to practice law in that state. Here is an example from the state of Texas.

State Bar of Texas Oath of Attorney

I do solemnly swear that I will support the constitution of the United States, and of this State; that I will honestly demean myself in the practice of the law, and will discharge my duties to my clients to the best of my ability. So help me God.

Source: State Bar of Texas, www.texasbar.com/Template.cfm?Section=Home&Template=/ContentManagement/ContentDisplay.cfm&ContentID=9721.

THE COURTROOM WORK GROUP

Not all courtrooms are the same. Different levels of jurisdiction (federal, state, and local) and different levels of responsibility (misdemeanors, felonies, and appeals) dictate different working arrangements among the participants in the courtroom work group. The following discussion of the courtroom work group is general and refers to the typical issues that arise in most courts.

The Participants

Although a certain adversarial atmosphere is present in the courtroom, those in the courtroom work group also exhibit a high level of cooperation.[3] Those working in the courthouse, and, ultimately, in the courtroom, come from vastly different backgrounds, agencies, and ideologies. As in the criminal justice system in general, those who work in the courthouse have different sets of funding sources, constituents, responsibilities, and goals. These people, who sometimes seem to be working at cross-purposes, are in many other ways cooperating to dispose of cases in a timely manner.[4] Consequently, there is a certain level of expectation of how each case will be settled based on the **going rate,** or, more precisely, on how other cases of a similar nature have been settled in the past by a given set of judges, prosecutors, and attorneys.[5]

> **going rate**
> A term describing how similar cases have been settled by a given set of judges, prosecutors, and attorneys.

In sociological terms, a certain routinization of work occurs whereby everyone (except the defendant) has a good idea about the ultimate outcome of the case. Nevertheless, each actor in the drama has a vested interest in seeing cases resolved according to his or her particular social and legal location within the courthouse. Let's review this variety of courthouse actors and reflect on how they affect the daily events in the courtroom.

LAW ENFORCEMENT   A variety of law enforcement officers interact daily within the courtroom work group. First is the courthouse security officer, who is responsible for protecting everyone in the courthouse.[6] Some jurisdictions might have metal-screening devices at the courthouse entrances to prohibit unauthorized people from carrying firearms into the courthouse. A second type of law enforcement officer working in the courthouse is the sheriff's deputy, who transports prisoners to and from jail. The courthouse usually has a holding pen where these deputies keep prisoners until their presence is needed in the courtroom. The bailiff is a court officer responsible for maintaining order in the courtroom.[7] In some jurisdictions, a bailiff works in the courtroom of a single judge. In other jurisdictions, bailiffs rotate from courtroom to courtroom as needed. Finally, there is a constant parade of law enforcement officers who come to the courthouse to testify in trials. Many courts have a senior law enforcement officer who coordinates with police agencies to ensure that officers do not spend all their time waiting in courthouse corridors for trials that might be canceled.

clerk of the court

The primary administrative officer of each court who manages nonjudicial functions.

court reporter

A court officer who records and transcribes an official verbatim record of the legal proceedings of the court.

court administrator

An officer responsible for the mechanical necessities of the court, such as scheduling courtrooms, managing case flow, administering personnel, procuring furniture, and preparing budgets.

bail agent

An employee of a private, for-profit company that provides money for suspects to be released from jail. Also called a bondsman.

child advocate

An officer appointed by the court to protect the interests of the child and to act as a liaison among the child, the child's family, the court, and any other agency involved with the child.

COURT SUPPORT STAFF   A number of courtroom support staffers work behind the scenes to ensure the smooth functioning of the court. The **clerk of the court** is an administrator with a large staff who keeps the court records and provides a sufficient pool of jurors for cases that go to trial. The **court reporter** makes a verbatim transcript of the proceedings. Given the ethnic diversity of many cities, various translators are employed by the court to ensure that defendants, victims, and witnesses can have their testimony translated into English.[8] Finally, the **court administrator** handles a variety of administrative tasks necessary for the functioning of the court, such as scheduling courtrooms, procuring furniture, improving case flow, creating calendars, and managing court personnel.[9]

CORRECTIONS   Probation officers perform two primary functions for the court. First, they interview offenders and write presentence investigation reports in which they review the case and make sentencing recommendations to the judge.[10] Second, the probation officer supervises offenders who are placed on probation to ensure that they are following the judge's orders and are not breaking any further laws. Depending on the jurisdiction, the court may directly employ the probation officer via a statewide department of corrections or by a local government or private probation department. In some jurisdictions, pretrial services personnel work with judges to help identify individuals who could be safely released from custody pending further court proceedings.[11] Finally, rehabilitation specialists identify drug and alcohol treatment programs for qualified offenders. Often, judges want to know whether there is a program willing to enroll an offender before such a sentence is mandated.[12]

THE PUBLIC   A number of individuals from the public sphere who have business with the court can be loosely identified as part of the courtroom work group. For-profit **bail agents** solicit offenders or their families to use their services. Suspects who cannot afford the entire amount of their bail can use a bail agent to get out of jail while awaiting trial.[13] Many news agencies have *reporters* covering the courthouse beat. Depending on their reputation for discretion, some of these reporters are allowed behind the scenes, where they participate in the informal workings of the courtroom work group. *Victim–witness program personnel*, including staff members of rape crisis centers, are other informal participants in the courtroom work group.[14] These individuals advocate on behalf of crime victims and may introduce victim impact statements to help the judge decide on an appropriate sentence.[15]

Juvenile courts often employ a **child advocate** to ensure that the best interests of the child, and not those of the state or the parents, are considered.[16] Many courts have members of the public who act as *court watchers*. These individuals might represent public-interest groups who advocate for better government, or they might simply be court aficionados who enjoy watching the courtroom action. Finally, perhaps the most important segment of the public that is constantly present in the courtroom are the *jurors*. Although no individual juror is a regular member of the courtroom work group, they are part of the proceedings and play an important role in the courts' decisions.

As we can see, the informal courtroom work group comprises a variety of individuals who represent many, and sometimes competing, interests.[17] All are instrumental in the workings of the courts and play important roles. However, the main actors in the courtroom work group have not yet been considered. Because the prosecutor, defense attorney, and judge play such prominent roles in the court, we will deal with each of them in greater detail.

The Prosecutor

The prosecutor has in many ways the most powerful position in the criminal justice system. The prosecutor functions as the major gatekeeper of the process and not only decides which cases are formally defined as criminal offenses, but also argues those cases in court.[18] The prosecutor's position is powerful because the exercise of discretion (the authority to decide which cases are inserted into the criminal justice system) rests with this office. With police officers pushing for harsh penalties for those whom they arrest, defense attorneys pleading for the best bargain they can get for their clients, and judges wanting to move the docket and dispose of cases quickly, the power of the prosecutor allows him or her to inject personal philosophy and political interests into the justice system (see Crosscurrents 9.1).[19] The prosecutor has the discretion to charge the case (or not), to decide what the charge will be, and to dismiss it if he or she so chooses. This pivotal actor has the most influence in plea bargaining.[20]

However, the discretion of the prosecutor is not completely unfettered. Even though the prosecuting attorney has sole discretion in deciding which cases to prosecute, which offenses to charge the defendant with, and what sorts of deals the government will agree to, prosecutorial behavior is limited. Especially during the trial stage of the proceedings, the prosecutor must act within firmly established parameters of procedural law. For instance, if the prosecutor knows of evidence that may show the defendant to be innocent, he or she must share that evidence with the defense attorney.[21] The converse of this obligation is not required. Defense attorneys are not expected to share evidence of their clients' guilt. The prosecutor must prove the case without the aid of the defense attorney and the defendant. This might seem somewhat unfair, but it is important to remember that the prosecutor has the resources of the state behind his or her efforts and that the Constitution protects the individual rights of the accused. Although the prosecutor represents the interests of the state (which includes the victim, law enforcement officers, and the ideal of justice), the idea of a free society under the law protects individuals from unfettered state power.[22]

Given the complexity of our court system with its various federal, state, and local jurisdictions, as well as its geographic hierarchy, it should not surprise us that the position of prosecutor also varies widely. It is useful to distinguish between prosecutors at the state and federal levels because their differences are as important as their similarities.

PROSECUTION AT THE FEDERAL LEVEL   The Department of Justice, or Justice Department, is at the top of the federal hierarchy of prosecution. The U.S. attorney general is a cabinet-level officer who is appointed by the president and confirmed by the Senate through its advise-and-consent function. Lawyers working for the Justice Department are protected from political influence by their civil service status. Because so many of them spend their whole careers working for the government, they become experts in their particular branch of the law.[23] The attorney general's office is responsible for a range of activities not associated with the prosecution of criminal cases.

- **Executive direction and management offices**   This includes the solicitor general, who argues all the government's cases before the Supreme Court and represents the interests of the executive branch in advising Congress on the crafting of legislation.
- **Litigation**   This part of the organization handles all courtroom matters including antitrust, civil, civil rights, criminal, environmental, tax, and the oversight of the U.S. attorneys' office in all the federal districts.
- **Investigatory and law enforcement agencies**   The Justice Department is responsible for the Federal Bureau of Investigation (FBI), the Drug Enforcement Agency (DEA), the U.S. Marshals Service, and the Federal Bureau of Prisons.
- **Policy and assistance offices**   These offices include the Bureau of Justice Assistance, the Immigration and Naturalization Service (INS), and other agencies that coordinate justice interests or provide assistance to other agencies or the public.

As we can see, the Justice Department is responsible for many activities that are not concerned with the prosecution of cases. Here, the discussion will be limited to the three offices of the Justice Department that directly affect the prosecutorial aspect

9.1

CrossCurrents

Prosecution or Persecution?

The criminal justice process is, unfortunately, not only about justice but about politics. Law enforcement officers, prosecutors, and judges all have their own agendas in addition to pursuing justice. One recent and egregious example of this occurred in March 2006 in Durham, North Carolina.

What has become known as the "Duke rape case" began when police found a woman passed out in a parked car near a Durham, North Carolina, grocery store at about 1:30 A.M. When she was taken into custody, she told police and medical officials that she had been raped while performing as a dancer at a party for the Duke University lacrosse team. The woman accused three players, whom she identified by first names, of forcing her into a bathroom at the house where she had gone to perform and sexually assaulting her for 30 minutes, as well as choking, kicking, and beating her.[1] The woman's story changed several times; at first, she claimed there had been 20 assailants, then two, then three. Physical examination showed no evidence of injuries consistent with rape.[2] The alleged victim at first accused the other dancer who had accompanied her to the party of stealing her money and assisting the players with the assault. That woman later told police that the alleged victim's story was false; however, she later recanted and said that a rape might have taken place.[3]

Two days later, police searched the house and interviewed the three team captains who resided there. The captains agreed to provide DNA samples. The next week, county district attorney Michael Nifong ordered 46 of the team members to provide DNA samples and to allow police to take their photographs.[4] After getting the team members' story, it appeared that the only uncontested facts about the case were that the woman and another dancer were hired by members of the Duke lacrosse team to perform for two hours for $400. The dancers left early, with the alleged victim appearing to be drunk, as some of the team members shouted racial epithets.[5]

The racial and social-class aspects of the case dominated: the accused were wealthy, young white men, and the victim was a young, black woman, who, if not impoverished, was certainly not as well off as the Duke lacrosse players. The accusations also stirred racial and class tensions in Durham. Although many small university-dominated towns have "town-and-gown" issues that pit a stable, older local population against a transient, young university population, Durham's population split is particularly acute. The town's local population is lower and middle income working class, and a large percentage are black, while its university population is wealthy, primarily white, and attending an expensive private school.

The case put Nifong in an interesting position. As an acting district attorney (he was appointed to the position in 2005 to replace a DA who left to became a Superior Court judge), Nifong was running in his first election that May.[6] The case seemed solid at first, and Nifong had the support of many of Duke's professors and students, as well as the media. But in the weeks after the three accused lacrosse players were arrested, the woman's story and Nifong's case began to come apart, with cracks appearing as early as April 2006.[7]

The woman had claimed 10 years earlier that she had been raped by three men, but her father told reporters that the rape never happened, and that his daughter never followed up the charge with authorities.[8] Apparently, at the police photo ID session in which the woman had identified her attackers, she was shown only players from the Duke lacrosse team.[9] None of the DNA samples taken from 46 of the team members turned up any matches with those taken from the alleged victim.[10] At some point, the news about the other dancer's telling police that the woman's story was a "crock" came out.[11] Finally, one of the alleged attackers produced cell phone records, testimony from a taxi driver, receipts, and a electronic entry time stamp to his dormitory room to show that he had already left the party while the rape was supposedly occurring.[12]

Even as the evidence mounted against the alleged victim's story, Nifong continued to vehemently pursue the case with the support of much of the public. The university canceled the remaining 2006 lacrosse season, and the team's coach resigned. Nifong won the May election.[13]

One of the most serious lapses committed by Nifong was his refusal to consider evidence that did not fit with his political ambitions. When the attorney for one of the young men asked to meet with Nifong and present exculpatory evidence, Nifong flatly refused. Later, a laboratory director testified that important evidence was withheld from defense attorneys for seven months and that Nifong had asked him to submit a report omitting that none of the DNA collected from the woman could be traced to any Duke lacrosse player.[14]

As the evidence against the young men disintegrated, Nifong was finally forced to drop the case. The rape charges against the players were dropped three days before Christmas in 2006, and the rest of the charges by April 2007.[15] According to legal experts, North Carolina's grand jury system contains a legal loophole that helped the case spin out of control: no records are kept of grand jury proceedings. This means there is no record of what prosecutors say to grand juries, and, therefore no way to hold them accountable for what they do say.[16]

In the end, Nifong was disbarred, cited for criminal contempt of court, and sentenced to a day in jail with a $500 fine.[17] The three falsely accused players were allowed to pursue a civil suit against Nifong after a federal judge lifted a stay that had protected the bankrupt Nifong. Also, 38 team members and nine of their parents sued Duke University and Durham officials, accusing school officials of withholding evidence that would have helped the players, as well as condoning their harassment.[18]

In an ambitious attempt to court the votes of a large segment of the Durham population, Nifong forgot his true mission of seeking unbiased justice. Although this might be a rare case of law enforcement officials going astray, it is difficult to know exactly how rare. One of the temptations of elected officials is to go too far in seeking votes and neglecting their real mission.

Think About It

1. Should Nifong have dropped the charges earlier? Should the charges have been filed at all?
2. Was 24 hours in jail and disbarment enough punishment for Nifong? Should he have been punished more, less, or not at all?
3. Discuss the role of politics and elections in this case.

[1]New York Times, "911 Calls Lead the Police to Duke's Lacrosse Team," March 30, 2006, D1.

[2]Evan Thomas and Susannah Meadows, "Doubts about Duke," Newsweek, June 26, 2006, 22; Duff Wilson and Jonathan D. Glater, "Prosecutor's Silence on Duke Rape Case Leaves Public With Plenty of Questions," New York Times, June 12, 2006, A13.

[3]Thomas and Meadows, "Doubts about Duke," 22.

[4]New York Times, "911 Calls," D1.

[5]Wilson and Glater, "Prosecutor's Silence," A13.

[6]Oren Dorell, "Duke Case Prosecutor's Media Whirl Raises Eyebrows," USA Today, first edition, May 2, 2006, A2.

[7]Susannah Meadows and Evan Thomas, "A Troubled Spring at Duke," Newsweek, U.S. edition, April 10, 2006, 42.

[8]Thomas and Meadows, "Doubts about Duke," 22.

[9]Wilson and Glater, "Prosecutor's Silence," A13.

[10]Ibid.

[11]Thomas and Meadows, "Doubts about Duke," 22.

[12]Wilson and Glater, "Prosecutor's Silence," A13.

[13]William Yardley, "Prosecutor in Duke Case Is Winner in Election," New York Times, late edition, May 3, 2006, A16.

[14]"A Rape Case Turns into an Ethics Case," St. Petersburg (FL) Times, January 2, 2007, 12A.

[15]David Aldridge, "Duke Lacrosse: After the Rape Scandal," Philadelphia Inquirer, City-D edition, March 4, 2008, A1.

[16]Patrik Jonsson, "Legacy of Duke Case: A Rein on Prosecutors?" Christian Science Monitor, September 14, 2007, 3.

[17]Aldridge, "Duke Lacrosse," A1.

[18]Kristen M. Daum, "Lacrosse Players Sue Duke over '06 Rape Case," Newsday, Nassau and Suffolk edition, February 22, 2008, A26.

of the criminal justice process. The offices of the solicitor general, the criminal division of the litigation branch, and the U.S. attorneys in the federal courts are all important representatives of the federal government's interests in prosecuting cases.

SOLICITOR GENERAL In addition to arguing on behalf of the federal government in proceedings before the U.S. Supreme Court, the solicitor general coordinates all the appeals of cases that went against the federal government in the lower courts. The solicitor general's office decides whether a case is important enough to the federal government to merit the time and resources required to file an appeal. The case must have a high degree of policy significance and a reasonable legal argument that will stand a good chance of success before the solicitor general's office will accept the case. The solicitor general also imposes on cases in which the federal government is not a direct participant but has some policy interest.[24] By filing an *amicus curiae* (friend of the court) brief, the position of the government can be argued in court even though neither party requests this information.[25]

DEPARTMENT OF JUSTICE CRIMINAL DIVISION The criminal division of the Justice Department coordinates the prosecution of all federal criminal statutes. It has a wide range of sections that deal with cases as varied as money laundering, terrorism, child exploitation, and obscenity. The criminal division prosecutes cases of national significance such as the Unabomber and the Oklahoma City bombing. Headquartered in Washington, D.C., the criminal division exercises nominal supervision over the U.S. attorneys' offices around the country.

U.S. ATTORNEYS There are 93 U.S. attorneys scattered across the country and other jurisdictions such as Guam, Puerto Rico, and countries that are considered territories of the United States. The U.S. attorneys enjoy wide latitude in deciding which criminal cases to prosecute, as well as in defending the United States in civil suits and in collection of debts owed to the federal government. There are more than 4500 assistant U.S. attorneys, and each jurisdiction handles both complex and simple cases. Some jurisdictions have higher caseloads for certain types of offenses. For example, jurisdictions on the U.S. border with Mexico prosecute more cases that involve drug smuggling or illegal immigration than do jurisdictions in the midwestern United States. Although the U.S. attorneys serve at the pleasure of the president and report to the attorney general, they often owe their jobs to senators or congressional representatives who recommended them for appointment.[26] Furthermore, with so many U.S. attorneys spread across the country, the criminal division of the Department of Justice has difficulty closely supervising them all and directing their discretion.

PROSECUTION IN STATE COURTS   State court systems are highly decentralized, with prosecution responsibility spread over state, county (or district), and local levels. This variety of organizational placements for prosecutors can result in an inefficient, overlapping, and often ineffective maze of responsibility for protecting the public's interests. Lawbreakers in large metropolitan areas might operate simultaneously in several jurisdictions, and prosecutors can be unaware of each other's efforts to bring them to justice. For instance, in the greater Atlanta, Georgia, area, six counties overlap the city limits. This results in competition, rivalries, and obstructions among law enforcement agencies and courts. Savvy attorneys can manipulate gaps between jurisdictions to broker advantageous circumstances for their clients.

Although considerable overlap in duties exists, the following three types of prosecutors are typically found in court systems across the United States.

STATE ATTORNEY GENERAL The state attorney general is the chief legal officer for a state, and the duties of this office are usually delineated in the state constitution. The state attorney general represents the state in legal actions in which the state is a party. In most states, the power of the state attorney general is limited in criminal matters. Because local prosecutors are elected by the citizens of their districts, the state prosecutor can provide only minimal supervision over their work. For the most part, the state attorney general exercises most of the office's power in the civil area of the law. A prime example of how state attorneys general prosecute civil cases on behalf of citizens is the lawsuits against the tobacco industry in the mid-1990s in which several states brought action against the major tobacco corporations.[27]

CHIEF PROSECUTOR The chief prosecutor is the most powerful person in the criminal justice system. Depending on the state, this officer of the court is called the district attorney, the state attorney, or simply the prosecuting officer. This individual is the chief law enforcement officer for the community and sits at the crossroads of the system between the police and the courts. There are more than 2000 chief prosecutors across the country with a combined staff of more than 65,000 assistant prosecutors, investigators, secretaries, and other support staff, such as victim–witness advocates. Because chief prosecutors are elected officers in 95 percent of the districts, they are much attuned to the local political scene.[28]

Working in the office of the chief prosecutor is a very sought-after position by new lawyers. Securing a job as an assistant district attorney has several advantages. First, the job has a salary, and for someone fresh from law school who has not had the opportunity to become established on the local legal scene, this is attractive. Even though some new attorneys can land jobs at large and prestigious law firms, the prosecutor's office carries a certain amount of status. The second reason why the prosecutor's office is attractive is that it affords new attorneys ample opportunity to practice courtroom law. As opposed to working in the research department of some large law firm writing briefs for the firm's partners, the assistant district attorney will soon be in the courtroom exercising a wide range of discretion and gaining valuable experience. The third reason why this is such a prized job for recent graduates is that it provides a high degree of visibility in the legal community. Assistant district attorneys are recruited into large law firms after they have established a name for themselves as effective courtroom warriors. Additionally, after prosecuting a few high-profile cases, some assistant district attorneys opt to enter politics. The exposure gained from this position can be parlayed into a political career. This is especially true in states where judges are elected and the prosecutor can position himself or herself as someone who is tough on crime.

Additional features of the position of chief prosecutor can enhance one's career. A certain amount of patronage is available in regions in which assistant district attorneys are appointed, as well as other support staff. Political parties also like to see one of their own in such a position in the hope that their affairs will not be too closely scrutinized.[29]

LOCAL PROSECUTORS Based at the city or county level, local prosecutors perform a wide range of duties that are concerned with either misdemeanor cases or the preliminary stages of felony cases. These are important actors in the criminal justice system because the vast numbers of cases they handle concern public drunkenness, petty theft, disorderly conduct, and minor assault. Depending on the size of the local jurisdiction, some of these local prosecutors work only part time.

THE PROSECUTOR AT WORK   Prosecutors engage in a variety of activities throughout the day. Much of the work of the prosecutor is invisible to the public, but this invisible work occupies most of the prosecutor's time and, more important, forms the bulk of activities that determine exactly how justice is dispensed in the courthouse. David Neubauer listed five categories of activities that divide the prosecutor's energies:[30]

1. **Fighting.**   Prosecutors must struggle to get a case in shape to take to court and ultimately to trial. The efforts of the law enforcement officer must be scrutinized to determine whether the case files are complete, and more important, whether the officer followed the procedural laws in arresting and interrogating the suspect. The prosecutor plans a legal strategy to present the strongest case possible and to deflect criticism from the defense. The prosecutor must have a good sense of how the judge and jury will react to the case, and must consider the psychological and sociological dynamics of witnesses, defendants, and others affected by the cases. In short, the prosecutor must battle to ensure that the case presented by the state is strong, complete, and coherent and satisfies the public's sense of justice.

2. **Negotiating.**   Only a small number of cases ever go to trial. Most are *plea-bargained*, meaning that the defense attorney and the prosecutor strike a deal for a plea of guilty or no contest in return for a lighter sentence. Plea bargaining has been the subject of much controversy because it appears to the public as though defendants can escape the full responsibility for their actions. We will discuss plea bargaining in greater detail in Chapter 10, but it is prudent to say here that this practice is absolutely vital to the functioning of the criminal justice system. Because so many defendants are guilty of the offenses the police charge them with, it is in their interests, as well as the interests of the state, to settle the case as quickly and as economically as possible. The state simply cannot afford the time and resources required to take every case to a jury trial, and guilty defendants cannot afford to expose themselves to the maximum sentence available under the law. Therefore, a deal is struck in which each party considers the weight of the evidence, the likelihood of a conviction, and the expenses that would be incurred by a trial, and they negotiate a settlement. The prosecutor represents the state and/or the victim in these negotiations and must make several tactical decisions to ensure that the government is getting the best deal possible and that, in a greater sense, justice is being served. Negotiating a plea is an

art, and experienced prosecutors must act like poker players, sometimes revealing their evidence and sometimes attempting to bluff the defense attorney into believing that the state's or victim's case is stronger than it actually is.

3. **Drafting.** It might be the least enjoyable part of being a prosecutor, but the drafting of legal documents is an important function for the workings of the criminal justice system. Prosecutors must be careful to lay a paper trail of their activities to ensure that cases can be upheld on appeal. Prosecutors must also prepare a number of documents that enable other actors in the criminal justice system to perform their duties. For instance, the prosecutor must draft the search warrant, specify what violations of the criminal codes defendants are charged with, and prepare documents that address motions made by the defense. The paperwork can be time consuming, distracting, and a downright pain in the neck, but for the prosecutor it is a vital part of the duties. Improperly prepared paperwork can have extremely negative ramifications that include letting guilty suspects escape justice.

4. **Counseling.** Because the prosecutor occupies such a pivotal position in the criminal justice system, he or she must contend with the emotional and psychological needs of victims, witnesses, law enforcement officers, and other officials who make up the courtroom work group. If a police officer's case is weak, the prosecutor must explain why it cannot be taken to trial, and the officer must be educated on the specific aspects of the law in which the case was inadequate. Victims might want the maximum penalty available under the law imposed on their assailant, but the prosecutors might be restrained by other factors and must counsel the victim on why the plea bargain was the best outcome possible given the circumstances of the case.[31] Additionally, the prosecutor spends a considerable amount of time advising victims, witnesses, and law enforcement officers on how to testify at trial. A poorly prepared witness can be fatal to the state's case, and although the prosecutor will not advise anyone to tell a lie, he or she might advise them to answer the defense attorney's questions as succinctly as possible and not provide extra information that could be used as ammunition against the prosecution's case.[32]

5. **Administering.** The prosecutor's office is a modern bureaucracy and suffers from the same strains as any large organization. Personnel issues include hiring, supervising, and firing assistant attorneys, secretarial staff, and investigators. The prosecutors must also play a large administrative role in keeping the cases moving by making sure victims and witnesses are interviewed, briefed, and available should they be needed to testify. Additionally, the prosecutor's office has to ensure that assistant district attorneys are available and present whenever one of the judges holds court.

Clearly, the prosecutor's work is varied and complex. As the primary representative of the state in the courtroom, the prosecutor must fight for justice and ensure that the interests of the victim, the police, and the public are addressed. Sometimes these demands can become complicated and even conflict. For example, the prosecutor might decide that a case involving a young person charged with assault is relatively minor and that the offender would best benefit from probation and restitution, while the victim of the assault, who lost his or her front teeth, demands that the defendant be incarcerated.

Becoming an assistant district attorney can be a major step in climbing the legal career ladder. In addition to some of the features of the job that we have already mentioned, the chance to argue cases in the courtroom is especially attractive. Because of the large caseloads in many prosecutors' offices, the new district attorney, often fresh out of law school, is thrown into a position of having to exercise considerable discretion, judgment, and power in the people's interest. This "on-the-job training" can be both stimulating and intimidating for a new prosecutor who must quickly learn to swim with the sharks of the legal environment. The quick learners survive by depending on the others in the courtroom work group to educate them on courtroom etiquette, protocol, and formal as well as informal procedures for a particular judge's court.[33]

As with any occupation, certain norms emerge that guide how cases are handled in the courtroom. However, the courtroom work group has some constraints that most organizations lack, constraints that make the work of the prosecutor difficult to learn and negotiate. Although each case must be decided individually, there are shared conceptions about how any one case should be decided. These shared conceptions arise from the history of what happened to similar cases that have been processed by the court in the past.[34] Legal variables such as the seriousness of the offense and the defendant's prior record (if any) are factored into the **disposition.** Additionally, organizational factors of the courtroom, such as the number of cases on the docket, the experience of the defense attorney, the presence or absence of the victim, and the remaining physical capacity of the local jail and the state prison system are all ingredients that affect the shared expectations of the courtroom work group. The assistant district attorney is expected to conform to the norms of the courtroom work group with each case or have a good reason for expending extra time and effort.

What happens when the prosecutor insists on spending too much time and resources on a case? Because those who work in the courtroom work group want to maintain a regular routine in which they get to eat lunch and go home at a reasonable hour, they exert subtle influences on prosecutors who are unwilling or unable to keep the docket moving. The judge may complain about the backlog of cases that develops when the prosecutor is too stingy in the plea bargains offered to defendants. If too many cases require trials, then the court administrator must find courtroom time; the clerk of the court must empanel a jury; the court reporter must be put on standby; and attorneys, especially private attorneys, must juggle other commitments. Everyone understands that trials are sometimes required, but they also understand that there is a going rate by which each case would normally be decided. When a prosecutor violates this well-understood norm, other members of the courtroom work group expect the case to be unique in some way. If it isn't, they complain. Promotions and reputations are gained according to conviction rates and how promptly and efficiently prosecutors dispose of cases; their role as major gatekeepers of the criminal justice process is evaluated by others in the courtroom work group.[35]

The prosecutor's office deals with a wide variety of issues that include not only prosecuting cases in courts but also representing the interests of the state in other areas of the legal community.[36] In large jurisdictions in which the caseload is tremendous, the prosecutor's office is divided into bureaus, special units, and programs that address specific concerns and issues that are problematic for the criminal justice system. For example, the Los Angeles County District Attorney's Office employs more than a thousand deputy district attorneys and hundreds of support personnel in a vast bureaucracy that includes the following programs:[37]

disposition
The final determination of a case or other matter by a court or other judicial entity.

- **Bad-check enforcement program** In addition to obtaining payment from individuals who write bad checks, this program counsels offenders and teaches them how to handle their personal finances. Bad-check writers pay for this program themselves.
- **Hard-core gang unit** This program works with local law enforcement to prosecute gang leaders and investigate serious gang-related crime.
- **Hate crimes unit** Hate crimes are connected to the victim's race, religion, national origin, sexual orientation, gender, or disability. These offenses are given special attention and resources.
- **Insurance fraud** Expert prosecutors and investigators pursue insurance fraud rings that operate massive workers' compensation and automobile scams.
- **Narcotics** A special prosecution unit works with the police to arrest major drug dealers, seize narcotics and dealer assets, and get dealers off the streets.

- **Sex crimes unit**   Rape and other sex offenses are prosecuted by this special program, which also assists victims.
- **A.C.T. (Abolish Chronic Truancy)**   This program places prosecutors in schools to work with students, parents, teachers, and administrators to intervene when juveniles skip school.
- **C.A.P.O.S. (Crimes Against Police Officer Section)**   This unit responds to offenses against police officers and emphasizes prosecuting cases in which officers are killed or injured. Prosecutors are called to the scene of offenses in which officers have been assaulted to ensure that proper procedures are followed so that the case will be upheld in court.
- **Speakers bureau**   This unit provides experts to meet with public groups to explain how the district attorney's office addresses criminal justice system issues. By providing this public education function, the speakers bureau represents the interests of the prosecutor's office at a number of venues in which organizations and the public interact.

These are just some examples of the types of programs that can be found in a large prosecutor's office. This division of labor allows attorneys to specialize in certain types of cases and allows the prosecutor's office to ensure that competent deputy district attorneys are assigned to difficult and complicated areas of the law.

The prosecutor clearly plays an important role in the criminal justice system. As we have previously stated, the prosecutor acts as a gatekeeper in deciding which cases are inserted into the criminal justice system. Additionally, the prosecutor engages in a wide variety of other activities to ensure that the people's interests are considered. In Chapter 10 we will deal in more detail with the prosecutor's role in plea bargaining and sentencing. Now we turn our attention to the prosecutor's adversary, the defense attorney.

The Defense Attorney

The defense attorney is responsible for protecting the interests of the accused and for presenting the case in the best possible light to ensure that the prosecution has adequately proved the charges. In an ideal world, the prosecutor would charge only the truly guilty, and the defense attorney would be successful in winning the cases of only the truly innocent. But alas, the world of the criminal courts is not perfect, and the struggle between the defense and prosecution too often arrives not at justice, but rather, at negotiated settlements that leave everyone feeling dissatisfied.[38]

The image of the defense attorney has two parts. On one hand, this officer of the court might be considered a valiant warrior against the injustice of the powerful and viewed as one of the stalwarts of freedom in our country. On the other hand, the defense attorney might be viewed as a liar, a cheat, and a twister of the truth who will do anything to prevent a guilty client from facing justice.[39] The truth is, of course, somewhere in the middle of these two extremes.[40] (See Focus on Ethics 9.1 for a related scenario.) The defense attorney is an important part of the criminal justice system, and if his or her role did not exist, we would have to invent some mechanism to compensate for its absence. Before we examine the profession of the defense lawyer in detail, let's dispense with the most fundamental and significant issue that surrounds how legal defense is conducted in the United States. Before any intelligent and significant analysis of the defense attorney can be undertaken, we need to examine the effects of money.

Not all defense attorneys are equally competent.[41] A host of variables divide the successful from the unsuccessful, the ethical from the vile, the connected from the disenfranchised, and the one you want to argue for your life from the one you would not even let contest your parking tickets. These variables are the result of such factors as the following:

- The law school the attorney attended
- The law firm the attorney is associated with

9.1   FOCUS on ETHICS

DIFFICULT DECISIONS FOR THE DEFENSE

As a defense attorney you have really grown to dislike your client. He is a liar, a cheat, and a drug dealer and has been accused of killing a police officer. The prosecutor does not know about half the offenses your client has committed and has presented a case that, although convincing to many, has a major flaw that you have detected that could set your client free. You are torn about what to do.

On one hand, you believe not only that your client deserves to go to prison for a long time, but also that your community would be a lot safer if he were taken off the streets. After all, you have a family that you want protected from this type of pathological criminal. On the other hand, you realize that the prosecution's responsibility is to make the case against your client and your obligation is to provide the best defense possible.

Unfortunately, the assistant district attorney has overlooked several pieces of critical evidence that can place your client at the scene of the crime and seal his fate. To complicate matters further, your firm's founding partners have all but assured you that if you can win the case, you will jump over 10 senior associates and be made a partner next year.

What Do You Do?

1. Win the case. Your duty is to represent your client first and foremost. It would be unethical to sabotage the case in any way or to give less than your best effort. Besides, this could be a major turning point in your career and could ensure your family's financial security.

2. Find an anonymous way of tipping the prosecutor off to the critical evidence. This man is too dangerous to be put back on the street, and your family's financial security is meaningless if dangerous offenders such as your client are roaming the streets of your community.

3. Resign from the case. Tell your senior partners that you cannot in good conscience represent such a despicable character. By making this choice, you realize not only that you risk the chance to make partner, but also that you could be fired.

4. What are your other options?

- How long the attorney has worked in a particular jurisdiction
- How many cases the attorney has previously tried before a particular judge
- The attorney's relationship and history with the prosecutor
- Whether the attorney is a private lawyer or a public defender
- Whether the attorney has other cases to settle with this prosecutor in the near future[42]

Given this long, but not exhaustive, list of variables that can influence an attorney's effectiveness, the single most important variable may well be how much money has been invested in getting the best representation possible. Although many reasonably priced private attorneys can provide an excellent defense, assembling the witnesses and legal and technical experts and constructing elaborate exhibits can become extremely expensive, and the client foots the bill for the cost of the defense (see Crosscurrents 9.2).[43]

In 2000, when Baltimore Ravens linebacker Ray Lewis was tried for murder in Atlanta following a Super Bowl party in a nightclub, he was able to provide his defense team with financial resources that most individuals could not muster. When the prosecution produced a witness who claimed he saw Lewis engage in the stabbings, the defense undermined the credibility of the witness by producing evidence of past lies. The hostile witness had been convicted of identity theft and running up exorbitant charges on credit cards. In a dramatic and effective courtroom maneuver, the defense attorney asked the witness if he had ever met the individual whose identity he had stolen and whose financial reputation he had besmirched, and then had that individual stand up in court to demonstrate to the jury that the witness had harmed a real person and not simply some abstraction. The Ray Lewis defense team had been able to fly this person across the country from California to Atlanta for the purpose of standing up in court for a mere 15 seconds to hammer home a point about the trustworthiness of a witness.[44] The average defendant, who is not a multimillionaire football player, would have been unable to finance such a legal tactic. Prosecutors

9.2 CrossCurrents

How Much Justice Can You Afford?

Being accused of breaking the criminal law can be expensive. Even for those who are not indigent, the expense of hiring a lawyer can seem astronomical and can place severe limits on just how effective a defense can be pursued. Lawyers cost money. Just how much money can shock even the most cynical of us.

At the extreme end are the legal fees that resulted from the contingency fees claimed by some private attorneys who represented states in suits against the tobacco industry. According to an editorial in the *Rocky Mountain News*, "In Maryland . . . one attorney claimed his 25 percent fee entitled him to more than $1.1 billion of the state's $4.6 billion settlement. That came out to $30,000 for each hour he claimed to have worked." Of course, criminal defense attorneys do not receive that level of compensation, but even at $100 to $400 an hour, the expense of a full trial with all of its preparation can run into tens of thousands of dollars. Other expenses in addition to attorney's fees could include the following:

- Psychiatric evaluations
- Expert witnesses
- Polygraph tests
- Travel expenses for witnesses
- Expenses associated with the preparation of courtroom visual aids such as diagrams, maps, and charts

Expenses such as these can severely deplete the savings of most people and cause them to go into debt. However, when the client is indigent and has to rely on a public defender, the expenses for the case can quickly become limited. In Bend, Oregon, a defense attorney billed the state $1,500 for plane fare for a witness from England. After interviewing the woman, the attorney decided she would not help the case. After the newspaper reported the story, the attorney paid the expense out of his own pocket. When the cost of a criminal offense soars to more than $100,000, even prosperous individuals have difficulty achieving full justice. When court-appointed public defenders are compensated with as little as $65 per hour, it is understandable that each client is not going to be the beneficiary of an extensive defense.

Finally, what happens when the client runs out of money in the middle of the case or desires an appeal? Defense attorneys have the expenses of maintaining an office and paying secretaries and can afford to do only limited *pro bono* (non-paying) work. The result is that the quality of justice one receives can depend on how deep one's pockets are.

Think About It

1. Should attorneys' fees be capped?
2. Should the state provide the best attorneys available to defendants who cannot afford them?
3. Should all attorneys work for the state? Should they all be private?

Source: "Put Cap on Fees From State Lawsuits," *Rocky Mountain News*, February 17, 2003, http://rockymountainnews.com/drmn/opinion/article/0,1299,DRMN_38_1749940,00.html; Charles E. Beggs, "District Attorneys Question Spending," Associated Press/Worldlink.com, www.theworldlink.com/articles/2003/02/14/news/news03.txt.

---

dropped the murder and aggravated assault charges against Lewis in exchange for his plea of guilty to misdemeanor obstruction of justice charges.

THE DEFENSE ATTORNEY AND THE COURTROOM WORK GROUP   Although the defense attorney's first obligation is to provide the best defense possible for the defendant, this duty does not always result in a full-blown jury trial in which the truth is revealed and justice is done to the satisfaction of all. Despite the defense attorney's commitment to the interests of the accused, other pressures mediate how aggressively the prosecutor's case is challenged.[45]

The attorney who engages in criminal defense work on a regular basis becomes part of the courtroom work group. Although ideally an adversary of the prosecutor, the defense attorney must develop a working relationship with the group to ensure that the group's goals are achieved. The wheels of justice never function smoothly, but the obstinate defense attorney who causes them to grind to a halt by contesting and protesting every routine point of law and procedural ruling will quickly find that the judge, prosecutor, court reporter, and others in the courtroom work group will be less flexible and accommodating in their dealings with that attorney and that attorney's

Football star Ray Lewis could afford a private attorney who was able to secure a dropped murder charge in exchange for a plea bargain. Here, Lewis is led from the courtroom after testifying against his co-defendant.
Source: CORBIS-NY

clients. An informal system of norms and relationships develops in the courtroom work group to efficiently move the docket and dispose of cases in accordance with expected outcomes. The dealings of the courtroom work group are best explained by two classic studies of the court conducted by David Sudnow and Abraham Blumberg.

David Sudnow provided us with his concept of "normal crimes," defined as cases that are considered in the context of how other, similar offenses were handled by the court.[46] Public defenders and prosecutors have a good idea what the sentence will be for a particular offense by considering how that infraction compares to the pattern of sentencing established by the court. For the offender to receive a more severe or a more lenient sentence than the going rate, the circumstances of the offense must be shown to be other than normal. Given this already established norm for sentencing, the public defender often encourages the defendant to plead guilty in return for a reduced sentence. When he or she takes a normal offense to trial, the public defender is looked on by the others in the courtroom work group as wasting the time and resources of the court. Consequently, in the interests of conforming to the expectations of the defense of normal crimes, the public defender acts as a facilitator of the criminal prosecution process rather than a zealous advocate of the defendant. This abdication of the responsibility to protect the offender's interests might seem wrong, but we will see in the next chapter that plea bargaining is a complicated and complex issue. In many ways, the public defender is getting the best possible deal for a client when the case is handled as a normal crime.

Part of the client's difficulty in evaluating the contributions of the defense attorney lies in determining what can be attributed to the attorney's expertise and what can be attributed simply to the normal routine of the courthouse. The attorney may be working hard for the client, doing legal research, negotiating strenuously with the prosecutors, and developing treatment plans with probation officers, but the client has limited knowledge of this. In fact, according to Abraham Blumberg, the dynamics of the courtroom work group aid the defense attorney in erecting a facade of competence even when the attorney is simply "acting" in an effort to impress the client.

Although Blumberg alerts us to some interesting dynamics of how courtrooms actually operate, we should be cautious about becoming too cynical. All organizations have distinctions between what Erving Goffman called *front-stage* and *backstage behavior*, in which participants act one way when they are on public display and another when they are surrounded only by trusted co-workers.[47] Courts are no exception, and

9.1 CASE IN POINT

ARGERSINGER V. HAMLIN

THE CASE	THE POINT
Argersinger v. Hamlin, 407 U.S. 25, 92 S.Ct. 2006 (1972)	*Defendants have the right to an attorney if an offense, regardless of its seriousness, is punishable by incarceration.*

Jon Argersinger, an indigent, was charged in Florida with carrying a concealed weapon. With no attorney present, Argersinger was tried by a judge and sentenced to 90 days in jail. The court did not appoint an attorney for Argersinger, which the state supreme court upheld, holding that the right to court-appointed counsel extended only to offenses punishable by more than six months' imprisonment. The U.S. Supreme Court reversed, holding that the right to counsel extended to defendants into any offense for which imprisonment can be imposed.

SCOTT V. ILLINOIS

THE CASE	THE POINT
Scott v. Illinois, 440 U.S. 367; 99 S.Ct. 1158 (1979)	*States may incarcerate offenders only if they have been represented by counsel; states are not obliged to appoint counsel for offenders who have not been sentenced to incarceration, even if incarceration is a possible punishment.*

Aubrey Scott was convicted of theft by a judge and fined $50, although the maximum penalty was a $500 fine and/or one year in jail. Citing *Argersinger*, Scott appealed, contending that the Sixth and Fourteenth Amendments required the state to provide him with an attorney. The U.S. Supreme Court affirmed the original opinion and clarified *Argersinger*, holding that offenders could be incarcerated only if they had been represented by counsel. As Scott was not sentenced to incarceration, and could not be because he had not been represented by counsel, the state was not obliged to provide him with counsel.

the defense attorney's dramatics performed for the benefit of the defendant do not differ substantially from how judges, prosecutors, or even professors or physicians act when they are attempting to put the best face on their actions. The message of Blumberg's critique is that the defense attorney is subject to organizational pressures from the other members of the court. The defendant needs to understand that although the defense attorney negotiates with the defendant's best interests in mind, sometimes the best interests of the defense attorney differ from those of the defendant.[48]

THE BEST DEFENSE: PRIVATE ATTORNEY OR PUBLIC DEFENDER? There is great variation in the quality of legal defense provided for individuals accused of breaking the law. An attorney's competence might depend on the level of the court, the geographic location, the resources of the client, and the way state and local governments fund indigent defense efforts. We commonly believe that private attorneys are automatically superior to those provided by the state, but in reality the issue is more complicated.[49]

Criminal defense work is not among the most lucrative specializations for private attorneys. In fact, only a few private attorneys can make a living practicing exclusively, or even primarily, criminal defense law. Many attorneys have more comprehensive practices in which they also practice tort law, family law, or business law.[50] Some of the most expensive and best attorneys confine themselves to specialties such as corporate law and seldom set foot in a courtroom. So although a private attorney looks prosperous, and therefore extremely competent, he or she might not be the best one to represent a drug dealer or someone facing a capital charge of homicide.[51]

However, many successful private attorneys are excellent defenders for criminal defendants. Many former prosecutors or public defenders who go into private practice regularly do criminal defense work. In this, they have an advantage in that they have been part of the criminal court's work group in the past and have already established relationships with the prosecutor's office and the judges. Depending on the reputation and experience of the private defense attorney, the cost of representation can be expensive. Because the private defense attorney is being paid by the client, the quality of the services rendered is expected to be superior to what is available from a public defender. Nevertheless, when an attorney is being paid by the hour, there is not a strong incentive to settle the case quickly. In fact, if we can believe Blumberg, the private defense attorney is likely to extend the case in order to charge a wealthy defendant as much money as possible.[52]

Public defenders have a precarious position in the criminal justice system. They are obligated to provide the best defense possible for the defendant, but the government pays their salary. Additionally, because of the large caseloads experienced by many public defender offices, the time and resources available are seldom sufficient to provide the extended defense services that the public defender would like.[53] It is difficult to generalize the work of public defenders because of the variation in how they are structured and financed. Each state has its own system for providing for the defense of indigent clients. (For more on the states' obligation to appoint attorneys for indigent defendants, see Case in Point 9.1.) These systems fall into three broad categories:[54]

ASSIGNED COUNSEL In small jurisdictions with limited resources, the judge may assign a practicing member of the bar to represent defendants who lack the financial means to hire a private lawyer. There are drawbacks to this method of assigning lawyers. A limitation in many jurisdictions is that the judge draws from a pool that consists of lawyers who volunteer.[55] This volunteer pool usually comprises young lawyers developing their courtroom skills or less successful lawyers willing to take the reduced court fee just to make a living. Even in jurisdictions in which all the attorneys are in the selection pool, the defendant might end up with an excellent real estate lawyer who is not familiar with the demands of criminal defense work.

CONTRACT SYSTEMS In a contract system, law firms bid for the business of all indigent defense work. The advantage of this system is that the firm's lawyers quickly become proficient in dealing with the prosecutor and the courtroom work group. Opponents of this system contend that because of the competitive bidding process, the low bidder ends up with a caseload that does not provide enough revenue for the support system of secretaries, investigators, and attorneys that is necessary for a vigorous defense of all cases.

PUBLIC DEFENDER Finally, about 37 percent of the jurisdictions have public defender systems in which a staff of full-time attorneys represents all indigent offenders. As a result of the *Gideon* decision (see Chapter 3), which requires states to provide for the legal defense of impoverished people, the public defender system has been adopted by most of the large jurisdictions and implemented statewide in 17 states. The advantages of having a full-time public defender staff are several. Attorneys who work in public defender offices quickly gain extensive experience working with the criminal law and become seasoned trial lawyers. Many attorneys like having a public defender office because it relieves their own firms of having to do *pro bono* work that drains their resources. Also, because of the permanence of public defender systems, relationships with other personnel in the criminal justice system have been developed so that the attorneys enter cases at an early stage, usually the initial hearing.[56]

The image of the public defender is sometimes cast in a negative light when compared to those of private lawyers. This image is, paradoxically, both accurate and misleading. Certainly, someone with sufficient financial resources can hire a lawyer who is experienced in criminal law and can provide the best legal defense money can buy.[57] However, many indigent offenders also receive excellent representation from competent, experienced, and dedicated public defenders. The successes of the public defender's office are not widely publicized. As Neubauer pointed out,

> The freedom to defend against the state cannot include the freedom to embarrass it. Hence, the complexity of the public defender's institutional role requires that the office not advertise its successes. McIntyre shows that the public defender's office deliberately retains its image of incompetency in order to guarantee its continued existence: Public defenders may practice good law, but they must do so in the darker shadows of repute.[58]

The Judge

Judges occupy a unique space in the criminal justice system. On one hand, they are looked on as the most powerful actors in the system, whose scorn is to be feared and mercy courted. On the other hand, judges are viewed as impotent referees who must act with neutrality, objectivity, and impartiality. They have neither the prosecutor's power of discretion nor the prestige or salary of a successful defense attorney. The term *judge* encompasses a range of responsibilities from the local justice of the peace to a Supreme Court justice (see Criminal Justice Reference 9.2).

Judges perform a wide range of duties in the administration of justice. They act as a check-and-balance to the discretion of zealous prosecutors, as impartial arbiters in the contest between law enforcement and defendants, and as decision makers in applying punishment or treatment to the guilty. Judges have a role to play at many points in the criminal justice system, including the following:

- **Signing search warrants**   Judges ensure that law enforcement officers do not violate suspects' rights against unreasonable searches by reviewing search warrants for evidence of probable cause (see Case in Point 9.2). Although there may be some question as to how adequately some judges actually perform these duties, their role here is to keep the police honest.
- **Informing defendants of charges**   At the initial-appearance stage of the criminal justice system, the judge informs the defendant of the charges that the law enforcement officer has filed.

9.2   CRIMINAL JUSTICE REFERENCE

The Code of Conduct for United States Judges

The Code of Conduct for U.S. judges was initially adopted by the Judicial Conference in 1973. The code applies to U.S. Circuit judges, district judges, court of international trade judges, court of federal claims judges, bankruptcy judges, and magistrate judges. The Tax Court, Court of Appeals for Veterans Claims, and Court of Appeals for the Armed Forces have also adopted this code.

The Code

Canon 1. A judge should uphold the integrity and independence of the judiciary.

Canon 2. A judge should avoid impropriety and the appearance of impropriety in all activities.

Canon 3. A judge should perform the duties of the office impartially and diligently.

Canon 4. A judge may engage in extrajudicial activities to improve the law, the legal system, and the administration of justice.

Canon 5. A judge should regulate extrajudicial activities to minimize the risk of conflict with judicial duties.

Canon 6. A judge should regularly file reports of compensation received for law-related and extrajudicial activities.

Canon 7. A judge should refrain from political activity.

Source: U.S. Courts, Code of Conduct for United States Judges, www.uscourts.gov/guide/v012/ch1.html.

- **Appointing counsel**   For indigent defendants, the judge appoints a defense attorney. In many states, this refers to the public defender who is appointed to that judge's courtroom. But in some jurisdictions, the judge appoints a private attorney whose turn it is to provide indigent defense.

- **Setting bail**   After hearing from the prosecutor who reviews the seriousness of the charges, the defendant's prior criminal history, and the likelihood that the defendant will appear at subsequent hearings, the judge gives the defense attorney an opportunity to rebut. The judge either sets a bail, releases the defendant on recognizance, or orders the defendant confined until trial.

- **Taking a plea**   At the arraignment phase of the process, the judge once again informs the defendant of the charges and allows the defendant to enter a plea of guilty, not guilty, or no contest.

- **Ruling on motions**   The judge rules on motions from the defense and the prosecution concerning the admissibility of evidence. These motions may concern illegal search and seizure issues, the interrogation of suspects without reading them their Miranda rights, or the use of police lineups.

- **Participating in or ruling on plea bargaining**   Some judges take an active role in deciding a plea bargain between the defense and the prosecution. Other judges simply approve or disapprove the negotiated decision.

- **Presiding at trial**   The judge's role in a trial is to ensure that the defendant's due process rights are respected, to rule on the admissibility of evidence, to instruct the jury as to which laws are applicable in the case, and to ensure that all parties, including spectators, conduct themselves properly.

- **Sentencing**   Passing sentence on the guilty is one of the most difficult duties of the judge. Although many cases provide clear-cut choices between incarceration and liberty, the range of options available to most judges is quite limited. Treatment options are scarce, and with prison overcrowding so serious in many states, judges are pressured to find dispositions other than incarceration in secure institutions.

9.2   CASE IN POINT

UNITED STATES V. L`EON

THE CASE	THE POINT
United States v. Leon, 468 U.S. 897, 104 S.Ct. 3405 (1984)	Evidence may be admitted if the fault for a bad warrant rests with the court and not with the police.

Police officers in Burbank, California, obtained search warrants for three residences and a number of cars owned by Alberto Leon, who was suspected of selling illegal drugs. The police seized large amounts of drug evidence, and Leon went to trial. Leon's defense argued that the poor quality of the information obtained by the police to initiate their investigation made for inadequate probable cause, thus invalidating their warrants. They argued that because the warrants were therefore invalid, the evidence against Leon should be excluded from the trial.

The state agreed that there were problems with probable cause, but it argued that the police had acted on the warrants in good faith and were unaware that the warrants were invalid. Both the district court and the California Supreme Court agreed, and the state appealed to the U.S. Supreme Court. The Supreme Court agreed that the warrants were invalid, but asserted that because the police had acted in good faith, the evidence against Leon should not be excluded.

In this case, the Supreme Court enacted a "good-faith" exception to the exclusionary rule, in which evidence may be admitted if the fault for a bad warrant rests with the court and not with the police. The exclusionary rule is designed to protect defendants against police mistakes, not judicial mistakes.

These duties illustrate the broad range of the role of the judge. In addition, there are other requirements of the job such as court administration, ceremonial duties, and, in some cases, campaigning for reelection. Because the roles of the judge are so varied, it is interesting to examine what types of individuals aspire to this job and what qualifications are required.

JUDICIAL SELECTION   What sorts of people become judges? Is it a job to which the best and the brightest aspire? Is the process of selecting judges adequate to weed out the incompetent, lazy, and intemperate in favor of the fair and wise? The answer to these questions is, It depends. It depends on which level of government we are considering. It depends on which level of judgeship we are discussing. And it depends on which selection method is used. More important than the selection method, however, is the question of whether any method produces better judges than other methods. After briefly reviewing the roads to a judgeship, we will address this issue.

EXECUTIVE APPOINTMENTS   At the federal level, judges are nominated by the president and confirmed by the Senate according to their advise-and-consent responsibility as stated in the Constitution. For the most part, this has been a routine rubber stamp of the president's wishes, but recently it has become quite politicized.[59] Controversial cases are subjected to lengthy Senate hearings (sometimes televised) in which the nominee is grilled by senators about his or her character, legal history, and views on certain controversial issues that will likely come before the courts. For example, abortion rights are often referred to as a "litmus test" in which the nominee's views will be ascertained. Perhaps the most spectacular of these hearings occurred when Clarence Thomas was nominated, and a former subordinate, Anita Hill, accused him of sexual harassment. Although the Senate eventually confirmed him and placed him on the Supreme Court, Thomas likened the experience to a "high-tech lynching." Such controversial hearings are uncomfortable for the president's party (and obviously for the nominee also).

A good deal of screening takes place to find candidates who reflect the worldview of the president, yet who are not controversial. The American Bar Association (see Criminal Justice Reference 9.3) plays a role in the selection process by ranking the candidates "exceptionally well qualified," "well qualified," "qualified," or "unquali-

9.3   CRIMINAL JUSTICE REFERENCE

American Bar Association

Founded in 1878 in Saratoga Springs, New York, the American Bar Association (ABA) is the world's largest voluntary professional organization. Currently, the ABA is based in Chicago, Illinois, and is operated as a private, not-for-profit corporation. With more than 400,000 members, the association represents about half of all the lawyers in the United States. Any practicing lawyer in good standing with a state or territory bar can join the ABA.

The ABA is governed by a president, a 39-member board of governors, and a 530-member house of delegates. Among other duties, the ABA accredits law schools and provides a variety of programs for lawyers and judges. The association states that its mission is "to be the national representative of the legal profession, serving the public and the profession by promoting justice, professional excellence and respect for the law."

In 1995 the United States sued the ABA for violating antitrust laws. The United States accused the association of using accreditation to elevate the salaries of law school faculty members by withholding accreditation from schools that would not meet a national salary average for its faculty. In settling the case, the ABA, among other concessions, agreed that it would no longer use compensation data in its accreditation process. The association currently accredits about 200 law schools in the United States and Puerto Rico.

Source: American Bar Association, www.abanet.org; *U.S.* v. *American Bar Association*, U.S. Department of Justice, Antitrust Case Filings, Antitrust Division, www.usdoj.gov/atr/cases/americ1.htm.

Supreme Court judges are nominated by the president and confirmed by the Senate. Occasionally this process can become contentious, such as when President George W. Bush nominated White House counsel and personal adviser Harriet Miers in 2005 to replace retiring justice Sandra Day O'Connor. According to the White House, Miers withdrew from the nomination over concerns that senators wanted records of discussions between the president and Miers.
Source: *Mandel Ngan / Getty Images, Inc.—Agence France Presse*

fied." For U.S. district court judges, the senators of the state in which the appointment is to be made are commonly consulted as a courtesy. If the senator finds the nominee unacceptable, senators from other states (particularly those in the same party) might vote against appointment. In this way, senators have both a formal and informal influence on the selection of judges in their state. At the state level, the legislature has no comparable advise-and-consent function, so governors have more leeway in the selection of judges. At both levels, the influence of party politics is significant.[60] See Criminal Justice Reference 9.4 for the ABA's guidelines for reviewing candidates for state judicial office.

ELECTION OF JUDGES In an effort to democratize judicial selection, nearly half of the states elect judges. It is assumed that judges who must stand for reelection will conform to the wishes of the people rather than the dictates of the elite.[61] For the most part, the campaigns for judgeships are of low visibility, and voters have little knowledge about the qualifications or temperament of the candidates. For this reason, incumbent judges have a distinct advantage over challengers especially when the title *Judge* is printed next to their names on the ballot. Some elections are hotly contested, especially state supreme court seats, where decisions can affect laws concerning insurance issues. Trial lawyers vie with insurance companies by channeling money into the campaigns of judges who will protect their interests.[62]

MERIT SELECTION In an effort to remove politics from the judicial selection process, court reformers have adopted a system called "merit selection," or, as it is sometimes known, the **Missouri Bar Plan.** In this type of selection process, a judicial nominating commission made up of lawyers and laypeople presents a short list of qualified candidates (usually three) to the governor, who makes the final decision. Judges are then required to face the voters after a short period of time (one year). Instead of running against another candidate, the vote is simply on whether the judge should be retained in office. Judges must stand for such reelection each term, but they are seldom removed because they essentially have no opponents and the voters seldom know of reasons why they should be removed.[63]

Each of the different methods of selecting judges has its merits. When judges are elected, they are considered more accountable to the voters and more likely to represent the interests of the average citizen rather than the elite of the legal profession. This admirable philosophy is pitted against the alternative of the appointment of judges, where, presumably free from catering to the voters, the judge can enjoy judicial independence and rule on the merits of the case. Some evidence supports the idea that the type of selection method influences the decisions of judges.[64] However, in terms of personal background characteristics there is little difference:

> From a broader perspective, methods of judicial selection have only marginal influence on the type of lawyers who become judges. Whether elected by the

Missouri Bar Plan

A judicial nominating commission presents a list of candidates to the governor, who decides on a candidate. After a year in office, voters decide on whether to retain the judge. Judges must run for such re-election each term. Also called merit selection.

9.4   CRIMINAL JUSTICE REFERENCE

American Bar Association Guidelines for Reviewing Qualifications of Candidates for State Judicial Office

These guidelines describe the minimum criteria for the evaluation of candidates for state and local judicial offices.

1. *Integrity.* A candidate should be of undisputed integrity.
2. *Legal Knowledge and Ability.* A candidate should possess a high degree of knowledge of established legal principles and procedures and have a high degree of ability to interpret and apply them to specific factual situations.
3. *Professional Experience.* A candidate should be a licensed, experienced lawyer.
4. *Judicial Temperament.* A candidate should possess a judicial temperament, which includes common sense, compassion,

decisiveness, firmness, humility, open-mindedness, patience, tact and understanding.

5. *Diligence.* A candidate should be diligent and punctual.
6. *Health.* A candidate should be in good physical and mental health.
7. *Financial Responsibility.* A candidate should be financially responsible.
8. *Public Service.* Consideration should be given to a candidate's previous public service activities.

Source: American Bar Association, "Guidelines for Reviewing Qualifications of Candidates for State Judicial Office," State of Nebraska Judicial Branch, www.supremecourt.ne.gov/commissions/aba-manual.shtml.

voters, appointed by the governor, or selected through merit plans, state judges are more alike than different. In terms of personal background characteristics such as prior political experience, ties to the local community, political party affiliation, and quality of legal education, the systems do not appear to produce very different types of judges.[65]

Perhaps the most important and notable change in the judicial selection process is the increase in the number of women and minorities appointed to the bench. The profile of the judge as a white male is being radically changed without affecting the other background characteristics such as judicial education. As more women go to law school and work their way up the ranks of prosecutors' offices and law firms, more of them are being elected or appointed as judges. To a large extent, the same can be said for minorities, but because of the underrepresentation of black lawyers, there are fewer black judges. In states in which judges are appointed, more minorities are on the bench than in states in which judges are elected.[66]

Defendants, Victims, and Witnesses

Those working in the criminal courts—judges, prosecutors, defense attorneys, bailiffs, clerks, and sheriff's deputies—learn the language, rituals, and protocols that dictate the pace and atmosphere of the court's daily routine.[67] These professionals must deal with civilians who are not knowledgeable about how the law is applied and how the courtroom works. Defendants, victims, and witnesses bring varying degrees of experience to the court and often leave with a sense of confusion, injustice, and bewilderment. It is useful to consider how each of these parties views the workings of the criminal court.

DEFENDANTS   Those who find themselves before a criminal court on felony charges are often the least able to understand the workings of the institution and feel powerless to affect the outcome of their case. Felony defendants are overwhelmingly male, young, poor, undereducated, and members of racial minorities.[68] Unless they are repeat offenders (and many are), they have little idea about what is happening to them as they are processed through the system. Many are illiterate and cannot comprehend even the simplest instructions or help their attorney prepare a defense.[69] Too many defendants come to court with problems that the criminal justice system is ill equipped to handle, such as drug addiction, mental illness, lack of education, or marital problems. Those who cannot secure bail before their appearance are attired in handcuffs, a jail jumpsuit, and slippers, which have the effect of stigmatizing them even further.[70] The middle-class worldview of those in the courtroom work group is unsympathetic to the plight of those whose fates are being decided. The entire ritual of the courtroom serves to intimidate the defendant and impress on him or her the gravity of the situation. It is little wonder that many who experience "their day in court" often come away with a feeling of injustice and alienation.[71]

VICTIMS   Perhaps the only ones more disillusioned by the workings and results of the criminal court than the defendants are the victims.[72] Because the charge of a felony pits the defendant against the state, the role of the victim is sometimes diminished. Especially when cases are plea-bargained, the victim's interests might be slighted. Victims see their particular case as being very serious and can become disillusioned when it is treated in the routine and bureaucratic manner that is the norm of the court.[73] Victims are perplexed when, in lieu of a trial, in which they expect to explain how they were injured by the behavior of the defendant, the prosecutor informs them that the case was settled with a disposition of probation rather than a long prison term. Many victims feel anger when they see defendants enjoying due-process rights while their voices remain unheard.[74]

WITNESSES   Those who witness crime or have other relevant testimony have less attachment to the case than does the defendant or victim. Witnesses have an important role to play, however, and they often experience frustration in dealing with the court. Being required to travel to the court to provide testimony and finding the case postponed or having to wait long periods in uncomfortable hallways can cause a good deal of distress for witnesses. Additionally, the loss of wages for time spent at court or having property that is kept for long periods of time as evidence can cause additional frustration. Perhaps the most stressful aspect of being a witness is the fear of retaliation from a defendant and the sense that criminal justice personnel are indifferent to the danger one feels.[75]

VICTIM–WITNESS PROGRAMS   The criminal justice system is not completely indifferent to the plight of victims and witnesses. Many jurisdictions have established victim–witness assistance programs to encourage cooperation in criminal cases and alleviate some of the inconvenience of appearing in court. Reducing the suffering caused by the offense and anticipating the confusion and frustration of dealing with the criminal justice system are the objectives of victim–witness programs.[76] Because each victim has different needs, programs are designed to provide a wide range of services, including the following:[77]

- **Crisis intervention**   Crime is a traumatic event for most victims. Especially in cases of violent crime, the victims and their families might need assistance in dealing with transportation to the hospital or court, notifying relatives, procuring money to buy meals after a robbery, and understanding how and when the criminal justice system will handle the case.

- **Follow-up counseling**   The traumatic nature of offenses such as sexual assault may require ongoing counseling until the case is brought to court and, in some cases, long afterward. Counseling services might be provided by victim–witness staff or by referral to a psychologist. Some programs have established support groups to help victims deal with the effects of crime.

- **Personal advocacy**   Often, the victim is too traumatized to effectively plead his or her side of the case to the police, prosecutor, judge, or others. The victim–witness staff member asserts the victim's interests in the repeated telling of the effect of the offense on the victim. Victims can grow tired of pleading their woes and might feel that others perceive them as whining. A professional staff member, however, can advocate for the victim's best interests.

- **Employer and landlord intervention**   Victimization can have far-reaching and long-lasting effects. If the offense was committed in a workplace or rental residence, the employer or landlord might see getting rid of the victim as a solution to future violence. The victim–witness staff member can intervene to convince the employer or landlord that the victim is just that, the *victim*, and that it would be morally unethical to fire or evict the victim.

- **Property return**   In cases of theft or armed robbery, the victim's stolen property can be used by the criminal justice system as evidence. Often the property is kept for long periods as the case winds through the court process. The victim–witness staff member can sometimes expedite the return of the property to the victim when the state has concluded the case.

- **Intimidation protection**   Victims and witnesses can be subject to intimidation from offenders or their families and friends. Sitting outside a courtroom waiting to testify can be frightening for the victim when the offender, who is out on bail, or the offender's family member is pestering him or her to drop the charge. Additionally, the defense attorney might give unsolicited advice to victims or witnesses that could border on intimidation.[78] The victim–witness staff member can act as a buffer for victims and witnesses and protect them from embarrassment or intimidation.

- **Referral**   The victim–witness staff member is knowledgeable about the community resources available to the victim. Often the trauma of the offense creates problems such as excessive drinking that can be helped with counseling. The victim–witness staff member can provide a referral.

- **Court orientation**   For many victims and witnesses, their case represents the first time they have had to go to a courthouse. Seemingly insignificant issues such as parking, finding the correct courtroom, and even what to wear are likely to be the subjects of questions for the uninitiated. Victim–witness staff members can answer questions and help prepare those who will be called to testify.

- **Court transportation and escort**   Victims and witnesses sometimes need transportation to the courthouse and support during the proceedings. The assistance of victim–witness program staff members might be deciding factors in getting them to court and avoiding a case dismissal.

- **Public education and legislative advocacy**   Victim–witness staff members speak to service organizations such as the Kiwanis, Rotary Club, and Chamber of Commerce to garner support for their programs and to educate the public on how the courts use victim–witness support services. Staff members may also talk to legislators about financial resources and to generate laws that support the roles of victims and witnesses in criminal proceedings.

Victim–witness programs provide a wide range of services to those who must help the criminal justice system by testifying in criminal trials. Unfortunately, the level of services provided varies widely across the country, especially between large urban courts and smaller ones. There is no mandate for the state or federal government to provide these services. Although everyone may agree that victim–witness programs are beneficial, they are not required in the way that legal counsel for indigent offenders is. In lean budget years, victim–witness programs are one of the "frills" that courts can cut to save money.

PRETRIAL RELEASE DECISIONS

The criminal justice system is not like a fast-food restaurant to which one can drive up and get instant justice. The process takes time, often a long time. Suspects may be kept in jail if they are dangerous, or released and told to come back to court when the system is ready to consider their case.[79] The court must somehow decide which option is appropriate for each suspect. The pretrial release decision is one of the most important crossroads of the criminal justice system. If innocent people are jailed for months before their cases are heard, then they are being punished unjustly, and if dangerous offenders are released, then they might continue to murder, rape, and rob.[80] Complicating this pretrial release decision is the overcrowded condition of many of the nation's jails. Courts have developed several types of systems for making this decision that attempt to ensure that the defendant will appear. These systems all involve some sort of bail-bond alternative:

- **Cash bond** The judge sets a bail of a certain amount of money the defendant must give to the court in exchange for release pending trial. If the defendant shows up for the court proceedings, then the entire amount is refunded. This cash bond ensures that the defendant will come back to prevent losing the money. However, if the bail is too low or the offense is really serious with a severe punishment likely, the defendant might flee anyway or "skip bail." The court then issues a warrant for the defendant's arrest, and the defendant is picked up and forfeits the bail. The Eighth Amendment says that "excessive bail shall not be required," but it is still difficult for many defendants to gather a large amount of cash in a short period.[81] Beginning in 1998, pretrial releases that required bail became more common than nonfinancial releases, such as release on recognizance. Defendants on financial release were more likely than those released on recognizance to appear in court.[82]

- **Property bond** By using a piece of property as collateral, defendants can avoid liquidating their assets to raise a cash bond. Property bond favors the well-off who have equity in property. Defendants who fail to appear before the court forfeit their property.

- **Release on recognizance (ROR)** The judge may release a defendant based on a promise to return to court. This is done for those accused of minor offenses and those who have ties to the community. ROR programs evaluate defendants on how long they have lived in the community, how long they have been employed, whether they have family nearby, and other factors in an effort to determine whether they are likely to flee.[83] A South American drug lord who has no local address would not be likely to be granted ROR.

- **Bail bond or surety bond** The most common method for securing bail is to use a bail agent. A *bail agent* is someone who promises to pay the defendant's

Bail is indispensable to the practice of pretrial release. This Bronx, New York, bail bond office is only a block from the courthouse.
Source: Joel Gordon / Joel Gordon
Photography

bail if he or she fails to appear for further court proceedings.[84] In exchange for the promise, the defendant pays the bail agent 10 percent of the bail as a fee and may put up some collateral. Thus, if the bail is $10,000, the bail agent makes $1000. The bail agent does not give the court the bail at that time, but must pay if the defendant fails to appear. The bail agent may then hire a bail enforcement agent (or "bounty hunter") to find the defendant and bring him or

9.3 CrossCurrents

Bounty Hunters: A Step Ahead of the Law

Bail enforcement agents, better known as bounty hunters, carry a mysterious and somewhat romantic reputation. Generally, the profession is poorly understood, which is not surprising. Bounty hunters do a dangerous job: tracking down and bringing in bail jumpers, while operating outside the boundaries of regular law enforcement.

Most states have few or no regulations governing bounty hunters. Thanks to an 1872 Supreme Court ruling in *Taylor* v. *Taintor*, bounty hunters enjoy more leeway than the police. Suspects who sign a contract with a bail bondsman are considered to be in the custody of the bail bondsman and, by extension, the bounty hunter. Therefore, bounty hunters are legally considered to be acting by private contract rather than enforcing government laws. Because of this extralegal status, bounty hunters are far more successful in bringing in fugitives than are law enforcement personnel. Many bounty hunters are private investigators, former police officers, or former soldiers. However, in most states, anyone can operate as a bounty hunter, free of training requirements or background checks.

This system sometimes leads to tragedy. On Christmas Eve 2002, in Richmond, Virginia, a bounty hunter looking for a fugitive broke into the wrong home and shot and killed a man unconnected with the case. Although the bounty hunter was charged with second-degree murder, breaking into what he thought was a suspect's home was not illegal. Agents in Virginia may enter a fugitive's residence without a search warrant and are not required to announce themselves before doing so. In a 1997 incident, Martin Tong of Kansas City, Missouri, was shot three times in his apartment by two bounty hunters who thought he was a fugitive. The bounty hunters had the correct address, but the man they were looking for had moved out of the apartment six months earlier, and it had since been leased to Tong.

The most recent federal attempt to regulate the profession was in 1999 with the Bounty Hunter Responsibility Act. More states are now pursuing or have enacted legislation to regulate bounty hunters.

State Bail Enforcement Agent Requirements

License Required	Restrictions	Few or No Restrictions
Arizona	Arkansas	Alabama
California	Colorado	Alaska
Connecticut	Delaware	Hawaii
Indiana	District of Columbia	Idaho
Iowa	Florida	Kansas
Louisiana	Georgia	Maine
Mississippi	Illinois	Maryland
Nevada	Kentucky	Massachusetts
New York	New Hampshire	Michigan
South Dakota	North Carolina	Minnesota
Texas	Ohio	Missouri
Utah	Oklahoma	Montana
West Virginia	Oregon	Nebraska
	South Carolina	New Jersey
	Tennessee	New Mexico
	Washington	North Dakota
	Wisconsin	Pennsylvania
		Rhode Island
		Vermont
		Virginia
		Wyoming

Source: American Bail Coalition Compendium of State Bounty Hunter Laws, www.americanbailcoalition.com/new_html/compendium.htm.

Think About It

1. Should bail enforcement agents be outlawed? Should they be given even more powers? Are they a "necessary evil"?
2. Would you consider working as a bail enforcement agent?
3. If you were a police officer, what view would you take of bail enforcement agents?

Source: Timothy Dwyer, "Working Justice System's Wild Side: Clients Who 'Skip' Keep Fairfax City Bail Bond Company on the Run," *Washington Post*, February 5, 2003, www.washingtonpost.com/ac2/wp-dyn?pagename=article&node=&contentId=A26920–2003Feb4; Susana Vera, "Bounty Hunters," Missouri Digital News, February 10, 1997, www.mdn.org/1997/STORIES/HUNTER.HTM.

her back to court (see Crosscurrents 9.3). If a bail agent thinks the defendant is likely to flee, the agent may revoke the bond and surrender the defendant to law enforcement.

Pretrial release is a controversial issue. It must balance two strongly held values: presumption of innocence and preventive detention. On one hand, we believe that someone should not be incarcerated until he or she has been found guilty by a court of law. However, given the nature of the criminal justice system and the inevitable delays caused by a crowded docket and constitutional guarantees of due process, both the guilty and the innocent could spend months in jail before a trial.[85] If the defendant is found guilty and sentenced to incarceration, the period of time spent in jail awaiting trial is credited toward the sentence. Sometimes the sentence is simply "time served," in which case the defendant is released having, in effect, served the sentence before the sentence was pronounced. In cases in which the defendant is acquitted or the charges dropped, the period spent in jail waiting for the courts to process the case is time lost. The defendant, who has suffered the pains of being detained, may feel a sense of injustice.

The issue of presumption of innocence must be weighed against the responsibility of the state to protect society by keeping truly dangerous people off the street while the court considers their cases. For example, in 2002 there was a case in the nation's capital in which two males, an adult and a juvenile, were arrested on suspicion of shooting and killing several people with a high-powered rifle. In the "D.C. sniper case," the court refused to grant any type of pretrial release because there was a reasonable fear that one of three bad things could happen.[86] First, because of the seriousness of the offenses, there was a fear that the defendants would attempt to flee the jurisdiction. Second, there was a reasonable concern that the defendants were still dangerous and could harm more people. Finally, because of the terror caused by the shootings, it was feared that the defendants might be injured or killed by irate individuals. In fact, these concerns are so pronounced in such cases that those who are awaiting trial on murder charges that carry the death penalty are not allowed bail.

As of 2004, murder defendants, as well as those charged with rape, robbery, burglary, and motor vehicle theft, were the least likely to be released (see Figure 9-1 for a look at the release rates of violent defendants versus other types of defendants). Other statuses affecting release were prior arrests, convictions, or currently serving probation or on parole. Defendants charged with fraud were the most likely to be released.[87]

There will always be a tension between the ideal of "innocent until proven guilty" and the need to protect society from potentially dangerous people. Law enforcement officers must meet high standards to place someone under arrest, so there is good reason to look carefully at putting the suspect back on the streets before the resolution

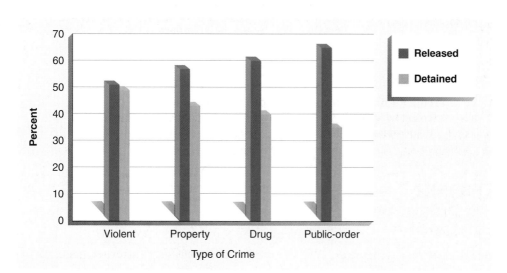

Figure 9-1   Percentage of Felony Defendants Released before and Detained until Case Disposition in the 75 Largest U.S. Counties, by Offense Type, 2004

Source: Sourcebook of Criminal Justice Statistics Online, Table 5.54.2004, www.albany.edu/sourcebook/pdf/t5542004.pdf.

of the case. In some cases, it is absolutely clear that the defendant is dangerous. In other cases it is not so clear, and law enforcement officials must make a judgment as to whether the suspect can be safely set free before trial. As the criminal justice system struggles with this balancing act, the possibility of class, racial, and gender bias must always be kept in mind.[88] Are impoverished black males being held in preventive detention because they pose a threat, or because of a stereotype held by those making the release decision?

SUMMARY

1. The *courtroom work group* refers to those who work in the courthouse. A great deal of cooperation is inherent in the daily routine of the court.

2. The pivotal position in the criminal court is that of the prosecutor. The prosecutor acts as a gatekeeper in deciding which cases are inserted into the system and which cases are dismissed.

3. At the top of the federal hierarchy of prosecution is the Department of Justice, or Justice Department. Three offices of the Justice Department affect the prosecutorial aspect of the criminal justice process: the offices of the solicitor general, the criminal division of the litigation branch, and the U.S. attorneys in the federal courts.

4. State court systems are decentralized, with prosecution responsibility distributed across state, county (or district), and local levels.

5. Three types of prosecutors are typically found in state court systems: the state attorney general, the chief prosecutor, and local prosecutors. The state prosecutor is the primary representative of the state in the courtroom.

6. According to David Neubauer, the prosecutor's workload can be categorized into the following:

fighting, negotiating, drafting, counseling, and administering.

7. The defense attorney is responsible for protecting the interests of the accused and ensuring that the prosecution has adequately proved the charges.

8. Each state has its own system for providing for the defense of indigent clients. These fall into three broad categories: assigned counsel, contract systems, and public defenders.

9. Judges act as a check-and-balance to the discretion of prosecutors, as impartial arbiters in the contest between law enforcement and defendants, and as decision makers in applying punishment or treatment to the guilty.

10. Because defendants, victims, and witnesses are unfamiliar with how the court works, they often find the courtrooms alienating. Many jurisdictions have therefore established victim–witness assistance programs to encourage cooperation in criminal cases.

11. The pretrial release decision is an important crossroads in the criminal justice system. Courts have developed several systems to help ensure the defendant's appearance: cash bond, property bond, release on recognizance (ROR), and bail agents.

KEY TERMS

bail agent 296
child advocate 296
clerk of the court 296

court administrator 296
court reporter 296
disposition 303

going rate 295
Missouri Bar Plan 313

REVIEW QUESTIONS

1. What is the "going rate"?
2. Who else can be found in courtrooms besides judges, attorneys, plaintiffs, and defendants?

3. Why is the prosecutor so powerful?
4. What else does the federal attorney general's office do besides prosecute criminal cases?

5. Do the U.S. attorneys have jurisdictions in only the 50 states?

6. What is the "invisible work" that occupies most of a prosecutor's time?

7. What are the two views the public has of defense attorneys?

8. Describe the three systems for providing legal defenses for indigent defendants.

9. What services might a victim–witness program provide?

10. Describe the systems that courts have for ensuring the appearance of a defendant.

SUGGESTED FURTHER READING

Baker, Mark. *D.A.: Prosecutors in Their Own Words*. New York: Simon & Schuster, 1999.

Bogira, Steve. *Courtroom 302: A Year Behind the Scenes in an American Criminal Courthouse*. New York: Vintage Books, 2006.

Davis, Angela J. *Arbitrary Justice: The Power of the American Prosecutor*. New York: Oxford University Press, 2007.

Feige, David. *Indefensible: One Lawyer's Journey into the Inferno of American Justice*. Boston: Little, Brown, 2006.

Suthers, John W. *No Higher Calling, No Greater Responsibility: A Prosecutor Makes His Case*. New York: Fulcrum, 2008.

Walker, Samuel. *Taming the System: The Control of Discretion in Criminal Justice, 1950–1990*. New York: Oxford University Press, 1993.

ENDNOTES

1. Josh Bowers, "Punishing the Innocent," *University of Pennsylvania Law Review* 156 (May 1, 2008): 1117.

2. Máximo Langer, "Rethinking Plea Bargaining: The Practice and Reform of Prosecutorial Adjudication in American Criminal Procedure," *American Journal of Criminal Law* 33 (July 2006): 223–299.

3. Kathryn Fahnestock and Maurice Geiger, "We All Get Along Here: Case Flow in Rural Courts," *Judicature* 76 (1993): 258–263.

4. Abraham S. Blumberg, "The Practice of Law as a Confidence Game," *Law and Society Review*, June 1, 1967, 15–39.

5. David Sudnow, "Normal Crimes: Sociological Features of the Penal Code in a Public Defender Office," *Social Problems* 12 (1965): 209–215.

6. "Review Cites 8 Steps to Boost Court Security," Crime Control Digest, March 24, 2006, 4.

7. N. Gary Holten and Lawson L. Lamar, *The Criminal Courts: Structures, Personnel, and Processes* (New York: McGraw-Hill, 1991), 109–110.

8. Stacey Laskin, "Dramatic Drop in Court Reporters Causes Alarm," *National Law Journal*, July 23, 2007, 6.

9. Ibid., 111–112.

10. John Rosecrance, "Maintaining the Myth of Individualized Justice: Probation Presentence Reports," *Justice Quarterly* 5 (1988): 235–256.

11. Gary A. Rabe and Dean J. Champion, *Criminal Courts: Structure, Process, and Issues* (Upper Saddle River, NJ: Prentice Hall, 2002). Chapter 7 has an excellent review of pretrial procedures.

12. Jennifer Eno Louden et al., "Supervising Probationers with Mental Disorder: How Do Agencies Respond to Violations?" *Criminal Justice and Behavior* 35 (July 1, 2008): 832.

13. Ronald Burns, Patrick Kinkade, and Matthew C. Leone, "Bounty Hunters: A Look behind the Hype," *Policing* 28 (January 1, 2005): 118–138.

14. Patricia Resick, "The Trauma of Rape and the Criminal Justice System," *Justice System Journal* 9 (1984): 52–61.

15. Robert Davis and Barbara Smith, "The Effects of Victim Impact Statements on Sentencing Decisions: A Test in an Urban Setting," *Justice Quarterly* 11 (1994): 453–469.

16. Ira Schwartz, *Justice for Juveniles: Rethinking the Best Interests of the Child* (New York: Lexington Books, 1989).

17. Erika Gebo, Nena F. Stracuzzi, and Valerie Hurst, "Juvenile Justice Reform and the Courtroom Workgroup: Issues of Perception and Workload," *Journal of Criminal Justice* 34 (July 1, 2006): 425–433.

18. William McDonald, "The Prosecutors' Domain," in *The Prosecutor*, ed. William McDonald (Newbury Park, CA: Sage, 1979).

19. Alissa Pollitz Worden, "Policymaking by Prosecutors: The Uses of Discretion in Regulating Plea Bargaining," *Judicature* 73 (1990): 335–340.

20. Talia Fisher, "The Boundaries of Plea Bargaining: Negotiating the Standard of Proof," *Journal of Criminal Law and Criminology* 97 (July 1, 2007): 943–1007.

21. *Brady* v. *Maryland*, 373 U.S. 83 (1963).

22. Bennett L. Gershman, "Why Prosecutors Misbehave," in *Courts and Justice: A Reader*, 2nd ed., eds. G. Larry Mays and Peter R. Gregware (Long Grove, IL: Waveland Press, 1999), 282–292.

23. Griffin Bell, "Appointing United States Attorneys," *Journal of Law and Politics* 9 (1993): 247–256.

24. Rebecca Sudokar, *The Solicitor General: The Politics of Law* (Philadelphia: Temple University Press, 1992).

25. Jeffrey Segal, "Amicus Curiae Briefs by the Solicitor General During the Warren and Burger Courts: A Research Note," *Western Political Quarterly* 41 (1988): 135–144.

26. Bell, "Appointing United States Attorneys."

27. "Key Events in State Suits against Tobacco Industry," CNN, November 16, 1998, www.cnn.com/US/9811/16/tobacco.timeline/

28. David W. Neubauer, *America's Courts and the Criminal Justice System*, 7th ed. (Belmont, CA: Wadsworth, 2002).

29. Ibid.

30. Ibid.

31. Michael Booth, "Victim Need Not Be Told of Plea Bargain," *National Law Journal*, July 16, 2007, 15.

32. Resa Baldas, "Hot-Button Words Are Iced in Court," *National Law Journal*, June 16, 2008, 1.

33. David Heilbroner, *Rough Justice: Days and Nights of a Young D.A.* (New York: Pantheon, 1990).

34. Sudnow, "Normal Crimes."

35. Pamela Utz, "Two Models of Prosecutorial Professionalism," in *The Prosecutor*, ed. William McDonald (Newbury Park, CA: Sage, 1979).

36. Joan Jacoby, *The Prosecutors' Charging Decision: A Policy Perspective* (Washington, DC: U.S. Department of Justice, 1977).

37. Los Angeles County District Attorney's Office, Office Overview, http://da.co.la.ca.us/oview.htm

38. David Lynch, "The Impropriety of Plea Agreements: A Tale of Two Counties," *Law and Social Inquiry* 19 (1994): 115–136.

39. William J. Price, "Make Sense of Your Client's Story," *Trial*, June 1, 2008, 66.

40. Rodney Uphoff, "The Criminal Defense Lawyer: Zealous Advocate, Double Agent or Beleaguered Dealer?" *Criminal Law Bulletin* 28 (1992): 419–456.

41. Stephen Bright, "Counsel for the Poor: The Death Sentence Not for the Worst Crime, but for the Worst Lawyer," *Yale Law Journal* 103 (1994): 1835–1884.

42. Michael J. McWilliams, "The Erosion of Indigent Rights: Excessive Caseloads Resulting in Ineffective

Counsel for Poor," *American Bar Association Journal* 79 (1993): 8.

43. Larry J. Cohen, Patricia P. Sample, and Robert E. Crew Jr., "Assigned Counsel versus Public Defender Systems in Virginia," in *The Defense Counsel*, ed. William F. McDonald (Beverly Hills, CA: Sage, 1983).

44. Laura Barandes, "Prosecutions Call Last Witness in Super Bowl Party Murder Trial," Court TV Online, June 7, 2000, www.courttv.com/archive/trials/raylewis/060700_ctv.html

45. Jerome Skolnick, "Social Control in the Adversary System," *Journal of Conflict Resolution* 11 (1967): 52–70.

46. Sudnow, "Normal Crimes."

47. Erving Goffman, *The Presentation of Self in Everyday Life* (Garden City, NY: Doubleday Anchor Books, 1959).

48. Brian Sullivan, "Canning Your Client," *ABA Journal* 94 (March 1, 2008): 46–52.

49. Roger Hanson, William Hewitt, and Brian Ostrom, "Are the Critical Indigent Defense Counsel Correct?" *State Court Journal* (Summer 1992): 20–29.

50. Carroll Seron, *The Business of Practicing Law: The Work Lives of Solo and Small-Firm Attorneys* (Philadelphia: Temple University Press, 1996).

51. Bright, "Counsel for the Poor."

52. Blumberg, "Practice of Law." "The real key to understanding the role of a defense counsel in a criminal case is to be found in the area of the fixing of the fee to be charged and its collection. The problem of fixing and collecting the fee tends to influence to a significant degree the criminal court process itself, and not just the relationship between the lawyer and his client" (p. 24).

53. McWilliams, "Erosion of Indigent Rights."

54. Alissa Pollitz Worden, "Privatizing Due Process: Issues in the Comparison of Assigned Counsel, Public Defender, and Contracted Indigent Defense Systems," *Justice Systems Journal* 14 (1991): 390–418.

55. Gail S. Goodman et al., "A Comparison of Types of Attorney Representation for Children in California Juvenile Court Dependency Cases," *Child Abuse and Neglect* 32 (April 1, 2008): 497.

56. Neubauer, *America's Courts*, 179–182.

57. Arye Rattner, Hagit Turjeman, and Gideon Fishman, "Public versus Private Defense: Can Money Buy Justice?" *Journal of Criminal Justice* 36 (March 1, 2008): 43.

58. Neubauer, *America's Courts*, 183.

59. Sheldon Goldman and Elliot Slotnick, "Clinton's Second Term Judiciary: Picking Judges under Fire," *Judicature* 82 (1999): 264–285.

60. Terry B. Friedman, "The Politicization of the Judiciary," *Judicature* 82 (July 1, 1998): 6–7.

61. Paul Brace and Brent D. Boyea, "State Public Opinion, the Death Penalty, and the Practice of Electing Judges:[1]," *American Journal of Political Science* 52 (April 1, 2008): 360–372.

62. Philip Dubois, *From Ballot to Bench: Judicial Elections and the Quest for Accountability* (Austin: University of Texas Press, 1980).

63. Richard Watson and Ronald Downing, *The Politics of the Bench and the Bar: Judicial Selection under the Missouri Nonpartisan Court Plan* (New York: Wiley, 1969).

64. Daniel Pinello, *The Impact of Judicial-Selection Method of State-Supreme-Court Policy: Innovation, Reaction, and Atrophy* (Westport, CT: Greenwood Press, 1995).

65. Neubauer, *America's Courts*, 202.

66. Ibid., 205.

67. Fahnestock and Geiger, "We All Get Along."

68. Marvin Free, *African Americans and the Criminal Justice System* (New York: Garland, 1997).

69. Arthur Rosett and Donald R. Cressey, *Justice by Consent: Plea Bargains in the American Courthouse* (New York: Lippincott, 1976).

70. John Irwin, *The Jail: Managing the Underclass in American Society* (Berkeley: University of California Press, 1985).

71. J. Dyer, *The Perpetual Incarceration Machine: How America Profits from Crime* (Boulder, CO: Westview, 1999).

72. Andrew Karnsen, *Crime Victims: An Introduction to Victimology*, 4th ed. (Belmont, CA: Wadsworth, 2001).

73. Emma Schwartz, "Giving Crime Victims More of Their Say: A Federal Law Has Created Tensions in the Legal System," *U.S. News & World Report*, December 24, 2007, 28.

74. Candace McCoy, *Politics and Plea Bargaining: Victims' Rights in California* (Philadelphia: University of Pennsylvania Press, 1993).

75. Kerry Healey, *Victim and Witness Intimidation: New Developments and Emerging Responses* (Washington, DC: National Institute of Justice, 1995).

76. Peter Finn and Beverley Lee, *Establishing and Expanding Victim-Witness Assistance Programs* (Washington, DC: National Institute of Justice, 1988).

77. William G. Doerner and Steven P. Lab, *Victimology* (Cincinnati, OH: Anderson, 1995), 53–54.

78. Elizabeth Connick and Robert Davis, "Examining the Problems of Witness Intimidation," *Judicature* 66 (1983): 438–447.

79. John Goldkamp, "Danger and Detention: A Second Generation of Bail Reform," *Journal of Criminal Law and Criminology* 76 (1985): 1–74.

80. Michael Corrado, "Punishment and the Wild Beast of Prey: The Problems of Preventive Detention," *Journal of Criminal Law and Criminology* 86 (1996): 778–814.

81. Michael J. Eason, "Eighth Amendment—Pretrial Detention: What Will Become of the Innocent?" *Journal of Criminal Law and Criminology* 78 (1988): 1048–1049.

82. Thomas H. Cohen and Brian A. Reaves, *Pretrial Release of Felony Defendants in State Courts* (Washington, DC: US Department of Justice, Bureau of Justice Statistics, 2007), 1, www.ojp.usdoj.gov/bjs/pub/pdf/prfdsc.pdf

83. Tim Bynum, "Release on Recognizance: Substantive or Superficial Reform?" *Criminology* 20 (1982): 67–82.

84. Mary Toborg, "Bail Bondsmen and Criminal Courts," *Justice System Journal* 8 (1983): 141–156.

85. Keith Hansen, "When Worlds Collide: The Constitutional Politics of *United States v. Salerno*," *American Journal of Criminal Law* 14 (1987): 155–225.

86. Robert Nagel, "The Myth of the General Right to Bail," *Public Interest* 98 (1990): 4–97.

87. Cohen and Reaves, *Pretrial Release of Felony Defendants*, 1.

88. Stephen Demuth, "Racial and Ethnic Differences in Pretrial Release Decisions and Outcomes: A Comparison of Hispanic, Black, and White Felony Arrestees," *Criminology* 41 (August 1, 2003): 873–907.

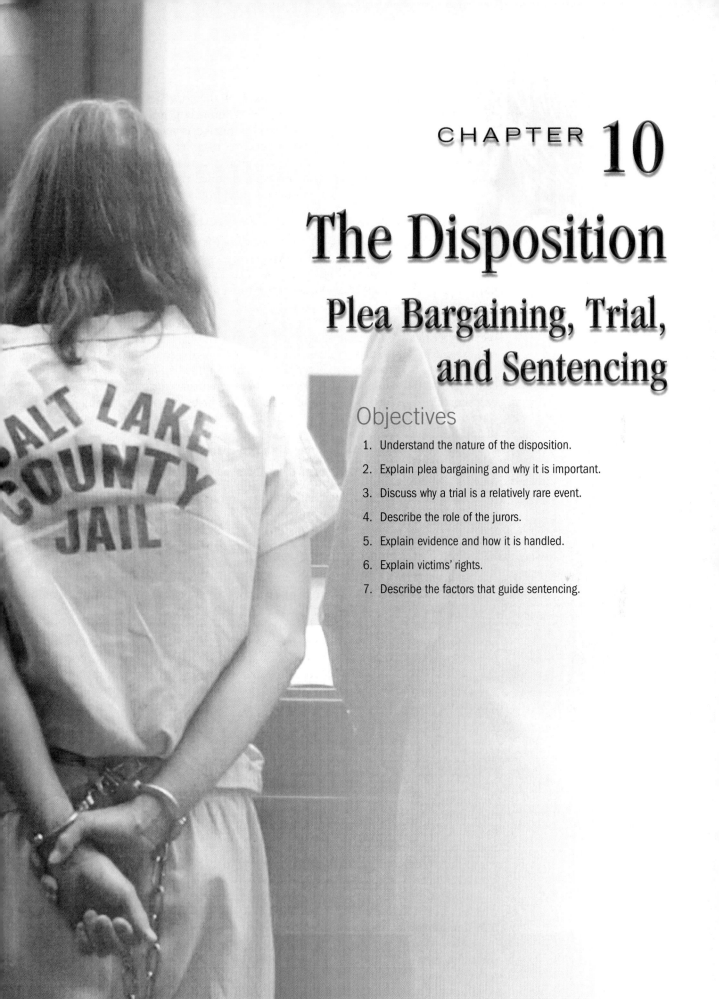

CHAPTER 10

The Disposition
Plea Bargaining, Trial, and Sentencing

Objectives

1. Understand the nature of the disposition.

2. Explain plea bargaining and why it is important.

3. Discuss why a trial is a relatively rare event.

4. Describe the role of the jurors.

5. Explain evidence and how it is handled.

6. Explain victims' rights.

7. Describe the factors that guide sentencing.

In the previous two chapters, we studied how the courts evolved and the rules of the various actors in the courtroom. The criminal courts also have several important decision points that determine how justice is meted out. These decision points are plea bargaining, trial, and sentencing. In order to fully appreciate how defendants proceed through the courts to acquittal or conviction, it is useful to consider the effect of each of these decision points on criminal cases.

The most dramatic and sensational decision point in the criminal justice system is the passing of the sentence. Rather like Judgment Day in the biblical sense, the passing of the sentence is considered the result of a deliberation process in which the evidence of the offense, the harm done to society (or other people), and the character of the defendant are weighed, and a sentence prescribing a punishment is announced.

The road to the disposition of a case is rocky and uncertain. Unlike the image presented by the media, the actions of the court are ponderous and fickle and often seem unfair. Defendants (even co-defendants) with identical charges, with similar prior records, appearing before the same judge, and with equal culpability might receive drastically different sentences.[1] Furthermore, sentencing disparity among judges, courts, states, or regions of the country all elicit a sense that justice is not uniform.[2] The luck of the draw in determining which judge handles a case or which prosecutor is assigned can mean the difference between incarceration or probation, a long or a short prison sentence, even life or death. It is little wonder that many people are wary of the criminal justice system when they see such vast disparities in the outcomes of apparently similar cases.[3]

This chapter will examine some of the mechanisms that the criminal justice system employs as part of its quest for justice. In part, we will argue that much of the process that many find so objectionable is required by law or is the inevitable result of funding limitations and political necessity. In turn, we look at the dynamics of the **plea bargain,** the process of the criminal trial, the concept of defendants' and victims' rights, and finally some of the broader issues concerned with sentencing patterns. In looking at these issues, we will come to appreciate how justice is determined in the criminal court. Despite the fact that reforms are desired and needed, they are difficult to enact because of the complicated and interdependent nature of the criminal justice system. Inserting a reform in one part of the system will have ramifications and unanticipated consequences in other parts of the system. For instance, enacting the popular notion that every offender should serve every day of every sentence would have a profound and negative effect on the prison system. There simply is not enough prison space to accommodate all the offenders serving all their time.[4] Consequently, the criminal justice system, particularly the courts, must prioritize how the precious resource of prison beds is allocated. This process of arriving at the sentence, therefore, is fraught with difficulties and dissension. Nowhere are these issues more blatant than in the practice of plea bargaining.[5]

PLEA BARGAINING

Plea bargaining is one of the features of the criminal justice system that most upsets the public. The prospect of an offender escaping the full measure of punishment flies in the face of many citizens' sense of justice.[6] Yet plea bargaining has become an essential feature of the criminal justice system.[7] If every defendant demanded a jury trial, the system would quickly grind to a halt under the oppressive weight of the caseload. Defendants' right to a speedy trial would become impossible to accommodate, and the state would spend vast amounts of money on obviously guilty defendants whose cases could otherwise be quickly disposed of. Additionally, without the reduced punishments inherent in the plea-bargaining process, the sentences meted out by judges would swamp the correctional system. In many ways, plea bargaining, in which the defendants plead guilty or *nolo contendere* (no contest) in exchange for a lighter sentence, benefits both sides.[8] Nevertheless, politicians are constantly calling to eliminate

plea bargain

A compromise reached by the defendant, the defendant's attorney, and the prosecutor in which the defendant agrees to plead guilty or no contest in return for a reduction of the charges' severity, dismissal of some charges, further information about the offense or about others involved in it, or the prosecutor's agreement to recommend a desired sentence.

The public defender explains to three defendants what rights the defendants give up if they enter into a plea bargain.

Source: Mikael Karlsson/Arresting Images

plea bargaining.[9] Law enforcement officials, victims of crime, and the public all consider plea bargaining as thwarting justice.[10]

Not all plea bargains are the same. A prosecutor might decide that one type of bargain serves the ends of justice better than another, and the defendant might reluctantly accept one type while really desiring an alternative. Although cases are negotiated in numerous ways, the following represents a useful way to differentiate among the types of plea-bargaining arrangements.[11]

1. **Vertical plea.**   This is perhaps the most advantageous plea for the defendant. By pleading guilty or *nolo contendere* to a lesser included charge, the defendant can reduce the potential for a harsh sentence. For instance, a homicide charge can be pleaded vertically downward to a manslaughter charge, thereby avoiding a potential death sentence and/or a longer prison term. The prosecutor might decide that the case does not have a sufficient quality of evidence to support a capital conviction and that a manslaughter plea would be better than an acquittal. Additionally, many drug cases are pleaded down to misdemeanors, which saves the offender from having a felony conviction on his or her record.

2. **Horizontal plea.**   In this case, the defendant pleads guilty to a charge in exchange for other charges being dropped. It is not unusual for a burglar to be charged with multiple counts of breaking and entering and to plead to one count in order to have the others dropped. The defendant is then vulnerable to the full penalty that one charge carries. In many cases, this arrangement is advantageous to the state because the judge might have passed concurrent sentences for the multiple charges.

3. **Reduced-sentence plea.**   The prosecutor and defense attorney, in consultation with the judge, might decide on a reduced sentence. For instance, if the charge carries a maximum five-year prison sentence, the agreement might be for a three-year sentence. This way, the defendant is assured of a specific less-than-maximum sentence, and the prosecutor gets a conviction without having to go to trial.

4. **Avoidance-of-stigma plea.**   One form of stigma is a legal stigma.[12] Several types of convictions do an extra measure of damage to a defendant's chances of receiving a light sentence. For instance, several states have "habitual offender" or "three-strikes-and-you're-out" statutes that carry mandatory severe penalties.[13]

Those convicted of relatively minor felonies sometimes find themselves facing life in prison because of offenses committed many years ago that also resulted in felony convictions. If the defendant's attorney is not successful in getting the charge reduced, the judge has no discretion in the case and must sentence the defendant according to the habitual-offender guidelines. This is a form of vertical plea, but because of the mandatory nature of these laws, the defendant has an extra incentive. Another type of avoidance-of-stigma plea concerns those facing sex-offense charges. Being adjudicated a sex offender can have long-term ramifications for the defendant even after the sentence has been served.[14] Conviction of a sex offense may lead to a defendant's identity being published in a public sex-offender database.

Plea bargaining is not concerned with determining guilt or innocence (see Focus on Ethics 10.1). Rather, it allows the defendant and the prosecution to efficiently determine the amount of punishment without the expense of a jury trial. Although this practice initially benefits both sides, plea bargaining is criticized from a number of quarters. Some view plea bargaining as being lenient on crime, whereas others see it as a weapon the prosecution can use to circumvent the defendant's rights.[15] In practice, highly disparate results are obtained by plea bargaining. Individuals in similar circumstances might receive widely varying punishments, as the proportionality of punishment to offense can become distorted by overcharging, draconian legislation, and political expediency. In practice, often no bargaining occurs because the prosecutor is in the position of the landlord with the only vacant apartment in town—"accept my terms or forget it." Increasingly, the prosecutor wields the sledgehammer with, for example, habitual-offender laws carrying life terms for relatively minor offenses.[16]

We would be remiss in our discussion of plea bargaining if we did not examine this in the larger context of the criminal justice system.[17] Plea bargaining affects the entire system. Diverse pressure (sometimes overt, sometimes subtle) is applied to the courts

---

10.1 FOCUS on ETHICS

LETTING THE BIG ONES GET AWAY

As an assistant prosecutor, you are under orders from the chief to rack up drug prosecutions to help make his reputation as a drug warrior in his campaign to run for Congress. You have been successful in putting several large-scale drug dealers behind bars, and you are in line for a promotion based on your high-profile success. In fact, when the total number of years for offenders' sentences is added up, your record is tied with your only competitor for the promotion. One of your current cases promises to vault you ahead if you can secure a reasonable plea bargain from the defense attorney.

Here's the problem: The drug dealer you have in your sights is a crafty and connected criminal. He has been charged before with several offenses and has always been able to squirm out of the clutches of the law. This time he has been caught with a kilo of cocaine at his girlfriend's house, and you have a perfect case if only she will testify against him. Because love makes fools of us all, she refuses to testify. She is pregnant with his child and does not want him to go to prison. His high-priced defense attorney comes to you with a deal. If you drop the charges against him, the drug dealer will testify that the cocaine belongs to his girlfriend. Because the girlfriend has had

shoplifting and bad-check convictions from several years ago, the state's mandatory minimum sentence statute will kick in, and you will be able to send her to prison for a 40-year term.

You really want to nail the drug dealer instead of the girlfriend, but she refuses to cooperate. She does not believe you when you tell her that her boyfriend has offered to roll over on her, and because the cocaine did not belong to her, she naively believes that she will not be prosecuted. Your chief prosecutor just wants a big conviction, and this one would ensure your promotion.

What Do You Do?

1. Teach her the most painful lesson of her life. Prosecute her for the cocaine and send her to prison for 40 years.
2. Dismiss the charges on both of them.
3. Explain your problem to the judge and ask her to try to talk some sense into the girlfriend.
4. Think of another creative way to try to bring justice to this case.

by both law enforcement agencies, who want their collars to serve prison time, and correctional administrators, whose institutions are already filled to capacity. Added to these outside pressures are the dynamics of the courtroom work group, which has established patterns of plea bargaining. Finally, the peculiarities of the case dictate just how wide a range of discretion can be applied. David Neubauer listed three fundamental issues that guide the practice of plea bargaining:[18]

1. **Presumption of factual guilt.**   By the time a case gets to the trial stage of the criminal justice system, its merits have been reviewed a number of times, and it has been deemed to be a legitimate arrest with a good chance of a conviction. In other words, most cases that get to this stage have a defendant who is guilty of some charge. The police officer believed there was reason to arrest; the prosecutor believed the case to be strong enough for a formal charge, and the judge in the preliminary hearing deemed that sufficient reason existed to move the case forward. Therefore, prosecutors and defense attorneys negotiate which level of offense the defendant will be charged with, what kind of evidence the state can produce, the nature of the victim, and the character of the defendant. There is little doubt, in most cases, that the defendant is actually guilty.

2. **Costs and risks of trial.**   Failing to successfully negotiate a plea is risky and costly for all involved. Trials can last days for simple cases and months for more complicated ones. During this time, the judge, clerk, bailiffs, prosecutor, public defender or private defense attorney, victim(s), and witnesses are all tied to the courtroom and cannot deal with the other pressing demands of their jobs. Because trials cost money for everyone concerned, given the scarcity of courtroom time, only a few cases are actually subjected to this legal process. Another reason why plea bargains are considered preferable to trials is risk: the prosecutor risks an acquittal in which a guilty defendant might go free; the defendant risks getting a more severe sentence if convicted; and the defense attorney risks damage to his or her reputation if a guilty verdict is returned. A plea bargain can leave everyone partially unsatisfied, but losing a trial involves bigger stakes and is to be avoided if possible.[19]

3. **What to do with the guilty.**   Plea bargaining increases the discretion of the prosecutor in crafting a sentence appropriate to the offender. If a case goes to trial, the defense attorney and the prosecutor lose their ability to influence the disposition. The willingness of an offender to enter a drug treatment program or to do community service can give the prosecutor justification in the plea-bargaining process to consider a full range of alternatives to incarceration. If the case goes to trial and the defendant is convicted, the courtroom work group presumes that the judge will select a more punitive disposition than would have been negotiated between the prosecutor and the defense attorney.

Other Benefits of Plea Bargaining

In addition to the previously mentioned reasons why a defendant may find it desirable to plea-bargain, there is the prospect of being allowed to enter a plea of *nolo contendere*, which translated from Latin means "I will not contest." In many ways, this is equivalent to entering a guilty plea in that the defendant waives the right to a jury trial and will be sentenced as though there had been a determination of guilt.[20] However, there are important differences between the *nolo contendere* plea and the guilty finding.

In many jurisdictions, the court allows the offender to enter a *nolo contendere* plea and holds the actual sentence in abeyance while the offender completes some type of diversion program, pays restitution, performs community service, or engages in some other court-ordered activity. Once this activity is successfully completed, the court drops the criminal charges, and the offender escapes the criminal justice system without a criminal record. This type of plea negotiation is used extensively with young offenders who commit relatively minor offenses. It allows the defendant to avoid the negative stigma of a criminal conviction and the frequent extralegal punishments of being denied access to schools or jobs.

Another benefit of being allowed to plead *nolo contendere* is that, unlike a guilty determination, this plea does not affect future civil court proceedings. If a defendant pleads guilty and/or is convicted, he or she has little leverage to contest a civil case. For example, if a defendant was involved in an accident while driving under the influence of alcohol and pleaded *nolo contendere* to the criminal charge, this plea could not be used as an admission of guilt by someone who may have been injured in that accident. The civil court case would need additional evidence such as witnesses or blood alcohol tests to determine culpability.

Should Plea Bargaining Be Abolished?

Although most practitioners in the criminal justice system realize that plea bargaining is an efficient and necessary process, the public is widely opposed to this practice. Many believe that offenders are cheating justice and obtaining less punishment than they deserve. Occasionally there are efforts to abolish plea bargaining and to require each case to be decided on its merits. Such efforts are usually short-lived; when plea bargaining is prohibited, a number of unintended consequences arise.[21]

- The first and most drastic result of eliminating plea bargaining is the increase in the number of cases that defense attorneys are willing to take to trial. When no consideration is allowed for a guilty plea, then there is no incentive for the defendant to waive the right to a jury trial. He or she might as well take a chance on acquittal before a jury if the sentence is going to be the same anyway.[22]

- Another consequence of abolishing plea bargaining is that the discretion inherent in the process is moved to another part of the criminal justice system, where it might not be as visible and thus subject to increased abuse or corruption. David Neubauer likened the criminal justice system to a hydraulic process in which efforts to control discretion at one stage cause it to be displaced to another stage. For instance, abolishing plea bargaining in a higher court could simply result in discretion being shifted to the charging decision made by the prosecutor at the preliminary hearing in the lower court.[23] Victims, witnesses, and the public have less opportunity to comprehend how the system is arriving at its dispositions, and consequently, may become even more disillusioned with the process.

- Finally, attempts to abolish plea bargaining may simply squeeze the prosecutor out of the process.[24] Defense attorneys can always attempt to negotiate directly with the judge to secure the best deal for the defendant. Judges faced with an increased caseload and under pressure to keep the docket moving are approachable by defense attorneys who can offer relief. One of the roles of prosecutors in the criminal justice system is to protect the interests of society. When they are excluded from the plea-bargaining process, they have more difficulty ensuring that all cases are being considered equally.

As students of the criminal justice system, we should realize that the law on the books and the law that is practiced in the courthouse are different. Although we tend to think that the criminal trial is the main activity of the court system, in reality, plea bargaining is responsible for deciding the disposition of most cases.[25] In many ways, plea bargaining is considered a "necessary evil" that leaves all involved without complete satisfaction. However, as courts are faced with caseloads that outstrip their resources, plea bargaining becomes a useful way of negotiating justice.

However, calls for plea-bargaining reform should not go unheard.[26] Opening the process to victims, law enforcement officers, and others who are affected by the sentence can make plea bargaining a more acceptable tool.[27] Plea bargaining is not going to go away. The challenge is to harness its potential to settle cases in a way that gives voice to all concerned.

THE TRIAL

A trial of a criminal defendant is actually a rare event. Because most cases are settled in the plea-bargaining process, only a few special cases actually end up in a jury trial. The question is, which ones are they? Certainly we would expect innocent defendants to assert their right to a trial. Also, sometimes the prosecution's deal is not favorable to the defendant, and the decision is made to roll the dice and go for "all or nothing." In any event, the trial, although rare, is an extremely pivotal point in the process because cases that fail to reach a plea bargain set the parameters for how justice is negotiated by the courtroom work group.

Trials follow a specific format that is dictated by law, custom, and the administrative procedures established by the federal government and the various states. In general, the trial process is conducted in the following steps:

1. Indictment
2. Defendant's plea
3. Prosecution opening statement
4. Defense opening statement
5. Witnesses and evidence presented
6. Defense closing arguments
7. Prosecution closing arguments
8. Judge's instructions to jurors about procedures
9. Judge's instructions to jurors about verdicts
10. Final verdict
11. Defendant released if acquitted or sentenced if convicted

The Pretrial Phase

Most cases never make it to a jury trial. A number of things must happen for a case to proceed through the system, and cases can be diverted at several points in the process, including the pretrial phase.[28]

- **Filing of charges**   Law enforcement agencies present information about the case and the suspect to the prosecutor, who decides whether formal charges will be filed. The suspect must be released if no charges are filed. A prosecutor can also decide to drop the charges later by entering a *nolle prosequi* (Latin for "we shall no longer prosecute"). A *nolle prosequi* must be made after charges are filed but before a plea is entered or a verdict returned. Usually, prosecutors must ask a judge's permission to enter a *nolle prosequi*.

- **Initial appearance**   The judge or magistrate informs the accused of the charges and decides whether there is probable cause for further detention, such as the suspect being considered dangerous or likely to flee. Although a pretrial release decision can be made at this point, it also may occur at other hearings or may be changed further along the process. If the offense is minor, the determination of the suspect's guilt and penalty, if required, can also occur at this point. For serious offenses, the suspect is asked whether he or she has retained counsel (a lawyer); if the accused is indigent, defense counsel is also assigned.

- **Grand jury**   This jury hears the prosecutor's evidence against the accused and decides whether it is sufficient to bring the accused to trial. If the grand jury

indictment

A written statement of the facts of the offense that is charged against the accused.

information

A formal, written accusation against a defendant submitted to the court by a prosecutor.

finds the evidence sufficient, it sends an **indictment** to the court. This system also works backward, in a sense. Instead of starting with a suspect and deciding whether to indict, a grand jury may be called to investigate possible criminal activity. If probable cause is found, the grand jury issues an indictment, called a *grand jury original*, naming the suspects. Police then try to apprehend and arrest the suspects named in the grand jury original. These investigations often target large, complex drug and conspiracy cases.

- **Indictments and informations** Some jurisdictions require grand jury indictments for felony cases. However, an accused may waive the indictment and accept service of an **information** instead. Misdemeanor cases may also proceed by the issuance of an information. Basically, an information may be used when a defendant has waived an indictment or when the offense is punishable by one year or less in prison.[29]

- **Arraignment** After an indictment or information has been filed with the trial court, the accused is scheduled for arraignment. There, the accused is informed of the charges, advised of his or her rights, and asked to enter a plea. Sometimes the prosecutor and the defendant negotiate a plea bargain, in which the defendant pleads guilty.

- **The plea** If the accused pleads guilty or *nolo contendere*, the judge either accepts or rejects the plea. No trial is held if the plea is accepted; the offender is sentenced either at this proceeding or at a later hearing. If the plea is rejected, the case proceeds to trial. For example, a guilty or *nolo* plea would go to trial if the judge believes that the accused is being coerced. If the accused enters a not-guilty plea, a date is set for the trial or the accused may request a bench trial (discussed later).

PRETRIAL MOTIONS Before the opening statement of the prosecution and the defense, each side may file pretrial motions that seek to gain the most favorable circumstances for their side and to limit the evidence the other side can present. Often the case is won or lost based on how the judge rules on the pretrial motions. Some of the more frequent motions include the following:

- **Motion for dismissal of charges** The defense may ask that the case be dismissed because the prosecution has failed to present a sufficient case that has all the elements necessary to charge the defendant with the offense or because the case has some critical weaknesses. This can happen at the beginning of the trial or at any point along the way. Often, this motion is presented after the prosecution presents its case.

- **Motion for continuance** This motion delays the trial. Often the defense or prosecution needs more time to prepare the case or to interview newly discovered witnesses. The defense is more likely to be granted such a continuance because the prosecution has an obligation to provide for a speedy trial.

- **Motion for discovery** The defense has a right to obtain documents and a list of witnesses that the prosecution plans to call.

- **Motion for severance of defendants** When more than one defendant is charged, each has his or her own defense attorney who might wish to separate the cases so that each defendant has his or her own trial. This is often done when a conflict of interest exists in which one defendant is more culpable than the other, or when the testimony of one defendant may incriminate others.

- **Motion for severance of offenses** Defendants charged with several offenses may ask to be tried separately on all or some of the charges. The judge usually makes this decision.

- **Motion for the suppression of evidence** The defense will attempt to prevent incriminating evidence from being presented in the trial. If the evidence was gathered illegally or a confession coerced by the police, the judge may rule it inadmissible (see Crosscurrents 10.1). The defense may raise a number of due-process issues that could result in motions to suppress evidence.

- **Motion to determine competency**   The defense can request that the judge rule that the defendant is not competent to stand trial. A defendant who cannot assist in the defense and does not understand the purpose and process of the proceedings might be mentally ill or mentally retarded. Often the court will order that a psychiatrist examine the defendant.

- **Motion for change of venue**   In offenses that draw a good deal of media coverage, the defense might claim that finding an impartial jury would be impossible. The court can move the case to another jurisdiction where those in the jury pool would not have heard about the case. Of course, offenses that receive national coverage make it impossible to find a jury pool anywhere in the country that has not been exposed to the case.

The prosecution or the defense can present other types of motions, but the preceding list illustrates how motions can be used to swing the advantage to a defendant.

10.1   *CrossCurrents*

Evidence That Can't Be Used: The Exclusionary Rule

When a defendant is set free because of a legal technicality, the exclusionary rule might be the reason. Although the exclusionary rule dictates that the police must follow procedural law when gathering evidence, the issue is decided in the courts. The prosecutor is prohibited from using evidence that was illegally obtained. The Supreme Court adopted the rule for three reasons:

1. If the courts used evidence that was illegally gathered, they would be participating in this violation of the defendant's rights. The rule of law must be respected in the courts if we are to have confidence in the quality of justice.

2. The exclusionary law deters law enforcement officers from attempting to break the law. If they know that their evidence will be thrown out of court, they are less likely to try to circumvent procedural laws.

3. The alternatives to the exclusionary rule are not feasible. Although a defendant might try to sue a law enforcement officer in civil court for damages stemming from police misconduct, this is a cumbersome and expensive process that is unlikely to have the desired effect of encouraging the police to play by the rules.

The exclusionary rule covers three types of evidence: the identification of suspects, confessions in which the Miranda rules apply, and searches in which the Fourth Amendment states that "the right of the people to be secure in their persons, houses, papers, and effects against unreasonable search and seizure, shall not be violated." The law allows for the suppression of evidence that violates the exclusionary rule. This is accomplished when the defense attorney files a suppression motion if the defendant was identified in a police lineup that was conducted improperly, gave a confession as a result of police misconduct, or was subjected to an illegal search.

The exclusionary rule is a controversial issue in the criminal justice system. To many people, it seems ludicrous to equate the offenses of the defendant with the mistakes made by law enforcement officers when they gather the evidence. The court has allowed some narrow exceptions when the police make mistakes in "good faith." Proposals to eliminate the exclusionary rule have included doing away with the Miranda warning requirement.

Think About It

1. Is the exclusionary rule a necessary check on overzealous law enforcement officers?
2. Do criminals enjoy too many rights and an unfair advantage because of the exclusionary rule?
3. In what ways might the exclusionary rule be modified so that defendants enjoy their constitutional rights but law enforcement officers are allowed to make reasonable mistakes without having their cases thrown out of court?

These motions set the tone and the limits of the trial and are extremely important even though they do not occupy a position of high visibility in the process.

Opening Arguments

The prosecution is the first to make an opening argument, with the goal of presenting the defendant as the most likely perpetrator. The prosecution will tell why it believes that the defendant is guilty. Actual evidence will not be presented at this time, but the prosecution will outline the case and alert the jury to the types of evidence that will be forthcoming. The goal of the opening statement is to convince the jury that the case against the defendant is strong and that the prosecution can be trusted to ensure that justice is being pressed in the name of the people. The defense attorney then gets a chance to counter the outline of the case presented by the prosecution. Again, evidence is not presented, but the defense attorney attempts to put a more favorable spin on the prosecution's arguments and also assure the jury that once it has seen all the evidence and heard all the facts, it will want to acquit the defendant on all charges.

Presentation of Witnesses and Evidence

The prosecution begins the presentation of the case by introducing evidence and witnesses. The goal is to carefully and fully explain the defendant's motive for breaking the law and his or her capability for carrying out the action. As the prosecution presents the case, the defense attorney may raise objections to the prosecutor's questions or a witness's answers.[30] The judge rules on these objections by either sustaining them or overruling them. The objections can be on points of procedural law or on the competency of a witness to answer a question. For instance, if a police officer claims the defendant was drunk, the defense attorney might object, claiming that the officer could not know for sure that this was the case. The prosecutor might then ask the police officer whether a breath test was administered to the defendant and what the result of that test was. Ideally, the process is designed to present the evidence and witness testimony in a factual and fair manner so that the jury can weigh them and reach its own conclusion.

One of the duties of an attorney is to present evidence to the jury.

Source: Getty Images, Inc. - Stockbyte Royalty Free

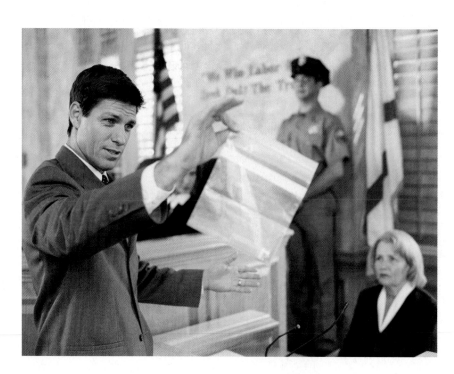

After the prosecution questions a witness, the defense attorney then has the opportunity to cross-examine. The right to cross-examine witnesses is derived from the Sixth Amendment of the Constitution and is one of the adversarial features of the trial. The defense attorney tries to **impeach** the witness by asking questions that help undermine the prosecution's case. Sometimes the defense attorney can be successful in soliciting information from the prosecution's witness that is favorable to the defendant. Once the defense attorney has cross-examined the witness, the prosecutor may ask additional questions under the right to **redirect examination.** In turn, the defense attorney can ask for a re-cross-examination. Often, this tactic is used later in the trial after other witnesses reveal new evidence.

After the state presents its case against the defendant, the defense attorney can ask the judge for a **directed verdict of acquittal.** Essentially, the defense attorney is asking the judge to rule that the prosecution has failed to present a compelling case documenting the defendant's guilt. Only in the most egregious cases would the judge be likely to make such a ruling, especially if the case is in a jury trial. However, it costs the defense nothing to make such a motion. In some cases, the judge might believe that the prosecution has failed so miserably to make a logical case that issuing a directed verdict of acquittal would not circumvent justice, but would save the court from having to sit through a trial with a foregone conclusion of acquittal.

Once the prosecution concludes the presentation of its evidence and witnesses, the defense is given the opportunity to present its own evidence and witnesses. Because the burden of proof rests with the prosecution, the defense attorney need only present evidence that raises a reasonable doubt about the defendant's guilt. If the prosecution had a witness from the state crime lab who testified about blood samples or hair fibers, the defense will counter with other scientists who will dispute the testimony. If the prosecution presented an eyewitness, the defense might attempt to impeach the testimony by showing that the witness's eyesight or memory is faulty. The prosecution is given the opportunity for cross-examination, and, of course, there may be redirect questions from the defense followed by re-cross-examination by the prosecutor. The intent is to give each side an equal opportunity to ask questions.

After each side has presented its evidence and witnesses, the court allows both sides to present a summation in which they attempt to account for all the facts in a closing argument designed to put the best possible spin on their case. The prosecution gets the last word before the jury because of its burden to prove the defendant's guilt beyond a reasonable doubt. New evidence may not be introduced at this stage of the trial because the opposing side does not have the opportunity to question it. Closing arguments can sometimes be flamboyant because the attorneys are not just presenting facts; they are trying to convince the jury that the defendant is good or bad, a solid citizen or a criminal, sympathetic or disgusting, guilty or innocent. It is during the closing arguments that television dramas have the culprit blurt out a confession or the defense attorney bring the jury to tears with a dramatic and heartfelt speech. In real life, the closing arguments are not nearly so theatrical, but they can be extremely interesting and moving.

EVIDENCE   To convict a defendant, the prosecutor must build a case based on evidence. Because the defendant enjoys a presumption of innocence, the prosecutor must prove **beyond a reasonable doubt** that the defendant is guilty. The term *beyond a reasonable doubt* is a legal yardstick that measures the sufficiency of the evidence. The prosecutor does not have to meet a standard of eliminating all doubt; lingering suspicions about the defendant's guilt might remain. The reasonable-doubt standard works in favor of the defendant, who needs only to raise questions about the quality of the prosecutor's case and does not have to prove anything.

In building the case, the prosecutor uses several different types of evidence. Some evidence is more convincing to the jury than other types, but the prosecutor's job is to weave a convincing pattern of evidence that demonstrates that the defendant is guilty as charged. Evidence must conform to a set of rules that ensures that the rights of the defendant are respected.[31] For instance, privileged communications between a

impeach
To discredit a witness.

redirect examination
The questioning of a witness about issues uncovered during cross-examination.

directed verdict of acquittal
An order from a trial judge to the jury stating that the jury must acquit the accused because the prosecution has not proved its case.

beyond a reasonable doubt
Refers to the highest level of proof required to win a case; necessary in criminal cases to procure a guilty verdict.

doctor and patient or between a lawyer and client are not admissible in court, nor is evidence that was illegally obtained by the police.[32] With these and other exceptions, however, the rules of evidence are geared toward obtaining the truth. Evidence is deemed trustworthy when every effort is made to ensure its veracity.

For example, original documents are required because copies are too easy to alter. Additionally, the court might judge young children or those suffering from mental illness to lack competence, so their testimony would be inadmissible. This is true also for hearsay evidence. *Hearsay evidence* is secondhand evidence in which someone reports that he or she heard someone else say something. Because it can be impossible to determine whether someone actually said what is reported, hearsay evidence is, as a rule, inadmissible in court. The prosecutor presents the best evidence available to the jurors, who then decide whether to believe it. Evidence can be classified in several ways:

- **Real evidence**   Real evidence consists of objects that can be readily observed. For instance, fingerprints, hair fibers, and blood can all be scientifically analyzed and certified by experts. Although opinions about the quality of the evidence or the chain of custody might conflict, there is a standard on which experts can agree. The courts are turning more and more to science to provide solid real evidence to determine guilt or innocence. The recent examples of death row inmates being released because of DNA evidence is a testament to how science can work both for and against the prosecution.

- **Testimony**   Testimony consists of statements by witnesses that are given under oath. Ideally, the prosecution can present witnesses who actually saw the defendant commit the offense. Lacking that eyewitness testimony, the prosecutor might present someone who can place the defendant in the proximity of where the offense was committed at about the same time. Additionally, much of the real evidence requires the interpretation of experts. For example, hair fibers do not speak for themselves, so the prosecution must elicit testimony from an expert who is competent to evaluate them in relation to how the prosecutor contends they are connected to the offense.

- **Direct evidence**   Both real evidence and testimony can be considered as direct evidence. Direct evidence is ascertainable by the five senses. For instance, eyewitness testimony is defined as the witness actually seeing the defendant do something. Hearing, smelling, touching, and tasting can also form the basis for direct evidence.

- **Indirect evidence**   Indirect evidence can also be termed *circumstantial evidence*. When the prosecution fails to find the "smoking gun," then circumstantial evidence that demonstrates that the defendant has bought a gun of the same caliber may be used to help establish the case. With enough circumstantial evidence, the prosecution can build a strong case. However, the defense has an easier time creating doubts with circumstantial evidence than with direct evidence.

The Case Goes to the Jury

Serving on a jury allows average citizens to participate in the criminal justice system in an important way that acts as a check-and-balance against government power. (For the requirements to be a juror on a federal case, see Criminal Justice Reference 10.1.) The jury can prevent an overzealous prosecutor from railroading a defendant through the criminal justice system. By having a jury composed of 12 citizens (this is the ideal number, but many states allow a jury of six for some types of cases) who consider the defendant's guilt, the dynamics of the courtroom work group are not as dominant as they would be if only criminal justice practitioners decided the cases.

The jury selection process is a complicated and uncertain procedure that results in juries that might be partial to either the prosecution or the defense. Certainly, each

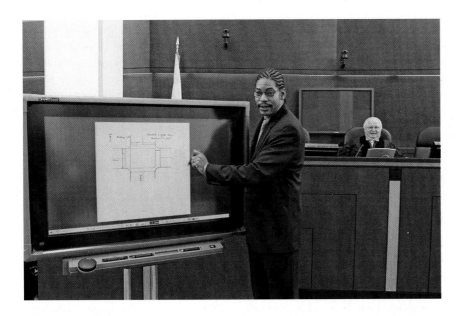

The level of technology has increased greatly in recent years. Although not all courtrooms have the budgets for such technology, many courts display evidence and exhibits using computer-based technology.

Source: Michael Newman/PhotoEdit Inc.

10.1 CRIMINAL JUSTICE REFERENCE

Federal Juror Qualifications and Exemptions

To qualify as a federal juror you must:

- Be a United States citizen
- Be at least 18 years of age
- Reside in the judicial district for one year
- Possess adequate proficiency in English
- Bear no disqualifying mental or physical condition
- Not be currently subject to felony charges
- Never have been convicted of a felony (unless your civil rights have been legally restored)

To be exempt from service, you must be:

- An active-duty member of the armed forces
- A member of the police or fire department

Certain public officials or others may qualify for exceptions based on individual court rules, such as members of voluntary emergency services or those who recently have served on a jury. Temporary deferrals may be granted because of hardship or extreme inconvenience.

The Terms of Jury Service
Length of Service

Length of service varies by court. Some courts require service for one day or for the duration of a single trial. Others require service for a fixed term of up to one month or more. Grand jury service may last up to 18 months.

Payment

Jurors are paid $40 per day. In some instances, jurors receive meal and travel allowances.

Employment Protection

By law, employers must allow employees time off (paid or unpaid) for jury service. The law forbids employers from firing, intimidating, or coercing employees because of federal jury service.

Source: Administrative Office of the U.S. Courts, Understanding the Federal Courts: 2003, 23–24, www.uscourts.gov/understand02/media/UFC99.pdf.

side attempts to influence the selection of the jury to ensure that its arguments find a sympathetic ear. The formation of a jury requires several steps:

- **Master jury list**   Each jurisdiction must develop a list of potential jurors. This list is compiled from voter registration records, driver's license lists, and utility customer lists. The goal is to develop a master jury list that is representative of the community in terms of race, gender, and social class.
- *Venire*   A list of names is randomly selected from the master jury list to form the *venire*, or the jury pool. The sheriff's office notifies these individuals by

venire
The list or pool from which jurors are chosen.

summons to appear at the courthouse for jury duty. Not all citizens who are summoned for jury duty report to the courthouse. In some jurisdictions, the nonresponse rate is as high as 20 percent. Furthermore, many citizens ask to be excused from jury duty because of the inconvenience and hardship it imposes. Judges vary widely in their patterns of excusing citizens from jury duty. Juries are selected from this final, reduced jury pool.

- *Voir dire*   The prosecutor and the defense attorney have some input into which members of the jury pool wind up on the jury for an actual case. The *voir dire* ("to see, to speak") consists of the questioning of prospective jurors to determine whether they have the necessary qualifications to serve. The questions cover possible previous relationships potential jurors may have had with those involved in the case (this includes the attorneys—for instance, the brother-in-law of the prosecutor would not be an appropriate candidate for the jury), knowledge about the case, attitudes about certain facts that could arise in the trial, and their willingness to be fair and impartial. The defense attorney or prosecutor can attempt to exclude someone from the jury by two means:

    1. **Challenge for cause.**   A potential juror can be excused if it is suspected that they cannot be objective—for instance, if someone made a statement in the newspaper about the case that clearly showed that he or she had already decided the defendant was guilty. Although challenges for cause are not often used and not often granted by the judge, this is an important safeguard against getting an obviously biased juror.

    2. **Peremptory challenge.**   Both the defense attorney and the prosecutor are allowed to have a certain number of potential jurors dismissed without having to provide reasons. For example, a defense attorney might decide that anyone who has experience working in the criminal justice system will not be sympathetic to the defendant and therefore may use peremptory challenges to exclude potential jurors who have been law enforcement officers, attorneys, criminology professors, or prison guards. However, using peremptory challenges to exclude individuals solely on the basis of race or sex is prohibited (see Case in Point 10.1).

Depending on the nature of the case, serving on a jury can be satisfying, or it can turn into an arduous task. Jurors can feel proud of doing their duty as citizens, or they can feel inconvenienced by the intrusion of jury duty on their lives. For instance, some juries are sequestered, and members are forced to live in a hotel and avoid watching television or reading the local newspaper. Some complicated and high-profile cases can cause jurors to lose months of work and exert a real hardship on their employers and families.

During the trial, jurors play a passive role. They must sit and listen to the prosecutor and the defense attorney present the case. They are not allowed to ask questions of the attorneys or the witnesses. Jurors who would like to have more control over their role and are not familiar with the legal procedures that underlie the trial process might find this role frustrating.[33] One feature that makes jury trials so interesting is that a conviction requires more than a majority vote. In fact, all the members of a jury must agree or it is considered a **hung jury.** When there is a hung jury, the prosecution has the option of trying the case again.

Not all cases get a jury trial. The exceptions are those in which the possible penalty is not serious (such as six months or less in jail), the defendant is a juvenile, or the defense requests a **bench trial.** A bench trial is held before a judge who decides for guilt or acquittal and passes sentence. A defense attorney may request a bench trial when the case involves very technical or emotional issues. Some believe that the chances are better for an acquittal when a professional judge decides rather than a jury comprising ordinary citizens who may be more likely to become confused by the evidence or biased because of the nature of the case.[34] For example, a defendant in a

voir dire

French for "to see, to speak." Refers to the questioning of jurors by a judge and/or attorneys to determine whether individual jurors are appropriate for a particular jury panel.

hung jury

A term describing a jury in a criminal case that is deadlocked or that cannot produce a unanimous verdict.

bench trial

A trial that takes place before a judge, but without a jury, in which the judge makes the decision. Sometimes called a court trial.

10.1	CASE IN POINT
	BATSON V. KENTUCKY

THE CASE	**THE POINT**
Batson v. Kentucky, 476 U.S. 79, 106 S.Ct. 1712 (1986)	*The Supreme Court established that the use of peremptory challenges to racially manipulate a jury violates the defendant's right to an impartial jury.*

During James Batson's trial on burglary charges, the prosecutor used peremptory challenges to exclude the four black jurors from the jury pool. The resulting all-white jury eventually convicted Batson, who was black, of second-degree burglary. On appeal, the Supreme Court ruled that the use of peremptory challenges to racially manipulate the jury violated the equal-protection rights of both Batson and the four excluded jurors. The case was remanded back to the trial court with the requirement that if "the prosecutor does not come forward with a neutral explanation for his action, our precedents require that petitioner's conviction be reversed."

child-abuse case might believe that the chances are better in a bench trial before a judge than in a jury trial. See Crosscurrents 10.2 for another reason why a defendant might choose a bench trial.

The Defense Doesn't Rest

Once the prosecution has presented the evidence, the defense attorney must make an important decision. The defense can claim that the prosecution has not proven beyond a reasonable doubt the guilt of the defendant and can decline to mount a defense. This is a risky gamble that defense attorneys do not often employ. The defense attorney might truly believe that the prosecution's case was fatally flawed, but the jury will make its own decision, and the defense attorney usually takes the opportunity to rebut the evidence presented.[35] A defense can use a number of strategies to counter the case presented by the prosecution. According to David Neubauer, the defense may consider at least five strategies:[36]

- **Reasonable doubt**   The defense has the right to confront the witnesses and evidence through cross-examination, then use this opportunity to attempt to poke holes in the case, thus raising a reasonable doubt about the defendant's guilt within the jury. By catching a witness in some contradicting testimony, or exposing how a witness may have a motivation to lie, the defense attorney attempts to weaken the prosecutor's case. When the defendant has no other plausible defense, this sometimes is the only strategy open to the defense attorney. According to Neubauer, this is the weakest type of strategy because it does not really give the jury "something to hang its hat on."

- **Defendant testimony**   The defendant is not required to testify. Although many jurors would like to see the defendant get on the witness stand and say, "I didn't do it," this strategy would give the prosecution the right to cross-examine. The Fifth Amendment protects defendants from self-incrimination, so the defense attorney must carefully weigh the risk of subjecting the defendant to questions from the prosecution against the problem of letting the jury wonder why the defendant does not take the stand to proclaim his or her innocence. One factor the defense attorney will consider is the believability of the witness and his or her likelihood to draw the jury's sympathy. In many cases defendants can do themselves much more harm than good by testifying. Although

Letting the Judge Decide

Why would a defendant waive a trial by jury in favor of a bench trial, that is, a trial by a judge? After all, doesn't one have a better chance with a jury of his or her peers than with a judge who might be far removed from a defendant's race and social class? Often the answer to that question is yes. However, the situation is sometimes different when the defendant's peers are not other regular citizens, but those who work within the criminal justice system.

At about 4 A.M. on a late November day in New York City, a young man who was to get married later that evening walked out of a Queens nightclub with two of his friends and got into a verbal altercation with another group of people. The two groups separated, and the three men got into their car. The man who was getting married drove the car half a block, turned a corner, and struck an unmarked police van that had several plainclothes officers inside. Police said the man then backed onto a sidewalk, hit a storefront's protective gate, almost struck an undercover officer, then hit the van again. The officers fired about 50 bullets at the man's car—hitting other cars and a nearby apartment window—striking the car at least 21 times.[1] By the time the shooting stopped, the young man was dead and his two friends were injured, one critically. Several police officers also sustained minor injuries. None of the men they were shooting at were armed.[2]

The undercover officers were part of a sting operation at the nightclub, which was suspected of narcotics and weapons violations, as well as prostitution. The police say that during the altercation between the two groups of men, a man in one of the groups shouted that he was going to get his gun. An undercover officer followed the group to their car and said that when the men got into the car, he pulled his gun, identified himself as a police officer, and told the men to stop.[3] When the car did not stop, the police officers started shooting.

Some witnesses say that that none of the officers identified themselves. Witnesses also disagree about the order in which the events took place, saying that the men tried to leave the club in their car; a shot was fired, then other officers started shooting.[4] Police experts said the number of shots pointed to "contagious shooting," which occurs when one officer feels threatened and begins shooting, and other officers on the scene shoot, too.[5]

The case also had a racial aspect, although New York City police denied any racial motivations for the shootings. The victims were black and Hispanic, whereas two of the officers were white, one Hispanic, and two black.[6]

Two of the officers were charged with first- and second-degree manslaughter; the third faced two misdemeanor charges of reckless endangerment.[7] Amid protests and intense media coverage, all three officers pleaded not guilty. When the case finally headed to trial in 2008, the defense lawyers asked for a change of venue, stating that their clients could not get a fair trial in Queens.[8] After an appeals court denied that request, the three detectives waived their right to a jury trial. In April 2008, two months after the trial began and only two weeks after the defense asked him to drop the charges, Queens Supreme Court Justice Arthur Cooperman acquitted the three officers.[9] Protests continued to roil for several months. In 2008, the young man's fiancée, as well as the two men who were injured, filed a wrongful-death lawsuit.

Although this case is a good example of why a defendant would choose a bench trial, it is also quite controversial. Many critics of the decidedly murky case say the officers' acquittal is merely a case of law enforcement protecting its own. Others believe such actions are necessary to protect civil servants who are more vulnerable to lawsuits. After all, if police officers had to fear a lawsuit every time they pulled their gun, then the locales that the police are sworn to protect, as well as the officers themselves, might be far less safe.

Think About It

1. How would the defendants have fared with a jury?
2. Does the outcome of this case harm the public's image of the criminal justice system? Why or why not?
3. Under what circumstances would you prefer a bench trial in front of a judge as opposed to a trial heard by a jury of your peers?

[1] Robert D. McFadden, "Police Kill Man after a Bachelor Party in Queens," *New York Times*, late edition, November 26, 2006, p. 1.

[2] "50 Bullets and a Death in Queens," *New York Times*, late edition, November 28, 2006, p. A22.

[3] Ibid.

[4] Michael Powell and Robin Shulman, "N.Y. Mayor Calls Shooting 'Inexplicable,'" *Washington Post*, final edition, November 28, 2006, A3.

[5] Michael Wilson, "50 Shots Fired, and the Experts Offer a Theory," *New York Times*, late edition, November 27, 2006, A1.

[6] McFadden, "Police Kill Man," 1.

[7] Michael Wilson, "Detectives in Bell Shooting Seek to Waive Trial by Jury," *New York Times*, January 25, 2008, late edition, B1.

[8] Michael Wilson, "Prosecutors Argue against Moving Bell Case From City," *New York Times*, late edition, January 18, 2008, B2.

[9] "517 Days That Gripped the City," *New York Daily News*, sports final edition, April 26, 2008, p. 12.

the direct examination by their own attorney can cast them in a positive light, this opens the door for the prosecutor to expose weaknesses in the character or in the alibi of the defendant.

- **Alibis**   The defense can present evidence that the defendant was somewhere else at the time of the offense. Having others testify that they saw the defendant miles from the scene of the offense at the time it was committed can raise doubt. According to Neubauer, some states require the defense to provide a list of witnesses who are going to present alibi testimony so that the prosecution can investigate their stories before the trial. The goal of the prosecutor is to catch the witnesses in contradictory testimony or to impugn their honesty by showing that they are friends of the defendant and are likely to be untruthful.

- **Affirmative defense**   An affirmative defense essentially says that the defendant committed the offense but had a good reason that excuses his or her culpability. Examples of an affirmative defense are self-defense, duress, and entrapment. In each of these instances, the question of reasonable doubt is not challenged. Rather, the focus of the case shifts to the defendant's having a good reason for committing the offense. Perhaps the most recognizable affirmative defense is the *insanity defense*, in which the defendant admits to the offense but contends that he or she should not be held responsible because of mental illness.[37]

- **Challenging scientific evidence**   When the prosecution presents scientific evidence, it must also summon experts to explain it to the jury. Often these experts are employees of the state or local crime laboratories that processed the evidence. The defense can present its own expert witnesses to cast doubt on the quality of the evidence or the interpretations of the prosecution's witnesses. The jury may be clueless about the issues in dispute and not really competent to distinguish which set of experts is correct. This situation favors the defense, which must raise only a reasonable doubt in the minds of the jury to secure an acquittal.[38] The effect of science in the courts has been subject to debate as to whether popular TV programs such as *CSI* have made jurors more demanding of the quality of physical evidence. This so-called CSI effect has not been shown to be any major influence in the expectations of most jurors.[39]

There are no right answers when it comes to picking the best tactic to defend against criminal charges. Practicing law is as much an art as it is a science, and pleading a case before a jury can involve a bit of theater. Some may compare this process to a game because of its adversarial nature and because it is bound by a set of complicated rules. However, the stakes are too high to think of a trial as a game. Its effect on the lives of the offenders, the careers of those in the courtroom work group, and the public's sense of justice make this stage of the criminal justice system an extremely serious endeavor.[40]

RIGHTS AND WRONGS IN THE COURTHOUSE

Thus far, we have reviewed an interesting and extensive set of decision points in which discretion is exercised by prosecutors, defense attorneys, judges, and even defendants. The administration of justice, then, is essentially the negotiation of justice. This reality leaves many observers with a negative view of the criminal justice system.[41] People want a degree of certainty in dealing with offenders and often complain that the crooks have more rights than the victims. In reviewing the legal standing of defendants, victims, witnesses, and those who work in the courthouse, we should consider how the criminal justice system evolved to its present incarnation and why the legal protection of the offender seems to occupy such a prominent space in the proceedings.

Scientific evidence has become an important factor in many cases. A fingerprint can tie a defendant to the crime scene.

Source: Courtesy Sirchie Fingerprint Laboratories, Inc., Youngsville, NC, www. sirchie.com.

"I Know My Rights"

The legal rights afforded defendants in criminal trials can be traced to the earliest codification of laws in Western societies. The Greeks and Romans developed some of the rudiments for the concept of judicial fairness, and early English common law further expanded the concept of rights of the accused. However, the rights enjoyed by defendants in criminal trials in the United States are derived directly from the Constitution, specifically from the first 10 amendments, or the Bill of Rights.

The power of the government to detain, arrest, incarcerate, or even execute must be controlled in ways that prevent overzealous criminal justice practitioners from turning the country into a police state.[42] The power of governments is immense, and documents such as the Bill of Rights help ensure that the United States remains a "government of laws, not of men."[43] Several provisions in the Bill of Rights speak directly to the rights of defendants in criminal trials:

- **Right to a speedy trial** The Sixth Amendment guarantees that the defendant shall not languish in jail for years before the state gets around to deciding the case. Of course, in practice, not everyone would agree that the process results in a speedy trial. The defense can delay a trial with requests for continuances in the hopes that witnesses will forget about the case. However, there is still the requirement that the prosecution make every effort to begin the trial under the speedy-trial principle.[44] Some detainees, such as the al-Qaeda participants captured in Afghanistan and held at the U.S. military base in Guantanamo Bay in Cuba, are not deemed by the federal government to be covered by the Constitution.

- **Right to confront witnesses** The Sixth Amendment also says the defendant shall have the opportunity to question those called to testify against him or her. This is an important right enjoyed by U.S. citizens that prevents the government and its citizens from abusing power. In totalitarian countries, the government could simply allege that someone accused the defendant, and the defendant would have no opportunity to challenge the testimony. Related to the right to confront hostile witnesses is the right of the defendant to call witnesses on his or her behalf. This helps ensure that the court hears the defendant's side of the case. However, the defense must always keep in mind that whenever it calls a witness to testify on behalf of the defendant, the prosecution will get a chance to cross-examine.

- **Right against self-incrimination**   When defendants refuse to testify and claim to "take the Fifth," they are invoking their right against self-incrimination as guaranteed by the Fifth Amendment. Although a jury may wonder why a defendant who is innocent would not testify, the refusal to take the stand is not supposed to be used against the defendant.

- **Right against excessive bail**   The Eighth Amendment provides that those accused and awaiting trial are to be allowed to post a reasonable bail unless the court finds that they are a danger to society or are likely to flee the jurisdiction and not return for further proceedings. Exactly what constitutes reasonable bail is a judgment call made by the court (see Case in Point 10.2). For those with no financial means, any bail could be hard to secure. However, thanks to bail bond companies that can free the defendant for one-tenth the bail and courts' increased use of release-on-recognizance (ROR) programs, the financial status of the defendant is not as large a factor as it has been in the past.[45]

- **Right to an impartial jury**   This right is another provision of the Sixth Amendment. In recent years, the races and sexes of jurors have been attacked as not representing a jury of peers who are likely to be impartial. Defendants and their attorneys are given some discretion in challenging potentially biased jurors.

Although this list of defendants' rights is not exhaustive, it illustrates some of the guards against abuse present within the criminal justice system (see Case in Point 10.3). Courts may not be totally successful in ensuring a fair trial, but many citizens believe that the courts coddle criminal defendants and that the rights enjoyed by offenders prevent justice from being enacted. In summary, the rights given to the accused are double-edged. Although these rights sometimes protect some guilty defendants from feeling the full effects of justice, they also help prevent many innocent citizens from being caught up in the gears of the system and punished for offenses they did not commit.

Victims' Rights

The victim can sometimes be the forgotten party in the criminal justice process. The rights of the offender have received substantial attention from the courts, but only relatively recently have efforts been made to empower the victim.[46] When a prosecutor charges a defendant, the offense is considered to be against the state even though there

---

10.2 CASE IN POINT

UNITED STATES V. SALERNO

THE CASE	THE POINT
United States v. Salerno, 481 U.S. 739, 107 S.Ct. 2095 (1987)	Denying bail and pretrial release to a suspect who may be a danger to society is constitutional.

Anthony Salerno was arrested in 1986 and charged with several RICO Act violations, as well as mail and wire fraud offenses, criminal gambling violations, and extortion. He was held under the Bail Reform Act of 1984 as too dangerous to release. After being convicted of the offenses and sentenced to 100 years in prison, Salerno appealed on the basis that his pretrial detention was unconstitutional. The U.S. Court of Appeals for the Second Circuit struck down as unconstitutional the provision of the Bail Reform Act in which a suspect may be denied bail because he or she is too dangerous to release.

Calling pretrial detention a "carefully limited exception" to the norm of liberty in U.S. society, the Supreme Court upheld Salerno's detention as constitutional, stating that it violated neither the due-process clause of the Fifth Amendment nor the excessive bail clause of the Eighth Amendment.

10.3 CASE IN POINT

FURMAN V. GEORGIA

THE CASE	THE POINT
Furman v. Georgia, 408 U.S. 238, 92 S.Ct. 2726 (1972)	The decision set forth that the administration of the death penalty constituted cruel and unusual punishment, not the death penalty itself.

William Furman, a black man, shot and killed a homeowner through a closed door while trying to enter the house at night. Furman, 26, pleaded insanity and was committed to the Georgia Central State Hospital for a psychiatric examination. The staff members who examined Furman concluded unanimously that Furman was mentally deficient with "psychotic episodes associated with Convulsive Disorder." They also said that although Furman was not currently psychotic, he also was not capable of helping his attorneys prepare his defense and needed further psychiatric treatment. Later, the hospital superintendent concluded much the same, but stated that Furman did indeed know right from wrong and was able to cooperate with his attorneys. Evidence that he was mentally unsound was presented at the trial, but Furman was convicted and sentenced to death. Furman appealed the conviction on the grounds that his Fourteenth Amendment rights were being violated. The Supreme Court concurred, saying that administration of the death penalty in Georgia was racially discriminatory and violated the Eighth and Fourteenth Amendments. In 1976 the court reversed its decision in *Gregg v. Georgia*.

GREGG V. GEORGIA

THE CASE	THE POINT
Gregg v. Georgia, 428 U.S. 153, 96 S.Ct. 2909 (1976)	The Supreme Court effectively reinstated the death penalty, finding that it did not constitute cruel and unusual punishment as long as its implementation was fair.

Troy Gregg was convicted of killing and robbing two men and sentenced to death. After *Furman v. Georgia*, the state implemented *bifurcated trials*, in which guilt or innocence is determined in the first stage, and the penalty is determined in the second. During the penalty phase, the jury is required to consider both mitigating and aggravating circumstances, and if aggravating circumstances are overriding, then the death penalty is to be imposed. Also, the law prescribed an automatic appeal. The Supreme Court found that all procedures were correctly followed and that all were constitutional and violated neither the Eighth nor the Fourteenth Amendment. Gregg's death sentence was upheld.

Four years earlier in *Furman v. Georgia*, the Supreme Court found the process by which the death penalty was imposed to be cruel and unusual. In this case, the court affirmed that the death penalty itself was not cruel and unusual, as long as its implementation was judged to be fair.

is most likely a human victim as well.[47] Victims get frustrated when they are not notified when the court hears cases, especially when the cases are plea-bargained.[48] The prosecutor and the judge make important decisions without the victim's input. In an effort to increase the victim's voice, many states have adopted victim-rights legislation.

Although not all states have passed such laws, the idea of treating victims and witnesses with more respect and consideration is taking hold in the criminal justice system. It would be unfair to contend that criminal justice practitioners have not always valued victims and witnesses. Certainly, they are not intentionally left out of the process because judges and prosecutors are mean-spirited or contemptuous of their input. The problems experienced by victims and witnesses are related to resources. With increased caseloads and few judges, prosecutors, secretarial support staff, and investigators, the workload of those in the courtroom work group leaves little time to ensure that victims and witnesses are being notified in a timely manner of all the changes in the docket and the status of cases and defendants. Certainly, the advent in recent years of victim–witness programs has helped alleviate some of the frustrations.[49] Laws like the ones in California, however, institutionalize these reforms and ensure that decent treatment of victims and witnesses is not always relegated to the bottom of the priority list when budgets get tight.[50]

SENTENCING THE OFFENDER

The criminal court process is twofold. The first part is concerned with determining the defendant's guilt. If the defendant is found guilty, or plea bargains for a *nolo contendere* or guilty plea, the second part of the court process begins. The defendant (now the offender) must be sentenced by the judge to an appropriate disposition. A range of philosophical concerns guides the sentencing process.[51] Depending on the nature of the case and the motivations of the judge, the goal of the sentence may be treatment, punishment, incapacitation, restitution, revenge, or deterrence.[52]

The philosophical intention of the judge is not the only factor that guides the sentencing decision (see Focus on Ethics 10.2). The availability of prison beds or treatment programs, the demeanor or remorsefulness of the defendant, and a host of factors that should have no bearing on the sentence, such as the offender's race, social and economic status, and gender, can all influence the type and severity of the disposition.[53] Therefore, the judge has considerable discretion in deciding the appropriate sentence for each offender. For the offender, then, it is a bit like gambling when he or she stands before the bench for sentencing and wonders whether the judge is in a good mood.[54]

A uniform pattern in sentencing would be comforting. If those who committed the most serious offenses and presented the greatest danger to society received the most severe sentences, the public's sense of justice would be satisfied (courts do try to lock up the most violent offenders; see Figures 10-1 and 10-2). However, when sentences for offenders with similar cases and prior records differ significantly, the courts appear to be arbitrary and capricious. At the heart of the matter is a long-standing

---

10.2   FOCUS *on* ETHICS

MAXIMUM MEL

You are the city's only female circuit court judge, and you are angry. Things have not been going right in your personal life or on the bench, and you have been taking out your anger on the hapless defendants who appear before you. Your daughter married a man 20 years her senior, and your son went to California to become an actor but instead is a waiter. Ever since you bleached your hair, the press has referred to you as the court's "blond bombshell," and several offenders to whom you gave probation have recently been caught running a stolen-car ring.

You have decided that you have had enough of law enforcement officers who fudge the facts, lawyers who twist the truth, reporters who spin the news, and offenders who look you right in the eye and lie. For the past three months you have made your decisions based on your instincts and your gut feelings, which has resulted in your sentencing just about everyone to the longest period of incarceration possible under the law. Your nickname around the courthouse is "Maximum Mel," and defense attorneys are afraid to bring their clients before your court.

The chief judge has politely suggested that your sentencing patterns are out of step with how other judges sentence. At the local bar association annual dinner, several judges jokingly said the state's prison system would soon be called "Mel's Big House." You are feeling pressure from others in the criminal justice system, but … the public loves you. In fact, one of the major political parties has suggested that you may be a good candidate for attorney general and maybe even governor. In some ways, you like the attention you are getting, but your mild-mannered husband asks if you have become burned out as a judge and suggests that maybe you should consider stepping down from the bench. You become angry with him and call your daughter to complain that no one appreciates strong women these days.

What Do You Do?

1. Is it possible that you have lost your sense of perspective?
2. Is it fair to the defendants who appear before you to sentence them to long prison sentences?
3. Do you need to consider your sentencing practices in light of how other judges sentence offenders?
4. Is it ethical to use your sentencing patterns as a stepping-stone to higher political office?
5. Would anyone be asking these questions if you were a man?

Figure 10-1 **Sentences of Violent Felons Convicted in State Courts during 2004**

Source: Matthew R. Durose and Patrick A. Langan, *Felony Sentences in State Courts, 2004* (Washington, DC: U.S. Department of Justice, Bureau of Justice Statistics, 2007), 3, www.ojp.usdoj.gov/bjs/pub/pdf/fssc04.pdf.

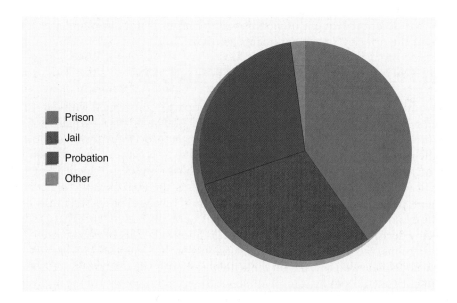

Figure 10-2 **Mean Sentence Length in State Courts During 2004 for Felons Sentenced to Prison, Jail, and Probation**

Source: Matthew R. Durose and Patrick A. Langan, *Felony Sentences in State Courts, 2004* (Washington, DC: U.S. Department of Justice, Bureau of Justice Statistics, 2007), 3, www.ojp.usdoj.gov/bjs/pub/pdf/fssc04.pdf.

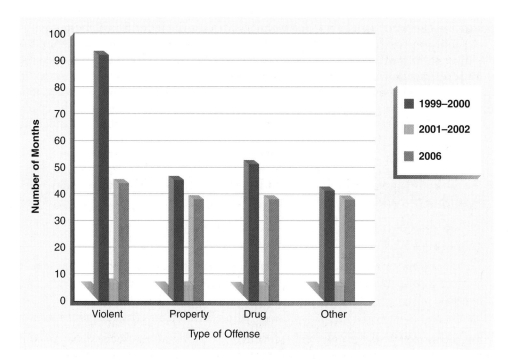

indeterminate sentence

A prison term that does not state a specific period of time to be served or date of release.

determinate sentence

A prison term that is determined by law and states a specific period of time to be served.

debate in criminology over whether the sentence should be geared toward the offense or fashioned to fit the offender's circumstances. This debate has spawned two types of sentences: **indeterminate sentences** and **determinate sentences.**[55]

Indeterminate Sentencing

Is the judge the best person to decide how long an offender should spend in prison? Even when a case is plea-bargained, is the courtroom work group the appropriate body to fashion a sentencing decision that affects not only the offender, but also the agencies that must carry out the sentence? Perhaps the prison is better able to decide which inmates deserve to be there and which are good probation and parole risks. Perhaps the trial, where passions are high and the details of the crime vivid, is not the time to decide how long the offender should be incarcerated. Perhaps society would be better served if the length of an offender's sentence were predicated on how well that offender adjusts to prison life and on how safe society would be once the offender is released.[56]

The indeterminate sentence takes these issues into consideration and leaves the discretion to the parole board to determine when the offender is ready to be released into the community. It views the judge as incapable of forecasting the future and predicting when the offender is no longer a threat to society. At its most extreme, the indeterminate sentence sends the offender to prison for somewhere between one year and life. Based on the offender's behavior in prison and his or her rehabilitation, the parole board picks a release date.

Based on the medical model of corrections, the indeterminate sentence considers the uniqueness of each offender's case and social background and is fashioned to address the diagnosed problems.[57] In a hospital it would be inconceivable to handle a patient with a broken leg in the same way as a patient who has had a heart attack. The indeterminate sentence applies the medical analogy to the criminal offender. By viewing unlawful behavior as a symptom of a social deficiency, the criminal justice system can prescribe a treatment, such as vocational training, drug or alcohol treatment, or therapeutic counseling.

The indeterminate sentence is attractive if we assume that criminal behavior is comparable to physical illness. We can prescribe individualized justice in the same way we do individualized medicine and develop a "treatment or a cure" for the antisocial behavior of the offender. The time it takes to apply a cure to each offender is different, so the prison sentences are not fixed. That way, the offender is not released too soon or kept in prison too long. The parole board, in consultation with the professional prison staff, determines when the offender has been rehabilitated and is safe to return to society.[58]

During the 1950s and 1960s, a progressive attitude in correctional circles advocated rehabilitation over punishment, and the indeterminate sentence enjoyed wide popularity. By shifting the discretion for deciding the length of incarceration from the judge to the prison staff and the parole board, the criminal justice system based treatment on the willingness of the inmate to take advantage of the rehabilitative services available. The indeterminate sentence was predicated on three assumptions:

1. The offender is sick, and the prison staff can diagnose the problem.
2. The prison can provide the necessary treatment to correct the problem.
3. The prison staff and parole board can accurately determine whether the inmate has been successfully treated and is ready to return to society.[59]

The indeterminate sentence was largely jettisoned in the 1970s and 1980s for four reasons. The first reason is that there was little evidence that any of the three aforementioned assumptions were warranted. Considering antisocial behavior to be analogous to physical illness and subject to diagnosis and treatment was not accurate in many cases. As offenders deemed to be rehabilitated continued to recidivate, citizens and politicians lost faith in the system.[60]

The second reason why the indeterminate sentence lost favor was the wide disparities in incarceration times. Particularly when extralegal factors such as race and social class were correlated with length of incarceration, the inexact science of indeterminate sentencing began to look like a smoke screen for discrimination and the influence of political power.[61]

The third reason why the indeterminate sentence lost support concerned its effect on prison inmates. If the sentence was to be determined by how well inmates appeared to be rehabilitated, then it was in their interest to play the game. The inmates learned to act rehabilitated to convince prison officials that they were ready to be released. They attended treatment programs, went to church, and developed the positive vocabulary of rehabilitation to attain their goal of release.[62]

Finally, some criminologists' interpretations of the research concerning recidivism did not reveal that participation in treatment programs significantly improved the inmates' prospects for avoiding a life of crime. Although the value of rehabilitation was, and continues to be, in dispute, the prevailing attitude was that it lacked evidence of effectiveness.[63] Consequently, the discretion for deciding how long the inmate would be incarcerated shifted from the prison staff and the parole board to the legislature and the prosecutor with the introduction of the determinate sentence.

Determinate Sentencing

The effectiveness of rehabilitation will be fully discussed in the chapters on corrections. For our purposes here, it is sufficient to say that there was widespread concern about its effectiveness and about the public's confidence in the criminal justice system. Although rehabilitation was considered a worthy goal, it was not deemed a sufficient foundation on which to base sentencing decisions. As legislators heard stories about liberal judges and parole boards, they decided to pass laws that restricted the discretion criminal justice decision makers could exercise in any individual case. Various state legislatures passed determinate- or fixed-sentence laws that stated that the length of time an inmate would serve would be determined not by the judge or the parole board but by the nature of the offense.[64] Sentencing grids or guidelines were developed that forced judges to apply sentences within a narrow range of variability.[65] In its purest form, a determinate sentence gives a fixed sentence to each inmate convicted of a particular offense. For example, an armed robbery conviction may call for a 30-year sentence. The judge has no discretion to make the sentence longer or shorter, regardless of the circumstances of the offense or of the offender. One form of determinate sentencing, the **presumptive sentence,** allows judges limited discretion to consider aggravating or mitigating circumstances and depart from the guidelines. Some states employ voluntary guidelines, which allow judges the same departures. See Figure 10-3 for an example of a state sentencing guidelines table.

presumptive sentence

A sentence that may be adjusted by the judge depending on aggravating or mitigating factors.

The perceived advantage of the determinate sentence is uniformity. Similar cases are treated in the same manner and, theoretically, such factors as social class, race, and gender do not affect the sentencing equation.[66] These efforts to remove discretion from the criminal justice system have produced some unintended consequences that some consider detrimental to the welfare of offenders and society.

First, determinate sentencing has removed the power to make decisions from those closest to the case. These participants are often in the best position to understand a case's complexities and weigh the conflicting interests of the welfare of society and the punishment of the offender. Second, legislators who espouse a get-tough-on-crime policy are not always sensitive to the limitations of the criminal justice system to bear the demands of long prison sentences for a vast number of inmates. A primary goal of a legislator is to get elected or reelected, and the making of effective criminal justice policy is often a casualty of the demands of political expediency. Even the most mundane criminal justice resources, such as prison beds, are limited. Legislators who restrict the discretion of criminal justice administrators to allocate those resources to the most pressing cases often are the same legislators who do not allocate sufficient budgets to the criminal justice system in the first place. In many ways, correctional officials are "left holding the bag" in that the legislature gives them an unreasonable workload and neither the resources nor the discretion to effectively handle their duties within acceptable limits.[67] The civil and human rights of inmates are infringed when prisons are overcrowded, but criminal justice decision makers, such as judges and parole board members, have little power to remedy the situation.[68]

Another detrimental effect of determinate sentencing is the shifting of power from the judge to the prosecutor.[69] By limiting the judge's discretion in imposing the sentence, determinate-sentencing laws increase the effect of the prosecutor's decision as to which charges will be filed. Defense attorneys unwilling to expose their clients to the long determinate sentences passed by the legislature are pressured to accept plea bargains to lesser included offenses or in exchange for avoiding the

CRIMINAL HISTORY ROW	
V	16+
IV	12–15
III	8–11
II	4–7
I	0–3

CRIME CATEGORY

		A	B	C	D	E	F	G	H	I	J	K
		1st Degree	2nd Degree	1st Degree	3rd Degree	1st Degree	2nd Degree	3rd Degree	2nd Degree	2nd Degree	3rd Degree	3rd Degree
		Murder	Death	Person	Death	Other	Person	Person	Other	Possession	Other	Possession
CRIMINAL HISTORY	V	24 YRS	8 YRS	10 YRS	48 MOS	84 MOS	60 MOS	36 MOS	30 MOS	20 MOS	20 MOS	18 MOS
	IV	22 YRS	7 YRS	9 YRS	42 MOS	78 MOS	45 MOS	30 MOS	24 MOS	18 MOS	18 MOS	16 MOS
	III	20 YRS	6 YRS	8 YRS	36 MOS	72 MOS	36 MOS	24 MOS	20 MOS	16 MOS	12 MOS	12 MOS
	II	18 YRS	5 YRS	7 YRS	24 MOS	66 MOS	30 MOS	20 MOS	18 MOS	14 MOS	10 MOS	10 MOS
	I	16 YRS	4 YRS	6 YRS	20 MOS	60 MOS	24 MOS	18 MOS	16 MOS	12 MOS	9 MOS	8 MOS

Mandatory Imprisonment — **Imprisonment** — **Intermediate Sanctions** — **Regular Probation** — *Misdemeanors*

CONSECUTIVE ENHANCEMENTS: 40% of the shorter sentence is to be added to the full length of the longer sentence.
CONCURRENT EHHANCEMENTS: 10% of the shorter sentence is to be added to the full length of the longer sentence.

Figure 10-3 **Utah Sentencing Guidelines Grid.** The score in the criminal history column (left) is tallied by scoring each offense in an offender's criminal history. Therefore, an offender with little or no criminal history would have a score of 3 or less and be assigned to the I row. An offender with more prior offenses would collect more "points" and be placed in a higher row. The periods specified within each cell are the typical length of incarceration if the offender is incarcerated. These periods do not apply if the offender is sentenced to an intermediate sanction or to regular probation.

Source: State of Utah, Utah Sentencing Commission, "2008 Adult Sentencing and Release Guidelines," 11, www.sentencing.utah.gov/Guidelines/Adult/AdultGuidelineManua12008.pdf.

stigma associated with drug or sex-offender convictions. The mandatory minimum sentences for these types of offenses provide the prosecutor with tremendous leverage in extracting plea bargains from defendants and their attorneys. Therefore, those in the best position to exercise discretion, the judge and the parole board, often find their hands tied by the determinate-sentencing laws. Determinate sentencing reduces criminal justice decision makers to clerks without the power to apply justice to the individual case and offender.

Mandatory Minimum Sentences

Mandatory minimum sentences are a form of determinate sentencing that has become widely used to address certain types of offenses that particularly rankle the public and receive little sympathy from the media or criminal justice practitioners (see Crosscurrents 10.3).[70] Typically, mandatory-minimum laws do not allow for probation and stipulate incarceration for a term not less than a specified number of years. Following are the types of offenses that are likely to carry mandatory minimums:

mandatory minimum sentence
A sentence determined by law that establishes the minimum length of prison time that may be served for an offense.

- **Weapons violations** Those who use a gun (or sometimes merely possess one) while committing a felony will find an additional prison term tacked on

CrossCurrents

Special Interest Laws

One of the interesting aspects of living in a democracy is the ability of groups and individuals to affect the making of laws. When a number of people begin to believe that the criminal justice system does not adequately respond to the needs of public safety, they have the freedom to demand through the democratic process that government listen and respond to their concerns. Politicians who want to be reelected ignore such organized groups at their peril. These groups have the goal of educating the public about their concerns and pressuring the criminal justice system to pay special attention to the harms done by the crimes they see as problematic. A few of the most notable examples of the power of special interest groups are as follows:

- *Drunk-driving laws.* Groups such as Mothers Against Drunk Driving (MADD) have influenced the passing of mandatory drunk-driving laws in a number of jurisdictions. Whereas before, a good defense attorney might have been able to get a well-heeled client off with a wink and a nod, now, because of the high-profile activities of groups such as MADD, judges have little or no discretion to dismiss these cases. Such efforts have also made the streets and highways safer because those who drink think twice about driving, knowing that DUI task forces are patrolling the roads. Knowing that judges are required to impose mandatory sentences influences people to drink less or desist from driving.[1]

- *Hate-crime laws.* Recently, laws have been enacted that call for additional charges for crimes in which a victim is selected because of race, ethnicity, sexual orientation, or gender. Extra punishments are given, and more resources are allocated to the investigation.

- *Sex-offender laws.* Perhaps the most feared and despised offenders are those charged with crimes of a sexual nature. Rapists, child abusers, and exhibitionists have been traditionally held in low regard by society, but recently a number of jurisdictions have passed laws that place extra surveillance on these offenders even when they are no longer under court supervision. For example, in Michigan those convicted of sex offenses have their names and addresses entered into a database that is available to the public via the Internet. Consequently, neighbors and law enforcement officials may be well aware when an offender with a history of sexual offending moves into a community. Although parents' desire to know when a child molester moves in next door is certainly understandable, some are concerned about the privacy rights of offenders who have served their prison terms and are now considered free. The stigma of "sex offender" can limit job opportunities of offenders who may have been successfully rehabilitated.

Think About It

1. Should some offenses require such special treatment?
2. Do these special-interest laws devalue other types of offenses?
3. What other behaviors do you think warrant the enactment of special laws that call for mandatory sentences?
4. Should judges be allowed more discretion in considering the circumstances of these crimes?
5. How do mandatory-sentencing laws affect the ability of criminal justice practitioners to efficiently use the resources of the system?

[1]Bureau of Justice Statistics, *Alcohol and Crime: An Analysis of National Data on the Prevalence of Alcohol Involvement in Crime* (Washington, DC: U.S. Department of Justice, Office of Justice Programs, April 1998), 5.

to the sentence. This guarantees that the case will not result in a probationary sentence.

- **Repeated drunk driving**   In some jurisdictions, those who persist in driving while intoxicated are sentenced to mandatory prison or jail time. Groups such as Mothers Against Drunk Driving (MADD) have been effective in changing laws that they deemed too lenient on repeat offenders.[71]
- **Drug-sales and drug-kingpin laws**   As a result of the nation's war on drugs, many jurisdictions, including the federal government, passed laws specifying mandatory prison time for the sale of illegal drugs. Some of these laws, aimed at drug kingpins, are especially punitive.
- **Three-strikes-and-you're-out laws**   Aimed at the habitual offender, these laws result in mandatory incarceration for those who have two prior felonies.

Judges are not allowed to consider the circumstances of the present offense and must sentence the offender to a prison term.

- **Truth in sentencing**   These laws specify that the offender must serve a substantial portion of the sentence before being released. These laws limit the flexibility of the parole board by ensuring that inmates spend most of the original sentence (often 85 percent) behind bars.[72]

Because the sentencing decision is such a high-profile event, it has become the primary way that citizens evaluate the quality of justice meted out by the system. This is unfortunate in many ways because sentencing is just one of many decision-making points in the system, and the reliance on this single event obscures the effects of the entire process (see Focus on Ethics 10.3). Efforts to limit the discretion of judges have been frustrated because of the inevitable shift of decision-making power to other points in the system.[73]

10.3   FOCUS *on* ETHICS

WHERE TO TRY A SNIPER?

Usually, an offense is prosecuted in the state in which it occurs, unless it is a federal offense. But what if an offense occurs in several states? And what if it is particularly heinous?

In October 2002, John Allen Muhammad, 41, and John Lee Malvo, 17, were arrested on suspicion of shooting and killing 10 people and wounding three with a sniper rifle. The murders were committed in Maryland, Virginia, and Washington, D.C. Authorities later discovered evidence that Muhammad and Malvo also committed murders in Washington State and Alabama. Authorities considered the evidence collected against the pair to be sound, so the question was not how to charge them, but where. The murders meant that three states and the District of Columbia could all claim jurisdiction in the case. Muhammad and Malvo were also accused of demanding a payment of $10 million to stop the shootings—considered extortion, a federal offense—giving federal prosecutors jurisdiction as well.

There is no law pertaining to such a situation, so the choice of where to prosecute Muhammad and Malvo fell to federal authorities, primarily because the two were in federal custody.

Other issues included the following:

- *Age.* Because John Lee Malvo was 17 years old at the time of the murders, he was considered a minor.
- *The death penalty.* Virginia, second only to Texas in executions, condemns minors. Maryland does not execute minors, nor does the federal government. Washington, D.C., has no death penalty at all.
- *Number and location of murders.* Maryland was the location of seven of the 10 sniper shootings. Three were in Virginia. Alabama and Washington state claimed one murder each.

Douglas Gansler, state's attorney in Montgomery County, Maryland, in which six people were murdered, said he would seek death for Muhammad and life in prison for Malvo. Virginia said it would seek execution for both.[1]

If you were a federal authority deciding this jurisdiction, what would you do? Here is a review: There is no law firmly governing jurisdiction in this case. The push for the death penalty is coming from all sides, and prosecutors from several states all have a rightful claim to try the accused. Some states had more evidence than others. With the exception of the District of Columbia, all have the death penalty, but not all have it for minors.

What Do You Do?

1. Is it ethical to try suspects in a jurisdiction because that jurisdiction will most likely hand down the most popular punishment?

2. What about when that punishment is execution, and one of the condemned is a minor?

Source: "Deciding Which Jurisdiction Should Prosecute Sniper Case," *Tampa Tribune*, October 30, 2002, http://tampatrib.com/News/MGAWJCLFW7D.html; Brandt Goldstein, "Who Gets to Prosecute the Sniper Suspects First?" *Slate*, October 29, 2002, http://slate.msn.com/?id=2073280; Laura Macinnis, "Sniper Suspect Muhammad Ordered Held Pending Trial," ABCNews.com/Reuters, November 5, 2002, http://abcnews.go.com/wire/us/reuters20021105_574.html; Sue Anne Pressley, "Procedural Questions Abound in Sniper Suspects' Legal Phase," *Salt Lake Tribune*, November 3, 2002, www.sltrib.com/11032002/nation_w/13116.htm.

[1] Lee Boyd Malvo was tried in Virginia and convicted of two counts of capital murder. In December 2003 he was sentenced to two life terms without parole. John Allen Muhammad, who was tried separately in Virginia, was convicted of capital murder and sentenced to death.

SUMMARY

1. Criminal trials are rare. Most cases are settled in the plea-bargaining process. Negotiations between the defense attorney and the prosecutor conclude most cases.

2. Plea bargaining has been the subject of a great deal of criticism from the public because it appears as though the offender is escaping full justice.

3. The rights of defendants in criminal trials are derived from the Constitution, specifically from the first 10 amendments, or the Bill of Rights. Several provisions in the Bill of Rights directly address the rights of defendants in criminal trials.

4. Before opening statements, each side may file pretrial motions to gain the most favorable circumstances and to limit the evidence from the other side.

5. The prosecution is the first to make an opening argument. The prosecution outlines the case and tells the jury of the types of evidence to be presented. The defense attorney then counters the prosecution's version of the case. No evidence is presented during opening arguments.

6. The prosecution then introduces evidence and witnesses and must prove beyond a reasonable doubt that the defendant is guilty.

7. The defense may object to the prosecutors' questions or the answers given by a witness. The defense then has the opportunity to cross-examine the witness. The prosecutor may then question the witness again, followed by questions from the defense.

8. After the prosecution presents its evidence and witnesses, the defense may present its own evidence and witnesses. The prosecution may cross-examine these witnesses, followed by redirect questions from the defense and re-cross-examination by the prosecution. Closing arguments follow, and the case goes to the jury.

9. Jury selection is subject to influence by the prosecution and defense through *voir dire*. The jury listens to the presentation of the case and then returns its verdict. A conviction or acquittal requires a unanimous vote.

10. Not all cases get a jury trial. The exceptions are those in which the penalty is not serious, those in which the defendant is a juvenile, and when the defense requests a bench trial. In a bench trial, a judge decides on guilt or acquittal and passes sentence.

11. If the defendant is found guilty, then he or she is sentenced by the judge. The two primary types of sentencing are indeterminate and determinate. The indeterminate sentence is fashioned to fit the offender, whereas the determinate sentence is fashioned to fit the crime.

12. Mandatory minimum sentences, a form of determinate sentencing, do not allow probation and specify incarceration for a term not less than a certain number of years.

13. To increase the voice and input of the victim, many states have adopted victim-rights legislation.

KEY TERMS

bench trial 338
beyond a reasonable doubt 335
determinate sentence 346
directed verdict of acquittal 335
hung jury 338
impeach 335

indeterminate sentence 346
indictment 332
information 332
mandatory minimum
  sentence 349
plea bargain 326

presumptive sentence 348
redirect examination 335
venire 337
voir dire 338

REVIEW QUESTIONS

1. What are the four types of pleas?

2. What are the steps of a trial?

3. Explain the major pretrial motions.

4. Describe the steps required in the formation of a jury.

5. What are *voir dire* and *venire*?

6. What are the two means by which a prosecutor can exclude a juror?

7. How is evidence classified?

8. What five strategies might a defense use to counter the prosecution?

9. What rights do defendants have in criminal trials?

10. Give an example of a victim's right.

11. Compare and contrast determinate and indeterminate sentences.

12. What are mandatory minimum sentences?

SUGGESTED FURTHER READING

Abramson, Jeffrey. *We the Jury: The Jury System and the Ideal of Democracy.* New York: Basic Books, 1994.

Carp, Robert A., Ronald Stidham, and Kenneth L. Manning. *Judicial Process in America.* Washington, DC: CQ Press, 2007.

Champion, Dean J., Richard D. Hartley, and Gary A. Rabe. *Criminal Courts: Structure, Process, and Issues.* Upper Saddle River, NJ: Prentice Hall, 2007.

Feeley, Malcolm. *The Process Is the Punishment: Handling Cases in a Lower Court.* Los Angeles: Sage, 1992.

Leo, Richard, and George Thomas. *The Miranda Debate: Law, Justice, and Policing.* Boston: Northeastern University Press, 2000.

Newman, Donald. *Conviction: The Determination of Guilt or Innocence without Trial.* Boston: Little, Brown, 1996.

ENDNOTES

1. John Hagan, "Extra-Legal Attributes and Criminal Sentencing: An Assessment of a Sociological Viewpoint," *Law and Society Review* 8 (1974): 357–381.

2. Thomas Austin, "The Influence of Court Location on Types of Criminal Sentences: The Rural-Urban Factor," *Journal of Criminal Justice* 9 (1981): 305–316.

3. Douglas Thomson and Anthony Ragona, "Popular Moderation versus Governmental Authoritarianism: An Interactionist View of Public Sentiments toward Criminal Sanctions," *Crime and Delinquency* 33 (1987): 337–357.

4. James Austin and John Irwin, *It's about Time: America's Imprisonment Binge*, 3rd ed. (Belmont, CA: Wadsworth, 2001).

5. Hedieh Nasheri, *Betrayal of Due Process: A Comparative Assessment of Plea Bargaining in the United States and Canada* (Lanham, MD: University Press of America, 1998).

6. Douglas Smith, "The Plea Bargaining Controversy," *Journal of Criminal Law and Criminology* 77 (1986): 949–957.

7. Arthur Rosett and Donald R. Cressey, *Justice by Consent: Plea Bargains in the American Courthouse* (New York: Lippincott, 1976).

8. William Rhodes, *Plea Bargaining: Who Gains? Who Loses?* (Washington, DC: Institute for Law and Social Research, 1978).

9. Michael Rubenstein and Teresa White, "Plea Bargaining: Can Alaska Live without It?" *Judicature* 62 (1979): 266–279.

10. Jay S. Albanese, "Concern about Variation in Criminal Sentences: A Cyclical History of Reform," *Journal of Criminal Law and Criminology* 75 (1984): 260–271.

11. N. Gary Holten and Lawson L. Lamar, *The Criminal Courts: Structures, Personnel, and Processes* (New York: McGraw-Hill, 1991).

12. Goffman, Erving, *Notes on the Management of a Spoiled Identity* (New York: Simon and Schuster, 1986).

13. Jeffery T. Ulmer, Megan C. Kurlychek, and John H. Kramer, "Prosecutorial Discretion and the Imposition of Mandatory Minimum Sentences," *Journal of Research in Crime and Delinquency* 44 (November 1, 2007): 427.

14. Linda A. Wood and Clare MacMartin, "Constructing Remorse: Judges' Sentencing Decisions in Child Sexual Assault Cases," *Journal of Language and Social Psychology* 26 (December 1, 2007): 343.

15. Greg M. Kramer, Melinda Wolbransky, and Kirk Heilbrun, "Plea Bargaining Recommendations by Criminal Defense Attorneys: Evidence Strength, Potential Sentence, and Defendant Preference," *Behavioral Sciences and the Law* 25 (July 1, 2007): 573.

16. B. Grant Stite and Robert H. Chaires, "Plea Bargaining: Ethical Issues and Emerging Perspectives," *Justice Professional* 7 (1993): 69–91.

17. Bradley S. Chilton, "Reforming Plea Bargaining to Facilitate Ethical Discourse," *Criminal Justice Policy Review* 5 (1991): 322–334.

18. David W. Neubauer, *America's Courts and the Criminal Justice System*, 7th ed. (Belmont, CA: Wadsworth, 2002).

19. Talia Fisher, "The Boundaries of Plea Bargaining: Negotiating the Standard of Proof," *Journal of Criminal Law and Criminology* 97 (July 1, 2007): 943–1007.

20. Neubauer, *America's Courts.*

21. David Lynch, "The Impropriety of Plea Agreements: A Tale of Two Counties," *Law and Social Inquiry* 19 (1994): 115–136.

22. Lynn Mather, *Plea Bargaining or Trial* (Lexington, MA: Heath, 1979).

23. Neubauer, *America's Courts.*

24. Thomas Church, "Plea Bargains, Concessions and the Courts: Analysis of a Quasi-Experiment," *Law and Society Review* 10 (1976): 377–389.

25. Jon'a F. Meyer and Diana R. Grant, *The Courts in Our Criminal Justice System* (Upper Saddle River, NJ: Prentice Hall, 2003).

26. Raymond Nimmer and Patricia Krauthaus, "Plea Bargaining Reform in Two Cities," *Justice System Journal* 3 (1977): 6–21.

27. Candace McCoy, *Politics and Plea Bargaining: Victims' Rights in California* (Philadelphia: University of Pennsylvania Press, 1993).

28. Bureau of Justice Statistics, "The Justice System: What Is the Sequence of Events in the Criminal Justice System?" http://ojp.usdoj.gov/bjs/justsys.htm.

29. United States Attorneys' Manual, "When an Information May Be Used," October 1997, www.usdoj.gov/usao/eousa/foia_reading_room/usam/title9/crm00206.htm.

30. David A. Bright and Jane Goodman-Delahunty, "Gruesome Evidence and Emotion: Anger, Blame, and Jury Decision-Making," *Law and Human Behavior* 30 (April 1, 2006): 183–202.

31. Henry J. Abraham, *The Judicial Process*, 7th ed. (New York: Oxford University Press, 1998).

32. Steven Schlesinger, *Exclusionary Injustice: The Problem of Illegally Obtained Evidence* (New York: Dekker, 1977).

33. Steve Tuholski, "When Facts Don't Fit, Some Jurors Make Up New Facts," *National Law Journal* (February 4, 2008): S3.

34. J. Don Read, Deborah A. Connolly, and Andrew Welsh, "An Archival Analysis of Actual Cases of Historic Child Sexual Abuse: A Comparison of Jury and Bench Trials," *Law and Human Behavior* 30 (June 1, 2006): 259–285.

35. Barbara Reskin and Christine Visher, "The Impacts of Evidence and Extralegal Factors in Jurors' Decisions," *Law and Society Review* 20 (1986): 423–439.

36. Neubauer, *America's Courts.*

37. Lincoln Caplan, *The Insanity Defense and the Trial of John W. Hinckley Jr.* (Boston: Godine, 1984).

38. Michael Freeman and Helen Reece, eds., *Science in Court* (Brookfield, VT: Ashgate, 1998).

39. Tom R. Tyler, "Viewing CSI and the Threshold of Guilt: Managing Truth and Justice in Reality and Fiction," *Yale Law Journal* 115 (March 1, 2006): 1050–1085.

40. William Brennan, "The Criminal Prosecution: Sporting Events or Quest for Truth?" *Washington University Law Review* (1963): 279–294.

41. Smith, "Plea Bargaining Controversy."

42. Richard Quinney, *Critique of Legal Order: Crime Control in Capitalist Society* (Boston: Little, Brown, 1974).

43. Chief Justice John Marshall in the Supreme Court's ruling on *Marbury* v. *Madison*, 5 U.S. 137 (1803), http://caselaw.lp.findlaw.com/scripts/getcase.pl?navby=case&court=us&vol=5&page=137.

44. "10th Circuit Says Speedy Trial Act Doesn't Allow Prospective Waiver," *Lawyers USA*, January 28, 2008, 1.

45. Sheila Royo Maxwell, "Examining the Congruence between Predictors of ROR and Failures to Appear," *Journal of Criminal Justice* 27 (March 1, 1999): 127–141.

46. Mary Achilles and Howard Zehr, "Restorative Justice for Crime Victims: The Promise, The Challenge," in *Restorative Community Justice: Repairing Harm and Transforming Communities*, eds. Gordon Bazemore and Mara Schiff (Cincinnati, OH: Anderson, 2001), 87–99.

47. Nils Christie, "Conflicts as Property," *British Journal of Criminology* 17 (1997): 1–15.

48. Valerie Finn-Deluca, "Victim Participation at Sentencing," *Criminal Law Bulletin* 30 (1994): 403–428.

49. Peter Finn and Beverley Lee, *Establishing and Expanding Victim-Witness Assistance Programs* (Washington, DC: National Institute of Justice, 1988).

50. Robert Elias, *Victims Still: The Political Manipulation of Crime Victims* (Thousand Oaks, CA: Sage, 1993).

51. Andrew von Hirsch, *Doing Justice* (New York: Hill & Wang, 1976).

52. Peggy Tobolowsky, "Restitution in the Federal Criminal Justice System," *Judicature* 77 (1993): 90–95. See also Christy Visher, "Incapacitation and Crime Control: Does a 'Lock em Up' Strategy Reduce Crime?" *Justice Quarterly* 4 (1987): 513–544.

53. Thomas Arvanites, "Increasing Imprisonment: A Function of Crime or Socioeconomic Factors?" *American Journal of Criminal Justice* 17 (1992): 19–38.

54. Elizabeth Moulds, "Chivalry and Paternalism: Disparities of Treatment in the Criminal Justice System," *Western Political Science Quarterly* 31 (1978): 416–440.

55. Tamasak Wicharaya, *Simple Theory, Hard Reality: The Impact of Sentencing Reforms on Courts, Prisons, and Crime* (Albany: State University of New York Press, 1995).

56. John Irwin, *Prisons in Turmoil* (Boston: Little, Brown, 1980). Irwin presents a scathing critique of the indeterminate sentence from a prisoner's point of view.

57. Ibid.

58. William Gaylin, *Partial Justice: A Study of Bias in Sentencing* (New York: Vintage Books, 1974).

59. Irwin, *Prisons in Turmoil*.

60. Steven P. Lab and John T. Whitehead, "From 'Nothing Works' to 'The Appropriate Works': The Latest Stop in the Search for the Secular Grail," *Criminology* 28 (1990): 405–418.

61. Hagan, "Extra-Legal Attributes."

62. James B. Jacobs, *Stateville: The Penitentiary in Mass Society* (Chicago: University of Chicago Press, 1977).

63. Francis T. Cullen and Karen B. Gilbert, *Reaffirming Rehabilitation* (Cincinnati, OH: Anderson, 1982).

64. Pamala L. Griset, *Determinate Sentencing: The Promise and the Reality of Retributive Justice* (Ithaca: State University of New York Press, 1991).

65. Jeffery Ulmer, *Social Worlds of Sentencing: Court Communities under Sentencing Guidelines* (Albany: State University of New York Press, 1997).

66. Darrell Steffensmeier, Jeffery Ulmer, and John Kramer, "The Interaction of Race, Gender, and Age in Criminal Sentencing: The Punishment Cost of Being Young, Black and Male," *Criminology* 36 (1998): 763–798.

67. Austin and Irwin, *It's about Time*.

68. William McDonald, Henry Rossman, and James Cramer, "The Prosecutorial Function and Its Relation to Determinate Sentencing Structures," in *The Prosecutor*, ed. William McDonald (Beverly Hills, CA: Sage, 1979).

69. John Harris and Paul Jesilow, "It's Not the Old Ball Game: Three Strikes and the Courtroom Workgroup," *Justice Quarterly* 17 (2000): 185–204.

70. Ibid.

71. Laurence H. Ross and James Foley, "Judicial Disobedience of the Mandate to Imprison Drunk Drivers," *Law and Society Review* 21 (1987): 315–323.

72. Paula Ditton and Doris Wilson, *Truth in Sentencing in State Prisons* (Washington, DC: Bureau of Justice Statistics, 1999).

73. Ulmer, Kurlychek, and Kramer, "Prosecutorial Discretion."

CHAPTER 11

History of Control and Punishment

Objectives

1. Understand why societies use control.

2. Compare and contrast ancient and modern methods of social control.

3. Describe the means of control in colonial America.

4. Discuss the eras in the development of the penitentiary.

5. Describe the contributions of Alexander Maconochie, Sir Walter Crofton, and Zebulon Brockway.

6. Describe the history of capital punishment.

7. Discuss the arguments for and against capital punishment.

Throughout history, societies have employed various means to encourage their members to adopt socially approved standards of behavior. Sociologists and anthropologists have revealed how societies construct folkways, norms, rules, and laws. Violations of these forms of social control bring reactions from mild rebuke to extreme violence as groups struggle to make members conform. This chapter presents a brief review of the history of social control with a special emphasis on the types of behavior that are now under the purview of the criminal justice system.

This is an interesting history, not only of the wide variety of methods of control (many of them brutal by today's standards) that have been used over the centuries, but also of how some of the ancient ways of controlling deviant behavior are still used in some form today.[1] To say that the history of social control illustrates progress in changing or correcting criminal behavior would be inaccurate. At most, we can say that although science and technology have introduced new methods of punishing or correcting criminal behavior, widespread dissatisfaction exists about the humaneness of current procedures, as well as scant evidence that they are any more or less effective than those used in earlier times.[2]

This chapter is divided into three sections. The first section covers how criminal behavior was managed before the advent of the prison. Here, the particular concern is with how society aimed to punish the offender by attacking the physical body of those who broke the law. Flogging, branding, mutilation, and other tortures were used to show everyone that antisocial behavior had dire consequences. The second section pertains to the history of the prison, particularly as it developed in the United States. Finally, the chapter places the controversial issue of capital punishment into historical context and discusses its present-day complexities. Specifically, we will look at arguments that defend capital punishment as well as those advocating its abolition.

BEFORE THERE WERE PRISONS

As we learned in our discussion of the history of the court, ancient societies did not have a well-defined criminal justice system that dealt with those who violated the law. In fact, society did not adopt the idea of a codified law until relatively recently. However, precursors of the criminal justice system developed in a patchwork fashion over time.[3]

In societies that existed before 700 C.E., justice was a private matter.[4] No criminal justice system existed to enforce societal rules, so it was up to the family, tribe, or group to enforce internal norms and to protect members from outside aggression. The blood feud, discussed in the chapters on the courts, was how justice was enforced. Retaliation for real or imagined crimes allowed aggrieved parties to settle scores with those who had offended them. Of course, the blood feud often resulted in a cycle of violence in which groups fought for years trying to balance the scales of justice. To limit the violence, societies began mandating that perpetrators compensate their victims with some type of payment.[5]

Corporal Punishment

One of the primary ways that individuals or societies extract revenge from the offender is through corporal punishment. Corporal punishment entails inflicting physical harm on the body. Pain is a sensation that everyone understands, and the idea behind corporal punishment is to inflict a carefully measured amount of pain considered proportional to the offense.[6] Despite the fact that individuals have varying tolerances to pain, using the body as a tool of the state to inflict pain, humiliation, and suffering on an offender has had wide acceptance throughout history. The infliction of pain can be traced to the earliest of societies.[7]

TORTURE   Torture, the infliction of severe or prolonged pain, is a method of coercion, revenge, and punishment used by many societies. Some societies use torture as a form of punishment for antisocial activity. Because torture is considered inhumane by many modern societies, officials often deny that torture is used or that a certain punishment constitutes torture.[8] However, even though some of the more gruesome forms of torture such as disembowelment or impaling are no longer used, other methods, such as long periods of solitary confinement, are common.[9] Numerous examples exist of the cruelty inflicted on individuals at the behest of the state. One of the better known and explicit depictions of torture as an act of justice is provided by Michel Foucault in *Discipline and Punish: The Birth of the Prison*. As punishment for attempting to assassinate King Louis XV in 1757, Robert-François Damiens was sentenced to be drawn and quartered. Foucault quoted the newspaper of the day thusly:

> The flesh will be torn from his breasts, arms, thighs and calves with red-hot pincers, his right hand, holding the knife with which he committed said [homicide], burnt with sulphur, and, on those places where the flesh will be torn away, poured molten lead, boiling oil, burning resin, wax and sulphur melted together and then his body drawn and quartered by four horses and his limbs and body consumed by fire, reduced to ashes and his ashes thrown to the winds.[10]

Drawing and quartering entails tying the arms and legs of the victim to four horses, which are then sent in different directions. Unfortunately for Damiens, four horses were not enough to accomplish this task, and two more horses were employed. Ultimately, his limbs were hacked apart to aid the straining horses. He remained conscious throughout this ordeal.

FLOGGING   Flogging (or whipping) is an age-old punishment. According to the Old Testament book of Deuteronomy, "If the wicked man be worthy to be beaten, that the judge shall cause him to lie down, and to be beaten before his face, according to his fault, by a certain number. Forty stripes he may give him. . . ."[11] The whips used had three separate thongs of leather, and each thong was of a different length. In effect, then, the 40 lashes actually numbered three times that. Often, the result was death.[12]

Flogging was used throughout history by the Egyptians and Romans, as well as in England, France, Germany, China, and the United States. In the slave-holding South before the Civil War, the whipping of slaves was a consistent form of punishment and control. The slave owner had considerable latitude in deciding how much a slave could be punished. However, the severity of the beatings was limited because a dead or disabled slave was not as valuable. Therefore, the slave owner sought methods of punishment that did not affect the slave's value:

> Where any spark of leniency showed itself the motive behind it was not humanity for the sufferer, but the fear that the market value of the slave might be

Flogging was a public form of punishment. Often people came to witness the spectacle for entertainment. Here, a man receives 30 lashes with the cat-o'-nine-tails.

Source: Courtesy of Image Works/Mary Evans Picture Library Ltd

lowered if signs of punishment were too obvious. For the slave-owner could not have it both ways: he could not indulge his sadistic pleasures and get the top market price for the maimed or crippled slave.[13]

With flogging, the amount of pain could be precisely meted out with the number of lashes. Tied to a post or a tree, the victim would often scream in pain each time the whip struck flesh; thus, whippings were used to intimidate others who might be tempted to break the rules.

BRANDING   In some societies, branding was used to show the community that criminals had been harshly and permanently punished. Branding identified criminals and prevented them from blending into the community. In colonial North America, repeat offenders were branded on the forehead.[14] Females, in lieu of physical branding, were required to wear identification on their clothing that signaled their transgressions. The most visible example comes to us through literature in Nathaniel Hawthorne's novel *The Scarlet Letter*, in which Hester Prynne wears the letter *A* embroidered on her dress to announce to the community that she had committed adultery.

Physical branding is a particularly extreme measure because it is a permanent stigma that forever labels the individual as an offender.[15] Today, we can see vestiges of the branding practice in prison tattoos that inmates proudly wear to show various aspects of their prison history. Additionally, some jurisdictions attempt to socially brand certain types of offenders (such as those accused of sex offenses) by requiring them to have bumper stickers on their cars so police and parents can identify them when they are near schoolyards.[16]

MUTILATION   Many societies used mutilation as a form of punishment. At times, it reflected the concept of proportionality in terms of the biblical dictate of "an eye for an eye." Those who blasphemed might have their tongues cut out. Those who stole might have their hands cut off.[17] Similarly, castration was used in many societies to punish those who committed sexual crimes. According to George Ryley Scott:

The torture associated with castration is of two kinds. In the first place, there is the intense agony and great danger to life which are inseparable from the operation performed in the crude manner customary among savage and primitive tribes (often involving complete ablation of the exterior genitals), where aseptic surgery is unknown and anesthetics are not employed. In the second place there is the psychological torture which cannot ever be effaced in the case of any man who is castrated against his will; so that where he succeeds in overcoming the physical dangers and suffering, he continues to suffer mentally as long as his life lasts.[18]

Mutilation existed in the penal code of every European country and was transported to the American colonies. It is difficult to find modern remnants of mutilation, although some may contend that the suggested chemical castration of sex offenders is a form of mutilation.

HUMILIATION   A number of societies used public humiliation and shaming techniques to punish a variety of crimes. In colonial North America, offenders were placed in stocks in the public square, where they were subject to the verbal and physical ridicule of the public. On some occasions, they were stoned while locked in these restraining devices. Some stocks required the offender to stand and support his own weight for long hours in the hot sun.[19] Humiliation techniques served a dual purpose. They exacted a degree of punishment on the offender while reinforcing community norms. Those who witnessed the humiliation of the offender were presumably less likely to engage in deviant behaviors themselves. Today, although we no longer put people in stocks, the criminal justice system employs a number of shaming and humiliation initiatives.[20] Offenders have been made to wear signs announcing their offenses, and some are required to address community groups. Others are made to do work that allows the rest of society to see them, such as picking up trash on the highways. In some jurisdictions, the names and/or pictures of drunk drivers or sex offenders are published in local newspapers or on the Internet.[21]

SHOCK DEATH   Before the invention of the prison, societies had difficulty developing punishments that were not too severe but that got the attention of the offender. Short of actually executing a person, the amount of fear that can be instilled in an offender is difficult to measure and inflict. One ingenious colonial era method of impressing an offender with the seriousness of the offense was termed "shock death":

> In the case of shock death, an offender would receive the sentence of death by hanging but would later be granted a reprieve. The reprieve, however, came only after the offender had proceeded through each and every ritual leading up to the execution. To elaborate, the offender would be led from the jail out to the gallows, with the mask placed over his head and the noose placed around his neck, and the wait for the trap door to open, ending his life. The sentenced offender could remain at the gallows for more than three hours, fully expecting to be executed. Finally, the noose and mask were removed and the offender was informed that his life had been spared.[22]

Such an ordeal would likely impress on the lawbreaker the ramifications of a life of crime. Such an extravagant charade is akin to psychological torture. It is easy to draw parallels from this account to how capital punishment is presently practiced with its multiple opportunities for appeals and stays of execution.

Economic Punishment

Although punishments on the offender's body were common before the use of prisons, a number of other dispositions featured extracting labor from the offender's body rather than pain.[23] In economic hard times, convict labor was a favorite mechanism both for punishment and getting the work of society done.

THE GALLEY   Before the development of sophisticated sailing techniques, ships were powered by wind and human labor. Some ancient societies used slaves or those who were captured during warfare. The French, Spanish, and Italians staffed their naval fleets with prisoners who were shackled to their oars and made to row large vessels long distances. This punishment was used primarily for those sentenced to death; however, in times of scarce labor, individuals convicted of lesser crimes were sent to the galley ships for a specified period of years. Galley service was extremely strenuous and dangerous and was feared almost as much as execution. Many individuals died as a result of the unsanitary conditions and extreme physical exertion required.[24]

WORKHOUSES   Throughout history, prisons have had a close relationship with the economic conditions of the times.[25] When labor is abundant, the prisons are full; when labor is scarce, either fewer people are incarcerated or the authorities find ways to exploit the offenders. With the waning influence of feudalism in the 16th century, many people left the large estates of wealthy landowners and migrated to the cities. This resulted in a large population of unemployed and restless individuals who threatened the cities' stability and peace. Thieves, prostitutes, and other "riffraff" had to be brought under control, so in London, Parliament established Bridewell, a place where the poor were put to work and supposedly learned good work habits. Workhouses for the poor easily became jails for petty offenders who were a societal nuisance. Gradually, the idea of locking up the rabble led to a proliferation of jails. Because they had no organizing principles, the jails were operated in the cheapest and most squalid manner imaginable.[26]

John Howard, elected to the post of high sheriff in Bedfordshire, England, in 1773, was appalled by the local jail's inhumane conditions. He toured other jails in both England and on the European continent and discovered English jails to be inferior in terms of living conditions and the way jailers treated the inmates. Based on his observations, Howard published *The State of Prisons in England and Wales* in 1777. Howard lobbied the House of Commons and was successful in getting Parliament to pass the Penitentiary Act of 1779, a major piece of reform legislation. This act addressed the living conditions of inmates, the need to make productive use of their labor, and humane treatment. In practice, the law failed to provide many of the desired reforms, but it did subtly change the nature and status of incarceration, removing it from the purview of local authorities and establishing the idea that the federal government has a responsibility to oversee conditions.[27]

EXILE AND TRANSPORTATION   Transporting offenders into exile in far-flung colonies served two primary purposes. First, it rid the mother country of a good number of "ne'er-do-wells," vagabonds, and petty offenders. Second, the colonies had a significant demand for the labor of the surplus population of the mother country. European countries such as England, France, and Spain transported offenders to the New World colonies to serve prison sentences or to work as indentured servants.

One interesting aspect of transportation is that it was done by private contractors. The contracts of the indentured servants were sold to these private contractors, who took the responsibility and risk of transporting the offenders to the colonies, where they sold the contracts to free colonists. The servants had little way of knowing what lay ahead of them. Their owners' attitudes varied widely, and some took advantage of illiterate individuals and kept them in servitude long after their original terms had expired.[28] The American Revolution in 1776 put an end to the practice of England sending offenders to the American colonies. Instead, the English housed their prisoners in large old ships, called *hulks*, that were anchored in harbors. Additionally, Australia became the preferred destination for English lawbreakers. Between 1787 and 1875, more than 135,000 felons were sent there.[29]

Offenders were transported to the New World at a high cost to their lives and health. The voyages were rigorous enough for the crew, but "passengers" were locked belowdecks in crowded and squalid conditions. By the time they arrived at their destination, many were dead or dying. It was a difficult way to start a term of punishment, not to mention a new life. Instead of rotting in a decrepit jail cell or on one of the stinking hulks, those who survived the trip were lent out as labor to free settlers,

11.1   FOCUS *on* ETHICS

TRANSPORTATION IN A CONTEMPORARY WORLD

Since the fall of the Soviet Union and the closing of the remote Siberian gulags where political prisoners were sent, transportation has not been a visible feature of corrections. What if the criminal justice system were to bring it back? A host of questions would arise for which answers are difficult to formulate without considering the profound moral, legal, and political issues. How would you address the following questions?

- Where would prisoners be sent today?
- Is it fair to dump our prisoners on another country?
- If you were an offender and told that you were to be transported and given a choice of destination, where would you most like to go? Where would you least like to go?
- What would be the purpose of transportation? Exile? Punishment? Deterrence? Retribution?

Here are some recent examples of policies related to the practice of transportation:

- U.S. judges used to routinely give young male offenders the option of going to jail or joining the military. Especially in times of war, these arrangements were seen as a way for a minor criminal to cleanse his record and

get a fresh start in life. Should this practice continue? Are violent offenders who we want as soldiers?

- In the late 1970s, Fidel Castro emptied the jails and mental institutions of Cuba and allowed these inmates to go to the United States in what was called the Mariel Boat Lift. Hundreds of Cubans were incarcerated in U.S. federal prisons even though they had not broken U.S. law. What eventually happened to these inmates? Should they have been incarcerated in the first place?
- After the United States invaded Afghanistan, hundreds of al-Qaeda and Taliban fighters were transported to the U.S. naval base in Guantanamo Bay, Cuba, and held indefinitely. Why were these prisoners not taken to the continental United States? What should have been done with them? Are they criminals or prisoners of war? What legal systems should they be held accountable to?

Transportation today is not a viable correctional practice because of these many questions. Perhaps if we needed colonists to work on distant planets or solar systems, we might try to revive this practice. Until then, it appears that incarceration will be our primary response to the criminal offender.

where they worked hard but had a chance for better living conditions. Those who did not get to work with free settlers were imprisoned in oppressive penal colonies such as Norfolk Island in the South Pacific.

We usually consider transportation to be an English idea, but other countries practiced banishment and transportation as well. Russia and the Soviet Union sent offenders to Siberia well into the 20th century.[30] (See Focus on Ethics 11.1 for a further look at modern transportation.)

PRISONS IN AMERICA

The history of punishment reveals a vast array of practices on which our modern prisons have drawn. In many ways, we can see how exile to another land has been replaced by social exile behind prison walls, and how modern prison industry programs have replaced workhouses. However, the real issues of the changing nature of punishments revolve around the idea of reform.[31] For better or worse, our prison efforts have been aimed at making the institution more effective, more humane, and more palatable to the public. What has resulted, however, have been serious, if unintended, consequences that have brought their own problematic issues. To understand how prisons in America have developed into today's bureaucratic institutions, we must trace their history from colonial times to the present with an eye toward how well-intended reforms have not worked out as planned.[32]

Control in the Colonies

The American colonies were faced with many of the same issues of social control as England, but some major differences between the two led to the unique development of American incarceration. Early penal institutions were under local control and

The Walnut Street Jail looms in the distance as a little church is drawn past it by a team of horses.
Source: The Granger Collection, New York

mixed various types of offenders; the accused were held with the convicted, civil violators with criminal offenders, and so on.

The idea of incarceration as the sole punishment for convicts took some time to develop. Corporal punishment, especially the stocks, or whipping was used in conjunction with jail to discourage crime. The Quakers in Pennsylvania suggested that incarceration and hard labor were preferable to corporal punishment. The state's penal code of 1786 allowed inmates to work on public projects while chained to cannonballs and dressed in brightly colored clothing. Because many objected to this public spectacle, the hard labor was moved behind the walls of the institution.

The Walnut Street Jail, in existence since 1776, demonstrated all the shortcomings of the early jails, such as housing men and women together and the guards selling alcohol to inmates. Used as a military prison in the Revolutionary War, it was converted in 1792 into the nation's first penitentiary, in which the most hardened convicts were kept in single cells. The Walnut Street Jail did not completely accomplish its goals of solitude and hard labor, but it did set the tone for the more formal prisons that would be built in the next century.[33]

The first institution to resemble a modern penitentiary was Castle Island in Massachusetts's Boston Harbor. Established by the Massachusetts legislature in 1785, it housed only convicted offenders from the state's various jails.[34] From 1785 to 1798, about 280 prisoners served time on Castle Island, with at least 45 escaping.

The theory and practice of prisons started in the United States with the Walnut Street Jail and Castle Island, but they were only the beginning. The 19th century brought a new era of true prisons, which would be tried and found wanting.[35]

Development of the Penitentiary: 1780–1860

Two prison systems that emerged in the United States during the first half of the 19th century attracted prison reformers across the nation and around the world. These systems, called the Pennsylvania System and the Auburn (New York) System (the names are based on their initial locations), emphasized regimens of silence and penitence.

PENNSYLVANIA SYSTEM   In 1829, the state of Pennsylvania opened a prison on the site of a cherry orchard outside Philadelphia. For years, the Eastern State Penitentiary,

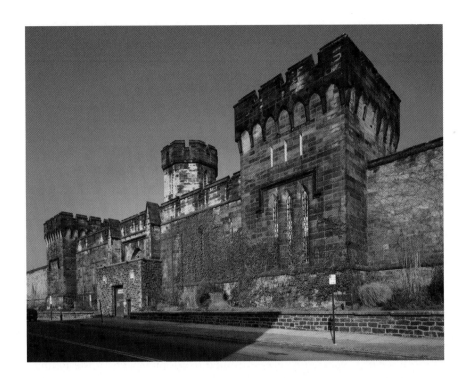

Built in 1822, Pennsylvania's Eastern State Penitentiary is now a historic site.

Source: Albert Vecerka. Courtesy of Eastern State Penitentiary Historic Site, Philadelphia, Pennsylvania

This 19th-century engraving depicts a silent-system work-shop at London's Millbank Prison.

Source: CORBIS-NY

called Cherry Hill by the locals, was characterized by the **separate-and-silent system,** by which it was reasoned that inmates would reflect on their offenses and reform. By keeping the inmates from seeing and talking to each other, the state hoped they would not contaminate each other with antisocial thoughts and behavior. Kept in solitary confinement, many inmates developed severe mental problems because of the oppressive boredom and lack of human contact. The inmates developed clever means of communicating (such as tapping codes on the water pipes in the cells), but for the most part, they were kept as separate as possible by the prison's limited resources.[36] However, as the prison became more crowded, double-celling became the norm and isolation was impossible. The separate-and-silent system was costly and soon met its demise, not only because of economics, but also because critics thought keeping anyone in isolation for so long was inhumane.

separate-and-silent system

A method of penal control pioneered by Philadelphia's Eastern State Penitentiary in which inmates were kept from seeing or talking to one another. This method is comparable to solitary confinement in modern prisons.

AUBURN SYSTEM   The Auburn Prison, opened in 1817 in New York, at first tried the separate-and-silent system. By 1823, it became apparent that this system caused more problems than it solved and that the mental and physical issues faced by inmates were more punishing than the administration thought reasonable. Therefore, although inmates were locked in separate cells each night, they were allowed to eat and work together during the day. They were forbidden to talk to each other, however. This **congregate-and-silent system,** which prohibited face-to-face contact, required prisoners to march in lockstep and keep their eyes downcast.[37]

Considerable debate surrounded these two prison systems. On one hand, the Pennsylvania System's supporters touted it as superior because it was easier to control prisoners, was more conducive to meditation and repentance, and avoided the cross-contamination inherent when inmates are together. By using such extreme procedures as having inmates wear hoods when outside their cells, the Eastern State Penitentiary administration believed it was facilitating the inmates' self-reflection and eventual reform.

In contrast, proponents of the Auburn model argued that their methods and techniques of incarceration were superior because they were a great deal cheaper, could provide better vocational training, and were less harmful to the inmates' mental health. Additionally, the Auburn model used a factory-oriented labor system as opposed to the craft-oriented labor system of the Eastern State Penitentiary. Although neither of these systems was totally copied in other jurisdictions, they did serve as models for other prisons. Reformers continued to adopt aspects of the Pennsylvania and Auburn models and introduced modifications that addressed changing political, economic, and social conditions.[38]

Age of Reform: 1860–1900

As innovative and well-meaning as these prison experiments were, they had their critics. Although the ideals of solitude, hard work, discipline, and reflection were attractive theoretically, in practice they produced a prison atmosphere that not only was

congregate-and-silent system
A style of control pioneered by the Auburn System, in which inmates were allowed to eat and work together during the day but were forbidden to speak and were locked alone in their cells at night.

This 19th-century torture punishment involved controlling an inmate's limbs with pulleys.

THE PULLEYS.

harmful to the inmate, but also created a public relations issue. English novelist Charles Dickens, who toured the Pennsylvania prisons, wrote:

> In its intention, I am well convinced that it is kind, humane, and meant for re-formation; but I am persuaded that those who devised this system of Prison Dis-cipline, and those benevolent gentlemen who carry it into execution, do not know what it is that they are doing. I believe that very few men are capable of estimating the immense amount of torture and agony which this dreadful pun-ishment, prolonged for years, inflicts upon the sufferers; and in guessing at it myself, and in reasoning from what I have seen written upon their faces, and what to my certain knowledge they feel within, I am only the more convinced that there is a terrible endurance in it which none but the sufferers can fathom, and which no man has a right to inflict upon his fellow creature.[39]

At the same time that the penitentiary was developed in the United States and copied by other nations, the practices of other nations affected U.S. corrections. While critics such as Dickens complained about the Pennsylvania and Auburn sys-tems in the United States, European countries were experimenting with techniques designed not just to punish, but to give the inmate a better chance at successfully re-turning to free society on completing the sentence. This new emphasis on social rein-tegration was called the *Irish System*, and although it was eventually tried in the post–Civil War United States, it was used for decades abroad. Here, we will focus on the three most well-known examples of the Irish System of reform: those developed by Alexander Maconochie, Sir Walter Crofton, and Zebulon Brockway.

ALEXANDER MACONOCHIE   Alexander Maconochie was a Scot who developed a sys-tem designed to make the inmate trustworthy, honest, and useful to society. A retired naval officer, he became superintendent of the penal colony at Van Diemen's Land (what is now called Tasmania). Here, Maconochie set about an experiment that sought to humanize prison life, but he was relieved of his duties before it could be fully implemented. In 1840, he was placed in command of another penal colony, this one on Norfolk Island off the eastern coast of Australia. Here, he imposed a system based on two fundamental beliefs:

1. Brutality and cruelty debase not only the subject, but also the society that deliberately uses or tolerates them for purposes of social control.

2. The treatment of a wrongdoer during his sentence of imprisonment should be designed to make him fit to be released into society again, purged of the ten-dencies that led him to his offense, and strengthened in his ability to withstand temptation again.[40]

Central to Maconochie's philosophy of incarceration was the indeterminate sen-tence, in which the offender would be released when the prison officials believed he was reformed. (As we will come to see later in the 20th century, the indeterminate sen-tence can work in the offender's favor or work to keep him or her incarcerated for an even longer time than a fixed term.) A **marks-of-commendation system** was instituted in which inmates earned the right to be released. Additionally, privileges, goods, and services could be purchased with marks given for good behavior. The marks system enabled inmates to progress through various stages of social control and was en-visioned to give inmates some control over the pains of incarceration. Although many of the ideas Maconochie incorporated into the Norfolk Island system had been sug-gested by others, including John Howard and Jeremy Bentham, Maconochie's rational and systematic implementation earned high praise from prison experts. However, the system set up on Norfolk Island was short-lived. Maconochie was recalled to England in 1844 and with him went the more humane treatment of inmates on Norfolk Island.

SIR WALTER CROFTON   In 1854, a decade after Maconochie left Norfolk Island, his progressive ways of treating inmates inspired Sir Walter Crofton, who was appointed

marks-of-commendation system

An incarceration philosophy devel-oped by Alexander Maconochie in which inmates earned the right to be released, as well as privileges, goods, and services.

Inmates at the Elmira Reformatory during the early 1900s.
Source: CORBIS-NY

director of the Irish prison system. Crofton liked both Maconochie's marks system and the progressive stages of social control. He added the concept of a completely open institution in which the inmates could gain experience in trust and avoiding temptation. Crofton is best remembered for instituting an early-release system called *ticket-of-leave*, in which inmates were given a conditional release and supervised by local police. If the inmates violated the conditions of their release, they were returned to prison.[41] (This idea will be more fully discussed in Chapter 13.)

ZEBULON BROCKWAY The ideas developed by Maconochie and Crofton were instituted by Zebulon Brockway at the reformatory in Elmira, New York. Brockway used the 500-bed facility to house young men between ages 16 and 30 who were first-time offenders. A three-grade program was used in which inmates entered at the second grade. An inmate was promoted to the first grade after six months of good behavior or demoted to the third grade if he failed to conform. Only those who were in the first grade were eligible for release (they were sentenced to an indeterminate term with only the minimum amount of time being fixed). An inmate needed a year of good marks before being eligible for parole. The Elmira Reformatory used volunteers, who can be thought of as forerunners of parole officers, to keep track of the released inmates. The important distinction between this accommodation and the Irish ticket-of-leave system is that the parolees were not supervised by police officers. This separation of law enforcement and correctional activities is an enduring feature of this early program.[42]

The reform movement had its drawbacks as well as successes. Penal reform did not progress in an uninterrupted manner from brutality to humane treatment because even the reformers, such as Zebulon Brockway, had some unattractive ideas. Brockway was known as a shameless self-promoter and often hid the less desirable conditions of the reform movement. The use of corporal punishment was such a stable feature of the Elmira Reformatory that Brockway was nicknamed "Paddler Brockway." In addition, the integrity of the classification system was difficult to maintain. Designed for young first offenders, the reformatories often housed seasoned offenders, and issues of violence, revolts, rape, smuggling, and arson often arose.[43]

For those who presented significant discipline problems, a form of solitary confinement was used. Brockway called this the "rest cure," but it included being shackled and fed nothing more than bread and water for months at a time. Although these problems eventually led to the demise of the reform movement, the idea of reform has become a recurring theme in corrections. Many of the ideals of the reform movement are

Convicts in Alabama break rocks with sledge hammers while working on the chain gang.

Source: Getty Images, Inc.-Liaison

at the foundation of modern prison systems. The repeated imperfect implementation of these reforms speaks not to the inadequacy of the reforms, but more to the economic, social, and political contexts that invariably frustrate the ideals of prison reformers.

Prison Labor and Public Works: 1900–1930

The idea that work is healthy for both the inmate and society is as old as the prison. The Pennsylvania System, which viewed too much labor as interfering with rehabilitative meditation, included a certain amount of craft work to be done by inmates in their cells. Other prison systems considered work wholly useful. Of particular interest is the degree to which work was viewed as a good thing in itself and when it was viewed as a means to other ends. Work was deemed beneficial in at least three ways:

1. **A good way to keep inmates occupied.**   By doing work (sometimes back-breaking work), the inmates have neither the time nor the energy to cause trouble.

2. **Rehabilitative value.**   Because most prisoners eventually return to society, they benefit from the activities of work. They practice good work habits and sometimes learn useful skills.

3. **Offsets the cost of incarceration.**   Inmate labor has been used to construct and maintain prisons, feed inmates, and at times make products that can be sold to other government agencies or even the outside society.

Many states have restrictive legislation that prevents prison labor systems from competing with businesses.[44] The advantage of free (or extremely cheap) labor gives prison labor systems an almost unbeatable competitive advantage. Therefore, many prison labor systems are restricted to making products to be used exclusively by the state government. For instance, prisoners in Georgia make office furniture that can be purchased by other state agencies. Some rural prisons grow vegetables or raise cattle that are used to feed inmates. (See Criminal Justice Reference 11.1 for more on this issue.)

These examples only partially reflect the variety of ways prison labor is used.[45] To fully appreciate the range of ways prison labor is used to produce wealth, we must consider whether the inmates are controlled and disciplined by public or private officials, who controls the sale of the products, and the size of the market.

The distinctions among these prison labor systems may be subtle at times, but they hold important ramifications for the inmates in terms of how they are treated and fed and what kinds of skills they develop. The oldest of these systems are the

11.1 CRIMINAL JUSTICE REFERENCE

Federal Prison Industries

Prison labor has come a long way since the days of chain gangs and license plate stamping. Although these forms of labor still exist, they have been joined by prison shops that produce clothing and textiles, office furniture, and electronics. Federal Prison Industries, or Unicor, is a government agency that trains and employs inmates to produce goods for sale to the federal government. In prisons around the country, inmates who are paid as little as 23 cents an hour produce bed linens, towels, office chairs and workstations, and filing cabinets. Unicor, established in 1934, has recently gone into the business of recycling old computer equipment and electronics.

Corrections officials say this work is good for inmates. They can earn money to buy small luxury items and pay any restitution they owe. It also gives them something to do and makes their time pass more quickly, officials say. The inmates seem to agree. As of 2002, Unicor employed about 21,000 inmates, and there is a waiting list for jobs. The private sector takes a dim view of Unicor, however. Unicor's goods are sold at market prices, and federal agencies must first check with Unicor for products before shopping the open market. Private companies also say inmates take jobs from law-abiding workers and that it is difficult to compete with an industry that can pay its workers less than a dollar an hour.

Unicor officials say their effect on private industry is negligible. Prison factories must factor in production hindrances that private industries do not. Tools and scrap materials must be tightly guarded and controlled, lest they become weapons. All outgoing vehicles must be searched, and lockdowns often halt work entirely. As a result, prison labor can't match the production of private labor.

Source: Rob Kirkbride, "Prison Factory Competes against Larger Office-Furniture Makers," Associated Press/*Grand Rapids Press* (Michigan), April 8, 2002, BC cycle.

public-works systems in which inmates work on projects owned by the state. Today, the most visible examples of public-works projects are the road crews that clean and maintain the right-of-way on state or county roads. Some sheriffs even dress these inmates in old-style prison stripes as a form of humiliation and shame, as well as so that they are identifiable by the public in case of escape.[46]

The type of prison labor system that authorities choose is always subject to political and technological conditions (see Criminal Justice Reference 11.2). Decades ago in southern states where counties rather than state governments controlled the prisons, the lease system was used extensively. Partly as a replacement for slave labor, this system allowed major landowners to employ inmates to do backbreaking work at wages that free people would not accept. Cotton in Georgia and turpentine in Florida are just two examples of crops for which prison labor was used.

Prison labor held a great appeal to both those who saw work as a form of treatment and those who saw work as a form of punishment. Today, with many prison systems experiencing overcrowding, prison labor is not used to the same degree as it was in the past. One of the by-products of overcrowding is the lack of staff to oversee the labor of prisoners. Keeping inmates in their cells for most of the day where they cannot put other inmates or staff members at risk is often easier than supervising them while they work. In many contemporary prisons, the only inmates doing any type of productive labor are those used to maintain the basic needs of the institution.[47]

Age of Rehabilitation: 1930–1970

Rehabilitating inmates has always been one of the goals of the criminal justice system, but not until around 1930 did U.S. prisons acknowledge that rehabilitation was a primary goal. Certainly as far back as Maconochie, some advocated the prison's role in reforming individuals, but the responsibility of the state for changing inmates' behavior was not widely recognized. Around 1930, several influences helped professionalize the field of corrections and allowed progressive reformers to advocate rehabilitation as a desirable and possible goal.[48]

11.2   CRIMINAL JUSTICE REFERENCE

Prison Labor Systems

Prison labor has had many uses and stemmed from several theories of corrections. Some prison labor was deemed rehabilitative in that inmates learned work habits and kept busy; some labor was deemed punitive because the work was backbreaking; and some labor was exploitive because inmates worked hard for someone else's profit. Over the years, several labor systems were used. Here are the rudiments of six of them:

- *Lease system.* Some states leased inmates to private businesses as a way of offsetting the costs of crime. The inmates were worked, guarded, and cared for by the private businesses. This system was controversial because the state no longer watched over the inmates, who were at the mercy of the private corporation or individual who paid the lease. Inmates were leased to sugarcane plantations and turpentine camps in the South and to coal mines and railroads in other parts of the country.

- *Contract system.* Under the contract system, the state was responsible for feeding and guarding the prisoners, and a private company contracted for their labor. This system was accomplished in or near the prison and had the advantage of keeping the machines going 24 hours as the inmates worked in shifts.

- *Piece-price system.* This was similar to the contract system, but instead of paying for the inmates' labor, the private contractor paid a set price for each piece of goods produced by the inmates. This way, the contractor pays for output rather than the number of hours worked.

- *Public-account system.* Under the public-account system, the state, rather than the private contractor, controlled the sale of the products. Like the previous systems, the public account system received criticism because it competed with the work of private businesses that were required to pay the going rate for labor and were at a considerable disadvantage when competing with inmate labor.

- *State-use system.* Goods produced by the state-use system are restricted to use by state agencies. Perhaps the best example of the state use system is the manufacturing of automobile license plates. This business is not found outside the prison, so no one can claim that the state has an unfair advantage. Some prisons grow food and raise cattle to feed inmates and other state workers, but do not sell their goods in the free marketplace.

- *Public works and ways system.* Much like the state use system, the public works and ways system's efforts are confined to the state and are not sold on the marketplace. With this system, inmates repair or construct public buildings, public roads, parks, and other public structures.

These various methods of employing prison labor have been subject to criticism from the outside over the centuries. However, in the hope of keeping the costs of incarceration reasonably low, states have used the labor of inmates in these various ways.

A primary reason why rehabilitation became important at this time was the change in how science regarded illness. This, in turn, affected how criminologists and correctional practitioners thought about criminality. The germ theory of medicine that absolved the sick person of responsibility for contracting an illness spread to corrections. Crime was no longer simply a choice made by the offender. The idea that outside influences contribute to criminality led theorists and correctional administrators to speculate on how antisocial behavior is transmitted among individuals. A medical metaphor that viewed offenders as "sick" developed, and rehabilitation efforts were dedicated to finding the causes of crime in the biological, psychological, and sociological deficiencies of the individual.[49] Once the cause could be diagnosed, it was a simple matter to prescribe a "cure" of drug or alcohol treatment, family or individual counseling, more education, or anger-management classes. The medical model, therefore, likens crime to disease and postulates that normal (law-abiding) behavior is within reach of all offenders and that the correctional practitioner can find the optimal treatment.

Another influence that led to the age of rehabilitation was the 1931 report of the Wickersham Commission. The Wickersham Commission prescribed a wide range of criminal justice reforms, including suggestions that rehabilitation should be attempted in earnest. The commission documented the failures of prison labor systems and the idleness of inmates in most prisons in its quest to solve the penitentiary's systemic problems. The Wickersham Commission did not present particularly new information, but the fact that it was a governmental fact-finding and policy-suggesting body gave its recommendations a legitimacy that previous reformers lacked.[50]

At the forefront of the prison rehabilitation movement was the Federal Bureau of Prisons, established in 1930. This agency eliminated political patronage in filling job vacancies, developed a better trained and more professional staff, and greatly improved the conditions of confinement.[51] Of particular interest to the rehabilitation movement were the new designs of prisons. Specifically, prisons were constructed with the goals of facilitating the classification and treatment of offenders. Bureau of Prison officials such as Sanford Bates, Austin MacCormick, and James V. Bennett were committed to treating offenders as individuals and keeping them occupied in productive activities, such as work and education.

Like many other prison reform movements, the rehabilitation movement in prisons was never fully accomplished.[52] Although the theoretical foundations of treating offenders was further refined during this time, a number of features intervened to prevent it from fully taking hold in prison systems and transforming how offenders were handled. One of the first limitations of the rehabilitation movement was lack of resources. Keeping inmates confined and preventing them from hurting each other and the staff soaked up most of the time, money, and creative energies of prison officials and staff. Treatment programs were considered luxuries in prison systems struggling to maintain the most minimal custody standards in states that would rather spend their limited tax dollars on more popular concerns such as education, infrastructure, and health care. In most prisons, the percentage of inmates who received any significant treatment was low. One observer called rehabilitation efforts during this time "token treatment," designed more for public relations purposes than for producing any real change in the attitudes and behaviors of inmates.[53]

Another reason why the rehabilitation era never fully developed into an effective method for changing the lives of inmates and reducing crime was the lack of consensus regarding whether it was or could ever be effective. In a major study of treatment programs, the unfortunate consensus was that "nothing works."[54] Even though this conclusion is more complex than initially reported, the correctional community jettisoned rehabilitation as an orienting perspective. Nevertheless, some claim that certain programs work for certain offenders, and that although nothing works for everyone, rehabilitation is still a worthy and attainable goal.[55]

The final reason why rehabilitation lost favor is the belief of some scholars that the medical model was a flawed metaphor for corrections. To view offenders as "sick" and in need of a "cure" was deemed problematic by many who favored a view that placed responsibility for antisocial behavior squarely on the shoulders of those who chose to violate the law. These scholars believed it more accurate to think of felons as lazy, unmotivated, poorly socialized, or exploitive. Their idea was that society did not need to "cure" inmates as much as inmates needed to learn that their unlawful behavior would have negative consequences. Therefore, they called for deterrence rather than rehabilitation.[56]

Retributive Era: 1970s to the Present

The movement away from the rehabilitation philosophy did not occur in a social vacuum. The events of the 1960s brought a number of changes in how our social institutions operated. A backlash to the political protests, reported widespread drug use, relaxation of sexual mores, and general disrespect for authority and tradition manifested in a number of ways that affected the prison.[57] One good example of how events outside the prison found their way inside was the politicization of inmates. As minorities, youth, and women outside prison walls challenged how society treated them, inmates challenged the conditions of their confinement inside the prison (see Case in Point 11.1).[58]

The courts traditionally had a "hands-off" policy concerning the operation of prisons, but in the 1960s they started to specify exactly which constitutional rights

11.1 CASE IN POINT

HOPE V. PELZER

THE CASE	THE POINT
Hope v. Pelzer, 536 U.S. 730 (2002)	*This case helped set guidelines for what constitutes cruel and unusual punishment in prison and the circumstances under which prison officials are liable.*

In 1995, Alabama inmate Larry Hope was handcuffed to a hitching post after fighting with a guard at a work site. Hope, who was ordered to remove his shirt, spent seven hours in the sun chained to the post. The guards gave him a couple of water breaks and no bathroom breaks. According to Hope, the guard gave water to some dogs, then kicked over the water cooler in sight of Hope, who watched the water spill onto the ground.

Hope filed suit against three guards.

The magistrate judge did not rule on the possibility of the Eighth Amendment violation, but ruled that the guards were immune to the suit because they were unaware of any constitutional violations. The Eleventh Circuit affirmed this judgment, but found that the hitching post violated the Eighth Amendment.

In reversing the decision, the Supreme Court agreed with the judgment about the Eighth Amendment violation, but disagreed that the guards were not liable. Justice John Paul Stevens wrote, "A reasonable officer would have known that using a hitching post as Hope alleged was unlawful." This part of the decision allowed Hope to file suit against the guards.

inmates forfeited in prison.[59] This led to major changes in areas such as food and disciplinary procedures. As prisoners organized to challenge the conditions of their confinement, a new, racial dimension appeared in the inmates' identity. The Black Panther Party and the Black Muslims agitated to have prisons recognize them as legitimate political organizations within the prison that spoke for minority inmates. The tensions caused by this politicization of the inmates made rehabilitation efforts difficult to accomplish. When Black Muslim inmates defined themselves as political prisoners, they became unwilling to adopt the "sick" label of rehabilitation and instead contended that society's institutions, particularly prisons, were deficient. In Stateville Prison in Illinois, this politicization attracted some of the most troublesome inmates to challenge the prison authorities:

> Whether troublemakers were attracted to Muslimism or whether attraction to Muslimism automatically defined an inmate as a troublemaker is difficult to resolve when posed in this way. The Muslims offered legitimacy and significance to the frustration, bitterness, and egotism of some of Stateville's most recalcitrant inmates. The officials countered by purging Muslims from their jobs, blocking their legitimate prison activities, and suppressing them whenever possible. Not surprisingly, many of the leaders ended up in segregation.[60]

With inmates rebelling against the conditions of their confinement, the courts questioning how prison officials did their jobs, and society losing faith in the promises of rehabilitation, a change in the basic philosophy of incarceration was inevitable. Retribution replaced rehabilitation as the primary goal of the prison. This had significant and widespread implications for how inmates were sentenced and what happened to them in prison.[61] Some of the changes were as follows:

- **Determinate sentences** Rehabilitation was no longer the main goal of the prison, and officials were no longer willing to certify when an inmate was safe to return to society. Therefore, indeterminate sentences were no longer desirable. In their place, fixed terms of incarceration were implemented based not on inmates' needs but on the seriousness of their offenses and prior criminal record.

In this way, inmates would be treated for what they did, rather than for some perceived deficiency in psychological makeup or social conditioning.[62]

- **Voluntary treatment**   With rehabilitation no longer a primary goal of incarceration, treatment services were offered on a voluntary basis. Prison administrators believed that treatment was more effective for those who sought it without coercion or conditions. When inmates participated in treatment to impress a parole board, their motivations were suspect. Inmates learned to "play the parole game" in the rehabilitation era.[63] Inmates who entered voluntary programs were considered more likely to be sincere in their desires to learn new skills, acquire an education, or seek drug treatment. Also, there were presumably fewer "jailhouse conversions" when attendance at religious services was not considered at parole hearings.

- **Abolition of parole**   One of the logical by-products of a system that abandoned indeterminate sentencing and compulsory treatment was the elimination of parole as an early-release mechanism. (Although this has not yet been accomplished, many critics want inmates to spend their entire sentence behind bars and view parole as "soft on crime." We will deal with parole issues later, but point out here that the current retributive era in corrections has brought about a reconsideration of parole.) Coupled with a surge in prison overcrowding, the elimination of parole is problematic, but several states have eliminated discretionary parole. However, parole's primary function, like that of the prison, has shifted from treatment to supervision.[64]

This brief history of social control highlights several themes. One is that many correctional practices that seem new and innovative are actually old gifts in new wrappers. The ideas of work as useful in reforming individuals, rehabilitation geared to the needs of the inmate, and the value of keeping inmates busy have all been used in various eras of corrections. What has changed are not the ideas themselves, but rather the resources and political will allocated to support those ideas. One may wonder whether rehabilitation has ever been given an honest chance. No jurisdiction has ever paid more than lip service to the idea of providing the counselors, modern conditions, and aftercare necessary to effectively change the behavior of criminals who have learned to survive by using a deviant lifestyle. In many ways, it is unrealistic to expect a 12-week program to overcome 25 years of poverty, discrimination, lack of education, and drug addiction. Yet all too often a 12-week program is all society can afford in an attempt to change the inmate. In a later chapter we will consider what community treatment efforts appear to be the most promising, but here we must recognize that rehabilitation is not a new idea and that there is still considerable room to develop and refine programs that address antisocial behavior.

CAPITAL PUNISHMENT

The history of social control requires that we consider the use of capital punishment as a method for compelling citizens to obey the law. This extreme form of control is controversial, with individuals and groups voicing impassioned opinions on both sides of the issue. Although whether the death penalty is cruel is subject to debate, from a historical point of view it is not unusual. Execution is much older than incarceration, and a fascinating number of ways have been devised to execute criminal offenders. We cannot do justice to all the issues and ramifications of the death penalty in the space available here, so we will content ourselves to briefly consider some of the basic arguments. Easy answers to the issues surrounding the death penalty are elusive because the research is still contested and because capital punishment is often viewed from a highly personal and subjective point of view. Therefore, the goal of this section is to simply frame the issues.

In *Ford v. Wainwright* and *Atkins v. Virginia* (see Case in Point 11.2), the court limited executions by determining that mental state must be considered when imposing a death sentence. Two primary reasons for this include deterrence and the condemned's understanding of the execution and the reason for it. According to the Supreme Court, executing a mentally ill or retarded offender will not deter other offenders who have similar incapacities. Also, there are questions about the justice of killing those who do not understand what they are alleged to have done or even that they are being put to death.

Capital Punishment in Historical Perspective

Historically, death is a common form of punishment. Sometimes, however, human life was considered too valuable to sacrifice for the sake of punishing a crime.

The Germans, as described by Tacitus, 60 years after the death of Christ, considered only treachery, desertion, cowardice and sexual perversion to be

---

11.2 CASE IN POINT

FORD V. WAINWRIGHT

THE CASE	THE POINT
Ford v. Wainwright, 477 U.S. 399 (1986)	*This decision banned the execution of the insane.*

In 1974, Alvin Bernard Ford was convicted of murder in Florida and sentenced to death. Although he appeared mentally sound during his trial and sentencing, as well as at the time of the offense, his behavior changed while he was on death row. Suspecting mental illness, his attorney had him examined by two psychiatrists, both of whom determined that Ford was not competent to undergo execution. The governor appointed three psychiatrists who interviewed Ford for 30 minutes in the presence of an eight-member panel. The psychiatrists agreed that although Ford had mental problems, he was fit for execution.

In April 1984, the governor signed Ford's death warrant without explanation or statement. A state court refused a hearing to reconsider Ford's competency. The Federal District Court denied a petition for an evidentiary hearing, and the Court of Appeals affirmed this.

The Supreme Court reversed the decision and remanded the case in June 1986. The court concluded that the Eighth Amendment prohibits the execution of the insane and that Florida's procedures in the matter were lacking.

ATKINS V. VIRGINIA

THE CASE	THE POINT
Atkins v. Virginia, 536 U.S. 304 (2002)	*This decision established limits for the execution of the mentally retarded.*

On August 16, 1996, Daryl Renard Atkins and William Jones abducted Eric Nesbitt at gunpoint. They took his money, then drove him to an automatic teller machine in his truck and forced him to withdraw more. They then went to an isolated area and shot Nesbitt eight times, killing him.

Jones and Atkins both testified at Atkins's trial. Their descriptions of the incident agreed, except that each blamed the other for actually killing Nesbitt. The jury found Jones's testimony more articulate and credited Atkins with the murder. During the trial's penalty phase, the state introduced the testimony of four victims of Atkins's earlier robberies and assaults. Atkins's defense relied on one witness, a psychologist who said Atkins was "mildly mentally retarded," a conclusion based, in part, on a standard intelligence test that indicated Atkins had an IQ of 59.

The jury sentenced Atkins to death. At a resentencing by the Virginia Supreme Court (the trial court had used a misleading verdict form), Atkins was again sentenced to death.

The U.S. Supreme Court reversed and remanded this decision, holding that executing mentally retarded offenders violates the "cruel and unusual punishments" clause in the Eighth Amendment. According to the Court, a "significant number of states" have rejected capital punishment for mentally retarded offenders, and that "the practice is uncommon" even in states that do. Justice John Paul Stevens wrote that, "The practice, therefore, has become truly unusual, and it is fair to say that a national consensus has developed against it." The Court cited evidence that an IQ of 70 or less indicates mental retardation.

crimes serious enough to be punished by death. In a society where every fighting man was a valuable asset, execution and mutilation could not reasonably be considered suitable punishments for lesser offenses, such as murder and theft; and so, Tacitus discovered, the German murderer or thief when convicted paid a fine "in a stated number of oxen or cattle. Half of the fine was paid to the King, half to the person for whom justice was being obtained or to his relatives."[65]

Nevertheless, over the centuries, authorities used a wide variety of methods to kill offenders (see Crosscurrents 11.1). Often the executions were part of a public spectacle designed to demonstrate the consequences of violating the law. Burning, crucifixion, drowning, boiling, flaying, beheading, being impaled, being thrown to the lions, and an infinite variety of other creative and grotesque techniques were used to kill people.[66] The aspect of torture is difficult to appreciate today when society takes great pains to give the appearance that executions are physically painless.

11.1   *CrossCurrents*

Killing Them Softly

The concept of killing those who offend societal norms is probably as old as humanity. For example, the book of Leviticus in the Bible states, "And he that killeth any man shall surely be put to death."[1] The reasons for such a stringent punishment are fairly clear-cut. They include retribution, revenge, and general and specific deterrence. Killing a person can be easier than expending resources to rehabilitate him or her. It is also a way for the state to show the extent of its power, organization, and control.

Before the 20th century, two major features of the death sentence were spectacle and pain. The spectacle aspect served many purposes, most of them related to the reasons for the sentence. Spectacle proved to the aggrieved party that justice had been done and assuaged the desire for revenge. It proved that the offender was dead, achieved specific deterrence, and provided a visual aid for general deterrence. Spectacle displayed the blunt power of the state and its willingness to see justice done. Finally, spectacle entertained the masses. Although this may not seem related to justice, the humiliation aspect could be considered part of the offender's sentence. In many cases, the last thing an offender would see would be a jeering crowd. According to an English writer, "An Execution that is attended with more lasting Torment, may strike a far greater Awe."[2]

The other feature of pre–20th century death sentence was pain. Pain was considered inextricably linked to punishment. Death was not enough. The offender was required to hurt while dying and hurt publicly. This can be linked to the crowd's need for revenge fulfillment and to the desire that the offender be humiliated, as well as injured. Some means of inflicting pain were slow; others, if the offender was lucky, were fast. Throughout the ages, the art of inflicting pain in pursuit of death became quite well developed.

Greeks and Romans

Although the death penalty and torture existed before the Greeks and Romans, these societies did much to impress their idiosyncrasies of it into Western thought. One of the most famous ancient executions was that of Socrates, who was made to drink poison. Although poisoning can be painful, torture did not seem to be a goal of Socrates' executioners. Other offenders were not so fortunate. One Roman method of execution was to tie the offender to a human corpse so that the rotting body would slowly and horribly kill the offender. The Romans are most infamous for crucifixion, a common method of execution, and forcing offenders to fight each other to the death or be killed by wild animals.

Europe

The favored methods of execution in Europe were hanging, beheading, and burning. Executions were later carried out by guillotine, a mechanized form of beheading, and firing squad. Again, pain, spectacle, and humiliation were considered important. One of the most fearsome executions was burning. Many offenders were burned alive; more fortunate ones were burned after being hanged. Burning was considered a punishment that punished beyond death because it destroyed the body, which would not receive a proper burial.

Execution by guillotine, Grenoble, France, 1929.

Source: Courtesy of the Library of Congress

Only much later in European history did authorities seek to reduce the offender's suffering (if not the humiliation), with the executioners themselves leading the way. Before the 19th century, death by hanging depended on the "short drop." A rope was tied to the offender's neck, and he or she was either dropped or hoisted a short distance, and death occurred by slow strangulation. In the 19th century, British hangmen discovered that a "long drop," letting the offender fall a long distance from a platform, would break the neck and cause a quicker, more humane death.[3]

In 1792, France popularized the use of the guillotine during the French Revolution. This mechanical device for lopping heads was used because it was considered humane, being quicker than hanging and less mistake-prone than an executioner wielding an ax or sword. However, concerns grew that a severed head might live and consciousness continue for several seconds or even minutes. Numerous experiments were done on severed heads, with reports of faces blushing when slapped or the victim's eyes responding to the sound of his or her name.[4] Despite the debate on this matter (which continues to this day), France continued to execute criminal offenders by guillotine until 1977. France abolished the death penalty in 1981.

Search for Humane Execution

The organized call for humane execution in the United States began in the 19th century. Although "long-drop" hangings were supposed to be less painful, they were not always carried out properly, resulting in slow, painful deaths. In response, gallows were redesigned and experiments were done. One contraption called the "upright jerker" used weights and pulleys to sharply draw the victim up, snapping the neck. The success of this method depended on the operator's skill and the condition of the machine itself. These were lacking in several cases, resulting in lingering asphyxiation and strangling rather than quick death.[5]

Electrocution

The late 19th century saw experiments with electricity move from the therapeutic to the punitive. Once it was discovered that electricity could kill, officials began searching for ways to use it to painlessly execute the condemned. Thomas Edison insisted in 1887 that the best method of electrical execution was via alternating current, the preferred current of his chief rival, George Westinghouse. Despite Westinghouse's protests,

The first execution by electrocution, of William Kemmler, for murder, at Auburn Prison, Auburn, New York, August 6, 1890.

Source: The Granger Collection

the first electrical execution was performed with his equipment on William Kemmler at New York's Auburn Prison in August 1890. Contrary to popular hopes and expectations, this execution was worse than hanging. The science of electrocution was poorly understood, and Kemmler's execution was botched. He survived the first 17-second jolt, so the executioners, panicking and struggling with the equipment, let the second burst go for more than a minute. Blood seeped through the broken capillaries on Kemmler's face as his flesh burned. Witnesses and officials were horrified.[6]

Despite this apparent failure, officials continued to experiment until they hit on a satisfactory combination of electricity and time. Less than a year after Kemmler's execution, four inmates were executed in one day in an electrocution marathon at Sing Sing Prison. All four executions were reported to have been clean and painless. By 1937, electrocution was the preferred method of execution by the federal government and many states.

Gas

The quest for humane execution continued during this era, pursued by those offended by hangings and botched electrocutions. Although it was established by 1896 that lethal gas could kill an inmate, interest did not pick up until 1921 when the Nevada legislature passed a bill allowing execution by gas.

One of the notions held by gas advocates was that the victims did not have to know they were being executed. These advocates specified that inmates should be asleep when the sentence was carried out, never knowing the exact date and time of their executions. This proved impractical for two major reasons: Executions required witnesses, and the inmate would have to live in a special gas-ready cell for several days, thus spoiling the surprise to some degree. Officials eventually settled on something resembling the modern gas chamber: a chair in a room with a window for spectators. In 1924, Chinese immigrant Gee Jon became the first inmate to die by gas. Unlike early episodes with the electric chair, Jon's execution went smoothly (although some later executions did not, with victims gasping and choking). At least 11 states had gas chambers by 1955.

Lethal Injection

Despite all the developments in humane execution, society has returned to the method used to kill Socrates: poison. Although the ability to inject poison into the veins has been around for a while, doing so via syringe was developed at about the time that society became squeamish about how its condemned died. Having an executioner touch a victim while killing him or her seemed too intimate.[7] However, once the process was automated, with executioners needing only to find a vein and turn on the chemicals, the method's relative frugality, simplicity, and painlessness

became apparent. The first lethal injection execution was performed by the state of Texas in 1982 on Charlie Brooks, without incident. As of 2008, lethal injection was the preferred method of execution in almost all states that had a death penalty, plus the military and federal government. A few states (see table) have alternatives to lethal injection, which either may be chosen by inmates or used if lethal injection is ever ruled unconstitutional.

Alabama, South Carolina, Virginia	Inmate can request electrocution
Arizona	Inmates sentenced before Nov. 15, 1992 may choose gas.
Arkansas	Inmates who committed their offense before July 4, 1983, may choose electrocution.
California	Choice of injection or gas.
Florida	Choice of injection or electrocution
Idaho	Uses a firing squad if injection is problematic.
Kentucky	Choice of injection or electrocution for those convicted after March 31, 1998
Maryland	Choice of injection or gas for those who committed their offense before March 25, 1994
Missouri	Injection or gas may be used
Nebraska	The Nebraska Supreme Court ruled electrocution unconstitutional in 2008; no other method currently in place
New Hampshire	Uses hanging if injection is problematic
Oklahoma	Electrocution if lethal injection becomes unconstitutional; firing squad if both lethal injection and electrocution become unconstitutional
Tennessee	Choice of injection or electrocution for those who committed their offense before December 31, 1998
Utah	Firing squad if lethal injection becomes unconstitutional

Source: Bureau of Justice Statistics, Capital Punishment, 2006, www.ojp.usdoj.gov/bjs/pub/html/cp/2006/tables/cp06st02.htm. Death Penalty Information Center, Methods of Execution, www.deathpenaltyinfo.org/methods-execution#state.

Think About It

1. Are painless executions more palatable or ethical than those that hurt the offender?
2. Instead of abolishing execution, should efforts be made, instead, to streamline it and make it more painless and efficient?

[1]Leviticus 24:17 (King James Version).

[2]George Olyffe, *An Essay Humbly Offer'd, for an Act of Parliament to Prevent Capital Crimes* (London: J. Downing, 1731), 6–7, in Stuart Banner, *The Death Penalty: An American History* (Cambridge, MA: Harvard University Press, 2002), 70.

[3]Robert M. Bohm, *Deathquest: An Introduction to the Theory and Practice of Capital Punishment in the United States* (Cincinnati, OH: Anderson, 1999), 73.

[4]Alister Kershaw, *A History of the Guillotine* (New York: Barnes & Noble Books, 1993), 81.

[5]Stuart Banner, *The Death Penalty: An American History* (Cambridge MA: Harvard University Press, 2002), 171–172.

[6]Ibid., 186.

[7]Ibid., 296.

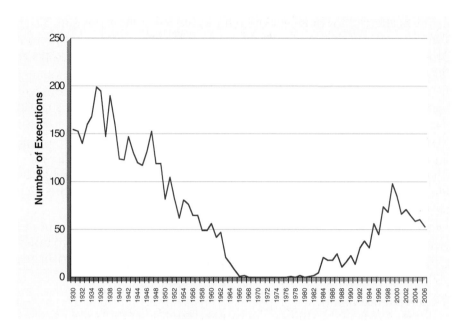

Figure 11-1   **Executions in the United States, 1930–2006**
Source: Thomas P. Bonczar and Tracy L. Snell, *Capital Punishment, 2002* (Washington, DC: Bureau of Justice Statistics, 2003), 11; Bureau of Justice Statistics, Capital Punishment, 2006–Statistical Tables, www.ojp.usdoj.gov/bjs/pub/html/cp/2006/tables/cp06st15.htm.

Methods of execution have changed to include more than the reduction of torture. The visibility of capital punishment has also evolved to the point that rather than have public ceremonies in which citizens can witness an execution, it is now done behind the walls of the prison with only a few corrections staff, families of the condemned and victim, and a few members of the press present.[67] See Figure 11-1 for the number of executions performed annually in the United States since 1930.

Arguments Supporting Capital Punishment

At the foundation of support for capital punishment is the deterrence argument. Two varieties of deterrence are used to justify the death penalty. Although considerable debate surrounds one of them, the other is obvious. **Specific deterrence** says that if a condemned individual is put to death, then he (most of those executed have been men) will never break the law again. There is no arguing with this logic. However, in practice only a small percentage of those who commit murder are ever executed. As a policy, then, specific deterrence is of limited value. On the other hand, **general deterrence** says that if murderers are executed, the rest of us will see the ramifications of this behavior and will refrain from murder ourselves because we fear the consequences. General deterrence allows us to have meaningful communities. Think of how chaotic our society would be, according to this perspective, if each of us had to be caught at our offenses and punished before we would engage in lawful behavior. Fortunately, most of us do not commit serious offenses even though we might be tempted. We understand by seeing others punished that we will be held accountable for our actions.

Although embracing the deterrence argument seems logical when considering most offenses and punishments, there is considerable debate as to whether it is useful when applied to murder and capital punishment.[68] Opponents of capital punishment say the general-deterrence argument is questionable for several reasons.

- Does the death penalty deter habitual offenders to the same degree that it deters the rest of us? For deterrence to be effective, we each must weigh the risks of getting caught and punished against the benefits of successfully committing the offense. Few circumstances exist in which most citizens would risk their lives, fortunes, and reputations for the possible benefits of an offense. In short, general deterrence works well on those who have something to lose, but may

specific deterrence
A method of control in which an offender is prevented from committing more crimes by either imprisonment or death.

general deterrence
A method of control in which the punishment of a single offender sets an example for the rest of society.

not be as effective for those who have little invested in the status quo. The idea that drug dealers who stand to gain thousands of dollars, professional assassins, young gang members, and jealous spouses rationally calculate the prospects of the death penalty is not assured.

- Does the death penalty deter better than other types of punishments? According to those who oppose the death penalty, the prospect of life in prison without parole is likely to deter as effectively as capital punishment.[69]

- Many murders are crimes of passion in which deterrence likely does not enter into the offender's motivation. Those in a blind rage may not consider the death penalty or may even reason that they are so incensed that only by exposing themselves to the ultimate punishment can they adequately express their outrage.[70]

- Deterrence is difficult to validate empirically because it is difficult to measure something that does not happen. Given the multiple variables that go into someone's decision to kill another person, it is extremely difficult to isolate the deterrent effect of death penalty laws.[71]

The deterrence argument is impossible to prove given our current laws. According to deterrence theory, we must do more than simply raise the severity of the punishment. Swiftness and certainty of punishment are also factors that offenders supposedly take into account when contemplating their offenses. In the case of the death penalty, neither swiftness nor certainty are guaranteed. Many executions occur 10 or more years after the offense (see Figure 11-2). Given the restrictive wording of statutes, plea bargaining, and the reluctance of some judges or juries to impose the death sentence, we can honestly say that under present conditions, deterrence theory has not had a fair opportunity to demonstrate its potential. To fully assess the effect of deterrence, we would need to see some fundamental changes in the criminal justice system. By making capital punishment mandatory for some offenses, limiting the number of appeals and time allowed for appeals, and thereby executing a larger number of offenders in a swift and certain manner, capital punishment laws would be perceived as having some teeth and could possibly provide a deterrent function.

Supporters of the death penalty point to the **just deserts** argument as a justification. This argument asserts that some people commit acts so heinous that only by killing them can a society fully express its values. In a sense, this argument maintains that some people deserve to be executed because of their antisocial behavior. This is a **retribution model** that embraces the "eye for an eye" concept that many believe is the basis of justice handed down throughout history and that is deeply ingrained in

just deserts

A philosophy that states that an offender who commits a heinous crime deserves death.

retribution model

A style of control in which offenders are punished as severely as possible for a crime and in which rehabilitation is not attempted.

Figure 11-2   Average Elapsed Time from Sentence to Execution

Source: Thomas P. Bonczar and Tracy L. Snell, *Capital Punishment, 2002* (Washington, DC: Bureau of Justice Statistics, 2003), 11; Bureau of Justice Statistics, Capital Punishment, 2006— Statistical Tables, www.ojp.usdoj.gov/bjs/pub/html/cp/2006/tables/cp06st17.htm.

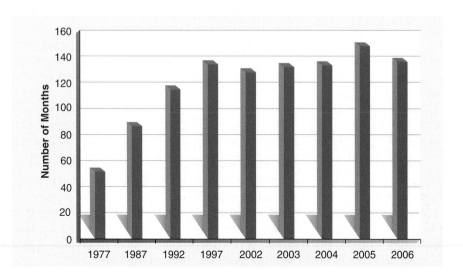

11.2 FOCUS *on* ETHICS

CAPITAL PUNISHMENT: SOME IMMODEST PROPOSALS

Almost everyone is dissatisfied with the death penalty for one reason or another. Liberals think it is applied in a discriminatory manner and that it fails to act as a deterrent. Conservatives say that it is used too sparingly and that the time between crime and execution is too long. Families of victims feel left out of the decision-making process, and murderers eventually believe that they are the ultimate victim. If we were to redesign how we execute people, what might we do differently? Here are some proposals that would change the face of capital punishment in the United States. How many of them would you vote for?

- *Take the guesswork out of who gets executed.* Make capital punishment mandatory for all first-degree murders. This would address two concerns. First, claims of racial, sexual, and social class bias would be eliminated because anyone convicted of a capital offense would receive the death penalty. An expensive lawyer, an emotional appeal, or a liberal judge could not intervene in such a process. Perhaps people would not kill if their conviction guaranteed the death penalty.
- *Limit the number and time frame of appeals.* The execution would take place one year after sentencing. This would discourage the defense from delaying the process. Perhaps people would not kill if death sentences were carried out promptly.

- *Make executions public.* This was once done to show people the consequences of crime. Now the execution has been moved behind prison walls, and only a few witnesses are allowed. If executions were televised, say at halftime of the Super Bowl when millions of people are watching, then everyone would have an opportunity to observe what happens to murderers. Major corporations might pay millions of dollars to sponsor such executions, and the money could be used for the victims' families.
- *To have the maximum deterrent effect, capital punishment should not be painless.* Instead of searching for humane ways to kill, the criminal justice system should bring back torture. Offenders would die in painful, protracted, and public ways.
- *Allow family members of victims to participate in the execution.* Victims' families should have a measure of retribution and revenge in the process. Allow a victim's family to pull the switch, for example.

What Do You Do?

1. Are these suggestions extreme? Ask your classmates, family members, and friends what they think. Is there agreement on how offenders should be executed?

2. How far have we come from the times when these proposals were practiced? Are you willing to go back?

many religious and philosophical teachings. Not to execute killers in some way cheapens the life of the victim, according to this perspective. This perspective speaks to some individuals who might take the law into their own hands if the government did not punish wrongdoers appropriately. The desire for revenge is a strong motivator for many, and the prospect of vigilante justice is always a concern. If the government fails to uphold the law and deal with offenders, then some individuals will act as their own judge, jury, and executioner. Lacking faith in the criminal justice system, the man who finds someone raping his daughter would be tempted to seek retribution by killing the rapist. Although rapists are not subject to the death penalty today, the point is that citizens must have confidence that justice will be done. For many, justice means that serious offenders "get what they deserve." See Focus on Ethics 11.2 for some controversial suggestions on how capital punishment could be handled.

Arguments against Capital Punishment

Those who oppose the death penalty do so for a variety of reasons.[72] Some religious people take to heart the Fourth Commandment found in the Old Testament of the Bible, which says, "Thou shall not kill." These individuals consider killing by the state, in the name of the people, as premeditated murder. Other capital punishment opponents point to the evidence on deterrence and conclude that capital punishment does not make society safer. Still others are concerned with the way some offenders are selected for capital punishment, while others escape it. They point to social class, race, and gender as factors that determine whether the death penalty is applied in a given case.[73] These are but a few of the concerns of those who oppose capital punishment. It is useful to explore some of these issues in more detail because they are inherently complicated and significantly important to our understanding of the criminal justice system.

An old axiom concerning capital punishment asks, "Why do we kill people to show people that killing people is wrong?" This statement is revealing on a number of levels, not the least of which is the perceived irony of the state modeling the very type of behavior it is attempting to discourage. The Italian criminologist Cesare Beccaria expressed much the same sentiments in 1761:

> The death penalty cannot be useful, because of the example of barbarity it gives men. . . . It seems to me absurd that the laws, which are an expression of the public will, which detest and punish homicide, should themselves commit it, and that to deter citizens from murder, they order a public one.[74]

Despite the fact that the death penalty has been modified over the centuries to inflict as little pain as possible, the process of execution is now so formalized, routinized, and bureaucratic that it has become a surreal procedure that some opponents consider a violation of the Eighth Amendment's proscription against cruel and unusual punishment. One vocal opponent who has studied the modern execution process is Robert Johnson, who wrote:

> The underlying function of death row confinement, then, is to facilitate executions by dehumanizing both the prisoner and, to a lesser degree, their executioners, making it easier for both to play their roles in the execution process. The confinement that produces these results is a form of torture. Indeed, the essence of torture is the death of a person—that is, his conversion into a subhuman object, a nonperson.[75]

Johnson is uncompromising in his condemnation of the brutal way the death penalty is applied in the United States. Its supporters, however, would contend that there is little problematic here. The death penalty, many people believe, should be brutalizing to the offender just as the offender was brutalizing to the victim. To be an effective deterrent, capital punishment should be unpleasant, according to its proponents. In fact, there are those who would return capital punishment to the days when it was a public spectacle in order to enhance what they believe to be its deterrent effects. Taken to an extreme, the death penalty could become a form of sport to entertain the public, raise money for the state, and demonstrate what happens to lawbreakers.

Many who might support capital punishment or are neutral on the subject find themselves opposing it because of a perceived unfairness in the way certain categories of people are selected (see Figure 11-3). In other words, it is not the idea of the death

Figure 11-3 Inmates under Sentence of Death by Race

Source: Thomas P. Bonczar and Tracy L. Snell, *Capital Punishment, 2002* (Washington, DC: Bureau of Justice Statistics, 2003); Bureau of Justice Statistics, Prisoners on Death Row by Race, www.ojp.usdoj.gov/bjs/glance/tables/drracetab.htm; Bureau of Justice Statistics, Capital Punishment, 2006–Statistical Tables, www.ojp.usdoj.gov/bjs/pub/html/cp/2006/tables/cp06st13.htm.

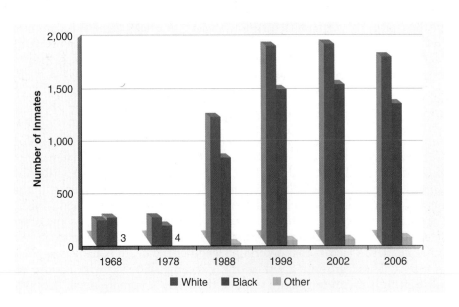

penalty they oppose, but rather the state's seeming inability to impose it in a fair and impartial manner. When minorities and people of lower social classes are executed, whereas many whites and wealthy people escape with imprisonment or less, the procedure's fairness is called into question. If everyone is equal under the law, then there should not be patterns of discrimination in how the death penalty is administered.[76] Unfortunately, the historical evidence is unambiguous. Blacks and Latinos are executed at a greater proportion than are whites. Another feature of racial bias is evident

---

11.2   CrossCurrents

The Innocence Projects

The criminal justice system is designed to ensure that the guilty are punished and the innocent go free. With so many cases going through the criminal justice systems in the federal government and all the states, sometimes mistakes are made. Judges and juries do their best to weigh the evidence presented by law enforcement and prosecutors to ensure that a just verdict is reached. Although it is inevitable that a number of guilty offenders will be acquitted, it is regrettable that from time to time individuals will be convicted of offenses they did not commit.

Many offenders have consistently contended that they did not commit the offenses for which they were convicted. Although the cynical among us may scoff at these protestations of innocence, DNA testing has recently revealed that some of these people have been falsely accused and wrongly imprisoned. Given the large caseloads of most prosecutors' offices, little effort is exerted to look at past cases to determine whether mistakes have been made. However, a number of programs across the country are initiating new looks at old cases to see whether justice has been served.

These programs, most often housed in law schools with law students doing the work, are called *innocence projects*. Fashioned after a project begun in 1992 by Barry Scheck and Peter Neufeld in New York City, these projects are devoted to freeing the wrongly convicted. A study at the University of Michigan estimates that between 1989 and 2003, 328 people have been exonerated. Most of these cases involve DNA evidence that establishes that the convicted individual was blameless.[1] There are many other cases that do not involve DNA in which a wrong conviction is more difficult to establish. However, many alleged offenders are getting a second serious look at their convictions.

In April 2008, James Lee Woodard, 55, was set free after 27 years in prison. Although he was released on a special bond pending a final hearing by the Texas Court of Criminal Appeals, he was given an apology by the judge for the tragedy of his unjust conviction. Woodard spent more time in prison for an offense he did not commit than any other individual on record. Even though he had an alibi, he was seen with the victim that day and became an immediate suspect. His attorney was not notified of the alibi witnesses, and one of them was killed three years after the offense. Additionally, another hostile witness recanted his testimony.[2] Alexis Hoff, a student at Texas Wesleyan University School of Law, initiated the review of this case. According to Larry Moore, an attorney in charge of the school's innocence project, the energy and enthusiasm of law students are what makes their innocence project feasible. Older and more established attorneys tend to become a bit jaded and cynical after years of working in the criminal justice system.[3]

The innocence projects are more than just efforts to free wrongly convicted people. Additionally, every time someone who is wrongly convicted is sent to prison, the real perpetrator has gone free. By demonstrating that the person sitting in prison is not guilty, the innocence projects alert law enforcement agencies to the need to reopen the investigation and attempt to find the real offender. A second important feature of the innocence projects is aimed at the victims of the offense. Those who are killed or seriously injured deserve to have the real perpetrator called to justice. For victims and their families, real closure cannot be obtained when the wrong person is punished.

Think About It

1. Is there an innocence project in your state?
2. Who should pay for DNA testing offenders who want to challenge their convictions?
3. Should the government pay for an innocence project in every state to look into questionable convictions?

[1]Amanda Buck, "Innocence Projects: Investigations of Wrongful Convictions Continue to Spread as Formal Programs," *IRE Journal* (May/June 2005).
[2]Ibid.
[3]Max B. Baker, "Top Criminal Defense Lawyer Thrilled with Challenge of Law School Program," *Fort Worth Star-Telegram*, September 17, 2007.

in how those who kill white victims are more likely to receive the ultimate sanction than are those who kill minorities.

> A black person convicted of an aggravated murder of a white in Florida between 1973 and 1977 was more than seven times more likely to receive a death sentence than was a black who killed a black. A white person convicted of an aggravated murder of a white was almost five more times likely to receive a death sentence than was a black who killed a black. A person convicted of aggravated murder of a white, whether the killer was a black or a white, was more likely to receive the death penalty than was a person of either race convicted of the aggravated murder of a black person.[77]

Is a white life more valuable than a black life? That is what the evidence on the racial bias of the death penalty suggests.[78] These kinds of patterns make those who might support the death penalty reconsider. The bulk of these studies that demonstrate this racial bias have controlled for other factors, such as the defendant's prior record; they show that race is a significant factor in deciding who is executed.[79]

Social class is also an influence. Because those with financial means can afford to hire private lawyers and employ investigators, the rich have a decided advantage over the poor when charged with capital offenses. This is not to say that many public defenders cannot mount a credible defense in a capital case (in fact, in some larger jurisdictions, the public defender's office is staffed with experienced and effective attorneys), but rather that the impoverished often lack the financial resources necessary to provide a first-class defense.[80]

Finally, a compelling reason for many people to object to the death penalty is the problem of executing the innocent (see Crosscurrents 11.2). Whereas defendants have numerous opportunities for appeal and review of their cases, condemned inmates do not. If a mistake is made in determining a defendant's guilt, a prison term, unlike death, can be rescinded. DNA evidence has exonerated several individuals who were convicted of capital crimes.[81] The situation in Illinois was so problematic that in 2000 Governor George Ryan, a conservative Republican, placed a moratorium on the death penalty. Before he left office in 2002, Ryan commuted the sentences of those on death row to life imprisonment. For Ryan, who had been a supporter of capital punishment, the prospect of killing innocent offenders outweighed the death penalty's assumed benefits.[82]

Is the Death Penalty Dead?

Although capital punishment is politically popular in the United States, there are repeated appeals to discontinue it.[83] Thirteen states do not even have a death penalty (see Criminal Justice Reference 11.3). Given the questions raised about its effectiveness,

11.3 CRIMINAL JUSTICE REFERENCE

States/Jurisdictions without a Death Penalty

Alaska	Minnesota
District of Columbia	North Dakota
Hawaii	Rhode Island
Iowa	Vermont
Maine	West Virginia
Massachusetts	Wisconsin
Michigan	

A lethal injection chamber. The curtains are opened during the execution to allow witnesses to observe the proceedings.
Source: CORBIS-NY

11.3   CASE IN POINT
BAZE V. REES

THE CASE

Baze v. Rees, 217 S.W.3d 207 (2006 Ky.)

THE POINT

The possibility that a method of humane execution would be incorrectly administered and cause the condemned pain does not violate the Eighth Amendment ban on cruel and unusual punishment.

Inmates on Kentucky's death row filed suit, claiming that the possibility that lethal injection protocols would not be correctly followed rendered such execution in violation of the Eighth Amendment ban on cruel and unusual punishment. The inmates allowed that lethal injection protocols correctly followed did not violate the Eighth Amendment. The Kentucky Supreme Court affirmed a lower court's decision that the existence of the possibility that the protocol would not be not followed—thus causing the condemned significant pain—did not violate the Eighth Amendment. The U.S. Supreme Court held that the inmates had been unsuccessful in demonstrating that the risk of pain from incorrectly following lethal injection protocols and the failure to adopt alternative methods constituted cruel and unusual punishment. However, the Court also held that if a successful alternative to lethal injection was discovered, one that reduced the risk of pain and was easily adopted, then a state's refusal to switch to that method would be a violation of the Eighth Amendment.

fairness, and morality, many people contend that capital punishment is not an enlightened policy for the country to pursue. Occasionally, it looks as though the courts will strike down this form of social control, but they seem to be unable to find the constitutional grounds to do so.

Recently, the Supreme Court upheld the constitutionality of lethal injection as a form of administering the death penalty in Kentucky (see Case in Point 11.3).[84] This ruling left the door open for states to continue their capital punishment practices.[85] However, the future promises even more challenges to capital punishment. The Supreme Court is in a pivotal position to decide policy on this issue. Those who are selected to fill vacancies on the Supreme Court are an important factor in whether capital punishment will be continued. For example, Justice Stevens celebrated his 88th birthday in April 2008 and will likely vacate his seat on the Supreme Court within the next few years. Justice Stevens was for many years a supporter of capital punishment, but eventually changed his mind on the issue.[86] As capital punishment cases continue to proceed to the U.S. Supreme Court, there will always be opportunities for new justices to make changes to the death penalty.

SUMMARY

1. Human societies can exist only if they employ rules and if most of their members follow those rules. Violations of the rules bring consequences ranging from mild rebukes to extreme violence as groups seek to make members conform.

2. Ancient societies did not have organized systems to deal with offenders. Corporal punishment, or inflicting physical harm on the body, was a primary means to control and extract revenge from offenders. The major formalized means of inflicting pain were torture, flogging, branding, mutilation, humiliation, and shock death.

3. Although corporal punishments were common before prisons, other dispositions used labor rather than pain. These dispositions included forcing offenders to work on galley ships and in workhouses and exiling them to foreign lands.

4. Early American institutions were locally controlled and imprisoned different types of offenders together. The first institution resembling a modern penitentiary was Massachusetts's Castle Island in Boston Harbor, established in 1785.

5. During the first half of the 19th century, two reform-type prison systems emerged: the Pennsylvania System and the Auburn System. Each emphasized regimens of silence and penitence.

6. European countries developed the Irish System, which was designed not just to punish, but to make the inmate more likely to return successfully to free society. The three most well-known examples were those developed by Alexander Maconochie, Sir Walter Crofton, and Zebulon Brockway.

7. Maconochie, who in 1840 ran the Australian penal colony of Norfolk Island, popularized the indeterminate sentence. Crofton, appointed director of the Irish prison system in 1854, instituted the early-release ticket-of-leave system. At the Elmira Reformatory in New York, Zebulon Brockway used volunteers, forerunners to parole officers, to keep up with released inmates.

8. The 20th century saw the idea that work was most useful for reforming offenders. The three major ideas were that work was a good way to occupy inmates, had rehabilitative value, and offset the cost of incarceration.

9. U.S. prisons did not acknowledge rehabilitation as a primary goal until around 1930. In criminal justice, a medical metaphor was developed in which "sick" offenders were to be "cured" by determining their biological, psychological, and sociological "symptoms."

10. The Wickersham Commission's 1931 report called for a wide range of reforms, including attempts at inmate rehabilitation. Limitations included lack of resources, the lack of consensus that treatment was effective, and the idea that the medical model was a flawed metaphor for corrections.

11. In the 1960s, inmates became politically active in demanding changes. The courts began to specify exactly what rights inmates had. This led to major changes in areas such as food and disciplinary procedures.

12. The retributive era began in corrections around 1970 and continues to the present. This era features replacing indeterminate sentencing with determinate sentencing, making treatment voluntary, and abolishing parole.

13. The most extreme and controversial form of control is capital punishment. Arguments for capital punishment include general and specific deterrence and retribution. Arguments against it include religious and spiritual concerns about killing; beliefs that it does not deter; race, gender, and class issues about who is selected for death; and fear of executing the innocent.

KEY TERMS

congregate-and-silent system 368
general deterrence 381
just deserts 382

**marks-of-commendation
system** 369
retribution model 382

separate-and-silent system 367
specific deterrence 381

REVIEW QUESTIONS

1. Is it true that modern corrections no longer use any form of ancient methods of control?

2. Why do societies resort to corporal punishment?

3. Which economic punishment was of particular use to European colonies?

4. Has prison reform been completely successful? A complete failure?

5. What group first suggested that incarceration and hard labor were preferable to corporal punishment?

6. What were the roles of the Walnut Street Jail and Castle Island in the development of U.S. penal institutions?

7. What reforms has Europe contributed to U.S. corrections?

8. What three ways has work been deemed beneficial to inmates?

9. What effect did the germ theory of medicine have on corrections?

10. What precipitated the move away from the rehabilitation philosophy?

11. What are three primary features of the retributive philosophy?

12. What are the primary differences between modern capital punishment and ancient capital punishment?

13. What effect will new U.S. Supreme Court justices have on capital punishment?

SUGGESTED FURTHER READING

Blomberg, Thomas G., and Karol Lucken. *American Penology: A History of Control*. New York: Aldine de Gruyter, 2000.

Garland, David. *Punishment and Modern Society: A Study in Social Theory*. Chicago: University of Chicago Press, 1990.

Hibbert, Christopher. *The Roots of Evil: A Social History of Crime and Punishment*. Birmingham, AL: Minerva Press, 1963.

Hughes, Robert. *The Fatal Shore: A History of Transportation of Convicts to Australia 1787–1868*. Suffolk, England: Pan Books, 1988.

Irwin, John. *The Warehouse Prison: Disposal of the New Dangerous Class*. Los Angeles: Roxbury, 2005.

Rothman, David J. *The Discovery of the Asylum: Social Order and Disorder in the New Republic*. Boston: Little, Brown, 1971.

ENDNOTES

1. Graeme Newman, *Just and Painful: A Case for the Corporal Punishment of Criminals* (New York: Macmillan, 1983). See especially Chapter 4, "The Limits of Pain: Barbarism and Civilized Punishments."

2. Karl Menningen, *The Crime of Punishment* (New York: Viking Press, 1968).

3. David Garland, "Penal Modernism and Postmodernism," in *Punishment and Social Control: Essays in Honor of Sheldon L. Messinger*, eds. Thomas G. Blomberg and Stanley Cohen (New York: Aldine de Gruyter, 1995), 181–209.

4. Thomas G. Blomberg and Karol Lucken, *American Penology: A History of Control* (New York: Aldine de Gruyter, 2000).

5. Christopher Hibbert, *The Roots of Evil: A Social History of Crime and Punishment* (New York: Minerva Press, 1963).

6. Newman, *Just and Painful*. In Chapter 3, Newman provides an interesting discussion about measuring human beings' pain thresholds.

7. George Ryley Scott, *The History of Corporal Punishment* (London: Senate, 1968).

8. Darius Rejali, *Torture and Democracy* (Princeton, NJ: Princeton University Press, 2007).

9. Rodney J. Henningsen, W. Wesley Johnson, and Terry Wells, "Supermax Prisons: Panacea or Desperation," in *Correctional Contexts: Contemporary and Classical Readings*, 2nd ed., eds. Edward J. Latessa et al. (Los Angeles: Roxbury, 2001), 143–150. These authors review the social costs of such prisons and conclude that inmates are made dysfunctional by them.

10. Michel Foucault, *Discipline and Punish: The Birth of the Prison* (New York: Pantheon Books, 1977).

11. Deuteronomy 25:1–2 (King James Version).

12. Scott, *History of Corporal Punishment.*

13. Ibid., 68.

14. Erving Goffman, *Stigma: Notes on the Management of Spoiled Identity* (Englewood Cliffs, NJ: Prentice Hall, 1963).

15. Harry Elmer Barnes and Negley K. Teeters, *New Horizons in Criminology*, 3rd ed. (Englewood Cliffs, NJ: Prentice Hall, 1959).

16. Fay Honey Knopp, "Northwest Treatment Associates: A Comprehensive Community-Based-Evaluation-and-Treatment Program for Adult Sex Offenders," in *Correctional Counseling and Treatment*, 4th ed., ed. Peter C. Kratcoski (Prospect Heights, IL: Waveland Press, 2000), 617–633.

17. Nagaty Sanad, *The Theory of Crime and Criminal Responsibility in Islamic Law: Shari'a* (Chicago: University of Illinois at Chicago, 1991).

18. George Ryley Scott, *A History of Torture* (London: Senate, 1994), 208–209.

19. Barnes and Teeters, *New Horizons.*

20. John Braithwaite, *Crime, Shame, and Reintegration* (Cambridge, England: Cambridge University Press, 1989).

21. Douglas Litowitz, "The Trouble with 'Scarlet Letter' Punishments," *Judicature* 81 (September 1, 1997): 52–57.

22. Blomberg and Lucken, *American Penology*, 31.

23. Martha H. Myers, *Race, Labor, and Punishment in the New South* (Columbus: Ohio State University Press, 1998).

24. Blomberg and Lucken, *American Penology*, 18.

25. David Garland, *Punishment and Modern Society: A Study in Social Theory* (Chicago: University of Chicago Press, 1990). See especially Chapter 4, "The Political Economy of Punishment: Rusche and Kirchheimer and the Marxist Tradition."

26. Pieter Spierenburg, "The Body and the State: Early Modern Europe," in *The Oxford History of the Prison*, eds. Norval Morris and David J. Rothman (New York: Oxford University Press, 1998), pp. 44–70.

27. Barnes and Teeters, *New Horizons.*

28. Scott Christianson, *With Liberty for Some: 500 Years of Imprisonment in America* (Boston: Northeastern University Press, 1998).

29. Harry E. Allen and Clifford E. Simonsen, *Corrections in America: An Introduction*, 9th ed. (Upper Saddle River, NJ: Prentice Hall, 2001), 21.

30. Aleksandr I. Solzhenitsyn, *The Gulag Archipelago: 1918–1956* (New York: HarperCollins, 1974).

31. Alexis M. Durham III, *Crisis and Reform: Current Issues in American Punishment* (Boston: Little, Brown, 1994).

32. David J. Rothman, *The Discovery of the Asylum: Social Order and Disorder in the New Republic* (Boston: Little, Brown, 1990).

33. Harry Elmer Barnes, *The Evolution of Penology in Pennsylvania: A Study in American Social History* (Montclair, NJ: Patterson Smith, 1968).

34. Phillip L. Reichel, *Corrections: Philosophies, Practices, and Procedures*, 2nd ed. (Boston: Allyn & Bacon, 2001), 72.

35. J. Hirsch, *The Rise of the Penitentiary: Prisons and Punishments in Early America* (New Haven, CT: Yale University Press, 1992).

36. Barnes, *Evolution of Penology.*

37. Barnes and Teeters, *New Horizons.*

38. Rothman, *The Discovery of the Asylum: Social Order and Disorder in the New Republic.*

39. Philip Collins, *Dickens and Crime* (Bloomington: Indiana University Press, 1962), 122–123.

40. J. V. Barry, *Alexander Maconochie of Norfolk Island* (Melbourne, Australia: Oxford University Press, 1958), 72.

41. Reichel, *Corrections*, 82.

42. Barnes and Teeters, *New Horizons.*

43. Blomberg and Lucken, *American Penology*, 76.

44. Glen H. Gildemeister, *Prison Labor and Convict Competition with Free Workers in Industrializing America 1840–1890* (New York: Garland, 1987).

45. Dario Melossi, *The Prison and the Factory: The Origins of the Penitentiary System* (Berkeley: University of California Press, 1980).

46. Kelly McMurry, "For Shame: Paying for Crime without Serving Time, but with a Dose of Humility," *Trial*, May 1, 1997, 12–14.

47. John Irwin, *The Warehouse Prison: Disposal of the New Dangerous Class* (Los Angeles: Roxbury, 2005).

48. Blake McKelvey, *American Prisons: A History of Good Intentions* (Montclair, NJ: Patterson Smith, 1977).

49. John Irwin, *Prisons in Turmoil* (Boston: Little, Brown, 1980). See especially Chapter 2, "The Correctional Institution."

50. Larry E. Sullivan, *The Prison Reform Movement: Forlorn Hope,* (Boston: Twayne, 1990).

51. John W. Roberts, "The Federal Bureau of Prisons: Its Mission, Its History, and Its Partnership with Probation and Pretrial Services," *Federal Probation* 61, no. 1 (1997): 53–58.

52. Francis T. Cullen, "It's Time to Reaffirm Rehabilitation," *Criminology and Public Policy* 5 (December 2006): 665–672.

53. James B. Jacobs, *Stateville: The Penitentiary in Mass Society* (Chicago: University of Chicago Press, 1977).

54. Robert Martinson, "What Works? Questions and Answers about Prison Reform," *Public Interest* 35: (1974):22–54.

55. Ted Palmer, "The 'Effectiveness' Issue Today: An Overview," in *The Dilemmas of Corrections: Contemporary Readings,* 4th ed., eds. Kenneth C. Hass and Geoffrey P. Alpert (Prospect Heights, IL: Waveland Press, 1999).

56. David Fogel, *We Are Living Proof: The Justice Model for Corrections* (Cincinnati, OH: Anderson, 1975).

57. Todd Gitlin, *The Sixties: Years of Hope, Days of Rage* (New York: Bantam Books, 1993).

58. Leo Carroll, *Lawful Order* (New York: Garland, 1998).

59. Jacobs, *Stateville.* See especially Chapter 5, "Intrusion of the Legal System and Interest Groups," pp. 105–137.

60. Ibid., 60.

61. Irwin, *Prisons in Turmoil.*

62. Pamala Griset, *Determinate Sentencing: The Promise and the Reality of Retributive Justice* (Albany: State University of New York Press, 1991). See also James Austin and John Irwin, *It's about Time: America's Imprisonment Binge,* 3rd ed. (Belmont, CA: Wadsworth, 2001).

63. Irwin, *Prisons in Turmoil.*

64. Robert Martinson and Judith Wilks, "Save Parole Supervision," in *Correctional Contexts: Contemporary and Classical Readings,* 2nd ed., eds. Edward J. Latessa et al. (Los Angeles: Roxbury, 2001), 422–427.

65. Hibbert, *Roots of Evil,* 3.

66. Edward Peters, *Torture* (New York: Blackwell, 1985).

67. Stuart Banner, *The Death Penalty: An American History* (Cambridge, MA: Harvard University Press, 2002).

68. Scott H. Decker and Carol W. Kohfeld, "The Deterrent Effect of Capital Punishment in the Five Most Active Execution States: A Time-Series Analysis," *Criminal Justice Review* 15 (1990): 173–191.

69. Marla Sandys and Edmund F. McGarrell, "Attitudes toward Capital Punishment among Indiana Legislators: Diminished Support in Light of Alternative Sentencing Options," *Justice Quarterly* 11 (1994): 651–677.

70. Robert M. Bohm, "Retribution and Capital Punishment: Toward a Better Understanding of Death Penalty Opinion," *Journal of Criminal Justice* 20 (1992): 227–236.

71. Robert M. Bohm, *Deathquest: An Introduction to the Theory and Practice of Capital Punishment in the United States* (Cincinnati, OH: Anderson, 1999). See especially Chapter 5, "General Deterrence and the Death Penalty," pp. 83–101.

72. Alison Tonks, "US States Experiment with Lethal Injections in an Ethical Vacuum," *British Medical Journal* 336 (June 21, 2008): 1401.

73. Samuel R. Gross and Robert Mauro, *Death and Discrimination: Racial Disparities in Capital Sentencing* (Boston: Northeastern University Press, 1989).

74. Cesare Beccaria, *On Crimes and Punishments,* trans. Henry Paolucci (Indianapolis, IN: Bobbs-Merrill, 1963), 50. First published in 1764.

75. Robert Johnson, *Deathwork: A Study of the Modern Execution Process* (Monterey, CA: Brooks/Cole, 1990), 136.

76. Elizabeth Rapaport, "The Death Penalty and Gender Discrimination," in *A Capital Punishment Anthology,* ed. Victor L. Streib (Cincinnati, OH: Anderson, 1993), 145–152.

77. Robert M. Bohm, *Deathquest II* (Cincinnati, OH: Anderson Publishing Co., 2003), 218.

78. Raymond Paternoster, "Prosecutorial Discretion in Requesting the Death Penalty: The Case of Victim-Based Discrimination," *Law and Society Review* 18 (1984): 437–478.

79. James R. Acker, "Impose an Immediate Moratorium on Executions," *Criminology and Public Policy* 6 (November 1, 2007): 641.

80. Jeffrey Reiman, *The Rich Get Richer and the Poor Get Prison: Ideology, Class, and Criminal Justice,* 6th ed. (Boston: Allyn & Bacon, 2001).

81. Michael L. Radelet, Hugo Adam Bedau, and Constance E. Putnam, *In Spite of Innocence: Erroneous Convictions in Capital Cases* (Boston: Northeastern University Press, 1992).

82. Mark P. Moore, "To Execute Capital Punishment: The Mortification and Scapegoating of Illinois Governor George Ryan," *Western Journal of Communication* 70 (2006): 311.

83. "Amnesty International Calls for End to Death Penalty in United States," *Preview Nation's Health* 38 (June/July 2008): 8.

84. Linda Greenhouse, "Justices Uphold Lethal Injection in Kentucky Case," *New York Times,* April 17, 2008, 1.

85. Carmen Gentile, "Florida: Inmate Is Executed," *New York Times,* July 2, 2008, 13.

86. Linda Greenhouse, "After a 32-Year Journey, Justice Stevens Renounces Capital Punishment," *New York Times,* April 18, 2008, 22.

CHAPTER 12

Contemporary Prison Life

Objectives

1. Understand how prisons are a "total institution."

2. Discuss inmate argot roles and the effect of prison gangs.

3. Describe how civilian work roles in the prison differ from those in society.

4. List some special job functions of correctional officers.

5. Discuss the "hands-off" doctrine.

6. Describe special problems or points of contention between inmate rights and institutional requirements.

7. Compare and contrast private prisons with government-run prisons.

The field of corrections includes many types of institutions and programs ranging from local jails to federal institutions. Included in this array of correctional efforts are diversion programs, probation programs, parole, and a host of secure institutions. However, when we think of corrections, usually the first thing that comes to mind is the prison. Prisons have been called various things over the years, including *dungeons*, *penitentiaries*, and *correctional centers*. Regardless of the terminology, the prison has been the central focus of corrections. Despite its history of questionable effectiveness, prisons are still the centerpiece of the criminal justice system's attempts to punish offenders and encourage them to change their behavior.

There are about 1200 state prisons and correctional institutions in the United States. These institutions take a number of forms and have a variety of titles. For example, Texas has a system of facilities called *state jails*. Other states have *correctional facilities* or *correctional institutions*, and many states have rehabilitative facilities, transitional facilities, work camps, boot camps, and inmate medical facilities. Several states have one or two facilities especially for women; all have one or more youth or juvenile institutions. The number of facilities a state has varies widely, as well. For example, Michigan has more than 50 state correctional facilities, whereas Utah has two; most states fall somewhere in between.[1] As of June 2007, state prisons housed nearly 1.4 million inmates and federal institutions nearly 200,000 (see Figure 12-1).

Over the centuries, the prison has developed into a unique institution that has become a fundamental feature in our criminal justice system. This chapter will examine the male prison in light of several important issues that illustrate how this institution affects not only the inmates, but also those who work in the prison. We will examine inmates' social roles and legal rights, the occupation of the correctional officer, the problems and dangers associated with incarceration, and finally the move to privatize this traditionally governmental service.

PRISON LIFE

total institution

A closed environment in which every aspect, including the movement and behavior of the people within, is controlled and structured.

The prison is what Erving Goffman called a **total institution.**[2] Much like the military, some religious monasteries, the secure mental health hospital, and tuberculosis sanatoriums, the prison is a closed institution in which everything is tightly controlled and highly structured. The inmates' ability to influence the conditions of their confinement is limited, and escaping is almost impossible. This total control of inmates' lives, including who their cellmates are, what they eat, and when they can bathe, is designed to help the prison run efficiently, maintain order, and deprive the inmate of

Figure 12-1   **Number of Inmates, as of June 30, 2007.**

Source: William J. Sabol and Heather Couture, *Prison Inmates at Midyear 2007* (Washington, DC: U.S. Department of Justice, Bureau of Justice Statistics, 2007), 1, www.ojp.usdoj.gov/bjs/pub/pdf/pim07.pdf.

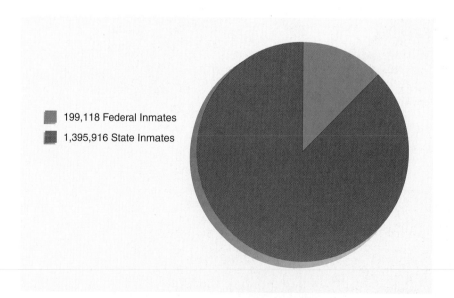

199,118 Federal Inmates

1,395,916 State Inmates

the discretion often taken for granted in free society. It is also designed to punish offenders by depriving them of goods and services, relationships with others, and, although unintentionally, their physical security. In an effort to protect society from criminal offenders, the prison places these potentially dangerous people together in a place where they can prey on one another, often in brutal ways.[3] Although confinement in a small cell may be uncomfortable to many, it is not the worst thing that can happen to a person. (In fact, to many, the closeness of walls can be comforting. The first thing Defoe's Robinson Crusoe did when stranded on a deserted island was to build himself a small structure the size of a prison cell so that he would feel secure.[4]) Instead, deprivations are largely what define a prisoner's lifestyle. Gresham Sykes, in his seminal book *The Society of Captives*, argued that maximum-security prisons make incarceration a painful experience by depriving inmates of some basic freedoms, stating that "the modern pains of imprisonment are often defined by society as a humane alternative to the physical brutality and the neglect which constituted the major meaning of imprisonment in the past."[5] Sykes further notes that the pains of imprisonment can be destructive to the psyche and pose profound threats to the inmate's personality and self-worth. Because of deprivation, we have come to believe that incarceration is a sufficient punishment and that physical brutality in the form of corporal punishment is not required to achieve justice. However, this does not mean that inmates do not experience brutality at the hands of each other. Sykes described five **pains of imprisonment** in this way:

pains of imprisonment
Deprivations that define the punitive nature of imprisonment.

1. **Deprivation of liberty.**   The inmate is confined to an institution and then further confined within that institution. This loss of freedom is the most obvious feature of incarceration, but to adequately understand its effect on the inmate, we must appreciate that not only does it include being restricted to a small space such as a prison cell, but also that this restriction is involuntary. Because friends and family are prohibited from visiting except at limited times, the bonds to loved ones are frayed, sometimes to the breaking point. Sykes goes on to say, "What makes this pain of imprisonment bite most deeply is the fact that the confinement of the criminal represents a deliberate, moral rejection of the criminal by free society."[6]

2. **Deprivation of goods and services.**   Inmates do not have access to the wide range of food, entertainment, and services that free people routinely enjoy.[7] To be sure, this deprivation is relative, and for some inmates "three hots and a cot" is an improvement over their disadvantaged lives on the outside. Having a dry

Meals are delivered through a slot in the door to inmates in solitary confinement. Often the food is cold by the time it reaches the inmate. This is one of the deprivations that results from not being allowed to mix with the general prison population.
Source: CORBIS-NY

place to sleep and a government-guaranteed calorie count is something that many in this world would consider an improvement in lifestyle. However, the inmates' perception is subjective and, according to Sykes, some inmates view the impoverishment that incarceration brings as the prison acting as a tyrant to deprive them of the goods and services they should reasonably have. More often, inmates may see their poverty as a consequence of their behavior and a result of their own inadequacies.

3. **Deprivation of heterosexual relationships.**   Living in a single-sex society such as a prison is stressful. The deprivation of heterosexual activities is one of the most visible and controversial because it sometimes leads to sexual deviation within the prison. We will not deal with this issue here, but will note that homosexual activities and rape are often associated with incarceration. This is particularly true in male prisons, where, as Sykes contended, the self-concept of men is bound up in their sexuality. By depriving men of the audience of females, their "self image is in danger of becoming half complete, fractured, a monochrome without the hues of reality."[8] In turn, without women to provide feedback for displays of masculinity, the inmates create an atmosphere that is sexually charged and difficult to negotiate. Men do not lose their sex drive when imprisoned; it is changed into a type of hypermasculinity that demands that some men be subservient to others.[9]

4. **Deprivation of autonomy.**   The inability to make decisions about some of the most basic tasks, such as walking from one room to another, is a particularly galling deprivation. Being subject to the rules, whims, and preferences of a bureaucratic staff that makes decisions that can appear to be arbitrary or mean-spirited is a humbling experience. Having to ask for everything reduces the inmate to the status of a child. Some inmates argue or bargain with the staff, but their position is so weak that they have little leverage in a well-run prison free of guard corruption. Finding ways to cope with this enforced lack of decision-making power occupies a good deal of the inmates' time and energy.

5. **Deprivation of security.**   This is perhaps the most disturbing pain of imprisonment. Most of those confined to a maximum-security prison have already proven themselves violent, aggressive, and untrustworthy. Having to cope with such cellmates can be an extremely anxious experience, even for those who are violent themselves. There are precious few places in the prison where one can feel secure. Inmates constantly test each other for physical or emotional weaknesses. Those without the courage or nerve to protect themselves are quickly victimized by others if they cannot find a protector.[10]

These pains of imprisonment define the prison experience. Even in the best-managed prisons, with well-trained guards and adequate resources, these deprivations are present. However, they are not unintended consequences. Prisons are meant to be uncomfortable for the inmates and are places that lack the niceties of home. Many people do not feel sorry for inmates who suffer these deprivations.[11] However, these pains of imprisonment are real to the inmates, and to understand prison dynamics, we must appreciate not only how these deprivations affect the inmates, but also how they cope with this lifestyle.

Inmate Subculture

argot roles

Specific patterns of behavior that inmates develop in prison to adjust to the environment.

According to Sykes, inmates compensate for the pains of imprisonment by adopting certain patterns of behavior called **argot roles.** An argot is a special language used by a particular group of people. Inmates have developed terms for the various roles they take on to adapt to imprisonment. According to Sykes, these names provide a map of the inmate social system and enable the inmates to engage in the "ordering and classifying of their experience within the walls in terms which deal specifically with the

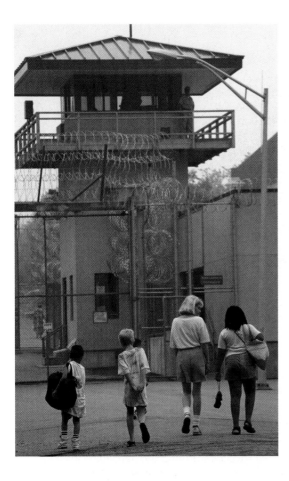

Security is a top priority in all prisons, and all visitors must obey strict rules and procedures. Here, children of inmates in New York State's maximum-security women's prison at Bedford Hills, New York, are on their way to visit their mothers.

Source: Kathy Willens/AP Wide World Photos

major problems of prison life."[12] Sykes listed and discussed these argot roles in the following manner:

- **Rats and center men**   In prison, information is a valuable commodity that the inmates guard jealously. Those who violate the inmate code and reveal to the administration information that can cause harm to another inmate or to the inmate population are called "rats" or "squealers." This is a serious accusation because of the physical and social consequences that can befall someone labeled in this way. There are two types of rats: those who reveal their identity in hopes of personal gain and those who remain anonymous but squeal on a competitor or to settle a grudge. A "center man" is not as vilified by the inmate population as the rat because his actions do not betray the inmate code. A center man is someone who too willingly obeys the rules, who takes the worldview of the administration or who publicly proclaims the virtue of the "rulers." The center man makes no secret of where his loyalties lie and is despised for his open disloyalty to the inmate subculture. However, inmates who adopt these roles do so to relieve the deprivation of autonomy and develop a way of influencing their world by squealing or ingratiating themselves to the prison administration.

- **Gorillas and merchants**   The deprivation of goods and services is partially relieved by the roles of "gorillas" and "merchants." The gorilla is the prison bully who takes what he wants from other inmates through physical force. Often, however, only the threat of force is necessary. The blatant willingness to use force can coerce other inmates to provide the gorilla with cigarettes, food, or gestures of deference, thus placing him at the top of the inmate pecking order. Gorillas can sometimes push inmates too far and find themselves stabbed for their efforts. Many inmates keep weapons as a line of last resort to protect themselves from these predators. The merchant, by contrast, does not use force

Inmates have a well-developed informal social system. In a situation in which resources are scarce, even the control of a basketball hoop may be a point of contention.

Source: Courtesy of CORBIS-NY

to get what he wants, but rather trades for it. The merchant does not engage in the reciprocal exchange of gifts that is common in other groups and that enhances the solidarity of equals. Rather, the merchant is concerned with his own material advantage and is willing to exploit the suffering of other inmates to advance his own standard of living. The roles of gorilla and merchant address the deprivation of goods and services.

- **Wolves, punks, and fags**   To relieve the lack of heterosexual relations, the roles of "wolves," "punks," and "fags" have emerged. A wolf is an individual who plays the masculine role in homosexual relations and uses force or the threat of force to make others submit. Regardless of the wolf's sexuality in the free world, he uses sex in the prison as a form of dominance to emphasize his masculinity. A punk is a weaker inmate who is forced to engage in homosexual relations against his will. By contrast, a fag is someone who is self-identified as a homosexual and who engages in extremely feminine patterns of behavior such as wearing makeup, walking in a feminine way, and playing games such as "stay away closer" and "hard to get but gettable." Although punks and fags differ in their motivations for homosexual activities, they are both held in low esteem by the other inmates. Inmates see the punk as lacking the inner core of toughness, whereas the fag is an overt symbol of femininity. In both cases, they are lower in the pecking order than the wolf, who exhibits masculine behavior. For the wolf, the deprivation of heterosexual relations can be substituted with the exploitation of weaker inmates, and thus his manhood can be redeemed in the prison's highly artificial society.

- **Ball-busters and real men**   "Ball-busters" are inmates who give the prison administration a hard time. They are verbally abusive, defiant, and blatantly disobedient. The ball-buster refuses to see the utter hopelessness of his position and clings to the vestiges of his manhood by defying the administration at every turn. In an effort to ease the deprivation of autonomy, the ball-buster forces guards to either put up with his abusive comments or discipline him. Other inmates see the ball-buster as a fool. Like a Don Quixote tilting at windmills, the ball-buster does not know when to pick his fights and ends up bringing down sanctions not only on himself, but often on the whole inmate population. For this reason, the ball-buster, although mildly amusing at times, is considered a liability by the other inmates because he can make life harder for everyone. The "real man," by contrast, is respected by the other inmates. The real man is the type of inmate most of us would like to think we would be if we were ever in prison. The real man does his time with his dignity intact. He is neither subservient nor aggressive, but "pulls his own time" with a strong and silent demeanor that suggests he is oblivious to the chaos around him. The real man refuses to let the prison strip him of his ability to control his emotions and behavior. He serves his sentence with integrity, respecting the inmate social system without exploiting others or bringing down the wrath of the administration on the general population.

- **Toughs and hipsters**   Violence is a consistent feature of the prison, and several of the argot roles we have discussed use violence or the threat of violence for various purposes. Whereas the gorilla uses violence for personal gain and the wolf to get sexual favors, the "tough" uses violence simply for the sake of violence. He is a touchy individual who will fight over any real or imagined slight or insult. The other inmates tend to give him a wide berth because he fears no one and demands that others placate him with deference. He is respected more than the gorilla because he is not a coward and will fight anyone, even if he is certain to lose. By contrast, the "hipster" is someone who "talks the talk but does not walk the walk." By this, we mean the hipster attempts to bluff and bully other inmates, but when real violence is imminent, he disappears. Each of these types is an adaptation to the deprivation of security that can exacerbate the pains of imprisonment for other inmates. While trying to maintain their own security through violence or the threat of violence, they create an atmosphere in the prison in which everyone must be careful not to offend others.

Sykes's system of argot roles presents an interesting and informative road map of the prison subculture, but some qualifications need to be considered. First, we must recognize that Sykes wrote his book 50 years ago, and prisons have undergone substantial change in the interim. To be sure, the names of the argot roles have mutated many times over, and modern inmates would probably have a difficult time with the titles assigned by Sykes. However, the basic problems of the inmate social structure (security, goods and services, etc.) remain, and inmates must still adapt to imprisonment. Second, each prison demonstrates its own variations of the inmate social structure. Sykes's argot roles, therefore, should be considered ideal types, rather than a scheme to explain all prisons across the decades. Sykes outlined some universal truths concerning the prison; the student of today must consider how these argot roles have evolved in the contemporary prison.

Finally, there has been considerable debate as to whether these roles are actually adaptations to the new environment of the prison or reflect roles that inmates occupied before they were incarcerated. John Irwin, a prominent scholar of the prison who has the added perspective of having served five years in California's institutions, contends that inmates come to prison with their identities already developed from their criminal involvement on the street. Irwin particularly described a "thief identity" that offenders who were thieves bring with them into the prison subculture; he suggested that the student of the prison should consider Sykes's argot roles from a more holistic perspective.[13]

Irwin's concerns can be extended to include the changing nature of the prison subculture as a result of the emergence of prison gangs. Many of the argot roles identified by Sykes have been overtaken by prison gangs. Now, instead of using argot roles to respond to the pains of imprisonment, inmates join prison gangs for security and to acquire goods and services.[14] Sykes's analysis is fascinating and worth contemplating, but we should consider it in light of the changing nature of the prison subculture.

Prison Gangs

To fully appreciate how the contemporary prison's informal inmate social structure shapes the lives of inmates and staff, we must consider the effect of prison gangs. Although not all correctional systems have severe gang problems, and not all gangs are

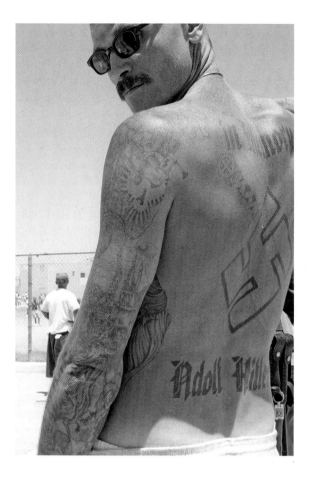

An ex–Aryan Brotherhood gang member walks through the prison yard at California's Calipatria State Prison. Calipatria State Prison holds general-population minimum-custody inmates, as well as Level 4 maximum-custody inmates who wish to participate in vocational/academic programs, prison industries, or support services. It is estimated that up to 97 percent of inmates in Level 4 prisons are in gangs.

Source: © Mark Allen Johnson/ZUMA Press

as violent as the ones we will discuss here, gangs are a concern because without proper vigilance, they can form and take partial control of any prison.

Here, we will discuss the California prison gang problem because it is the most serious in the nation and because a great deal of material has been written about it. The signature feature of the California prison gang structure is that it is based on race. Although not every inmate is affiliated with a gang, those who are stick to their own races. Christian Parenti described several gangs:[15]

- **Mexican Mafia**   The oldest of the prison gangs, the Mexican Mafia, has been traced to the 1950s when a group of Mexican juveniles from Los Angeles was incarcerated together in the Deuel Vocational Institution in Tracy, California. They began preying on white and black inmates by extorting and robbing them. They also attacked Mexican inmates from northern California, especially from cities such as Fresno and Sacramento, whom they considered to be "farmers." The prison authorities, in an effort to destabilize this cadre of troublemakers, dispersed them to prisons all across the state where, unfortunately, they recruited other Mexicans from southern California. The Mexican Mafia, or "La Eme," eventually appropriated the number 13 (*M* is the 13th letter in the alphabet). The gang became a vertically integrated organization that had considerable power not only in the prison, but also on the streets of Los Angeles. For example, according to Parenti, during the post–Rodney King gang truce in Los Angeles in 1993, La Eme ordered an end to drive-by shootings because too many innocent civilians were getting killed. Gang members were ordered to "take care of business with honor and dignity" and not shoot regular people.

- **La Nuestra Familia**   This Mexican gang draws its members from northern California and is constantly at odds with La Eme. In recent years, some of this gang's younger members have spun off and created the Northern Structure, which, in addition to feuding with La Eme, has also clashed with the old guard of La Nuestra Familia. Together, La Nuestra Familia and the Northern Structure represent the largest prison gang in the state. It has gone to great lengths to detail its military structure and educate new gang members about its code of honor, how to identify the enemy, and how to resist interrogations. Those who are released are instructed to set up "regiments" back on the streets of their hometowns, but how successful the gang is in "calling the shots" of what happens on the outside is not really clear.

- **Black Guerrilla Family**   This gang of black inmates originates from the 1960s, when members of the Black Panther Party such as Huey Newton, George Jackson, and Eldridge Cleaver were incarcerated in California prisons. Back then, the inmates were extremely political and adopted a Marxist rhetoric that cast them as political prisoners of an unjust capitalist state. They espoused revolution, but as the years passed, a number of them traded political aspirations for more pragmatic ones. They became gangsters in their own right and instead of robbing drug dealers, they became drug dealers. Today the Black Guerrilla Family is composed of black lifers. Younger black inmates who join gangs are more likely to be affiliated with inmates who belonged to the Bloods or Crips street gangs.

- **Aryan Brotherhood**   These white gang members employ Ku Klux Klan symbols and Nazi swastikas as evidence of their racial identity. Formed partly in response to the increasing dangers posed by Chicano and black gangs, the Aryan Brotherhood is among the most violent and fights hard for its share of prison-yard drug dealing, extortion, and prostitution scams.[16] Parenti reported that the Aryan Brotherhood has, on occasion, aligned itself with La Eme in its ongoing conflict with La Nuestra Familia to the extent of conducting assassinations. The Aryan Brotherhood has spawned franchises around the country in other prisons, but its control of these other gangs is more symbolic than real. Gangs in other states develop their own mythologies that reference Celtic and Norse cultures in addition to the Ku Klux Klan and Nazis.

This list of gangs is incomplete and, to a great extent, already dated because of the changing nature of gang identity and the efforts of prison officials to combat gangs. Gangs mutate over time, changing their names and leadership, but racial identification is a constant. One may think that the prisons could stop gang activity by isolating leaders, punishing those who display gang insignia, and transferring those who refuse to cooperate. These techniques have been partially successful in the short run, but the diffusion of gang activity to other prisons has complicated efforts at gang control.[17]

Parenti somewhat cynically suggested that it is not entirely in the prisons' interests to eliminate gang conflict. Prison officials reportedly keep gangs in a state of perpetual conflict by allowing rival gang members to use the exercise yard at the same time. At California's Corcoran institution, this practice was routinely a source of amusement for the guards. According to Parenti, not only were rival gang members placed in the same yard, but when the ensuing fight took place, the guards placed bets on which inmate would win. These "gladiator fights" were videotaped:

> At the micro-level, COs (also known as "screws" or "bulls"), were staging fights as a form of sadistic diversion, even videotaping the fights for later viewing, and gathering to watch the contests from gun towers. But this local practice, which occurred in other prisons as well, was given a veil of legitimacy by the CDC's integrated yard policy, which mandates the mixing of rival gangs and races in the name of teaching tolerance and testing prisoners' "ability to get along in a controlled setting." Not surprisingly, fist fights and stabbings were, and still are, epidemic throughout the system.[18]

For the most part, prison officials are forced to make difficult decisions in attempts to stem gang violence. On one hand, they attempt to segregate inmates from members of rival gangs and different races to avoid violence. On the other hand, they hope to allow inmates to learn to get along with one another and promote the values of diversity espoused in society. Charges of discrimination can be leveled when inmates are racially separated, but when inmates are allowed access to each other and violence ensues, there can be charges of failing to protect the weak. One solution has been to build extremely expensive prisons where all the inmates are separated from one another in a modern version of the separate-and-silent system.[19]

Supermax Prisons

supermax prison

An extremely secure type of prison that strictly limits inmate contact with other inmates, correctional staff, and the outside world.

The modern **supermax prison** is based on the federal penitentiary at Marion, Illinois, which the Bureau of Prisons opened six years after the closure of Alcatraz in 1963. Like Alcatraz, Marion was a high-security institution, designed to hold the federal system's most dangerous inmates. The prison added the "H unit" in 1972, a special facility within the institution that held Marion's most troublesome inmates. As inmate violence at Marion intensified throughout the 1970s, prison administrators added a maximum-level unit to provide for the long-term separation of violent inmates.

Marion became the first standalone supermax prison in the United States in the fall of 1983, when two correctional officers were killed in one day. The prison's administration locked down the facility permanently, confining all inmates in their cells for 23 hours a day. Throughout the 1980s and 1990s, other federal and state institutions assumed the supermax model. Today, at least 44 states have at least one standalone supermax prison or a prison with a supermax unit, with about 55 supermax prisons or units nationwide.[20] An excellent example of such an institution is Pelican Bay State Prison.

PELICAN BAY STATE PRISON   Pelican Bay is a maximum-security state prison located in Crescent City, California. What makes this supermax prison a good example for study is the way it recalls the separate-and-silent systems in the first prisons in Pennsylvania and Auburn, New York.

Constructed in 1989, relatively shortly after the conversion of the federal penitentiary in Marion, Illinois, the Pelican Bay prison architecture is designed to ensure almost total isolation of inmates as well as minimal contact with the staff. The prison itself is such a bleak, stark, and monotonous environment that inmates suffer severe disorientation, depression, and suicidal behavior.[21] High, gray concrete walls surround the exercise yards and totally block out the surrounding national forest.

The maximum-security prison is a secure institution where most inmates are placed in individual cells. Privileges are limited and boredom is constant.

Source: CORBIS-NY

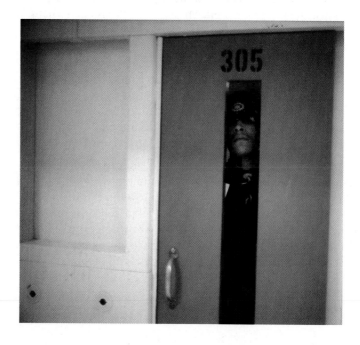

Inmates are confined to their cells with no work, recreation, or contact with anyone other than a cellmate who is equally deprived. When going to the shower (three times a week) or the exercise yard, the inmates are shackled and can move only with the escort of two baton-wielding correctional officers. The prison's security housing unit (SHU) is the end of the line for the state's most recalcitrant inmates. It is reserved for those who have proven unable to live in a general population prison. Most of these inmates belong to gangs. Although the prison is designed to house just over 2000 inmates, its population as of 2008 was about 3400.[22]

The prison at Pelican Bay is successful in a number of ways. It keeps the most dangerous offenders securely incapacitated, ensuring both their safety and the safety of the prison staff. This is a significant feat because it usually takes some degree of cooperation from the inmates to run a truly safe prison. Pelican Bay maintains order mechanically by using technology and prison design, giving inmates absolutely no opportunity to assemble outside their cells. However, this total control comes at a price. This type of prison is extremely expensive to operate, demanding a high degree of technology (see Crosscurrents 12.1 for more criticisms of supermax prisons). Most states can afford to use such a specialized maximum-security institution for only a small percentage of extremely dangerous offenders.[23] For the bulk of the prison population, less expensive prisons, with less control of the inmates, are the norm. Another important expense of the Pelican Bay-type prison, however, is the ultimate effect it has on the inmate who will eventually be released into society. Craig Haney finds these psychological consequences of isolation problematic:

> My own [Haney's] review of the literature suggested these documented negative psychological consequences of long-term solitary-like confinement include: an impaired sense of identity; hypersensitivity to stimuli; cognitive dysfunction (confusion, memory loss, ruminations); irritability, anger, aggression, and/or rage; other-directed violence, such as stabbings, attacks on staff, property destruction, and collective violence; lethargy, helplessness and hopelessness; chronic depression; self-mutilation and/or suicidal ideation, impulses, and behavior; anxiety and panic attacks; emotional breakdowns and/or loss of control; hallucinations, psychosis and/or paranoia; overall deterioration of mental and physical health.[24]

Prison Riots and Violence

The prison is a delicate social system that includes not only inmates, but also guards and administrators, and to a lesser extent, the legislators and politicians responsible for funding and personnel decisions. Although inmates are presumed to be powerless in

At the Maricopa County Jail in Phoenix, Arizona, prisoners who refuse to cooperate or are violent are isolated and strapped into a restraining chair. The hood protects officers and staff from being bitten and spit upon. The county has been sued by the family of a prisoner who died after being restrained in this chair.

Source: Andrew Lichtenstein, CORBIS-NY

What's Wrong with Supermax Prisons?

What do you do with the worst-behaved inmates? In state and federal institutions throughout the nation, there are extremely dangerous individuals who are a threat not only to the general public, but also to other inmates and correctional staff. The solution of this problem has been the development of the supermax prison. This type of correctional institution maintains its inmates in a form of solitary confinement that allows an extra degree of safety for staff and other inmates. Supermax inmates are typically kept in their cells for 23 hours a day and are allowed only one hour of exercise in an enclosed cage that does not allow physical contact with other inmates. Supermax inmates are fed through a slot in the steel door of their cells, and when they must move in the institution, they are shackled and guarded by at least two correctional officers.[1]

Defining the supermax prison is difficult. It is more of a concept than an identifiable category of a prison. In 1996, the National Institute of Corrections defined supermax prisons as "a stand-alone unit or part of another facility [that] is designated for violent or disruptive inmates. It typically involves up to 23-hour per day, single-cell confinement for an indefinite period of time. Inmates in supermax housing have minimal contact with staff and other inmates."[2]

Maintaining a supermax prison is both labor intensive and expensive. One would think that it is reserved only for extreme cases when no other options are available. However, although only 1 to 2 percent of the nation's 2 million inmates are held in the nation's 55 supermax prisons, this still represents 20,000 inmates. The cost of building a supermax prison is about $75,000 per cell as compared to about $25,000 for each cell in an ordinary prison. Supermax prisons cost more than $1 billion over their life span of 30 to 40 years.[3]

According to Jeffrey Ian Ross, supermax prisons have proliferated for a number of reasons:

- Many prisons have had staff members attacked or killed by unruly inmates.
- Rehabilitating dangerous inmates is difficult, or, with present resources, impossible. According to Ross, this is at least partly because serious attempts were jettisoned in response to the war on crime.
- As prison populations have grown, it has become increasingly difficult to keep all inmates safe. Supermax prisons are a way to isolate dangerous or troublesome inmates.
- The practice of minimum sentencing has led to many inmates serving extremely long periods of incarceration with little hope of parole.

With little incentive to obey prison rules, many of these inmates have become even more dangerous.

- Prison administrators found supermax prisons to be a good way of increasing budgets and power within state governments. Ross suggests that the careerism of some correctional administrators has been responsible for the surge of supermax prisons. The costs associated with building supermax prisons are substantially more than those for maximum-security prisons. This inflates the budgets of state correctional systems and gives administrators control over greater resources. Criminologist Nils Christie uses the term "prison industrial complex" to describe how the growth of correctional systems has become a goal in and of itself.[4]
- Finally, supermax prisons gave institution administrators an option to deal with not only the most violent and hardened criminals, but also those who were persistent rule breakers, high-profile serial killers, gang leaders, and spies or terrorists.

The effects of incarceration on inmates can be severe. In the supermax prison, where isolation is the norm, this problem is even more acute. Long periods of solitary confinement have stripped many inmates of any ability to civilly interact with others, severely damaging their chances of adjusting to society when they have served their sentences.[5]

The future of supermax prisons is in doubt. Although there might be a continuing need for this type of secure incarceration, it is also evident that states have invested too much money in building supermax prisons. According to Ross, states such as Wisconsin and Maryland have not been able to fill the beds of the supermax prisons with the types of inmates for which they were envisioned. Consequently, inmates who do not require this extreme level of security are sent to these extremely expensive prisons. In times when states are experiencing financial difficulties, the cost of building, maintaining, and operating supermax prisons is quickly losing political favor. Other essential services such as education, highway construction, and health insurance are competing for the public dollar.

Although supermax prisons provide visible evidence that society is serious about being tough on crime, they may simply be too expensive to maintain. Regardless, there is a still a category of inmate that is colloquially known as the "worst of the worst." Critics of those who criticize supermax prisons point out that these inmates are not going to go away simply because we want them to. They still must be confined and closely guarded, usually for long periods of time, and, for now, there are few alternatives.

Think About It

1. Should states continue to build and maintain supermax prisons even though they are expensive?
2. Some critics of supermax prisons say that the need for so many indicates societal problems, and that more money should be spent to rehabilitate offenders rather than to build more supermax prisons. Do you agree or disagree? Why?
3. In your opinion, does keeping an inmate in a cell for 23 hours a day constitute cruel and unusual punishment?

[1]Sam Torres, review of *Supermax Prisons: Their Rise, Current Practices, and Effects on Inmates,* by Jesenia Pizarro and M. K. Vanja Stenius, *Federal Probation* 84 (June 2003): 248–264, www.uscourts.gov/fedprob/December_2004/reviews.html.

[2]Daniel P. Mears, "Evaluating the Effectiveness of Supermax Prisons" (Washington, DC: Urban Institute, Justice Policy Center, 2006).

[3]Ibid.

[4]Nils Christie, *Crime Control as Industry* (London: Routledge, 1993).

[5]Jeffrey Ian Ross, "Supermax Prisons," *Society* 44 (March 2007): 60–64.

their captivity, they often employ a number of techniques to address the conditions of their confinement. Inmates may write letters to correctional officials, complain to their congressional representatives, petition the parole board, file briefs in the courts, or simply act out in ways that range from bothersome to seriously violent. Some of these techniques are more effective than others. The bottom line, however, is that regardless of how frustrated inmates may feel in a correctional institution, they cannot walk away. Those of us in society can drop out of school, move out of our parents' houses, quit our jobs, or dump our significant others when we have "had enough." Inmates do not have these options. Being incarcerated means that problems and frustrations can accumulate until a breaking point is reached. This breaking point can be a mental collapse, a fight with a fellow inmate, violence against a guard, or simply retreating from prison life by being so ornery that solitary confinement is required.[25] These are daily occurrences in the prison and, for the most part, they are handled with established procedures that are understood by all involved. (See Figure 12-2 for homicide rates among state inmates.)

On rare occasions, the inmate's frustrations are shared by others, and the authority of the institution is seriously challenged. Inmates acting together can overwhelm the guards and take over the institution in a full-scale prison riot in which people are killed and injured and property destroyed. Sociologists use the term *collective behavior* to explain how the actions of the individual are transmitted into group actions that can go well beyond what any of the individuals in the group intended.[26] This "herd mentality"

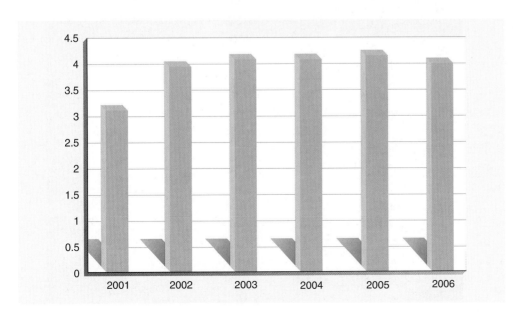

Figure 12-2 Homicide Rates among State Inmates, 2001–2006.

Source: Bureau of Justice Statistics, State Prison Deaths, 2001-2006, www.ojp.usdoj.gov/bjs/dcrp/tables/dcst06spt1.htm; Paige M. Harrison and Allen J. Beck, *Prisoners in 2004* (Washington, DC: U.S. Department of Justice, Bureau of Justice Statistics, 2005), 2, www.ojp.usdoj.gov/bjs/pub/pdf/p04.pdf; William J. Sabol, Heather Couture, and Paige M. Harrison, *Prisoners in 2006* (Washington, DC: U.S. Department of Justice, Bureau of Justice Statistics, 2007), 2, www.ojp.usdoj.gov/bjs/pub/pdf/p06.pdf.

can cause even law-abiding citizens to engage in destructive actions. (A good example of this would be the riots that sometimes occur after sports championships.)[27]

In the prison, collective behavior can not only have deadly consequences, but also temporarily invert the social structure and shatter the bonds of social control.[28] With the administration no longer controlling the institution, the oppressed become king, the protected become vulnerable, and anyone caught in the middle can become a victim. The prison's most antisocial individuals are, for a limited time, free to wreak havoc. A number of studies on the causes and prevention of prison riots have made it clear that despite many commonalities, each institution has its own limitations, atmosphere, and vulnerabilities.[29] Rather than attempting a comprehensive review of prison riots, we will focus on two very different but infamous examples of what can happen when things go terribly wrong in the prison.

ATTICA PRISON RIOT   The 1971 Attica prison riot may be the most famous because so much has been written about it. It has been the subject of at least four major books—one written by the then-commissioner of corrections, one by an inmate, and two by outside observers. Additionally, it was investigated primarily by the McKay Commission, which interviewed guards, inmates, state police, National Guardsmen, reporters, and former governor Nelson Rockefeller. In total, more than 2600 interviews were conducted. The official McKay Commission report was 500 pages long.[30]

Attica Prison opened in upstate New York in 1931. It was considered a state-of-the-art prison at the time and boasted of being both "escape-proof" and a "paradise for convicts." Neither of these proclamations turned out to be the case.[31] To understand the riot's causes, we must examine the social dynamics both inside and outside the prison as they existed in 1971. The United States was embroiled in a number of social conflicts during this period. Many citizens had high expectations that opportunity and social justice would be available to all and were frustrated when conditions did not improve quickly enough. Social movements concerned with civil rights, women's liberation, and opposition to the ongoing Vietnam War placed the government on the defensive and brought scrutiny to many social institutions. Universities were challenged to make their curricula more relevant; traditional family values were challenged by communal living and sexual relations without commitment; and the government's foreign policy was protested by people from a wide variety of backgrounds.

In prisons nationwide, this age of protest was embraced by inmates who thought the conditions of their incarceration were unjust, inadequate, or unconstitutional.

The 1971 Attica Prison riot left 39 dead over a period of four days.

Source: AP Wide World Photos

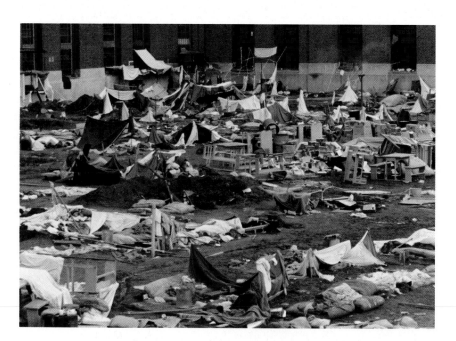

12.1   CRIMINAL JUSTICE REFERENCE

The Demands Collected by the Inmates during the Attica Prison Riot

1. Provide adequate food and water and shelter for this group.
2. Replace Superintendent Mancusi immediately.
3. Grant complete administrative and legal amnesty to all persons associated with this matter.
4. Place this institution under federal jurisdiction.
5. Apply the New York State minimum wage law to all work done by inmates. STOP SLAVE LABOR.
6. Allow all New York State prisoners to be politically active, without intimidation or reprisal.
7. Allow true religious freedom.
8. End all censorship of newspaper, magazines, letters, and other publications from publishers.
9. Allow all inmates on their own to communicate with anyone they please.
10. When an inmate reaches conditional release, give him a full release without parole.
11. Institute realistic, effective rehabilitation programs for all inmates according to their offense and personal needs.
12. Modernize the education system.
13. Provide a narcotics treatment program that is effective.
14. Provide adequate legal assistance to all inmates requesting it.
15. Provide a healthy diet; reduce the number of pork dishes; serve fresh fruit daily.
16. Reduce cell time, increase recreation time, and provide better recreation facilities and equipment.
17. Provide adequate medical treatment for every inmate, engage either a Spanish-speaking doctor or interpreters who will accompany Spanish-speaking inmates to medical interviews.
18. Provide a complete Spanish library.

Source: Bert Useem and Peter Kimball, *States of Siege: U.S. Prison Riots 1971–1986* (New York: Oxford University Press, 1991), 236.

Additionally, as John Irwin tells us, there was a major change in the collective self-concept of minorities. The "black is beautiful" idea signaled a newfound pride in racial status and persuaded many to reject the second-class treatment they believed prison officials meted out to people of color.[32] Against this backdrop of challenges to institutional authority, Attica Prison imploded in 1971. Was Attica different from other prisons of the time? Probably not. But an assessment by Useem and Kimball succinctly described the state of Attica:

> Life at Attica was terrible. The McKay Commission devoted 71 pages to discussing how bad it was and all the ways in which it was bad. The cells were cramped, the food was barely edible or nutritious, the medical care was unsatisfactory, the recreation was minimal, the job assignments were boring and unrewarding, and the atmosphere was depressing and degrading.[33]

Yet Useem and Kimball did not consider the prison's conditions as the major reason for the riot. Other prisons had inmate politicization and lacked an adequate physical plant like Attica, but such devastating riots did not occur at these prisons. However, the Attica administration adopted policies that exacerbated the sense of hopelessness and injustice there. For instance, the rules of the prison were mutable, unwritten, arbitrarily enforced, and frustrating to even the best-behaved inmates. Usually, in such situations, the guards and the inmates negotiate which behaviors are acceptable and which are not. But at Attica, according to Useem and Kimball, the guards' job assignments were reorganized in 1970. The result was that the guards no longer had stable assignments that allowed them to get to know the inmates and work out what constituted acceptable behavior. Instead, all 400 of the guards were rotated on an apparently random basis. To avoid rule infractions, inmates would need to know the predilections of each guard. This lack of consistent rule enforcement discouraged a stable environment.

Another feature unique to Attica was the inmates' political savvy. Before the riot, the inmates had communicated with inmates in other New York correctional institutions; negotiated with the commissioner of correctional services, Russell Oswald; and successfully engaged in a sit-down strike in the metal shops and won a tripling of their wages. In retaliation, the prison moved the leaders of this peaceful protest to other prisons.

The Attica prison riot is instructive because the inmates were able to present a united front and negotiate as a group (see Criminal Justice Reference 12.1 for their demands). The inmates established an order of discipline and formulated and presented demands to prison officials. Additionally, after the first wave of violence (in which one correctional officer and three inmates were killed), inmates protected hostages from further violence. More than 1600 inmates took control of the prison yard, and after an initial celebration, the serious work of organizing the siege and negotiating with authorities got underway. Of particular interest was the introduction of outside observers to act as negotiators.[34] Negotiating with prisoners became problematic in that their demands would change radically and become unreasonable (some inmates wanted to be transported out of the country). With the introduction of press coverage, a circuslike atmosphere developed. Negotiations eventually broke down for a number of reasons, and the administration, using correctional officers and National Guardsmen, stormed the prison and reestablished control in a violent paramilitary operation that resulted in the deaths of 29 inmates and 10 correctional officers who were being held hostage. (Autopsy reports revealed that all the hostages were killed by gunfire, which is significant because the inmates had no firearms.)

The Attica prison riot is known for the way the inmates cooperated to maintain the discipline of their social system under great stress and uncertainty. The riot is also famous for the inability of the state to bring a peaceful resolution and its botched retaking of the prison by correctional officers and National Guardsmen who were not trained for such operations.[35] In terms of brutality, however, the Attica prison riot pales in comparison to the New Mexico prison riot.

NEW MEXICO STATE PENITENTIARY RIOT   In 1980, 33 inmates died in a riot at the New Mexico State Penitentiary in Santa Fe. Although no guards were killed, 12 were severely beaten and raped. The major difference between the Attica riot and the New Mexico riot was the lack of social cohesion among the inmates. Unlike Attica, where the inmates displayed a certain amount of control and coordination, the New Mexico inmates killed with abandon and without regard for the existing inmate social system. According to Bert Useem,

> No group of inmates attained clear leadership status. Control over hostages, walkie-talkies, and negotiations was fragmented, personalistic, and ephemeral. Some inmates, alone or in groups, took advantage of the situation to rape, torture, and mutilate other inmates. One inmate had his head cut off with a shovel; another died from a screw-driver driven through his head; several were immolated in their cells when inmates sprayed lighter fluid on them; and still others were tortured to death with acetylene torches. No inmate group made a serious attempt to prevent this.[36]

The New Mexico prison riot caused great anxiety in institutions across the nation about the consequences of prison disturbances. Although the place of an inmate in the prison social structure may have prevented victimization in the past, this riot showed that when all the bonds of social control are cast aside, a prison riot can be deadly for anyone.[37] In the few days the inmates controlled the prison, everyone lived in terror. Only the strong and the lucky escaped unscathed.

A number of new features in contemporary prisons make riots less likely and, if they do happen, less deadly. Today, it is easier to segregate prisoners who cause trouble, not only because prison systems have more options in moving inmates to other prisons, but also because staffs keep better records and communicate more often about the emotional state of the inmate population.[38] Prison officials are also better at discovering and reacting to problems before they can escalate into a riot situation.

Stanford Prison Experiment

In 1971 Stanford psychology professor Philip Zimbardo created an experiment to test the effects of prison life on inmates and staff. For this experiment he recruited 24 young men to act as inmates and guards in a makeshift prison. The experiment was scheduled to last two weeks. It ended in six days. Dr. Christina Maslach, who witnessed the student prison in its last stages, told a symposium of the American Psychological Association in 1996, "I was sick to my stomach. . . . I was having a hard time watching what was happening to these kids."[1]

In August 1971, in Palo Alto, California, police arrested nine young men in their homes. The men were students who had answered a newspaper ad offering to pay them $15 a day to participate in an experiment on prisons. The arrestees were part of a group of 24 men who had been randomly split into two parts: guards and inmates. Before the experiment, all had taken tests to determine that they were mentally healthy.

The nine men who had been assigned as inmates were booked and fingerprinted at a real jail, then blindfolded and driven to the Stanford campus to a "prison" located in the basement of a school building. The students assigned as guards received no training, only uniforms and instructions to control the prison as they saw fit without using violence. The prison cells were created by removing the doors of laboratory rooms and replacing them with steel bars and cell numbers. The prison had no windows, and no clocks were allowed. Other modifications included the addition of secret videotaping equipment and the conversion of a small closet into a solitary confinement chamber. The cells were bugged via an intercom system.

At the prison, the new inmates were greeted by the "warden," who established the seriousness of the inmates' offenses and their status as inmates. The inmates were strip-searched and deloused. Although the experimenters did not expect that these students would actually introduce contraband or lice, this procedure was done to imitate real prison procedures and to humiliate the student inmates. The inmates wore only dresslike smocks (no underwear) printed with their ID numbers and rubber sandals. Each inmate had a heavy chain bolted to each ankle, and his head was covered with a nylon stocking. The chain, smock, and stocking are not features in actual prisons, but they were introduced to quickly stimulate a sense of humiliation and oppression. For example, the inmates were called only by their ID numbers and could refer to themselves only by their numbers.

The experiment got underway with nine guards and nine inmates (the remaining six men remained on call if replacement guards or inmates were needed). The guards were divided among three eight-hour shifts, overseeing the inmates, who were divided among three small cells. The guards began the simulation by counting the inmates several times a day, including waking the inmates for counts at 2:30 A.M. The guards also devised, with no input from the staff who ran the experiment, the punishment of push-ups, often placing their feet on the backs of inmates sentenced to do them.

By the second day, the inmates staged a revolt, removing their stocking caps and numbers and barricading themselves inside their cells. The guards dealt with this by calling in the three standby guards and having the night shift remain at the prison. They forced the inmates away from their cell doors with blasts from a fire extinguisher, entered the cells, and stripped the inmates. The leaders of the rebellion were forced into solitary confinement, while the remaining inmates were harassed. To break inmate solidarity, the guards set up a "privilege" cell in which the three inmates least involved in the rebellion were allowed to wash, dress, and eat a special meal in front of the other inmates, who were not allowed to eat. After a few hours, the guards put the innocent inmates back in the regular cells and the scheming inmates in the privilege cell, setting up confusion and distrust among the inmates. A staff consultant who had been a former inmate in a real penitentiary confirmed that such divide-and-conquer tactics were actually used by correctional officers.

According to Zimbardo, the guards continued to increase the humiliation, coercion, and dehumanization of the inmates. For example, they would not allow any bathroom visits after 10 P.M. "lights-out," forcing the inmates to urinate and defecate in buckets in their cells. Occasionally, the guards would not allow inmates to empty these buckets. Although it may seem that the guards were overplaying their roles for the researchers, some guards were caught on videotape continuing to abuse the inmates even when they thought the researchers were not watching.

The inmates became so stressed that the staff released five of them early, but not easily. The staff themselves, according to Zimbardo, had already begun thinking like prison officials. When one inmate began to show signs of mental distress, they thought he was trying to "con" the staff. Instead of offering him release, the guards asked him to inform on the other inmates in exchange for better treatment. He was released only when his signs of distress increased. The staff also manipulated the inmates' parents and friends who came on visiting day. After sprucing up the prison and the inmates, they forced the visitors to comply with an assortment of rules much like those in a real prison. Although some of the parents complained, they all complied, even though some remarked that they had never seen their sons looking so stressed or fatigued.

The psychologists who ran the experiment were not immune to its effects, either. Zimbardo admitted becoming so consumed by his role as a prison official that he tried to quash a rumored mass escape plot by going to the Palo Alto police and asking to use their old jail to hold the student inmates. (The police turned down the request, much to Zimbardo's frustration.) When the escape plot did not materialize—after the prison staff had gone to a lot of trouble to thwart it—the guards and staff increased the harassment and humiliation. Even a former prison chaplain, a Catholic priest invited in to evaluate the situation, fell completely into his role. On interviewing individual inmates, he even offered to get lawyers for them. Even more surprising was the inmates' parents' reactions. Many of them took the priest's advice and called the staff to request attorneys to bail their sons out of "jail."

According to Zimbardo, "By the end of the study, the prisoners were disintegrated, both as a group and as individuals. There was no longer any group unity; just a bunch of isolated individuals hanging on, much like prisoners of war or hospitalized mental patients. The guards had won total control of the prison, and they commanded the blind obedience of each inmate. At this point it became clear that we had to end the study. We had created an overwhelmingly powerful situation—a situation in which inmates were withdrawing and behaving in pathological ways, and in which some of the guards were behaving sadistically."[2]

Zimbardo's experiment became legendary and, because of the ethical questions it raised, was among the last of its kind. Not only did it shed light on human behavior, but it also raised questions of what constitutes good ethics in experiments using human subjects.

Think About It

1. Did this experiment help increase our understanding of human behavior, or was it too flawed?
2. Should more experiments like this be allowed?

[1]Kathleen O'Toole, "The Stanford Prison Experiment: Still Powerful after All These Years," Stanford University News Service, January 8, 1997, www.stanford.edu/dept/news/relaged/970108prisonexp.html.

[2]Philip G. Zimbardo, Stanford Prison Experiment, www.prisonexp.org.

A cellblock at the New Mexico State Penitentiary after the end of 36 hours of rioting in February 1980.
Source: CORBIS-NY

(See Crosscurrents 12.2 for a controversial look at how incarceration can affect inmates, staff, and administrators).

In addition to creating more professionally trained prison administrations, most prisons have developed special units to deal with explosive situations. Like the special weapons and tactics (SWAT) units in law enforcement, prisons have implemented

Officers prepare to enter the cell of an unruly inmate at Nebraska's Tecumseh State Correctional Institution.

Source: *Michael Karlsson/Arresting Images*

special operations response team (SORT) units to handle situations such as hostage taking and an inmate who refuses to leave his or her cell. Wearing helmets and protective clothing and armed with shields and batons, the team overwhelms and disarms troublesome inmates. The SORT unit marches to the cell block in double-time, chanting and banging their batons against their shields to psychologically intimidate the problem inmate and to display to other inmates that the prison can quickly marshal sufficient force to quell any disturbance.[39]

WORKING IN THE PRISON

Guards, medical technicians, treatment specialists, administrators, secretaries, and clergy all contribute to the prison dynamic. Most of these occupations are found in society, but unique demands are placed on those who serve in these positions in the prison. For instance, a secretary in most organizations is encouraged to promote good customer relations. In the prison, the consumer of the service is the inmate, and secretaries are cautioned to be wary, emotionally distant, and suspicious of every request, motive, and kindness offered by the inmate. Working in an environment in which the potential for violence, escape, and duplicity are constant is not for everyone. Those who work in the prison perform a job that, although important, is not always appreciated.

By far the most prevalent and problematic of these jobs is the correctional officer or guard. Lucien Lombardo, a respected scholar of the prison, has looked at the work of the correctional officer and found that, contrary to the popular media image, the job has many variations. Lombardo listed seven variations of correctional officer job assignments:[40]

1. **Block officers.** These officers not only are responsible for the security of the housing block, which can contain 300 to 400 inmates, but also must see that the

12.1 FOCUS on ETHICS

CONNED BY THE CONS

You have known for a long time that your older brother Mike is not the brightest bulb on the Christmas tree. He always seemed to find a way to let his good intentions go astray and end up in some kind of disaster. Now it looks as if his latest scheme is going to bring you down with him unless you make a difficult decision.

Mike has worked at the county jail for three years and has risen to the rank of sergeant and is supervisor over the visiting center. Because of his connections, you were recently hired as a guard and work directly under him as a security officer in charge of searching visitors. Mike has wide discretion in this post in determining what types of visits are granted to inmates and is usually pretty good about making sure high-risk offenders do not get contact visits with their families. Lately, however, you have noticed that several members of a violent gang have been getting more visits than normal and that these contact visits extend well past the normal visiting hours. Furthermore, Mike has just purchased a new extended-cab pickup truck that must have cost close to $25,000, money you know he does not have because he still owes money to you. Troubled, you suspect that Mike has been taking money from inmates in exchange for letting them smuggle drugs inside the jail.

Today, Mike came to you and confessed that he was in big trouble. It seems that the drugs he has allowed in the jail have become the reason for a pending all-out gang war, and he fears not only for his life but also for yours and your family's. A rival gang of the one he has been helping has put a contract out on Mike, you, and your parents. Mike says that the only way to solve this problem is to smuggle a gun inside the jail and let his gang friends "take care of business." Mike needs your cooperation in overlooking the gun, which will be carried in by a gang leader's girlfriend. She will have it hidden in a big pocketbook, and you are to do a careless search and allow her inside the jail with this loaded gun.

What Do You Do?

1. Do you value your loyalty to your brother more than your integrity to the job?

2. Should you attempt to protect your parents by going along with Mike's plan?

3. Given Mike's limited intelligence, are you certain that even if the plan works it will solve any problems?

4. What are your other options?

---

daily work and activities are done in an orderly way. This includes ensuring that inmates are fed, get their medical and rehabilitative treatment programs, are released into the exercise yard at the appropriate time, and get their mail. This is all done in a noisy and hectic environment in which the officer may be surrounded by inmates with varying demands. The block officer must ensure the maintenance of a healthy balance of security and social services. According to Lombardo, the administration can frustrate the work of the block officer by changing the prison's rules or routine. These officers must then translate the reasoning behind the sudden changes to inmates who get upset with alterations of their routine.

2. **Work-detail supervisors.** Every function of the prison that requires inmate labor must be supervised by a correctional officer, including commissary, clothing, library privileges, and recreational activities. This job can be rewarding or frustrating. Control of scarce resources can be accompanied by pressures from inmates as well as other correctional officers to stretch the limits of discretion to do favors (see Focus on Ethics 12.1). Although this gives officers some bargaining power with the inmates, it also is a source of tension because the work-detail officers are accountable to the administration for getting the work of the prison done. These officers, who are evaluated on how well they can get 10 felons to do their work, are in a vulnerable position.

3. **Industrial shop and school officers.** These officers perform security and order-maintenance functions by supervising inmates engaged in work or school activities provided by civilians. When things go right, this can be a stable and relatively safe assignment, but if a teacher fails to show up one day, the officer may have to supervise 50 inmates who have nothing to do for two hours. The teachers get the socially rewarding tasks of educating inmates, but the school officer must maintain the discipline required for learning to occur. Imagine teaching a class of 50 220-pound fifth-graders.

The duty of some correctional officers is to stand at post at important locations within the prison. This officer is responsible for monitoring a vital prison checkpoint.

Source: CORBIS-NY

4. **Yard officers.** Lombardo made the interesting observation that the yard is the closest thing to the street in the prison environment. The block is the inmate's home, and the school or work assignment keeps the inmate busy, but the yard is where the greatest potential for trouble exists. Yard officers are often the most inexperienced, and their primary job is to be constantly alert for signs of trouble.

5. **Administrative building assignments.** These officers have little contact with the inmates and perform a variety of administrative functions in the prison. They control security gates; handle the storage of weapons; field telephone calls from the outside; and supervise the visitation of friends, attorneys, and relatives.

6. **Wall posts.** Some officers watch from a tower what is going on inside the prison yard and on the outside perimeter. This duty is devoid of the anxiety of dealing with inmates at close quarters, but it can be boring. The important part of the job is to protect innocent people, especially fellow guards.

7. **Relief officers.** These officers have no steady assignment but rather fill in for other officers who take days off or go on vacation. The job can be stressful because, without a regular post, the officers have not developed working relationships with inmates. Like substitute teachers, these officers are constantly tested by inmates wanting to determine the boundaries of acceptable behavior. Written job descriptions exist for every post in the prison, but the relief officer must quickly learn any of these jobs while simultaneously performing it for the first time.

Although the exact posting of the correctional officer dictates the type of duties he or she performs, some general functions are performed in every correctional institution. Over the years, bureaucratization has increased the number of specialist guards, but these general functions are still pertinent to the overall nature of the correctional officers' work. Lombardo identified these functions as follows:

- **Human services** Officers perform a variety of services for inmates, either as a formal part of their duties or because of informal relationships they develop with certain inmates. Some officers complain about being reduced to babysitters because some inmates are incapable of dealing with these issues themselves, or as a result of their captivity, are prevented from handling the little problems they would normally deal with on the outside. Some inmates may also be mentally ill and require extra attention (see Crosscurrents 12.3). Although human-services work can be a headache for the officer, it can also provide a sense of satisfaction. The three aspects to human-services work are providing goods and services, acting as a referral agent or advocate, and playing a role in inmates' institutional adjustment.

- **Order maintenance** Correctional officers maintain the social order in prison by earning the inmates' trust and cooperation. By enforcing rules in a consistent and evenhanded manner, and by showing inmates respect and allowing them a certain level of dignity, the correctional officer can help establish an atmosphere in which inmates feel not only secure, but also that their world is predictable and controllable. By maintaining order in subtle ways, as well as with the threat of punishments, the officer can reduce the level of tension in the cell block.

- **Security** Another function officers perform is security. This is a passive function in which the officer watches to ensure that inmates are not acting out. The primary focus of the security function is to keep the inmates inside the institution.

- **Supervision** The physical maintenance of the prison is accomplished by correctional officers' supervision of inmates. Because the inmates lack the moral obligation to do the work themselves, the officers are responsible for seeing that the work is done efficiently and safely.

COURTS AND THE PRISON

Should inmates have legal rights while they are incarcerated? This might seem like a silly question. Inmates are viewed as having forfeited their rights as citizens, and many people believe that one of the consequences of incarceration is that the inmate is stripped of the privileges and legal protections that citizens have. Some people, however, believe that inmates should not lose all of their rights. Inmates are still under the protection of the Constitution. Their legal rights, although necessarily attenuated, are not totally restricted. The rights lost by inmates should be only those consistent with their confinement and the maintenance of institutional safety. These different perspectives make for an interesting debate, but we will confine ourselves here to examining how the courts have treated this issue.

hands-off doctrine
The judicial attitude toward prisons before the 1960s in which courts did not become involved in prison affairs or inmate rights.

Before the 1960s, the courts cultivated a **hands-off doctrine** toward inmates' rights.[41] It was thought that offenders had legal rights granted to them in the arrest and trial phases of the criminal justice system and that incarceration was primarily an administrative matter concerning the internal workings of the prison and not subject to a great degree of judicial oversight. There were a few significant reasons for this hands-off doctrine. First, the decisions made about the conditions of confinement were viewed as a technical matter that judges were not educationally equipped to consider. Second, because of the separation of powers, decisions about prisons were considered a matter for the executive branch of government, not the judicial branch. Third, the public did not really care about what went on in the prison and were content to allow prison administrators wide latitude in the treatment of inmates. Finally, the treatment of prisoners was considered a product of privileges rather than legal rights. For these reasons, the courts were historically reluctant to involve themselves with the conditions of confinement.[42]

The social upheavals of the 1960s influenced many aspects of society. The prison felt the ramifications of the protests of marginalized people in much the same way that the rest of society was affected by the civil rights and women's movements. Inmates and those concerned with the welfare of inmates began to petition the courts to address several issues they deemed problematic. For instance, in Stateville Prison

12.3 CrossCurrents

Incarceration and the Mentally Ill

One of the most controversial issues in criminal justice is how to deal with mentally ill offenders. A tried-and-true method has never existed to treat mentally ill offenders. As of 2005, more than half of all prison and jail inmates reported a mental health problem. Nearly a quarter of both state and jail inmates who had a mental health problem had served three or more prior incarcerations. Jail inmates had the highest rate of mental health disorder symptoms, followed by state and federal inmates (see the figure).

Historically, mentally ill offenders have been thrown together with healthy offenders and locked up in dungeons, jails, and dank asylums, and hanged on gibbets without cognizance of or concern for the fact that had they received the proper medical treatment, they might not have broken the law at all. This was especially true before the development of mental health science in the early 20th century. However, now that diseases of the mind and brain are a bit more understood, the treatment of mentally ill offenders is still much the same. They go to prisons and jails. They receive inadequate treatment or no treatment. They are executed. According to government statistics, five times as many mentally ill people are in prisons and jails than in mental hospitals, and 16 percent of all inmates are mentally ill.

In Fairfax County, Virginia, advocates say that up to 200 seriously mentally ill people are in prison at a time. Some are charged with violent offenses, and others are there for minor things such as loitering. What they have in common is that they might not be in the lockup at all had they received the right treatment and/or medication. Paradoxically, the only way many mentally ill offenders, especially the indigent, can get treatment is by going to prison or jail, where they have access to doctors and medication.

Experts say that the move toward incarceration rather than treatment began in the 1950s, when many mental institutions were closed in favor of community-based programs. Many communities, however, lack the resources or the organization to treat the mentally ill. For example, the U.S. Department of Health reported that in 1955 a total of 558,922 patients were in public mental hospitals. By 1998, with the U.S. population booming, that number had dropped to 57,151.

Think About It

1. Are mentally ill offenders treated unfairly, or is a crime a crime that should be punished accordingly?
2. Should some of the funding that goes to build more prisons go to building more mental hospitals?

Source: William Branigin and Leef Smith, "Mentally Ill Need Care, Find Prison without Treatment, Many Cycle In and Out of Jail," *Washington Post*, November 25, 2001, www.washingtonpost.com/ac2/wp-dyn/A10740–2001Nov24; Doris J. James and Lauren E. Glaze, *Mental Health Problems of Prison and Jail Inmates* (Washington, DC: U.S. Department of Justice, Bureau of Justice Statistics, 2006), 1, 3.

in Illinois, Christian inmates were allowed to read the Bible, but Muslim inmates were forbidden to possess the Qur'an.[43] Prison officials were successfully sued in *Cooper* v. *Pate* (1964) (see Case in Point 12.1), which began a new era in prison litigation. This new interventionist doctrine resulted in the courts considering a wide variety of issues in the prison and fundamentally changing the relationship between the

12.1	CASE IN POINT

COOPER V. PATE

THE CASE	THE POINT
Cooper v. Pate, 378 U.S. 546 (1964)	This case helped end the judicial "hands-off" doctrine toward prisons by allowing inmates to sue for civil rights violations.

Thomas Cooper, an inmate at the Illinois State Penitentiary, claimed that because of his religious beliefs as a Muslim he was not allowed to possess the religious literature that he wanted and was denied privileges. Two lower courts granted motions to dismiss the case. However, the Supreme Court reversed this judgment, allowing Cooper's suit to continue.

courts and corrections. Inmates found the courts receptive to their complaints about the arbitrary ways prisons were operated. Prison administrators were forced to treat inmates in a more uniform manner, keep better records, and run their institutions according to well-defined and ascertainable criteria.[44]

What was the source of this newfound concern for the rights of inmates? From where did the courts draw their authority to enter into the realm of inmate rights? Inmates' lawyers turned to several places in the Constitution to persuade the courts to reconsider prisons.

Eighth Amendment

The Eighth Amendment states, in part, ". . . nor cruel and unusual punishments be inflicted." There is considerable debate as to what should be considered cruel or unusual. The courts have ruled on thousands of cases in which prison administrators were faulted for a wide variety of policies such as food issues, heating, and discipline. Although we cannot list and discuss all these issues, one scholar has suggested that the court has not provided a clear statement about what constitutes "cruel" or "unusual." Rather, the court has provided a general statement in which it likens a given situation to that which "amounts to torture, when it is grossly excessive in proportion to the offense for which it is imposed, or that is inherently unfair; or that is unnecessarily degrading, or is shocking or disgusting to people of reasonable sensitivity" (*Holt v. Sarver*, 309 F. Supp. 362) (ED Ark. 1970).[45] Additionally, there is an ongoing debate as to whether modern capital punishment can be considered cruel and unusual under the Eighth Amendment.[46]

Fourteenth Amendment: Due Process

When the prison administration changes an inmate's status, such as placing him or her in segregation for disciplinary reasons, should this concern the court? On one hand, the court system is overburdened as it is and has little time to consider cases involving the internal workings of the prison. On the other hand, inmates can be abused by prison officials and need somewhere to turn to have their concerns heard. The Fourteenth Amendment says that the due process granted to citizens by the Constitution is also applicable to the states. Because of the concept of incorporation, states cannot restrict rights granted by the federal government. The courts determined in *Wolff v. McDonnell* (see Case in Point 12.2) that inmates are allowed some level of due process.

12.2   ## CASE IN POINT

WOLFF V. MCDONNELL

THE CASE	THE POINT
Wolff v. McDonnell, 418 U.S. 539, 94 S.Ct. 2963 (1974)	This case defined the processes required for prison disciplinary proceedings.

In Nebraska, prisoners earned good-time credits under a statute that granted mandatory sentence reductions for good behavior, which were revocable only for serious misconduct. In this case, inmates at a state prison challenged their institution's practice of revoking these good-time credits without adequate procedures. In *Wolff*, the Supreme Court set forth minimum requirements of procedural due process for prison inmates:

1. Advance written notice to the inmate of the charges
2. A written statement as to the evidence relied on and the reasons for the disciplinary action taken
3. An impartial hearing
4. An opportunity for the inmate to call witnesses and present documentary evidence in defense, as long as it does not endanger institutional security

However, *Wolff* does not require that the inmate be allowed to confront and cross-examine witnesses or be granted the right to counsel.

Fourteenth Amendment: Equal Protection

The equal protection clause has also been used to help define inmates' rights. Although we might be tempted to think that equal protection means that inmates with similar circumstances are to be treated alike by the courts and the prison, we would be mistaken. Legal officials still have tremendous latitude to use discretion in fashioning punishments and rehabilitation programs to fit the perceived needs of offenders. The Fourteenth Amendment addresses racial and gender-based discrimination in the prison. Individuals cannot be treated differently based on their race or because they are male or female.[47] Discrimination that is prohibited in society is not permitted in the correctional institution. Cases that involve religious freedom are also applicable here in that the prison cannot allow certain religions to be practiced while excluding others.[48] Of course, given the multiplicity of religions, there are some limits as to just how far the prison can go in accommodating inmates' needs. For security, economic, and commonsense reasons, not all inmates can practice all of their desired religious requests. For instance, the prison cannot keep kitchens open 24 hours a day to feed inmates who might have different eating concerns based on religion, nor can prisons cater to the exact requests for the specialty foods of all religions.[49] Nevertheless, prisons are obligated to make reasonable efforts to address the different legitimate religious needs of a substantial number of inmates.

Prisons are a unique environment, and the expectations of privacy granted by the Constitution and its amendments are only partially available to inmates. For instance, the standards of privacy in the home do not extend to the prison cell.[50] Although the inmate lives in the cell, there is no constitutional guarantee that it cannot be searched for contraband. The prison has a security imperative to make the institution safe for other inmates and staff that overrides any demand for privacy. Cells may be searched without warning (prior notice would give the inmate time to dispose of drugs, weapons, or other contraband), as may inmates' personal effects such as books, papers, clothing, and mail.

The inmate's body is also a point of contention, according to the courts. Under what circumstances, and to what degree, can the inmate's body be searched? The inmate's body has only slightly more protection than does the cell and personal effects. The courts have deemed routine strip and body-cavity searches necessary for the institution's safety.[51] However, body-cavity searches that are abusive, nonhygienic, or unreasonably degrading are prohibited. The right to privacy of the body has also been brought up as a concern where there are male guards and female inmates or female guards and male inmates. It sounds reasonable to prohibit cross-sex supervision of inmates, but the courts consider the matter in a more involved way. For instance, although modesty and privacy are important concerns, the cost of same-sex guards for the prison might be prohibitive. Additionally, male inmates might object to a homosexual guard watching them shower, or female inmates might feel uncomfortable having a lesbian guard. The courts have determined that there are simply too many such possibilities for potential embarrassment to get involved.

Courts have an additional reason to be reluctant to intervene in gender issues. To prohibit women from supervising male inmates would violate women's rights under Title VII and the equal protection clause.[52] Women cannot be excluded from large parts of the institution and from core duties of the correctional officer simply because of their sex. Certainly, institutions may establish reasonable efforts to diminish cross-sex supervision, but the legitimate demands of institutional security, efficiency, and worker rights all permit this practice.[53]

The courts have also considered the issues of what mail the inmates may receive and with whom and how they can have outside visitation. Prison officials have wide discretion in limiting the mail and publications that inmates can send and receive.[54] The institution must demonstrate how restrictions are consistent with the needs of security and efficiency of the prison. Likewise, the issue of visits from outsiders is a concern.[55] Mail from those with a personal or professional relationship with the inmate are generally allowed. Links to family, lawyers, clergy, and the like are important contacts that the court allows. However, the type of visitation that is allowed varies considerably by institution. Jails and prisons are constantly threatened by contraband that some visitors try to bring into the prison. Therefore, personal visits may be restricted by separating the visitor and inmate with a glass barrier and having them communicate by telephone. Contact visits, in which inmates and visitors are allowed to touch, have been deemed problematic by the courts and not a constitutional right. There is also no right to conjugal visitation.[56] Such visitation may help maintain the marital bond while the inmate is incarcerated, but it is up to the state to allow this practice, which is usually permitted for only a few inmates.[57] An extreme case of the issues surrounding inmates' bodies concerns medical care and how much effort should be made to save their lives, especially if the inmate is condemned (see Focus on Ethics 12.2).

PRIVATE PRISONS

Interest in privatizing prisons began around the mid-1970s, and the first modern private prisons opened in the early 1980s.[58] A number of factors that had their roots in the social revolutions of the 1960s contributed to this trend. By the mid-1970s, the United States was reeling from the loss of the Vietnam War, economic recession, gas and oil shortages, major paradigm shifts in civil society, and a skyrocketing crime rate. All of the cures for social ills that seemed to have worked before the 1960s had become useless. To Americans, that bewildering entity known as "the government" had become unpopular, and probably not without good reason. It had participated in an unpopular war; President Nixon had left office in disgrace, only to be pardoned by his successor; the cities were crumbling; and the country itself seemed to be at the mercy of such foreign powers as OPEC and Iran's Ayatollah Khomeini.[59] The government, many Americans believed, could no longer do anything right, including run prisons.

As crime rates rise and states grapple with growing inmate populations (see Figure 12-3), the idea has taken hold that private firms can handle inmates more inexpensively and more efficiently. Prison privatization also agrees with a new form of political conservatism that took hold with the election of President Ronald Reagan. One idea was that capitalism could solve a variety of problems because an open market

12.2   FOCUS *on* ETHICS

KEEPING THE CONDEMNED ALIVE

Horacio Alberto Reyes-Camarena needs a kidney. His dialysis treatment reportedly costs $121,000 a year, and his doctor believes he is a good candidate for a transplant. Because the state of Oregon pays for his medical care, he is at the top of the transplant list ahead of those who cannot afford a transplant. Reyes-Camarena is also on death row. He has been there since 1996, when he was convicted of repeatedly stabbing two women, one of whom died from her wounds.

Acute medical care for prisoners is a controversial subject, with many opponents citing cost as a major factor. Oregon has suffered massive budget cuts affecting such essential services as health care for the poor and education. However, even in a difficult economy, states say they are bound to provide the medical care that inmates need, regardless of the cost. A California inmate received a $1 million heart transplant, and another received a $120,000 kidney transplant. A Georgia prisoner received heart bypass surgery that cost $70,000. Because Reyes-Camarena is on death row, his case is even more complicated. Not only is the procedure he is slated for—and the drugs that follow—expensive, but he is also dipping into a highly limited resource: donated organs.

Opponents of such procedures question saving the life of a man who is going to die with an organ that could have saved someone else's life. They also point to poor, law-abiding citizens who do not even qualify for placement on organ transplant lists because they cannot afford the antirejection drugs, as well as a state already ravaged by a desperate economy. Supporters of lifesaving procedures for inmates say states have a responsibility to fund the health care of those it convicts. Also, denying necessary health care to death-row inmates could be construed as violating the cruel and unusual punishment provision of the Eighth Amendment. Doctors, as well, have an ethical responsibility to treat those who are sick, regardless of social status.

As of July 2008, more than 99,000 Americans were waiting for an organ transplant, according to the United Network for Organ Sharing.

What Do You Do?

1. Should death-row inmates receive organ transplants?
2. Should life-sentence inmates receive organ transplants?
3. How far should states go in providing medical care to inmates?

Source: Bryan Robinson, "Death-Row Privilege: Condemned Prisoner May Get Kidney Transplant While Law-Abiding Citizens Wait," ABCNews.com. May 28, 2003, http://abcnews.go.com/sections/us/GoodMorningAmerica/deathrow_transplant030528.html; United Network for Organ Sharing, www.unos.org.

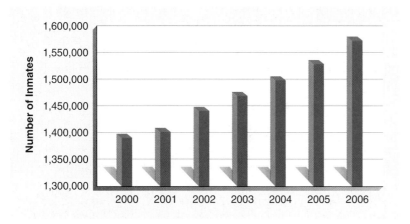

Figure 12-3 **The Increasing Imprisonment Rate: Prisoners under State or Federal Jurisdiction, 2000–2006.**
Source: William J. Sabol, Heather Couture, and Paige M. Harrison, *Prisoners in 2006* (Washington, DC: U.S. Department of Justice, Bureau of Justice Statistics, 2007), 1, www.ojp.usdoj.gov/bjs/pub/pdf/p06.pdf.

forced the providers of any good or service to produce the most "bang for the buck." During the next few decades, three companies—the Corrections Corporation of America, Wackenhut Corrections Corporation, and Correctional Services Corporation—became the major providers of private correctional services in the United States.

- **The Corrections Corporation of America (CCA)**   The Corrections Corporation of America, currently the largest provider of private prison services in the United States, was founded in 1983. Working off the idea that the government "can't do anything very well,"[60] CCA expanded quickly. As of 2003, the company operated 65 U.S. jails and prisons, housing about 78,000 inmates. Its revenues in 2007 were $1.5 billion.[61]

- **Wackenhut Corrections Corporation (WCC)/Geo Group** Wackenhut Corrections Corporation was founded as a division of the large, multinational Wackenhut Corporation in 1984. WCC, which operated facilities in Australia, Canada, New Zealand, South Africa, Scotland, and England, ran 35 facilities in the United States. Wackenhut designed, built, financed, and managed prisons, as well as providing immigration and detention services for the U.S. Department of Homeland Security and U.S. Marshals. By 2008, Wackenhut spun off its private prison business, and the firm became known as the Geo Group. Geo Group reported in 2008 that it was planning five new facilities and expanding four others among its current 62 facilities, bringing in another $140 million in annual revenue.[62] The Geo Group's revenue at the end of 2006 was $860.8 million.[63]

- **Correctional Services Corporation** Started in 1993, Correctional Services Corporation operated 11 adult correctional facilities and 18 juvenile facilities in 14 states.[64] The Geo Group acquired the company in 2005.[65]

Although private correctional facilities have become big business, they have met with mixed success. State and local facilities still take in the bulk of inmates (Figure 12-4). According to Charles Logan, the arguments both for and against private prisons are quite numerous.[66] Following are some arguments Logan listed for private prisons:

- **Money** According to Logan, private contracting makes "true costs highly visible." Private enterprise can run prisons more cheaply than the government can because government agencies have an incentive to grow in order to inflate their budgets. Corporations can operate a large number of prisons across several jurisdictions, which local and state agencies cannot do, allowing for economy of scale. The profit motive of private prisons demands less waste and more suppliers, which allows facilities to spend money wisely and avoid shortages.

- **Better employee control** Workers for private enterprises are more easily hired and fired than government workers, so private prisons can adjust staff sizes more quickly when needed. Staff members are less likely to strike because they are more likely to be fired. Administration and staff have more incentive to do a good job and treat inmates fairly because their jobs are more directly at stake. Also, contracting, according to Logan, may "reduce overly generous public employee pensions and benefits," as well as promote more effective personnel management and lower absenteeism and employee turnover.

- **Flexibility and accountability** Stockholders and corporate boards add another layer of review to decision making, while being immune to some of the political

Figure 12-4 **At the end of 2006, 2.26 million inmates were held in state and federal prisons and local jails. This was an incarceration rate of 751 inmates per 100,000 U.S. residents.**
Source: William J. Sabol, Heather Couture, and Paige M. Harrison, *Prisoners in 2006* (Washington, DC: U.S. Department of Justice, Bureau of Justice Statistics, 2007), 4, www.ojp.usdoj.gov/bjs/pub/pdf/p06.pdf.

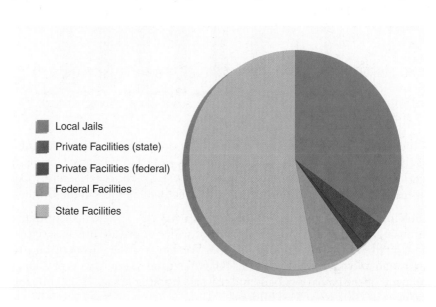

- Local Jails
- Private Facilities (state)
- Private Facilities (federal)
- Federal Facilities
- State Facilities

pressures inherent in governments. Prisons can be built more quickly and cheaply and designed for more efficient operation. Competition with other private prison firms encourages higher quality and lower costs. By transferring inmates across jurisdictions, optimum residence levels can be maintained at all facilities.

Logan gave the following arguments against private prisons:

- **Money**   The first duty of a for-profit operation is to make a profit. Therefore, a private prison must necessarily put profit ahead of inmate welfare. Private prisons would "cut corners" to save money without concern for inmates' rights or welfare. Also, if the prison company goes bankrupt or is not meeting its profit needs in a given market, it could pull up stakes, leaving a jurisdiction without facilities. In the end, private prisons are more expensive because their profit margins are added to other costs.

- **Labor**   Private prisons threaten the jobs, benefits, professionalism, and tenure of public employees. Staff members have less incentive to do a good job because they are less secure and paid less. This increases the risk of strikes and high employee turnover.

- **Control**   Private enterprise morally should not have the degree of control over human beings that incarceration requires. Private prisons might make government prisons more difficult to manage by housing only the best-behaved offenders and refusing the difficult ones. Prison corporations might lobby to build more prisons, thus increasing society's dependence on imprisonment and weakening the use of alternatives such as parole. A poorly staffed or understaffed facility jeopardizes public safety. Private prison corporations are less accountable to the public than those governed by legislatures comprising elected officials. Lastly, another layer of managerial involvement introduces new opportunities for corruption.

The final judgment on private prisons remains to be seen. The news is rife with their failures: escapes, employee and inmate maltreatment, closings, and falling stock prices. Some evidence even suggests that they cost only marginally less than government-run prisons.[67] Additionally, there is little evidence that private prisons do a better job of reducing recidivism. According to Andrew Spivak and Susan Sharp, private prison inmates in Oklahoma had a greater chance of returning to prison than those held in state prisons.[68] Another factor that might limit the growth of private prisons is the new emphasis on faith-based initiatives that seek to fund religious-oriented prison programs. The federal government has developed a policy that provides public money for these types of programs in public institutions, and, as the overall prison population levels off, there is less demand for private prisons.[69]

SUMMARY

1. The prison is a fundamental feature of the U.S. criminal justice system. The prison is a closed institution where everything is tightly controlled and structured, and one that dominates almost every aspect of inmates' lives. These controls help maintain efficiency and order and deprive the inmate of discretion.

2. According to Sykes, historically, inmates have compensated for the pains of imprisonment by adopting argot roles. Many of these argot roles have been overtaken by prison gangs that many inmates join for security and to acquire goods and services.

3. Two of the most infamous prison riots were the Attica riot of 1971 and the New Mexico riot of 1980.

4. One recent solution to increased violence and gang problems has been to totally segregate the worst-behaved inmates in supermax prisons.

5. The specialization of correctional officers has increased, but their basic function has remained the same: to control and supervise prison inmates.

6. Inmates are protected to some extent by the Constitution. The rights lost by inmates should be consistent with their confinement and institutional safety.

7. Before the 1960s, the courts cultivated a hands-off doctrine toward inmate rights, considering incarceration primarily a prison administrative matter. After the 1960s, inmates and those concerned with their welfare petitioned the courts to address several issues, specifically referring to the Eighth and Fourteenth Amendments. Other points of contention include inmate privacy regarding the prison cell and physical body, the people with whom inmates may have contact, and issues concerning the genders of correctional officers.

8. In the early 1980s, the first modern private prisons were created. During this period, many believed that private enterprise could manage prisons more effectively and cheaply than the government. Despite criticism, more than a hundred private prisons are currently operating in the United States.

KEY TERMS

argot roles 396
hands-off doctrine 414

pains of imprisonment 395
supermax prison 402

total institution 394

REVIEW QUESTIONS

1. List the five pains of imprisonment.

2. Name three general types of inmate argot roles.

3. What difficulties do prison staff and officials face in dealing with prison gangs?

4. Along what lines do prison gangs tend to be divided?

5. How are supermax prisons successful? In what areas do they fall short?

6. What are some of the causes of prison riots?

7. What are the seven variations of correctional officer job functions, according to Lombardo?

8. What were the reasons for the courts' hands-off doctrine?

9. To what constitutional amendments did inmates turn to draw the courts' attention?

10. What led to the development of private prisons?

11. Give arguments for and against private prisons.

SUGGESTED FURTHER READING

Austin, James, and John Irwin. *It's about Time: America's Imprisonment Binge*. 3rd ed. Belmont, CA: Wadsworth, 2001.

Durham, Alexis M. III. *Crisis and Reform: Current Issues in American Punishment*. Boston: Little, Brown, 1994.

Goffman, Erving. *Asylums: Essays on the Social Situation of Mental Patients and Other Inmates*. Garden City, NY: Anchor Books, 1961.

Parenti, Christian. *Lockdown America: Police and Prisons in the Age of Crisis*. New York: Verso, 2000.

Silberman, Matthew. *A World of Violence: Corrections in America*. Belmont, CA: Wadsworth, 1995.

Useem, Bert, and Peter Kimball. *States of Siege: U.S. Prison Riots 1971–1986*. New York: Oxford University Press, 1991.

ENDNOTES

1. The numbers of facilities were counted by the author at each state's department of corrections site.

2. Erving Goffman, *Asylums: Essays on the Social Situation of Mental Patients and Other Inmates* (Garden City, NY: Anchor Books, 1961).

3. Tonisha R. Jones and Travis C. Pratt, "The Prevalence of Sexual Violence in Prison: The State of the Knowledge Base and Implications for Evidence-Based Correctional Policy Making," *International Journal of*

Offender Therapy and Comparative Criminology 52 (June 2008): 280–295.

4. Victor H. Brombert, *The Romantic Prison: The French Traditions* (Princeton, NJ: Princeton University Press, 1978).

5. Gresham M. Sykes, *The Society of Captives: A Study of a Maximum Security Prison* (Princeton, NJ: Princeton University Press, 1974), 64.

6. Ibid., p. 65.

7. Kris Axtman, "The Newest Prison Contraband: Cell-phones," *Christian Science Monitor* 96 (June 11, 2004): 1.

8. Sykes, *Society of Captives*, 72.

9. Cindy Struckman-Johnson and David Struckman-Johnson, "A Comparison of Sexual Coercion Experiences Reported by Men and Women in Prison," *Journal of Interpersonal Violence* 21 (December 2006): 1591–1615.

10. Sykes, *Society of Captives*. Sykes devoted his entire Chapter 4 to the pains of imprisonment.

11. Michael Windzio, "Is There a Deterrent Effect of Pains of Imprisonment?" *Punishment and Society* 8 (July 2006): 341–364.

12. Sykes, *Society of Captives*. Chapter 5 is devoted to a full explication of these argot roles. A different set of roles appear in women's prisons. See Rose Giallombardo, *Society of Women: A Study of Women's Prison* (New York: Wiley, 1966).

13. John Irwin and Donald Cressey, "Thieves, Convicts and the Inmate Culture," *Social Problems* (Fall 1962): 142–155.

14. James B. Jacobs, *Stateville: The Penitentiary in Mass Society* (Chicago: University of Chicago Press, 1977).

15. Christian Parenti, *Lockdown America: Police and Prisons in the Age of Crisis* (New York: Verso, 2000). See especially Chapter 10, "Balkan in a Box: Rape, Race War, and Other Forms of Management," pp. 182–210.

16. Tori Richards, "Murder Trial Yields Sharply Conflicting Portrayals of White Prison Gang," *New York Times*, July 14, 2006, 16.

17. Marie Griffin, "Prison Gang Policy and Recidivism: Short-Term Management Benefits, Long-Term Consequences," *Criminology and Public Policy* 6 (May 2007): 223–230.

18. Parenti, *Lockdown America: Police and Prisons in the Age of Crisis*, 172.

19. Jeffrey Ian Ross, "Supermax Prisons," *Society* 44 (March 2007): 60–64.

20. Sam Torres, review of *Supermax Prisons: Their Rise, Current Practices, and Effects on Inmates*, by Jesenia Pizarro and M. K. Vanja Stenius, *Federal Probation* 84 (June 2003): 248–264, www.uscourts.gov/fedprob/December_2004/reviews.html.

21. Craig Haney, "Infamous Punishment: The Psychological Consequences of Isolation," in *Correctional Contexts: Contemporary and Classical Readings*, 2nd ed., eds. Edward J. Latessa et al. (Los Angeles: Roxbury, 2001), 172.

22. Pelican Bay State Prison, www.cdcr.ca.gov/Visitors/Facilities/PBSP.html.

23. James Austin and John Irwin, *It's about Time: America's Imprisonment Binge*, 3rd ed. (Belmont, CA: Wadsworth, 2001). See especially Chapter 6, "Super Max," pp. 117–137.

24. Craig Haney, "The Psychological Impact of Incarceration: Implications for Post-Prison Adjustment," paper presented at the national policy conference of the U.S. Department of Health and Human Services: The Urban Institute, January 2002, http://aspe.hhs.gov/hsp/prison2home02/Haney.htm.

25. Ibid.

26. Ralph S. Turner and Lewis M. Killian, *Collective Behavior*, 3rd ed. (Englewood Cliffs, NJ: Prentice Hall, 1987).

27. Gustave Le Bon, *The Crowd* (New York: Viking Press, 1960). First published in 1895; see also Ladd Wheeler, "Toward a Theory of Behavioral Contagion," *Psychological Review* 73 (March 1966): 179–192.

28. Vernon B. Fox, *Violence behind Bars: An Explosive Report on Prison Riots in the United States* (New York: Vantage Press, 1956).

29. Randy Martin and Sherwood Zimmerman, "A Typology of the Causes of Prison Riots and an Analytical Extension to the 1986 West Virginia Riot," *Justice Quarterly* 7 (1990): 711–737; See also John Pallas and Robert Barber, "From Riots to Revolution," in *The Politics of Punishment*, ed. Erik Olin Wright (New York: Harper & Row, 1973), 237–261.

30. New York State Special Commission on Attica, *Attica: The Official Report of the New York State Special Commission on Attica* (New York: Bantam Books, 1972). This was commonly referred to as the McKay Report after its chairman, Robert B. McKay.

31. Russell Oswald, *Attica: My Story* (New York: Doubleday, 1972); Richard X. Clark, *The Brothers of Attica* (New York: Links, 1973); Tom Wicker, *A Time to Die* (New York: New York Times Books, 1975); Herman Badillo, *A Bill of No Rights: Attica and the American Prison System* (New York: Outerbridge & Lazard, 1972).

32. John Irwin, *Prisons in Turmoil* (Boston: Little, Brown, 1980).

33. Bert Useem and Peter Kimball, *States of Siege: U.S. Prison Riots 1971–1986* (New York: Oxford University Press, 1991).

34. Wicker, *A Time to Die*.

35. "The Attica Case, Revisited: Lawyers Speak Out," *New York Times*, September 24, 2006, 11.

36. Bert Useem, "Disorganization and the New Mexico Prison Riot of 1980," *American Sociological Review* 50 (October 1985): 680.

37. Ibid., 677–688.

38. Eliot S. Hartstone et al., "Identifying and Treating the Mentally Disordered Prison Inmate," in *Correctional Contexts: Contemporary and Classical Readings*, 2nd ed., eds. Edward J. Latessa et al. (Los Angeles: Roxbury, 2001), 380–393.

39. Matthew Silberman, *A World of Violence: Corrections in America* (Belmont, CA: Wadsworth, 1995), 122–124.

40. Lucien X. Lombardo, "Guards Imprisoned: Correctional Officers at Work" in *Correctional Contexts: Contemporary and Classical Readings*, eds. Edward J. Latessa et al. (Los Angeles: Roxbury, 2001), 153–167.

41. Jacobs, *Stateville*, 105.

42. These reasons are best articulated by Philip L. Reichel, *Corrections: Philosophies, Practices, and Procedures*, 2nd ed. (Boston: Allyn & Bacon, 2001), 517.

43. Jacobs, *Stateville*, 107.

44. James Bennett, "Who Wants to Be a Warden?" *New England Journal of Prison Law* 1 (1974): 69–79.

45. Reichel, *Corrections*, 522.

46. "Is Death Penalty Cruel? " *New York Times*, April 30, 2006, 13.

47. *Lee v. Washington*, 390 U.S. 333, 88 S.Ct. 994 (1968); *Holt v. Sarver*, 309 F. Supp. 362 (ED Ark. 1970).

48. *Cruz v. Beto*, 405 U.S. 319, 92 S.Ct. 1079 (1972).

49. *Cooper v. Pate*, 378 U.S. 546, 84 S.Ct. 1733 (1964).

50. *Hudson v. Palmer*, 468 U.S. 517, 104 S.Ct. 3194 (1984).

51. *Bell v. Wolfish*, 441 U.S. 520, 99 S.Ct. 1861 (1979).

52. *Grummett v. Rushen*, 587 F.Supp. 913 (1984).

53. *Johnson v. Phelan*, 69 F.3d 144 (1995).

54. *Thornburgh v. Abbot*, 490 U.S. 401, 109 S.Ct. 1874 (1989).

55. *Kentucky Department of Corrections v. Thompson*, 490 U.S. 454, 109 S.Ct. 1904 (1989).

56. *Tarlton v. Clark*, 441 F.2d 384 (1971).

57. Rachel Wyatt, "Male Rape in U.S. Prisons: Are Conjugal Visits the Answer?" *Case Western Reserve Journal of International Law* 37 (March 2006): 579–614.

58. David Shichor, *Punishment for Profit: Private Prisons/Public Concerns* (Thousand Oaks, CA: Sage, 1995), 13–14.

59. OPEC is the Organization of the Petroleum Exporting Countries. Its current members are Algeria, Indonesia, Iran, Iraq, Kuwait, Libya, Nigeria, Qatar, Saudi Arabia, the United Arab Emirates, and Venezuela. As for the Ayatollah Khomeini, in November 1979, Iranian militants supporting Khomeini took 70 Americans captive at the U.S. embassy in Tehran. The ordeal lasted 444 days.

60. David Shichor and Michael J. Gilbert, *Privatization in Criminal Justice: Past, Present, and Future* (Cincinnati, OH: Anderson, 2001), 209, as quoted in E. Bates, "Prisons for Profit," in *The Dilemmas of Corrections: Contemporary Readings*, 4th ed., eds. Kenneth C. Haas and Geoffrey P. Alpert (Prospect Heights, IL: Waveland Press, 1998).

61. Corrections Corporation of America 2002 Annual Report, 4, www.shareholder.com/cxw/downloads/2002ar.pdf.

62. Randy Diamond, "Boca Raton, Fla.–Based Geo Group's Profit up 10 Percent in 4th Quarter," *McClatchy-Tribune Business News*, February 14, 2008.

63. Geo Group, www.thegeogroupinc.com/corporate.asp.

64. Business Wire/Yahoo, "Correctional Services Corporation Announces Financial Results for First Quarter 2003," May 14, 2003, http://biz.yahoo.com/bw/030514/145413_1.html.

65. "The GEO Group, Inc. Announces Closing of Acquisition of Correctional Services Corporation," www.prnewswire.com/cgi-bin/stories.pl?ACCT=104&STORY=/www/story/11–07–2005/0004209738.

66. Charles H. Logan, *Private Prisons: Cons and Pros* (New York: Oxford University Press, 1990), 41–48; www.ucc.uconn.edu/~wwwsoci/proscons.html.

67. U.S. General Accounting Office, "Private and Public Prisons: Studies Comparing Operational Costs and/or Quality of Service," www.gao.gov/archive/1996/gg96158.pdf.

68. Andrew L. Spivak and Susan F. Sharp, "Inmate Recidivism as a Measure of Private Prison Performance," *Crime and Delinquency* 54 (July 2008): 482–508.

69. Richard F. Culp, "The Rise and Stall of Prison Privatization: An Integration of Policy Analysis Perspectives," *Criminal Justice Policy Review* 16 (December 2005): 412–442.

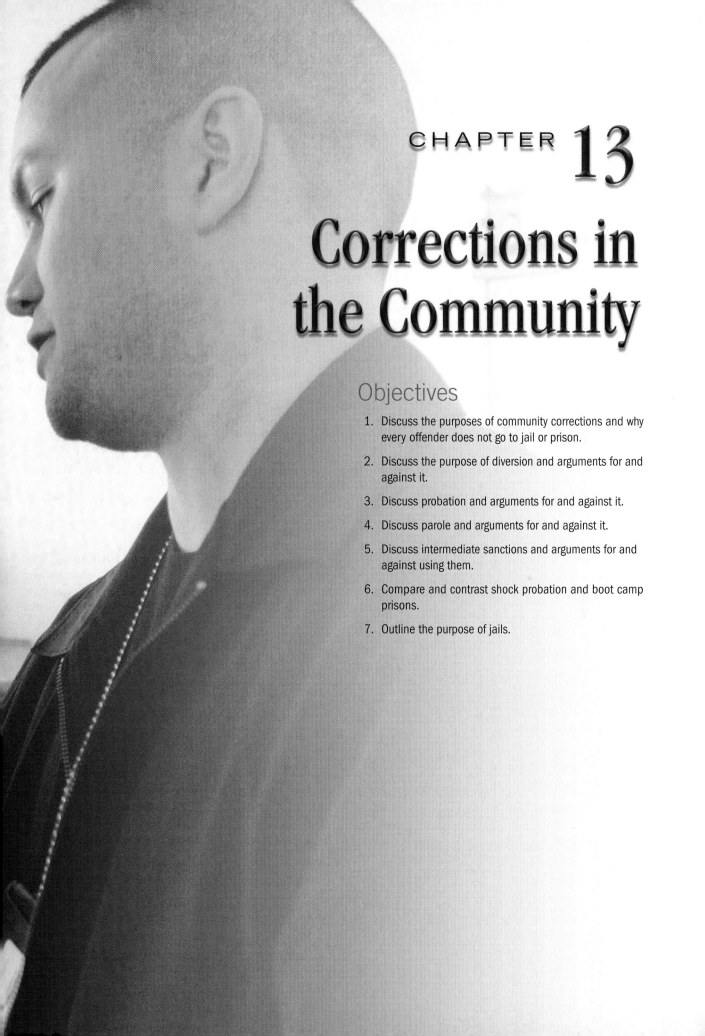

CHAPTER 13

Corrections in the Community

Objectives

1. Discuss the purposes of community corrections and why every offender does not go to jail or prison.

2. Discuss the purpose of diversion and arguments for and against it.

3. Discuss probation and arguments for and against it.

4. Discuss parole and arguments for and against it.

5. Discuss intermediate sanctions and arguments for and against using them.

6. Compare and contrast shock probation and boot camp prisons.

7. Outline the purpose of jails.

Sentencing offenders to long prison terms, although politically feasible and desirable in terms of protecting the community, is expensive. The cost of incarcerating large numbers of offenders has overwhelmed the ability for federal, state, and local governments to pay for it.

Caught between the conflicting demands of protecting the community and keeping taxes low, government agencies are attempting to find new community corrections programs. How does society send a message to criminal offenders that they will be dealt with seriously and at the same time make the criminal justice response cost-effective? The answer that many jurisdictions have come up with is community corrections. By partially restricting freedoms, requiring participation in treatment programs, and imposing fines, community corrections attempts to provide not only a deterrent effect but also a rehabilitative one.

There are many alternatives to prison for dealing with criminal offenders. Some of these alternatives, such as corporal or capital punishment, are no longer used to the degree they were in the past and, in many circumstances, have been abandoned altogether. Attacking the offender's body is not generally accepted as progressive or effective crime control policy. (Although some advocate a return to corporal punishment, they are not finding an audience in the general public or legislators.)[1] Therefore, society seeks other policies and programs that provide meaningful ways to deal with offenders.

Although not as highly visible as prisons, community corrections account for a major portion of the correctional efforts of the contemporary criminal justice system.[2] This chapter will briefly review four related community corrections strategies: diversion programs, probation, parole, and intermediate sanctions. The historical and philosophical underpinnings of attempts to reform and/or incapacitate offenders outside the prison will also be discussed.

COMMUNITY CORRECTIONS IN CONTEXT

Why do we treat and punish offenders within the community? Why not just send them all to prison so we will not have to worry about them? The answers to these questions are both simple and complex. Simply put, we cannot afford to incarcerate everyone who violates the law.[3] It is not possible to build enough prisons to house all the offenders, and, if the truth be known, there would be precious few of us not in prison who would be available to work and pay the taxes to incarcerate the majority.[4] One of the functions of the criminal justice system is to remove offenders who pose a continued threat and place them in the relatively few prison cells. (See Crosscurrents 13.1 for why this is a more troubling issue than it sounds.)

A more complex answer to the question of why every offender is not locked up is that, for the most part, prisons work only in a limited and partial manner. As we have discussed before, the criminal justice system has multiple goals: incapacitation, retribution, and to a lesser extent, rehabilitation.

- **Incapacitation** Prisons are good at achieving the goal of incapacitation. That is, for the limited time offenders are behind bars, they are not free to break any more laws outside the prison. Of course, offenders might break the law within prison by victimizing other inmates or correctional workers, but this depends on how effective the prison is in keeping internal order. Also, as we learned in the last chapter, prison gang members may order fellow gang members to commit offenses on the outside, but the chance of this occurring might be less than if the offender were free.

- **Retribution** The goal of retribution is to punish the offender for transgressions of the criminal law. Prisons are somewhat successful in accomplishing this goal, but for financial reasons related to prison overcrowding, the public is generally unsatisfied with the amount of punishment they believe the offender is getting when they hear stories about "country club prisons" and early parole.[5]

13.1   *CrossCurrents*

Probation and Parole: Controversial Issues Left, Right, and Center

- On a Monday morning in July 2007, Jennifer Hawke-Petit walked into a bank where she had a joint account with her husband, Dr. William A. Petit Jr., and withdrew $15,000. Waiting for her in a nearby parking lot was Stephen Hayes, 44, a career burglar on parole who had regularly been in and out of prison since 1980. At the Petits' home a few miles away, Joshua Komisarjevsky, 26, another paroled burglar whom Hayes had met in a halfway house, waited with Dr. Petit, and the couple's two daughters, Hayley, 17, and Michaela, 11. During the bank transaction, Mrs. Hawke-Petit told the teller that her family was being held hostage and would be killed if anyone called the police. After Mrs. Hawke-Petit left, a bank employee called 911. Shortly thereafter, at about 9:45 A.M., several police and SWAT team officers began circling the Petits' home. Meanwhile, Dr. Petit, his hands still bound, escaped through a rear basement door to a neighbor's house. Minutes later, Hayes and Komisarjevsky dumped gasoline on Ms. Hawke-Petit, who had been strangled to death, and the Petits' two daughters, who were tied to their beds, alive, and set the house on fire. Shortly before 10 A.M., Hayes and Komisarjevsky stole the family's SUV, crashed into several nearby police cruisers set up as roadblocks, and were captured. They had started the fire to try to eliminate DNA evidence of the rape of Ms. Hawke-Petit and the sexual assault of Michaela. By the time firefighters entered the house, both Hayley and Michaela Petit had died of smoke inhalation. Dr. Petit was the only survivor.[1]

- Carla, an impoverished single mother in Americus, Georgia, received a traffic citation for failing to completely stop at two stop signs. In Americus, where probation is handled through a private company, those who cannot pay their fines immediately are placed on probation with a private company that supervises misdemeanor and traffic offenders. Carla, who held only a minimum-wage job in a south Georgia community where high-paying jobs are not plentiful, was ordered to pay a $200 traffic fine plus the private probation office's supervision fees. In the ensuing weeks, still struggling to pay the fines, Carla gave birth to her second child prematurely via cesarean. She had trouble with the wound from the operation and was told to stay in bed while it healed. Carla says she repeatedly called her probation officer trying to give her weekly reports, but the officer issued a warrant anyway. Later, Carla received a letter from the probation office stating that she was $245 behind. Two months later, the amount due went up to $690, more than three times her original fine.[2]

These are two controversial cases of what critics would point out as the failure of the nation's parole and probation system. Those who say the system is too lenient point to the Petit case as a tragic example of how too many dangerous offenders are paroled. Those who believe that the system is unduly harsh cite stories like Carla's. Although each of these criticisms has some truth, both are partially the result of two problems that are not going to go away: limited budgets and limited prison space. So many people are processed through the criminal justice system that states are hard-pressed to afford either the costs of incarcerating offenders or supervising them on probation or parole.

Since the Petit murders, Connecticut legislators have been pressured to crack down on parole programs. An online petition advocating passage of a state "three-strikes" law similar to California's, which requires mandatory long sentences for offenders convicted of three felonies, collected more than 40,000 signatures. Such a law, many say, would have ensured that Komisarjevsky, with 21 felony convictions and Hayes, with 17, would never have been paroled. Although neither man had convictions involving violence, one judge had described Komisarjevsky as "predatory."[3] In October 2007, Governor M. Jodi Rell suspended parole temporarily for violent inmates until new parole laws could be constructed. With Connecticut's prison population swelling, some state legislators worried that the system would crack under the strain of a measure that still would not have affected Komisarjevsky and Hayes, who had been classified as nonviolent offenders. To cover that issue, Connecticut reclassified burglary of an occupied home as a violent offense.[4]

In January 2008, with parole still suspended, Connecticut legislators made home invasion punishable by 10 to 25 years in prison, with a minimum five-year sentence for burglaries at night.[5] As of mid-2008, Connecticut resisted passing a three-strikes law, although the legislature was still debating it.

Although Connecticut's stiffer penalties may keep more offenders like Komisarjevsky and Hayes in prison, the problem remains of where to put them. One way of keeping cells available for serious and violent offenders is probation: as you will recall from the chapter, "parole after, probation instead." However, many states' probation and parole agencies are as overburdened as the prisons and jails. Therefore, some states have contracted private probation agencies for certain types of offenders. The system is designed to pay many of its own costs by charging probationers for their supervision. This collections system has been deemed to work so well that many state agencies are now using it. In 2005, Washington state collected about $25 million in offender fees. One Georgia judge has said that such fees are a roundabout way to make impoverished people pay for the costs of their appointed legal representation.[6]

Besides the $30–$40 that private probation companies charge for supervision, other charges include application fees for public defenders, drug-test fees, therapy fees, court costs, restitution, laboratory fees, halfway-house fees, and fees for surveillance devices such as ankle bracelets. According to the American Bar Association, several states charge indigent defendants to apply for a public defender.[7] As with a credit card bill, interest and other charges are assessed on unpaid fees.[8] That is how Carla in Americus, Georgia, ended up owing three times her original fine. Although the system keeps minor offenders from doing time and recoups some of the costs of supervision, it also digs a hole for impoverished offenders that many say they will never get out of.

Think About It

1. The release of nonviolent offenders, charging probationers the costs of their supervision, and assessing fees for criminal justice services are efforts to reduce prison crowding as well as criminal justice costs. Are these solutions working?

2. Many nonviolent offenders who broke laws concerning illegal drugs are serving multidecade sentences with no chance of parole. Should the law be changed to allow some of these offenders out of prison to make space for offenders like Joshua Komisarjevsky and Stephen Hayes?

3. What problems could arise from allowing private companies to profit from supervising probationers?

[1]Manny Fernandez and Alison Leigh Cowan, "When Horror Came to a Connecticut Family," *New York Times*, late edition, August 7, 2007, A1.

[2]Celia Perry, Justine Sharrock, and Michael Mechanic, "Probation for Profit," *Mother Jones*, July 1, 2008, 57–58.

[3]"The Wrong Answer in Connecticut," *New York Times*, editorial, late edition, September 2, 2007, A18.

[4]Ihsan Taylor, "Halting Parole Spurs Concerns of Fallout," *New York Times*, late edition, October 7, 2007, CT6.

[5]Joe Wojtas, "Cracking Down on Home Invasion," *New York Times*, March 30, 2008, LI3.

[6]Adam Liptak, "Debt to Society Is Least of Costs for Ex-Convicts," *New York Times*, February 23, 2006, www.nytimes.com/2006/02/23/national/23fees.html.

[7]James Downing and the Spangenberg Group, *Public Defender Application Fees: 2001 Update* (West Newton, MA: American Bar Association, 2002), www.abanet.org/legalservices/downloads/sclaid/indigentdefense/pdapplicationfees2001-narrative.pdf.

[8]Liptak, "Debt to Society."

- **Rehabilitation** Finally, the goal of rehabilitation might not be met because of the spartan conditions of confinement within most institutions, which seem to release inmates who are more antisocial than when they first went to prison.[6] In a sense, then, prisons might not enhance public safety because they tend to embitter, harden, and alienate inmates.[7] Consequently, efforts are made to limit the deleterious effect of prisons by finding alternatives to incarceration for all but the most dangerous offenders.

At the heart of the community corrections movement are some assumptions about the nature of crime and the benefits of using community resources to address the problems of crime. These assumptions include the following:

- Prison is a highly artificial society. Conformity in prison is not always a good indicator of the inmate's ability to adjust to the free world.

- The total control of the prison does little to prepare inmates to take responsibility for their actions.

- Because the community has resources that are unavailable in the prison, the likelihood of rehabilitation is enhanced.

- The community can provide support networks to the offender that do not exist in prison. With the help of spouses, parents, children, and clergy who have already established bonds with the offender, the offender has a greater chance of leading a law-abiding life.

- The offender can contribute to the financial upkeep of his or her family and, if gainfully employed, pay taxes. Additionally, some community corrections programs require offenders to pay for the cost of their supervision.

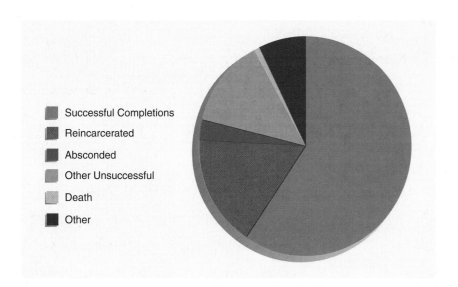

Figure 13-1   **Adults Leaving Probation, 2005**
Source: Lauren E. Glaze and Thomas P. Bonczar, *Probation and Parole in the United States, 2005* (Washington, DC: U.S. Department of Justice, Bureau of Justice Statistics, 2004), 6, www.ojp.usdoj. gov/bjs/pub/pdf/ppus05.pdf.

- Successful Completions
- Reincarcerated
- Absconded
- Other Unsuccessful
- Death
- Other

- The state spends less money on offenders in community corrections programs than it does incarcerating them. The cost of providing prison cells is extremely high, and the state can address many more offenders by handling them outside the prison setting.

- The state can accurately identify which offenders are dangerous and need secure incarceration and which ones are safe to release into the community with supervision.

- The number of trained probation and parole officers is sufficient to adequately supervise the offenders who are selected for community corrections programs.

Is it safe to make these assumptions about the efficacy of community corrections? For the most part, the answer is yes. Millions of offenders have successfully served sentences in community corrections programs during which, in addition to not breaking any more laws, they have completed treatment programs, supported their families, paid their taxes, reentered societal life, and made contributions to the community (see Figure 13-1 for the number of adults who have successfully completed probation).[8] Many notable failures have occurred, however, in which offenders in the community have killed, raped, or robbed and caused criminal justice officials to look incompetent and careless with whom they allowed to go free.[9] Therefore, tension always exists about the wisdom of using community corrections. Despite this, community corrections will always be with us. Only the degree to which they are used is controversial. Which and how many inmates or offenders should be released into the community, and what level of supervision they are going to be subjected to, are the only real remaining questions. Despite calls for such radical initiatives as abolishing parole, those who understand the corrections situation in the United States appreciate that some other early-release mechanism is necessary.[10]

DIVERSION

Offenders can be diverted to alternative programs at a number of points in the criminal justice system. These programs are based on *labeling theory*, which suggests that the more limited the offender's penetration into the criminal justice system is, the less likely the offender will be to adopt a criminal self-concept and continue to commit offenses. Diversion programs are especially popular when dealing with the first-time offender who has committed a relatively minor offense.[11] Typically, the offender's charges are held in abeyance while he or she completes some type of treatment program or community service, or simply continues to stay out of trouble for a specified

Group counseling sessions can be productive for many inmates. It is difficult to fool others who have similar experiences. These inmates are participating in a substance abuse meeting at the Julia Tutwiler Prison in Alabama.

Source: A. Ramey/PhotoEdit Inc.

One feature of many diversion programs is community service. Here, offenders paint fences.

Source: Janine Wiedel Photolibrary.

period of time.[12] Once the conditions of the diversion program are completed, the offender is released from supervision without a conviction on his or her record.

Sometimes this brief encounter with the criminal justice system is enough to get the attention of young offenders who are then successful in avoiding further contact with the law. For many young people who have college aspirations or hope for a career in law, medicine, or teaching, a clean record is crucial (see Focus on Ethics 13.1). Many prosecutors and judges also do not want to soil the record of young people who commit minor offenses. They see diversion programs as a method for sorting out the ones who respond immediately and those who will continue to be problems for the criminal justice system.[13]

Although diversion programs limit the number of people who enter the criminal justice system, they are not without critics. Given the present state of prison overcrowding and the heavy caseloads that probation officers carry, were it not for diversion programs, the state would dismiss the cases of many first-time offenders who commit minor

13.1 FOCUS *on* ETHICS

STUDYING FOR YOUR DRUG TEST

You are graduating from college next semester, and you are just starting your job search. You have an excellent résumé that includes a 3.5 grade-point average, leadership in several important campus organizations, and an honorable mention as an all-American in your favorite sport. Additionally, you have a clean criminal record and have done an internship at the local police department, where your supervisor has said she would be happy to write a glowing letter of recommendation for you. In short, you are on the fast track for a good job in the criminal justice system, and you have set your sights on a federal agency such as the FBI, the DEA, or one of the agencies connected with Homeland Security.

Here is the problem: Up until last year you had wanted to go to law school, so you were never worried about a history of drug use. Although you were never involved with any seriously harmful drugs such as heroin or methamphetamine, you did smoke your share of marijuana. You justified your drug use by saying that your grades actually improved when you smoked, so there must not be that much harm in it. Now your friends and professors are telling you that to get a sensitive job in the federal government you will have to reveal your drug history on a written form, pass a polygraph test in which they will ask about drugs, and take random drug tests.

What Do You Do?

1. Lie on the form and say that your marijuana use happened more than five years ago, before you came to college.
2. Try to discover ways to successfully lie on the polygraph test.
3. Tell the truth and hope they believe that you have turned over a new leaf and will no longer be involved in drug use.
4. Stop using drugs, go to law school, and try to get the federal job after being drug-free for a few years when you have your law degree.

offenses.[14] At a time when prosecutors must develop priorities as to what cases to pursue, diversion programs provide an attractive alternative to doing nothing. However, the overall effect of these diversion programs is to widen the net of social control. By that, we mean that the state controls more and more people who, with one more minor slipup, could find themselves entangled deeply within the criminal justice system. It is one thing to be caught with a misdemeanor quantity of marijuana, but when the offender fails to attend a drug-counseling program and return the diversion officer's phone calls, the resulting revocation of diversion can mean incarceration.[15] Some programs have so many restrictions that clients are almost sure to violate at least some of them. Thomas Blomberg and Karol Lucken called this "stacking the deck." Instead of diverting offenders from the system, some programs, with their multitude of conditions and requirements, actually suck the offender into a deeper quagmire of legal problems.[16]

PROBATION

Probation is a chance for offenders to stay out of prison or jail if they promise to be good. At any given time, there are more probationers than inmates or parolees (see Figure 13-2), with state probationers far outnumbering federal probationers (see Figure 13-3). Probationers are not completely free, however. They must agree to certain terms set by the judge, such as performing public-service work, abstaining from alcohol, getting therapy, and reporting regularly to a probation officer.[17] Those who violate these agreements are usually incarcerated for the term for which they were initially eligible. Probation is a widely used sentencing alternative because it accomplishes several positive outcomes. Depending on how one views the criminal justice system, one or more of these outcomes might be more attractive than others. Here, we will consider the practice of probation from the relative viewpoints of the key actors in the criminal justice system.

- **How the offender views probation**   Probation can seem like a good deal for the offender. When faced with the prospect of going to prison, many offenders embrace the prospect of probation like a lifeline. Probation allows the offender

Figure 13-2   **Persons under Correctional Supervision, selected years, 1998–2006**

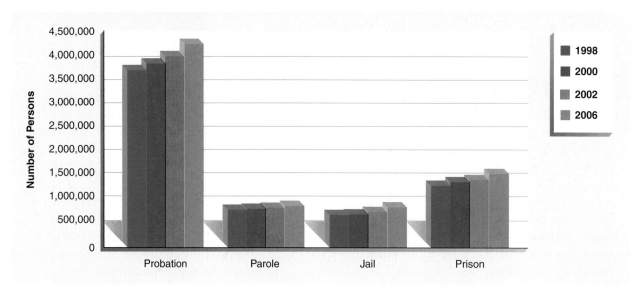

Source: Lauren E. Glaze and Thomas P. Bonczar, *Probation and Parole in the United States, 2006* (Washington, DC: U.S. Department of Justice, Bureau of Justice Statistics, 2007), 2, www.ojp.usdoj.gov/bjs/pub/pdf/ppus05.pdf.

Figure 13-3   **Number of Adults on State and Federal Probation, 2006**
Source: Lauren E. Glaze and Thomas P. Bonczar, *Probation and Parole in the United States, 2006* (Washington, DC: U.S. Department of Justice, Bureau of Justice Statistics, 2007), 3. www.ojp.usdoj.gov/bjs/pub/pdf/ppus05.pdf.

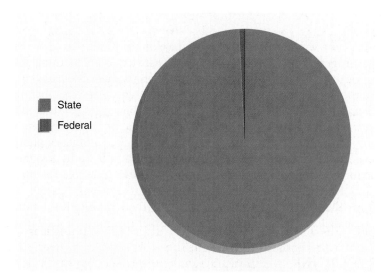

to remain at home, at work, and safe from the pains of imprisonment. Compared to life in prison, the restrictions of probation seem like a minor irritant. However, the conditions of probation do affect the offender's freedom and, after a while, can seem frivolous and nitpicky. Reporting to the probation officer on a weekly or monthly basis; abstaining from alcohol; and seeking permission to move to a different residence, change jobs, or travel outside the county can cause resentment and alienation.[18] These conditions must be taken seriously because their violation can bring swift and certain punishment from the state. Probationers do not enjoy the same legal rights as other citizens, and revocation, even after many successful years, could result in receiving the entire prison sentence for which one was initially eligible. Because the time served on probation does not count toward the new prison sentence, the sword of Damocles is always hanging over the probationer's head.

- **How the prosecutor views probation**   The prosecutor's first and foremost concern is to win the case. Having decided to file the charge against the offender, the prosecutor wants to dispose of the case in a positive way as efficiently as possible. Although often under pressure from the victim to seek prison time, the prosecutor has considerable discretion in fashioning plea bargains with defense attorneys.[19] Probation is a sanction that the prosecutor can point to as a victory even though it required little time or resources. As a plea-bargaining tool, probation allows the prosecutor to avoid costly trials for a large percentage of cases. Additionally, prosecutors may embrace probation when the facts of the case are weak and the case would likely result in a dismissal if it went to trial.

- **How the defense attorney views probation**   The defense attorney, just like the prosecutor, views probation as a victory. By keeping the offender out of prison, the defense attorney can claim to have preserved the offender's liberty with some reasonable compromises, such as the conditions of probation. The defense attorney is not overly concerned with the conditions because, for the most part, they will not hurt the offender and may serve as positive influences. Being required to get more education or alcohol counseling are not violations of fundamental human rights, and the defense attorney is not likely to object to such requirements.[20]

- **How the judge views probation**   Judges are under tremendous pressure from the public to punish offenders despite the fact that the prisons are full. Probation allows the judge to impose a sentence that is less expensive than prison and, to some degree at least, satisfies victims and other citizens that the offender did not escape punishment. The judge can make probation more palatable to those who want punishment by adding special conditions such as drug testing, home confinement, and increased supervision. We will discuss these intermediate punishments in greater detail at the end of this chapter, but we note here that they are used to give probation more teeth and to satisfy the need to punish criminals.

- **How reformers view probation**   Probation offers the offender a variety of treatment and community service activities. Community resources such as schools, mental health centers, hospitals, and opportunities for gainful employment are offered that cannot be duplicated in the prison. If used judiciously, these resources can provide the ingredients for successful rehabilitation and reintegration of the offender. Perhaps the major benefit of probation as seen by reformers is the avoidance of the deleterious effects of prison. By keeping the offender away from hardened, long-term inmates, the criminal justice system can instill productive work habits and positive social skills.

- **How politicians view probation**   As with many issues, politicians talk out of both sides of their mouths on the issue of probation. On one hand, many politicians adopt a tough-on-crime stance and advocate sending vast numbers of offenders to prison for incredibly long sentences. On the other hand, these same politicians do not provide the funds needed to build enough prisons, hire enough probation officers, or establish effective community corrections treatment services. To them, probation is a cheaper way to punish than the prison. However, politicians can be expected to condemn parole when some parolee commits a heinous offense while under supervision.

Probation means many things to many people. The emphasis of probation in any given jurisdiction may vacillate between its twin goals of supervision and treatment. Because it is such a fundamental feature of the criminal justice system, however, it will always be used in one form or another.

Probation Officers at Work

The probation officer's job requires a variety of skills, a strong sense of self-worth, and a tolerance for other people not doing what is expected of them (see Focus on Ethics 13.2). The probation officer spends time in the courtroom, in the office, and

GOING OUT ON A LIMB

As a probation officer you have a reputation of being pretty tough with your clients. However, every once in a while, someone comes along whom you are willing to take a chance on. You have been burned a couple of times before by probationers who promised one thing and did the opposite, but this time you think you have a client who warrants your trust and help.

James is a gifted athlete who has NFL written all over him. He is a college freshman who is on scholarship but was implicated in a brawl at a rock concert where several people were brutally beaten and hospitalized. Although the degree of James's involvement is unclear, his lawyer arranged a plea bargain for probation with the stipulation that the coach would allow James to remain on scholarship and play that season. Everyone, including you when you did the presentence investigation, believed James was a worthwhile risk for probation because of his bright future.

However, as James's probation officer you have come to suspect that he is developing an entitled attitude and believes that because he is a football star, he need not abide by the conditions of his probation or listen to you when you try to give him advice. Specifically, James is missing classes, will not return your phone calls, has had beer in his dormitory refrigerator even though he is not of drinking age, and violates the court-ordered curfew of midnight on weekends. You have tried to correct the problem by contacting his coach and advising him of your concerns, but you are finding that the longer the football season goes on, the less anyone—James, his coaches, the judge, or your supervisor—cares about your complaints. Most of the issues are minor technical violations, but you have just recently noticed a hostile attitude in James both on the field and off. Today, his girlfriend shows up at your office with a black eye and a tale about violence, gunplay, and steroids. This weekend is the big game against the cross-state rival, and everyone knows that James must do well for the team to win. You are afraid he might not make it to the weekend without hurting somebody unless you take action.

What Do You Do?

1. Go to James's dorm room and have a face-to-face, heart-to-heart talk with him.

2. Go to the coach and threaten to get the judge to revoke James's probation before the game if he doesn't shape up.

3. Go to the judge and express your concerns and essentially place the whole issue in his lap, thereby covering your own rear end.

4. Say nothing until after the game and hope that once the pressure of football is off, James will start to behave in a more appropriate way.

---

out in the field visiting clients where they work and live. Each probation department has standards for monitoring offenders, and each probation officer works out how to accomplish the job's multiple demands. Many probation officers love this work because its discretion and flexibility allow them to use their particular administrative, interpersonal, and investigative strengths to help offenders and protect society. The duties of the probation officer are many, but three universal functions define the occupation: investigation, supervision, and service.

presentence investigation

The report prepared by a probation officer to assist a judge in sentencing; also be called a presentence report.

INVESTIGATION The probation officer spends a lot of time gathering information for decision makers throughout the criminal justice system. The offender's case file contains data gleaned from police reports; prosecutors' files; and interviews with offenders, victims, witnesses, neighbors, teachers, and peers. The most time-consuming and significant report that the probation officer writes is the **presentence investigation** (PSI).[21]

The United States has a bifurcated court process. The first goal of the proceedings is to determine the defendant's guilt or innocence. This is sometimes done by means of a criminal trial. However, the criminal trial is used sparingly; most cases are settled through plea bargaining.[22] With plea bargaining, the judge does not have the opportunity to become familiar with the case or the defendant, so in the second part of the case proceedings, the sentencing, the judge has little information on which to base a sentence. Typically the judge postpones the sentencing judgment while the probation department conducts a presentence investigation.[23]

During the presentence investigation the probation officer collects information about two important aspects of the case: the legal history of the incident and the offender's social history.

- **Legal history**   The legal history offers the judge two primary items to help make an informed sentencing decision. The first item is a complete report on the offense. The probation officer summarizes the police report, provides the offender's version of the incident, and includes additional perspectives from the victim or other interested parties. The goal is to give the judge a good idea of the offense's impact on the victim and the community.[24] This is especially useful when the case has been plea-bargained because the final charge might not reflect the seriousness of the offense or the dangerousness of the offender. For example, in a case of spousal abuse, the husband may have been able to plead a savage beating down to a simple assault charge. This reduced charge limits the sentence, but the judge is well served in knowing exactly what happened and how violent the husband can be. With this knowledge, the judge can decide to impose special conditions of probation, such as attending anger management classes. Additionally, this part of the presentence investigation alerts the judge to the dispositions of any co-defendants and to any further charges that might be hanging over the offender. The second item of the legal history is the offender's prior record. Is this the first time the defendant has violated the law or the fifteenth? Has probation been attempted before, and if so, did the defendant successfully complete the probationary term without violating its conditions? Is there a pattern of increasing severity to the defendant's offenses? Did the Peeping Tom become a flasher who now is convicted of rape? Have other interventions such as alcohol and drug treatment been successful? The answers to all of these questions help the judge determine the risk of putting this offender back on the street.

- **Social history**   The offender's social history also helps the judge craft an appropriate sentence. The probation officer gathers information on the offender's education, family, work situation and employment history, physical and mental health, and military history. If any of these factors are related to the case, the probation officer may describe in great detail how the offender may have special issues that require consideration. For example, if the offender has been convicted of child abuse, it would be important for the judge to be aware of his employment as a fourth-grade teacher and his volunteer work for the Boy Scouts. In gathering this information, the probation officer includes names, addresses, phone numbers, and other information on family members, places of employment, peers, victims, and witnesses. This information is important not only for the case at hand, but to develop a record of attachments that can be used by future probation officers to monitor the offender. For example, sometimes the old phone number of a former girlfriend becomes the one link to a probationer who has disappeared.

The probation officer questions the client on all of these issues and then spends a great deal of time attempting to verify the truthfulness of the answers. Some clients forget important details of their past; some try to put a positive spin on their actions, and some look the probation officer right in the eye and lie. A forthcoming and honest offender may find a more receptive judge than one who continues to demonstrate that he or she cannot be trusted. The presentence investigation is the probation officer's opportunity to provide the judge not only with facts, but also with information on the offender's attitude. Because this document can determine whether the defendant goes to prison or is placed on probation, the probation officer must be fair to both the defendant and society.[25]

SUPERVISION   Once an offender is placed on probation, the probation officer advises him or her about what is expected. Each probation system has standard conditions. Typically, these include instructions on how often to report; restrictions on changing jobs, residences, or schools without prior approval; and proscriptions on alcohol consumption, drug use, and consorting with known felons. The probationer must also cooperate with the probation officer and follow all lawful instructions. These standard conditions give the probation officer wide latitude in controlling the probationer's lifestyle. However, because of high caseloads, most officers cannot systematically ensure that all the conditions are being followed.

The judge may also apply special conditions to a particular case. For instance, in the case of a child abuser, the judge may prohibit him from loitering around schools or playgrounds.[26] Other special conditions may include community service. For example, an accountant convicted of a DUI may be required to provide free tax advice to senior citizens, or a college student involved in a hit-and-run accident may be required to speak at high schools and confess to her lack of judgment and the remorse she has for the harm she did to the victim. The probation officer must ensure that these activities are accomplished.

The supervision function of the probation officer's job accomplishes two goals. On one hand, supervision is a form of punishment in which the probationer's life is disrupted by the many conditions of probation. This disruption obviously pales in comparison to the disruption of going to prison, but still, reporting to the probation officer and asking permission for simple things such as leaving the state to go on vacation can become tiresome after a couple of years. Second, the supervision function is a form of surveillance designed to protect society by alerting the probation officer that the probationer is drifting back into unlawful behavior.[27]

Because prisons are crowded, the court must place on probation some offenders who pose a risk to society. Therefore, the surveillance function of probation is important.[28] To determine the level of risk for each offender, probation departments measure the type of offense, legal record, social history, and drug and alcohol use to determine the level of supervision and the frequency of probation-officer contacts. The determination of probation risk is an internal management issue for probation departments and not a legal issue in which offenders are protected by the court. The risk assessment instrument does have some built-in bias. For instance, younger offenders are automatically assigned more risk than older offenders. Similarly, juvenile and adult first-offender offenses are usually treated more leniently by the courts, but in probation risk assessments, they are counted against the offender as stringently as any other offense.[29] Probationers have reduced legal rights, and the courts have intervened only sporadically to limit the discretion of probation officers and judges.

The probationer's risk level dictates how much he or she will be watched. Typically, probation officers allocate more attention to new offenders until they can determine that they are adjusting to their status. If the probationer follows instructions and reports when required, attends school and/or holds down a steady job, and fulfills the standard and special conditions of probation, then the supervision is relaxed.

In an ideal world, there would be enough probation officers to ensure that every probationer is living a law-abiding life and following the conditions of probation. However, because of a lack of funding, many probationers get away with numerous minor violations, and some of them continue to maintain a criminal lifestyle. This is a precarious practice, however, because probation officers have surveillance powers that police officers lack. If the probation officer suspects that a probationer is engaged in criminal activity, then a search of the residence, car, or person can be conducted without the benefit of Fourth Amendment requirements of probable cause. When one is placed on probation, it is understood that permission is automatically given for the probation officer to conduct almost unlimited surveillance. Because probation is a conditional release, probationers must agree to limited legal rights (see Criminal Justice Reference 13.1).

When a probationer is caught committing a new offense or violating the conditions of probation, the case goes back to the judge (see Case in Point 13.1). This is where things get dicey for the probationer. Although the court must afford the offender all the required legal rights for the new crime, this new crime will also be considered a probation violation. The legal requirements necessary to revoke the

13.1   CRIMINAL JUSTICE REFERENCE

Standard Conditions of Probation for Federal Offenders

1. The defendant shall not leave the judicial district or other specific geographic area without the permission of the court or probation officer.

2. The defendant shall report to the probation officer as directed by the court or probation officer and shall submit a truthful and complete written report within the first five (5) days of each month.

3. The defendant shall answer truthfully all inquiries by the probation officer and follow the instructions of the probation officer.

4. The defendant shall support the defendant's dependents and meet other family responsibilities.

5. The defendant shall work regularly at a lawful occupation unless excused by the probation officer for schooling, training, or other acceptable reasons.

6. The defendant shall notify the probation officer at least ten (10) days prior to any change of residence or employment.

7. The defendant shall refrain from excessive use of alcohol and shall not purchase, possess, use, distribute, or administer any controlled substance, or any paraphernalia related to any controlled substance, except as prescribed by a physician.

8. The defendant shall not frequent places where controlled substances are illegally sold, used, distributed, or administered, or other places specified by the court.

9. The defendant shall not associate with any persons engaged in criminal activity, and shall not associate with any person convicted of a felony unless granted permission to do so by the probation officer.

10. The defendant shall permit a probation officer to visit the defendant at any time at home or elsewhere and shall permit confiscation of any contraband observed in plain view of the probation officer.

11. The defendant shall notify the probation officer within seventy-two hours of being arrested or questioned by a law enforcement officer.

12. The defendant shall not enter into any agreement to act as an informer or special agent of a law enforcement agency without the permission of the Court.

13. As directed by the probation officer, the defendant shall notify third parties of risks that may be occasioned by the defendant's criminal record or personal history or characteristics, and shall permit the probation officer to make such notifications and to confirm the defendant's compliance with such notification requirement.

14. The defendant shall pay the special assessment imposed or adhere to a court-ordered installment schedule for the payment of the special assessment.

15. The defendant shall notify the probation officer of any material change in the defendant's economic circumstances that might affect the defendant's ability to pay any unpaid amount of restitution, fines or special assessments.

Source: U.S. Probation/Pretrial, Northern District of Indiana, www.innp.uscourts.gov/Forms/Standard_Conditions_for_Offenders.pdf.

---

probation and sentence the offender on the old charge are far less rigorous than those needed to convict and sentence the offender on the new charge. Additionally, any plea bargaining the offender does on the new charge can affect his or her probation status. For example, suppose Joe is on probation for five years for assault and has successfully completed four years of the sentence when he is arrested for selling drugs to an undercover narcotics officer. Because he cooperated with the police by ratting out all his drug-using friends, he strikes a deal with the prosecutor on the drug charge for probation. However, Joe's prior charge of assault, because it was in another jurisdiction, has an entirely different judge who determines that his plea bargain on the drug charge is an admission of guilt and a violation of his conditions of probation. Consequently, Joe's probation is revoked, and the judge sentences him to five years in prison based on the assault charge. When Joe gets to prison, he is alarmed to find that his new cellmate is one of his friends, incarcerated as a result of his testimony. Oops.

Most violations of the technical conditions of probation do not result in revocation. Judges are reluctant to send people to jail because they failed to report to their probation officers or moved to a new apartment without prior permission. In fact, judges do not want to be bothered with minor issues and depend on the probation officer to chastise the offender. On some occasions, the probation term may be extended for an offender who cannot follow instructions, or new, more restrictive conditions may be applied until it is clear that compliance is forthcoming.[30]

The probation officer must document his or her supervision of offenders because there is always the possibility that one will commit a serious crime and not only make the officer look incompetent, but open the officer to professional liability. If the probation officer did not follow the protocols of the office and failed to require the probationer to abide by the conditions of probation, then the offender's victims might be able to sue.[31] Say, for instance, that as a probation officer, you unknowingly permitted a child molester to move to a new residence that happened to be next to an elementary school, and that for seven months you never visited the probationer, who was using a puppy to lure children into his yard, where he sexually abused them. It would be reasonable for an attorney representing the children's parents to argue that as society's watchdog, you should have known your probationer lived next to the school. The attorney may also examine your case records and find that you have not followed office procedures and made the required home contacts. Because you are responsible for making a reasonable effort at supervision, your case records must reflect a good-faith effort to comply with the preestablished reporting standards. In this case, losing your job may be the least of your worries.

One management technique to ensure that dangerous offenders are provided with an adequate level of supervision is to give their cases to probation officers with reduced caseloads, who can then be required to make more contacts. These reduced-caseload strategies are called **intensive-supervision probation** (ISP). Because this practice is similar to the parole function, we will discuss it in greater detail later in this chapter.

intensive-supervision probation
A form of supervision that requires frequent meetings between the client and probation officer.

Service   One reason why individuals decide to work in corrections is to help people. Although investigation and supervision occupy most of probation officers' time, they are still expected to provide some level of service to offenders who need help. Sometimes new probation officers are disillusioned when they discover the impediments to providing the help they believe is needed. These impediments include the following:

- **High caseloads**   Because probation officers must supervise so many cases, they have little time to establish a personal rapport with each client.
- **Many offenders do not want the help and extra attention of the probation officer**   Some officers are surprised that the very clients they are trying to help are liars, cheats, and con artists. Some of these officers become cynical after being betrayed a few times and replace their naiveté with an equally ineffective bitterness.
- **Sparse resources**   Mental health centers, drug treatment institutes, and all sorts of people-helping programs have been jettisoned because of budget cuts at every level of government. This can be frustrating to both the probation officer and the probationer. Sometimes a "treatable moment" appears when the probationer is motivated to seek help; however, being placed on a six-month waiting list can mean a lost opportunity.

It is unfortunate that the service aspect of the probation officer's job is so limited. Some may argue that rehabilitation is a secondary activity, but evidence suggests that appropriate placement in a decent treatment program can have a positive effect. Although the investigation and supervision aspects of probation will always be the primary focus, the service component may well be the most important for the long-term behavior change of the offender and ultimately the protection of society.

Private Probation

With probation caseloads rapidly expanding, many states have found it difficult to provide enough probation officers to adequately supervise everyone who is on probation. At least 12 states have contracted out probation services for misdemeanor cases.[32] Presumably, these offenders require little in the way of supervision as compared to people convicted of felonies, and relieving state probation officers of this responsibility seems to be an attractive way to focus resources on more serious offenders.

13.1 CASE IN POINT

MEMPA V. RHAY

THE CASE	THE POINT
Mempa v. Rhay, 389 U.S. 128, 88 S.Ct. 254 (1967)	Felony defendants must be allowed to have an attorney during hearings when probation may be revoked or a deferred sentence imposed.

Jerry Mempa, an indigent, was convicted of riding in a stolen vehicle. His sentence was deferred, and he was given two years' probation. A few months later, Mempa was accused of being involved in a burglary, and the prosecution recommended that his probation be revoked. At the hearing, Mempa was not appointed an attorney, asked about his previous court-appointed attorney, or asked whether he wanted another attorney. Mempa's probation officer testified that Mempa had been involved in the burglary, but that Mempa had denied it. The probation officer was not cross-examined. Mempa then admitted to his involvement in the burglary. Without questioning Mempa further, the court revoked his probation and sentenced him to 10 years in the penitentiary as per state law, but recommended that he serve only a year.

Six years later, in 1965, Mempa, still in prison, filed a writ of *habeas corpus* with the Washington Supreme Court, claiming that he had been deprived of his right to counsel at the probation revocation hearing. The state court denied the petition, and he appealed to the Supreme Court. The Court agreed with Mempa and wrote that according to the Sixth Amendment, felony defendants must be allowed counsel during hearings when probation might be revoked or a deferred sentence imposed, even if counsel had been present during the original trial at which the sentence was deferred. The decision was reversed and remanded.

Private probation involves contractual agreements between the state government and companies owned by private individuals whereby misdemeanor probationers are assigned by the judge to be supervised by agencies that are not part of a formal state government. These private agencies may charge probationers a cost-of-supervision fee that helps offset their personnel costs and overhead. Additionally, this cost-of-supervision fee allows the private agency to make a profit. Although figures are not available as to how much profit is realized, it is potentially substantial.

There is considerable debate about the ethical issues of this type of for-profit probation, but it is not unlike the example of private prisons. When traditional government activities are privatized, it is assumed that the service will be less expensive and more effective. To this end, states have developed guidelines and requirements that dictate how private probation agencies supervise misdemeanor cases.[33] These requirements specify such activities as how often the probationers are contacted, the collection of fines and cost-of-supervision fees, and the provision for treatment alternatives. Some states also contract the treatment to private agencies.

Private probation has a number of advantages and disadvantages. Even though private probation is not widespread, it can be expected that more states will adopt this practice as their budgets become stressed.

private probation
A form of probation supervision that is contracted to for-profit private agencies by the state.

Advantages

- **Cost** The cost of supervising individuals on private probation is borne by the probationer. In a sense, this is a "user fee" similar to toll roads or impact fees charged to real-estate developers. The idea is for those who use the service to assume the cost of the service.

- **Effectiveness** By shifting the burden for misdemeanor offenders to private agencies, state agencies can more effectively supervise and treat more serious felony offenders. Furthermore, misdemeanor offenders receive a greater degree of contact with probation officers, especially considering that the private agency has an incentive of collecting the cost-of-supervision money. Most misdemeanor offenders do not require substantial counseling or rigorous supervision, so the high caseloads of these private agencies are not considered problematic.

- **Public perception**   Under traditional probation, misdemeanor offenders often fall through the cracks. There simply are not enough resources available to provide the type of supervision that the public and victims of crime expect. With private probation agencies, it is clear to all that those convicted of misdemeanors literally pay a price.

DISADVANTAGES

- **Staff qualifications**   Most traditional probation officers are required to have a four-year university degree. Many private agencies have no educational requirement, and people with a high-school diploma are put in charge of a large number of offenders. Most traditional probation officers get intensive in-service training when they join the agency. Private probation agencies offer little or no training. Although many private probation officers are dedicated and effective in their jobs, the lack of standards and guidelines make this type of arrangement problematic. Because it is such a new type of correctional service, there are no uniform standards.[34]

- **Profit motive**   The primary missions of traditional probation are to protect the public and provide treatment for their clients. In private probation agencies, the first order of business is that the organization make money. This profit motive can conflict with the basic reasons why misdemeanor probation was established in the first place.

- **Ethical concerns**   Some people have raised concerns about the ethical position of punishment for profit. The government has a monopoly on the legitimate use of correctional coercion, and outsourcing it to private agencies is deemed questionable. A relevant analogy would be the employment of mercenaries to fight in the nation's wars. Public safety is a basic government responsibility, and many believe that it should remain in the hands of the government and be accountable to the public.[35]

- **Social-class bias**   Charging misdemeanor probationers cost-of-supervision fees has a differential effect depending on individual financial capabilities. Those who have enough money to meet their basic needs might be inconvenienced by the added expense, but those who are unemployed or living a paycheck to paycheck may find the cost of freedom more than they can afford. Some agencies charge up to $50 per month for the cost of supervision, which can mean the difference between successfully completing the probation or being brought back before the judge on a technical violation.[36]

The use of private probation in the United States will continue to be a controversial issue. As state governments seek more efficient ways to provide services without raising taxes, the outsourcing of misdemeanor probation is a tempting strategy. Very little reliable criminological research is available to assess the quality of private probation or its acceptance by the public. This practice will be of interest to scholars for many years as it matures into a more common feature of the correctional system.

PAROLE

The origin of the word *parole* is French. *Parole d'honneur*, which means "word of honor," was used in wartime when prisoners of war were released on their promise not to engage in further fighting.[37] The practice grew from the experiences and reforms discussed in Chapter 11 on the origins of the prison. Reformers such as Alexander Maconochie (marks system), Sir Walter Crofton (ticket-of-leave), and Zebulon Brockway contributed to the idea that the penal system should help the offender in

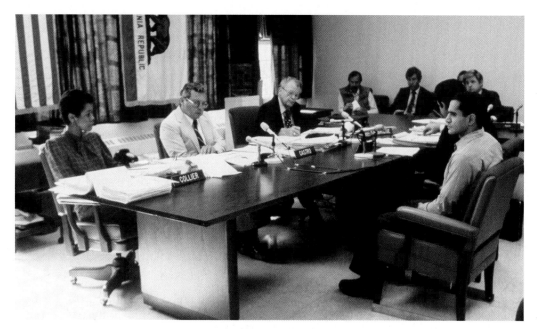

Parole board members want to hear a good post-parole plan that includes a supportive residence and a viable job. Here, parole board members listen to Sirhan Sirhan, who assassinated Robert F. Kennedy, explain why he should be released.
Source: CORBIS-NY

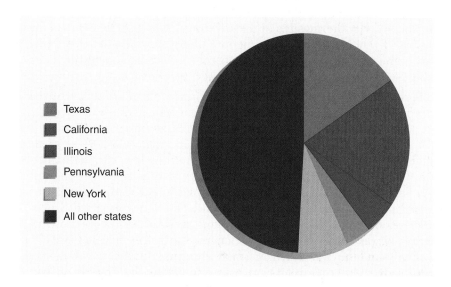

- Texas
- California
- Illinois
- Pennsylvania
- New York
- All other states

Figure 13-4 **Major State Parole Supervising Agencies** As of 2006, five agencies supervised half of the nation's parole population
Source: Thomas P. Bonczar, *Characteristics of State Parole Supervising Agencies, 2006* (Washington, DC: U.S. Department of Justice, Bureau of Justice Statistics, 2008), 2. www.ojp.usdoj.gov/bjs/pub/pdf/cspsa06.pdf.

the transition back into society. Today, there are 52 parole supervising agencies in the United States, 17 of which handle only parolees, and 35 of which handle both parolees and probationers. As of 2006, these state agencies had nearly 65,000 full-time and 2,900 part-time employees.[38] Currently, five agencies supervise half of the nation's parole population (see Figure 13-4).

Many people use the terms *probation* and *parole* interchangeably. Although they do have many similarities, significant differences make these corrections practices distinct and worthy of separate consideration. Both deal with offenders in the community, but they differ in a number of distinctive ways.

- **Probation instead, parole after** The primary difference between parole and probation is the point at which it occurs in the criminal justice process. Probation is a sentencing option that allows offenders to be placed under community corrections supervision *instead* of being placed in prison. Parole, on the other hand, is a form of early release that happens *after* the offender has served part of the prison sentence. For a comparison of the number of state and federal parolees at the end of 2006, see Figure 13-5.

Figure 13-5 **Number of Adults on State and Federal Parole, 2006**

Source: Lauren E. Glaze and Thomas P. Bonczar, *Probation and Parole in the United States, 2006* (Washington, DC: U.S. Department of Justice, Bureau of Justice Statistics, 2007), 5, www.ojp.usdoj.gov/bjs/pub/pdf/ppus06.pdf.

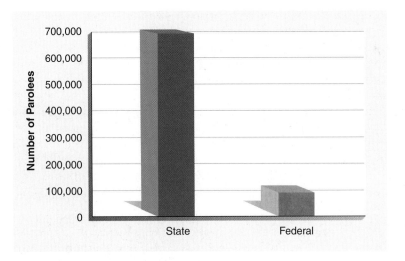

- **Governing authority** Although there is considerable variation across the United States in the bureaucratic placement of the probation and parole functions, probation is usually attached to the judiciary, with the judge being the primary decision maker. Parole is extended by the executive branch of government and is under the auspices of the governor. Of course, there are many variations on this theme. In some jurisdictions, the agency that supervises parolees is part of the executive branch, but the parole board is an independent decision-making panel that is presumably free of political influence.

- **Parolees and probationers are different types of clients in terms of risk factors, community ties, and social needs** Generally, parolees have committed more serious offenses, have readjustment issues after being incarcerated, and might not have the same support from family and friends because of weakened social bonds caused by long periods of incarceration. This may certainly be the case for many offenders; however, whether the client is on probation or parole depends on the last offense he or she was convicted of. Many individuals, especially the most problematic ones, have been on multiple probations and paroles. Therefore, it is misleading to judge the level of risk as higher for those on parole than for those on probation. In some ways, parolees may be more cooperative because they have already had a taste of prison life and are willing to abide by the conditions of their release in order to maintain their liberty.

- **Probation and parole officers have different mandates and responsibilities** Again, depending on the jurisdiction, there are different expectations of probation and parole officers. In some states, parole officers carry firearms and arrest parole violators, whereas the probation officer would call the police to do any dangerous work.

When to Parole

The complicated decision of when to grant parole is based on three competing principles. First, there is the political issue of how much time the offender should spend in prison to satisfy the public demand for retribution and punishment. By paroling inmates too early, the parole board risks losing the confidence of politicians and society, who start to question whether prison is a sufficient deterrent and punishment. In fact, some states have abolished parole and others have greatly modified the discretion of parole boards by assigning fixed sentences to several types of offenses. For an example of a state's parole process, see Criminal Justice Reference 13.2.

A second and competing principle when deciding whether to grant parole is the rehabilitation issue.[39] Can a parole board accurately determine when someone is emotionally ready to be released from prison? We have already discussed indeterminate sentencing, in which the offender is sentenced to serve an unspecified time: the prison officials and parole board are responsible for deciding when, based on the medical model, the inmate is "cured." However, ascertaining when an inmate is safe to release is difficult, and because of prison overcrowding, few resources are allocated for treatment programs.[40]

The third principle driving the parole decision is the limited number of prison beds. States simply cannot afford to keep everyone incarcerated for as long as they have been sentenced. To let new offenders in the front door of the prison, they must release others out the back door. With these complicating principles in mind, the parole board attempts to make rational, fair, and informed decisions on when to grant parole. These decisions are based on a number of factors:

1. **Time served.**   The parole board does not have unlimited discretion in the release decision. The length of the imposed sentence controls, in part, when the inmate may first be eligible to be considered for parole. Another factor is the consideration of the time the inmate served in jail awaiting trial (in some cases this could be a year or more).

2. **Prison adjustment.**   In many states, inmates are granted **good time** for behaving in prison, which can reduce the sentence by up to one-third. Some inmates can significantly reduce their sentence by earning **meritorious time** for completing treatment programs or educational degrees while in prison. By taking advantage of opportunities for self-betterment, inmates can demonstrate that they can compete for jobs or have acquired the social skills necessary to function in society.

3. **Pre-parole plan.**   A plan is developed for the inmate's release. A parole officer (either one assigned to the institution or one in the jurisdiction where the parole will be served, or both) develops a plan with the inmate and family members (or those who will be involved with the inmate on release). This plan specifies where the inmate will live, how the inmate will survive financially, and what supervision level and treatment programs will be required. One reason for the denial of many paroles is an insufficient parole plan. If the parole board does not see a reasonable support network for the inmate, they will instruct all involved to develop a comprehensive plan before the next parole hearing. The longer an offender stays in prison, losing contact and trust with family and friends on the outside, the more difficult it is to develop these plans.[41]

4. **Offender interview.**   The parole board (or hearing officers acting in its name) interviews the offender before the parole decision to get a feel for the attitude, demeanor, preparedness, and sincerity of the offender. In these hearings, the parole board inquires about the offender's remorse, prison experiences, parole plan, and sensitivity to criticism. The parole board asks pointed and personal questions to see how the inmate reacts to authority figures. Some inmates are defiant, but most attempt to determine what the hearing officers want to hear and then provide it.

5. **Victim-impact statements.**   The parole staff contacts the victim(s) of the offense committed by the inmate and asks them to comment on how they suffered as a result of the inmate's actions and how the release of the inmate will affect them. Some victims who have been especially traumatized may write impassioned statements that sink any chance of parole. On some occasions, victims— or in homicide cases, their relatives—show up at every parole hearing to ensure that the parole board is aware of their opposition to the offender's release.[42]

As you can see, the decision to grant parole involves many factors and is difficult to predict in many cases. One is never sure how the hearing officer or the parole board will respond to evidence, but some established policies and a given board's track record suggest what the "going rate" is for most parole authorities.[43] Because so many

good time

The time deducted from an inmate's prison sentence for good behavior.

meritorious time

Time deducted from an inmate's sentence for doing something special or extra, such as getting a GED.

13.2 CRIMINAL JUSTICE REFERENCE

State of California Lifer Parole Process

- Only inmates sentenced to life in prison (an indeterminate sentence) with the possibility of parole may receive suitability hearings. Some life inmates are sentenced without the possibility of parole. All California inmates who are not serving life sentences or determinate sentences are released on parole after serving the sentence.
- Inmates serving life sentences become eligible for parole hearings automatically, one year before their minimum eligible parole date. Inmate suitability for parole is determined by the parole board.
- Inmates might receive many parole hearings before they are found suitable for release. Inmates convicted of murder can be denied parole for up to five years at a time. Inmates serving a life sentence for offenses other than murder can be denied parole for up to two years at a time.
- Parole hearings do not decide guilt. The purpose of a parole hearing is to determine whether or when an inmate can return to society.
- Some of the factors the parole board considers include the following:
    Counseling reports and psychological evaluations
    Behavior in prison
    Vocational and/or educational accomplishments in prison
    Involvement in self-help therapy programs
    Parole plans, including the inmate's expected residence and means of support on release

- Inmates are entitled to legal counsel, which may be a private attorney or one appointed by the parole board.
- The district attorney county may make a presentation opposing or supporting parole.
- Victims or their families are entitled to present a 15-minute victim-impact statement.
- Any person may submit information concerning any inmate or parolee. Written comments are included in the inmate's or parolee's file.
- If denied parole, the inmate's next hearing is scheduled.
- If granted parole, the decision is subject to review, which includes a review by the parole board staff within 120 days to determine whether there are any errors of law or fact
- Possible review by the governor within 30 days. The governor may allow the decision to stand, actively approve the decision, modify the decision, or refer the decision back to parole board for reconsideration. Reversal of a decision is optional in murder cases only.

Source: Edited from the California Department of Corrections and Rehabilitation, Lifer Parole Process, www.cdcr.ca.gov/Parole/Parole_Process.html.

cases are heard each year, patterns develop according to the length of time served and the appropriateness of the parole plan, so that even though an inmate has a parole hearing, parole likely will not be granted until a few more years have passed.

Reentry and "Making It"

Most prison systems attempt to prepare the inmate for reentry into society. Generally, about as many state inmates successfully complete parole as return to prison (see Figure 13-6). Some programs can last up to a year and include mechanisms of gradual reintegration such as furloughs and work release. Other programs last only weeks and include mock job interviews and/or studies to prepare for getting a driver's license. Regardless of how the prison prepares the inmate, at least three major adjustments stand as obstacles to successful reentry. One of these obstacles involves changes in the inmate, and the others involve changes in the world to which he or she is returning.

1. **Prisonization.**[44] Life in prison is lived according to rigid rules established by both the administration and the inmate social system. The inmate quickly learns the boundaries of appropriate behavior and lives a life of predictability, routine, and boredom. The inmate is not required, or permitted, to make decisions, exercise judgment, be creative, or experiment in relationships or daily life. Some inmates find comfort in this atmosphere in which all important decisions and even most unimportant decisions are made for them. When these inmates are released, they are overwhelmed by the magnitude of decisions they must make. For example, whereas in prison deciding what to eat involves sticking

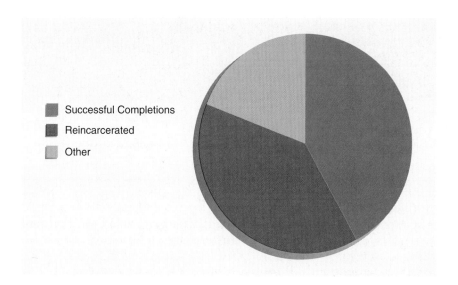

Figure 13-6   **Adults Leaving State Parole, 2006**
Source: Lauren E. Glaze and Thomas P. Bonczar, *Probation and Parole in the United States, 2006* (Washington, DC: U.S. Department of Justice, Bureau of Justice Statistics, 2007), 10, www.ojp.usdoj.gov/bjs/pub/pdf/ppus05.pdf.

- Successful Completions
- Reincarcerated
- Other

out a tray and assessing what is plopped on it, in the free world the menu options can be daunting. The prison has a soup of the day (sometimes it is the soup of every day), but the grocery store has almost 100 soups of different brands, flavors, and sizes. Multiply the soup decision by the vast array of foods in the store, and the former inmate can experience decision overload. Other concerns have greater consequences than the choice of soup. The interpersonal skills needed to survive in prison are not always conducive to getting along with co-workers in society. The necessity to demonstrate a willingness to use violence that can keep one alive in prison is problematic in the workplace, where supervisors and co-workers are used to giving and taking criticism without worrying about their physical safety.

2. **Weakened social ties.**   The Taoists say that you never stick your toe into the same river twice. This principle reflects a major problem of reentry. The world that the inmate left behind is not the same as the one he or she returns to. People have moved on with their lives, and the inmate must reestablish social bonds that have been weakened, twisted, or broken by incarceration.[45] Spouses, children, parents, friends, and bosses might act very differently and be wary of how the offender has been affected by prison. At its most extreme, these changes in social bonds include divorce or estrangement from spouses and rejection by children. The inmate often comes home to find that his or her former status as authority figure, breadwinner, and confidant has been usurped by someone else. While in prison, a mother might remember her children in a highly romanticized way, but on release she may return home to find them hostile, bitter, and attached to a new stepmother. The assumed social location of the inmate that was frozen in time by incarceration thaws out on release and melts into a puddle of disillusionment, anomie, and alienation.

3. **Stigmatization.**[46]   Erving Goffman defined one type of stigma as a "blemish of individual character" and included imprisonment as one of the conditions that individuals must carry around with them for a lifetime and constantly fight to overcome. This stigma is both legal and social. The legal stigma involves, depending on the jurisdiction, losing the right to vote, to parent, to hold public employment, to serve on a jury, to hold public office, and to possess a firearm, and could mean being required to register as a felon. Perhaps these restrictions are understood by the former inmate who concedes that there is a continuous price to pay for criminal activity. However, the social stigma can be even more frustrating. The stigma of "ex-con" can be as debilitating as that of "convict." For the offender who has served a sentence and has paid for his or her offenses, the continuing discrimination and prejudice seem unjust. One is never allowed

13.2	CASE IN POINT
	MORRISSEY V. BREWER

THE CASE	THE POINT
Morrissey v. Brewer, 408 U.S. 471, 92 S.Ct. 2593 (1972)	*The Supreme Court provides minimum due-process requirements for the revocation of parole.*

John Morrissey had his parole revoked after he allegedly violated several of its conditions, including not reporting his residence to his parole officer, buying a car using a false name and driving it without permission of his parole officer, using a false name to obtain credit, and lying to police after a traffic accident. Morrissey was sent back to prison, whereupon he appealed the revocation of his parole. The Supreme Court set forth the following requirements for revocation of parole.

1. The parolee must receive written notice of the alleged violations.
2. The parolee must be advised of the evidence against him or her.
3. A preliminary hearing must be held in which officials determine whether there is probable cause that the parolee has violated any parole conditions.
4. The parolee must have the chance to be heard and to present supporting witnesses and evidence.
5. The parolee may cross-examine any witnesses against him or her, unless cause is found for not allowing such confrontations.
6. A second hearing must be held in which the facts are judged by a "neutral and detached" hearing committee.
7. If parole is revoked, a written statement must be provided describing the reasons and the evidence used.

These requirements were later made applicable to both parole and probation revocation hearings.

master status

A personal status that overwhelms all others.

to make a fresh start and also carries a **master status** that overwhelms all of his or her positive attributes and accomplishments.[47] Once parents hear that the new boyfriend is a convicted rapist, there is no convincing them that he has mended his ways, learned his lesson, paid his debt to society, or is in any way a suitable future son-in-law.

Those on parole face many of the same challenges as those on probation. Being under the supervision of the state means that restrictions are placed on the offender. Conditions of parole are not significantly different from conditions of probation, but include the requirement to maintain contact with the parole officer and get permission to change residences, change employment, and travel outside the jurisdiction. For both probation and parole, a number of other tactics require examination if we are to truly appreciate how community corrections have developed over the years. Because of overcrowding in the prison systems and the concurrent heavy caseloads faced by probation and parole officers, the criminal justice system has developed intermediate sanctions designed to make probation and parole more effective, more stringent, and more palatable to the public, who demand that offenders be held accountable for their actions (see Case in Point 13.2).[48]

INTERMEDIATE SANCTIONS

Intermediate sanctions are sentencing alternatives available to the judge who finds regular probation too lenient and prison too severe.[49] If prisons were not so crowded, many offenders who receive intermediate sanctions might actually be incarcerated. With the pressures for parole boards to release inmates early to make room for new offenders, some of these intermediate sanctions are also employed at the parole stage of the criminal justice process.

Intermediate sanctions give the criminal justice system a broader range of mechanisms of social control and enhance the public's perception that crime does not pay. Although some of these newer intermediate sanctions are problematic, the critics' concerns are being addressed, and the courts are becoming cognizant of the issues that must be resolved. Here are some of the more notable intermediate sanctions.

Intensive-Supervision Probation

Intensive-supervision probation (ISP) is simply what probation used to be before the advent of unreasonably high caseloads for probation officers.[50] ISP is actually a form of triage in which offenders deemed the most problematic are allocated extra supervision. Probation officers assigned to these troublesome offenders are given small caseloads and are expected to have more frequent contact with clients. It is believed that if probation officers can concentrate on those who need help or really pose a threat to society, then they can recognize emerging problems and intervene quickly. Because it is more structured, ISP differs in several ways from regular probation:

- ISP clients have about four times as much contact with probation officers. More contacts occur at the probationer's home or place of work. Some regular probationers only have to report as little as one or two times a month, and home visits may occur as infrequently as once every six months.
- ISP clients are more likely to be required to participate in electronic home monitoring and random and/or alcohol testing.
- There are more unannounced job-site or home visits.
- ISP clients are more likely to be brought before the court for technical violations.
- ISP clients are more likely to be required to maintain full-time employment or vocational training, as well as have community-service requirements.
- Curfews are more strict. Some ISP clients must request permission to leave their homes or place of work at any time.
- ISP officers' caseloads are lower, typically 20 or fewer clients, although some might be as high as 40. Regular probation caseloads usually range from 30 to more than 100 probationers per officer.

The focus of the intensive-supervision probation program is up to the individual agency. Some are treatment-oriented, whereas others are more concerned with surveillance. A 2006 review of 34 studies of intensive-supervision probation programs found that programs that used some form of treatment saw a 21.9 percent reduction in recidivism on average, whereas surveillance-oriented programs did not affect recidivism at all.[51]

A number of tools are available to the intensive-supervision probation officer to aid in detecting wrongdoing. One of the most controversial of these tools is drug testing.

Drug Testing

Testing probationers or parolees for illegal drug use is a technological solution to a human problem. Rather than relying on behavioral cues or lifestyle changes to detect drug use, the officer can require that clients, on either a routine or random basis, submit a sample of urine for analysis.[52] Because one of the conditions of freedom is to refrain from the use of illegal drugs, and because probation and parole are conditional-release practices, the client has a choice of cooperating or going to prison. Most offenders cooperate and retain their liberty, live with their families, hold down a job, and escape the pains of imprisonment. Submitting a urine sample, although humiliating and insulting, seems a small price to pay for staying out of prison. This is not to say, however, that offenders do not attempt to frustrate the system by masking their drug use. Probationers use a range of techniques to deceive authorities. These techniques include submitting someone else's urine, eating or drinking various items that mask the presence of drugs, and missing or delaying tests until drugs have been diluted in the body. Probation and parole authorities counter these deceptions by increasing the sophistication of the drug tests (for example, using hair strands instead of urine), surprising the clients with random tests, and closely monitoring the administration of the tests.

House Arrest and Electronic Monitoring

House arrest is an old concept that has appeal today because it allows offenders to maintain family ties, work to support themselves and pay taxes, take advantage of community resources such as school and counseling services, and save the state the cost of incarceration.[53] Typically offenders are required to stay home except when they are attending approved activities such as employment, school, treatment programs, or religious services. They are especially restricted during the evening hours, when most offenses take place and when they can expect unannounced calls or visits from their probation officer. Although some citizens are concerned about some home-confined offenders being a danger to the community, for the most part, these probationers are selected because they are low-risk and have relatively stable residences in which to be confined. Electric monitoring is often used to supplement house arrest but is also used with other programs.[54]

Like drug testing, electric monitoring uses technology to address human concerns.[55] In this case, a device attached to the offender's ankle alerts authorities when it is moved too far from its transmitter. If the offender can slip off the electronic bracelet and leave it next to the transmitter, then he or she is free to roam at will, safe in the knowledge that the probation officer believes he or she is still home. Another limitation of electronic monitoring is that it can only tell the probation officer that the offender is at home, not what the offender is doing. Offenses such as child abuse, spouse battering, or drug sales could be happening, and the probation officer would have no clue.

In many ways, technological devices may lull us into thinking that offenders are adjusting to their limited freedoms when they are still engaging in serious offenses.

Electronic monitoring is a cost-effective method to keep track of offenders on house arrest. It allows offenders to live at home, continue employment, and stay out of prison.

Source: Dwayne Newton/PhotoEdit Inc.

Therefore, these tools should be considered merely as a supplement to face-to-face supervision, rather than as a replacement for the traditional probation or parole officer. As this type of technology becomes more sophisticated, it is interesting to speculate how it could be used to supervise criminal offenders. It is already possible to implant a small transmitter under the offender's skin and use a satellite to track his or her movements.[56] This way, probation officers can tell whether the offender is at home, at work, or at a bar with other offenders. Implanted monitoring devices may one day be able to report the offender's blood alcohol level or whether illegal drugs are present in the body.[57]

Fines

Although the use of fines has been a consistent feature of the U.S. criminal justice system for a long time, other countries have used them more. For some types of offenses, especially some economic offenses, fines are an appropriate sanction.[58] For other types of offenses, the public does not think offenders should be able to "buy their way out of trouble." Fines are often used in conjunction with other types of sanctions, such as short periods of incarceration.[59]

Fines have several advantages as a criminal sanction. Fines used as an alternative to incarceration are not only less expensive to administer, but bring extra money to the criminal justice system's budgets. In fact, many probation systems require their clients to pay cost-of-supervision fines as a condition of probation, thus offsetting a major portion of the expense.[60] A final advantage of fines is the message that is sent to the public that offenders sometimes do "pay for their crimes." A large fine levied on a tax cheat or an unscrupulous businessperson gives the public a sense of justice.

The downside of using fines as a criminal sanction involves fairness. Poor people can barely afford to support their families, and adding fines to the sentence places a hardship on them that wealthy offenders do not experience. For this reason, in addition to having fixed fines for certain offenses, some countries have instituted a "day fine" system in which the offender is fined in proportion to how much money he or she makes. The idea is that the fine would be based on how much the offender is paid for one day of work and then multiplied by the degree of punishment the court wants to administer. Consequently, someone who makes $100,000 a year would pay 10 times the fine of someone who makes $10,000 a year. Although this fine system may be more equitable than a fixed-fine system, wealth still has its advantages. Someone who makes $10,000 a year has little discretionary money. Every dime is used for rent, food, health care, and other necessities. However, for offenders making $100,000 a year, even though their houses may cost more and their children may go to more expensive schools, a certain economy of scale works in their favor and allows them to pay a percentage of their income without suffering as much as impoverished offenders.

Boot Camp Prisons

A recent addition to the intermediate arsenal of criminal sanctions is the **boot camp prison.** The philosophy behind boot camp prisons is that juvenile delinquents and young offenders can be shocked into adopting conforming behaviors. This idea has its roots in the "scared-straight" programs of the 1970s in which young offenders were taken to adult prisons and verbally assaulted by inmates in the hope that they would be so afraid of going to prison that they would be "scared straight."[61] A documentary film titled *Scared Straight* became the primary exposure to this policy for many politicians and decision makers. The practice spread to many states where inmates, with good intentions, screamed at the kids and made graphic suggestions about what was going to happen to them if they continued their lives of crime and landed in prison. The appeal of the scared-straight programs was the idea that an afternoon in a prison could, by fear and intimidation, overcome years of parental neglect, poor school

boot camp prison
A short-term prison that uses military boot camp training and discipline techniques to rehabilitate offenders; often used for young offenders.

Boot camp prisons emphasize discipline, physical conditioning, and regimentation. In theory, this provides inmates with the ability to control their behavior. At this Montana boot camp prison, a new inmate is intimidated by drill instructors on intake day.
Source: Eastcott-Momatiuk

performance, involvement in a criminal lifestyle or gang activity, social disorganization, and poverty. This quick, cheap, and highly visible program seemed almost too good to be true. It was. The shock of being yelled at by inmates was discovered to wear off quickly. Scared-straight programs were a wonderful public relations tool for corrections but of little lasting value in changing the behavior of young offenders.

The continuing search for a correctional panacea through fear and intimidation has led to the creation of the boot camp prison. Patterned after the military boot camp experience, these prisons are designed to address a number of issues thought to benefit the correctional mission.

- **Identity**   Erving Goffman described how each of us has an identity kit that we use to construct how we present ourselves to the outside world. How we style our hair, the clothes we wear, the makeup we apply to our faces, and the cars we drive are all selected to communicate a certain impression. Much of our identity is based on how successfully we manage that impression.[62] The purpose of the military boot camp experience is to strip its participants of their ability to project this impression and force them to conform to rules that govern not only how they look, but also how they act. A disparate group of young people enter boot camp, and by the time they graduate, they have been transformed into soldiers. The key to this transformation is not just stripping their previous identities, but also reconstructing their senses of self as military people.

- **Discipline**   Many young offenders (actually, many young people) lack self-discipline and do not work hard at school or in their jobs and cannot compete successfully in a fast-paced society. The boot camp prison is intended to instill good work habits and discipline in these offenders. Critics of boot camp prisons contend that discipline and self-discipline are not the same thing. The boot camp prison can discipline offenders and make them conform to rigid supervision on the outside, but young offenders need self-discipline.[63] Although the military model looks attractive in forcing individuals to conform to a group ethos, a major distinction exists between the mission of the military and that of the prison. The military takes basically good young people and teaches them how to kill people or perform duties that expedite killing people. The goal of the prison is to take people who have broken the law, some of them violently, and correct this antisocial behavior.

- **Cost**   Cost is the issue that drives the boot camp prison movement. With a 90-day program, each prison bed can be used for four offenders in a year, substantially reducing costs. Given the number of offenders that states are required to handle and the great expense of the traditional prison, the boot camp concept looks like an attractive alternative, even if it does not demonstrate a lower recidivism rate.[64]

- **Punishment** Citizens do not want offenders to "get away" with breaking the law. They want to see something "done to" the prisoners, and the boot camp prison fulfills this desire in a highly visible and satisfying way.[65] The media shows "drill instructors" yelling and harassing young offenders, giving the boot camp prison an image of being a severe punishment and possibly having a deterrent effect on young people. No one can accuse the boot camp prison of being a country club. Except for its short duration, it satisfies the desires of the public that inmates serve a hard and spartan sentence devoid of frills and comforts.

Shock Probation

Another program that employs fear as a main feature is **shock probation.** In these programs, the probation officer and the judge play a confidence game on the offender. The offender receives a bogus sentence of jail or prison time, and then, after he or she has been incarcerated for 30 to 90 days, the judge converts the sentence to probation.[66] Because offenders think they are going to be imprisoned for a long time, the sudden release is presumed to encourage them to "turn over a new leaf" and to "start fresh" a new life of law-abiding and conforming behavior. There is a certain commonsense appeal to shock probation, but on closer examination, it has some flaws that make it, like scared-straight programs, a better public relations tool than corrections program. Incarcerating offenders for 30 to 90 days ruptures any stability they have. They lose their jobs, drop out of school, and sever ties with significant social networks. However, on release after their short stay, they are expected to instantly pick up the pieces of their shattered lives. The shock probation programs may also make the courts look hypocritical and duplicitous and further alienate and label the offender. When used sparingly with carefully selected offenders, this sanction has some corrections value, but for most offenders, probation or a short, planned incarceration is a better option.

Intermediate sanctions include several ways to make the sentence that stands between probation and prison more effective, more severe, and more politically popular. These sanctions are driven by a high crime rate with few traditional alternatives, a desire on the part of well-intentioned people to provide more effective community corrections services, and simple economics. If used intelligently, intermediate sanctions provide useful alternatives to incarceration at a low cost and without endangering the community.

However, intermediate sanctions are susceptible to compromise by the problem of net-widening.[67] Unless their use is monitored closely, intermediate sanctions can be diverted from their intended targets—those who require intense supervision—and used on trivial, frivolous, and petty offenders who would normally be released. On one hand, judges want to "teach a lesson" to small-time thieves or marijuana users and place them in programs that capture their attention and alter their lifestyles. On the other hand, because these programs are evaluated constantly and must demonstrate successful recidivism rates, judges tend to select those who are the most likely to complete the sanction successfully. The result is that a greater proportion of citizens are brought under social control by the state, and scarce resources are frittered away on petty offenders instead of being directed at those who pose a genuine threat to society.

JAILS

No survey of community corrections would be complete with out a discussion of local jails. Jails, a fundamental component of the corrections system, are a vital and crucial institution. Jails are connected to the law enforcement, courts, and correctional systems and serve as a major focal point in the administration of justice. Jails are

shock probation
The practice of sentencing offenders to prison, allowing them to serve a short time, and then granting them probation without their prior knowledge.

controlled by either the local sheriff or a jail administrator under the auspices of county or city administrators.[68] Control of the jail can often be a political issue because it is such an important part of the community, the local criminal justice system, and the local power structure. How the jail is placed organizationally can have a major effect on how it is funded, who is detained there, and the quality of justice.[69]

The jail serves two major functions (see Criminal Justice Reference 13.3 for a complete list of functions). First, it holds suspects who have been arrested and are awaiting disposition of their cases. Judges and prosecutors decide whether suspects can be safely released before court hearings, so many people spend short periods behind bars ranging from a few hours to a few weeks. Other offenders spend months behind bars awaiting trial or release. The factors that determine how much time is spent in jail before trial include the gravity of the offense, the offender's reputation and ties to the community, and money. The second major function of the jail is the confinement of misdemeanor offenders who have been sentenced to less than one year of incarceration. In some jurisdictions, these sentenced offenders may serve their time on weekends and live at home during the week while maintaining their employment and family ties. Sentenced offenders often act as trustees and clean the courthouse, mow the grass, shovel sidewalks, or help feed and service the inmates awaiting disposition of their cases. The local jail can also be connected to a larger local corrections system that includes work-release programs (see Figure 13-7), road crews, stockades, and local

Figure 13-7 Number of People under Jail Supervision by Confinement Status, 2006

Source: Paige M. Harrison and Jennifer C. Karberg, *Prison and Jail Inmates at Midyear 2006* (Washington, DC: U.S. Department of Justice, Bureau of Justice Statistics, 2006), 21, www.ojp.usdoj.gov/bjs/pub/pdf/pjim06.pdf.

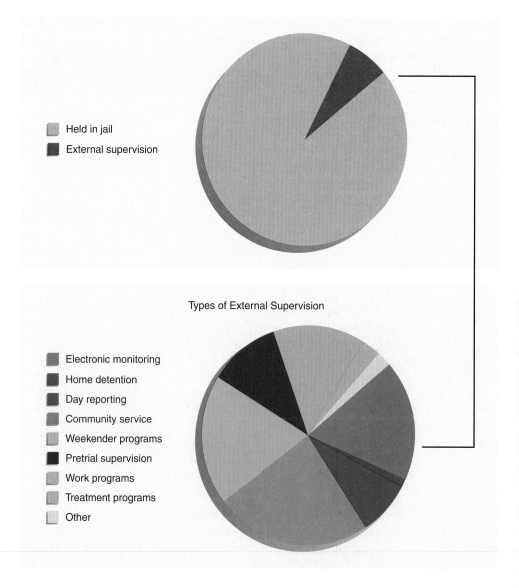

13.3   CRIMINAL JUSTICE REFERENCE

What Jails Do

- Receive individuals pending arraignment and hold them awaiting trial, conviction, or sentencing
- Hold inmates sentenced to short terms (generally less than 1 year), and readmit probation, parole, and bail-bond violators and absconders
- Temporarily detain juveniles pending transfer to juvenile authorities
- Hold mentally ill offenders pending their movement to appropriate health facilities
- Hold individuals for the military, for protective custody, for contempt, and for the courts as witnesses
- Release convicted inmates to the community on completion of sentence, and transfer inmates to federal, state, or other authorities
- House inmates for federal, state, or other authorities to alleviate crowding
- Sometimes operate community-based programs as alternatives to incarceration

Source: Paige M. Harrison and Jennifer C. Karberg, *Prison and Jail Inmates at Midyear 2002* (Washington, DC: U.S. Department of Justice, Bureau of Justice Statistics, 2003), 7, www.ojp.usdoj.gov/bjs/pub/pdf/pjim02.pdf.

probation departments. There is a wide variety of local corrections structures around the country, each with its own concerns, funding issues, and punishment philosophies.

Some see the jail as a place where society's "rabble" can be placed to improve the appearance of city streets.[70] The homeless, the drug users, the drunks, and the mentally ill are all susceptible to being swept into the jail for real or imagined infractions of the law.[71] Citizens demand that the police keep the streets safe for everyone, and those who appear to pose a security threat are quickly incarcerated in the local jail. This is not to say that jails are being used inappropriately, but rather that law enforcement is under tremendous pressure to maintain order, and jails are where those without community ties or resources often end up. Law enforcement's job would be much easier and jails less crowded if more community resources existed to help those in desperate financial or social trouble.[72]

SUMMARY

1. Community corrections are a way to punish offenders without incarceration. Society cannot afford to incarcerate everyone who violates the law.

2. Prisons achieve the goals of incapacitation, retribution, and rehabilitation in only a limited manner.

3. The four interrelated community corrections strategies are diversion programs, probation, parole, and intermediate sanctions.

4. Offenders can be sent to alternative programs at a variety of junctures in the criminal justice system. Diversion programs are popular for the minor, first-time offender.

5. Probation is a widely used sentencing alternative. Probation is a chance for offenders to go free if they agree to certain restrictions and/or requirements set by a judge.

6. Probation officers are responsible for presentence investigations, monitoring offenders on probation, and assisting them in getting help, such as treatment programs.

7. Parole is for offenders who are leaving prison after serving a partial sentence. Parolees face much of the same restrictions and requirements as those on probation.

8. The decision of when to grant parole is based on three principles: retribution, rehabilitation, and prison space. Offenders returning to society face three primary obstacles: prisonization, weakened social ties, and stigmatization.

9. Intermediate punishments are sentencing alternatives between probation and incarceration. The more notable intermediate sanctions are

intensive-supervision probation, drug testing, house arrest and electronic monitoring, fines, and boot camp prisons.

10. The boot camp is based on the military model. Boot camp prisons are an attempt to shock young offenders into adopting conforming behaviors. Another program that employs fear as a main feature is shock probation, in which the offender receives a false sentence in jail or prison, but is released on probation after 30 to 90 days of incarceration.

11. Jails are fundamental to the corrections system. Connected to the law enforcement, courts, and corrections systems, jails hold suspects awaiting disposition and misdemeanor offenders sentenced to less than a year of incarceration. The local jail may also be connected to a larger local corrections system that includes work-release programs, road crews, stockades, and local probation departments.

KEY TERMS

boot camp prison 451
good time 445
intensive-supervision
  probation 440

master status 448
meritorious time 445
presentence investigation 436

private probation 441
shock probation 453

REVIEW QUESTIONS

1. What are the three primary goals of the criminal justice system?

2. At the heart of the community corrections movement are some assumptions about the nature of crime. What are these assumptions?

3. What is the relationship between diversion and labeling theory?

4. What are the three main responsibilities of the probation/parole officer?

5. What is in the presentence investigation, and what purpose does it serve?

6. The decision concerning when to grant parole is based on what three principles?

7. What early concept of shock incarceration is the boot camp prison based on?

8. What is intensive-supervision probation?

9. Why are cost-of-supervision and other criminal justice–related fees controversial?

10. What two major functions do jails serve?

SUGGESTED FURTHER READING

Austin, James, and John Irwin. *It's about Time: America's Imprisonment Binge*. 3rd ed. Belmont, CA: Wadsworth, 2001.

Clear, Todd R., and Harry Dammer. *The Offender in the Community*. Belmont, CA: Wadsworth, 2000.

Cullen, Francis T., and Karen Gilbert. *Reaffirming Rehabilitation*. Cincinnati, OH: Anderson, 1982.

Morris, Norval, and Michael Tonry. *Between Prison and Probation: Intermediate Punishments in a Rational Sentencing System*. New York: Oxford University Press, 1991.

National Research Council, *Parole, Desistance from Crime, and Community Integration*. Committee on Community Supervision and Desistance from Crime, Committee on Law and Justice, Division of Behavioral and Social Sciences and Education. Washington, DC: National Academies Press, 2007.

Walters, Scott T., Michael D. Clark, Ray Grigerich, and Melissa Meltzer. *Motivating Offenders to Change: A Guide for Probation and Parole*. Washington, DC: National Institute of Corrections, 2007.

ENDNOTES

1. Graeme Newman, *Just and Painful: A Case for the Corporal Punishment of Criminals* (New York: Macmillan, 1983).

2. Belinda Rodgers McCarthy, Bernard J. McCarthy Jr., and Matthew C. Leone, *Community-Based Corrections*, 4th ed. (Belmont, CA: Wadsworth, 2001).

3. Jane Browning, "Coming to Terms with Prison Growth," *Corrections Today* 69 (October 2007): 18–19.

4. We are not suggesting that everyone is a criminal, but rather that almost all of us have committed crimes for which we could have been brought into the criminal justice system and punished with a period of incarceration. Our drug use, DUI, and income tax creativity has largely gone undiscovered, and hence we maintain our freedom and conventional lifestyles.

5. This is especially true of the federal prisons that incarcerate white-collar offenders. Although the prisons are still uncomfortable circumstances, the media has dubbed them "Club Fed," giving federal prison a somewhat distorted view. See Jennifer Senior, "You've Got Jail," New York Metro.com, www.newyorkmetro.com/nymetro/news/crimelaw/features/6228/.

6. John Irwin, *Prisons in Turmoil* (Boston: Little, Brown, 1980).

7. Sasha Adamsky, "When They Got Out," Atlantic Online, June 1999, www.theatlantic.com/issues/99jun/9906prisoners.htm.

8. Francis T. Cullen and Karen E. Gilbert, *Reaffirming Rehabilitation* (Cincinnati, OH: Anderson, 1982).

9. Eric W. Hickey, *Serial Murderers and Their Victims*, 3rd ed. (Belmont, CA: Wadsworth, 2002). See Hickey's profile of Henry Lee Lucas on p. 194.

10. Todd R. Clear and Harry R. Dammer, *The Offender in the Community* (Belmont, CA: Wadsworth, 2003), 226.

11. Thomas G. Blomberg, "Diversion and Social Control," *Journal of Criminal Law and Criminology* 68 (1977): 274–282.

12. Jeffrey Draine, Amy Blank Wilson, and Wendy Pogorzelski, "Limitations and Potential in Current Research on Services for People with Mental Illness in the Criminal Justice System," *Journal of Offender Rehabilitation* 45 (July 2007): 159–177.

13. Kristie A. Blevins, Francis T. Cullen, and Jody L. Sundt, "The Correctional Orientation of 'Child Savers': Support for Rehabilitation and Custody among Juvenile Correctional Workers," *Journal of Offender Rehabilitation* 45 (July 2007): 47–83.

14. James Austin and Barry Krisberg, "Wider, Stronger, and Different Nets: The Dialectics of Criminal Justice Reform," *Journal of Research in Crime and Delinquency* 18 (1981): 165–196.

15. Kathy G. Padgett, William D. Bales, and Thomas G. Blomberg, "Under Surveillance: An Empirical Test of the Effectiveness and Consequences of Electronic Monitoring," *Criminology and Public Policy* 5 (February 2006): 61–91.

16. Thomas G. Blomberg and Karol Lucken, "Stacking the Deck by Piling Up Sanctions: Is Intermediate Punishment Destined to Fail?" *Howard Journal of Criminal Justice* 33, no. 1 (1994): 62–80.

17. Heather Barklage, Dane Miller, and Gene Bonham, "Probation Conditions versus Probation Officer Directives: Where the Twain Shall Meet," *Federal Probation* 70, no. 3 (December 2006): 37–41.

18. Ricky N. Bluthenthal et al., "Perspectives on Therapeutic Treatment from Adolescent Probationers," *Journal of Psychoactive Drugs* 38 (December 2006): 461–471.

19. Douglas Thomson, "How Plea Bargaining Shapes Intensive Probation Supervision," *Crime and Delinquency* 36 (1990): 146.

20. Dane C. Miller, Richard D. Sluder, and J. Dennis Laster, "Can Probation Be Revoked When Probationers Do Not Willfully Violate the Terms or Conditions of Probation?" *Federal Probation* 63, no. 1 (June 1999): 23.

21. John Rosecrance, "Maintaining the Myth of Individualized Justice: Probation, Presentence Reports," *Justice Quarterly* 5 (1988): 235–236.

22. David Sudnow, "Normal Crimes: Sociological Features of the Penal Code in a Public Defender Office," *Social Problems* 12 (1965): 255–276.

23. Marilyn West, "A Few Words about Interviewing in Presentence Investigations," in *Correctional Assessment, Casework, and Counseling*, 3rd ed., ed. Anthony Walsh (Lanham, MD: American Correctional Association).

24. Anthony Walsh, ed., *Correctional Assessment, Casework, and Counseling*, 3rd ed. (Lanham, MD: American Correction Association), 106.

25. Anthony Walsh, "The Role of the Probation Officer in the Sentencing Process: Independent Professional or Judicial Hack?" *Criminal Justice and Behavior* 12 (1985): 289–303.

26. Fay Honey Knapp, "Northwest Treatment Associates: A Comprehensive Community-Based-Evaluation-and-Treatment Program for Adult Sex Offenders," in *Correctional Counseling and Treatment*, 4th ed., ed. Peter C. Kratcoski (Prospect Heights, IL: Waveland Press, 2000), 617–633. For instance, Knapp reported, "One

of the most creative things we do with flashers who exhibit in their cars is to have them put their names on the front, back, and sides of the car" (p. 624).

27. Fay S. Taxman, "Dealing with Technical Violations," *Corrections Today* 57 (1995): 46–53.

28. Nancy Rodriguez and Vincent J. Webb, "Probation Violations, Revocations, and Imprisonment," *Criminal Justice Policy Review* 18 (March 2007): 3–30.

29. Jeffrey J. Shook and Rosemary C. Sarri, "Structured Decision Making in Juvenile Justice: Judges' and Probation Officers' Perceptions and Use," *Children and Youth Services Review* 29 (October 2007): 1335–1351.

30. Ibid.

31. R. V. Del Carmen and J. A. Pilant, "The Scope of Judicial Immunity for Probation and Parole Officers," *Perspectives* (American Probation and Parole Association) (Summer 1994): 14–21.

32. Christine S. Schloss and Leanne F. Alarid, "Standards in the Privatization of Probation Services," *Criminal Justice Review* 32 (2007): 233–245.

33. Ibid.

34. Ibid.

35. Celia Perry, Justine Sharrock, and Michael Mechanic, "Probation for Profit," *Mother Jones* (July 2008): 57–58.

36. Ibid.

37. Clear and Dammer, *Offender in the Community*, 182–183.

38. Thomas P. Bonczar, *Characteristics of State Parole Supervising Agencies, 2006* (Washington, DC: U.S. Department of Justice, Bureau of Justice Statistics, 2008), 1–2, www.ojp.usdoj.gov/bjs/pub/pdf/cspsa06.pdf.

39. Melinda D. Schlager and Kelly Robbins, "Does Parole Work?— Revisited: Reframing the Discussion of the Impact of Postprison Supervision on Offender Outcome," *Prison Journal* 88 (June 2008): 234–251.

40. Irwin, *Prisons in Turmoil*.

41. Catherine Cuellar, "Investing in Second Chances: An Innovative Program Helps Prison Inmates Make a Fresh Start—and a Business Plan," *Sojourners Magazine* 37 (July 2008): 20–24.

42. Robert C. Davis and Carrie Mulford, "Victim Rights and New Remedies: Finally Getting Victims Their Due," *Journal of Contemporary Criminal Justice* 24 (May 2008): 198–208.

43. In some states, such as Kentucky, violent offenders must serve 85 percent of their sentences.

44. Donald Clemmer, "The Prison Community," in *Correctional Contexts: Contemporary and Classical Readings*, 2nd ed., eds. Edward J. Latessa et al. (Los Angeles: Roxbury, 2001), 83–87.

45. Clear and Dammer, *Offender in the Community*, 213–214.

46. Erving Goffman, *Stigma: Notes on the Management of Spoiled Identity* (Englewood Cliffs, NJ: Prentice Hall, 1963), 4.

47. D. Stanley Eitzen and Maxine Baca Zinn, *Social Problems*, 6th ed. (Boston: Allyn & Bacon, 1992), 305.

48. Schlager and Robbins, "Does Parole Work?"

49. Norval Morris and Michael Tonry, *Between Prison and Probation: Intermediate Punishments in a Rational Sentencing System* (New York: Oxford University Press, 1990).

50. Joan Petersilia, "Conditions That Permit Intensive Supervision Programs to Survive," *Crime and Delinquency* 36 (1990): 126–145.

51. Christopher T. Lowenkamp et al., "Adhering to the Risk and Need Principles: Does It Matter for Supervision-Based Programs?" *Federal Probation* 70, no. 3, (December 2006), www.uscourts.gov/fedprob/December_2006/adhering.html.

52. Beau Kilmer, "Does Parolee Drug Testing Influence Employment and Education Outcomes? Evidence from a Randomized Experiment with Noncompliance," *Journal of Quantitative Criminology* 24 (March 2008): 93–123.

53. P. J. Hofer and B. S. Meierhoefer, *Home Confinement: An Evolving Sanction in the Federal Criminal Justice System* (Washington, DC: Federal Judicial Center, 1987).

54. Padgett, Bales, and Blomberg, "Under Surveillance."

55. A. K. Schmidt, "Electronic Monitors: Realistically, What Can Be Expected?" *Federal Probation* 55, no. 2 (1991): 47–53.

56. See "Microchips: The New Surrogate Parents?" FoxNews.com, www.foxnews.com/story/0,2933,58945,00.html; "What Are Those Microchips That People Put in Their Dogs?" Howstuffworks.com, http://science.howstuffworks.com/question690.htm.

57. Brad Heath, "Electronic Monitoring Now Includes Sweat Sniffers, Screeching Black Boxes," *USA Today*, November 6, 2006.

58. Diana Marszalek, "Jail and Fines Proposed for Theft of Recyclables," *New York Times*, May 25, 2008, 2.

59. Sally Hillsman, Barry Mahoney, George Cole, and Bernard Auchter, *Fines as Criminal Sanctions* (Washington, DC: National Institute of Justice, 1987).

60. Dale Parent, *Recovering Correctional Costs Through Offender Fees* (Washington, DC: National Institute of Justice, 1990).

61. James O. Finckenauer, *Scared Straight and the Panacea Phenomenon* (Englewood Cliffs, NJ: Prentice Hall, 1982).

62. Roberta C. Cronin, *Boot Camp Prisons for Adult and Juvenile Offenders: Overview and Update* (Washington, DC: U.S. Government Printing Office, 1994).

63. Erving Goffman, *The Presentation of Self in Everyday Life* (Garden City, NY: Doubleday, 1959).

64. John R. Fuller, *Criminal Justice: A Peacemaking Perspective* (Boston: Allyn & Bacon, 1998), 136–139.

65. James Austin and John Irwin, *It's about Time: America's Imprisonment Binge*, 3rd ed. (Belmont, CA: Wadsworth, 2001), 167–169.

66. Clear and Dammer, *Offender in the Community*, 255–256.

67. Dale K. Sechrest, "Prison 'Boot Camps' Do Not Measure Up," *Federal Probation* 53, no. 3 (1989): 15–20.

68. Brandon K. Applegate and Alicia H. Sitren, "The Jail and the Community: Comparing Jails in Rural and Urban Contexts," *Prison Journal* 88 (June 2008): 252–269.

69. Thomas G. Blomberg, "Beyond Metaphors: Penal Reform as Net-Widening," in *Punishment and Social Control*, eds. Thomas G. Blomberg and Stanley Cohen (New York: Aldine de Gruyter, 1995): 45–61.

70. Stan C. Proband, "Jail Populations Up—Racial Disproportions Worse," *Overcrowded Times* 4, no. 4 (1993): 4.

71. John Irwin, *The Jail: Managing the Underclass in American Society* (Berkeley: University of California Press, 1985).

72. Michael Welch, "Social Junk, Social Dynamite and the Rabble: Persons with AIDS in Jail," *American Journal of Criminal Justice* 14, no. 1 (1989): 135–147.

CHAPTER 14

Juvenile Delinquency and Juvenile Justice

Objectives

1. Understand why the modern criminal justice system treats juvenile delinquents differently than it treats adult criminal offenders.

2. Understand the position and role of children in pre-20th-century times.

3. Discuss the concept of *parens patriae*.

4. Understand the problems of the child-saving movement.

5. Describe the reforms in juvenile justice at the beginning of the 20th century.

6. Discuss the societal issues that can cause children to come in contact with the juvenile justice system.

7. Describe the general structure of the juvenile justice system.

 One of the most stable features of crime is that a great deal of it is committed by youths. There are a number of reasons for this that we will discuss in this chapter. However, we should always keep in mind that even though many young people break the law, they desist once they get older and become more legitimately involved in society. In many ways crime is a young person's game.

Although offenses such as embezzlement, insider trading on stocks, and corporate malfeasance are usually committed by older offenders, much of the crime problem, especially street crime, is more likely to involve juveniles.[1] There are several commonsense reasons for the historically stable relationship between youth and crime. We will not dwell on them here—the subject is a university course in its own right—but this chapter will highlight some of the themes of youth crime. The modern criminal justice system even has a legal term for a child who has broken the law: **juvenile delinquent.** That the term is a modern invention is important when considering the history of children. The concept of juvenile delinquency did not exist before the 20th century. As discussed later in this chapter, children who broke the law in earlier times were punished as adults or turned over to their parents for discipline. Of course, these days, juvenile delinquents are handled differently from adult offenders. It is not only a matter of degree, but rather involves a completely different system with its own philosophy, courts, and correctional system.[2] In fact, the juvenile justice system is a parallel, and sometimes competing, system of justice.

Much of the dissatisfaction that many Americans have with the justice system is caused by the perceived liberal tendencies of the juvenile justice system. However, although the juvenile justice system is based on a progressive philosophy, the handling of juvenile delinquents is often punitive.[3] One of the themes in this chapter is that the juvenile justice system has changed its focus from one of rehabilitation to one of deterrence and punishment. This should not be surprising given the public's concern for rising crime rates, drug abuse, and gang violence. The problems youths experience today are different from those of a generation ago and require new ways of addressing crime and deviance. Although the juvenile justice system is not solely to blame for the problems of young people, it is responsible for addressing issues that have not been resolved by families, schools, and the community. Therefore, this chapter will illustrate both the promise and the problems of the juvenile justice system, with consideration of how it contrasts with the criminal justice system.

CHILDHOOD AND THE LAW

The concept of childhood is relatively new. In contemporary times, the age of an individual dictates the rights and responsibilities granted by society. In the past, many societies did not make such differentiations based on age, and everyone was more or less treated in a similar manner. The transition from child to adolescent and from adolescent to adult was much more abrupt and was not assisted by schools, the media, or family traditions.

The historical treatment of children is interesting because there is still some debate as to whether young people were always "treated as children" or whether they were treated as little adults.[4] For instance, the French social historian Philippe Ariès argued that in medieval times children were treated as adults from the time they were toddlers. Although this view of European medieval childhood has been revised (medieval children, in fact, did have childhoods that we would recognize as true childhoods, and medieval parents were just as delighted by small children as we are now), young people in those societies quickly learned to pull their weight and were expected to act and behave in a responsible manner from an early age. By today's standards, the concept of adolescence that we call "teenage" did not exist. Young men were quickly apprenticed into the workforce, and young women were often married into another family. In many societies, young men went to war at an early age and were expected to carry an adult's burden before they were fully developed physically, emotionally, and financially.

Before the creation of a separate juvenile justice system, parents whose children were arrested had little recourse. Placing children in the adult criminal justice system often meant they would be victimized by older offenders. In this 19th-century drawing, a mother pleads with police officers to release her son.
Source: CORBIS-NY

How did medieval laws treat children? This is difficult to answer because a great deal of variation existed. Generally, the authority for dealing with children resided with the parents, primarily the father, and not the state. In his book *Medieval Children*, Nicholas Orme states:

> The topic of children and the law, then, was a complicated one. It differed according to status, gender, and property. There was no single age of responsibility or majority. . . . Children . . . might suffer imprisonment, and be executed from about the age of ten in exceptional cases. The formal demarcations between childhood and adulthood were often placed lower than they are today, between the ages of twelve and fifteen.[5]

As previously mentioned, when a child broke the law, the courts held the parent accountable rather than the youth. This may seem like a good deal for the child, but we must remember that the child was considered the responsibility and property of the parent, and the state was powerless to intervene in the youth's discipline and up-bringing. So although the youth did not answer to the law, he or she did answer to the father, who wielded unlimited authority to punish the child as brutally as he wished. Thus, although the state did not recognize children as responsible, parents were not hindered by child welfare laws in how they disciplined their children.

Gradually, the status of the child began to improve in many societies. One factor was the increased availability of education. No longer only for the rich, schools became a major socializing factor.[6] Associated with schools was the apprenticeship movement, in which young people were placed in the care of craftsmen who taught them trades. This relationship was recognized by the law, and apprenticed youths were committed to work for their employers until age 21. For some youths, however, the apprenticeship lasted too long, and they often struck out on their own before completing their obligations. For instance, Benjamin Franklin was apprenticed to his brother to learn printing skills, but ran away from Boston to Pennsylvania because his brother treated him badly and had fewer skills as a printer.[7]

In 19th-century England, poor children were put to work at an early age. Here, children work in a forge in deplorable working conditions.

Source: Getty Images Inc.—Hulton Archive Photos

poor laws

Seventeenth-century laws that turned over vagrants and abandoned children to landowners or shopkeepers as indentured servants.

chancery court

"Court of equity." In England, these were established, in part, to assist when common law courts failed to resolve a case. These courts were favorable to vulnerable individuals, especially children.

parens patriae

Latin for "father of the country." Refers to the philosophy that the government is the ultimate guardian of all children or disabled adults.

Another factor that helped the status of children in England was the establishment of the **poor laws** in the 16th century. Passed partly as a means of social control aimed at ridding the streets of destitute and homeless children, poor laws allowed for the placement of these children in the homes of the wealthy or in the shops of merchants as servants and workers. Thus, the youths learned a trade and were looked after in safe housing with adequate food rather than having to beg on the street. Those who were not placed in homes might have found themselves in a poorhouse or workhouse where they were required to work. Although this was a less attractive alternative, for the most part, these youths were separated from adult inmates and protected to a degree.[8]

A third factor in the gradual change in the legal status of children in England was the establishment of **chancery courts.** Orphans were appointed guardians to protect their inheritance rights until they reached the age of majority and could legally take care of their own affairs. The concept of *parens patriae* was established whereby the king could intervene in the interests of children. The term means "father of the country," but has come to refer to the right of the king (government) to take a protective role in overseeing children's welfare.[9] This important principle allows modern courts to take children away from unfit parents and to establish standards for education and welfare.

Juveniles in the Early United States

In colonial America, little distinction was made between the offenses committed by adults and those committed by children. Certainly no special mechanism was set up to handle juvenile delinquents. Parents were responsible for the actions of their children, and when those actions became especially egregious, the community used the same punishments for young people as it did for adults.[10] Corporal punishments and public shaming techniques, such as confinement in stocks, were the primary means of social control for both adults and children. In some cases, banishment from the community or even capital punishment was used. The cases did not have to be especially serious:

> Children over the age of seven were subject to the criminal law. In some colonies, children who disobeyed their parents or stole a silver spoon from their masters received the death penalty. Cases are rare, but there have been a few examples of death. As late as 1828, in New Jersey, a boy of 13 was hanged for an offense committed when he was 12.[11]

In some colonies, such as Virginia, the exploitation of children was used to remedy periodic labor shortages. According to Barry Krisberg and James Austin, contractors in England promised young people wealth and happiness in the New World and signed them to commitments as **indentured servants.** These contracts were then sold to New World landowners, and the young people found themselves obligated to years of indentured work on large plantations with little hope of self-improvement. Some youths were kidnapped or were victims of contractual fraud. Orphans were taken from English poorhouses and shipped to the colonies to work as indentured servants. Although some did eventually achieve a viable lifestyle, many others found the arrangement little more than severe punishment for being young, destitute, and illiterate. Furthermore, according to Krisberg and Austin, American Indian children were kidnapped and brought into colonist households as servants and indoctrinated with the colonists' language, religion, and customs. Of course, one of the most deplorable exploitations of children happened when African children were brought to the United States as part of the slave trade.[12]

The Industrial Revolution of the late 18th century demanded even more from children. Because the factories required a steady stream of young and immigrant workers, little attention was focused on the social welfare of those who were brought into the labor force. In fact, many families depended on the labor of their children for their most basic needs, and the idea of child welfare was tied to his or her economic viability. Families had large numbers of children to work on the farm and contribute to the family's upkeep. Before modern birth control and a low infant mortality rate, the American family was much larger than it is today.

The influx of immigrants in the 19th century brought some fundamental changes in the concept of children and childhood. Waves of European immigrants flooded into the cities, each new wave challenging the customs, ideas, and practices of the ones that had come before. As immigrant adults filled the factories, their children presented challenges to the community in terms of socialization, delinquency, and schooling. New institutions were created to deal with this challenge of the "dangerous classes."[13] (See Criminal Justice Reference 14.1 for a timeline of juvenile justice in the United States.)

indentured servant
From the 17th to 19th centuries, a person who came to the American colonies/United States and was made to work for a period of time, usually seven years.

Houses of Refuge

The first house of refuge was established in New York City in 1825. Over the next 60 years, states designed similar types of institutions to correct the wayward habits of deviant young people. Houses of refuge were considered a major reform at the time, but the public perception and the stark reality of these institutions were often at odds. Intended as a safe haven from the life of the streets and from abusive or neglectful parents, houses of refuge were often dangerous places where older children preyed on younger children. The houses were operated by religious people who had good intentions but were also prejudiced and biased. Girls were considered sexually promiscuous, and black youths of both sexes were treated less favorably than white youths. Although the primary mission of the houses was to provide education and training for delinquent and neglected youth, they often employed the practice of "placing out," in which boys were sent to work on farms or on dangerous sea vessels, and girls were sent into the homes of respectable ladies to serve and learn. At times, groups of children were placed on "orphan trains" (even though many were not actually orphans) and sent west to frontier families to work on their farms and ranches.[14] Life could be difficult for many of these children, and they were often exploited for their labor or their sexuality. Children would run away from their newly assigned homes and duties and would gather in large cities, where they would make a living based on petty crime.

The houses of refuge had the goal of improving the lives of impoverished children, but there was an underlying concern, as well, with the socialization of immigrant children. Workers in houses of refuge failed to understand the variety of

14.1   CRIMINAL JUSTICE REFERENCE

Juvenile Justice in the United States

- *Colonial era–early 19th century:* Juveniles are tried as adults and court records are open to the public. Public shaming is common and convicted offenders are often forced to wear the initial letters of their offenses around their necks or sewn to their clothes (such as a T for thief).
- *1828:* James Guild, age 12, is hanged for killing a woman.
- *1899:* After years of calls for a separate justice system for children, Illinois establishes the first juvenile court system.
- *1925:* Forty-six of the 48 states have established a juvenile court or juvenile probation program.
- *1966–1967:* The U.S. Supreme Court holds, in *Kent v. United States* and *In re Gault*, that due process applies to juvenile court proceedings.

- *1994:* Illinois requires courts to make public the addresses of juveniles convicted of serious felonies.
- *1994:* The federal omnibus crime law requires the release of some juvenile-record information.
- *1995:* According to the *GAO Report,* 44 states and the District of Columbia facilitate the transfer of juveniles to adult courts.
- *1995:* Legislatures in more than 12 states open juvenile records to schools, victims, state agencies, and others. Legislatures in 10 states permit public access to juvenile records in specific circumstances.

Source: Privacy and Juvenile Justice Records: A Mid-Decade Status Report, (Washington, DC: U.S. Department of Justice, Bureau of Justice Statistics, 1997), 33–34, www.ojp.usdoj. gov/bjs/pub/pdf/pjjr.pdf.

Houses of refuge had the task of helping poor children. They also helped socialize immigrant children into the language and customs of the United States. Pictured here are scenes from the New York House of Refuge on Randall's Island, 1868.

Source: CORBIS-NY

HOUSE OF REFUGE, RANDALL'S ISLAND, NEW YORK.

cultures brought by immigrant families. They considered new customs and ideas to be deviant and sought to "rescue" the children. Unfortunately, the houses of refuge not only systematically failed to reform wayward children, but they also were such dangerous and substandard institutions that by the end of the 19th century they were abandoned as newer reforms were sought.[15]

Juvenile Court

Turning delinquent and neglected youths over to the well-meaning individuals who ran the houses of refuge eventually came to be considered ineffective and sometimes counterproductive. Clearly, the criminal law had failed to meet the needs of children and families. A new reform, in which the responsibility for children's welfare was removed from the adult criminal court, began at the dawn of the 20th century. In 1899, the first juvenile court was established in Cook County, Illinois, with the mandate to process cases of children between ages 8 and 17.

The social forces that led to the development of the juvenile court were entwined with the rapid social changes happening in the United States and the desire of many to preserve established values. Thus, the term *child savers* was attached to the civic-minded and middle-class women who extended their maternal ideas about the innocence of children into public services and carved out the role of the social worker in the juvenile court.[16] These reformers, according to C. Wright Mills, were primarily white, middle-class, Protestant, rural Americans who believed that the problems of the cities were caused by social disorganization.[17] By extending the *parens patriae* philosophy, in which the state assumes the ultimate responsibility for the welfare of children, the juvenile court stripped young people of their legal rights (many of which have since been restored) and operated in what the reformers believed was the best interests of the child. This philosophy led to the development of what are today the major differences between the modern criminal court and the juvenile court:

- **Focus on rehabilitation**   The juvenile court operates on the idea that antisocial children can be redeemed. Rehabilitation instead of punishment is the primary concern. Juveniles are not subject to capital punishment, and instead of a sentence, the case receives a disposition. (In 2005, the U.S. Supreme Court decided in *Roper* v. *Simmons* that offenders who were younger than 18 at the time of their offenses cannot be executed.) At the beginning of the reform movement, many believed that by keeping juveniles out of jails and reform schools, they would not be subjected to further pressures and temptations to break the law. Additionally, there was a belief that officials knew how to change the behavior of delinquent youth. It was assumed that antisocial behavior was a result of individual deficiencies and that people could be "treated" and thus cured of their propensity for this behavior.

- **Informal hearing**   The juvenile case is conducted as a **hearing** instead of a trial. The adversarial process is absent, and the court workers and judge determine how to best serve the needs of the child by correcting or counteracting social deficiencies such as inadequate schooling, poverty, poor neighborhoods, faulty parenting, and alcohol abuse.

- **Individualized justice**   Each juvenile case is treated according to its own merits. There is little effort to produce uniform dispositions because each child has a different set of problems and a different network of social support. The idea is to craft the disposition to the child instead of the offense. This focus on individualized justice ignores underlying structural issues of poverty, racism, and gender inequities. Then again, it allows society to focus on the presumed individual deficiencies of children and not address the underlying social fabric of the community.

- **Private hearings**   Juvenile hearings are closed to the public and the press, and after a period of time, juvenile court records are expunged. Deviant behavior committed as a juvenile is not to be counted against the offender when he or she becomes an adult.

The juvenile court has its critics. Its basis, the child-saving movement, which attempted to work for the best interests of young people, has been criticized on a

hearing
A session that takes place without a jury before a judge or magistrate in which evidence and/or arguments are presented to determine some factual or legal issue.

number of grounds. Anthony Platt, in his examination of the history of the juvenile court, was especially harsh in his comments when he said the child savers should not be considered libertarians or humanists for the following reasons:

1. Their reforms did not herald a new system of justice but rather expedited traditional policies that had been informally developing during the 19th century.

2. They implicitly assumed the "natural" dependence of adolescents and created a special court to impose sanctions on premature independence and behavior "unbecoming" to youth.

3. Their attitudes toward delinquent youth were largely paternalistic and romantic, but their commands were backed by force. They trusted in the benevolence of government and similarly assumed a harmony of interest between delinquents and agencies of social control.

4. They promoted correctional programs requiring longer terms of imprisonment, long hours of labor and militaristic discipline, and the inculcation of middle-class values and lower-class skills.[18]

Widespread dissatisfaction with the juvenile courts led to a number of reforms during the 20th century. Foremost among these reforms was the move to restore some of the legal rights that had been taken from juveniles with the benign intention of doing what was best for them. Because of a number of concerns, such as law enforcement officers misleading juveniles about the consequences of admitting to offenses, perfunctory court hearings that failed to adequately consider the interests of the child, reform schools that were little better than prisons, and the public's overall impression that the juvenile justice system fostered more crime than it prevented, the courts moved to reinstate some of the **due-process rights** of children. In a number of cases, such as *Kent* v. *United States* (1966), *In re Gault* (1967), *In re Winship* (1970), *McKeiver* v. *Pennsylvania* (1971), and *Breed* v. *Jones* (1975), the courts provided that juveniles have the rights to be given notice of charges, a lawyer to represent their interests, the ability to confront and cross-examine witnesses, and the privilege against self-incrimination (see Case in Point 14.1 for *Winship* and *Gault*). Another reform that took root in the 1960s and 1970s was the move to deinstitutionalize delinquent and neglected children. Rather than incarcerate youths in prisonlike reform or training schools, community correctional practices such as foster homes, halfway houses, and extended probation-like supervision were employed.[19]

Linked to the move to deinstitutionalize juveniles were efforts to divert them from the justice system. By referring youths to programs that addressed their educational, counseling, and drug treatment needs, diversion sought to avoid contact between casual offenders and more seriously troubled youngsters. Based on labeling theory (discussed in Chapter 3), diversion programs attempted to prevent young offenders from thinking of themselves as criminals by immersing them in conventional schools, activities, and close contact with their families.[20]

CHILDREN AND SOCIETY

Each new generation of children has slightly different opportunities and faces different challenges and dangers than prior generations.[21] Although adolescence has always been a time of experimentation and boundary testing, the consequences of some of this deviant behavior today is more dangerous and is met with stiffer sanctions. Some of the most pressing and intractable issues facing young people today include the following:

- **Violence**   Violence has always been a feature of human societies, but it is particularly pervasive in U.S. culture today. Juveniles can be expected to commit a substantial portion of violence. Sociologist Elijah Anderson, in his acclaimed book *Code of the Street: Decency, Violence, and the Moral Life of the Inner City*, contended

due-process rights
Guarantees by the Fifth, Sixth, and Fourteenth Amendments of the U.S. Constitution establishing legal procedures that recognize the protection of an individual's life, liberty, and property.

14.1   CASE IN POINT

IN RE WINSHIP

THE CASE

In re Winship, 397 U.S. 358, 90 S.Ct. 1068 (1970)

THE POINT

If incarceration or loss of freedom is possible, a case against a juvenile must be proved beyond a reasonable doubt.

Twelve-year-old Samuel Winship was accused of entering a locker and stealing $112 from a woman's purse in New York City in 1967. He was charged as a juvenile delinquent because, according to the New York Family Court Act, if the theft had been committed by an adult, it would have constituted larceny. The act defined a juvenile delinquent as "a person over seven and less than 16 years of age who does any act, which if done by an adult, would constitute a crime."

During the stage in which Winship was determined to be a delinquent, the judge admitted that the prosecution might have been unable to prove Winship guilty beyond a reasonable doubt. However, the judge rejected Winship's contention that the Fourteenth Amendment required such proof, even in such adjudication stages. The question was whether proof beyond a reasonable doubt of an act—which if committed by an adult would be considered a criminal offense—was required to establish Winship as a juvenile delinquent.

Winship was adjudicated delinquent and ordered to a training school for at least 18 months up to a maximum of six years, until he reached his 18th birthday. The Supreme Court eventually heard Winship's appeal and reversed the ruling because the reasonable-doubt standard had not been considered in a case in which the defendant was subject to incarceration or loss of freedom.

IN RE GAULT

THE CASE

In re Gault, 387 U.S. 1, 87 S.Ct. 1428 (1967)

THE POINT

Juveniles' right to an attorney and the right to confront accusers and protection from self-incrimination are established.

In 1964, 15-year-old Gerald Gault and another boy were accused of making an obscene telephone call to a female neighbor. Gault was arrested without the knowledge of his parents, who were both at work, and questioned by police at the jail. He was held in detention for four or five days, then released to his parents. In the court proceedings, Gault was not allowed to cross-examine his accuser, who was never present, or to testify on his own behalf, nor was he advised of his rights. He was sentenced to the Arizona State Industrial School until he was 21. No appeal was permitted in juvenile cases in Arizona at that time. In 1967 the Supreme Court reversed the decision on appeal and established that juveniles have a right to an attorney, as well as the right to confront accusers and protection from self-incrimination.

---

that the willingness to use violence must be displayed in some neighborhoods in order to be respected. Those who do not understand or employ the code of violence are likely to become victims of young people who see violence as their only method of achieving respect and self-esteem.[22] When the community is plagued by gang activity, the violence becomes even more deadly, with drive-by shootings and gang fights making death likely.[23] The streets are not the only violent threat to young people, however. As the violence at Colorado's Columbine High School in 1999 so graphically demonstrated, children are at risk in school. In reaction to Columbine and other high-profile school shootings, all schools now have specific contingency plans for dealing with disturbed students, staff members, or outside individuals who bring weapons to campus.[24]

- **Alcohol and drug problems**   Drinking a few beers and smoking some marijuana are considered normal rites of passage for young people in many circles; however, the criminal justice system has been encouraged to severely punish these offenses as a way of deterring young people from abusing harder drugs. With the availability of cocaine (particularly crack cocaine), heroin, methamphetamines,

Reform schools were harsh environments where children were forced to grow up early. The faces in this picture, taken at a London reform school in 1850, show that youths were forced to take life seriously at a young age.

Source: CORBIS-NY

Ecstasy, and performance-enhancing steroids, the drug scene has become more dangerous.[25] Additionally, because of the well-intentioned war on drugs, the violence associated with the drug trade has escalated to the point that a drug deal might get one killed more quickly than the drug itself. The problems of drug and alcohol addiction are significant, and the treatment resources are often inadequate.[26] Consequently, society's response to the drug problem often is encapsulated in Nancy Reagan's famous 1980s "Just Say No!" antidrug campaign in which abstinence was the preferred and only message given to young people.[27]

- **Sexuality and sex abuse**   Society gives children mixed messages about sexuality. Our media are saturated with messages of sexuality in both entertainment and advertising, much of it directed at teenagers, yet we restrict the pleasures and responsibilities of sex to adults.[28] In spite of the prohibition of sex for children, we find they are often victimized by adults, even family members.[29] It is little wonder that sexuality is one of the primary obstacles young people have in developing a healthy self-concept. Because we prohibit young people from engaging in sexual relations and limit the amount of education we make available to them on responsible ways to engage in sex, we are finding that they are woefully ignorant of the dangers posed by HIV and other sexually transmitted diseases.[30] Consequently, children often do not seek medical treatment for sex-associated problems, such as a pregnancy, until it is too late. On many different levels, then, children and teenagers are victims of sex-related crimes and society's response to the sexuality of children.[31]

- **Runaway and kidnapped children**   Family stress causes a number of children to lose their homes and families. For a variety of reasons, many children leave home at an early age and attempt to make their own way in the world. Sometimes this means taking a bus to a big city where adult predators called "chicken hawks" sometimes pick them up and introduce them to a life of prostitution and drug abuse.[32] Other children live on the streets and panhandle for a living or flirt with criminal lifestyles involving larceny, burglary, and drug sales. Without the guidance of parents or responsible guardians, these children miss valuable schooling, do not learn occupational skills and good working habits, and grow up to be criminals or vagabonds.[33] Other children are kidnapped from

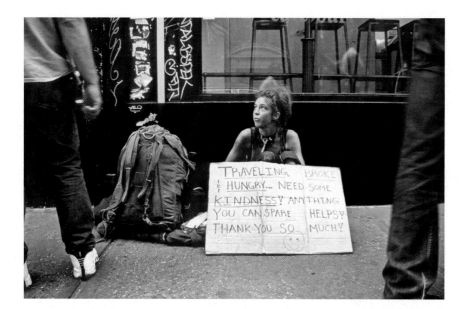

Runaway homeless children and teenagers are vulnerable to a host of dangers.

Source: Jeffrey Greenberg/The Image Works

their homes by a parent engaged in a nasty separation or divorce. Taken to another state, forced to use a different name, and completely cut off from the parent who was awarded legal custody, these children have their lives ripped apart by a parent who believes he or she is doing the right thing.

- **Anomie and nihilism**   As adolescents bridge the span of rights and responsibilities between childhood and adult society, they are often confused about their place in the world. This is an expected, and in many ways positive, feature of adolescence. As they try on new roles and discard others, teenagers experiment with peer groups, families, and society. However, it can also be a time of great risk. Sometimes teenagers take their newfound freedoms to extremes, and in the quest to try something different, make mistakes with irrevocable consequences. On the more innocent end of this concern is body modification: tattoos and body piercing. As a way of rebelling against conventional society, tattooing has lost much of its shock value. It has become a mainstream fashion statement embraced by movie stars and athletes. As a fad, however, tattooing has long-term implications that may restrict or affect future decisions. Tattooing the name of your boyfriend on your arm at 16 might look like a bad idea at 18 after you have broken up and gone off to separate universities. On a more serious level are teenagers who embrace violent, racist, or nihilistic groups. When one's identity is defined by opposition to conventional values, often little positive is left on which to build an identity that has the power to withstand the passing fashion of the day. For instance, neo-Nazi or criminal lifestyles are ill equipped to provide a foundation for adulthood.[34]

These are just a few of the issues that put children at risk. The transition from childhood to adulthood in modern times is fraught with such risks, and although most young people successfully navigate this passage, many others are caught in the cross-currents of rapid social change, underfunded institutions, predatory adults, and youth-serving agencies that lack a clear vision or are politically motivated. We turn now to an examination of the juvenile justice system and how it both serves the needs of young people and produces some unintended consequences that put youth at additional risk.

Types of Youths in the Juvenile Justice System

The modern juvenile justice system is responsible for dealing with a variety of issues affecting children's lives. Controlling antisocial behavior is the most visible of these duties, but it is only part of the system's mission. When controlling antisocial behavior is necessary, this usually means that the other parts of the system, and indeed other

The juvenile court has jurisdiction over children who are neglected by their parents.

Source: Eugene Richards / Magnum Photos, Inc.

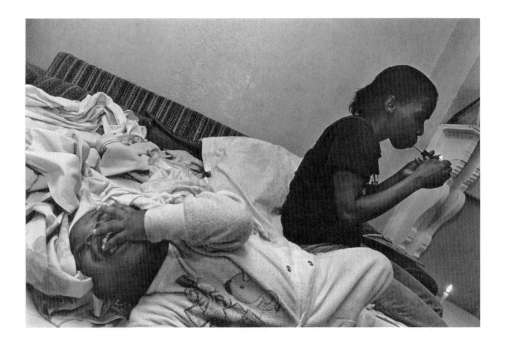

institutions in society, have failed to meet the needs of youngsters.[35] The juvenile justice system is responsible for dealing with the following types of children:

- **Incorrigible children**   Some parents cannot control their children, particularly as they become teenagers and are lured by the temptations of the street. When children disobey their parents, refuse to go to school, leave home for days at a time, or physically abuse their parents and siblings, the court may remove them from their homes and find alternative living arrangements. Sometimes parents give up on their children and ask the court to take them. (See Focus on Ethics 14.1 for a scenario involving incorrigible children and laws meant to prevent the sexual abuse of children.)

- **Dependent children**   When children are abandoned or orphaned, the state becomes responsible for their welfare. Usually, the first option is to place the child with a relative, but if no suitable relative is available, the court seeks a foster home and oversees adoption requests.

- **Neglected children**   Some parents are unconcerned, careless, or incapable of providing the physical, emotional, and economic care that children require. The juvenile justice system must ensure that neglected children are given adequate food, shelter, clothes, and schooling. Sometimes this means working with the parent(s) to monitor the family living conditions, and sometimes it means removing the child from the home and placing him or her in a more suitable environment.

- **Status offenders**   A number of behaviors are considered legitimate for adults, but deviant for children. These are known as **status offenses.** For instance, because of mandatory-education laws, children are required to attend school until age 16, whereas there is no such requirement of those older than 16 (this age may vary in some states). Underage drinking laws are another example of a status offense. Those under 21 are subject to arrest for consuming alcohol, whereas adults are free to drink as much as they want as long as they do not violate other laws, such as being drunk in public or driving an automobile while intoxicated. Running away from home, violating curfew, and breaking other age-determined laws make juveniles subject to a range of restrictions that do not affect adults.

status offense

An act that is considered a legal offense only when committed by a juvenile and that can be adjudicated only in a juvenile court.

- **Delinquent children** Children must obey all the laws that apply to adults, with limited exceptions.[36] As a general rule, children are subject to the same laws as adults. On breaking them, children are brought into the juvenile justice system, just as adults are brought into the criminal justice system. However, what happens to them once arrested can be very different. In serious cases, the child's case may be transferred to adult court (this will be discussed in greater detail later in this chapter).

Children do not exist in a vacuum, and they are not independent. Therefore, the juvenile court has control not only over children, but also over their parents and siblings. Often children's problems are not their own doing but are caused by parents who will not or cannot provide a suitable home. To appreciate the causes and prevention of juvenile delinquency, we should consider the social context of the lives of children.

Juvenile Delinquency in Context

One can almost predict which children will get into trouble with the law.[37] Some children exhibit early signs of maladjustment, alienation, and an inability to cope with even the minimal demands of conventional behavior. Some individual characteristics of children, such as mental illness or physical disability, are difficult to address, which makes it difficult for them to successfully interact with society in a law-abiding manner. However, the state can successfully address some consistent social issues that affect the juvenile delinquency rate. In this section, we consider how the quality of some of society's institutions and issues may be connected to the problem of juvenile delinquency.

GOOD SCHOOLS, BAD SCHOOLS   Some schools are better than others. Because public school funding depends on local property taxes, and control of the schools is invested in local school boards, a distinct correlation between the quality of a school and the affluence of the community exists.[38] This situation confronts Americans with a disturbing balance of values. On one hand, we say "no child will be left behind" and that we want to provide a quality education for all.[39] On the other hand, we want the schools to be accountable to local authorities, not state or federal bureaucrats. However, with high dropout rates, social promotion, overcrowded classrooms, and dangerous and violent students, our schools are an institution in crisis that all too often contributes to the delinquency rate.[40] If all schools could provide academically challenging and interesting lessons in a safe and secure environment, more children would be able to take advantage of the opportunities that education provides for success in conventional society.[41]

POVERTY   Children are more likely to live in poverty than are adults, and the effects of not having health care and educational opportunities as a child are difficult to compensate for in later life. One of the most disturbing features of American society is the cycle of poverty that plagues some families and communities.[42]

Poverty is related to delinquency in two ways.[43] First, some children engage in delinquent activity to secure physical and economic needs. Stealing food, selling drugs to help support the family, and shoplifting clothes are all responses that the delinquent may believe are necessary to survival. Another category of poverty-related delinquency is related not to what the youth needs, but to what the youth wants. The idea of conspicuous consumption is not lost on young people, and although few of them get everything they want, those in poverty have little hope of an increased allowance, a significant gift, or breaking down the willpower of parents with increased whining and complaining. When all of a family's resources are devoted to maintenance, no discretionary money is available for designer clothes, musical instruments, video games, or other items that children from more affluent families acquire. There is tremendous peer pressure on young people to acquire the clothes, jewelry, and electronic equipment that marks them as middle class. Even though their families might not be able to afford

FOCUS on ETHICS

KIDS AND SEX

In August 2003, the *Milwaukee Journal Sentinel* reported that a girl and her boyfriend, both 14 years old, were caught nude in bed by the girl's mother. The teens were not at all scared or remorseful but incensed that the mother would invade their privacy. The teens even challenged the mother to call the police, which she did. The case went to court. The boy was charged with attempted second-degree sexual assault, a felony, and the girl with fourth-degree sexual assault, a misdemeanor.

The boy's defense lawyer contended that the law prohibiting juveniles from having sex was written to protect children from being abused and exploited by adults, not to prohibit consensual sex between children. The prosecutor disagreed and said that although similar cases had been handled informally in the past, the teens' attitude dictated that they be charged with the crimes. Both youths came from troubled backgrounds and experienced attention deficit disorder and parental abandonment. Additionally, each refused to follow the rules of a "deferred prosecution agreement"; the charges were brought because they were stubborn and uncooperative.

What Do You Do?

1. Should teenagers be allowed to have sex with other teenagers?
2. Do teenagers have the right to privacy, even from their parents?
3. Does the government have any business regulating consensual sex?
4. Should the attitude of the teenagers be held against them? If they are simply being honest and telling the court and parents to leave them alone, should they be prosecuted?
5. At what age should teenagers be allowed to engage in sexual relations without intervention by the juvenile justice system?
6. Is it possible that more damage is done to these teenagers by punishing them than by ignoring their behavior?

Source: Jamaal Abdul-Alim, "Teens Have Right to Have Sex, Lawyer Argues," *Milwaukee Journal Sentinel*, August 20, 2003, www.jsonline.com/news/metro/aug03/163688.asp.

such luxuries, many young people consider these items necessities. The cost of cigarettes, fast food, and entertainment outstrip the ability of impoverished families to provide the image that the children desire. Consequently, breaking the law in the form of dealing drugs, larceny, and prostitution becomes an alternative to the pains of poverty.

FAULTY FAMILIES A child's family life can affect his or her chances of delinquency. Although the ideal family structure is popularly considered an intact nuclear family in which both biological parents are in the home and provide the love and emotional support necessary to raise well-adjusted children, in the United States more than half of families have a different structure. Blended families, single-parent families, and foster families together outnumber traditional nuclear families, and in many instances are as successful in meeting the needs of children.[44] Family structure does not tell the whole story, however. Some intact families might be dysfunctional, in which case the children might be better off if the parents separate.[45] Although family structure can be related to economic viability, it does not reveal the interpersonal dynamics happening inside families that are more important to our understanding of delinquency. Parental drug or alcohol abuse; sexual, emotional, or physical abuse of the children; lack of positive role modeling; and a host of other problems may indicate more about family life than the convenient and easily measured factor of family structure.[46]

Today, the period of a child's dependence on parents has been extended until the completion of high school and sometimes beyond. In the tough economy of the new century, the term *boomerang kids* has emerged to refer to children who return to their parents' homes after graduating from college and failing to find a job that can support them independently.[47]

NEIGHBORHOODS The community is one context in which juveniles develop attitudes and values that ultimately contribute to unlawful behavior. In an ideal world, the community is a supportive network of government and private organizations that provide stimulating after-school programs, healthy recreational opportunities, and a safe environment in which young people can thrive without worrying about physical violence, illegal drugs, and predatory adults.

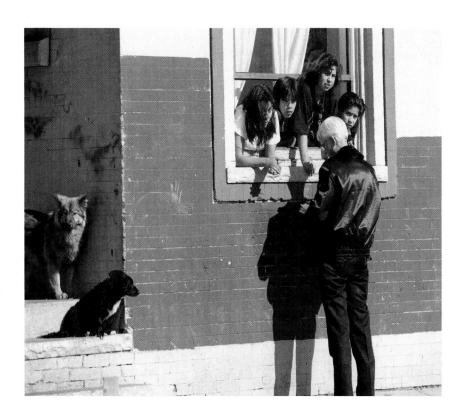

A Denver patrol officer talks with some children about a shooting that happened in front of the apartment where they live.

Source: Kent Meireis/The Image Works

Unfortunately, not all communities can provide these safeguards. Much like our schools, our communities are a reflection of the material wealth of those who are willing to contribute to their welfare. Taxes, charitable contributions, and community fund-raising activities all work with other institutions such as schools, churches, and industry to provide a support network for young people. In many communities, opportunities are divided along socioeconomic lines.[48] As some communities can no longer afford to fund park programs, pay the liability insurance costs of organized youth activities, and ensure the safety of public functions, more and more recreational activities are being provided by private companies for profit.[49] Whereas the children of the wealthy attend music lessons, soccer practice, gymnastics instruction, and advanced academic tutoring sessions, the children of the less affluent often are consigned to television or the streets. Whereas the community once provided low-cost Little League baseball and summer camps, now these activities are expensive and, in some communities, completely absent.

In difficult economic times, communities might be unable to afford many of the support activities normally associated with preventing delinquency. Cash-strapped communities must use their limited tax dollars to provide basic services such as police and fire protection, road maintenance, hospitals, libraries, and building inspections. Everyone may agree that youth support systems are beneficial and worthy activities, but sometimes they are too low on the list of priorities to fund adequately. This engenders a downward spiral in the quality of life in the community and results in fewer opportunities for children to grow up in a supportive and healthy environment.

It is certainly not our intention here to indict all families, schools, and communities as neglecting children and causing delinquency. There is, of course, a wide range of quality in these institutions. Some are exemplary and provide extremely beneficial services for young people.[50] Rather, our point here is that not all of the blame can be laid at the feet of the individual youngster. Delinquency occurs in a social context, and we must understand not only the context, but also how some children through privilege, good luck, or special skills can overcome the disadvantages of deficient institutional support.

THE DARK FIGURE OF JUVENILE DELINQUENCY   As discussed in Chapter 2, the measurement of crime is an inexact endeavor. Because a large percentage of crime goes unreported and a substantial amount of it can never be attributed to any individual or group, we can only approximate the true nature of the picture of crime. Although we use multiple methods such as self-report studies, victimization studies, and official statistics, such as the *Uniform Crime Reports* reported by the Federal Bureau of Investigation, we do know that the actual amount of crime in the country can never be definitively measured.

When dealing with juvenile delinquency, this inability to accurately comprehend the true nature of the problem is even more acute. In addition to the many reasons why people do not report crime, there are additional reasons why much juvenile delinquency never finds its way into official statistics or reports. These reasons include the following:

- **Adults are unaware of the offense**   Often, fights between youths never become known by adults who have the ability or desire to report it. Young people sometimes get in a fight after school, and even though the combatants may return home bloodied and bruised, they might not tell their parents about the injuries. These conflicts are not defined by youth as crime, and they may have good reasons not to make their parents aware of the problem. Perhaps a youth was the one who picked the fight in the first place and expects little or no sympathy from his or her parents. Consequently, much of this behavior goes unreported by the traditional measures of crime.

- **Some delinquency and status offending is consensual**   Drinking alcohol underage, drug use, and sexual activity are all behaviors that would be included in the juvenile delinquency and status-offending picture if they could be reported. Because these activities are often entered into freely by juveniles, there is little incentive, and great disincentive, to make parents, teachers, or law enforcement officials aware of these transgressions.

- **Status offenses are difficult to identify**   A number of offenses apply only to juveniles. These status offenses include underage drinking, truancy, running away, and incorrigibility. It is difficult, however, to define exactly when some of these behaviors are status offenses. For instance if a 14-year-old runs away from home and is gone for two weeks but reconciles with the parents, should this be counted as a running away? At what point does disobeying one's parents and being a general pain in the neck become incorrigibility? Finally, schools have a great deal of discretion, and their policies allow for working with students to keep them attending school before declaring them as truant. For this reason, one school district's policy may result in more truancy being recorded than another school district's, although the behaviors of the youths are identical.

- **Adults choose not to report**   Many minor transgressions by youths are not reported by adults because they do not want youngsters to be inserted into the juvenile justice system. In order to avoid the label or stigma of "juvenile delinquent," teachers and law enforcement often give out a stern warning for minor misbehavior in the hopes that they were simply youthful transgressions and not an indicator of a pattern of delinquency. As you will recall from our discussion of labeling theory, it is often deemed wise to overlook and minimize the deviant behavior of young people so that they are not officially labeled as delinquent and, furthermore, don't come to think of themselves as problem children. The idea here is to prevent the negative label from becoming a self-fulfilling prophecy.

These reasons why much juvenile delinquency and status offending is not reported should not blind us to the fact that a great deal of it is, and that it is a substantial problem. Efforts to measure juvenile delinquency have become more sophisticated over the years, and because these measures show some stability in levels and trends, we can approximate how serious a problem juvenile delinquency is. According to the 2006 *Uniform Crime Reports*, 1,240,985 violent offenses were known to be committed by

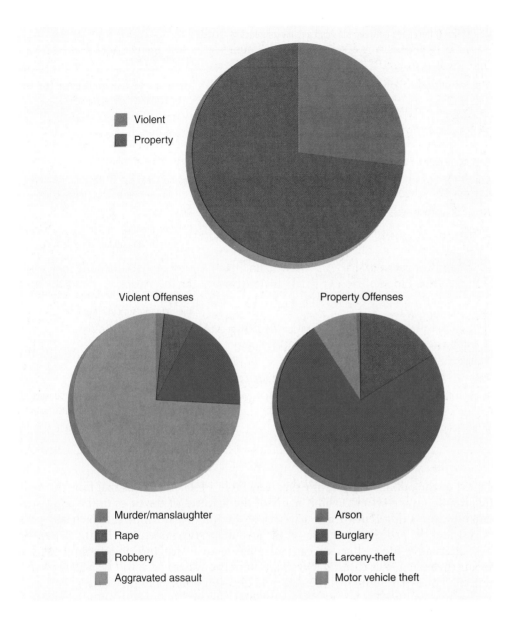

Figure 14-1   **Number of Property and Violent Offenses Cleared by Arrest or Exceptional Means, Involving Persons under 18 Years of Age**

Source: FBI, *Uniform Crime Reports: Crime in the United States, 2007,* Number of Offenses Cleared by Arrest or Exceptional Means, Table 28, http://www.fbi.gov/ucr/cius2007/data/table_28.html.

people under age 18. Most of these were aggravated assaults, followed by robbery. Relatively few were murders/nonnegligent manslaughters and rapes. However, most juvenile delinquency comprised property offenses: 8,851,465. The most common of these were larceny/theft followed by burglary and motor vehicle theft. See Figure 14-1.[51]

We must remember that these figures represent only known offenses and not the actual level of juvenile delinquency. Still, they are useful figures because they indicate the volume of cases that the juvenile justice system must handle. Regardless of how much delinquency juveniles are involved in, the juvenile court and juvenile corrections systems only has to deal with those who are identified by the police and taken into custody. We now turn to the specific types of problems that lead children to the juvenile justice system.

THE JUVENILE JUSTICE SYSTEM

In organizational structure, the juvenile justice system is parallel to the criminal justice system. This can be confusing because these two systems, although distinctly different in many of their goals, philosophies, and practices, also have points of convergence in which they share personnel, interact on certain cases, and are jointly

Table 14-1   Differences between the Adult and Juvenile Justice Systems

Issue	Adult System	Juvenile System
Status in question	The defendant's guilt in breaking a law	The child's delinquency in breaking a law or committing a status offense
Searches	Protections exist against unreasonable searches of one's person, home, and possessions.	Protections against unreasonable searches are limited.
Self-incrimination	Both children and adults are protected.	
Goal of proceedings	The defendant is assumed innocent until proven guilty.	The best interests of the child, whether guilty or innocent, are paramount.
Nature of proceedings	Adversarial	Remedial
Arrests	Warrant required	Children are not arrested but taken into custody via petition or complaint.
Representation	Both children and adults have the right to an attorney.	
Trials	Open to the public	There are no trials, but closed hearings. The right to a jury trial does not exist.
Result on conviction or finding of delinquency	Convicted adults are punished with possible rehabilitation and/or treatment.	Children are protected and r ehabilitated.
Treatment	No right to treatment	Right to treatment
Release	Via bail or release on recognizance (ROR)	Parental or guardian custody
Public records	The results of the trial and judgment remain on public record.	Records are sealed and may be destroyed once the child reaches a certain age.
Incarceration	Prison or jail	Children are held or incarcerated in nonadult facilities.

blamed by the public for the crime rate (see Table 14-1). The cases that flow through the juvenile justice system exhibit many of the features of the cases in the adult system; however, a different vocabulary is used to signify what happens at each stage. As we consider the processing of cases in the juvenile justice system, we must be alert for these alternative terms. Because each state has its own structure and method of processing juvenile justice cases, the description of the system here will be a general and simplified one that highlights the common decision points and practices.

Entering the Juvenile Justice System

referral

Similar to a "charge" in the adult system in which an authority, usually the police, parents, or the school, determines that the youth needs intervention from the juvenile court.

Cases are inserted into the juvenile justice system by a process called a **referral.** There are two types of referrals. The first type of referral can come from schools, parents, or child welfare agencies that believe the child is at risk from others, as in cases of child abuse or delinquency. A parent may turn the child over to the juvenile court because of incorrigibility or because the parent lacks the necessary resources to provide an adequate home. A child welfare agency may turn the child over to the jurisdiction of the court if both parents are incarcerated and no proximate or appropriate relative is available to care for the youth. The second type of referral to the juvenile court comes from law enforcement agencies. This type of referral is the functional equivalent of an arrest. Depending on the youth's age and the seriousness of the delinquency, the processing of the child can closely resemble the arrest of an adult, although the process is often very different. Based on the philosophy of doing what is best for the child, many large law enforcement agencies have specialized juvenile units that are familiar with the community resources available to treat the youth. Often as many as one-third of the juvenile cases handled by law enforcement agencies are diverted from the juvenile justice system, and the youths are either released or funneled into alternative programs.[52] Of the two types of referrals, the law enforcement referral is the most common by a large margin. Typically, law enforcement referrals account for up to 69 percent of the cases entered into the juvenile justice system (see Figure 14-2).[53]

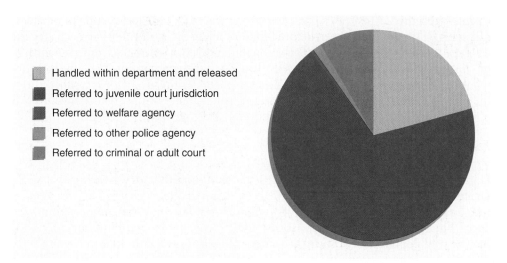

Figure 14-2   **Police Disposition of Juveniles Taken into Custody, 2007**
Source: Federal Bureau of Investigation, *Uniform Crime Reports: Crime in the United States, 2007,* www.fbi.gov/ucr/cius2007/data/table_68.html.

Legend:
- Handled within department and released
- Referred to juvenile court jurisdiction
- Referred to welfare agency
- Referred to other police agency
- Referred to criminal or adult court

Prehearing Detention

Law enforcement agencies are discouraged from holding juvenile delinquents in adult jails while the case is processed. Federal regulations require that youths be held no more than six hours and that they be kept out of sight and sound of adult inmates. After six hours, youths must be transferred to a juvenile agency that can provide secure detention.

Intake

The intake function is a major **gatekeeping** decision point. An intake officer, who is responsible to the juvenile probation department and/or the juvenile court judge, reviews the case to determine whether evidence is sufficient to prove the allegation. This review is often in the form of a preliminary hearing in which the youth and his or her parents are questioned about the youth's understanding of the offending behavior and the willingness and ability of the parents or guardian to correct that behavior. The youth may be released at this point if the evidence is weak; however, the burden of proof is low.[54] Consequently, a finding by the intake officer that sufficient reason exists to pass the case forward is enough to keep the case under the purview of the court.

The intake officer, in conjunction with the probation department, may establish an informal way of handling the case that, if successfully completed, could allow the youth to escape formal processing and the resultant paper trail of legal transgressions.[55] A **consent decree** may be written at this point, in which the youth agrees to some conditions for a specified period of time. These conditions may include restitution to a victim, drug or alcohol counseling, attendance at school, or maintaining a curfew. Once the youth successfully completes the conditions, the case is dismissed. Because these conditions are often monitored by the probation department, this procedure is often called **informal probation.** This type of processing allows the case to be diverted from the system without formal charges being filed. If the youth fails to comply with the conditions, the case goes back into the system.[56]

Determining Jurisdiction

Once an intake officer decides that the case should be processed through the normal juvenile justice system and not diverted into informal probation, it is decided whether the case will remain in the juvenile court or be transferred to adult court. The states have a variety of mechanisms for making this decision. The prosecutor may file the case in criminal court, or the intake officer may file a petition waiver to transfer the case.[57] The decision is based on two factors: the seriousness of the delinquency and the history and demeanor of the offender. Only very serious offenses, such as homicide, are bound over

gatekeeping
Points, or "gates," in the criminal and juvenile justice systems at which crucial decisions are made about a case.

consent decree
When the parties to a lawsuit accept a judge's order that is based on an agreement made by them instead of continuing the case through a trial or hearing.

informal probation
A period during which a juvenile is required to stay out of trouble or make restitution before the case is dropped.

to criminal court.[58] Most cases involving youths stay under the jurisdiction of the juvenile court. If the youth has been before the court many times and has shown a disregard for the authority of the judge and probation staff, waiver to the adult criminal court may be deemed an appropriate way to handle the case. If the youth is not amenable to treatment and continues to commit criminal acts while under the juvenile court supervision, the prosecutor may decide to kick the case up to the adult criminal court, in which the protection of society is considered as important as the welfare of the youth.[59]

Adjudicatory Hearing

adjudicatory hearing

The process in which a juvenile court determines whether the allegations in a petition are supported by evidence.

Within a specified period (this varies by state), an **adjudicatory hearing** is held to determine whether the youth committed the delinquent acts charged against him or her. This hearing is the equivalent of a criminal trial but with some important differences. First, the juvenile hearing is a quasi-civil proceeding (not criminal) and therefore may be confidential. Only official and interested parties are allowed in the court. The facts of the case and, most important, the names of juvenile delinquents and victims may be kept from the media. Second, the adjudicatory hearing is conducted by a judge who also acts as a jury. Third, the youth, if guilty, will be adjudicated delinquent, shifting the focus of the case from the delinquent act to the rehabilitation of the youth.

Because of the legal reforms of the 1960s and 1970s, juvenile delinquents enjoy many of the rights afforded adults in the criminal court, including the right to have an attorney, the right to confront and cross-examine hostile witnesses, the right to present witnesses in defense, and the right against self-incrimination. Furthermore, the standard of proof in an adjudicatory hearing is set at the highest standard: beyond a reasonable doubt. Although youths have the right to an attorney, this right can be waived by the youth or the parents. This makes for a somewhat confusing situation. Attorneys are supposed to exercise independent professional judgment on behalf of their clients, but sometimes the juvenile's best interests conflict with the wishes of the parents, who pay the attorney's fee. Also, the juvenile system, to further set it apart from the adult system, has its own terminology. Therefore, in the adjudicatory hearing (trial), the **petitioner** (prosecutor) attempts to prove the youth delinquent and in need of **commitment** (incarceration), whereas the **respondent** (defense attorney) challenges the facts of the case.

petitioner

A person who files a lawsuit; also called a plaintiff.

commitment

An order by a judge on conviction or before a trial that sends a person to jail or prison. Also, a judge's order that sends a mentally unstable person to a mental institution.

respondent

The party who must reply to a petitioner's complaint. Equivalent to a defendant in a lawsuit.

Although not an **adversarial process,** the adjudicatory hearing does have many of the aspects of the trial. Because of the restored legal rights of juveniles, the case is no longer handled as juvenile cases were when the juvenile courts were originally established.[60] Remember, the welfare of the juvenile must now be balanced with his or her legal rights when the case is processed.

Disposition

adversarial process

A term describing the manner in which U.S. criminal trial courts operate; a system that requires two sides, a prosecution and a defense.

The disposition of the juvenile case can be compared to the handing down of the sentence in criminal court. The disposition can take two paths: residential placement (confinement) in a secure facility or referral to probation or a similar nonresidential program. As a rule, placement in a residential facility is reserved for those adjudicated for the most serious offenses. The term **residential placement** sometimes means being placed in a community halfway house or a foster home. However, residential placement often means the juvenile is sent to a training school or reform school that is little different in appearances from a prison. Although the youth is confined with other youths, residential placement can, in many ways, be compared to "hard time" in an adult institution.

residential placement

Any sentence of a juvenile delinquent to a halfway house or other community home in which the juvenile is closely monitored, but allowed to leave for work or school.

A disposition of juvenile probation can be linked to a set of conditions that require the youth to participate in treatment programs, additional schooling, or public service activities.[61] Again, the philosophy of the juvenile justice system is geared toward rehabilitation, but in forcing the juvenile to engage in multiple activities, the distinction between rehabilitation and punishment can appear blurred to the offender.[62] In some cases, youths can be sentenced to adult facilities in which relatively young adults are confined. Some youths are so advanced in antisocial lifestyles that officials believe that

Figure 14-3   Juvenile Justice System Case Flow

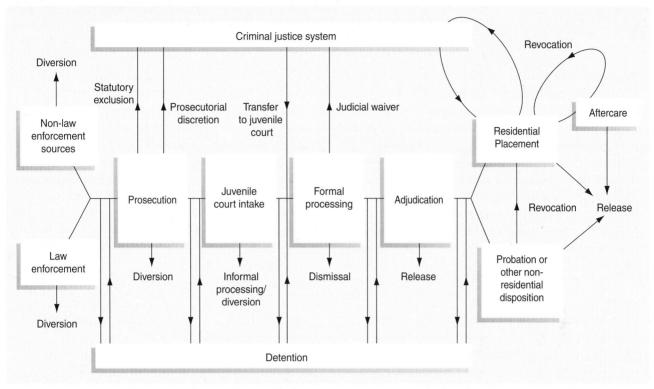

Source: U.S. Department of Justice, Office of Juvenile Justice and Delinquency Prevention, Statistical Briefing Book Case Flow Diagram, http://ojjdp.ncjrs.org/ojstatbb/structure_process/case.html.

keeping them in institutions for juveniles would not provide the proper security and that these recalcitrant youths provide negative examples for other young offenders.

Aftercare

To ease the transition of the youth from residential treatment back into the community, the court may order some type of *aftercare*. This can be thought of as similar to the parole function in the criminal court. Aftercare may consist of a number of programs designed to address the youth's problems, including drug or alcohol treatment, counseling, attending school on a regular basis, or employment. The key to aftercare programs is the ability of the court to ensure the offender's accountability. If the youth fails to complete the aftercare requirements, the juvenile corrections worker may recommend another period of confinement.[63]

Figure 14-3 shows that juveniles can be diverted from the system at many points. However, this does not mean that they are not under some type of social control. The case is being *held in abeyance* until the youth successfully completes the diversion program or other court requirements. Sometimes this is as easy as going one year without getting into trouble again. If the court's orders are completed, the case is dismissed, but if the youth violates the law or ignores the directives of the diversion program, he or she again faces a judge who might order more draconian forms of control. See Focus on Ethics 14.2 for a look at how this form of social control can engulf not only delinquents and status offenders, but whole families.

PROBLEMATIC ISSUES IN JUVENILE JUSTICE TODAY

Despite the good intentions and concerns of the many people working in the juvenile justice system, some issues remain that have not been resolved in a way that makes youths more controllable or society any safer. In fact, in some ways, the juvenile

FOCUS *on* ETHICS

WIDENING THE NET OF SOCIAL CONTROL

The juvenile court is responsible for safeguarding the welfare of children, including protecting them from abusive or neglectful parents. You are a juvenile court judge who has been struggling with a particularly difficult case involving a 14-year-old boy who continually smokes marijuana, shoplifts, and recently has been running with a local gang and terrorizing other children with threats of violence. The experienced caseworker who has been working hard to help this young man has told you that the source of much of the problem is his parents and his family's dynamics. The boy ignores his mother's instructions and argues with his father. You order the family to see a psychologist who specializes in family matters, but the father refuses to cooperate and contends that the problem is not himself but the "rotten" boy and has discontinued therapy. After several attempts to resolve the situation, you order the boy placed in foster care because you believe the father is an unfit parent and a negative influence.

This boy has a 12-year-old brother whose behavior is exemplary. He is an honor student, star athlete, and all-around good kid. You order the 12-year-old out of the home also because the father is recalcitrant and continues to refuse to cooperate with the courts. Your thinking is that if he is a poor father for one child, he is probably a poor father for the other and that your duty is to place both boys in foster care for their own well-being. The 14-year-old seems to be responding well to his new home, but the 12-year-old has become a problem. He runs away from home, is in danger of being dropped from the honors program because of slipping grades, and refuses to discuss his new problems with the psychologist. You are so angry with the father because of his attitude that you do not want to allow the 12-year-old to return to the home, but you are worried that your actions have resulted in a good kid going bad.

What Do You Do?

1. Let the 12-year-old return to the home and keep pressuring the father to participate in family therapy.

2. Keep both children in foster care until the father starts to cooperate.

3. Return both boys to the home and let the situation run its course. You tried to help, but now it is the father's problem. If his sons end up in prison, it is not your fault.

4. Order the 12-year-old to live with you so that you can show the father that you care about children and are willing to go to great lengths to ensure that they are protected.

---

justice system and our society in general have not addressed delinquency in a comprehensive and effective way. All the institutions that deal with children are partially responsible for this failure. The juvenile justice system is the institution of last resort and so looks more ineffective than the school, family, or community. If those other institutions were fulfilling their missions more completely, however, there might be fewer delinquent children. Therefore, any real reform of the juvenile justice system must be linked to the way these other institutions interact with law enforcement, the juvenile court, and treatment programs. To a large extent, the solution is better funding, but other issues may be more politically feasible than raising taxes and allocating more funds to schools, recreational programs, treatment alternatives, or more police officers. To reform the juvenile justice system, the following issues should receive greater scrutiny and consideration.

Chronic Offenders

Given the broad reach of statutes criminalizing the behavior of youths, we can expect many to come in contact with the juvenile justice system as they test the boundaries of appropriate behavior, seek to establish their identities, and have a bit of fun. The "boys will be boys" behavior is not what concerns us most because boys (and girls) will generally outgrow much of this deviant behavior.

A small percentage of youth, however, are long-term, chronic, and consistent law violators.[64] According to one landmark study, 6 percent of the juvenile delinquent population was responsible for 52 percent of all offenses. Furthermore, these 627 boys out of a total sample of 9,945 accounted for 71 percent of the homicides, 82 percent of the robberies, and 64 percent of the aggravated assaults. These boys were tracked from birth until their 18th birthdays, and two significant predictors of chronic offending stood out in the findings. First, the gravity of the first offense suggested that those who start with relatively major offenses are more likely to become chronically delinquent and that those who receive severe punishment are most likely to end up living a life of crime.[65] These findings are not surprising, but they do suggest that arrest and going to the juvenile court did little to deter these youths from further delinquency. Because research has shown that these youths share a number of factors such as behavior problems, poor grades, drug or alcohol use, family problems (such as criminal parents), abuse or neglect, and patterns of stealing or running away, the solution to chronic delinquency is necessarily complex, broad-based, and expensive. Although it may be tempting to identify the chronic delinquent early and implement treatment or punishment before the behavior gets deadly, there are some ethical issues with intervention based on what is expected of the youth rather than on what he or she has actually done.[66]

Youth Gangs

Another predictor of chronic delinquency is membership in a youth gang. Gangs have become a favorite theme of the media. Much of the music of youth today is influenced by gang ideas, and even middle-class youth adopt the accoutrements of gangs in dress, tattoos, and using gang signs. Graffiti in cities and towns of all sizes across the country suggest some level of gang influence.[67] Regardless of the perceived growth and diffusion of youth gangs, they remain a particular problem in the largest cities, where there are contested neighborhoods, a critical mass of disenfranchised youth, and a long history and tradition of gang activity. There so are many types of youth gangs that it becomes difficult to construct a general definition other than that they engage in criminal or delinquent activity. This broad concept, however, would include some fraternities on college campuses. Youth gangs can be focused around drug distribution, turf protecting, robbery, extortion, or any number of other illegal behaviors. At their most extreme, gangs are highly organized, have members who remain active well into their adult years, are connected with prison gangs, and have hundreds of members.

Race is another dimension of many gangs.[68] California has Hispanic gangs, black gangs, Asian gangs, and white gangs. This list is misleading, however, because the number and types of gangs can be subdivided in any number of ways. For instance, Asian gangs can be subdivided into Filipino, Chinese, Indochinese (Vietnamese, Cambodian, Laotian, Thai, and Hmong), Korean, Japanese, and Pacific Islander (Samoan, Fijian, Guamanian, and Hawaiian) gangs. There is a constantly shifting loyalty among gangs; sometimes certain ethnic groups oppose each other one month and then merge to confront another group the following month. Law enforcement agencies have established gang units and have recruited as officers people from many of the nationalities that contribute to the U.S. gang problem.[69]

Gangs are not only composed of young males. Many young females are affiliated with male gangs or belong to all-female gangs. Here, two girls from rival gangs in Los Angeles fight.

Source: Luis Romero/AP Wide World Photos

Although we typically think of the gang problem as being a male issue, research shows that females are also active in gangs. Previously, female gang activity was thought to be supportive of male gangs, but today, full-fledged female gangs provide many of the functions for their members that make gangs so attractive to males. From a feminist point of view, the social liberation of women and girls has enabled them to become more actively engaged in gang and criminal pursuits.[70] However, we should not make too much of this liberation hypothesis. The opportunity that young women have to form their own gangs does not reflect a greater freedom of choice. Often, they are forced to enter gang life to protect themselves in a community that has lost (or never had) social viability. Female gang activity is not a step forward for women but rather an unintended consequence of so many young men going to training schools and prisons and leaving a void in the drug markets and power relationships on the street. As young women move to fill this void by engaging in gang activity, they are not only in danger of being further victimized by males, but also in danger of victimizing each other and exposing themselves to the oversight of the juvenile justice system.

Finally, although youth street gangs have been involved in crime for a long time, the effect of the drug culture since the 1970s has radically changed the nature of many of these gangs and greatly increased the amount of lethal behavior associated with gang activity. Simply put, the expressive gang activities of fighting, graffiti, and turf protection have been replaced to some extent by lucrative drug sales. Given the amount of money involved in the drug trade, neighborhood gangs are driven to act more like organized-crime groups.[71]

Conditions of Youth Confinement

The types of institutions available for young offenders vary widely across the country. Even when a state has a range of sentencing options, overcrowding often means there is no room in the most appropriate type of confinement. As of 2003, more than 300 juvenile delinquents were in custody for every 100,000 juveniles in the nation.[72]

CASE IN POINT

14.2

SCHALL V. MARTIN

THE CASE	THE POINT
Schall v. Martin, 467 U.S. 253, 104 S.Ct. 2403 (1984)	As long as procedures protect a juvenile's rights, detention of a juvenile is constitutional if it protects the juvenile and society from offenses he or she might commit before trial.

On December 13, 1977, in New York City, 14-year-old Gregory Martin was arrested at 11:30 P.M. and charged with first-degree robbery, second-degree assault, and criminal possession of a weapon. Martin lied to the police about where he lived and was confined in jail.

Martin came under the jurisdiction of the state's family court and made his initial appearance on December 14, accompanied by his grandmother. It was determined that at the time of his arrest, Martin possessed a loaded weapon, gave a false address to police, and was away from his home at a late hour, all of which the judge cited as a lack of supervision. The New York Family Court Act allows for pretrial detention of an accused juvenile delinquent if there is a "serious risk" that the juvenile "may before the return date commit an act which if committed by an adult would constitute a crime." Because of the evidence at the time of his arrest, Martin was held until his hearing on December 27–29.

At the hearing, Martin was found guilty of the robbery and criminal possession charges. He was adjudicated delinquent and placed on probation for two years. From the time of his arrest to the conclusion of the hearing, he had been detained for 15 full days. His attorney appealed the finding on grounds that the detention violated the due-process clause of the Fourteenth Amendment. However, the Supreme Court upheld Martin's detention as constitutionally valid, stating that the New York Family Court Act provided adequate procedures to guard the juvenile's rights and that it protected "both the juvenile and society from the hazards of pretrial crime."

(See Case in Point 14.2 for a landmark case concerning juvenile confinement.) Four types of public facilities are available in many states:

- **Adult prisons**   Some young offenders convicted of serious offenses may be kept here. Juvenile delinquents are kept separate from adult inmates, but because of security risks and the harm they may do to other youths, they are often placed in the most restrictive confinement possible. For many of these dangerous delinquents, this means protective custody in what amounts to solitary confinement.

- **Ranches and camps**   Ranches and forestry camps enable juvenile delinquents to work outside on public lands. The intent is to provide positive work experiences so that the youth will be able to find gainful employment when released. Additionally, by being away from the temptations of urban life and the confines of a training school, the more normal summer-camp-like experience of these types of detention are thought to be less stigmatizing and deleterious to the self-concept of the youth.[73] Most ranches and camps are privately operated.[74]

- **Boot camp prisons**   Patterned after military basic training camps, these short-term (usually 90-day) programs are designed to teach hard work, discipline, and obedience. They are physically and mentally rigorous and relatively inexpensive when compared with a training school. Although these programs are popular, critics point out the high potential for abuse and that the programs are no more effective in preventing recidivism than traditional programs.[75] Boot camp prisons are more likely to be operated by the government than by private interests.[76]

- **Traditional training schools**   These often overcrowded and understaffed programs are where the more serious delinquents are incarcerated for longer periods of time. Some training schools physically resemble adult prisons; others have the appearance of a college campus.[77]

In addition to these four types of public institutions are a number of public and private residential placement facilities, with juveniles in their mid- to late teens comprising most of these placements (see Figure 14-4). Although private facilities hold less than half as many youths as public facilities, there are more than twice as many privately operated juvenile facilities in the United States, and more than half of these are group homes. Private facilities hold fewer delinquents than public facilities, but more status offenders.[78] These programs offer the court, the parents, and the youths an alternative to traditional confinement. Although private programs can be expensive, some can offer exceptional educational and counseling opportunities. However, some of the private programs are extremely controversial; at those located in other countries, the legal rights of young offenders can be extremely limited.

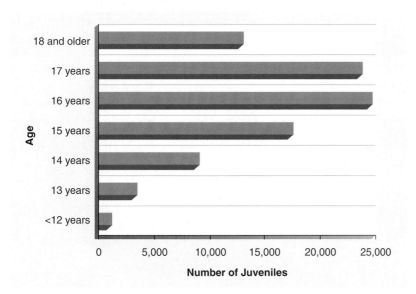

Figure 14-4   Juveniles in Public and Private Residential Placement Facilities, by Age, 2006

Source: Adapted from Melissa Sickmund, T. J. Sladky, and Wei Kang, Census of Juveniles in Residential Placement Databook, 2008, www.ojjdp.ncjrs.gov/ojstatbb/cjrp/.

Boot camp institutions are patterned after military basic training. Critics claim that these programs are no more effective than traditional methods of reforming juvenile offenders.

Source: CORBIS-NY

Much like adult prisons and jails, security is an issue at many youth facilities. The level of security varies with the type of facility, but generally the most secure facilities hold the most troublesome delinquents. Private facilities, which typically house less-serious delinquents, were far less likely to lock youths in their sleeping rooms than public facilities. The facilities most likely to use razor wire to secure the grounds were detention centers, training schools, and boot camps. Locked doors and gates are most typically used for juveniles being held for offenses such as homicide, sexual and aggravated assault, robbery, arson, and technical violations. The use of fences, walls, and equipment such as surveillance cameras is becoming more common in juvenile facilities.[79] However, the Juvenile Justice and Delinquency Prevention Act of 2002 does not allow status offenders to be placed in secure facilities for long terms. One aspect of security is the ability of the facility to protect some youths from themselves. Most youths go to facilities that screen for mental health problems, suicide risk, and substance abuse.[80] However, by far, the most common cause of fatalities among state-confined youths is suicide (see Figure 14-5).

Figure 14-5 **State Juvenile Correctional Facility Deaths, 2002–2005**

Source: U.S. Department of Justice, Bureau of Justice Statistics, www.ojp. usdoj.gov/bjs/dcrp/tables/juvtab1.htm.

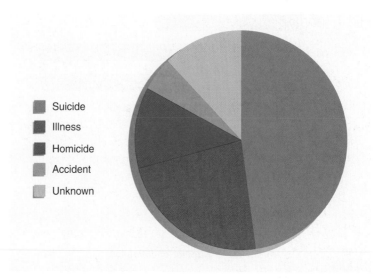

- Suicide
- Illness
- Homicide
- Accident
- Unknown

Treating Children as Adults

One of the outgrowths of the get-tough-on-crime approach has been to treat serious juvenile delinquents as adult offenders (see Criminal Justice Reference 14.2). Rather than handling these cases in juvenile courts, which are geared toward the needs of the child, these cases are waived to the criminal court, where the protection of society is paramount. It is argued that the most serious juvenile delinquents require a minimum criminal sentence that is not available in juvenile court. Critics of the waiver process point out that sending a juvenile to adult court does not always ensure the protection of the public because the child might serve only a fraction of the sentence imposed by the criminal court. Additionally, the criminal court may not have the treatment alternatives for young offenders that are available in juvenile court.[81] Finally, there is evidence of a racial bias in who gets waived to criminal court, with young black males being disproportionately selected.[82] (Although waiver to criminal court is a controversial topic, the practice has been around for decades. See Case in Point 14.3).

What is the right balance between protecting children and holding them accountable for their actions? To answer this question, we must consider the presumed advantages and disadvantages of having a separate juvenile justice system for juvenile delinquents. The advantages of the juvenile justice system are as follows:

- The philosophy of the juvenile justice system is different from that of the adult criminal justice system. Whereas the adult system seeks to deter crime and punish offenders to promote public safety, the juvenile justice system acts in the best interests of the child.

- The juvenile justice system seeks to reduce the stigma of deviant behavior. By shielding the names of juvenile delinquents from the press, keeping hearings private, and allowing for the purging of juvenile records, the juvenile justice system seeks to prevent youths from being labeled "bad kids."

- By having a separate juvenile justice system, young offenders are kept apart from adult criminals who may abuse them, exploit them, or teach them negative behaviors and attitudes.

14.3   CASE IN POINT
KENT V. UNITED STATES

THE CASE

Kent v. United States, 383 U.S. 541, 86 S.Ct. 1045 (1966)

THE POINT

In its first juvenile case, the Supreme Court ruled that a juvenile's due-process rights are denied when his or her case is waived to criminal court without a formal hearing.

In 1961, in the District of Columbia, 16-year-old Morris Kent was charged with entering the apartment of a woman, then robbing and raping her. Kent had been adjudicated delinquent in 1959 after being charged with a series of housebreakings and attempted purse snatchings. Kent admitted to the robbery and rape, and the juvenile court judge waived Kent to criminal court. The case went to the U.S. district court for the District of Columbia, where Kent was convicted of several counts of housebreaking, but not the rape "by reason of insanity."

The Supreme Court reversed his conviction, objecting to the casual manner in which juvenile cases were waived to criminal court and the broad discretion judges had in these decisions. The Court held that for a juvenile case to be waived to an adult court, a hearing must be held, with the juvenile having access to counsel. Also, the juvenile and/or his or her attorney must have access to the juvenile's records on which the waiver decision is being based, and the judge must state the reasons for the waiver in writing. They ruled that, in Kent's case, his right to due process was denied when he was not allowed such a formal hearing on the waiver.

- By addressing the social, emotional, and educational needs of young offenders, the juvenile justice system seeks to help them gain the necessary skills to become productive members of society.
- The juvenile justice system protects young offenders from receiving the harsh punishments meted out by the adult criminal justice system.

Those who are dissatisfied with the juvenile justice system point to the following disadvantages:

- Youths who commit serious offenses are treated too leniently. A 17-year-old who commits murder or rape does as much harm to society as a 20-year-old and deserves to be punished as severely. Many people believe that juveniles can appreciate the consequences of their unlawful behavior and should be held accountable.
- There is a great inconsistency between the punishments meted out in the juvenile justice system and those meted out in the adult criminal justice system. For citizens to have confidence in law enforcement and the courts, the punishments need to be more uniform.
- Juvenile delinquents are not afforded all the due-process rights that are available in the criminal justice system. Although the juvenile court is supposed to be working in the best interests of the child, some believe that certain cases are dealt with more harshly because the youth does not have the full protection of the legal rights granted to adults.

In many cases, it is a tough call as to whether the juvenile justice system promotes or hinders the application of justice and the best interests of the child. The compromise that has been crafted is that of waiving particularly serious cases to the adult court.

Zero Tolerance

zero-tolerance policies
Policies of agencies in which the strict letter of the law or rule is followed without question or room for individual discretion on the part of the authority.

Public officials and school administrators have a responsibility to ensure the safety of those entrusted to their care. However, catastrophic incidents are still possible, such as the incident at Columbine High School in which two students killed 12 students, a teacher, and themselves. Anyone in a position of responsibility must prepare policies and procedures for these infrequent but devastating incidents. Administrators looking to balance public safety with personal freedoms must always err on the side of safety. In this quest to protect those in their charge, many administrators have enacted **zero-tolerance policies** that are sometimes counterproductive to the welfare of children.[83] In an attempt to protect young people, many have been made victims of policies that appear to be designed to eliminate judgment and discretion on the part of administrators and teachers. This is done to shield schools and administrators from legal liability should violence occur. Unfortunately, the result is that zero tolerance takes the rules to extremes. For example, in Greeley, Colorado, two students were suspended from school because they were playing with a water gun, which violated the policy of having a gunlike facsimile.[84] Zero-tolerance policies rob teachers and administrators of their right to use professional judgment and can end up hurting innocent youths and lowering the respect we all have for our institutions.[85]

THE FUTURE OF JUVENILE JUSTICE

What is the future of the juvenile justice system? Specifically, can we identify trends that are likely to influence how juvenile delinquents and dependent or neglected children are dealt with in the coming decades? There are reasons to be optimistic that we will become more effective in meeting the needs of youths and prevent them from becoming involved in delinquent activity. There are equally compelling reasons to be concerned that many youths will be victimized by abuse and neglect and that delinquency, and ultimately criminal behavior, will occur at relatively high levels.

14.2 CRIMINAL JUSTICE REFERENCE

Tried as an Adult

All states have provisions for trying juveniles as adults. Some states lower the age for juvenile jurisdiction to 15 or 16 rather than 17 or 18. Other methods by which juveniles may be sent to adult criminal court are *judicial waiver*, *statutory exclusion*, and *direct filing* (or *concurrent jurisdiction*). In 34 states, juveniles who have been tried as adults must be processed by the criminal justice system rather than the juvenile justice system for any offenses thereafter.[1]

Judicial Waiver

A judge sends the juvenile to adult court. The three types of judicial waiver are discretionary, mandatory, and presumptive.

- *Discretionary waiver.* Transfer of the juvenile to adult court is at the judge's discretion.
- *Mandatory waiver.* Automatic transfer to criminal court on the basis of the youth's age and the gravity of the offense.
- *Presumptive waiver.* The burden of proof shifts from the state to the juvenile, who must contest being transferred to adult court.

States with judicial waiver as of 2004 (states in bold have once an adult, always an adult provisions):

Discretionary waiver: **Alabama**, Alaska, **Arizona**, Arkansas, **California**, Colorado, **Delaware**, **District of Columbia**, **Florida**, Georgia, **Hawaii**, **Idaho**, **Illinois**, **Indiana**, **Iowa**, **Kansas**, Kentucky, Louisiana, **Maine**, **Maryland**, **Michigan**, **Minnesota**, **Mississippi**, **Missouri**, **Nevada**, **New Hampshire**, New Jersey, **North Carolina**, **North Dakota**, **Ohio**, **Oklahoma**, **Oregon**, **Pennsylvania**, **Rhode Island**, South Carolina, **South Dakota**, **Tennessee**, **Texas**, **Utah**, Vermont, **Virginia**, **Washington**, West Virginia, **Wisconsin**, Wyoming

Mandatory waiver: Connecticut

Discretionary and mandatory waiver: Delaware, Georgia, Illinois, Indiana, Kentucky, Louisiana, New Jersey, North Carolina, North Dakota, Ohio, Rhode Island, South Carolina, Virginia, West Virginia

Discretionary and presumptive waiver: Alaska, California, Colorado, Washington, D.C., Illinois, Kansas, Maine, Minnesota, Nevada, New Hampshire, New Jersey, North Dakota, Pennsylvania, Rhode Island

Discretionary, presumptive, and mandatory waiver: Illinois, New Jersey, North Dakota, Rhode Island

No judicial waiver: Massachusetts, Nebraska, New Mexico, New York

Direct Filing (Concurrent Jurisdiction)

A prosecutor has the discretion to file charges in either juvenile or adult court. States with concurrent jurisdiction as of 2004 are as follows:

Arizona	Arkansas	California
Colorado	D.C.	Florida
Georgia	Louisiana	Michigan
Montana	Nebraska	Oklahoma
Vermont	Virginia	Wyoming

Statutory Exclusion

Also called *legislative waiver*, **statutory exclusion** comes from a state's legislature and does not require a juvenile court hearing. It automatically excludes some juveniles from juvenile court, and they go directly to adult court. Criteria include age, type of offense, and prior record. Statutory exclusion is used most for particularly heinous offenses, such as murder and aggravated rape. Some states without concurrent jurisdictions may also use statutory exclusion for minor violations such as traffic, fish or game, and local ordinance. Twenty-nine states had statutory exclusion provisions as of 2004:

Alabama	Illinois	Montana	South Carolina
Alaska	Indiana	Nevada	South Dakota
Arizona	Iowa	New Mexico	Utah
California	Louisiana	New York	Vermont
Delaware	Maryland	Oklahoma	Washington
Florida	Massachusetts	Oregon	Wisconsin
Georgia	Minnesota	Pennsylvania	
Idaho	Mississippi		

Source: OJJDP Statistical Briefing Book, April 25, 2002, http://ojjdp.ncjrs.org/ojstatbb/.

[1]Howard N. Snyder and Melissa Sickmund, *Juvenile Offenders and Victims: 2006 National Report* (Washington, DC: U.S. Department of Justice, Office of Juvenile Justice and Delinquency Prevention, 2006), 110.

- With the graying of America, resources will be diverted from programs that serve young people to programs that serve the elderly. This will be a factor of generational politics in which the baby boom generation will ensure by the sheer power of their voting numbers that Social Security will become a greater economic responsibility for society.

- Programs for children will continue to become privatized. Families with discretionary income will be able to provide the soccer camps, music instruction, extra

statutory exclusion
Provisions that exclude, without hearing or waiver, juveniles who meet certain age, offense, or past-record criteria from the jurisdiction of the juvenile court.

tutoring, and/or drug treatment that their children need. Those who must rely on government programs will find these programs continuing to disappear. Small communities will not be able to afford the insurance premiums to keep parks open, cover the risks of Little League baseball or gymnastics programs, or even fund field trips for schools.

- The juvenile justice system will continue to transfer young offenders to criminal courts. A disproportionate number of those selected for accelerated punishment will continue to be youths who have minority status, are impoverished, and are from the inner city.

- The age of dependency will continue to increase. Today, the period of a child's dependence on parents has been extended until the completion of high school and sometimes beyond.

- Technology can level the playing field. As the price of computers decreases and a greater percentage of children can use them, we might witness a revolution in the way children learn. Instead of being totally dependent on their schools, now most children will be "wired to the world" and able to supplement their schoolwork and possibly compensate for inadequate home situations and exploitive media. Children will be able to find information on their own and make decisions based on a larger foundation of knowledge.

- Trends suggest that the juvenile justice system may be shifting its emphasis away from the punish-or-treat dichotomy. Innovative restorative justice programs are appearing in many jurisdictions. This movement toward treating crime and delinquency in a more holistic manner will be covered more comprehensively in Chapter 16.[86]

SUMMARY

1. Juvenile delinquents are handled differently from adult offenders. Juveniles have an alternate, parallel justice system with its own philosophy, courts, and correctional system.

2. The juvenile justice system is based on a progressive philosophy of acting in the best interests of the youth.

3. In medieval England, the authority for dealing with children resided with the parents and not the state. In 16th-century England, the poor laws allowed impoverished children to be employed in homes and shops. The concept of *parens patriae* was established whereby the king could act to intervene in the interests of children.

4. In colonial North America, little distinction was made between offenses committed by adults and those committed by children. Parents were responsible for their children's actions.

5. The first house of refuge was established in New York City in 1825, and states designed similar types of institutions over the next 60 years. By the end of the 19th century, these were abandoned in favor of newer reforms.

6. In the 20th century the responsibility for children was removed from the adult criminal court. In 1899, the first juvenile court was established in Cook County, Illinois, with a mandate to process cases of children between ages 8 and 17.

7. The major differences between the modern adult criminal court and juvenile court are a focus on rehabilitation, the informal hearing, individualized justice, and private hearings. Widespread dissatisfaction with the juvenile courts led to more reforms, among these being the restoration of some of the legal rights that had been taken from juveniles.

8. One reform instituted during the 1960s and 1970s was the move to deinstitutionalize delinquent and neglected children. Rather than incarcerate them in prisonlike reform or training schools, community correctional practices such as foster homes, halfway houses, and extended probation-like supervision were employed.

9. The modern juvenile justice system is responsible for dealing with a variety of issues affecting children's lives such as incorrigibility and neglect, as well as those who are status offenders and those who are delinquent.

10. Connected to the problem of juvenile delinquency is the quality of some of society's institutions and issues such as schools, poverty, neighborhoods, and faulty families. Some of the most pressing issues facing young people include violence, alcohol and drugs, sex and sexual abuse, running away, depression, and nihilism.

11. The problem of the dark figure of crime is even more acute when considering juvenile delinquency. Reasons why much juvenile delinquency never finds its way into official statistics include the following: adults are unaware of the offense; some juvenile delinquency is consensual; some offenses are difficult to identify; and adults choose not to report.

12. The stages of the juvenile justice system are entry via referral, prehearing detention, intake, determining jurisdiction, the adjudication hearing, the disposition, and aftercare.

13. Four types of public facilities are available in many states: adult prisons, ranches and camps, boot camp prisons, and traditional training schools. A number of private facilities are also available.

14. To reform the juvenile justice system, the following issues should receive greater scrutiny and consideration: chronic offenders, youth gangs, the conditions of youth confinement, the treatment of children as adults, and zero-tolerance policies.

15. Several trends are likely to influence how juvenile delinquents and dependent or neglected children are likely to be dealt with in the coming decades. These include a growing elderly population that will need increasing amounts of resources, the privatization of youth programs, the continuing transfer of juveniles to adult criminal courts, and the increasing age of child dependency.

KEY TERMS

adjudicatory hearing 482
adversarial process 482
chancery court 466
commitment 482
consent decree 481
due-process rights 470
gatekeeping 481

hearing 469
indentured servant 467
informal probation 481
juvenile delinquent 464
parens patriae 466
petitioner 482
poor laws 466

referral 480
residential placement 482
respondent 482
status offense 474
statutory exclusion 491
zero-tolerance policies 490

REVIEW QUESTIONS

1. What are the four major differences between modern adult criminal courts and juvenile courts?

2. What is the significance of England's poor laws?

3. Where and under what circumstances was the first juvenile court established?

4. What is a status offense?

5. How is the dark figure of crime related to juvenile delinquency?

6. What are the four primary types of confinement for juvenile delinquents?

7. What is zero tolerance? What are good reasons for its use? What are bad reasons for its use?

8. What are the juvenile system's counterpart terms to *prosecutor*, *defense attorney*, *trial*, and *incarceration*?

9. What rights do juvenile defendants have in common with adult defendants?

10. What is the driving philosophy of the juvenile justice system?

SUGGESTED FURTHER READING

Anderson, Elijah. *Code of the Street: Decency, Violence, and the Moral Life of the Inner City.* New York: Norton, 1999.

Currie, Janet. *The Invisible Safety Net: Protecting the Nation's Poor Children and Families.* Princeton, NJ: Princeton University Press, 2006.

Fuller, John Randolph. *Juvenile Delinquency: Mainstream and Crosscurrents.* Upper Saddle River, NJ: Pearson Prentice Hall, 2009.

Laub, John H., and Robert J. Sampson. *Shared Beginnings, Divergent Lives: Delinquent Boys to Age 70.* Cambridge, MA: Harvard University Press, 2003.

Platt, Anthony. *The Child Savers: The Invention of Delinquency.* Chicago: University of Chicago Press, 1969.

Shelden, Randall G. *Controlling the Dangerous Classes: A Critical Introduction to the History of Criminal Justice.* Boston: Allyn & Bacon, 2001.

ENDNOTES

1. Howard N. Snyder and Melissa Sickmund, *Juvenile Delinquents and Victims: 1999 National Report* (Washington, DC: U.S. Department of Justice, Office of Juvenile Justice and Delinquency Prevention, 1999).

2. Mary Clement, *The Juvenile Justice System: Law and Process* (Boston: Butterworth-Heinemann, 1977).

3. Donna M. Bishop, "Injustice and Irrationality In Contemporary Youth Policy," *Criminology and Public Policy* 3 (November 2004): 633–644.

4. Nicholas Orme, *Medieval Children* (New Haven, CT: Yale University Press, 2001).

5. Ibid., 327.

6. William Glaser, *Schools without Failure* (New York: Harper & Row, 1969).

7. H. W. Brands, *The First American: The Life and Times of Benjamin Franklin* (New York: Anchor Books, 2000).

8. Lawrence Stone, *The Family, Sex, and Marriage in England: 1500–1800* (New York: Harper & Row, 1977).

9. Larry J. Siegel, Brandon C. Welsh, and Joseph J. Senna, *Juvenile Delinquency: Theory, Practice, and Law*, 8th ed. (Belmont, CA: Wadsworth, 2003). See Chapter 1, "Childhood and Delinquency."

10. John Sutton, "Inventing the Stubborn Child," in *Juvenile Delinquency*, 2nd ed., eds. Joseph G. Weis, Robert D. Crutchfield, and George S. Bridges (Thousand Oaks, CA: Pine Force Press, 2001), 5–6. Sutton presents a 1646 law that states if the parents turn a stubborn child over to the court, the child can be put to death.

11. Clement, *Juvenile Justice System*, 9.

12. Barry Krisberg and James Austin, *Reinventing Juvenile Justice* (Newbury Park, CA: Sage, 1993).

13. Randall G. Shelden, *Controlling the Dangerous Classes: A Critical Introduction to the History of Criminal Justice* (Boston: Allyn & Bacon, 2001).

14. Leslie Wheeler, "The Orphan Trains," *American History Illustrated* 18 (1983): 10–23.

15. David J. Rothman, *The Discovery of the Asylum: Social Order and Disorder in the New Republic* (Boston: Little, Brown, 1971).

16. Anthony Platt, *The Child Savers: The Invention of Delinquency* (Chicago: University of Chicago Press, 1969).

17. C. Wright Mills, "The Professional Ideology of Social Pathologists," *American Journal of Sociology* 49, no. 3 (1943): 165–180.

18. Platt, *Child Savers*, p. 176.

19. Clement, *Juvenile Justice System*.

20. Thomas G. Blomberg, "Diversion and Accelerated Social Control," *Journal of Criminal Law and Criminology* 68, no. 2 (1977): 274–282.

21. Neil Howe and William Strauss, *Generations: The History of America's Future, 1584 to 2069* (New York: Morrow, 1991).

22. Elijah Anderson, *Code of the Street: Decency, Violence, and the Moral Life of the Inner City* (New York: Norton, 1999).

23. Randall G. Shelden, Sharon K. Tracy, and William B. Brown, *Youth Gangs in American Society*, 3rd ed. (Belmont, CA: Wadsworth, 2004), 116.

24. "How Safe Are Our Schools?" *American School Board Journal* 194, no. 12 (December 2007): 12.

25. Carlos F. Ríos-Bedoya et al., "Children Taking Risks: The Association with Cocaine and Other Drug Use by Young Adulthood," *Addictive Behaviors* 33 (September 2008): 1154–1161.

26. Alexandra Marks, "In Drug War, Treatment Is Back," *Christian Science Monitor*, July 14, 2000, http://search.csmonitor.com/durable/2000/07/14/p1s1.htm.

27. Janelle Brown, "Saying No to Propaganda," *Salon*, March 12, 2002, www.salon.com/mwt/feature/2002/03/12/propaganda/.

28. Diane E. Levin and Jean Kilbourne, *So Sexy So Soon: The New Sexualized Childhood, and What Parents Can Do to Protect Their Kids* (New York: Ballantine, 2008).

29. Cathy Spatz Widom, "Childhood Sexual Abuse and Its Criminal Consequences," *Society* 33, no. 4 (1996): 47–53.

30. Joan R. Cates, "Education on Sexually Transmitted Infections: Finding Common Ground among Youth, Parents, Providers and Policy Advocates," *Sex Education* 8, no. 2 (May 2008): 129–143.

31. Patricia Hersch, "Coming of Age on City Streets," *Psychology Today*, January 1988, 31–37.

32. Daniel J. Campagna and Donald L. Poffenberger, *The Sexual Trafficking of Children* (South Hadley, MA: Auburn, 1988).

33. Les B. Whitbeck and Danny R. Hoyt, "Depressive Symptoms and Co-occurring Depressive Symptoms, Substance Abuse, and Conduct Problems among Runaway and Homeless Adolescents," *Child Development* 71 (May 2000): 721.

34. Kevin Young and Laura Craig, "Beyond White Pride: Identity, Meaning, and Contradiction in the Canadian Skinhead Subculture," in *Deviance and Deviants: An Anthology*, eds. Richard Tewksbury and Patricia Gagné (Los Angeles: Roxbury, 2000), 304–316.

35. See Jerome H. Skolnick and Elliott Currie, *Crisis in American Institutions*, 2nd ed. (Boston: Little, Brown, 1973), v. Here Skolnick and Currie "examine the roots of current social problems in the fundamental structure of American society as a whole."

36. For instance, a 15-year-old and a 14-year-old who have sex are treated much differently than is a 25-year-old who has sex with a 14-year-old.

37. Nancy Weishew and Samuel Peng, "Variables Predicting Students' Problem Behaviors," *Journal of Educational Research* 87, no. 5 (1993): 5–17.

38. Jonathan Kozol, *The Shame of the Nation: The Restoration of Apartheid Schooling in America* (New York: Three Rivers Press, 2006).

39. Christopher Hickman, "No Child Left Behind and the Transformation of Federal Education Policy, 1965–2005," *Congress and the Presidency* 35, no. 1 (Spring 2008): 107–110.

40. Julius Menacker, Ward Weldon, and Emanuel Hurwitz, "Community Influences on School Crime and Violence," *Urban Education* 25, no. 1 (1990): 68–80.

41. Janice Joseph, "School Factors and Delinquency: A Study of African-American Youths," *Journal of Black Studies* 26 (1996): 340–355.

42. Annette Lareau, *Unequal Childhoods: Class, Race, and Family Life* (Berkeley: University of California Press, 2003).

43. Janet M. Fitchen, "The Single-Parent Family, Child Poverty, and Welfare Reform," *Human Organization* 54 (1995): 355–362.

44. Judith S. Wallerstein and Sandra Blakeslee, *Second Chances: Men, Women, and Children a Decade after Divorce* (New York: Ticknor & Fields, 1989).

45. Christopher R. Browning and Edward O. Laumann, "Sexual Contact between Children and Adults: A Life Course Perspective," *American Sociological Review* 62 (1997): 540–560.

46. James C. Howell, *Preventing and Reducing Juvenile Delinquency: A Comprehensive Framework* (Thousand Oaks, CA: Sage, 2003), 123–129.

47. Jean E. Veevers and Barbara A. Mitchell, "Intergenerational Exchanges and Perceptions of Support within 'Boomerang Kid' Family Environments," *International Journal of Aging and Human Development* 46, no. 2 (February 1998): 91.

48. Nancy Kleniewski, *Cities, Change, and Conflict with Infotrac: A Political Economy of Urban Life* (Belmont, CA: Wadsworth, 2002).

49. BBC News, "Summer Schemes Slash Youth Crime," August 21, 2001, http://news.bbc.co.uk/1/low/uk/1506876.htm.

50. Suzanne Le Menestrel and Daniel F. Perkins, "An Overview of How Sports, Out-of-School Time, and Youth Well-Being Can and Do Intersect," *New Directions for Youth Development* 2007, no. 115 (Fall 2007): 13–25.

51. FBI, *Uniform Crime Reports: Crime in the United States, 2006*, Number of Offenses Cleared by Arrest or Exceptional Means, Table 28, www.fbi.gov/ucr/cius2006/data/table_28.html.

52. Alexes Harris, "Diverting and Abdicating Judicial Discretion: Cultural, Political, and Procedural Dynamics in California Juvenile Justice," *Law and Society Review* 41, no. 2 (June 2007): 387–428.

53. Leona Lee, "Factors Influencing Intake Disposition in a Juvenile Court," *Juvenile and Family Court Journal* 46, no. 1 (1995): 43–62.

54. Douglas C. Dodge, *Due Process Advocacy* (Washington, DC: U.S. Department of Justice, Office of Juvenile Justice and Delinquency Prevention, 1997).

55. Eyitayo Onifade et al., "Risk Assessment: Identifying Patterns of Risk in Young Offenders with the Youth Level of Service/Case Management Inventory," *Journal of Criminal Justice* 36, no. 2 (May 2008): 165–173.

56. James Austin and Barry Krisberg, "Wider, Stronger, and Different Nets: The Dialectics of Criminal Justice Reform," *Journal of Research in Crime and Delinquency* 18, no. 1 (1981): 165–196.

57. James Howell, "Juvenile Transfers to the Criminal Justice System: State of the Art," *Law and Policy* 18, no. 1 (1996): 17–60.

58. Benjamin Steiner and Emily Wright, "Assessing the Relative Effects of State Direct File Waiver Laws on Violent Juvenile Crime: Deterrence or Irrelevance?" *Journal of Criminal Law and Criminology* 96 (Summer 2006): 1451–1477.

59. James L. Loving and Nicholas S. Patapis, "Evaluating Juvenile Amenability to Treatment: Integrating Statutes and Case Law into Clinical Practice," *Journal of Forensic Psychology Practice* 7 (January 2007): 67–78.

60. Joseph B. Sanborn Jr., "The Right to a Public Jury Trial—A Need for Today's Juvenile Court," *Judicature* 76, no. 4 (1993): 230–238.

61. Grant Grissom, "Dispositional Authority and the Future of the Juvenile Justice System," *Juvenile and Family Court Journal* 42, no. 1 (1991): 25–34.

62. Erika Gebo, "Do Family Courts Administer Individualized Justice in Delinquency Cases? " *Criminal Justice Policy Review* 16 (June 2005): 190–210.

63. John Whitehead and Steven Lab, "Meta-Analysis of Juvenile Correctional Treatment," *Journal of Research in Crime and Delinquency* 26 (1989): 276–295.

64. Kimberly Kempf-Leonard, Paul E. Tracy, and James C. Howell, "Serious, Violent, and Chronic Juvenile delinquents: The Relationship of Delinquency Career Types to Adult Criminality," *Justice Quarterly* 18 (2001): 449–478.

65. Paul Tracy, Marvin Wolfgang, and Robert Figlio, *Delinquency in Two Birth Cohorts: Executive Summary* (Washington, DC: U.S. Department of Justice, 1985).

66. Brigitte Bouhours and Kathleen Daly, "Youth Sex Offenders in Court: An Analysis of Judicial Sentencing Remarks," *Punishment and Society* 9 (October 2007): 371–394.

67. Wayne S. Wooden, "Tagger Crews and Members of the Posse," in *The Modern Gang Reader*, eds. Malcolm W. Klein, Cheryl L. Maxson, and Jody Miller (Los Angeles: Roxbury, 1995), 65–68.

68. Matthew T. Heriot and Barbara "Sunshine" Parker, "Native American Youth Gangs: Linking Culture, History and Theory for Improved Understanding, Prevention and Intervention," *Journal of Ethnicity in Criminal Justice* 5 (December 2007): 83–97.

69. Shelden, Tracy, and Brown, *Youth Gangs*.

70. Jody Miller, *One of the Guys: Girls, Gangs, and Gender* (New York: Oxford University Press, 2001).

71. Jerome H. Skolnick, "Gangs and Crime Old as Time; But Drugs Change Gang Culture," in *The Modern Gang Reader*, eds. Malcolm W. Klein, Cheryl L. Maxson, and Jody Miller (Los Angeles: Roxbury, 1995), 222–227.

72. Howard N. Snyder and Melissa Sickmund, *Juvenile Offenders and Victims: 2006 National Report* (Washington, DC: U.S. Department of Justice, Office of Juvenile Justice and Delinquency Prevention, 2006), 201.

73. Thomas Castellano and Irina Soderstrom, "Therapeutic Wilderness Programs and Juvenile Recidivism: A Program Evaluation," *Journal of Offender Rehabilitation* 17, no. 1 (1992): 19–46.

74. Snyder and Sickmund, *Juvenile Offenders and Victims: 2006 National Report*, 218.

75. Margaret Beyer, "Juvenile Boot Camps Don't Make Sense," *American Bar Association Journal of Criminal Justice* 10, no. 1 (1996): 20–21.

76. Snyder and Sickmund, *Juvenile Offenders and Victims: 2006 National Report*, 218.

77. Patricia Puritz and Mary Ann Scali, *Beyond the Walls: Improvising Conditions of Confinement for Youth in Custody* (Washington, DC: U.S. Department of Justice, Office of Juvenile Justice and Delinquency Prevention, 1998).

78. Snyder and Sickmund, *Juvenile Offenders and Victims: 2006 National Report*, 196, 198, 218.

79. Ibid.

80. Ibid., 225.

81. Lisa M. Flesch, "Juvenile Crime and Why Waiver Is Not the Answer," *Family Court Review* 42 (July 2004): 583–596.

82. J. Fagan, E. Slaughter, and E. Hartstone, "Blind Justice: The Impact of Race on the Juvenile Justice Process," *Crime and Delinquency* 53 (1997): 224–258.

83. Lawrence T. Kajs, "Reforming the Discipline Management Process in Schools: An Alternative Approach to Zero Tolerance," *Educational Research Quarterly* 29 (June 2006): 16–27.

84. Randy Cassingham, "Losing My Tolerance for Zero Tolerance," *This is True*, www.thisistrue.com/zt.html.

85. Fiona Morgan, "Deadly Consequences," *Salon*, http://dir.salon.com/news/feature/2001/03/09/shooting/index.html.

86. Although some controversy exists about the restorative justice practice, it is accepted most in the juvenile justice system.

CHAPTER 15

Victimless Crimes

Objectives

1. Discuss why drug use, gambling, and sex work are controversial issues.

2. Explain the concept of victimless crimes.

3. Discuss why Prohibition was a failure.

4. Discuss the concept of the war on drugs.

5. Compare and contrast arguments for and against drug legalization and/or decriminalization.

6. Discuss why some forms of gambling are legal and sanctioned by the state, whereas other forms are not.

7. Discuss how gambling and prostitution exist in a legal and social gray area, in which some forms of these activities are illegal and others are not.

sex work

The exchange of coital or sex-related activities for payment.

victimless crimes

Behaviors such as gambling or prostitution that are deemed undesirable because they offend community standards rather than directly harm people or property.

The criminal justice system has a broad mandate to enforce all the laws the legislature passes. The making of law is inherently a political process in which various interest groups influence the process and have laws enacted that reflect their values. For the most part, this is not a problem because a wide consensus exists on the desirability of most laws. It would be difficult to find anyone who opposes the proscriptions on rape, murder, and robbery. Although most of us are shocked by the idea, some pedophiles believe that consensual sex between adults and children should be legalized, and they attempt to have their views considered by lawmakers.[1] So far, the pedophiles have not been successful in normalizing this behavior and having it legalized because most of society deems it deviant and harmful to children. A number of illegal behaviors, however, do not have a strong consensus favoring their proscription. Many people knowingly and willingly break the laws prohibiting these behaviors because they believe they pose little harm or because they realize they can make money by engaging in them. This chapter will cover three of these activities: drug use, gambling, and **sex work**.[2]

Drug use, gambling, and sex work are controversial issues because they challenge the values and religious beliefs of many people. Others, however, see them as consensual activities that do not harm anyone other than those who choose to engage in them. There is an old saying, "My right to wave my fist in the air ends where your nose begins." That is to say, as long as I do not harm you with my fist waving, you should not care, and you certainly should not pass a law against it. Drug use, illegal forms of gambling, and prostitution are considered by many people to be **victimless crimes** because, unlike armed robberies, these crimes have no direct victim.[3] However, not everyone agrees with the claim that these behaviors are victimless, pointing to the drug addict who robs a house to pay for drugs, or the gambler who wipes out the joint checking account she has with her husband, or her husband who brings home a sexually transmitted disease he caught from a prostitute. Those in favor of legalizing these behaviors counter these claims by pointing out that burglary is already a criminal offense and that spending money from a joint checking account is something husbands and wives do all the time. These illegal behaviors are not the problem: the wife who cannot be trusted with the checkbook, the husband who is unfaithful, or the junkie who is addicted to drugs are the problems. These people believe that better ways exist to deal with these problems than making them illegal.[4] In fact, many argue that criminalizing these behaviors causes social harm.[5]

We will not resolve these issues here because they are matters of values. Rather, we will examine the profound and wide-ranging influence that drug use, illegal gambling, and prostitution exert on the criminal justice system. These activities drain resources from the detection and prosecution of other crimes, create opportunities for selective enforcement that undermines the trust of many in the criminal justice system, and provide large amounts of cash that can be used to corrupt criminal justice officials.[6] Therefore, we examine each of these behaviors not to pass judgment on the morality of those who choose to engage in them, but merely to understand and appreciate their effect on the criminal justice system.

DRUG USE AND ABUSE

The use and trafficking of illegal drugs is the most controversial issue facing the criminal justice system today.[7] In 2006, police made more arrests for drug abuse violations, about 1.9 million, than for any other offense.[8] The resources dedicated to the detection, prosecution, and punishment of the illegal drug user and seller have stretched the ability of the federal, state, and local criminal justice systems to such a point that they must establish priorities as to which offenses to pursue.[9] Simply put, drug use and drug-related offending is so prevalent that criminal justice officials must overlook some offenses to concentrate resources on the control of other types of offending. How did the drug problem get to be this way? Can the criminal justice system solve the problems associated with illegal drug use? What alternatives does the war on drugs propose?

Drug Abuse

What do we mean by *drug abuse*? Drugs have a range of legitimate, beneficial uses. The pharmaceutical industry has been responsible for eradicating diseases, relieving chronic pain, and addressing a wide range of health issues. Certainly no one would advocate getting rid of all drugs. Yet there is a problem with the use of drugs in some contexts that constitutes drug abuse. Many drugs have been made illegal because they are subject to abuse. However, other drugs, such as alcohol, tobacco, and caffeine, can be abused, yet they remain legal. Therefore, for our purposes, we will use Howard Abadinsky's definition of drug abuse: "ingesting a psychoactive substance that is illegal to possess or that is taken in quantities that are clearly harmful."[10]

This definition is widely, although not completely, accepted. Some contend that moderate use of marijuana is not drug abuse, but it would be deemed so by this definition because marijuana is illegal. We employ Abadinsky's definition while recognizing this controversy, but also understanding that if we are to consider drugs' effect on the criminal justice system, we must also recognize that illegality is an indispensable feature of a working definition of drug abuse.

A Short History of Drug Use and Drug Laws in the United States

Although patterns of drug and alcohol use have varied widely throughout history and across different societies, it is important to our understanding of the criminal justice system to consider how these patterns were established and how they changed in the United States. The large quantities of alcohol that early Americans consumed presented what we would today consider a social problem. Because it was so ingrained in colonial society, however, there was little effort to control it. Drinking alcohol was integrated into daily life because it was safer than drinking the water.[11] In his book *The Alcoholic Republic: An American Tradition*, W. J. Rorabaugh reported that between 1790 and 1830 the United States was considered a nation of drunkards:

> Alcohol was pervasive in American society; it crossed regional, sexual, racial, and class lines. Americans drank at home and abroad, alone and together, at work and at play, in fun and in earnest. They drank from the crack of dawn to the crack of dawn. At nights taverns were filled with boisterous, mirth-making tipsters. Americans drank before meals, with meals, and after meals. They drank while working in the fields and while traveling across half a continent. They drank in their youth, and, if they lived long enough, in their old age. They drank at formal events such as weddings, ministerial ordinations, and wakes, and on no occasion—by the fireside of an evening, on a hot afternoon, and when the mood called.[12]

Some groups, such as the Quakers, saw the problems associated with high levels of alcohol consumption, but the government did not take a moral stand on the issue. Instead, it adopted a laissez-faire attitude toward alcohol consumption and intervened only in taxing drugs and alcohol. In 1791, Congress passed an excise tax on whiskey that met with opposition from farmers west of the Appalachians who believed that the federal government did not have the right to tax the states. In what came to be known as the Whiskey Rebellion, federal revenue agents were attacked and sometimes tarred and feathered until President George Washington was forced to call in the militia to impose the power of the government on citizens who refused to pay the tax.[13]

A good example of the government's reluctance to regulate drug use can be found in the history of opium in the United States. In the mid-1880s, many Chinese were brought to the United States for labor on large projects such as the building of the railroads. They brought with them opium, the trade of which had made many American

Alcohol was used heavily in the American colonies and the early United States. The effect of alcohol abuse caused many citizens to worry about the safety of their communities.

Source: CORBIS-NY

A government inspector is tarred and feathered during the Whiskey Rebellion in 1794. Farmers objected to the government's collecting taxes on those who produced whiskey.

Source: The Granger Collection

and British merchants rich. The opium addiction of some of these Chinese was not considered a significant problem as long as it was confined to the Chinese. But when this drug use spread to other parts of society, it suddenly was deemed a serious social problem.[14] For instance, in San Francisco's Chinatown:

> The practice spread rapidly and quietly among this class of gamblers and prostitutes until the later part of 1875, at which time authorities became cognizant of the fact . . . that many women and young girls, and also young men of

respectable family, were being induced to visit the dens, where they were ruined morally and otherwise, a city ordinance was passed forbidding the practice under penalty of heavy fine or imprisonment or both.[15]

As opium smoking decreased over the years, other drugs took its place. During the Civil War, morphine, a highly addictive opium extract, was widely used to combat pain and dysentery. Eventually, so many soldiers became physically dependent on it that its addiction earned the epithet "the army disease." Cocaine was used to treat morphine addiction, until it was realized that cocaine was just as habit forming.[16]

Because cocaine and morphine were considered legal drugs, they found their way into all sorts of patent medicines. Advertised as therapeutic medicines, these concoctions contained large percentages of alcohol and other habit-forming drugs. Although they tended to give short-term relief for a wide range of ailments, the unsuspecting public was simply getting drunk or stoned on these supposed medicines. Traveling hucksters prescribed these patent medicines for "whatever ails you" and found an especially eager audience in respectable women who, instead of going to the bar or saloon, would go home and get drunk on their "medicine."

Drug Control Legislation

In the 20th century a steady progression of laws attempted to protect people from the harmful effects of drugs. These laws, although not wholly effective, shaped and reflected the attitudes and policies that the general public developed over the years. In 1906, Upton Sinclair published his muckraking exposé of the meatpacking industry, *The Jungle*.[17] This book provided graphic descriptions of the unsanitary conditions in slaughterhouses and included stories of how dead rodents were routinely tossed into processed beef. Congress responded by passing the Pure Food and Drug Act of 1906, which required producers of food and drugs to clearly list what their products contained. Furthermore, this law made it illegal to transport across state lines mislabeled or adulterated food or drugs. This law crippled the patent medicine business. Once people could see what was in these products, they could make informed choices and avoid them.[18]

The Pure Food and Drug Act of 1906 did not criminalize drugs. Selling and consuming narcotics was still legal; they just had to be labeled accurately. The goal of this legislation was not to protect people from themselves but to ensure that incompetent or unscrupulous merchants did not take advantage of unsuspecting individuals. The next major piece of drug legislation was the Harrison Act, passed by Congress in 1914. This law was designed "to provide for the registration of, with the collectors of internal revenue, and to impose a special tax upon all persons who produce, import, manufacture, compound, deal in, dispense, or give away opium or coca leaves, their salts, derivatives, or preparations, and for other purposes."[19] The Harrison Act did not make the use and sale of narcotics illegal, but it did ensure that the government collected taxes from those who trafficked in drugs.

Soon, however, the courts ruled that prescribing narcotics to addicts even to maintain their comfort was not a legitimate medical practice (*Webb* v. *United States* [1919]), although this stance was softened somewhat in *Lindner* v. *United States* (1925). For the next 50 years, the United States inched toward the criminalization of narcotics and other drugs, including marijuana, through court cases and legislation. The 1951 Boggs Act increased penalties for violating drug laws and, for the first time, regulated both narcotics and marijuana in a single federal law.[20] In 1956, President Eisenhower signed the Narcotics Control Act, which increased both penalties and federal authority.[21] These pieces of legislation were the U.S. government's first coherent stab at criminalizing specific classes of drugs and prohibiting their sale and use. The Controlled Substances Act of 1970 set forth the drug schedules currently used to classify drugs, and the United States completed its move from allowing the use of any drug by anyone to regulating drugs for tax purposes to outlawing them completely.

Early efforts to demonize marijuana, such as this 1935 movie poster, were not only inaccurate but counterproductive. Those who tried the drug found their experiences differing widely from the negative propaganda.
Source: CORBIS-NY

To fully appreciate how drug use is a crime dictated by societal values as much as the need for the public good, we must consider the country's experience with the prohibition of alcohol in the early 20th century. On January 16, 1919, the Eighteenth Amendment was ratified, and Congress passed the National Prohibition Act (also known as the Volstead Act), which funded the Prohibition Bureau of the Treasury Department.[22] Prohibition was a monumental failure. Not only did it fail to prevent the use of alcohol, but it also provided an opportunity for corruption and organized crime. Speakeasies, bootlegging, and political payoffs became ingrained in society, and the selective enforcement of alcohol laws resulted in an overall disregard for the law. The criminal element infiltrated law enforcement agencies, and citizens became cynical not only about the liquor laws but about government in general.[23] Prohibition was regarded as a "great experiment" that not only failed to achieve its goals but produced the unintended consequences of undermining the criminal justice system by stimulating corruption, making romantic figures out of bootleggers and lawbreakers, and straining citizens' trust in their government.[24] Although most people might have agreed that alcohol produced problems for individuals and society, not many were prepared to give it up. Alcohol use was (and is) part of the social fabric, and a significant percentage of the population either wanted the freedom to engage in social drinking or saw an opportunity to make a great deal of money by violating the laws against smuggling, distribution, and sales.[25]

Prohibition ended in 1933, but the country was not ready to go back to the days of completely unregulated drugs and alcohol. In fact, by 1937 the Treasury Department's Bureau of Narcotics considered marijuana a serious problem that required national legislation. The Marijuana Tax Act resulted from a campaign by Bureau of Narcotics chief Harry Anslinger to demonize the drug by calling it the "devil drug," "assassin of youth," and the "weed of madness."[26] Whereas opium had been introduced by the Chinese, marijuana found its way to the United States by way of Mexico. Even though marijuana had been known since colonial days, particularly in the form of hemp used to make rope, the recreational use of marijuana was linked to Mexican culture and used to stigmatize Mexicans as dangerous.[27]

When drugs affected only the marginal populations of society, such as Chinese and Mexican immigrants, they were not deemed serious social problems. However, as drugs moved into the middle and upper classes, they received the attention of the criminal justice system. In the 1960s, rampant drug use accompanied protest movements concerned with civil rights, women's rights, and the Vietnam war.[28] Drug use was considered another repudiation of the dominant value system, and the criminal justice system reacted harshly. Although there were (and continue to be) efforts to decriminalize marijuana, people who used other drugs, particularly heroin and cocaine, were vigorously prosecuted and punished.

One may legitimately ask why recreational drugs are still demonized so long after the 1960s. Why haven't the "baby boomers," who used drugs then, sought to legalize or at least greatly decriminalize some drugs now that their generation is in its prime years of political and social power? The answer is complex. On one hand, recreational drug use can be considered a form of youthful rebellion. As people grow older and take responsible roles in society, they no longer feel the need to act out. Furthermore, seeking to protect their own children and grandchildren, baby boomers have limited the availability of drugs. Many enjoyed their own reckless youths, but they consider themselves lucky to have escaped the downsides of drug use: addiction, criminal records, and death.[29] See Crosscurrents 15.1 for a look at the cycle of drugs and drug law enforcement throughout the past few decades.

The War on Drugs

The problems of illegal drug use in the last part of the 20th century fundamentally altered the criminal justice system. Politicians, law enforcement officials, teachers, and parents developed policies that figuratively waged a "war on drugs." Although the war metaphor may be somewhat misleading, it illustrates the lengths to which our leaders are willing to go to control drug use. Few people defend the use of illegal drugs; however, a public policy debate continues about how the government should handle this problem.[30] Concerns have emerged from both conservative and liberal quarters about how the war on drugs challenges our constitutional liberties. There is considerable evidence that the war on drugs has had a negative effect on minorities. For instance, the different penalties for crack cocaine versus powder cocaine have had a detrimental impact on blacks. The result is that those arrested and convicted for drug offenses have been disproportionately people of color, who have been incarcerated at a much greater rate than would normally be expected.[31] Additionally, many believe that the war on drugs strains the trust between parents and children, alters the relationship between students and schools, and erodes the respect citizens have for the criminal justice system. The war on drugs is being waged on many fronts (see Crosscurrents 15.2).[32] The following examples illustrate how the criminal justice system is simply one part of the web of social control:

- **Testing children for drug use**   One of the fronts on which the war on drugs is being waged is at the consumer level. Theoretically, if the demand for drugs can be reduced, then the price of drugs will fall and fewer people will engage in drug trafficking. A vast number of prevention programs are aimed at changing the attitudes of young people who are considering drug use. One need only watch television to see public service announcements directed at children or their parents describing the dangers of drug use and how to prevent it. There are also well-meaning efforts to stem drug use by detecting it. Parents and schools are encouraged to look for signs of drug use by monitoring children's friends and the music they listen to, and by searching their children's rooms or school lockers. In extreme cases, children are tested for drug use.[33] Home drug-testing kits are marketed to parents who suspect drug use in their children, and some schools test athletes and anyone else who participates in official extracurricular activities.[34]

- **Increased penalties for drug use or sales**   Legislatures around the country, including Congress, have greatly increased many of the penalties for drug use or sales. These increased penalties are based on the deterrence principle—that

The Drug du Jour

The history of drug laws of the United States reflects an interesting and disturbing pattern. As new drugs are introduced to American culture, they are first met with a sense of curiosity, concern, and then moral panic. Long before the real effect of the drugs can be established, anecdotal information is used to spread dismay and fear about the influence these drugs have on citizens, especially on children. The result has been a patchwork of drug laws that lack any sense of proportionality or fairness and typically are aimed at marginalized groups in society.

As we have previously discussed, the history of opium and Chinese workers in the United States led to new laws banning that substance, and the connection between marijuana and Mexican laborers stimulated the country to attempt to control cannabis. The failed policies of Prohibition in the 1920s and 1930s further reflected how drug laws were fashioned according to the morality of certain groups in society. One of the underlying agendas in the construction of our drug laws has been the attempt to control the "dangerous classes" of society.[1] These dangerous classes are usually identified as young people, people of color, or immigrants.

The more recent history of drug legislation has been directed at a broader spectrum of society. As drug use and abuse has spread into middle-class, rural, or mainstream society, drug laws have been aimed at suppressing the negative effects of addiction. However, it is necessary to look at each drug individually to comprehend how drug legislation has been motivated by various agendas.

- *Cocaine.* Cocaine is an expensive drug. It is used primarily by upper-middle-class white people for recreational purposes. Although there are many noted cases of cocaine addiction that have had devastating effects on individuals, most cocaine users save it for social situations such as parties and concerts. Although the prolonged use of cocaine can be extremely damaging to the human body, its proponents contend that its moderate use as a recreational drug does not necessitate the stringent enforcement of laws prohibiting this drug. In many ways, cocaine legislation and enforcement has been aimed at international dealers and not particularly at middle- and upper-middle-class consumers.
- *Crack cocaine.* The laws and enforcement dealing with crack cocaine are very different from those concerning powder cocaine. Crack cocaine is relatively cheap compared to powder cocaine and has been the drug of choice for many lower-class Americans. A moral panic developed over crack cocaine in the late 1980s and early 1990s, asserting that it is more addictive than powder cocaine and more destructive to society. Black people were especially affected by crack-cocaine laws because of the vastly different penalties associated with powder cocaine and crack cocaine. In many jurisdictions, the penalties for crack cocaine were 10 times as punitive as those for powder cocaine. Additionally, mandatory-minimum sentences prevented judges from using discretion in arriving at a appropriate disposition for these cases. Critics of the criminal justice system alleged that these disparities are racist in nature and perpetuate and exacerbate racial inequalities.[2]
- *Ecstasy.* Ecstasy or MDMA is a drug that is popular on the music scene and has raised alarms among parents and law enforcement. Although it might have some legitimate medical uses, it is used as a recreational drug by young people attending concerts, who claim that it allows them to experience the music in a more personal and in-depth manner. Sometimes called the "love drug," it has the advantage of making people more tolerant and passionate toward those around them.[3]
- *Methamphetamine.* The most recent panic involves methamphetamine. It can be argued that the popularity of methamphetamine is a result of the effective policies that prevent cocaine and marijuana from entering the country from overseas. Methamphetamine can be cooked up in crude laboratories and is composed of many common household chemicals and over-the-counter drugs. The problem has become so widespread that many states have introduced legislation to limit the sale of some cold and allergy medicines. Many of these drugs are now no longer on the supermarket shelves but must be purchased from a pharmacist. The government keeps track of how much of these substances are purchased by individuals and limits the amount of any individual transaction.[4] Outlets have sprouted up in both urban and rural areas, and the government has an extremely difficult time keeping up with methamphetamine dealers. It can be an extremely profitable drug because it requires little in the way of expertise to manufacture.[5] One popular method of trying to combat methamphetamine is the showing of before-and-after pictures of users. The physical toll that methamphetamine takes can be shocking, and the publication of these pictures is intended to warn people of the destructive nature of the drug. One of the more alarming

features of methamphetamine has been the way it has infiltrated rural areas that previously did not experience drug problems. Consequently, politicians are feeling pressure to increase efforts to stem this drug from constituents who had previously considered drugs an urban problem.

- *OxyContin.* Although OxyContin is a drug that is abused by a small, select group of people, it has gotten quite a bit of attention. OxyContin is a controlled Schedule II drug, which means it is legal but ". . . requires registration, record keeping, distribution restrictions, dispensing limits, manufacturing security and reports to the DEA."[6] This drug is most often prescribed as a painkiller, but some users have found that it can give a quick and effective high. The pills are manufactured in a time-release formula, but abusers often chew, snort, or inject the drug for a quicker, more intense experience. Several high-profile celebrities such as radio host Rush Limbaugh have become addicted to this drug, which has raised its public awareness and, in many cases, its popularity.[7]

The crafting of U.S. drug laws has occurred over many decades. They are result of the social concerns and political pressures of particular times. There has not been an objective and uniform appraisal of the harm done by drugs, which has resulted in critics contending that the laws are biased against certain groups of people and, in some cases, outright racist. If drug laws reflected the actual harm to society, alcohol and tobacco would certainly be outlawed rather than simply regulated.[8]

Think About It

1. It seems that just as the criminal justice system is able to control one type of drug through legislation, law enforcement, and incarceration, another is developed. Should the criminal justice system change its approach to the control of drugs?
2. Has restriction of the purchase of cold and allergy medications been effective in controlling methamphetamine production?
3. Are legal drugs just as dangerous as illegal drugs? Why or why not?

[1]Randall G. Shelden, *Controlling the Dangerous Classes: A Critical Introduction to the History of Criminal Justice* (Boston: Allyn & Bacon, 2001).

[2]The Sentencing Project, www.sentencingproject.org/crackreform.aspx.

[3]Leslie Iverson, *Speed, Ecstasy, and Ritalin: The Science of Amphetamines* (New York: Oxford University Press, 2008).

[4]Matt Wagner, "Meth in Crosshairs of Cluster of New Bills," New Leader.com, January 15, 2006.

[5]Frank Owen, *No Speed Limit: The Highs and Lows of Meth* (New York: St. Martin's Press, 2007).

[6]OxyContin Abuse, www.oxycontinabuse.org/.

[7]Clay Lambert, "OxyContin Rushes into State's Drug Lexicon," *San Francisco Examiner*, October 7, 2003, http://opioids.com/oxycodone/rushlimbaugh.html

[8]Phillip J. Cook, *Paying the Tab: The Costs and Benefits of Alcohol Control* (Princeton, NJ: Princeton University Press, 2007).

is, individuals will eventually consider the cost (in terms of long imprisonment) too high when measured against the temporary pleasure associated with drug use. Debate is considerable about whether this strategy works. Certainly an increased number of inmates are serving time for drug trafficking and sales, but real questions remain about whether the streets are any safer because of these laws. Many question whether addicts can be deterred from drug use.[35] Others examine the market dynamics of the drug trade and question whether increased penalties simply mean higher prices for drugs and greater profits for drug dealers.[36] Finally, we may question whether increased penalties for drug offenses make the job of police officers more dangerous. When a drug dealer is facing life in prison, is he or she more likely to attempt to resist arrest? With stakes so high, in terms of both the money to be made and freedom to be lost, one of the unintended consequences of the war on drugs has been increased violence.[37]

- **Drug forfeiture laws** When law enforcement discovers that an individual's private possessions are being used in the drug trade, those possessions may be confiscated by the state. Have you ever wondered why some DARE drug prevention police officers have sleek muscle cars? Those cars used to belong to drug dealers who were caught with drugs in their cars, and the state used drug forfeiture laws to take them. In addition to cars, the police have taken boats, airplanes, homes, and large quantities of cash from drug dealers. Although this seems to be a legitimate practice—after all, those who rob banks or embezzle money should not be able to keep their ill-gotten gains—the forfeiture laws are broad enough to invite abuse. For instance, if you are stopped on the highway

Weight loss, apparent stress, and opportunistic infections are some of the visible consequences of using methamphetamine.

Source: Faces of Meth Program

and you fit the profile of a drug runner, the police have the latitude to confiscate any large amount of cash you have even if you have no drugs in your possession.[38] An additional concern about these drug forfeiture laws is the way that some law enforcement agencies might be tempted to overextend their mandate in order to seize cash and property that can be used by their agencies. For financially strapped local governments, the ability to confiscate the property of those engaged in drug use or drug sales can be a source of income. Some scholars question whether such "policing-for-profit" is desirable.[39]

These brief examples show that there is a difference of opinion about how the drug war is being prosecuted. Some people believe that the war on drugs is more harmful than the drugs themselves. In critiquing the war on drugs, Elliott Currie wrote:

> Reasonable people may debate the details. But there is no denying the fundamental realities: the American drug problem continues to tower above those of the rest of the industrial world, and it does so despite a truly extraordinary experiment in punitive control. We have unleashed the criminal-justice system against drug users and dealers with unprecedented ferocity, but drugs continue to destroy lives and shatter communities outside the Third World. And now the drug war itself contributes to that destruction—first in the incarceration of vast numbers of the young in what should be the start of their most productive years; and again in the depletion of resources that could otherwise be used to deal with the deeper problems of devastated communities.[40]

Drug Treatment

In addition to the war metaphor, the criminal justice system also addresses the problem of drugs from a medical perspective. Although it is illegal to possess and distribute certain drugs (see Table 15-1), it is not illegal to be a drug addict. Therefore, addiction is treated as a physical and psychological issue.[41] If individuals are compelled to continue drug use because of addiction, then the offenses associated with that addiction will continue as long as drug users remain trapped in the cycle of dependency. Treating the addiction is an important step in reducing the offenses associated with drug use.[42] As long as individuals physically need illegal drugs, there will always be those who are willing to engage in the highly lucrative drug trade. Few treatment programs are available for those who do not have the means to pay for private hospitalization, and government programs for the serious drug user are scarce and can have waiting lists that delay treatment until long after the user's motivation

15.2 CrossCurrents

A War on Many Fronts

The criminal justice system is not the only institution that is fighting the war on drugs. Because illegal drugs affect all aspects of society, the war is being waged on many fronts. Those who use illegal drugs, whether convicted or not, often find their lives changed in ways they never considered when they chose to get high at a party, while driving, or at home while watching cartoons. Following are some of the ways prior drug use can come back to haunt a person:

- *Driver's license.* Much like driving under the influence of alcohol, driving while on drugs can be used as a reason to deprive someone of driving privileges. However, unlike in the case of alcohol, there is no test to measure the driver's impairment. The Breathalyzer can distinguish when drivers have a blood alcohol level of .08, which is used as a benchmark to determine when someone cannot safely operate a motor vehicle. However, the mere presence of drugs in the body is all that is needed to make this judgment. Therefore, someone who smoked marijuana two days ago could be charged with driving under the influence even though the behavioral effects of the drug have worn off.

- *Extracurricular activities.* Some school districts test students for illegal drug use and prevent those found with drugs in their bodies from participating in sports. In addition to sports, other districts prohibit students who use drugs from participating in any type of school-sponsored activities, including cheerleading, band, and newspaper staff.

- *Military.* In the all-volunteer military, those who use drugs can be prevented from joining. This is especially true of the National Guard and the Reserves. Those already in the military will find themselves subject to the laws of the Uniform Code of Military Justice, which has broad discretion in the investigation and prosecution of drug use. Because the military has the important mission of national security, it must ensure the readiness of its personnel and take drug violations seriously.

- *Law enforcement.* Like the military, law enforcement agencies and other units of the criminal justice system screen candidates and

employees for drug use. If officers are going to enforce the drug laws, it seems reasonable to expect those officers to obey them as well. Otherwise they could have a conflict of interest and, even more important, could be susceptible to blackmail.

- *Political office.* Those who have used drugs might find their pasts coming back to haunt them when they run for political office. Even if they were never arrested for illegal drug use, the mere reporting of such indiscretion must be explained. During the 1960s many young people used drugs, and such politicians as Al Gore, Bill Clinton, George W. Bush, and Newt Gingrich have had to explain their transgressions. Several times, candidates for appointed jobs such as the Supreme Court have withdrawn when drug use was discovered in the background check.

- *Property forfeiture.* The government has confiscated cars, boats, houses, and airplanes that have been used in the drug trade. Additionally, large amounts of cash that belonged to suspects involved in the drug business have also been taken and legally kept by law enforcement agencies.

These examples demonstrate that the criminal justice system is not the only institution fighting the drug war. Those who use illegal drugs face consequences at a number of points in their lives. In some ways, those who make a mistake might find that society continues to persecute them long after the criminal justice system has provided its punishments. They could even have a difficult time reentering conventional society. Therefore, students, especially those who want a career in the criminal justice system, should seriously weigh any illegal drug use against the possible long-term consequences.

Think About It

1. In what other ways does society discourage the use of illegal drugs?
2. Has the drug war gone too far? Not far enough?
3. If you could repeal one law concerning drugs, what would it be?
4. If you could create one law concerning drugs, what would it be?

has waned.[43] The criminal justice system is good at detecting and arresting drug users but often fails to provide the treatment necessary to prevent recidivism.[44]

One important aspect of drug treatment is the need to consider the environment to which the client will return after the treatment. (See Focus on Ethics 15.1 for a scenario.) Although some users may respond to treatment in a controlled setting, such as an inpatient hospital, it is an entirely different matter when they return to their

Table 15-1   **Drug Schedules**

Schedule	Substances
Schedule I (no medical use; high abuse)	heroin, mescaline, psilocybin, LSD, marijuana, hashish, peyote, Ecstasy, Quaaludes, synthetic heroin
Schedule II (some medical use; high abuse)	methadone, morphine, cocaine, amphetamine, methamphetamine, PCP, opium, Ritalin
Schedule III (medical use; moderate abuse)	codeine, anabolic steroids, barbiturates
Schedule IV (medical use; low abuse)	Xanax, Valium, Darvon
Schedule V (medical use; low abuse)	cough syrups

Schedule I

1. High potential for abuse.
2. No currently accepted medical use in treatment in the United States.
3. A lack of accepted safety for use of the drug or other substance under medical supervision.

Schedule II

1. High potential for abuse.
2. Currently accepted medical use in treatment in the United States or a currently accepted medical use with severe restrictions.
3. Abuse may lead to severe psychological or physical dependence.

Schedule III

1. Potential for abuse less than the drugs or other substances in Schedules I and II.
2. Currently accepted medical use in treatment in the United States.
3. Abuse may lead to moderate or low physical dependence or high psychological dependence.

Schedule IV

1. Low potential for abuse relative to the drugs or other substances in Schedule III.
2. Currently accepted medical use in treatment in the United States.
3. Abuse may lead to limited physical dependence or psychological dependence relative to the drugs or other substances in Schedule III.

Schedule V

1. Low potential for abuse relative to the drugs or other substances in Schedule IV.
2. Currently accepted medical use in treatment in the United States.
3. Abuse may lead to limited physical dependence or psychological dependence relative to the drugs or other substances in Schedule IV.

Source: U.S. Drug Enforcement Administration, www.usdoj.gov/dea/.

homes and neighborhoods where all the circumstances that encouraged their initial drug use still exist. For treatment to have long-term success, a number of conditions should be considered. Elliott Currie specified several goals that treatment programs should strive for:[45]

1. **Taking treatment seriously.**   Many treatment programs, including those in correctional institutions and private hospitals and those connected with the courts, provide only token treatment. The resources are meager, the commitment is insufficient, and there is no realistic plan or focus. To have quality service and effective results, a certain level of funding and accountability is required. Currie advocated rigorous standards of evaluation and modification of programs based on what is found to be effective.

2. **Making treatment user-friendly.**   To get addicts involved in treatment programs, the programs should regard them as partners in the treatment process rather than as criminals or deviants. Drug treatment is not something that can be imposed; rather, it must accommodate clients' social and emotional needs. The success of drug treatment depends on the individual client's ability to explore

his or her reasons for drug use, the feelings and vulnerabilities that continue to make addiction possible, and his or her relationships and dependence on others. To be effective, drug treatment should foster a helping relationship rather than a punitive one.

3. **Linking treatment with harm reduction.** Drug treatment can be partially successful in several ways. Although the goal is to free the user from drug dependency, this should be viewed as a process, not an event. On the road to complete independence from drugs are steps that can make the drug use less deleterious to the user and others. For instance, because of the problems of HIV and AIDS, drug users can participate in educational programs that promote safe-sex practices and more sanitary drug usage. One particularly controversial harm-reduction strategy is to give addicts new syringes or bleach kits to clean their needles. Some people believe this is a tacit encouragement of drug addition by the government, but others believe it is a humane intermediate step in the treatment process. If the addict dies of AIDS and/or continues to spread the infection, the harm done by the outright prohibition policy is greater than the reduced harm of helping drug users pursue their habits in a more sanitary way.

4. **Making aftercare a priority.** When someone is locked away in a secure institution, it is not difficult to provide detoxification and counseling practices and demonstrate a healthy rate of success. The difficult part of drug treatment occurs when the user is released from custody and must return to the street, where he or she is faced with the temptations that initiated the drug use. Currie advocated that addicts need to be provided with help in negotiating the "increasing inhospitable housing and labor markets, as well as the criminal justice system."[46]

5. **Linking treatment with work.** Treating the addiction is only one part of successful rehabilitation. To become a fully functioning member of society again (or sometimes for the first time), the person must have the skills to compete in the job market. This can be an awesome task because many hard-core addicts have lost their social and work skills. At the very least, they must be retrained in such basic skills as constructing a résumé and locating employment opportunities, as well as in making themselves presentable to future employers. Such concerns as dressing appropriately, punctuality at interviews and work, and maintaining a stable residence are instrumental in maintaining long-term employment and successful drug abstinence.

The life of the hard-core drug user is a difficult one fraught with hardship, danger, loss of loved ones, poverty, and the ultimate possibility of an early death. Given a realistic choice, many addicts would like to kick their habits and return to conventional society. Unfortunately, for many, no realistic choice exists because not enough treatment programs are available for those without the money or insurance for private hospitalization. The result of the nation's failure to provide adequate treatment for drug addiction has been a continued healthy market for illegal drugs and an overburdened criminal justice system that must divert resources from other types of offenses.[47] Is there another way for society to deal with the drug problem that will be more effective in reducing the harm done to society and those who find themselves addicted to drugs?

The Decriminalization and Legalization Debate

The war on drugs has not rid the nation of illegal drugs. Some critics argue that the war on drugs has been such a monumental failure that the war has become a more serious problem for society than the drugs themselves.[48] We will not directly address this point here because the answer to whether the cure is worse than the disease is as much a political and social question as it is an empirical one.[49] The answer is bound up in each person's value system and cannot be decided by counting the number of addicts, counting the amount of money spent on prisons, or measuring the spread of

15.1   FOCUS *on* ETHICS

BETTER, BUT STILL BAD

As a probation officer, sometimes your victories are incomplete. You have worked hard with Winston to make sure he stays off drugs and out of trouble. You and Winston have had your moments, but you have been firm and consistent, and you seem to have won a certain amount of his respect. Winston has a long record of dealing drugs and has been in and out of treatment for his addiction to crack cocaine. For the past several months, he has been passing his drug tests, showing up for his required appointments, and holding down the best job he has ever had as a mailroom clerk at a large publishing house. He seems to be on the right track.

On your latest home visit, you discover that Winston and his new girlfriend, Karol, have been smoking marijuana. As a matter of fact, when you walk into their living room, the pungent stench is so strong that the cats, who normally flee when they see you, only yawn. Winston cannot talk in complete sentences, and Karol plows through an entire box of cookies as you read them the riot act. It is late, and you are mad, so you order Winston to be in your office at 8:00 A.M. When Winston arrives at 9:30 the next morning, he is contrite. You are already doing the paperwork to have him arrested for violation of probation as he tries to convince you that he deserves another chance. He is persuasive as he argues that smoking marijuana is the only way he can stay off crack. He claims that he has been cheating on his drug tests to disguise his marijuana smoking, but that he has been crack free for several months. He is convinced that if he gives up the marijuana, he will go back to smoking crack. Karol, who came with him, testifies that he is doing everything else right and that if given a chance, he will be able to eventually give up the marijuana also. Because she is a middle school English teacher, you believe she has been a good influence on Winston.

What Do You Do?

1. Revoke his probation and take Winston back before the judge, where he will face the prospect of going to prison.

2. Give him another chance and simply ignore his marijuana smoking because, in an odd way, it seems to be helping him stay off crack.

3. Give him another chance but insist that he quit smoking marijuana and double up on his drug testing to make sure he is not cheating.

4. Insist that he dump his girlfriend, Karol, because she smokes marijuana with him and you want to take that temptation away.

5. Report Karol to the school board because she is teaching middle school students while she is an active marijuana user.

---

infectious diseases. It is also useful to consider carefully the terms *drug decriminalization* and *drug legalization* because they mean different things. Therefore, without advocating any of these ideas here, we simply present some of the possibilities and distinctions of drug decriminalization and **legalization**.

legalization
The total removal of legal prohibitions on specific acts that were previously proscribed and punishable by law.

LEGALIZATION   Society has an interest in discouraging the use of recreational drugs. The lessons taught by Prohibition appear to be that the outright banning of a substance demanded by the public does not work.[50] Now, although alcohol continues to cause significant social harm, it is restricted to people of a specified age, sold through a variety of controlled mechanisms depending on local and state laws, heavily taxed, and regulated in such a manner that organized crime is no longer a major factor in its sale and consumption. Alcohol is a legal but regulated substance that continues to be problematic for the criminal justice system but has generally been accepted as a moderate social risk.[51] The alcohol industry is a multi-billion-dollar enterprise that has its own lobbyists who are effective in keeping it legal.

Could the legalization of drugs follow a structure similar to that of alcohol? The answer is probably no, because there are so many different drugs that each would have to be considered according to its potential harm. Just as states have different rules for the sale of beer and wine as opposed to liquor, a variety of rules would be needed to regulate the sale of recreational drugs. Furthermore, the legalization of drugs would probably be incremental, and some drugs would remain illegal. In the following section we consider some of the issues surrounding the legalization of drugs.

- **Marijuana**   Perhaps the drug that stands the best chance of being legalized is marijuana. It appears to be the least physically harmful of the recreational drugs and is advocated by some to be useful as a medicine (see Case in Point 15.1). Several states, including California and Arizona, have passed laws making marijuana legal under a doctor's prescription for the treatment of some conditions

15.1   CASE IN POINT

UNITED STATES V. OAKLAND CANNABIS BUYERS' COOPERATIVE ET AL.

THE CASE	THE POINT
United States v. Oakland Cannabis Buyers' Cooperative et al., 532 U.S. 483 (2001)	The distribution of marijuana, even for medical purposes and with approval by a state's citizens, is prohibited under the Controlled Substances Act.

In 1996 voters in California approved Proposition 215, the Compassionate Use Act. The act legalized the medical use of marijuana in California for seriously ill patients who provided a doctor's recommendation. The Oakland Cannabis Buyers' Cooperative distributed marijuana to people who qualified under Proposition 215. The United States sued to stop the cooperative's activities under the Controlled Substances Act, which prohibits the distribution, manufacture, and possession with intent to distribute a controlled substance.

The district court ordered the cooperative to cease its activities and rejected its arguments of the necessity of medical marijuana. The Ninth Circuit court reversed and remanded this ruling on appeal. The case then went to the U.S. Supreme Court, which in turn reversed and remanded the Ninth Circuit's decision. The Court ruled in part, "There is no medical necessity exception to the Controlled Substances Act's prohibitions on manufacturing and distributing marijuana."

The Oakland Cannabis Buyers' Cooperative is currently enjoined from dispensing medical marijuana.

An American tourist uses a water pipe to smoke marijuana at a coffee shop in Amsterdam, the Netherlands. In 2000, the Dutch parliament adopted a resolution to legalize the production of marijuana and supply it to coffee shops.

Source: Getty Images, Inc - Liaison

such as the nausea associated with chemotherapy. The penalties for possession of marijuana vary widely from state to state (see Table 15-2). Although federal law supersedes the state laws at the present time, this issue continues to be debated. However, it is a big leap from medical marijuana to the legalization of the recreational use of marijuana. Some issues make complete legalization problematic, not the least of which is how it would be regulated. Because marijuana is grown in every state and can be grown indoors as well, it would be difficult for the

Table 15-2   **Penalties in Selected States for Possession of Marijuana, 2006**

State	Amount	Charge	Incarceration	Fine
California	28.5 g or less	Misdemeanor	None	$100
	More than 28.5 g	Misdemeanor	6 months	$500
	28.5 g or less on school grounds while school is open	Misdemeanor	10 days	$500
	More than 28.5 g on school grounds while school is open	Misdemeanor	6 months	$500
D.C.	Any amount	Misdemeanor	6 months	$1000
Florida	20 g or less	Misdemeanor	1 year	$1000
	More than 20 g	Felony	5 years	$5000
Illinois	2.5 g or less	Misdemeanor	30 days	$1500
	2.5–10 g	Misdemeanor	6 months	$1500
	10–30 g	Misdemeanor	1 year	$2500
	30–500 g	Felony	First offense 1–3 years; subsequent 2–5 years	$25,000
	500–2000 g	Felony	2–5 years	$25,000
	2000–5000 g	Felony	3–7 years	$25,000
	More than 5000 g	Felony	4–15 years	$25,000
Maine	Usable amount with proof of doctor's recommendation	None	None	None
	Less than 1.25 oz	Civil violation	None	$550
	More than 1.25 oz	Misdemeanor	1 year	$2000
Maryland	Any amount	Misdemeanor	1 year	$1000
New York	25 g or less (first offense)	Civil citation	None	$100
	25 g or less (second offense)	Civil citation	None	$200
	25 g or less (subsequent offense)	Misdemeanor	5 days and/or fine	$250
	25 g–2 oz	Misdemeanor	3 months	$500
	2–8 oz	Misdemeanor	1 year	$1000
	8–16 oz	Felony	4 years	$5000
	16 oz–10 lb	Felony	7 years	$5000
	More than 10 lb	Felony	15 years	$5000
Texas	2 oz or less	Misdemeanor	180 days	$2000
	2–4 oz	Misdemeanor	1 year	$4000
	4 oz–5 lb	Misdemeanor or Felony	180 days–2 years	$10,000
	5–50 lb	Felony	2–10 years	$10,000
	50–2000 lb	Felony	2–20 years	$10,000
	More than 2000 lb	Felony	5–99 years	$50,000

Source: California Health and Safety Code, sec. 11357–11362.9; D.C. Codes 48–904.01; Florida State Code, Title XLVI, sec. 893.13; Illinois Compiled Statutes, chap. 720/550, sec. 4; Maine Revised Statutes, Title 22, chap. 558, sec. 2383; Maryland Code, Title 5, sec. 601; New York State Consolidated Laws, sec. 221; Texas Statutes, chap. 481.

government to control its production and sale. Especially problematic would be the prospect of the government levying some sort of sales tax on marijuana that could be used to offset whatever social problems increased marijuana use might produce. One possibility would be for marijuana to be sold and taxed as are cigarettes. Presumably, individuals would be willing to pay the price for marijuana that has a consistent dose, is packaged in a safe way, and can be obtained legally.

• **Other drugs could be legalized with more stringent regulation**   For instance, heroin or cocaine could be controlled by the medical profession and given to people who had a legitimate need. If completely legalized, these drugs could be dispensed with the requirement that users be monitored and treated to control their addictions. Although the pressure to legalize these harder drugs is minimal, some claim that people should be free to use them as long as their drug use does not hurt others.

- **Drug legalization may reduce crime**   Those who are under the influence of drugs may continue to commit certain offenses as a result of their intoxication, but the offenses directly associated with the drug trade would be eliminated because dealers would no longer be fighting over territory, and interactions between buyers and sellers would be routinized. Additionally, with the price of drugs lowered because of legalization, users would not have to rob and steal to maintain their drug habits.

- **Drug legalization may have a positive effect on the criminal justice system**   With the burden of enforcing unpopular drug laws lifted from the system's mandate, the police would be able to focus their resources on violent crime. Another expected benefit would be the reduced opportunities for corruption of criminal justice personnel with the vast amounts of money generated by the illegal drug trade.

- **Legal drugs may be more difficult for juveniles to obtain**   Presently, many juveniles are recruited into the drug trade because the juvenile justice system treats offenders more leniently than the criminal justice system. In many communities today, underage youth find obtaining marijuana easier than buying beer. Effective regulation could be a better way to separate juveniles and drugs than prohibition.

- **Respect for the law may be increased with the legalization of drugs**   Presently, thousands of people use illegal drugs in a manner that does not harm others and allows them to pursue their careers and family life without problems. "Social users" of recreational drugs develop cynical attitudes toward the criminal justice system and government in general because of the risks they must take to engage in what they believe is private behavior.

Of course, legalizing drugs would certainly have a downside. Depending on which drugs are legalized and how they are regulated, increased drug use would likely result in threats to public safety, loss of productivity, and accidental-overdose cases. These are debatable concerns, but all are beyond the scope of this discussion. However, the harms associated with keeping drugs illegal are also of concern, and a public debate about our drug laws could be healthy for society. James Q. Wilson, a noted criminologist, argues that legalizing drugs would not accomplish all the benefits of reduced violent crime that its proponents commonly claim. Furthermore, Wilson suggested that other consequences to legalization should be considered before drug policies and laws are altered. He suggested that the number of addicts who no longer have to steal to pay black-market prices for drugs would be offset by the possible increase in the total number of addicts. Because these addicts would be difficult to employ, they would still have to resort to stealing to support themselves.[52]

DECRIMINALIZATION   In the current political atmosphere, the prospect for the legalization of drugs, even marijuana, seems dim. However, another strategy could serve as a compromise between the demonization of drug use and the war on drugs. **Decriminalization** of drugs would greatly reduce the penalties for drug use. For instance, possession of small amounts of marijuana is a misdemeanor in many jurisdictions, whereas selling larger amounts remains a felony. Many consider it a waste of expensive resources to incarcerate the occasional marijuana user who is better handled by fines, probation, and community-service sentencing options.[53]

Decriminalization allows the criminal justice system to escape the expense of enforcing stringent drug laws and allows other institutions to help deter drug use. Schools, the workplace, and recreational programs can still prohibit drug use even though the criminal justice system no longer wages a full-scale drug war. Those who are employed

decriminalization
The emendation of laws or statutes to lessen or remove penalties for specific acts subject to criminal prosecution, arrest, and imprisonment.

in good jobs have much to lose from even a misdemeanor conviction if they work in a drug-free workplace that has the option of firing employees who consume illegal drugs. Decriminalization makes a certain amount of sense for the criminal justice system, which would be relieved of expending large amounts of money, personnel, and other resources on a drug war but at the same time need not completely surrender the moral high ground of combating drugs.[54] Decriminalization allows society to discourage illegal drug use without having to attempt to stamp it out completely.

The Police and Drugs

Until U.S. policies on legalization or decriminalization of drugs change, the police must deal with the laws and realities that shape the contemporary drug scene. (For arrest trends by drug type, see Figure 15-1.) This mandate for law enforcement is crucial in many respects because it requires the police to pursue numerous goals in controlling illegal drugs, including the following:

- Addressing the violence associated with street-level drug dealing (in many respects, pursuing this goal means dealing with gangs and preventing the emergence of powerful organized criminal groups)
- Controlling the offending of drug users
- Addressing the health, economic, and social well-being of drug users
- Restoring the quality of life in urban communities by ending street-level dealing
- Providing programs to help keep juveniles from experimenting with drugs
- Dealing with the problems inherent with the large amount of money in the illegal drug trade, such as police corruption and the integrity of the criminal justice system[55]

These goals require that law enforcement agencies fundamentally change their structure, training, recruitment, and allocation of resources. The issues of dealing with illegal drugs mean establishing narcotics bureaus, employing community cooperation, targeting politically sensitive neighborhoods or subcultures, and convincing the citizenry that law enforcement is walking the fine line of combating drugs without violating the legal and civil rights of drug users.[56] It is probably unrealistic to expect law enforcement agencies to fulfill all of these goals alone. Other institutions such as schools, families, and human-service agencies must also do their part in discouraging drug use. Unfortunately, law enforcement must deal with the problems of illegal drugs after other institutions have failed.

Figure 15-1   Number of Arrests by Drug Type, Selected Years, 1982–2007

Source: Federal Bureau of Investigation, *Uniform Crime Reports: Crime in the United States,* www.ojp.usdoj.gov/bjs/dcf/tables/drugtype.htm and www.fbi.gov/ucr/cius2007/arrests/index.html.

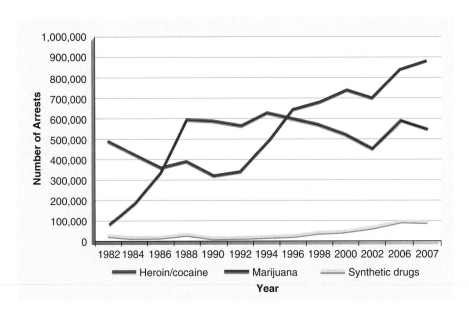

GAMBLING

Much as with drug use, Americans have ambivalent attitudes toward gambling (see Focus on Ethics 15.2). In a strict and limited sense, gambling can be considered a consensual and victimless activity; however, many segments of society question the economic, moral, and social ramifications of gambling. A particularly interesting fact about gambling today is that our attitudes, laws, and incentives concerning gambling are in a state of flux.[57] Legalized gambling has spread across the country as state and local governments have tried to capitalize on the public's desire to risk a little to gain a lot even though the odds are astronomically against them. For the criminal justice system, gambling, whether legal or illegal, has important ramifications; its inclusion as a topic of interest here demonstrates how crimes are socially defined.[58]

Gambling in the United States has undergone a radical transformation in the past 30 years. Once confined to Nevada and New Jersey, casinos now operate in many states and more ambiguous locations such as rivers and offshore (see Table 15-3). Additionally, a number of American Indian reservations have built casinos. Even more illustrative of the changing attitudes toward gambling in this country is the spread of government-sponsored lotteries. Even in the southern loop of the Bible Belt, states such as Florida, Georgia, and South Carolina have instituted lotteries to raise money.[59]

15.2   FOCUS *on* ETHICS

ROLLING THE DICE

You are a state representative. The northeastern area of the state where your hometown is located lost its manufacturing base in the late 1980s, affecting almost everyone you know. Your friends' parents lost their jobs, and after high school, most of your friends had to leave to find work. The big textile mills moved to other countries, devastating your hometown. For the past 20 years, the town has limped along on the revenues produced by a few small businesses and fast-food outlets near the freeway.

However, things are beginning to change. Your town is only 50 miles from one of the fastest-growing cities in the nation, and the city's growth is spreading toward your hometown. Even though the townsfolk never really recovered from the loss of their jobs, at least their local taxes remained low. Now developers are plunking in high-priced subdivisions to attract people who are tired of living in the city but still work there. As a result, the cost of living in your hometown is rising quickly without new jobs. Everyone is unhappy, and the old-timers are bitter about all the changes.

One morning, your grandfather, who made his first million selling real estate in the county, calls you with an idea. He wants to help bring in a casino. He says it will bring money to the area through tourism and provide jobs for the locals. Casinos are not legal in your state, and he is pressuring you to sponsor legislation that will legalize casino gambling, including card rooms, slot machines, and table games. Your mother, on the other hand, is against casinos. As a paralegal, she has dealt with more than a few divorces and bankruptcies caused by gambling addictions. She is convinced that casino gambling will not only exacerbate

those problems, but also bring corruption and crime to your vulnerable little town. You also know that bringing in a casino will mean that the county would have to rewrite or dispose of most of its alcohol restrictions, something that several large, influential local churches oppose. You point out to your grandfather that casino gambling is not an economic cure-all and refer him to several moribund racetracks in the next state and a struggling new lottery in another nearby state. He replies that casino gambling has done wonders for places such as Branson, Missouri, and you have to agree.

Your town sorely needs jobs, and although the new housing developments have created a few, it is mostly minimum-wage work at a couple of new gas stations. The commuters who live in the new developments spend most of their money in the city, not in your hometown.

What Do You Do?

1. Tell your grandfather that you will give his plan some thought but in the meantime hope that the city's rapid economic development will eventually spread to your hometown and bring some new jobs with it.

2. Study statistics on gambling addiction and crime and tell your grandfather that you will not support casino gambling.

3. Agree with your grandfather and start pushing for laws that will allow casinos. You believe that a slight rise in crime is natural in a developing area and that the increased revenues and jobs will offset any social problems.

Table 15-3 Types of Legalized Gambling by State

State	Charitable Gaming	Commercial Casinos	Indian casinos	Lottery	Pari-mutuels	Racetrack Casinos
Alabama	•		•		•	
Alaska	•		•			
Arizona	•		•	•	•	
Arkansas	•				•	
California	•		•	•	•	
Colorado	•	•	•	•	•	
Connecticut	•		•	•	•	
Delaware	•			•	•	•
D.C.	•			•		
Florida	•		•	•	•	•
Georgia	•			•		
Hawaii						
Idaho	•		•	•	•	
Illinois	•	•		•	•	
Indiana	•	•		•	•	•
Iowa	•	•	•	•	•	•
Kansas	•		•	•	•	
Kentucky	•			•	•	
Louisiana	•	•	•	•	•	•
Maine	•			•	•	•
Maryland	•			•	•	
Massachusetts	•			•	•	
Michigan	•	•	•	•	•	
Minnesota	•		•	•	•	
Mississippi	•	•	•			
Missouri	•	•	•	•	•	
Montana	•		•	•	•	
Nebraska	•		•	•	•	
Nevada	•	•			•	
New Hampshire	•			•	•	
New Jersey	•	•		•	•	
New Mexico	•		•	•	•	•
New York	•		•	•	•	•
North Carolina	•		•	•		
North Dakota	•		•	•	•	
Ohio	•			•	•	
Oklahoma	•		•	•	•	•
Oregon	•		•	•	•	
Pennsylvania	•	•		•	•	•
Rhode Island	•			•	•	•
South Carolina	•			•		
South Dakota	•	•	•	•	•	
Tennessee				•	•	
Texas	•		•	•	•	
Utah						
Vermont	•			•	•	
Virginia	•			•	•	
Washington	•		•	•	•	
West Virginia	•			•	•	•
Wisconsin	•		•	•	•	
Wyoming	•		•		•	

Source: Compiled and adapted from American Gaming Association, www.americangaming.org/Industry/factsheets/general_info_detail.cfv?id=15.

From the perspective of the criminal justice system, the spread of legalized gambling can be viewed as a double-edged sword. On one hand, by making gambling legal, the government has taken the management of the enterprise out of the hands of organized crime and provided a level of regulation that ensures that gamblers are afforded a standard of fairness and honesty in the administration of the games. Additionally, gambling has moved from back alleys and dingy garages to well-lit, safe, and physically comfortable casinos and riverboats, as well as to local convenience stores and the Internet. Gamblers are free from the constant threat of robbery, assault, and arrest that characterized the lifestyle of illegal gambling. In short, gambling has become a much safer activity since it has been legalized, and thousands of people incorporate it into their vacations and recreational pursuits.

Gambling remains problematic for the criminal justice system in other respects, with illegal gambling requiring the attention of criminal justice agencies. Betting on sporting events; illegal gambling on the Internet; and privately run video poker games, numbers running, and animal fighting still exist in many parts of the country. Legalized gambling also brings some concerns to the criminal justice system. Although casinos are typically well lit and have their own security, the surrounding area can be risky. According to Robert Goodman's *The Luck Business: The Devastating Consequences and Broken Promises of America's Gambling Explosion*, the neighborhoods in which casinos are located experience negative effects in terms of lower property values and urban decay. Along with the casinos come pawnshops, used-car lots, bars, and other businesses that drive down property values and drive out the residents of previously stable communities.[60]

Perhaps the most distressing unintended consequence of legalized gambling is the increase in the number of gamblers who become addicted to the activity (see Table 15-4) and continue to gamble with money they cannot afford to lose. Problem gamblers present a number of concerns for the criminal justice system as well as society. According to Goodman, the debts of problem gamblers affect the public as a whole because these gamblers have no money to pay their bills, taxes, or other debts, and often declare bankruptcy. Other gamblers, to get the money they owe, commit offenses such as writing bad checks, fraud, embezzlement, drug dealing, and stealing.[61]

According to the Council on Compulsive Gambling of New Jersey, compulsive gamblers accrue a high level of debt, with the average being around $40,000. One

Table 15-4   Diagnostic Criteria for Pathological Gambling

Diagnostic Criteria	Behavior Patterns
Preoccupation	Is preoccupied with gambling (e.g., preoccupied with reliving past gambling experiences, handicapping or planning the next venture, or thinking of ways to get money with which to gamble)
Tolerance	Needs to gamble with increasing amounts of money to achieve the desired excitement
Withdrawal	Is restless or irritable when attempting to cut down or stop gambling
Escape	Gambles as a way of escaping from problems or relieving dysphoric mood (e.g., feelings of helplessness, guilt, anxiety, or depression)
Chasing	After losing money gambling, often returns another day to get even ("chasing one's losses")
Lying	Lies to family members, therapists, or others to conceal the extent of involvement with gambling
Loss of control	Has made repeated unsuccessful efforts to control, cut back, or stop gambling
Illegal acts	Has committed illegal acts (e.g., forgery, fraud, theft, or embezzlement) to finance gambling
Risked significant relationship	Has jeopardized or lost a significant relationship, job, or educational or career opportunity because of gambling
Bailout	Has relied on others to provide money to relieve a desperate financial situation caused by gambling

Source: National Gambling Impact Study Commission, final report (June 1999); American Psychiatric Association information in U.S. General Accounting Office, *Impact of Gambling: Economic Effects More Measurable than Social Effects* (Washington, DC: Author, 2000), 43, www.gao.gov/new.items/gg00078.pdf.

estimate of insurance-related fraud that could be linked to compulsive gambling was estimated at $1.3 billion a year. Additionally, those who experience problems controlling their gambling debts are reported to have a suicide rate 5 to 10 times higher than the rest of the population.[62]

An emerging issue with gambling has been the explosion of Internet sites that allow one to wager money on a wide range of activities. Many of these sites are offshore; the globalization of the Internet allows people to connect to servers in locations as far-flung as the Caribbean islands, the Isle of Man, and sites in Asia. Because these offshore gambling sites are not regulated by the U.S. government, there is no way to ensure their credibility or for the U.S. government to collect taxes. In October 2006, President George W. Bush signed into law the Unlawful Internet Gambling Enforcement Act. Financial instituions are responsible for enforcing the law, which prohibits the use of credit cards, checks, and electronic fund transfers to place and settle bets made on the Internet. As a result, many Internet betting companies went out of business, stopped allowing U.S. customers to place bets, or simply halted operations in the United States.[63] Citibank, Bank of America, Fleet, and Chase Manhattan are some of the major credit card providers that already prohibited the use of their services for betting online. EBay, which acquired the Internet payment company PayPal in 2002, made the banning of gambling transactions one of the terms of its purchases.[64]

Technology in gambling presents new challenges to law enforcement efforts to control the industry. With shifting attitudes toward the morality of gambling, the criminal justice system's philosophy in addressing the issue has changed from one of keeping people from harming themselves by engaging in immoral activities to one of making sure that the government gets its taxes from the gambling economy. As gambling quickly changes from a public moral issue to an economic one, the criminal justice system is being forced to modify its response. Like drug use, gambling has become a moving target for the criminal justice system. Society's attitudes change, new laws are enacted, and new technologies are introduced that alter the way the criminal justice system must respond. Overall, some positive features have accrued with the move to legalize gambling in so many states. The underworld crime and corruption generally associated with the gaming industry has been replaced by corporations that integrate gambling with hotel and entertainment concerns and provide a relatively regulated, safe, and fair product.[65]

However, even as legalized gambling has relieved the criminal justice system of some problems, it has created or exacerbated others. Robert Goodman argued that legalized gambling did not simply give those who already gambled a legitimate place to safely conduct their activities, but rather created a whole new class of gambler. In fact, governments are spending a good deal of money on promotional materials and commercials to keep gamblers interested in gaming products. Rather than protecting citizens from gambling operators who could take advantage of them, the government now has a vested interest in encouraging gambling to fill the public coffers. One result of this move to promote gambling has been the trend of individuals in the lower economic brackets to use gambling as an investment rather than entertainment. Poor people spend a higher percentage of their income on gambling than do those in the middle class. The ultimate result of such patterns is a transfer of wealth from the pockets of the poor to the government.[66] In states such as Georgia, where the lottery pays for college tuition through a cleverly titled program called the Hope Scholarship, impoverished families are paying the college tuition for middle-class families.[67]

SEX WORK

In addition to controlling illegal drug use and gambling, the criminal justice system has a mandate to enforce laws that regulate sexuality. Although most Americans would agree that the government should not be concerned with the private behavior of consenting adults, the criminal justice system still must deal with a number of behaviors that society has deemed problematic. When sexual activity is exploitive or harmful, or when sex is used as a commodity and is bought and sold, the government has a legitimate obligation and appropriate authority to intervene.[68] Although there is debate about the exact role of the government, there is a long and well-established history of restricting sexual activity. The remainder of this chapter will review three types of sexual behaviors that are currently being contested in American society and the way the criminal justice system responds to them.[69] These offenses all revolve around the concept of selling sex. In part, they are crimes of values, and in part they are economic crimes that are committed without the government being able to set standards, regulate access, and/or impose taxes. These issues—prostitution, exotic dancing, and pornography—are termed "nuisance" sex offenses and illustrate the ambivalence on the part of society and the criminal justice system. Other serious sex offenses such as rape, child molestation, and sex-related homicide are beyond the scope of this chapter. There is little or no difference of opinion on whether society should condone or prohibit these behaviors.[70]

Prostitution

Prostitution is the practice of engaging in sexual activity in exchange for money. Although the popular concept of prostitution is that of a female prostitute and a male customer, other variations are common. Prostitution is illegal in just about every jurisdiction in United States, with the most well-known exception being Nevada, which has state-licensed brothels (see Case in Point 15.2).[71] Estimating the scope of the practice of prostitution is difficult. Official arrest records show that in 2006 more than 79,000 people were arrested for prostitution and commercialized vice, but this represents only a fraction of those who engage in the practice.[72] Because prostitution is essentially a consensual activity, there is no victim to alert law enforcement. Most arrests for prostitution are a result of proactive police stings in which police officers pose as prostitutes or customers and arrest those who express a desire to engage in the activity.[73]

Not all prostitutes are equally problematic for the criminal justice system. A hierarchy of prostitution reflects both an economic and social dimension, as well as a public safety dimension, to the practice of selling sex. According to N. Jane McCandless, prostitution has a four-level occupational hierarchy:[74]

1. **Call girl or male escort.** At the top of the hierarchy is the call girl or male escort who works for an escort service. These women and men command high fees, up to hundreds of dollars a night, and can screen their clients. Often they have several repeat customers, and the date might include activities other than

15.2 CASE IN POINT

NYE COUNTY V. PLANKINTON

THE CASE	THE POINT
Nye County v. Plankinton, 94 Nev. 739, 587 P.2d 421 (1978)	*This Nevada Supreme Court case demonstrates the continuing debate over the legalization of sex work in the only state where sex work is legal. It also demonstrates the movement of a controversial activity from extralegal toleration into a state's legal code.*

In 1977, officials of Nye County, Nevada, tried to close a brothel, Chicken Ranch, on the basis that it constituted a public nuisance. During this period, brothels in the county—where several were already operating—were not required to be licensed. The owner of Chicken Ranch, Walter Plankinton, sued, pointing to a 1971 law prohibiting the legalization of prostitution in counties with a population above a specified limit. According to Plankinton, this law, NRS 244.345, implicitly negated the assertion that brothels are public nuisances *per se*. The Nevada Supreme Court agreed, and Chicken Ranch continues to operate.

sex, such as dinner, going to plays or movies, or attending functions where presentable companions are desired. These types of prostitutes are often indistinguishable from a regular date. Occasionally, a male or female prostitute finds a rich customer who is willing to pay for exclusive access and lease an apartment for him or her to live in that the customer can visit at will.

2. **Strippers and exotic dancers.**   Next on the occupational hierarchy of prostitution are strippers or exotic dancers (this is not to imply that all dancers are prostitutes). These men and women—although they are usually women—may have some type of arrangement with the management of the bar that allows them to solicit customers in return for a financial kickback from the transaction. Additionally, the management ensures that other prostitutes are not allowed to compete in the bar. These prostitutes have some discretion in which customers they choose.

3. **House girls.**   House girls are prostitutes who work in brothels. Although brothels are legal only in Nevada, these institutions are common in many cities and are able to function because the criminal justice system turns a blind eye toward them. The brothels are run by a madam, and the girls get a percentage of the fee. The advantage of a brothel for a prostitute is that the madam recruits and screens the customers, provides the room for the tryst, provides a level of security and rules, and deals with law enforcement. The disadvantages for the prostitute include not being able to select the customer, having to give up a sizable percentage to the madam, and being told when to work and how many customers per night to see.

4. **Streetwalkers.**   At the lowest end of the spectrum are *streetwalkers*. These women and men publicly solicit customers on street corners, in parks, and outside bars or hotels. They command the least payment and cannot afford to be selective in whom they choose for customers. Often they are controlled by pimps and have little control over the money they earn. Among their greatest concerns are their exposures to police officers who continually arrest them and their customers, thus upsetting their businesses. More important, streetwalkers are at high risk for sexually transmitted disease, physical violence from customers, and abuse from pimps.

According to McCandless, a new and even lower level of prostitute works in crack houses and trades sex for drugs. This prostitute's primary goal is to stay intoxicated. While under the influence of drugs, she will be extremely promiscuous in her choice of sex partners, sloppy in practicing safe sexual techniques, and likely to be the victim of rape and physical violence.

When discussing the public's ambivalence concerning prostitution, we must be careful to specify which of these strata we are considering. Many individuals consider any type of sex-for-money transaction morally wrong, but others are more tolerant of what consenting adults do in private. At the lower end of the prostitution hierarchy, however, are some public safety concerns that fall under the mandate of the criminal justice system.[75] Many times, the act of prostitution is not a consensual one, and the prostitute is forced by pimps, boyfriends, or organized crime to act against his or her will. At the global level, young women and men are smuggled into the prostitution trade. Additionally, sex tourism has become a multimillion-dollar business in which some travel agencies sponsor tours to impoverished countries so that the tourist can engage in sex with extremely young girls or boys.[76] Many distressing issues clearly surround the practice of prostitution. Like drugs and gambling, prostitution resists efforts to suppress it.

Is there another way to reduce the social harm caused by prostitution? Thus far, we have reviewed the not-so-successful attempts to legalize drugs and the largely successful moves to legalize gambling. In that vein, a small constituency would like to see prostitution legalized (see Crosscurrents 15.3). Current laws prohibiting prostitution seem to be ineffective, invite selective enforcement, and push the practice into the shadows where regulation is impossible and exploitation inevitable. Those who advocate the le-

15.3 CrossCurrents

Legitimizing Sex Work

Values change in societies. Many forms of gambling that were once prohibited are now not only permitted, but used by the government to generate revenue. Currently there is also a heated debate about legalizing or decriminalizing drugs. But what about sex work? Will prostitution become legalized and regulated by the government? Many people advocate such ideas. In fact, sex workers around the world are lobbying for recognition of sex work as a legitimate occupation that should be brought into mainstream society. For example, in Australia certain forms of prostitution are legal with some restrictions. In the United States a group of exotic dancers in San Francisco won the right in 1996 to unionize and negotiate with their employer. Organizations such as the Network of Sex Work Projects focus on such issues as the following:

- **Health and safety.** Sex work is a hazardous occupation in which pimps, law enforcement officers, and customers may abuse sex workers. Additionally, health risks, such as AIDS and other sexually transmitted diseases, plague the sex industry.
- **Rights.** Sex workers advocate that they should be entitled to the same human, civil, and labor rights that are afforded to other workers.

- **Ethics.** When research is done on sex workers, they are entitled to the same protections as other subjects. These include informed consent, knowledge about experimental drugs, and privacy.

If sex workers succeed in introducing their concerns into mainstream society, many things would change. Prostitutes would be allowed to advertise their services, write legitimate business expenses off their taxes, set consistent pay rates based on objective criteria (such as amount of time or services rendered), and openly lobby legislative bodies for worker protections such as health insurance and overtime.

Think About It

1. Should sex work be treated like any other occupation?
2. Are the concerns of sex workers also women's issues?
3. What do you think a feminist response would be to the proposal to legitimize sex work?
4. What unanticipated consequences might arise from such a proposal?
5. Where would the most opposition to legitimizing sex work come from? Women? Men? Religious groups? Law enforcement officials?

Source: Live Nude Girls Unite!, www.livenudegirlsunite.com/.

---

galization or decriminalization of prostitution suggest the following benefits:

- **Women would have control over their own sexuality**   They would not be under the control of pimps or madams who take a large percentage of their earnings. They would be allowed to work out of their own homes without worrying about the police arresting them.
- **Customers would be able to find sex without worrying for their physical safety**   Sex would simply be another commodity that could be found through advertising, and the customer would not need to cruise through unsafe areas looking for sex.
- **Prostitutes could be licensed and checked for sexually transmitted diseases**   Public health could be improved by addressing the problems of unsafe sex, intravenous drug use, and violence, variables that are not measured when prostitution is illegal.
- **The government would collect taxes from legal prostitution and use that money to address the consequences that legal prostitution might bring**   Additionally, prostitutes could develop employment benefits such as unions, pension plans, health insurance, and lobbyists so that their concerns could be discussed in the open.
- **The profession would be destigmatized**   Prostitutes would be able to receive loans to finance their businesses, be able to advertise, and be free from extortion by public officials.[77]

Whether the legalization of prostitution in the United States would provide these benefits and whether either society or prostitutes would be better off with such a change is an open question. However, prostitution is legal in many countries and subject to a wide variety of laws and regulatory practices. Rather than venture an opinion here, we simply suggest that, much as with drugs and gambling, the sale of sexual behavior is contested in our society. Additionally, prostitution continues to be a concern for the criminal justice system, and because its elimination is unlikely, selective and uneven enforcement of prostitution laws will continue to affect those with the least power in society, particularly women.

Although we typically think of prostitutes as female, some are male. These activities are almost exclusively same-sex transactions and are typically at the lower end of the occupational hierarchy. In *The Times Square Hustler: Male Prostitution in New York City*, Robert McNamara detailed the lives of a cohort of young male prostitutes. McNamara described how these street hustlers reached a working relationship with law enforcement officers in which the officers would tell the youths to "get lost," "move it," and "hit the road." The youths would move a short distance away and then continue their hustling activities. The officers and the youths each realized that the other had a job to do and cooperated in allowing each other to pursue their occupations. The youths were respectful of officers and moved when told. The officers kept the youths from loitering in one place for too long, but did not make arrests, write citations, or hassle the youths too much as long as they showed respect to the police officers. This accommodation is important to the appreciation of law enforcement's attitude toward sex work, as well as gambling and drug use. Certain levels of deviance are tolerated as long as the authority of the police is not directly challenged and as long as the behavior remains consensual and not exploitive.[78]

One interesting finding in McNamara's study concerned how the street hustlers viewed their sexuality. Although they engaged in homosexual activity to support themselves, most of these youths did not consider themselves homosexual. The viewed their behavior as "just a job" and seemed able to compartmentalize their feelings and self-concepts. Many of these youths had girlfriends, or even wives and children, and were committed to heterosexual relationships away from work.

Strippers and Exotic Dancers

Stripping and exotic dancing are other forms of sex work that operate within the purview of the criminal justice system. These activities are bound by varying sets of rules and regulations that span legal jurisdictions. Many communities pass laws that

Prostitution is often called a victimless crime because it involves consensual behavior. However, prostitution can produce victims when juveniles are involved or when prostitutes are exploited by pimps. Here, young male prostitutes stand on a street corner.

Source: Jana Birchum

forbid establishments from offering exotic dance as entertainment, but other communities, typically ones that want to attract business conventions, permit strip clubs. For law enforcement agencies, these establishments often mean an increase in drug sales, prostitution, drunken assaults, and muggings. The activities inside the strip clubs are also monitored to ensure that the fine points of the law, such as no touching with the hands during a lap dance, are observed.[79]

Although some strippers use exotic dancing as a way to recruit clients for prostitution, many do not engage in prostitution at all. Most strippers find that they can earn a man's money (the clients are predominantly male) without actually engaging in sex. Researchers have used the term *counterfeit intimacy* to describe how exotic dancers provide a facsimile of sex without actually touching, caring about, or meeting the desires of strip-club customers. This can cause problems when drunken clients believe they have paid a lot of money and have received "only the sizzle and not the steak."[80]

Pornography

Pornography is another form of sex work that has implications for the criminal justice system. Two issues concerning pornography are the most problematic for some people. The first concern comes from those who find pictures or descriptions of nakedness and sexual activity immoral. Although public fashions change and partial nakedness is deemed appropriate according to context (i.e., bikinis at the beach or dresses on prom night), some individuals are offended by what appears regularly on television, in motion pictures, and in the print media. What passes as popular culture in the 21st century is considered lewd and vulgar by some. There is more consensus about what is offensive when certain "adult" magazines are considered and even more agreement regarding the content of hard-core pornographic movies. A continuum of obscenity appears to exist, and individuals have their own opinions about what should be considered objectionable. This difference of opinion will always cause tension about what is allowed in the media, and free speech rights will continue to be a contested issue in regard to pornography.

A second concern of those who object to pornography is the link between sex and violence. Some pornography is highly sexist, racist, and homophobic. For some people, the humiliation of others (particularly women and children) is stimulating. Some feminists link pornographic objectification of women with violence against women. It is true that certain strains of pornography cater to those who find pleasure in seeing other people suffer.[81] At the extreme end of the pornographic continuum is the "snuff film," the stuff of urban legends in which a victim is allegedly killed.

The tension that exists in the policing of pornography centers on the difference between erotica and obscenity. Distinctions can be made among the following:

- Violent pornography
- Nonviolent but dehumanizing pornography
- Erotica (material that is nonsexist and nonviolent)

In attempting to regulate the types of pornography and erotica available to adults, the criminal justice system walks a fine line between enforcing laws and encroaching on citizens' legal behavior. To a large degree, the exact definition of pornography is open to interpretation. In *Jacobellis* v. *Ohio* (1964), Justice Potter Stewart illustrated this difficulty in defining obscenity by saying only, "I know it when I see it." (See Case in Point 15.3 for another landmark obscenity case.) If we leave the interpretation of what is obscene to each individual, we cannot have workable laws governing pornography. In some way, the criminal justice system needs guidance in defining, detecting, and enforcing these activities when there is so much difference of opinion on the part of the public.

15.3 CASE IN POINT

MILLER V. CALIFORNIA

THE CASE	THE POINT
Miller v. California, 413 U.S. 15 (1973)	The Supreme Court set forth a new three-part test for obscenity.

Marvin Miller sent sexually explicit advertisements for four books, *Intercourse*, *Man-Woman*, *Sex Orgies Illustrated*, and *An Illustrated History of Pornography*, and a film titled *Marital Intercourse* to addresses on a mass-mailing list. The list recipients had not specifically requested sexually explicit materials. Miller was arrested after a restaurant owner and his mother complained about receiving the advertisements in the mail. Miller was convicted under California's obscenity law, which made mailing obscene material a criminal offense, and his conviction was confirmed on appeal. The case went to the U.S. Supreme Court, which set forth the three-part test for obscenity that is used today:

1. Whether "the average person, applying contemporary community standards" would find that the work, taken as a whole, appeals to the prurient interest
2. Whether the work depicts or describes, in a patently offensive way, sexual conduct specifically defined by the applicable state law
3. Whether the work, taken as a whole, lacks serious literary, artistic, political, or scientific value

Two aspects of this decision are particularly important. First, it allows a jury to use community standards, not national standards, to determine obscenity. The second is that it discarded a previous requirement that obscene material be "utterly without redeeming social value" (*Memoirs* v. *Massachusetts* [1966]) and exchanged it for the stricter requirement that obscene material need only lack "serious literary, artistic, political, or scientific value."

---

community standards

Practices, acts, and/or media accepted by a given social group who share a geographic area and/or government.

Historically, the solution to this lack of consensus has been a reliance on **community standards**. This explains why such wide variations exist across the country in what types of sexually explicit material is available. When each city or small town can determine what materials can be sold in stores, then the sexual sensibilities of those residents can be respected. Sex work, such as prostitution and exotic dancing, as well as the sale of pornographic magazines, can be discouraged through arrests, fines, and the revocation of business licenses. However, in the 21st century, community standards have collided with the globalization of the media. Pornography, like many other products, is available in a variety of easily procured formats. Following are some issues the criminal justice system faces as the delivery of obscene materials matures with the overall improvement of communications:

- **Stores that sell sex**   Law enforcement has a relatively easy time dealing with business establishments that sell so-called dirty magazines or sex aids and sex toys. Some local laws require convenience stores to shield the covers of men's magazines, place the magazines behind the sales counter where minors cannot see them, or prohibit the sale of certain materials altogether. A visit to the store by a police officer can quickly reveal which stores are in compliance with the law and which are not. Citations can be written, arrests made, and trials held within the community. These cases can be handled without exposing the magazines' producers to state or federal courts.

- **Pornography and the mail**   Local law enforcement has no way of policing what is delivered to private homes in the mail. Therefore, the federal government uses the U.S. Postal Service to control some pornography. Postal inspectors investigate the illegal distribution of a wide range of products, including pornography, that is delivered via the mail. Not only can the producers and distributors of pornographic materials be arrested and fined, but so can the customers. Some people argue that the government has no business interfering with what citizens order through the mail, but the government has a clear and compelling mandate to ensure that guns, drugs, and other items such as child pornography are not using the Postal Service to violate the law.

- **The Internet and sex**   The Internet has introduced a new challenge in the law's attempt to control pornography. In what has quickly become a multi-million-dollar industry, Internet pornography is practically impossible for local law enforcement agencies to control. They have no way of knowing whether any of the citizens in their jurisdiction are consuming the pornography, and the producers and distributors of pornography reside in other states or countries. Although Internet filters are available for parents to control the types of sites their children can access, these filters are resisted by First Amendment advocates who believe that libraries and universities should provide unfettered Internet access. The laws dealing with the Internet are evolving, and it could be several years before stable patterns of social control of online pornography emerge.[82]

SUMMARY

1. The criminal justice system has a broad mandate to enforce all the laws passed by the legislature. A wide consensus exists on the desirability of most laws; however, a number of illegal behaviors do not have a strong consensus favoring their proscription. Drug use, gambling, and sex work are controversial because they challenge the values and religious beliefs of many people. Others see them as consensual activities that do not harm anyone other than those who choose to engage in them.

2. The first popular drug in the United States was alcohol, and the government intervened only to collect taxes.

3. In the 1800s, although the use of opium, morphine, and cocaine was deemed problematic, these drugs were ingredients in many patent medicines. In the 20th century, laws were passed to control these drugs.

4. The Pure Food and Drug Act of 1906 required food and drug purveyors to label what their products contained.

5. The 1914 Harrison Act imposed a tax on opium and cocaine.

6. In 1919, the ratification of the Eighteenth Amendment prohibited the use and sale of alcohol. Prohibition, largely considered a failure, ended in 1933.

7. In 1937, the government began to control the use and sale of marijuana.

8. The criminal justice system has since turned to treating drug offenders as well as punishing them. Some critics of the war on drugs suggest that taxation, decriminalization, and legalization are preferable to drug prohibition. While the war on drugs persists, law enforcement continues to pursue a variety of strategies to deal with enforcing the laws banning drugs.

9. Some states and communities allow almost any form of gambling, whereas others are more restrictive. Many states operate lotteries, and casinos have also become more common.

10. Internet-based gambling is problematic because some sites are located outside the United States, and the government cannot collect taxes or regulate it.

11. Although many people consider gambling harmful, especially to those addicted to the behavior, the consumer activity it stimulates has been deemed beneficial by many communities.

12. Three types of sexual behaviors currently being contested in U.S. society involve the selling of sex: prostitution, pornography, and exotic dancing. These represent either crimes of values or economic crimes in which the government is unable to set standards, regulate access, and/or impose taxes.

13. Prostitution, the practice of engaging in sexual activity in exchange for money, is illegal in every U.S. jurisdiction with the exception of Nevada, which has state-licensed brothels.

KEY TERMS

community standards 526   legalization 512   victimless crimes 500
decriminalization 515   sex work 500

REVIEW QUESTIONS

1. What is drug abuse?

2. What legislative acts and cases led to the criminalization of drugs?

3. What are some of the means of social control used in the war on drugs?

4. What goals should drug treatment programs strive for, according to Elliott Currie?

5. What are some of the arguments for legalizing and decriminalizing drugs?

6. How has legalized gambling been transformed in the last 30 years?

7. What forms of gambling remain illegal?

8. What is the occupational hierarchy of prostitution, according to N. Jane McCandless?

9. What would be the possible benefits of legalizing prostitution?

10. Considering the rapid development of computers and the Internet, what challenges face the criminal justice system in controlling pornography?

SUGGESTED FURTHER READING

Currie, Elliott. *Reckoning: Drugs, the Cities, and the American Future.* New York: Hill & Wang, 1993.

Donziger, Steven R., ed. *The Real War on Crime: The Report of the National Criminal Justice Commission.* New York: Harper Perennial, 1996.

Goodman, Robert. *The Luck Business: The Consequences and Broken Promises of America's Gambling Explosion.* New York: Free Press, 1995.

McNamara, Robert. *The Times Square Hustler: Male Prostitution in New York City.* Westport, CT: Praeger, 1994.

Spector, Jessica. *Prostitution and Pornography: Debate about the Sex Industry.* Palo Alto, CA: Stanford University Press, 2006.

Whisnant, Rebecca, and Christine Stark, eds. *Not for Sale: Feminists Resisting Prostitution and Pornography.* New York: Spinifex, 2005.

ENDNOTES

1. Edward Brongersma, "Boy-Lovers and Their Influence on Boys: Distorted Research and Anecdotal Observations," in *Deviance and Deviants: An Anthology*, eds. Richard Tewksbury and Patricia Gagné (Los Angeles: Roxbury, 2000), 83–98.

2. Sex work is the behavior of engaging in the selling of sex-related behaviors as an occupation. There are many types of sex work, but we will be primarily concerned here with prostitution, exotic dancing, and pornography.

3. Robert F. Meier and Gilbert Geis, *Victimless Crime? Prostitution, Drugs, Homosexuality, Abortion* (Los Angeles: Roxbury, 1997).

4. Andrew Hathaway, "Marijuana and Lifestyle: Exploring Tolerable Deviance," in *Deviance and Deviants: An Anthology*, eds. Richard Tewksbury and Patricia Gagné (Los Angeles: Roxbury, 2000), 152–160.

5. Steven R. Donzigen, ed., *The Real War on Crime: The Report of the National Criminal Justice Commission* (New York: Harper Perennial, 1996).

6. Elliott Currie, *Reckoning: Drugs, the Cities, and the American Future* (New York: Hill & Wang, 1993).

7. David L. Carter, "An Overview of Drug-Related Misconduct of Police Officers: Drug Abuse Narcotic Corruption," in *Drugs, Crime, and the Criminal Justice*

System, ed. Ralph Weisheit (Cincinnati, OH: Anderson, 1990), 79–109.

8. Federal Bureau of Investigation, *Uniform Crime Reports: Crime in the United States, 2006*, www.fbi.gov/ucr/cius2006/arrests/index.html.

9. Lynn Zimmer, "Proactive Policing against Street-Level Drug Trafficking," in *Drugs, Crime, and Justice: Contemporary Perspectives*, eds. Larry K. Gaines and Peter B. Kraska (Prospect Heights, IL: Waveland Press, 1997), 249–274.

10. Howard Abadinsky, *Drug Abuse: An Introduction*, 2nd ed. (Chicago: Nelson-Hall), 3.

11. In H. W. Brands's *The First American: The Life and Times of Benjamin Franklin* (New York: Anchor Books, 2000), Brands tells of how Franklin as a young man was able to drink the water of Philadelphia without getting sick and was then able to work more efficiently than his co-workers, who drank alcohol all day long (p. 71).

12. W. J. Rorabaugh, *The Alcoholic Republic: An American Tradition* (New York: Oxford University Press, 1991,) 21.

13. Oakley Ray and Charles Ksir, *Drugs, Society, and Human Behavior*, 6th ed. (St. Louis, MO: Mosby, 1993).

14. Dean Latimer and Jeff Goldberg, *Flowers in the Blood: The Story of Opium* (New York: Watts, 1981).

15. Ray and Ksir, *Drugs, Society*, 39.

16. Howard Wayne Morgan, *Drugs in America: A Social History, 1800–1980* (Syracuse, NY: Syracuse University Press, 1981).

17. Upton Sinclair, *The Jungle* (New York: Bantam, 1981). First published in 1906.

18. Edward Brecher, *Licit and Illicit Drugs* (Boston: Little, Brown, 1972).

19. Ray and Ksir, *Drugs, Society*, 59.

20. Charles E. Faupel, Alan M. Horowitz, and Greg S. Weaver, *The Sociology of American Drug Use* (Boston: McGraw-Hill, 2004), 45–48.

21. Abadinsky, *Drug Abuse*, 75.

22. Edward Behr, *Prohibition: Thirteen Years That Changed America* (New York: Arcade, 1996).

23. Ibid. See especially Chapter 13, "Chicago," pp. 175–193.

24. Norman H. Clark, *Deliver Us From Evil: An Interpretation of American Prohibition* (New York: Norton, 1976).

25. Harvey A. Siegal and James A. Inciardi, "A Brief History of Alcohol," in *The American Drug Scene: An Anthology*, 3rd ed., eds. James A. Inciardi and Karen McElrath (Los Angeles: Roxbury, 2001), 52–57.

26. Harry J. Anslinger and Courtney Ryley Cooper, "Marijuana: Assassin of Youth," in *The American Drug Scene: An Anthology*, 3rd ed., eds. James A. Inciardi and Karen McElrath (Los Angeles: Roxbury, 2001), 89–94.

27. Martin Booth, *Cannabis: A History* (New York: Picador, 2005).

28. Todd Gitlin, *The Sixties: Years of Hope, Days of Rage* (New York: Bantam Books, 1993), 427.

29. Richard Fields, *Drugs in Perspective: A Personalized Look at Substance Use and Abuse*, 4th ed. (Boston: McGraw-Hill, 2001). See especially Chapter 5, "Substance Abuse and Family Systems," pp. 148–163.

30. Peter B. Kraska, "The Unmentionable Alternative: The Need for and the Argument against the Decriminalization of Drugs," in *Drugs, Crime, and the Criminal Justice System*, ed. Ralph Weisheit (Cincinnati, OH: Anderson, 1990), 111–137.

31. Doris Marie Provine, *Unequal under Law: Race in the War on Drugs* (Chicago: University of Chicago Press, 2007).

32. Ralph Weisheit, "Declaring a 'Civil' War on Drugs," in *Drugs, Crime, and the Criminal Justice System*, ed. Ralph Weisheit (Cincinnati, OH: Anderson, 1990), 1–10.

33. A number of companies sell and market technologies designed for parents to monitor the activities of their children. Drug-testing kits, hidden cameras, and GPS systems on cars are all available to consumers. See www.spyparent.net.

34. Janelle Brown, "When the Drug War Invades the Chess Club," *Salon*, June 28, 2002, www.salon.com/mwt/feature/2002/06/28/boyd_interview/.

35. Duane C. McBride et al., "US Public Health Agency Involvement in Youth-Focused Illicit Drug Policy, Planning, and Prevention at the Local Level, 1999–2003," *American Journal of Public Health* 98 (February 2008): 270–277.

36. James F. Quinn and Zach Sneed, "Drugs and Crime: An Empirically Based, Interdisciplinary Model," *Journal of Teaching in the Addictions* 7 (April 2008): 16–30.

37. Peter B. Kraska and Victor E. Kappeler, "Militarizing American Police: The Rise and Normalization of Paramilitary Units," in *The Police and Society: Touchstone Readings*, 2nd ed., ed. Victor E. Kappeler (Prospect Heights, IL: Waveland Press, 1999), 463–479.

38. J. Mitchell Miller and Lance H. Selva, "Drug Enforcement's Double-Edged Sword: An Assessment of Asset Forfeiture Programs," in *Drugs, Crime, and Justice*, eds. Larry K. Gaines and Peter B. Kraska (Prospect Heights, IL: Waveland Press, 1997), 275–296.

39. John L. Worrall and Tomislav V. Kovandzic, "Policing for Profit? Answers from Asset Forfeiture," *Criminology and Public Policy* 7 (2008): 219–244.

40. Currie, *Reckoning*, 33–34.

41. Michele J. Elison, *Improving Substance Abuse Treatment: An Introduction to the Evidence-Based Practice Movement* (Thousand Oaks, CA: Sage, 2007).

42. Alexandra Marks, "In Drug War, Treatment Is Back," *Christian Science Monitor*, July 14, 2000, http://search.csmonitor.com/durable/2000/07/14/p1s1.htm.

43. Jamie F. Chriqui et al., "State Policies Matter: The Case of Outpatient Drug Treatment Program Practices," *Journal of Substance Abuse Treatment* 35 (July 2008): 13–21.

44. Todd R. Clear, Val B. Clear, and Anthony A. Braga, "Correctional Alternatives for Drug Offenders in an Era of Overcrowding," in *Drugs, Crime, and Justice*, eds. Larry K. Gaines and Peter B. Kraska (Prospect Heights, IL: Waveland Press, 1992), 375–395.

45. Currie, *Reckoning*. See Chapter 5, "Redefining Treatment," pp. 213–279.

46. Ibid., 253.

47. Michael Massing, *The Fix* (New York: Simon & Schuster, 1998).

48. Jerome H. Skolnick, "Rethinking the Drug Problem," in *Drugs, Crime, and Justice*, eds. Larry K. Gaines and Peter B. Kraska (Prospect Heights, IL: Waveland Press, 1997), 403–426.

49. Doug Husak and Peter de Marneffe, *The Legalization of Drugs (For and Against)* (New York: Cambridge University Press, 2005).

50. Behr, *Prohibition*.

51. Stanton Peele and Archie Brodsky, "Gateway to Nowhere: How Alcohol Came to Be Scapegoated for Drug Abuse," in *The American Drug Scene: An Anthology*, 3rd ed., eds. James A. Inciardi and Karen McElrath (Los Angeles: Roxbury, 2001), 58–63.

52. James Q. Wilson, "Against the Legalization of Drugs," in *The American Drug Scene: An Anthology*, 3rd ed., eds. James A. Inciardi and Karen McElrath (Los Angeles: Roxbury, 2001), 440–449.

53. Clear, Clear, and Braga, "Correctional Alternatives."

54. Faupel, Horowitz, and Weaver, *Sociology of American Drug Use*, 263.

55. Mark H. Moore and Mark A. R. Kleinman, "The Police and Drugs," in *Drugs, Crime, and Justice*, eds. Larry K. Gaines and Peter B. Kraska (Prospect Heights, IL: Waveland Press, 1997), 227–248.

56. Lynn Zimmer, "Proactive Policing."

57. Jess Marcum and Henry Rowen, "How Many Games in Town? The Pros and Cons of Legalized Gambling," *Public Interest* 36 (Summer 1974).

58. Florida Department of Law Enforcement, *The Questions of Casinos in Florida—Increased Crime: Is It Worth the Gamble?* (Tallahassee: Author, 1994).

59. Peter Passell, "Lotto Is Financed by the Poor and Won by the States," *New York Times*, May 21, 1989.

60. Robert Goodman, *The Luck Business: The Devastating Consequences and Broken Promises of America's Gambling Explosion* (New York: Free Press, 1995).

61. Ibid., 48.

62. Arnold Wexler and Sheila Wexler, "Compulsive Gambling: The Hidden Addiction," *Counselor*, December 1992.

63. Frank Ahrens, "New Law Cripples Internet Gambling," *Washington Post*, October 14, 2006, final edition, A1.

64. Margaret Kane, "eBay picks up PayPal for $1.5 billion," CNET News, July 8, 2002, http://news.com.com/2100-1017-941964.html.

65. John M. Findlay, *People of Chance: Gambling in American Society from Jamestown to Las Vegas* (New York: Oxford University Press, 1986).

66. Paul Della Valle and Scott Farmelant, "A Bad Bet: Who Really Pays for the Massachusetts Lottery's Success?" *Worcester Magazine*, January 27, 1993.

67. Vicki Abt, James F. Smith, and Eugene Martin Christiansen, *The Business of Risk: Commercial Gambling in Mainstream America* (Lawrence: University Press of Kansas, 1985), 66.

68. Belina Brooks-Gorden, *The Price of Sex: Prostitution, Policy, and Society* (London: Willan, 2006).

69. Donal E. J. MacNamara and Edward Sagarin, *Sex, Crime, and the Law* (New York: Free Press, 1977).

70. Eric W. Hickey, *Serial Murderers and Their Victims*, 3rd ed. (Belmont, CA: Wadsworth, 2002).

71. Alexa Albert, *Brothel: Mustang Ranch and Its Women* (New York: Ballantine, 2001).

72. Federal Bureau of Investigation, *Uniform Crime Reports, Crime in the United States 2006*, www.fbi.gov/ucr/cius2006/data/table_29.html.

73. William H. Daly, "Law Enforcement in Times Square, 1970s–1990s," in *Sex, Scams, and Street Life: The Sociology of New York City's Times Square*, ed. Robert P. McNamara (Westport, CT: Praeger, 1995), 97–106.

74. N. Jane McCandless, "Prostitution as an Occupation," in *The Encyclopedia of Criminology*, ed. Richard Wright (forthcoming).

75. Jody Miller and Martin D. Schwartz, "Rape Myths and Violence against Street Prostitutes," in *Deviance and Deviants: An Anthology*, eds. Richard Tewksbury and Patricia Gagné (Los Angeles: Roxbury, 2000), 73–82.

76. Heather Montgomery, "Sex Tourism and Child Prostitution in Asia," in *Investigating Deviance: An*

Anthology, eds. Bruce A. Jacobs and Barry Glassner (Los Angeles: Roxbury, 2002), 289–291.

77. Robert F. Meier and Gilbert Geis, "The Social Organization of Prostitution," in *Investigating Deviance: An Anthology*, ed. Bruce A. Jacobs (Los Angeles: Roxbury, 2001), 232–241.

78. Robert P. McNamara, *The Times Square Hustler: Male Prostitution in New York City* (Westport, CT: Praeger, 1994).

79. Adrienne Packer, "Critics Say Lap-Dance Law Does Not Sit Well," *Las Vegas Sun*, August 6, 2002, www.lasvegassun.com/sunbin/stories/sun/2002/aug/06/513814372.html.

80. Carol Rambo Ronai and Carolyn Ellis, "Turn-Ons for Money: Interactional Strategies of the Table Dancer," in *Investigating Deviance: An Anthology*, ed. Bruce A. Jacobs (Los Angeles: Roxbury, 2002), 273–288.

81. Kathleen Barry, *Female Sexual Slavery* (New York: New York University Press, 1979). See especially Chapter 9, "Pornography: The Ideology of Cultural Sadism," pp. 205–252.

82. Keith F. Durkin and Clifton D. Bryant, "Exotic Cyberspace: The Internet and 'Logging On' to Sex," in *Investigating Deviance: An Anthology*, ed. Bruce A. Jacobs (Los Angeles: Roxbury, 2001), 242–253.

CHAPTER 16

Present and Emerging Trends

The Future of Criminal Justice

Objectives

1. Discuss the significance of the war metaphor when it is applied to crime.

2. Compare and contrast the war on terrorism with the war on crime.

3. Discuss how terrorism has affected Americans' perception of civil rights.

4. Discuss the USA Patriot Act.

5. Discuss the Department of Homeland Security and its relationship to the criminal justice system.

6. Compare and contrast peacemaking criminology with the war metaphor for dealing with crime.

7. Discuss restorative justice and its relationship to peacemaking criminology.

8. Describe the peacemaking pyramid.

9. Discuss the principles of restorative justice.

What is the future of criminal justice? This interesting question will doubtless be answered by many of the people taking this class. It is hoped that after reading this book, many students will decide to engage in further study of criminal justice. One of the most interesting benefits of being a criminal justice major is participating in a vigorously changing discipline. As social problems wax and wane, political parties demand new programs, the economy fluctuates, and new strategies to reduce crime are implemented, the criminal justice system continues to change. The student of criminal justice can look forward to a career that will encourage innovation, reward success, recognize hard work, and foster creativity. But which of the many paths in criminal justice should one pursue? Where is the criminal justice system headed, and what can the student of the discipline do to prepare for the future? This chapter will suggest that there are two emerging trends: war and peace. These two trends, however, are in competition and present a bit of a dilemma to the future criminal justice practitioner.

WAR AND PEACE IN THE CRIMINAL JUSTICE SYSTEM

It is useful to think about the criminal justice system as struggling between the extremes of waging war on criminals and making peace with citizens. This view is not simply two sides of the same coin, but rather represents a fundamental difference in how the government relates to and reacts to unlawful behavior.

Without taking a stand one way or another, this chapter will introduce the history of the trends of war and peace and review several of the major initiatives pursued by each. The primary concern is to accurately and fairly reflect the promise and potential problems of each of these perspectives. Additionally, we must recognize the risk of creating a false dichotomy. We may be able to reconcile these war and peace perspectives, and the ultimate answer for developing a criminal justice system effective in reducing crime while protecting the rights of citizens may draw from both of these perspectives. In the meantime, however, we find the criminal justice system careening into the future while simultaneously pursuing a war on crime and developing alternative approaches that emphasize mediation, reconciliation, and the preservation of individual legal, civil, and human rights.[1]

The next generation of criminal justice practitioners—lawyers, judges, police, victim–witness program staff members, and a host of others who work in or with the criminal justice system—will be responsible for determining the nature, tone, and philosophy of how we deal with those who break the law. At another even more important level, however, the next generation of citizens will determine the nature of the substantive law. We may find that the rules, mores, customs, expectations, and laws of tomorrow are very different from those of today. In fact, each generation is faced with new problems and equipped with new technologies, making the past an unreliable guide for policy. This does not mean we should not learn from the past, but rather that we should keep an open mind and recognize issues and trends that require a response by those engaged in the vital work of criminal justice.

The Wars on Crime and Drugs

War is a convenient and slippery term to use when referring to the work of the criminal justice system. It is easy to understand and easy to promote as a crime-fighting policy. Criminals are the enemy, and we should use any and all resources to defeat the enemy. Because the enemy robs, rapes, steals, and sells illegal drugs, we are justified by the principle of self-defense to use warlike strategies, tactics, and weapons to fight crime.

But is fighting crime the same as fighting a war? Are we as a nation willing to endure the consequences of treating the crime problem as a war problem? The answers to these questions are elusive because so much emotion is involved in fighting drugs and terrorism that reasoned and sober reflection on preventing crime becomes difficult. Although many citizens applaud the idea of fighting a war against criminals, the war concept becomes problematic when applied to the criminal justice system in the United States:

> Among the characteristics implied in the notion of coping with a problem by declaring war on it are extra effort, expediency, ruthlessness, sacrifice, and subordination of the individual. It is the last mentioned characteristic that is especially troubling to students of justice and to the mind of a liberal, at least the old-fashioned liberal who regards the rights of the individual as paramount.[2]

Before the war on terrorism, there was a war on crime, a war on drugs, and a war on poverty. These wars are still being pursued without a realistic end in sight. In fact, so much money and so many resources have been spent on these wars that it is safe to conclude that the United States has not been able to make much of a dent in these social problems, much less win any war against them. Although dealing with these problems is appropriate and noble, *war* is a misleading metaphor. In a traditional war between nations, national security and citizens' lives and lifestyles are at risk. For example, in World War II Americans sacrificed their fortunes, lives, and lifestyles to defeat a well-defined enemy who had committed aggressive acts against our allies and the United States. However, when we use the term *war* to describe a movement to stem crime, we mean that the government and citizenry are willing to allocate some resources to prevent or reduce a set of social problems. A war on drugs or a war on crime lacks a clear, identifiable external enemy. Hitler, the Axis, the North Vietnamese, and other peoples designated as the enemy have been relatively easy to demonize and hate. However, a war on drugs means that, in addition to attacking Colombian drug cartels, we must attack U.S. citizens who sell, buy, and consume illegal drugs. This becomes even more precarious when our children, siblings, classmates, or friends are at the business end of this declared war. The war metaphor becomes a problem when it means using military tactics, reasoning, and resources to arrest U.S. citizens for rather ordinary and conventional offenses.[3] (See Focus on Ethics 16.1 for a scenario.)

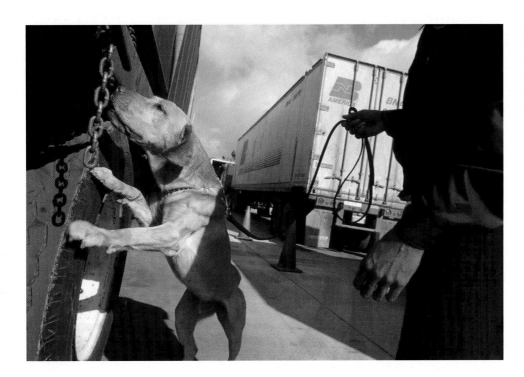

U.S. customs inspectors use drug-sniffing dogs to check for illegal contraband at the Otay Mesa Border Crossing in San Diego, California, one of the nation's busiest borders.

Source: Aurora Photos, Inc.

The Constitution has provisions to protect citizens from an overzealous criminal justice system. The Bill of Rights along with a long history of court cases interpreting the meanings of the framers of the Constitution have greatly limited what the criminal justice system can and cannot do in pursuit of lawbreakers. Recent Supreme Court cases have illustrated that the protections of the Constitution and the law are subject to change when circumstances demand a new way of considering crime and protecting the United States. For example, during World War II, the courts allowed the internment of U.S. citizens of Japanese descent because of the perceived seriousness of the war threat. However, the question posed by wars on drugs and crime is, Are drugs and crime so harmful that Americans must give up legal and civil rights to allow the police greater flexibility in performing their duties? For the most part, the answer to this question has been no. Drugs and crime are certainly problems, and some citizens' rights have been abbreviated, but the problem does not rise to the level of war in which citizens feel so threatened that they would forfeit most their rights. However, the events of September 11, 2001, have changed that to some degree.[4]

The War on Terrorism

Under normal circumstances, the police and the military are, for the most part, different. They share such characteristics as organizational structures, ranks, the carrying of weapons, and the wearing of uniforms, but their goals are different. A law enforcement officer is sworn to keep the peace and protect citizens. A soldier is obligated to attack an enemy. In fact, one of the criticisms of the war-on-crime metaphor is that it puts police officers in the position of being soldiers and, therefore, citizens in the position of being enemies. Under normal circumstances, the goals and targets of the military and the police do not intersect. Terrorism has changed this, however, and the primary point of intersection, unfortunately, is citizens.[5] There is, of course, a flipside to this quandary. The military actions of the United States in Iraq and Afghanistan have placed U.S. soldiers in the position of having to act as an occupational force. One of the missions of the military is to ensure social order and keep the peace. In many ways, U.S. soldiers are forced to engage in activities similar to domestic law enforcement even though they have never been formally trained.

16.1   FOCUS on ETHICS

COULD YOU BE A TERRORIST?

Why did the terrorists of the September 11 events commit suicide by flying planes into the World Trade Center and the Pentagon? Certainly they had issues with the United States, but an almost unbelievable level of commitment is required to take one's own life to make such a political statement. Over the past 50 years a number of people have committed acts of domestic terrorism in the United States against the government or civilian targets. Under what circumstances (if any) would you resort to violence against your country? Imagine the following scenarios:

1. The government suspends the Bill of Rights and imprisons individuals for real or imagined criticisms of its policies.

2. The government declares your religion to be undesirable and forbids church attendance, the display of religious symbols, and praying. Violations are subject to fines or imprisonment.

3. The government eliminates taxes for the rich and increases them to 70 percent for the middle class.

4. The government decides that people of your religion, ethnic heritage, race, or political persuasion are no longer desirable and institutes a program to send you back to your country of origin, even though your family has been in the United States for well over a hundred years.

What Do You Do?

1. If the government treated you in such a way and abolished the traditional mechanisms for redress, such as courts and petitions, would you resort to violence to preserve your cherished values?

2. Can you understand how others might have resorted to terrorism?

3. What do you think when you see a bumper sticker that says, "You can have my gun when you pry it from my cold dead fingers"?

Although terrorists have always existed, this phenomenon was encountered most potently by the United States in the Vietnam war. U.S. soldiers were trained to kill an enemy, soldiers of the North Vietnamese army or the Viet Cong. However, because the war was a civil war, the enemy was often hard to discern. An enemy soldier would not necessarily be wearing a uniform, and could be an old man, woman, or child as easily as a young man. The enemy was everywhere, and that meant that all of the citizens of Vietnam, North and South, could be considered enemies.

Although in the United States terrorists have been stereotyped as men of Middle Eastern descent, a terrorist can emerge from any political group. (Some of the Taliban inmates at Guantanamo Bay are Australian and British.)[6] This poses a problem for those responsible for keeping nonviolent, law-abiding citizens safe on a daily basis. Who is the enemy? This question is changing the nature of law enforcement and its relationship with government security agencies and the military.

As mentioned earlier, the police are reactive, whereas soldiers are proactive. Police respond to crimes; soldiers seek out and neutralize enemy soldiers. The criminal justice system is reactive as well. It deals with those who are inserted into the system by way of breaking a law, and those defendants are innocent until proven guilty. A common complaint about the criminal justice system is that it cannot act until a law is broken. For instance, a person who is suspected of being a violent sex offender cannot be arrested for thinking about attacking another person. He or she can be arrested only after the attack. Many would argue that this is too late, but from a purely statistical point of view, only a few people have been harmed by the sex offender.

Currently, society is willing to accept this statistical safety in return for a set of personal freedoms and rights. However, terrorism presents another statistical problem. All too frequently, an act of terrorism hurts a vast number of people. Nearly 3000 people died in the World Trade Center attack.[7] Most citizens would accept the trampling of some freedoms and rights if the attack's perpetrators could have been arrested while planning it. This type of proaction, however, is military in style and philosophy.

Terrorism, then, is causing law enforcement and the criminal justice system to sustain some fundamental changes and alliances. The question remains just what those changes will be. How will law enforcement become more like the military? The war on drugs has already nudged the police in that direction, with increased latitude

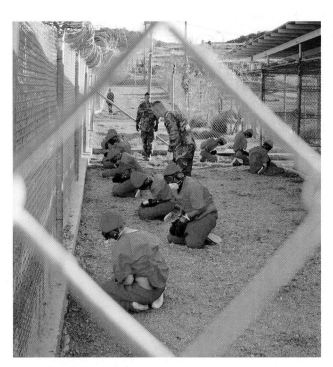

The war on terrorism has forced the government to take extraordinary strides to deal with those suspected of plotting or committing terrorist acts. Pictured here is Camp X-Ray in Guantanamo Bay, Cuba, where many of those who fought against the United States in Afghanistan were incarcerated.

Szource: AP Wide World Photos

for drug stings and search-and-seizures. How will the legal system deal with citizens who have not broken a law but have, say, donated money to an organization that funds another organization that is suspected of committing terrorist acts in a faraway country, or who have browsed plans for making pipe bombs on the Internet? George Orwell coined a term for this type of activity—and described its punishment—in his novel *1984:* **thoughtcrime**.[8] Thought crimes might be one of the new challenges to law enforcement, the legal system, and the civil rights of U.S. citizens.

In many ways, the war on terrorism is different from the war on crime or the war on drugs. (See Figure 16-1 for the structure of terrorist organizations.) The terrorist attacks on the Pentagon and the World Trade Center inspired a new wave of patriotism. The events of September 11 represent the greatest loss of life on U.S. soil caused by an outside aggressor since the Revolutionary War. At this point, it is worth considering some of the differences between the war on terrorism and the other social problems that we have been discussing.

- **The war on terrorism has a clear and identifiable outside enemy**   Well, sort of. This enemy is stereotyped as a Middle Eastern male of the Muslim faith. Although Osama bin Laden is the poster boy for the extreme terrorist, a popular concept in the United States is that almost anyone of Middle Eastern descent could be a terrorist.[9] However, that should not blind us to the fact that some individuals and groups have serious issues with the policies, culture, and economic nature of the United States. We must keep in mind, therefore, that domestic terrorism is also a serious threat.

- **The war on terrorism is political rather than social**   Whereas drugs and crime are considered problems that can be solved by tinkering with social service agencies and the criminal justice system, terrorism occupies an international realm outside the purview of traditional U.S. state and local

thoughtcrime

A term coined by George Orwell in his novel 1984, in which the act of thinking about breaking a law is a criminal offense.

Figure 16-1 **Basic Structure of Terrorist Organizations**
Source: The White House, National Strategy for Combating Terrorism (Washington, DC: 2003), 6, www.whitehouse.gov/news/releases/2003/02/counter_terrorism/.pdf

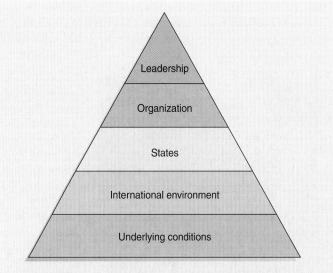

Structure of Terror
• At the base, underlying conditions such as poverty, corruption, religious conflict, and ethnic strife create opportunities for terrorists to exploit.
• The international environment defines the boundaries within which terrorists' strategies take shape.
• Terrorists must have a physical base from which to operate.
• The terrorist organization's structure, membership, resources, and security determine its capabilities and reach.
• The terrorist leadership provides the overall direction and strategy that link all these factors and thereby breathes life into a terror campaign.

agencies. To effectively deal with international terrorist threats, we will have to use instruments of national defense, including the military.[10] Using the military to deal with routine, domestic drug arrests and crime is prohibited by the Constitution and takes extraordinary permissions from the courts and Congress.

- **The war on terrorism uses military weapons** The tools of the criminal justice system are used to address drugs and crime, but terrorism requires resources not available to local and state law enforcement agencies. Although many law enforcement agencies have become more militaristic by establishing SWAT teams that wear black outfits and carry automatic weapons, most police activities do not require the warlike approach and equipment needed to fight the war on terrorism.[11]

- **An outside terrorist enemy does not enjoy U.S. legal protections** Terrorists are treated in a more efficient and determined way than are other types of lawbreakers. They are not subject to constitutional protections, and although this is hotly debated, it would appear that they are not privileged to the protections normally afforded to prisoners of war. The members of Afghanistan's Taliban political party who are being held at the naval base at Guantanamo Bay, Cuba, are being denied basic legal rights. So far, they are not officially charged with any criminal offense, are not allowed to have attorneys, and have no legal recourse to protest their imprisonment. As "enemy combatants," they appear caught in a no-man's-land between being criminal offenders and being soldiers.[12] (See Crosscurrents 16.1.)

- **Terrorists firmly believe that their cause is just** Most offenders and drug dealers would readily admit that their activities are illegal. Terrorists, on the other hand, believe that their acts are justifiable, and in many cases, spiritually ordained.[13] The role of law enforcement is greatly complicated when lawbreakers have little regard for human life, either theirs or others, and are willing to participate in suicide bombings. The normal techniques of making targets more difficult to strike and escape do not work when the perpetrator has no intention of escaping.[14]

The war on terrorism accelerates the war metaphor of the criminal justice system's responses to crime in other ways, but these points are sufficient to illustrate how different terrorism is from conventional crime. The differences in the motivations, techniques, and consequences of terrorist crime demand that it be addressed differently.[15] By employing the war metaphor, criminal justice practitioners can use a range of laws, equipment, surveillance techniques, and funding resources that are unavailable for controlling normal crime. For better or worse, the new emphasis on terrorism will make dramatic changes in the criminal justice system that will be influential for years to come. Before we look at these changes, let us consider in greater detail just how the events of September 11 affected the resolve of Americans to fight terrorism.

SEPTEMBER 11, 2001 Some people question whether the terms *war on crime* and *war on drugs* are simply rhetorical devices created by politicians to give the illusion that the government takes these social problems seriously. There is no such ambiguity about the war on terrorism, however. It is clear, so far, that Americans are willing to cede greater authority to government agencies to prevent terrorism.[16] The events of September 11, 2001, showed the world that large-scale terrorism can be brought anywhere, including New York City and Washington, D.C.

From the terrorists' point of view, September 11 was a resounding tactical success. The terrorists hijacked four planes from three airports and flew three of those planes into high-profile targets, killing thousands of people. The fourth plane crashed in a field in Pennsylvania. Officials speculate that this fourth plane was headed for Washington with a likely target of the Capitol building or the White House. The nation had not seen such a coordinated attack since Pearl Harbor. The difference with September 11, however, was that the terrorists used the nation's own airliners to

Legal Rights at Guantanamo Bay

One of the consistent criticisms of the war on terror has been the suspension of legal rights for "enemy combatants." The U.S. government has determined that those captured on the battlefield in Afghanistan and Iraq are not entitled to rights normally given to prisoners of war or U.S. citizens. By housing these individuals at a U.S. Navy base in Guantanamo Bay, Cuba, the administration has effectively kept suspected terrorists in a legal limbo that prevents them from challenging the reasons and conditions of their confinement.

The Supreme Court recently ruled in *Boumediene* v. *Bush* that these detainees are now entitled to the constitutional right of *habeas corpus*, which means they can challenge the legal basis of their detention in federal court. According to Human Rights Watch, it is unclear exactly what this will mean for the detainees. At the very least it means that some semblance of due process will be afforded them, but it is doubtful that they will be released anytime in the near future. There is considerable public pressure on the U.S. government to close down the Guantanamo Bay prison and give the detainees a hearing to determine whether they are legally held. The court held that Guantanamo cannot be a "law free zone" where lawyers and the press are kept away from the detainees.[1]

At one point, the prison held 750 detainees from more than 40 countries, many of whom have been there for more than five years without access to legal counsel. Reports of abuse have been circulating in the media for years, and in 2006 there were three suicides.[2] Furthermore, conditions of confinement are so spartan that many inmates have experienced mental health problems including hallucinations, anxiety disorders, and severe depression. According to Salon.com:

> More than half of the 270 detainees currently at Guantánamo—including many who are slated for release or transfer—are housed in high-security facilities akin to U.S. "supermax" prisons. They spend all but two hours a day in small cells with no natural light or fresh air. Their meals are slipped through a slot in the door, and they are given little more than a single book and the Koran to occupy their time. Even their limited "recreation" time—which is sometimes provided in the middle of the night—generally takes place in single cell cages so that detainees can't physically interact with one another. None of these detainees have been allowed visits by family members, and very few have been able to make phone calls home.[3]

The future of the prison at Guantanamo Bay is uncertain. Public pressure is growing to close it down and provide a more humane form of detention and legal rights. Exactly what will become of these detainees remains in doubt. The home countries of some of them do not want them back, and it is difficult to find other countries willing to accept suspected terrorists. In many respects these are "men without a country," as the legal problems of releasing them are significant. Many wonder whether they have the requisite mental health to adjust to freedom after being incarcerated for more than six years in extremely difficult conditions.

Think About It

1. Should the detainees be allowed to challenge their detention?
2. Should the detainees be returned to their home countries, whether those countries want them or not?
3. Should the detainees be held indefinitely?
4. Are the rights guaranteed by the U.S. Constitution for U.S. citizens only?

[1] James Ross, "Supreme Court to Bush: You're Not above the Law," Human Rights Watch, June 13, 2008, http://hrw.org/english/docs/2008/06/13/usint1912.
[2] "Profile: Guantanamo Bay," BBC News, October 17, 2006, http://news.bbc.co.uk/2/hi/americas/4720962.stm.
[3] Jennifer Daskal and Stacy Sullivan, "The Insanity inside Guantánamo," *Salon*, June 10, 2008, www.salon.com/news/feature/2008/06/10/guantanamo_mental/.

wreak havoc. Looking back at September 11, we can see many issues that contributed to the tragedy.

- **Airport security** Some airports in Europe enjoy a high degree of security, and some airlines such as Israel's El-Al are particularly vigilant; however, airport security in U.S. cities before September 11 was geared toward a different sort of threat. In the 1960s, there was a spate of airline hijackings in which guns were used to force planes to divert to other cities or countries. Disgruntled Cubans who wanted to go home performed several of the hijackings. The

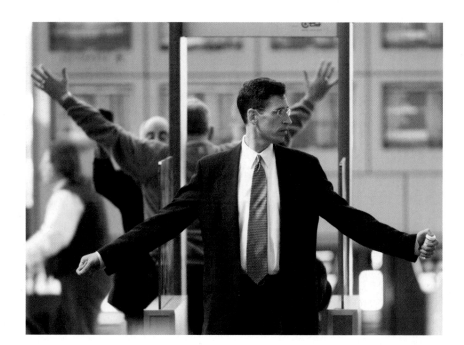

The U.S. government has increased security measures at airports as a result of September 11. Here, passengers are checked at a security checkpoint in O'Hare International Airport.
Source: Corbis/Bettmann

United States' response was to electronically search passengers for metal weapons. Although more drastic actions were contemplated, such as a physical search of everyone wanting to get on a plane or the use of sky marshals to ride "shotgun" on every flight, the government and the airline industry agreed to limit the public's inconvenience to walking through metal detectors. This system worked quite well in the United States for many years. Hijackings were almost nonexistent, and the public learned to accept the minimal intrusions on their privacy in exchange for safety. So what went wrong on September 11? The hijackers were able to smuggle relatively small, unobtrusive box cutters (plastic knives with razor blades) onto the planes.

- **Passengers' response**   We can only speculate about the initial minutes of each of these hijackings, but clearly they were well planned and well executed. The crew was overpowered and probably killed, and the passengers were forced to the rear of the planes. Before September 11, the conventional wisdom was to allow professionals to handle hostage situations. Most likely the passengers expected the hijackers to make their demands known to authorities and hoped that some deal could be made for their release. The passengers probably did not initially realize that the hijackers were on a suicide mission and that their cooperation only facilitated the hijackers' goals.

- **Rights of aliens**   The freedoms enjoyed by Americans made us vulnerable to the September 11 attacks. It is only because of our geographic distance from those who would do us harm that we do not experience even more terrorism. One of the pressing issues that Americans face in combating terrorism is the loss of privacy. Our agencies of immigration, customs, and law enforcement did not communicate with each other very well before September 11. In fact, communications within the FBI were so compartmentalized that field agents who found suspected terrorists taking flying lessons on large jets could not get that information to other agents who were responsible for tracking terrorists.[17] It was reported that these men were not interested in learning how to take off or land the aircraft; they simply wanted to learn to control the jet in the air. In an effort to protect the privacy of citizens, and to a large extent, noncitizens, our agencies did not share vital information that would have alerted the right officials about the pending hijackings.

Terrorism is an international problem. Rescue workers cover up bodies near a bomb-damaged passenger train following a number of explosions on trains in Madrid, Spain, on March 11, 2004.

Source: AP Wide World Photos

The events of September 11 changed the way we prepare for terrorism and, to an even greater extent, changed our criminal justice system. Several federal agencies have been reorganized into the Department of Homeland Security. Other agencies, such as the FBI, have been given increased responsibility in combating terrorism. Less visible, but more pervasive, has been the effect on local and state agencies. Because local law enforcement and emergency service agencies are likely to be the "first responders" to terrorist acts, they have taken on new responsibilities requiring additional training, improved equipment, and more money. The net effect of this new mandate has been both a blessing and a curse for local agencies.[18] On one hand, some extremely positive benefits have emerged from this new responsibility. First, the status of law enforcement officers, firefighters, and emergency service technicians has received a boost. Rather than being taken for granted, those who risk their lives on a daily basis are being recognized for the public service they perform.

A second beneficial by-product of September 11 has been the increased attention and resources allocated to local agencies. Even though many communities are discovering that funding the new initiatives demanded by federal legislation is difficult, there has been a substantial upgrading in the training, coordination, and equipment available to local agencies. Given that terrorist events are rare, this new level of competence can be expected to significantly address more conventional crime problems in many jurisdictions.

A third and longer-term effect of the war on terrorism is that the criminal justice system is experiencing an influx of new and talented personnel at all levels. As an employer, the criminal justice system competes with other employers for the best talent. Before September 11, criminal justice salaries often were not competitive, although the work was dangerous. Now criminal justice programs at many universities are experiencing an influx of students. There is a new urgency and status associated with serving and protecting the public, with nothing but solid support for the mission of domestic police and fire personnel.[19]

THE PATRIOT ACT   The response of Congress to the terrorist attacks of September 11 was to pass the USA Patriot Act. Officially titled the "Uniting and Strengthening America by Providing Appropriate Tools Required to Intercept and Obstruct Terrorism Act," the Patriot Act gives the government greater latitude over a broad range of concerns that specify the rights of citizens, aliens, and government agents.[20] Moreover, the act toughens penalties for those who assist terrorists and provides financial relief for victims of terrorism, including public safety officers and their families. Two particularly sweeping and controversial components of the Patriot Act are of concern to students of the criminal justice system: the reorganization and retasking of federal law enforcement and the implications for civil liberties and legal rights.

DEPARTMENT OF HOMELAND SECURITY There has been a great deal of speculation that the September 11 terrorist attacks could have been prevented if our criminal justice system had communicated more efficiently. Some people believe that enough information was in the hands of officers from different agencies and that a coordinated and centralized command structure could have collated this information and prevented the attacks. Whether this is true is not of concern here because the mere suggestion that the attacks were preventable moved the president and Congress to restructure the federal government by creating the cabinet-level Department of Homeland Security. The intent of this action was to ensure that these agencies were organizationally allied in the most efficient and productive manner to combat terrorism.[21]

The overall effect of the creation of the Department of Homeland Security will not be known for several years, but it is interesting to observe which agencies managed to retain their independence and which ones were brought under the auspices of the new department. For instance, the two agencies that seemed to be the most likely candidates to be brought into the Department of Homeland Security were the Federal Bureau of Investigation (FBI) and the Central Intelligence Agency (CIA). Each has a mandate to protect the United States from terrorism, with the FBI being responsible for activities within our borders and the CIA being responsible for activities in other countries that may threaten the United States. Of course, the nature of the threats often overlap, and there has been considerable friction between the FBI and CIA over the years as to which agency is responsible for which threats.[22] However, it has been suggested that these two agencies did not share vital information that could have prevented September 11.

Neither of these agencies was included in the reorganization. Why? There are two plausible answers, and the truth probably contains elements of each. The first lies within the nature of the agencies' basic missions. Preventing terrorism is only a small (albeit significant) part of what the FBI and CIA are mandated to do. By being under the Department of Homeland Security, they could lose their authority to decide how best to deploy their resources. This is a reasonable explanation for allowing these agencies to retain their independence and their current organizational placement; however, over the next few years, it will be crucial to monitor how well each agency works with the Department of Homeland Security. The second reason why the CIA and FBI have remained independent is political. These are mature agencies that, over the years, have developed networks with politicians, a large number of loyal alumni, and their own organizational culture. Placing them under the Department of Homeland Security would have required more of a political battle than was desired after September 11. (See Figure 16-2 for the organization chart of the Department of Homeland Security.)

The agencies that were brought into the Department of Homeland Security came from many different organizational cultures tasked with a wide range of activities only tangentially related to terrorism. The result is that the new department will need several years to design procedures and lines of communication to enable these disparate agencies to function in the coordinated manner envisioned by Congress. For instance, the Secret Service, formerly part of the Treasury Department and responsible for protecting the president and dealing with counterfeiting and other currency crimes, is now part of the Department of Homeland Security and has had to shift some of its attention to the broader issues of terrorism. Similarly, agencies such as the Plum Island Animal Disease Center, once attached to the Department of Agriculture, is now part of the Department of Homeland Security. It is reasonable to

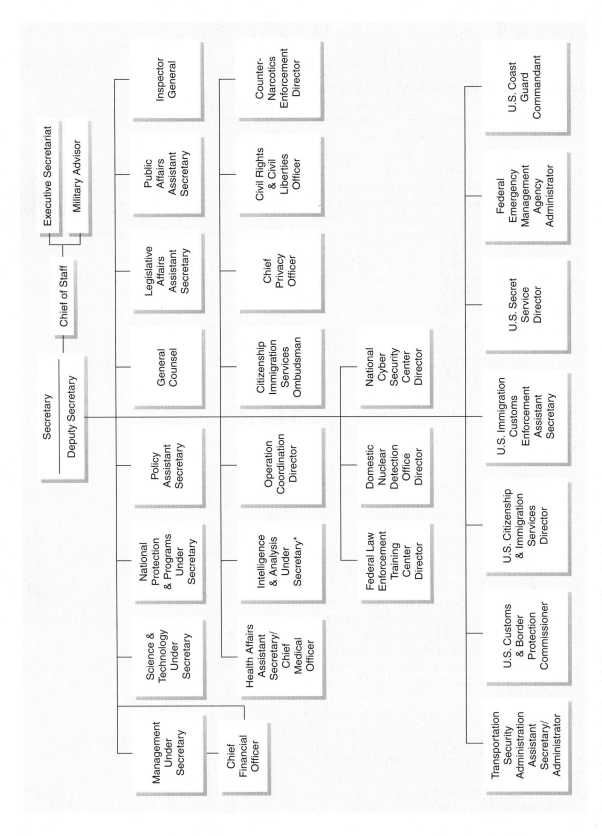

Figure 16-2 Organization of the Department of Homeland Security

Source: Department of Homeland Security, www.dhs.gov/xabout/structure/editorial_0644.shtm.

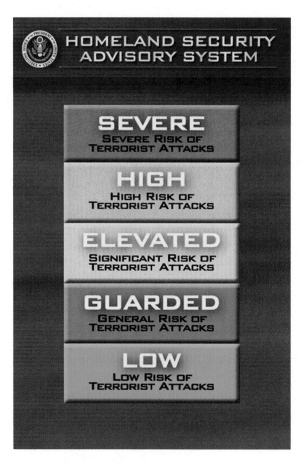

The Department of Homeland Security's color-coded terrorism warning system lists five national threat levels. Check the Department of Homeland Security's website at www.dhs.gov to see what the national threat level is today.

Source: AP Wide World Photos

speculate that much of the center's emphasis will be shifted toward investigating the weaponized use of anthrax and away from its mission dealing with other concerns of animal disease. These issues of reorganization might never be problematic, but a major adjustment period of several years will be required before the formal and informal mechanisms of government are established in the way that the president and Congress envisioned when they created this new department.

PRIVACY ISSUES   The Patriot Act not only restructured law enforcement agencies, but also greatly expanded the government's authority to gather information. In the wake of September 11, this seemed to make a great deal of sense. If U.S. intelligence efforts are more efficient and effective, we may be able to prevent future attacks. However, the act has its critics, some of whom believe that the Patriot Act gives the government too much authority to snoop into citizens' private affairs and that it greatly weakens the protections provided by the Bill of Rights. Following are two of the most controversial aspects of the Patriot Act:

1. **Judicial review.**   The Crime Control and Safe Streets Act of 1968 and the Foreign Intelligence Surveillance Act of 1978 limit the government's ability to conduct domestic surveillance. They provide that government agents must obtain approval from a federal judge before using wiretaps or other means of electronic eavesdropping. This sounds reasonable, but judicial review has been practiced in different ways. In criminal cases, judges are more reluctant to grant wiretaps than in foreign surveillance cases. Because the Patriot Act is concerned with terrorism, some people think the government will abuse the authority to wiretap and use it indiscriminately against U.S. citizens for activities that transcend terrorism and/or are simply normal offenses. This is particularly sensitive when we consider the links of the illegal drug trade to terrorism. Although Congress

wants to fight terrorism, the Patriot Act can be used on the local level to wiretap street-level marijuana dealers without adequate judicial review. Additional surveillance issues concern the act's provisions that authorize law enforcement to check the records of bookstores and libraries to see what people are reading. For instance, this provision would allow law enforcement officers to find out who is reading library books on how to build a nuclear bomb or biological weapon. Although these provisions may seem reasonable to some, before the Patriot Act, the government had to convince a judge that there was probable cause to suspect an individual. Now, under the Patriot Act, government officials can go on fishing expeditions to discover what ordinary citizens are reading. Other records, including financial, travel, medical, video rental, and phone records, are also subject to these warrantless searches.

2. **Secret searches.**   The Patriot Act authorizes government agents to search homes and property without prior or subsequent notification that the residence has been searched. This authority might be a wonderful aid to law enforcement in prosecuting the war against terrorism; however, it is also a threat to citizens' individual liberties. The Patriot Act is so broadly written that these powers may legitimately be used against citizens suspected not of terrorism but of regular criminal activity. These Patriot Act provisions give the appearance of creating a police state rather than protecting a free democracy. Although extreme violations of rights have not yet occurred, the legal provisions that allow for such police behavior are of concern to constitutional scholars and are being challenged in the courts.[23]

The Patriot Act was hastily passed as a reaction to the terrorist events of September 11. Two primary motivations propelled it through Congress. The first motivation was cosmetic. Politicians were eager to demonstrate their outrage at the horrendous attacks and to demonstrate to their constituents that they had the backbone and resolve to fight terrorism. The second motivation was just as sincere but more substantive. The security of the United States was exposed as inadequate in a new age of terrorism, and Congress was anxious to shore it up. Whether the Patriot Act provisions are enough to provide this additional security or are even a step in the right direction remains to be seen. What is apparent at this juncture, however, is that controversy over how to fight terrorism without infringing on citizens' rights will continue.

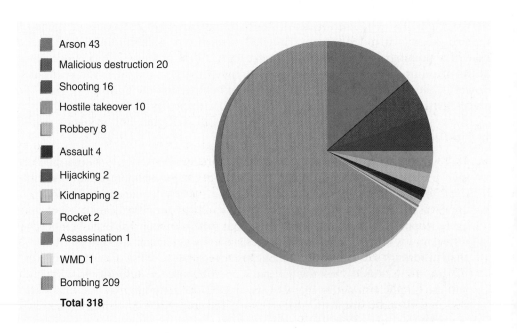

Figure 16-3   Terrorism by Event, 1980–2005

Source: Federal Bureau of Investigation, *Terrorism 2002–2005*, 11, www.fbi. gov/publications/terror/ terrorism2002_2005.pdf

Arson 43

Malicious destruction 20

Shooting 16

Hostile takeover 10

Robbery 8

Assault 4

Hijacking 2

Kidnapping 2

Rocket 2

Assassination 1

WMD 1

Bombing 209

Total 318

HOW TERRORISM IS CHANGING THE CRIMINAL JUSTICE SYSTEM   The war on terrorism is deeply changing the criminal justice system. Despite the fact that terrorism has struck relatively few jurisdictions, the threat has affected the whole United States, and local criminal justice systems nationwide have had to alter their funding priorities to prepare for the day they hope will never come. (For a historical look at the total number of terrorist events in the United States from 1980 to 2005, see Figure 16-3). For the most part, however, life will go on, and law enforcement officers will continue to pursue those who are suspected of breaking the law. However, the war on crime and the war on drugs will be both hindered and aided by the war on terrorism.

- **Unfunded mandates**   When terrorism strikes national targets, it also hits local governments hard. The New York City fire and police departments were the first responders to the World Trade Center attacks on September 11. The loss of life and resources will affect these agencies for years and have forced other local police and fire departments to institute a whole new level of training and preparedness. Although the risk of terrorism is relatively low for most cities, especially on the scale of September 11, each city government has had to develop contingency plans. These plans include mechanisms to communicate and coordinate with other agencies at the local, state, and federal levels. Communications equipment, specialized suits to handle chemical and biological hazards, specialized training for police and fire personnel, and increased security for essential services such as the water supply and symbolic targets such as the St. Louis Arch and the Golden Gate Bridge have stretched the resources of local and state governments. The federal government is being flooded with requests by local governments for more money to fund these new duties.[24]

- **Increased capacity**   For the first time since the legislation establishing the Law Enforcement Assistance Administration in 1968, the criminal justice system has moved to the head of the line in the allocation of government resources. Because domestic terrorism is relatively rare, the personnel, equipment, and intelligence that have been established to fight it can be used to fight normal crime. Local criminal justice systems are experiencing an infusion of personnel positions, weapons, communications equipment, and training that can be used to respond to local crime concerns.[25] Furthermore, morale has improved as the contributions of local police and firefighters are reflected in the heroism of the first responders of September 11. The relatively low pay and low status of these occupations are being offset by the appreciation of citizens who are thankful for the sacrifices these public servants make.

PEACEMAKING CRIMINOLOGY AND RESTORATIVE JUSTICE

The recent history of the United States' approach to dealing with crime clearly illustrates the war metaphor. Critics of this approach ask whether the war metaphor is the most effective way to address the complex problems of crime. Is the crime situation getting better? Are our communities safer? Are prisons doing their job by reducing the criminal tendencies of those they release through either deterrence or rehabilitation? The answers to these questions are mixed. Critics of the war metaphor contend that, in many ways, the tough-on-crime approach, although politically attractive, may cause even more crime. By concentrating on deterrence and incapacitation as primary crime-control strategies, the United States has become a country with both a high crime rate and an expensive and punitive criminal justice system (see Crosscurrents 16.2 for the current situation on California's death row). Critics suggest that the high crime rate and the war approach are related and ask the question, What would the crime situation be like if we had a less punitive and more rehabilitative criminal justice system?

Paying for the Death Penalty

California is discovering that the war on crime is costly. The amount of money needed for law enforcement agencies, courts, and prisons to operate in a state that is already in financial crisis puts all agencies in a position of desperation. This financial burden is felt particularly acutely on the state's death row.

Faced with expanding its death row at the San Quentin prison, California is looking at a cost overrun of more than $40 million. The project is expected to cost at least $395 million, and politicians, as well as the public, are questioning whether the state can afford such an expense to house inmates who have been sentenced to die. The state prison system represents about 10 percent of a $100 billion state budget, which diverts money away from other more popular causes:

> "This is a giant black hole," said Sen. Gloria Romero, D-Los Angeles, chairwoman of the Senate public safety committee. "It's a never-ending gravitational force that'll continue to suck away money that should be spent on local government, education, health and human services and higher education."[1]

One of the problems that California is experiencing is the inability to execute inmates in a timely fashion. The state has executed only 13 inmates since the death penalty was reinstated in 1976, causing death row to grow out of control.[2] The average time it takes for a condemned inmate to be executed in California has more than doubled in the last decade. The wait to be executed averages nearly 20 years, and housing a death row inmate costs about $90,000 more per year compared with other inmates.[3]

The dysfunctional nature of California's death row has raised numerous legal and ethical problems. Because the state cannot carry out executions in a reasonable time, Eighth Amendment concerns of cruel and unusual punishment are raised. The argument is that sitting in a cramped cell on death row for 20 years constitutes a violation of the right to reasonable conditions of confinement.

Think About It

1. Why is the death penalty so expensive in California?
2. If California cannot execute condemned inmates in a reasonable time, what should be done with them?
3. Should the citizens of California be made to pay for such an expensive criminal justice system at the expense of education, infrastructure, and social programs?

[1]Matthew Yi, "Death Row Cost Overrun: $40 Million," *San Francisco Chronicle*, July 30, 2008, www.sfgate.com/cgi-bin/article.cgi?file=/c/a/2008/07/30/MNIH121H7J.DTL.
[2]Randy Dotinga, "As California Looks to Expand Death Row, a Flap over Where to Build It," *Christian Science Monitor*, July 15, 2008, www.csmonitor.com/2008/0716/p02s01-usju.html.
[3]Kevin Johnson, "Prisoners' Time Spent on Death Row Doubles," *USA Today*, July 24, 2008, www.usatoday.com/news/nation/2008-07-23-Death-row-time_N.htm.

peacemaking criminology
A theoretical perspective that focuses on nonviolence, social justice, and reducing the suffering of both the victim and the offender.

restorative justice
An alternative justice model that uses community programs to repair the harm done by offenders.

One alternative to the war metaphor is the peacemaking approach. The remainder of this chapter will detail the theoretical developments of **peacemaking criminology** and also delineate its practical applications through the **restorative justice** movement. This section will suggest that the emerging perspectives of peacemaking criminology and restorative justice provide a promising strategy for dealing with crime. The peacemaking perspective might never fully replace the war-on-crime metaphor, but it mediates some of the more destructive tactics that are the consequences of addressing crime with the war metaphor. The promise of the peacemaking perspective is that it holds out long-lasting solutions not only to the problems of crime, but also for the issues and controversies that create crime. Peacemaking criminology and restorative justice implemented in the optimal manner ease the increasing pressures on the criminal justice system by employing alternate mechanisms for resolving social conflict. The criminal justice system should be the institution of last resort for resolving social problems, and the peacemaking and restorative justice movements provide the intermediary processes that can resolve issues in ways that do not require the expense and resources of the traditional criminal justice process. We will first address the theoretical foundations of peacemaking criminology, then turn to restorative justice as a practical model for implementing peacemaking principles.

Peacemaking criminology is not a particularly new concept. In fact, many of its principles, such as social justice, nonviolence, and rehabilitation, have been advocated for centuries and, for the most part, have been discarded by the modern criminal justice system. The accuracy of this criticism is immaterial here because the foundations of peacemaking criminology have never been subjected to empirical examination or given an honest opportunity to demonstrate their promise. Although some regard peacemaking criminology as utopian and naive, its principles are worth considering given the failure of the war metaphor to solve many of the problems of crime. Therefore, this section will present the theoretical traditions from which peacemaking criminology has developed and present some of the contributions made by current criminologists to refine the perspective to address contemporary issues of crime and justice.

In 1991, Harold Pepinsky and Richard Quinney edited a book titled *Criminology as Peacemaking*.[26] This work gathered the ideas of scholars who were concerned with developing a more effective approach to the problems of crime, an approach that was aimed at reducing the suffering of both victims and offenders. Pepinsky and Quinney gave voice to a new movement in criminology circles that rejected the violence done by the criminal justice system and sought to improve the quality of justice for society by addressing the needs of victims and offenders. Both academic criminologists and criminal justice practitioners have embraced the resulting peacemaking perspective. *Criminology as Peacemaking* envisioned peacemaking criminology as developing from three intellectual traditions: the religious and humanist tradition, the feminist tradition, and the critical tradition.

Religious and Humanist Tradition

One of the consequences of living in such a pluralistic country as the United States is the dislocation felt by citizens from some of the ancient-wisdom traditions embodied in religion. Because of the establishment clause in the Constitution dictating that there is no state religion, much of the comfort of religious teachings has been absent in civil society. This is as it should be in a pluralistic society based on the premise that each of us should be able to believe and practice in our own manner, but much has been lost as our institutions turn a blind eye to the benefits of faith.

Peacemaking criminology recognizes the contributions to meaningful communities and individual well-being that religion can supply and argues that the criminal justice system should be aware of the transformative power of religion.[27] Religious perspectives such as Buddhism, Christianity, Hinduism, Islam, Judaism, and American Indian traditions all encompass principles that are important contributions to the peacemaking perspective. The ideas of living in meaningful communities characterized by harmony, mutual cooperation, and peace is central to most major religions. Additionally, although each religion puts its own spin on the cosmic questions of why we are here and what happens after death, they all provide a prescription for following a path of kindness, respect, and healthy living.[28] The promise for reclamation of the soul is an important part of religious life that is often neglected or rejected by the secular criminal justice system. Some critics contend that religious zealots have divided peoples and waged war over the centuries, but the promise of peace and individual salvation is still a powerful motivator for a great many people and something the contemporary criminal justice system can employ to help deal with the problems of criminal behavior.

Pepinsky and Quinney also recognized that humanist traditions contribute to the foundations of peacemaking criminology. Humanists believe that it is possible to live a moral life without religious theory. Based on the concept that people are basically good and will cooperate for the benefit of all if society's institutions are fair, humanists embrace many of the same social concerns as do religious individuals, except without the idea of supreme guidance. Regardless of the religious or humanist particulars, Pepinsky and Quinney pointed to these intellectual traditions as being an important part of the cultural fabric by which people live their lives. By recognizing and incorporating these intellectual traditions into peacemaking criminology, its advocates believe that offenders and victims can witness how the solutions to crime are integrated into a larger pattern of righteous living.

Feminist Tradition

Feminism has a history of resisting the patriarchy in which societal rights and responsibilities are allocated according to gender roles. Feminism advocates a criminal justice system that is blind toward sex and in which women and men are treated with respect, equal opportunities and consequences, and fairness. The war metaphor, which relies on domination and power, is antithetical to the feminist perspective. The feminist model suggests that the criminal justice system's laws, biases, and personnel have been historically supportive of an unjust attitude that supports a privileged position in society for men. Feminists argue that the criminal justice system must be examined for sexist practices and chauvinistic attitudes in law enforcement, the courts, and correctional institutions. Most important, feminists want their share of the power, but contend that they would exercise it differently, repudiating the culture of domination that they believe is a large part of the masculine world.[29]

Critical Traditions

In addition to critiquing the contributions of gender inequality to the dysfunctions of the criminal justice system, critical traditions consider other social characteristics such as social class, age, and race. Historically, the most pressing concern of critical criminologists has been the influence of social class on the quality of justice in society and more particularly in the criminal justice system. Karl Marx laid the groundwork for critiquing capitalist societies and their inherent contradictions in allocating wealth and power. One of the central tenets of capitalism is the prospect of upward mobility whereby those willing to work hard, play by the rules, and defer gratification can "pull themselves up by their bootstraps" and realize the dream of financial independence. According to Marx, this goal is a product of false consciousness whereby the precious few who do attain the goal serve as an unrealistic example that keeps most of us slaving away at low-paying jobs that serve only the interests of those who own and control the means of production.[30]

Another characteristic that critical theorists deem problematic is that of age. Rights and responsibility in most societies are allocated according to age. This tradition is well-meaning, but it reinforces the interests of those who already control society. For instance, those under age 18 are not allowed a voice in making the law, but are subject to a vast number of statutes that do not apply to adults. Although laws denying young people the right to drive, vote, or drink alcohol supposedly exist to protect them, they are enforced by a system that does not allow them the same constitutional guarantees afforded to the adults who passed the laws.

Each of these intellectual traditions contributes to peacemaking criminology to make it an overarching perspective that can be used not only to reform the criminal justice system but also to address problems on both the personal and social levels. The peacemaking perspective is applicable to four levels of analysis (see Figure 16-4).

- **Intrapersonal**   Religious intellectual traditions speak to the need for personal peace. The cause of much of the crime and violence in society is the torment experienced by offenders who cannot find inner peace and security and strike out at others as a way to ease their pain. Programs in prisons not only rely on religious services to attend to individuals' personal development but also encourage such activities as meditation, weight lifting, and yoga as ways for inmates to develop self-discipline and a healthy self-concept.

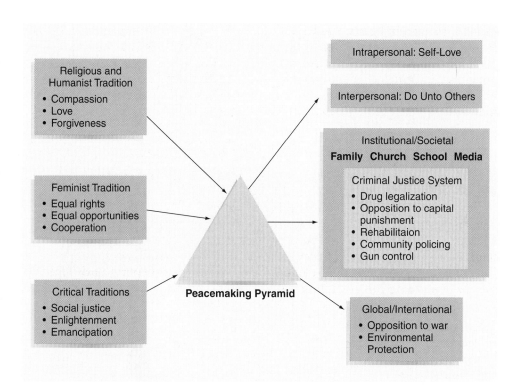

Figure 16-4 **Peacemaking and the Criminal Justice System in Context**

- **Interpersonal**   The peacemaking perspective is especially concerned with the interpersonal level of analysis in which the Golden Rule, "Do unto others as you would have others do unto you," applies.

- **Societal and institutional**   The institutional and societal level of the peacemaking perspective is where peacemaking criminology can be applied. Laws and institutions are a reflection of how people live their personal lives. According to the peacemaking perspective, people should strive to ensure that schools, families, workplaces, and especially the criminal justice system do not violate fundamental principles of living.

- **International and global**   Finally, the peacemaking perspective can be applied on the international and global level. Relationships between nations all too often erode to wars and economic sanctions. Although a strong national defense is required for protection against unstable despots, strong nations must constantly guard against the temptation to use power simply because they can.

This brief overview of the scope of the peacemaking perspective illustrates that it is more than a midlevel theory to control crime. The peacemaking perspective is a way to engage all aspects of an individual's life as well as a prescription for a society to dispense economic and social justice. We turn now to exploring the actual principles that underlie the peacemaking perspective.

The Peacemaking Pyramid

Although peacemaking can be envisioned in a number of ways, the peacemaking pyramid is intended to show that the components build on one another to form a solid and stable approach to the problems of crime (see Figure 16-5). The pyramid depicts a set of increasingly important ideas that draw from the intellectual traditions.

NONVIOLENCE   At the base of the pyramid is the principle of nonviolence. In considering the history of injustice, we can see how Jesus Christ, Leo Tolstoy, Mohandas Gandhi, and Dr. Martin Luther King Jr. used nonviolence to confront institutional injustice in a positive way. For example, in the United States, the civil rights

Figure 16-5   **Peacemaking Pyramid**

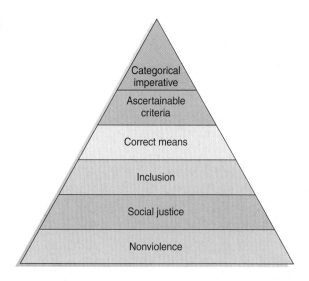

Categorical imperative

Ascertainable criteria

Correct means

Inclusion

Social justice

Nonviolence

Mohandas Gandhi promoted nonviolent social protest. His philosophy has inspired many peacemaking criminologists who advocate social change. This statue of Gandhi is in Atlanta, Georgia.

Source: PhotoEdit Inc.

movement was led by King, who employed the teachings of these other peacemakers to challenge the institutionalized racism of the southern states. By not resorting to violence, King led the Southern Christian Leadership Conference in a series of demonstrations that revealed not only the injustices of the law, but also how the law relied on violence for its enforcement. King used nonviolence to expose the violence inherent in the system.

Because of the unique mission of the criminal justice system, particularly that of law enforcement, a certain level of defensive violence is required. According to the principles of the peacemaking perspective, however, this violence must be proportional, used as a last resort, and continually evaluated in every situation to determine whether better alternatives were available. The goal of nonviolence as an instrument of the criminal justice system is to break the cycle of self-perpetuating violence that afflicts U.S. society.

SOCIAL JUSTICE   The criminal justice system should also strive toward social justice. A system that merely reinforces the power wielded by those who enact and enforce the laws does not serve the best interests of all citizens. When sexist or racist policies

Dr. Martin Luther King Jr. led the civil rights movement in the United States in the 1950s and 1960s. Like Gandhi, he advocated nonviolent social protest against discriminatory and racist laws.
Source: Courtesy of CORBIS-NY

are tolerated as part of the criminal justice system, it cannot be considered peacemaking even if it is done in a nonviolent manner. For example, if police officers respond to a domestic violence complaint and can persuade the husband to stop beating his wife and children, nonviolence has been attained. But if that man still psychologically and economically dominates and controls the family in a manner to the detriment of the well-being of the wife and children, then social justice has not been attained. The remedy for such a situation, then, is not only police response, but counseling and public education. Unfortunately, the limitations of the criminal justice system prevent it from ensuring that social justice is always considered. Criminal justice practitioners, however, can be trained to be aware of how advocating for social justice may help craft long-term solutions to problems.

INCLUSION   In the current criminal justice system, the product of justice is imposed on the defendant with little input from the victim, the victim's family, the community, or even the defendant. As covered later in this chapter when we discuss restorative justice, a peacemaking solution often requires that the criminal justice system seek the cooperation, counsel, and commitment of all affected parties. Currently, the prosecutor represents the state, and this effectively denies the victim an opportunity to be heard. Additionally, even though most criminal offenses reflect a dispute between the victim and the offender, the current system leaves little room for any kind of negotiation or resolution. The principle of inclusion suggests that the victim, the victim's family, the offender's family, representatives from local law enforcement, representatives of the community, and the offender work together to craft a sentence that fully resolves the dispute. In this way, the offender becomes bonded to the sentence; it is not something that is simply imposed. Moreover, because both the offender and victim have worked together to find a solution, they are more likely to be satisfied that justice has been done.

CORRECT MEANS   *Correct means* is a term coined by Gandhi that suggests that a good solution to the problems of crime can be attained only by processes that embody the principles of peacemaking. Gandhi is reputed to have said, "There is no path to peace; peace is the path." Applied to the criminal justice system, the principle of **correct means** suggests that offenders be supplied their constitutional and civil rights. Additionally, law enforcement officers and court and correctional personnel need to abide by procedural law and institutional guidelines to ensure that offenders are treated fairly, equitably, and without rancor or deception. The intent here is not

correct means
A peacemaking criminology term coined by Gandhi that describes how the problems of crime can only be attained using processes that embody peacemaking principles.

to limit the ability of law enforcement officers to pursue their duties, but to ensure that in enforcing the law, they also abide by the law. Good ends obtained by faulty means will, in the long run, only weaken the ability of the criminal justice system to achieve justice.

ASCERTAINABLE CRITERIA   Often individuals caught up in the criminal justice system, whether offenders or victims, have a difficult time understanding why decisions are made, who is advocating their best interests, or even what the legalistic language used by attorneys and judges means. As discussed in Chapter 9, the courtroom work group has an agenda of its own that often leaves the ordinary citizen confused about how and why the sentence was determined. **Ascertainable criteria** means that everyone involved should have a clear understanding of the rules and procedures the criminal justice system employs. This may slow the court process as offenders are educated about their various options and the ramifications of accepting one plea bargain over another, but the overall result is that the offenders will feel greater accountability for the decisions they make.

CATEGORICAL IMPERATIVE   **Categorical imperative** is a term associated with the philosopher Immanuel Kant, who postulated that individuals should decide the course of their actions according to the axiom "Act only according to the maxim whereby you can at the same time will that it should become a universal law."[31] When applied to the peacemaking perspective, this means that every decision should have an underlying moral logic to it that would allow that decision to be applied to other cases at other times. This, of course, means that racial or sexist bias should be eliminated, but it does not mean that justice need be mechanical or absolutely uniform. Individualized justice allows for discretion, but the categorical imperative dictates that decisions should have a defensible reason that promotes an overarching goal of not only justice, but social justice arrived at by correct means.

Is the peacemaking perspective simply a warmed-over version of liberal philosophies? (See Focus on Ethics 16.2 for a scenario.) Is it unrealistic, utopian, and naive? Is it the equivalent of giving in to the criminal element and turning the asylum over to the lunatics? Actually, no. The peacemaking perspective does not excuse crime or erase the culpability of offenders. Rather, it aims to craft institutions and policies that repair the harm caused by crime and reduce the suffering of victims, families, offenders, and the greater community. Because most human relationships are ongoing— that is, family members will continue to live together, neighbors will continue to

ascertainable criteria
A peacemaking criminology term that states that everyone involved in a criminal justice process should understand the rules and procedures employed by the system.

categorical imperative
A term associated with the philosopher Immanuel Kant. When applied to peacemaking, it means that every decision should be logical enough to be applied to other cases at other times.

16.2   FOCUS on ETHICS

HOW MUCH COULD YOU FORGIVE?

One of the primary concerns of peacemaking criminology is the issue of forgiveness. To heal the harms caused by crime over the long run, the victim and the offender should reconcile. This is often difficult, especially in cases of violent injury or death. Yet it does happen. Some of the family members of those killed in the Oklahoma City bombing did not want Timothy McVeigh executed because their religious faith forbade such a policy. Through restorative justice practices, some offenders who demonstrated true remorse have been forgiven by their victims' families.

Suppose someone murdered a member of your family and, after a period of time, expressed remorse and asked for you forgiveness. Could you forgive this person? If you are a religious person, what does your faith have to say about forgiveness? Is forgiveness something you might be able to develop after many years?

What Do You Do?

1. Is peacemaking criminology a nice theory but something that cannot be realistically expected of victims and their families?

2. If you made a big mistake and killed someone in a car wreck while you were drunk, could you ask the forgiveness of your victim's family?

3. Does someone who is truly remorseful deserve forgiveness?

dwell next door to each other, and offenders will remain in the community or return to it—solving the underlying problems that lead to crime is more effective than simple punishment. Many additional benefits are associated with the peacemaking perspective, including developing more integrated communities, giving individuals skills and tools to advance themselves, and providing a more inclusive sense of justice.

Much of what the peacemaking perspective advocates is already ingrained in the criminal justice system. The peacemaking perspective provides a philosophical foundation for practices that recognize the promise of believing that people are basically good and that our institutions can achieve better results by modeling the types of behavior we demand of our offenders. For instance, when the state kills through capital punishment, it has a brutalizing effect on society, according to the peacemaking perspective. Abusive behavior by the police alienates not only the victim, but also those who witness the event.[32] Programs that promote the rehabilitation of offenders have been a consistent feature in the criminal justice system for decades, but because of the drain of resources caused by the war on crime, they have been neglected, underfunded, and made politically unpopular. But just how has the peacemaking perspective been implemented in the criminal justice system? One major strategy for injecting the principles of peacemaking is the restorative justice movement.

Restorative Justice

Restorative justice is a way to apply peacemaking criminology to the criminal justice system and to the community.[33] Whereas peacemaking might seem theoretically vague or idealistic, restorative justice has concrete evidence that its philosophy works in the real world (see Crosscurrents 16.3 for an alternate view). By highlighting the principles of restorative justice and reviewing some of the types of programs in which it has been effective, our goal here is to demonstrate that restorative justice and peacemaking are serious endeavors that deserve consideration as alternatives to the war-on-crime perspective.

Restorative justice forces us to consider the problems of crime in a different manner than do the traditional methods.[34] According to the principles of restorative justice, the criminal justice system is just a small part of society's response to crime. The possibility of making substantive changes in our crime picture is limited if we depend primarily on the formal criminal justice system. Restorative justice practices involve the community and, most important, establish and strengthen programs within the community to respond not only to crime, but also to some of the underlying conditions that contribute to crime.[35] The principles of restorative justice were aptly delineated by Ron Claassen from the Center for Peacemaking and Conflict Studies at Fresno Pacific University:[36]

1. Crime is primarily an offense against human relationships and secondarily a violation of the law (since laws are written to protect public safety and fairness in human relationships).

2. Restorative justice recognizes that crime (violations of persons and relationships) is wrong and should not occur, and also recognizes that after it does, there are dangers and opportunities. The danger is that the community, victim(s), and/or offender(s) emerge from the response further alienated, more damaged, disrespected, disempowered, feeling less safe and less cooperative with society. The opportunity is that injustice is recognized; equity is restored (restitution and grace); and the future is clarified so that participants are safer, more respectful, and more empowered and cooperative with society.

3. Restorative justice is a process to "make things as right as possible," which includes: attending to needs created by the offense, such as safety and repair of injuries to relationships and physical damage resulting from the offense, and attending to needs related to the cause of the offense (addictions, lack of social or employment skills, lack of moral or ethical base, etc.).

4. The primary victim(s) of a crime is/are the one(s) most impacted by the offense. The secondary victims are others impacted by the crime and might include family members, friends, witnesses, criminal justice officials, community, etc.

5. As soon as immediate victim, community, and offender safety concerns are satisfied, restorative justice views the situation as an opportunity to teach the offender and an opportunity to encourage the offender to learn new ways of acting and being in the community.

6. Restorative justice prefers responding to the crime at the earliest point possible and with the maximum amount of voluntary cooperation and minimum coercion, since healing in relationships and new learning are voluntary and cooperative processes.

7. Restorative justice prefers that most crimes are handled using a cooperative structure, including those impacted by the offense, to provide support and accountability. This might include primary and secondary victims and family (or substitutes if they choose not to participate), the offender and family, community representatives, government representatives, faith/community representatives, school representatives, etc.

8. Restorative justice recognizes that not all offenders will be cooperative. Therefore, an outside authority must make decisions for uncooperative offenders. The actions of the authorities and the consequences imposed should be tested by whether they are reasonable, restorative, and respectful (for victim(s), offender(s), and community).

9. Restorative justice prefers that offenders who pose significant safety risks and are uncooperative be placed in settings where the emphasis is on safety, values, ethics, responsibility, accountability, and civility. They should be exposed to the impact of their offense(s) on victim(s), invited to learn empathy, and offered learning opportunities to become better equipped with skills to be a productive member of society. They should continually be invited (not coerced) to become cooperative with the community and be given the opportunity to demonstrate this in appropriate settings.

10. Restorative justice requires follow-up and accountability structures utilizing the natural community as much as possible, since keeping agreements is the key to building a trustful community.

11. Restorative justice recognizes and encourages the role of community institutions, including the religious/faith community, in teaching and establishing the moral and ethical standards that build up the community.

Perhaps the most distinguishing aspect of restorative justice is its goal of widening the response to crime to include the community. In our rambling, suburbanized society, much of the functions of the community have been lost. Many people are socially and emotionally closer to co-workers, old friends via cell phones and e-mail, or even strangers thousands of miles away through Internet chat rooms than to their neighbors or family members. Many of us know little about our neighbors only a few doors away, yet these people share our concerns about safety, criminal activity, and community resources. Restorative justice establishes programs that connect the government with community programs to provide alternative mechanisms to respond to crime. Programs such as neighborhood justice centers, victim-compensation agencies, rape crisis centers, and juvenile court conferencing circles all seek to provide ways to reduce the harms caused by crime and to heal the rift between offenders and victims. Restorative justice programs include the following:

- **Victim–offender reconciliation programs (VORPs)**   When the traditional criminal justice system handles a case, the offender and victim sit on opposite sides of the courtroom and listen while attorneys argue about the quality of

16.3   CrossCurrents

The Downside of Restorative Justice

We would be remiss in this chapter if we did not give voice to some of the criticism that has been leveled at peacemaking criminology and restorative justice programs. These concepts, although appealing from a theoretical point of view, are little tested as public policies. They have yet to stand the test of time or be applied to multiple jurisdictions in a successful way. It has long been the experience of the criminal justice system that a good program with a dedicated staff often is less successful when transferred to another city where the staff members view it as a job as opposed to a noble experiment. Some of the concerns that will need to be rigorously considered before restorative justice and alternative conflict-resolution programs become widely accepted are as follows:

- *Due process.* Once someone agrees to participate in a restorative justice or alternative dispute-resolution program, certain legal rights are dismissed. Although these programs strive to ensure that everyone is treated fairly and that everyone's voice is heard, the prospect of facing a legal proceeding without the benefit of an attorney or without the right to protections from inadmissible evidence is a daunting prospect. It takes a leap of faith that justice will be done. The criminal justice system, with all of its imperfections, has developed over centuries and has established a vast complex of rules and procedures to protect individual rights. It is too soon to tell just how equably these new justice programs will protect individuals' rights.

- *The guise of neutrality.* The adversarial criminal justice case is under the control of a neutral judge. Third-party mediators are neutral in theory, but many times they may lack the training necessary to ensure that everyone gets a fair shake. Sometimes, the aggressive and the verbal can be persuasive and get their points fully considered, whereas the shy and reticent are intimidated.

- *Individuality.* One of the problems of the criminal justice system that is shared by alternative programs is that the situation is considered a conflict between individuals when it could consist of broader concerns. When the problem is institutional racism, social inequality, or age discrimination, the solutions arrived at by individuals mediating their differences do not address the underlying concerns that led to the dispute.

- *Connections to the community.* Courts have evolved over the years, and the people who work in them have a certain level of training and in most cases are professionals. Judges and attorneys have law degrees and devote their professional lives to upholding a code of ethics that is supervised by the American Bar Association and various state bar associations. Additionally, the courts are accountable to citizens because judges are elected or appointed by others who are elected. Grassroots alternative dispute-resolution programs recruit their personnel from a variety of backgrounds. Many times these well-meaning individuals have little training and may be completely ineffective in helping disputants craft reasonable solutions. There is a serious question of adequate oversight when amateurs are in charge.

Think About It

1. Are these concerns more serious than the concerns we have about the functions of the courts?
2. Is having an attorney a reasonable assurance that one's best interests will get a fair hearing in court?
3. Is abridging people's rights acceptable as long as they are happy with the solution?
4. Are judges really accountable to the community, or could the volunteers and professionals who staff restorative justice programs provide the same level of response to community needs?

Source: Joseph A. Scimecca, "Conflict Resolution and a Critique of 'Alternative Dispute Resolution,'" in *Criminology as Peacemaking*, eds. Harold E. Pepinsky and Richard Quinney (Bloomington: Indiana University Press, 1991), 263–279; Sharon Levrant, Francis T. Cullen, Betsy Fulton, and John F. Wozniak, "Reconsidering Restorative Justice: The Corruption of Benevolence Revisited," *Crime and Delinquency* 45, no. 1 (1999): 3–27.

evidence, the believability of witnesses, culpability, and legal procedures. The entire trial often takes place without the victim and offender ever exchanging words. In plea-bargained cases, the victim and offender may never even be in the same room. Victim–offender reconciliation programs place these parties together with a trained mediator who facilitates an interaction that allows for a more satisfying result. Victims can put a human face on their losses and explain to offenders the extent of their injuries. Offenders are given an opportunity to explain their motivations and mitigating circumstances. As each side learns more about the humanness and circumstances of the other, they can craft solutions that accomplish three goals: identifying the injustice, making things right, and establishing mechanisms for future actions. Sometimes all the victim wants is to tell his or her story to the offender and receive a sincere apology. Sometimes the offender welcomes the opportunity to confess his or her transgressions without fear that the court will use it to impose a harsh sentence. Most important, when the offender and victim will have an ongoing relationship, such as when they are neighbors or family members, the mediator can suggest ground rules so that disputes can be avoided and issues can be worked out before they mushroom into bad feelings.

- **Family group conferencing**   These programs, which were pioneered in New Zealand and Australia, use a mediator to enable everyone connected to an offense to develop a solution that is acceptable to all. In addition to the victim and the offender, there is a representative of law enforcement, a representative of the community, and others with an interest in the case such as family members. Offenders are not simply sentenced; they are included in a process that determines an equitable solution. In this way, offenders feel accountable for carrying out the decision because they had a hand in it and could express their side of the story.

- **Victim–offender panels (VOPs)**   Often the victim does not want to meet with the offender. Other times, it is simply not feasible because the case has already been settled and the offender is incarcerated. However, the potential still exists to educate offenders about the damage they have done through victim–offender panels. In cases such as rape or drunk driving, a victim may talk to a group of offenders who had nothing to do with his or her case. The idea is to let a victim of the type of offense committed by the offender explain how he or she has suffered so that the offender can appreciate how angry a victim can become and reflect on how his or her own offense hurt another victim. The traditional criminal justice system often does not have time for the procedures that allow offenders to understand how their actions harmed others. Especially in cases that are plea-bargained, the offender misses the chance to consider the effect of his or her actions on the victim.[37]

SUMMARY

1. The war concept as applied to criminal justice is problematic. A war on drugs or a war on crime lacks a clear, identifiable external enemy.

2. The police and the military share organizational structures, ranks, the carrying of weapons, and the wearing of uniforms, but their goals are different. A law enforcement officer is sworn to keep the peace and protect citizens. A soldier is obligated to attack an enemy.

3. Some of the differences between the war on terrorism and the other social problems are that the war on terrorism has a clear and identifiable outside enemy; it is political rather than social; it involves military weapons; an outside terrorist enemy does not enjoy U.S. legal protections; and terrorists firmly believe that their cause is just.

4. Several federal agencies have been reorganized into the Department of Homeland Security.

5. Local law enforcement and emergency service agencies are likely to be the "first responders" to terrorist acts and have taken on new responsibilities requiring additional training, improved equipment, and more money.

6. The official title of the USA Patriot Act is the "Uniting and Strengthening America by Providing Appropriate Tools Required to Intercept and Obstruct Terrorism Act."

7. Two controversial components of the Patriot Act are of concern to students of the criminal justice system: the reorganization and retasking of federal law enforcement and the implications for civil liberties and legal rights.

8. Two of the most controversial aspects of the Patriot Act are judicial review and secret searches.

9. An alternative to the war metaphor is the peacemaking approach. Peacemaking criminology is not a new concept. Many of its principles, such as social justice, nonviolence, and rehabilitation, have been advocated for centuries.

10. Peacemaking criminology developed from three intellectual traditions: the religious and humanist tradition, the feminist tradition, and critical traditions.

11. The peacemaking perspective is applicable to four levels of analysis: intrapersonal, interpersonal, societal and institutional, and international and global.

12. The steps of the peacemaking pyramid are nonviolence, social justice, inclusion, correct means, ascertainable criteria, and categorical imperative.

13. Restorative justice is a way to apply peacemaking criminology to the criminal justice system and the community. Restorative justice programs include victim–offender reconciliation programs, family group conferencing, and victim–offender panels.

KEY TERMS

ascertainable criteria 554
categorical imperative 554

correct means 553
peacemaking criminology 548

restorative justice 548
thoughtcrime 539

REVIEW QUESTIONS

1. How are law enforcement officers different from soldiers? How are they alike?

2. How is terrorism changing the mission of the criminal justice system?

3. What are some of the differences between the war on terrorism and other social problems?

4. What issues contributed to the September 11 tragedy?

5. What are some of the agencies that were incorporated into the Department of Homeland Security?

6. What are some of the controversial aspects of the Patriot Act?

7. How will the war on crime and the war on drugs be hindered by the war on terrorism? How will they be helped?

8. What traditions contribute to peacemaking criminology?

9. What are the four levels of analysis to which peacemaking is applicable?

10. What are examples of restorative justice programs?

SUGGESTED FURTHER READING

Barak, Gregg. *Violence and Nonviolence: Pathways to Understanding.* Thousand Oaks, CA: Sage, 2003.

Christie, Daniel J., Richard V. Wagner, and Deborah Du Nann Winter, eds. *Peace, Conflict, and Violence: Peace Psychology for the 21st Century.* Upper Saddle River, NJ: Prentice Hall, 2001.

Frampton, Mary, Ian Lopez, and Jonathan Simon. *After the War on Crime: Race, Democracy, and a New Reconstruction.* New York: NYU Press, 2008.

Simon, Jonathan. *Governing through Crime: How the War on Crime Transformed American Democracy and Created a Culture of Fear.* New York: Oxford University Press, 2007.

Van Ness, Daniel W., and Karen Heetderks Strong. *Restoring Justice*, 3rd ed. Cincinnati, OH: Anderson, 2006.

Western, Bruce. *Punishment and Inequality.* New York: Sage, 2007.

ENDNOTES

1. Lynn Hunt, *Inventing Human Rights: A History* (New York: Norton, 2008).

2. Eugene H. Czajkoski, "Drugs and the Warlike Administration of Justice," *Journal of Drug Issues* 20, no. 1 (1990): 125–129.

3. Eva Bertram, Morris Blackmon, Kenneth Sharpe, and Peter Andreas, *Drug War Politics: The Price of Denial* (Berkeley: University of California Press, 1996).

4. Amitai Etzioni, *How Patriotic Is the Patriot Act?: Freedom versus Security in the Age of Terrorism* (London: Routledge, 2008).

5. David Cole and James X. Dempsey, *Terrorism and the Constitution: Sacrificing Civil Liberties in the Name of National Security* (New York: New Press, 2006).

6. Clark Butler, *Guantanamo Bay and Judicial-Moral Treatment of the Other* (West Lafayette, IN: Purdue University Press, 2007).

7. National Commission on Terrorist Attacks, *The 9/11 Commission Report* (New York: Norton, 2004).

8. George Orwell, *1984* (New York: New American Library, 1961). First published in 1949.

9. This stereotype of terrorists as being only from the Middle East is both unfair and misleading. It is unfair because only a tiny fraction of the people from Middle Eastern countries have engaged in terrorist acts. Furthermore, millions of Americans of the Islamic faith and/or of Middle Eastern descent are unjustly suspected of having terrorist tendencies. This stereotype is misleading because terrorists come from many different backgrounds. For instance, Timothy McVeigh, who blew up the Murrah Federal Building in Oklahoma City, was an army veteran who had no ties to the Middle East. In the hours after the explosion there was much speculation that it was done by Arab terrorists, and this caused great concern in the Arab community.

10. Rob de Wijk, "The Limits of Military Power," in *Terrorism and Counterterrorism*, eds. Russell D. Howard and Reid L. Sawyer (Guilford, CT: McGraw-Hill/Dushkin, 2002), 482–494.

11. Egon Bittner, *The Functions of the Police in Modern Society* (Cambridge, MA: Oelgeschlager, Gunn, & Haim, 1980).

12. Joseph Margulis, *Guantanamo Bay and the Abuse of Presidential Power* (New York: Simon & Schuster, 2007).

13. Mark Juergensmeger, "The Religious Roots of Contemporary Terrorism," in *The New Global Terrorisms: Characteristics, Causes, and Controls*, ed. Charles W. Kegley (Upper Saddle River, NJ: Prentice Hall, 2003), 185–193.

14. Bruce Hoffman, "The Logic of Suicide Terrorism," in *Defeating Terrorism*, eds. Russell D. Howard and Reid L. Sawyer (Guilford, CT: McGraw-Hill/Dushkin, 2004), 103–113.

15. James S. Corum, *Fighting the War on Terror: A Counterinsurgency Strategy* (New York: Zenith Press, 2007).

16. Patricia H. Brady, "The Impact of the September 11, 2001 Terrorist Attacks on Civil Liberties," in *Understanding Terrorism: Threats in an Uncertain World*, eds. Akorlie A. Nyatepe-Coo and Dorothy Zeisler-Vralsted (Upper Saddle River, NJ: Prentice Hall, 2004), 175–182.

17. CNN, "Senators Question 'Phoenix Memo' Author," May 21, 2002, www.cnn.com/2002/US/05/21/phoenix.memo/index.html.

18. Jeffrey H. Norwitz, "Combating Terrorism: With a Helmet or a Badge," in *Terrorism and Counterterrorism: Understanding the New Security Environment, Readings and Interpretations*, eds. Russell D. Howard and Reid L. Sawyer (Guilford, CT: McGraw-Hill/Dushkin, 2002), 470–481.

19. Stephen Lambert and Debra Regan, *Great Jobs for Criminal Justice Majors* (New York: McGraw-Hill, 2007).

20. Brady, "Impact of September 11."

21. Paul Viotti, Michael Opheim, and Nicolas Bowen, *Terrorism and Homeland Security* (New York: CRC Press, 2008).

22. Bob Graham and Jeff Nussbaum, *Intelligence Matters: The CIA, the FBI, Saudi Arabia, and the Failure of America's War on Terror* (Lawrence: University Press of Kansas, 2008).

23. Walter M. Brasch, *America's Unpatriotic Acts: The Federal Government's Violation of Constitutional and Civil Rights* (New York: Lang, 2005).

24. Martin Kady, II, "Localities Get the Bill For Beefed-Up Security," *CQ Weekly* 62 (April 10, 2004): 852–853.

25. This point can be legitimately debated. The funds going to local and state law enforcement agencies are not uniformly applied. Some jurisdictions, such as Washington, D.C., and New York City, have more likely targets, whereas others have few targets of symbolic value.

26. Harold E. Pepinsky and Richard Quinney, *Criminology as Peacemaking* (Bloomington: Indiana University Press, 1991).

27. Richard Quinney, "The Way of Peace: On Crime, Suffering, and Service," in *Criminology as Peacemaking*, eds. Harold E. Pepinsky and Richard Quinney (Bloomington: Indiana University Press, 1991), 3–13.

28. Floyd H. Ross and Tynette Hills, *The Great Religions by Which Men Live* (Greenwich, CT: Fawcett, 1956).

29. M. Kay Harris, "Moving into the New Millennium: Toward a Feminist Vision of Justice," in *Criminology as Peacemaking*, eds. Harold E. Pepinsky and Richard Quinney (Bloomington: Indiana University Press, 1991), 83–91.

30. Ian Taylor, Paul Walton, and Jock Young, *The New Criminology: For a Social Theory of Deviance* (New York: Harper & Row, 1973).

31. Immanuel Kant, "The Categorical Imperative," in *Morality in Criminal Justice: An Introduction to Ethics*, eds. Daryl Close and Nicholas Meier (Belmont, CA: Wadsworth, 1995), 45–50.

32. John Randolph Fuller and John Wozniak, "Peacemaking Criminology: Past, Present, and Future," in *Taking Stock: The Status of Criminological Theory*, eds. Francis T. Cullen, John Paul Wright, and Kristie R. Blevins, (New Brunswick, NJ: Transaction, 2006).

33. David R. Karp and Todd R. Clear, eds., *What Is Community Justice: Case Studies of Restorative Justice and Community Supervision* (Thousand Oaks, CA: Sage, 2002).

34. Howard Zehr, *Changing Lenses: A New Focus for Crime and Justice* (Scottdale, PA: Herald Press, 1990).

35. Gordon Bazemore and Mara Schiff, *Restorative Community Justice: Repairing Harm and Transforming Communities* (Cincinnati, OH: Anderson, 2001).

36. Ron Claassen, *Restorative Justice—Fundamental Principles*, paper presented at the National Conference on Peacemaking and Conflict Resolution, May 1995; revised May 1996 at the UN Alliance of NGOs Working Party on Restorative Justice, 1996). © 1996 by Ron Claassen. Printed by permission. www.fresno.edu/pacs/docs/rjprinc.html.

37. Michael Braswell, John Fuller, and Bo Lozoff, *Corrections, Peacemaking, and Restorative Justice: Transforming Individuals and Institutions* (Cincinnati, OH: Anderson, 2001).

Glossary

A

actual-seizure stop An incident in which police officers physically restrain a person and restrict his or her freedom.

actus reus "Guilty deed"; the physical action of a criminal offense.

adjudicatory hearing The process in which a juvenile court determines whether the allegations in a petition are supported by evidence.

adversarial process A term describing the manner in which U.S. criminal trial courts operate; a system that requires two sides, a prosecution and a defense.

alibi A defense that involves the defendant(s) claiming not to have been at the scene of a criminal offense when it was committed.

amicus curiae A brief in which someone who is not a part of a case gives advice or testimony.

anomie A condition in which a people or society undergoes a breakdown of social norms and values.

argot roles Specific patterns of behavior that inmates develop in prison to adjust to the environment.

arraignment A court appearance in which the defendant is formally charged with a crime and asked to respond by pleading guilty, not guilty, or nolo contendere.

arson Any willful or malicious burning or attempt to burn a dwelling, public building, motor vehicle or aircraft, or personal property of another.

ascertainable criteria A peacemaking criminology term that states that everyone involved in a criminal justice process should understand the rules and procedures employed by the system.

Assize of Clarendon A 12th-century English law that established judicial procedure and the grand jury system.

atavisms The appearance in a person of physical features thought to be from earlier stages of human evolution.

authority The right and the power to commit an act or order others to commit an act.

B

bail agent An employee of a private, for-profit company that provides money for suspects to be released from jail. Also called a *bondsman*.

bailiff An officer of the court responsible for executing writs and processes, making arrests, and keeping order in the court.

behaviorism The assessment of human psychology via the examination of objectively observable and quantifiable actions, as opposed to subjective mental states.

bench trial A trial that takes place before a judge, but without a jury, in which the judge makes the decision. Sometimes called a *court trial*.

beyond a reasonable doubt Refers to the highest level of proof required to win a case; necessary in criminal cases to procure a guilty verdict.

bill of indictment A declaration of the charges against an accused person that is presented to a grand jury to determine whether enough evidence exists for an indictment.

Bill of Rights The first 10 amendments to the U.S. Constitution, which guarantees fundamental rights and privileges to citizens.

blood feud A disagreement whose settlement is based on personal vengeance and physical violence.

bobbies A slang term for the police force created in 1829 by Sir Robert Peel's Metropolitan Police Act, derived from Bob, the short form of Robert.

boot camp prison A short-term prison that uses military boot camp training and discipline techniques to rehabilitate offenders; often used for young offenders.

Bow Street Runners A police organization created circa 1748 by magistrates Henry Fielding and his brother Sir John Fielding whose members went on patrol, rather than sitting at a designated post.

broken-windows theory The idea that untended property or deviant behavior will attract crime. This theory is used as a justification for clearing the streets of homeless people, drunks, and unruly teens, even when no law has been broken.

burglary Breaking into and entering a structure or vehicle with intent to commit a felony or a theft.

C

case law *See* common law.

categorical imperative A term associated with the philosopher Immanuel Kant. When applied to peacemaking, it means that every decision should be logical enough to be applied to other cases at other times.

chancery court "Court of equity." In England, these were established, in part, to assist when common law courts failed to resolve a case. These courts were favorable to vulnerable individuals, especially children.

chemical castration Anti-androgen drugs, usually administered by injection, that have the effect of lowering the testosterone level and blunting the sex drive in males.

Chicago school Criminological theories that rely, in part, on individuals' demographics and geographic location to explain criminal behavior.

child advocate An officer appointed by the court to protect the interests of the child and to act as a liaison among the child, the child's family, the court, and any other agency involved with the child.

circuit A judicial district established within a state judicial system or the federal judicial system.

circuit court A court that holds sessions at intervals within different areas of a judicial district.

civil law The law that governs private rights as opposed to the law that governs criminal issues.

classical school of criminology A set of criminological theories that uses the idea of free will to explain criminal behavior.

clearance rate The number of offenses that have been solved by the police.

clerk of the court The primary administrative officer of each court who manages nonjudicial functions.

Code of Hammurabi An ancient code instituted by Hammurabi, a ruler of Babylonia, dealing with criminal and civil matters.

commitment An order by a judge on conviction or before a trial that sends a person to jail or prison. Also, a judge's order that sends a mentally unstable person to a mental institution.

common law   Laws that are based on customs and general principles and that may be used as precedent or for matters not addressed by statute.

community policing   A policing strategy that attempts to harness the resources and residents of a given community in stopping crime and maintaining order.

community standards   Practices, acts, and/or media accepted by a given social group who share a geographic area and/or government.

compurgation   In medieval German and English law, a practice by which a defendant could establish innocence by taking an oath and having a required number of people swear that they believed the oath.

concurrence   The coexistence of actus reus and mens rea.

congregate-and-silent system   A style of control pioneered by the Auburn System, in which inmates were allowed to eat and work together during the day but were forbidden to speak and were locked alone in their cells at night.

consent decree   The parties to a lawsuit accept a judge's order that is based on an agreement made by them instead of continuing the case through a trial or hearing.

constable (*comes stabuli*)   The head of law enforcement for large districts in early England. In the modern United States, a constable serves areas such as rural townships and is usually elected.

corporate crime   Offenses committed by the officers of a corporation who use that corporation's business to pursue illegal activity in the name of the corporation.

corpus delicti   "Body of the crime"; the criminal offense.

correct means   A peacemaking criminology term coined by Gandhi that describes how the problems of crime can be attained using only processes that embody peacemaking principles.

county stockade   A component of a county corrections system that usually holds offenders who have already been sentenced.

court administrator   An officer responsible for the mechanical necessities of the court, such as scheduling courtrooms, managing case flow, administering personnel, procuring furniture, and preparing budgets.

Court of the Star Chamber   An old English court comprising the king's councilors that was separate from common-law courts.

court reporter   A court officer who records and transcribes an official verbatim record of the legal proceedings of the court.

courts of appeals   Intermediate courts that dispose of many appeals before they reach the Supreme Court.

crime rate   The number of Crime Index offenses divided by the population of an area, usually given as a rate of crimes per 100,000 people.

D

dark figure of crime   A metaphor that describes crime that is unreported and never quantified.

decriminalization   The emendation of laws or statutes to lessen or remove penalties for specific acts subject to criminal prosecution, arrest, and imprisonment.

determinate sentence   A prison term that is determined by law and states a specific period of time to be served.

differential association theory   A theory developed by Edwin Sutherland that states that crime is learned.

directed verdict of acquittal   An order from a trial judge to the jury stating that the jury must acquit the accused because the prosecution has not proved its case.

discretion   The power of a judge, public official, or law enforcement officer to make decisions on issues within legal guidelines.

disposition   The final determination of a case or other matter by a court or other judicial entity.

district courts   Courts of general jurisdiction that try felony cases involving federal laws and civil cases involving amounts of money over $75,000.

double jeopardy   Prosecution in the same jurisdiction of a defendant for an offense for which the defendant has already been prosecuted and convicted or acquitted.

double marginality   A term that refers to the multiple outsider status of female and minority police officers.

due-process rights   Guarantees by the Fifth, Sixth, and Fourteenth Amendments of the U.S. Constitution establishing legal procedures that recognize the protection of an individual's life, liberty, and property.

E

electronic monitoring   A form of intermediate punishment in which an offender is allowed to remain in the community but must wear an electronic device that allows the authorities to monitor his or her whereabouts.

F

false consciousness   The idea that the attitudes held by the lower class do not accurately reflect the reality of that class's existence.

felony   An offense punishable by a sentence of more than a year in state or federal prison and sometimes by death.

frankpledge system   An early form of English government that divided communities into groups of 10 men who were responsible for the group's conduct and ensured that a member charged with breaking the law appeared in court.

G

gatekeeping   Points, or "gates," in the criminal and juvenile justice systems at which crucial decisions are made about a case.

general deterrence   A method of control in which the punishment of a single offender sets an example for the rest of society.

geographic jurisdiction   The authority of a court to hear a case based on the location of the offense.

going rate   A term describing how similar cases have been settled by a given set of judges, prosecutors, and attorneys.

good time   The time deducted from an inmate's prison sentence for good behavior.

grabbable area   The area under the control of an individual during an arrest in an automobile.

grass-eaters   A slang term from the 1971 Knapp Commission report on police corruption in New York City, describing officers who accept bribes but do not actively pursue them.

H

habeas corpus   A writ issued to bring a party before the court.

hands-off doctrine   The judicial attitude toward prisons before the 1960s in which courts did not become involved in prison affairs or inmate rights.

hearing   A session that takes place without a jury before a judge or magistrate in which evidence and/or arguments are presented to determine some factual or legal issue.

hedonistic calculus   An individual's mental calculation of the personal value of an activity by how much pleasure or pain it will incur.

hierarchical jurisdiction   The authority of a court to hear a case based on where the case is located in the system.

hue and cry   In early England, the alarm that citizens were required to raise on the witness or discovery of a criminal offense.

hundred-man   The head of a group of 10 men who served as an administrator and judge.

hung jury   A term describing a jury in a criminal case that is deadlocked or that cannot produce a unanimous verdict.

I

impeach   To discredit a witness.

inchoate offense   An offense comprising acts necessary to commit another offense.

indentured servant   From the 17th to 19th centuries, a person who came to the American colonies/United States and was made to work for a period of time, usually seven years.

indeterminate sentence   A prison term that does not state a specific period of time to be served or date of release.

indictment   A written statement of the facts of the offense that is charged against the accused.

infancy   In legal terminology, the state of a child who has not yet reached a specific age; almost all states end infancy at age 18.

informal probation   A period during which a juvenile is required to stay out of trouble or make restitution before the case is dropped.

information   A formal, written accusation against a defendant submitted to the court by a prosecutor.

inquest   In archaic usage, considered the first type of jury that determined the ownership of land. Currently, a type of investigation.

insanity defense   A defense that attempts to give physical or psychological reasons that a defendant cannot comprehend his or her criminal actions, their harm(s), or their punishment.

intensive-supervision probation   A form of supervision that requires frequent meetings between the client and probation officer.

J

just deserts   A philosophy that states that an offender who commits a heinous crime deserves death.

juvenile delinquent   A person, usually under age 18, who is determined to have committed a criminal offense or status offense in states in which a minor is declared to lack responsibility and cannot be sentenced as an adult.

L

labeling theory   A perspective that considers recidivism to be a consequence, in part, of the negative labels applied to offenders.

larceny/theft   A form of theft in which an offender takes possessions that do not belong to him or her with the intent of keeping them.

legalistic style   A mode of policing that emphasizes enforcement of the letter of the law.

legalization   The total removal of legal prohibitions on specific acts that were previously proscribed and punishable by law.

lower courts   Sometimes called inferior courts, in reference to their hierarchy. These courts receive their authority and resources from local county or municipal governments.

M

magistrate court   The lowest level of the federal court system, created in 1968 to ease the caseload of the U.S. district courts.

Magna Carta   "Great Charter"; a guarantee of liberties signed by King John of England in 1215 that influenced many modern legal and constitutional principles.

mandatory minimum sentence   A sentence determined by law that establishes the minimum length of prison time that may be served for an offense.

marks-of-commendation system   An incarceration philosophy developed by Alexander Maconochie in which inmates earned the right to be released, as well as privileges, goods, and services.

master status   A personal status that overwhelms all others.

meat-eaters   A slang term from the 1971 Knapp Commission report on police corruption in New York City describing officers who actively seek out situations that can produce financial gain.

mens rea   "Guilty mind"; intent or knowledge to break the law.

meritorious time   Time deducted from an inmate's sentence for doing something special or extra, such as completing a GED.

Metropolitan Police Act   Created in 1829 by Sir Robert Peel, the first successful bill to create a permanent, public police force.

misdemeanor   A lesser offense punishable by a fine and/or jail time for up to one year.

Missouri Bar Plan   A judicial nominating commission presents a list of candidates to the governor, who decides on a candidate. After a year in office, voters decide on whether to retain the judge. Judges must run for such re-election each term. Also called *merit selection*.

N

National Incident-Based Reporting System (NIBRS)   A crime-reporting system in which each separate offense in a crime is described, including data describing the offender(s), victim(s), and property.

Neighborhood Watch   A community policing program that encourages residents to cooperate in providing security for the neighborhood.

neutralization theory   A perspective that states that juvenile delinquents have feelings of guilt when involved in illegal activities and search for explanations to diminish that guilt.

no-bill   The decision of a grand jury not to indict an accused person as a result of insufficient evidence.

nolo contendere   Latin for "I do not wish to contend." The defendant neither admits nor denies committing the offense, but agrees to be punished as if guilty.

O

observational learning   The process of learning by watching the behavior of others.

operant conditioning   The alteration of behavior by rewarding or punishing a subject for a specified action until the subject associates the action with pleasure or pain.

organized crime   Illegal activity by a group that is set up specifically to break the law in pursuit of profit.

P

pains of imprisonment   Deprivations that define the punitive nature of imprisonment.

parens patriae   Latin for "father of the country." Refers to the philosophy that the government is the ultimate guardian of all children or disabled adults.

peacemaking criminology   A theoretical perspective that focuses on nonviolence, social justice, and reducing the suffering of both the victim and the offender.

penal codes   A code of laws that deals with crimes and the punishment for them.

petitioner   A person who files a lawsuit; also called a *plaintiff*.

pillory   A wooden frame with holes for securing the head and hands that was used to secure and expose an offender to public derision.

plea bargain   A compromise reached by the defendant, the defendant's attorney, and the prosecutor in which the defendant agrees to plead guilty or no contest in return for a reduction of the charges' severity, dismissal of some charges, further information about the offense or about others involved in it, or the prosecutor's agreement to recommend a desired sentence.

policeman's working personality   A term coined by Jerome Skolnick to refer to the mindset of police who must deal with danger, authority, isolation, and suspicion while appearing to be efficient.

poor laws   Seventeenth-century laws that turned over vagrants and abandoned children to landowners or shopkeepers as indentured servants.

positivist school of criminology   A set of criminological theories that uses scientific techniques to study crime and criminal offenders.

precedent   A prior legal decision used as a basis for deciding a later, similar case.

prejudicial error   An error affecting the outcome of a trial.

presentence investigation   The report prepared by a probation officer to assist a judge in sentencing; also called a *presentence report.*

presentence report   An account prepared by a probation officer that assists the sentencing court in deciding an appropriate sentence for a convicted defendant.

presumptive sentence   A sentence that may be adjusted by the judge depending on aggravating or mitigating factors.

preventive detention   The jailing of a defendant awaiting trial, usually in order to protect an individual or the public.

***prima facie* case**   A case established by evidence sufficient to establish the fact in question unless it is rebutted.

private probation   A form of probation supervision that is contracted to for-profit private agencies by the state.

probable cause   A reason based on known facts to think that a law has been broken or that a property is connected to a criminal offense.

problem-oriented policing   A style of policing that attempts to address the underlying social problems that contribute to crime.

procedural law   Laws that prescribe the methods for their enforcement and use.

Prohibition   The period from January 29, 1920, to December 5, 1933, during which the manufacture, transportation, and sale of alcoholic beverages was made illegal in the United States by the Eighteenth Amendment.

R

racial profiling   Suspicion of illegal activity based on a person's race, ethnicity, or national origin rather than on actual illegal activity or evidence of illegal activity.

rape   Sexual activity, usually sexual intercourse, that is forced on another person without his or her consent, usually under threat of harm. Also sexual activity conducted with a person who is incapable of valid consent.

rational choice theory   A theory that states that people consciously choose to break the law on realizing that the offense's benefits probably outweigh the negative consequences.

reasonable stop standard   A Supreme Court measure that considers constitutionality on whether a reasonable person would feel free to terminate an encounter with law enforcement personnel.

reasonable suspicion   A suspicion based on facts or circumstances that justifies stopping and sometimes searching an individual thought to be involved in illegal activity.

redirect examination   The questioning of a witness about issues uncovered during cross-examination.

referral   Similar to a "charge" in the adult system in which an authority, usually the police, parents, or the school, determines that the youth needs intervention from the juvenile court.

residential placement   Any sentence of a juvenile delinquent to a halfway house or other community home in which the juvenile is closely monitored, but allowed to leave for work or school.

respondent   The party who must reply to a petitioner's complaint. Equivalent to a defendant in a lawsuit.

restorative justice   An alternative justice model that uses community programs to repair the harm done by offenders.

retribution model   A style of control in which offenders are punished as severely as possible for a crime and in which rehabilitation is not attempted.

robbery   The removal of property from a person by violence or by threat of violence.

rule of four   A rule that states that at least four of the nine Supreme Court justices must vote to hear a case.

S

seizure   The collection by police officers of potential evidence in a criminal case.

separate-and-silent system   A method of penal control pioneered by Philadelphia's Eastern State Penitentiary in which inmates were kept from seeing or talking to one another. This method is comparable to solitary confinement in modern prisons.

serial murder   Homicides of a sequence of victims committed in three or more separate events over a period of time.

service style   A mode of policing that is concerned primarily with serving the community and citizens.

sex work   The exchange of coital or sex-related activities for payment.

sexual assault   Sexual contact that is committed without the other party's consent or with a party who is not capable of giving consent.

sheriff (shire reeve)   The *shire reeve* led the English shire's military forces and judged cases.

shock probation   The practice of sentencing offenders to prison, allowing them to serve a short time, and then granting them probation without their prior knowledge.

show-of-authority stop   An incident in which police show a sign of authority (such as flashing a badge) and the suspect submits.

social control theory   A theory that seeks not to explain why people break the law, but instead explores what keeps most people from breaking the law.

socialization   A process by which individuals acquire a personal identity and learn the norms, values, behavior, and social skills appropriate to their society.

sociological imagination   The idea that we must look beyond the obvious to evaluate how our social location influences how we perceive society.

somatotyping   The use of body types and physical characteristics to classify human personalities.

specific deterrence   A method of control in which an offender is prevented from committing more crimes by either imprisonment or death.

stare decisis   The doctrine under which courts adhere to legal precedent.

state courts   General courts and special courts funded and run by each state.

status offense   An act that is considered a legal offense only when committed by a juvenile and that can be adjudicated only in a juvenile court.

statute   A law enacted by a legislature.

statutory exclusion   Provisions that exclude, without hearing or waiver, juveniles who meet certain age, offense, or past-record criteria from the jurisdiction of the juvenile court.

statutory law   The type of law that is enacted by legislatures, as opposed to common law.

statutory rape   Sexual activity conducted with a person who is younger than a specified age or incapable of valid consent because of mental illness, mental handicap, intoxication, unconsciousness, or deception.

stop   A temporary detention that legally is a seizure of an individual and must be based on reasonable suspicion.

stop-and-frisk   A term that describes two distinct behaviors on the part of law enforcement officers in dealing with suspects. To conduct a lawful frisk, the stop itself must meet the legal conditions of a seizure. A frisk constitutes a search.

strain theory   The theory that the causes of crime can be connected to the pressure on culturally or materially disadvantaged groups or individuals to achieve the goals held by society, even if the means that those goals require the breaking of laws.

street crime   Small-scale person offenses such as single-victim homicide, rape, robbery, assault, burglary, and vandalism.

strict liability   Responsibility for a criminal offense without intention to break the law.

subject-matter jurisdiction   The authority of a court to hear a case based on the nature of the case.

substantive law   The law that defines rights and proscribes certain actions (crimes).

supermax prison   An extremely secure type of prison that strictly limits inmate contact with other inmates, correctional staff, and the outside world.

T

terrorism   The use or threat of violence against a state or other political entity in order to coerce.

Thames River Police   A private police force created by the West India Trading Company in 1798 that represented the first professional, salaried police force in London.

thoughtcrime   A term coined by George Orwell in his novel *1984*, in which the act of thinking about breaking a law is a criminal offense.

tort law   An area of the law that deals with civil acts that cause harm and injury, including libel, slander, assault, trespass, and negligence.

total institution   A closed environment in which every aspect, including the movement and behavior of the people within, is controlled and structured.

trial by ordeal   An ancient custom in which the accused was required to perform a test to prove guilt.

true bill   The decision of a grand jury that sufficient evidence exists to indict an accused person.

U

U.S. Supreme Court   The "court of last resort." The highest court in the United States, established by Article III of the Constitution, hears only appeals, with some exceptions.

Uniform Crime Reports (UCR)   An annual publication by the Federal Bureau of Investigation that uses data from all participating law enforcement agencies in the United States to summarize the incidence and rate of reported crime.

use of force   The legal police use of violence to enforce the law. Excessive use of force is considered police brutality.

utilitarianism   A theory associated with Jeremy Bentham that states that people will choose not to break the law when the pain of punishment outweighs the benefits of the offense.

V

venire   The list or pool from which jurors are chosen.

victim precipitation   A situation in which a crime victim plays an active role in initiating a crime or escalating it.

victimization survey   A survey that attempts to measure the extent of crime by interviewing crime victims.

victimless crime   Activities such as gambling or prostitution that are deemed undesirable because they offend community standards rather than directly harm people or property.

voir dire   French for "to see, to speak." Refers to the questioning of jurors by a judge and/or attorneys to determine whether individual jurors are appropriate for a particular jury panel.

W

war on drugs   A policy aimed at reducing the sale and use of illegal drugs.

warrant   A judicial writ that authorizes a law officer to perform a specified act required for the administration of justice, such as an arrest or search.

watch-and-ward system   An early English system overseen by the constable in which a watchman guarded a city's or town's gates at night.

watchman style   A mode of policing that emphasizes the maintenance of order and informal intervention on the part of the police officer rather than strict enforcement of the law.

writ of certiorari   An order from a superior court calling up for review the record of a case from a lower court.

X

XYY syndrome   A condition in which a male is born with an extra Y chromosome.

Z

zero-tolerance policies   Policies of agencies in which the strict letter of the law or rule is followed without question or room for individual discretion on the part of the authority.

zero-tolerance policing   This form of policing punishes every infraction of the law, however minor, with an arrest, fine, or other penalty so that offenders will refrain from committing more serious offenses.

Case Index

Subject Index